D0086669

Courtesy of the Devereux Foundation, Devon, Pennsylvania

TEACHING THE EXCEPTIONAL CHILD

LUCIANO L'ABATE
Professor of Psychology,
Georgia State University, Atlanta

LEONARD T. CURTIS
Professor of Special Education,
Georgia State University, Atlanta

Hydrocephaly - 42
Down's - 1st page, 82
Symptoms 53

W. B. SAUNDERS COMPANY
PHILADELPHIA • LONDON • TORONTO • 1975

W. B. Saunders Company: West Washington Square
Philadelphia, PA 19105

12 Dyott Street
London, WC1A 1DB

833 Oxford Street
Toronto 18, Ontario

Library of Congress Cataloging in Publication Data

L'Abate, Luciano, 1928–

Teaching the exceptional child.

Bibliography: p.

Includes index.

1. Exceptional children – Education. I. Curtis, Leonard T., joint author. II. Title.

LC3965.L32 371.9 74–4575

ISBN 0–7216–5588–2

Teaching the Exceptional Child ISBN 0-7216-5588-2

© 1975 by W. B. Saunders Company. Copyright under the International Copyright Union. All rights reserved. This book is protected by copyright. No part of it may be reproduced, stored in a retrieval system, or transmitted in any form or by any means, electronic, mechanical, photocopying, recording, or otherwise, without written permission from the publisher. Made in the United States of America. Press of W. B. Saunders Company. Library of Congress catalog card number 74-4575.

Print No.: 9 8 7 6 5 4 3 2 1

Dedicated to Bess L'Abate and Anne Curtis.

PREFACE AND ACKNOWLEDGMENTS

This text is designed to be used in basic level, broad-coverage special education courses. We have tried to achieve an appropriate balance between etiology and remediation. Our purpose has been to provide regular classroom teachers as well as teachers of exceptional children with the fundamentals of analysis and remediation of all exceptionalities. We have employed a practical approach in order to help teachers with specific implementation of particular problems and situations, both in and out of the classroom, and have tried to follow as much as possible an information-processing approach, even though this emphasis may not appear consistently throughout the book. It is clear that existing psychodynamic, psychophysiological, or behavioral approaches alone are insufficient to deal with all the complexities of exceptionalities in children.

Our intent has been to write a book about teaching children with exceptionalities rather than for exceptional children. We feel strongly that children with exceptionalities are children *first* and that their exceptionalities, whatever the type and the intensity, should be a secondary consideration. Their exceptionality may be a form of labeling that we consider unfortunate because it pigeonholes the child in a fashion we consider negative and often degrading. In fact, why not use assets rather than liabilities to categorize children with exceptionalities? Since such an approach is obviously unsuitable at the present time, we want to stress throughout the book that the state of being a child—*childhood*—is our primary consideration.

We are indebted to those who generously provided photographs for this book. We would especially like to thank Dr. Harold S. Barbour and Marion DeBrosse, The Woods Schools, Langhorne, Pennsylvania; Jon E. Olexy, John M. Barclay, and Nicholas Korff, The Devereux Foundation, Devon, Pennsylvania; Mrs. Alan M. Bonnem, The Children's Hospital of Philadelphia; Margaret Zecher, Overbrook School for the Blind, Philadelphia; and Mrs. Ruth Carpenter, Shaw Center for Exceptional Children, DeKalb County Public Schools, Atlanta.

We are grateful to Enya Sullivan for reviewing the section on suicide in childhood and adolescence; to Robert W. Wildman II for helping with bibliographical entries and page proof; and to Sherry Harbin for working on the Glossary. To Linda Griffis, Barbara Taylor, Jim Beverly, Bunny Hopson, and Mary Pickett goes our gratitude for their untiring dedication in typing and retyping of the entire manuscript.

This book could not have been completed without the careful proofreading by Bess L. L'Abate, who gave most generously of her time beyond the call of duty or of need.

CONTENTS

Section I

INTRODUCTION

CHAPTER 1

EXCEPTIONALITIES IN CHILDREN

(From Smith, D. W., and Wilson, A. A.: The Child With Down's Syndrome. Philadelphia, W. B. Saunders, 1973.)

The main purpose of this book is to provide the regular classroom teacher and the special education teacher with a practical introduction to the identification, evaluation, and management of the child who is considered "exceptional." It is, of course, a truism that all human beings are unique, but in the case of the exceptional child there is a serious deviation from that which is considered "normal" in terms of intellectual, psychological, or sociocultural factors. In more technical terms, a child may be considered exceptional if he or she is recognizably different from the generally accepted norms in terms of the affective, cognitive, or psychomotor areas of human behavior. Owing to the great number of children placed in one or more categories of exceptionality, the bulk of their education will, for most purposes, be the responsibility of the regular classroom teacher. It is our aim to present basic concepts by which the regular classroom teacher, as well as the special education teacher, may provide a more adequate education for the child who is "different."

This book will focus on the interaction between teacher and pupil, with a basic assumption that all children are worthy of good teaching. Educational procedures must shift from a mass method of instruction to an individual mode which might be properly called the facilitative mode. A considerable amount of this text will be devoted to the techniques and methods by which a teacher may make this all-important shift.

Since the very earliest days of American education, the philosophy stated in textbooks and in speeches has been that in the United States all children are entitled to an adequate education. Recent court decisions (Diana vs. State Board of Education, 1970; Pennsylvania Association for Retarded Children vs. Commonwealth of Pennsylvania, 1971) in California and Pennsylvania seem to indicate that the public is accepting this idea. The basic assumption of this book is that it is possible to provide appropriate education for even the exceptional child under the general rubric of regular American education (Kirk, 1972; Zedler, 1974; Ross et al., 1974; Abeson, 1974).

MAJOR ASSUMPTIONS

For many years, special education for the exceptional child has been based on the following assumptions:

1. All students are capable of learning some type of worthwhile knowledge. While this sentence may sound like a cliché, it is fundamental to the educational system of those who work with exceptional children. Intrinsic to all work with exceptionalities is the assumption that every child has the potential for making some contribution to society.

2. All students have an intrinsic value. An anathema to the field of

special education is the concept of the "poor little child." Basic goals in working with exceptionalities are to provide the opportunity for each child to acquire all the competencies, skills, knowledge, and understanding of which he, as an individual, is capable, and to accept him as an individual of value, for himself, apart from any other characteristics.

3. The majority of students with exceptionalities can be taught skills, knowledge, and attitudes that will enable them to function independently in an adult society. Much evidence exists to indicate that these children, generally speaking, are capable of learning the skills which will enable them to be gainfully employed and to become contributing taxpayers to their society.

4. The child with exceptionalities is more like the normal child than he is different from the normal child.

5. The teacher of exceptional children should be carefully trained to start working with children at their individual levels of intellect. Special education has literally accepted this as a basic premise upon which to operate.

6. A close corollary to the preceding assumption is that all children should be provided with individualized instruction. The very fact that a child is exceptional forces the teacher to individualize instruction to provide this child with the skills that are necessary to become economically self-sufficient.

7. Children with some degree of intellectual retardation need more instruction in a *concrete mode* than do normal children. There is much evidence that the lower the intellectual level, the greater the need for concrete instruction as opposed to instruction on an abstract level. This is not to say that retarded children do not have the ability to abstract, because there is clear evidence that retarded children have this ability to some extent.

8. Because of the short attention span of many exceptional children, instruction sessions should be limited to include only as much information as the child can absorb.

Figure 1–1 Concrete mode of instruction through play-acting.

9. Exceptional children must be provided with more specific cues while learning academic subjects, since they are usually not as capable as the normal child in learning to generalize from specifics.

10. The teacher of exceptional children should make a detailed and specific analysis of each child's mode of learning, in terms of which learning styles are more appropriate and which *modalities* are more involved in the learning process. This analysis involves individual assessment of the child and individual prescriptions for him.

11. Evidence indicates that most exceptional children are able to learn appropriate social behavior in terms of the normal population. Exceptionality is no longer an excuse for social maladaptation.

12. Exceptional children have been found to be most seriously deficient in the areas of reading and arithmetical reasoning.

CLASSIFICATIONS OF EXCEPTIONAL CHILDREN

Programs for the exceptional child have typically been provided by various governmental agencies according to the following classifications.

The Visually Handicapped Child

The visually impaired child is one who has a significant loss of vision varying from mild to total blindness. For educational purposes, the usual practice is to classify such children as partially sighted or blind. The partially sighted child is usually able to function in a normal classroom provided that some visual aids are made available. The totally blind are frequently placed either in special schools or in special classes within the public school system.

The Hearing Handicapped Child

It is customary to divide those who are hearing handicapped into two categories, the hard of hearing and the deaf. As with the visually impaired, the less handicapped children are usually taught within the normal educational system.

The Mentally Retarded Child

The *mentally retarded* child is one who is mentally subnormal as determined by an assessment of intellectual factors. It is customary to divide the mentally retarded for educational purposes into the *trainable mentally retarded* (TMR) and the *educable mentally retarded* (EMR). Most states now provide some type of public schooling for both levels of mental retardation.

The Gifted Child

The gifted child is one who is significantly superior in terms of intellectual ability. The actual IQ score and criteria for determining giftedness vary from state to state and from area to area.

The Behaviorally Disordered Child

The area of behavioral disorders encompasses emotional disturbances, social maladaptation, and psychoses. Programs for behaviorally disordered children vary from modification of the regular classroom to placement in a state institution for the mentally ill.

The Orthopedically Handicapped Child

The orthopedically handicapped child is one who, either through congenital factors or acquired characteristics, suffers from a loss or deformity of a part of the body or from the inability to use a part of his body. Such children often are required to attend special schools, although many schools now make some provisions for certain types of physical handicaps.

The Speech-Defective Child

The speech-defective child possesses some type of atypical speech pattern which may be mild, moderate, or severe. The speech problem may be organic, developmental, or psychological in origin. Care for those who are speech-defective is usually provided through the use of speech therapists who travel from school to school to work with such children.

The Brain-Damaged Child

The category of brain-damaged children includes a large variety of intracranial deficits, ranging from severe to minimal. Severely brain-damaged children may be easily recognized; however, there are large numbers of children with minimal brain damage who are difficult to identify and to properly evaluate in the classroom.

Other Handicapping Conditions

A general category is used to cover those children who have health problems of such a nature as to require some minor or major educational adjustment. This category may include children with tuberculosis, heart conditions, or general loss of vitality. Children with such conditions are frequently placed in instructional programs for the homebound.

Two large categories of exceptionality are not included in the preceding classification of exceptionalities traditionally considered to be within the realm of special education. Such a delimiting of the term "exceptional" seriously misinterprets reality. We would like to propose that the slow learner and the culturally deprived, or culturally different, be added to the field of exceptionalities. The needs of these two groups of children have not been adequately met by many segments of American public education. The great number of children included in these two categories poses many logistical problems in terms of providing appropriate educational procedures. However, the extent of the problem must not cause us to exclude these exceptionalities from consideration. The fact is that both the culturally deprived and the slow learner provide more than their share of "failures" in the current school scene. Suggestions as to methods which might, to some degree, allow a more adequate education for these children will be discussed in a later chapter.

INCIDENCE OF EXCEPTIONALITIES IN CHILDREN

It is difficult to determine the incidence of exceptionalities. No comprehensive survey has ever been conducted by the federal government or any other agency. Part of the problem stems from the fact that the incidence of any exceptionality is to some extent a function of its definition. All exceptionalities vary from very mild to very severe, and where the cutoff point is placed will, to a large measure, determine the final number of individuals who will be labeled as exceptional. The number of cases of speech defects, for example, has been reported to be anywhere from 2 to 20 per cent of all school children (Kirk, 1972). Reasonably estimating the incidence of emotional disturbances and learning disorders poses an even greater difficulty. There has been a tendency to underestimate the incidence of any exceptionality for purposes of state or federal legislation because of the amount of money involved.

It is important, however, to report some general type of incidence figures. According to figures issued by the Bureau of Education for the Handicapped in July, 1968, there were approximately 7,083,500 handicapped individuals, the ages ranging from birth to age 19. Table 1–1 lists the Bureau's estimated percentages of handicapped school age children and includes the percentages of the various handicapped children who were not receiving special service as of the Bureau's 1970 report. The number of handicapped children receiving some type of special service falls far below even the incidence figures shown here. The preceding figures should be considered absolute minimums. For a more detailed examination of the problem of incidence, the reader is referred to the discussions of each exceptionality in this book. At this point, it should suffice to state that the actual incidence is probably much greater than the listed figures, particularly if one includes those individuals with a mild condition.

These figures did not include the gifted, the slow learner, or the culturally deprived. According to a normal distribution curve, one might expect some 16.0 per cent of the school-age population to fall into the slow learning category, while 2.5 to 3.0 per cent of the school-age population would be called gifted. It is not possible to make any sort of a reasonable estimate of the culturally different, since this type of exceptional child may already have been listed as a slow learner or in other exceptional categories.

The major point to be considered is that the total number of such children far exceeds the capacity of the self-contained classroom in special education. In fact, it would probably be advantageous for the current category system to be somewhat modified to provide appropriate education for all American children. Many problems ensue whenever one attempts to place a particular child in a given category. Children tend to be handicapped in more than one area, and, thus, labeling a child as mentally retarded or emotionally disturbed, for instance, tends to ignore the fact that the child may also possess speech problems or sensory difficulties. A more serious criticism of the current

TABLE 1–1 PERCENTAGES OF HANDICAPPED SCHOOL AGE CHILDREN AND THOSE NOT RECEIVING SPECIAL SERVICE.*

Exceptionalities	*Percentage of School Population, 5 to 19 Years of Age*		*Percentage of Handicapped Not Receiving Special Service*
Speech impaired	3.5		49
Emotionally disturbed	2.0		87
Mentally Retarded	2.3		48
Hard of hearing Deaf	0.5 0.075		79
Crippled or otherwise health impaired	0.5		67 85
Visually impaired	0.1		66
Multihandicapped	0.06		62
Total percentage of school-age exceptionalities	9.035	Total percentage of handicapped not receiving service	62

*Data courtesy of Bureau of Education for the Handicapped, August, 1970.

category system is based on the emotional problems that may result from placing a label on a child. The child labeled "mentally retarded" may in many cases be placed in a divergent system of education that will forever preclude his re-entry into the mainstream of American education. In addition, a child's concept of himself may be damaged considerably if he is placed in a category which has serious derogatory implications. Figure 1–2 indicates how a child's academic performance depends on a variety of factors.

Many children in the public schools are not keeping pace with the academic work of the regular school curriculum, and many also exhibit a variety of problems in making appropriate social adjustments. The causes of such behavior are complex; labeling a child "mentally retarded" or "emotionally disturbed" may be just one aspect of the problem. All behavioral problems tend to involve many factors. Thus, a teacher must assess and evaluate each factor as it contributes to the malfunction of a given child in a particular classroom. The degree to which each factor listed in Figure 1–2 contributes varies from child to child and probably from moment to moment. Some tasks may require more of the *psychomotor* or the *affective processes*. The model simply states that, at any given moment, a particular child will function according to a complex of ecological factors which interact within the social-cultural environment. The model implies the need for an evaluation of each child and an educational prescription written in accordance with the needs, prior experiences, strengths, and weaknesses of each child. The child with impaired vision or hearing requires a particular type of approach, while the child with good vision and hearing but who comes from an environment that is totally alien to current American educational practices requires an en-

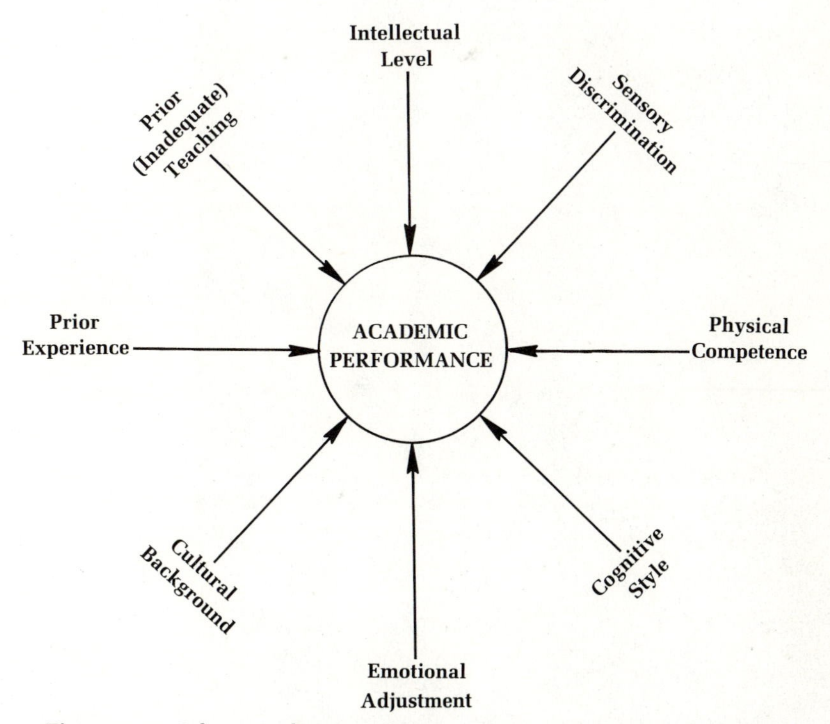

Figure 1–2 Schematic diagram of factors affecting academic performance.

tirely different approach. The relation between the child's exceptionality and all the other influencing factors must be taken into account if appropriate educational procedures are to be instituted.

HISTORICAL BACKGROUND

Interest in the exceptional child extends into the very earliest writings of man. As early as 1500 B.C., when Thebes ruled ancient Egypt, a document entitled The Theban Papyrus was published. This document discussed the care and treatment of individuals whose exceptionalities were intellectual. The development of the care and treatment of exceptionalities should properly be called evolutionary, rather than revolutionary. Primitive man was ambivalent toward deviant individuals. At times, they were regarded as beings cursed by the gods. The term "*idiot*" came into being in ancient Greece and was originally applied to all types of deviance. It literally means peculiar or different. The general tone of the early Greek writings would indicate that the word was used in a somewhat contemptuous fashion. It was fairly common practice in ancient times to abandon the deviant infant on a hillside to die, and the problem of the care and treatment of the adult deviant was thereby lessened.

Figure 1–3 Demonic possession as shown by artistic productions. Detail of Raphael's "Transfiguration." (Courtesy of The Bettmann Archive.)

Figure 1-4 G. Fungai's painting of St. Catherine of Sienna casting the devil out of a woman. (Courtesy of The Bettmann Archive.)

The Romans treated the deviant individual in a more tolerant way. Although the attitude toward the deviant was a paternalistic one, the common fate of many deviants in Rome was to serve as a sort of entertainer or buffoon for the rich and powerful.

Early concern with the deviant was not restricted to the Western World. In ancient China, Confucius wrote about a type of deviant that he called the "weak minded." Confucius also regarded the retarded as having a claim on society, since he felt that society must assume responsibilities for those individuals who were unable to care for themselves.

The coming of Christianity failed to bring about a resolution of the problem of caring for exceptional children. The Justinian Code did attempt to make some provisions for care and treatment, but the law was often ignored. Early attempts to care for the deviant individual centered on the concept of compassion. Such care was typically provided by the monasteries of the time. In general, the word "idiot," which was the term applied most commonly, was reserved for extreme cases. In modern terms, one might say that the ancient world was concerned with the individual who presented an almost totally dependent care pattern. Such individuals would probably be classified by the modern diagnostician as those having IQ's below 50.

During the Middle Ages there was vacillation and, at times, a regression in terms of the attitudes toward and treatment of exceptionality. Exceptional individuals achieved the status of fools and jesters in the royal courts of the day, while some were regarded as beings possessed by the devil. The most common treatment in such cases was the scourging of the individual in an attempt to drive out the devil.

Starting with the twelfth century, the kings of England made the care and treatment of idiots a matter of royal concern in that all such individuals were automatically made wards of the king. Most commonly, a deviant individual possessing certain physical disabilities was employed by the king as a jester or fool. At times, those who were intellectually retarded were regarded as "infants of God."

Although there were periodic attempts in the Middle Ages to enforce legally the care and treatment of exceptional individuals, such persons were frequently seen wandering over the countryside with little assistance being provided for them by the authorities. In other words, they were given the right to beg. This attitude, to some extent, may be observed on the streets of some countries today.

The Protestant Reformation was characterized by an even less enlightened attitude regarding the care and treatment of exceptional individuals. Both Luther and Calvin considered intellectual retardation to be essentially evil and said that individuals so "possessed" were filled with Satan.

The right of care for the deviant was recognized in Belgium in the thirteenth century, when many deviants were taken into the homes of the people. The seventeenth century is noteworthy for the work of Saint Vincent de Paul (1576–1600) and the Sisters of Charity, who founded many homes devoted to the care of intellectual retardates. The famous Bictre was founded at this time. Later, the institution became specialized in the care and treatment of psychiatric exceptionalities.

The modern era began with the work of Pedro Ponce de Leon (1520–1584) in the care of the deaf. The first organized work for the blind was that of Valentine Hauy (1745–1822), who in 1785 established a school for the blind in Paris.

Figure 1–5 Medieval court jester. (Courtesy of The Bettmann Archive.)

Advances in the study of intellectual retardation came later. The first modern case study of work with retardation was that of the well-known case of Victor, the so-called wolf boy. In 1799, Victor was discovered wandering in the woods in the south of France. The child was brought to Paris where Philippe Pinel (1742–1826), an alienist, classified him as an "idiot" and, thus, beyond any hope of rehabilitation. However, Jean Gaspard Itard (1775–1838), a physician, disputed Pinel's opinion and undertook to rear the boy. Itard was convinced of the importance of sensory input and felt that the basic problem with Victor was his prior lack of appropriate sensory input. Itard felt that Victor would be restored to normal functioning if he was provided with intensive sensory experiences.

During the first year of treatment, Victor made little progress, and Itard shifted somewhat in his treatment without ever making any formal admission of the failure of his original theory. After four additional years of treatment, in which Itard sought to teach Victor reading, writing, and speech, Itard gave up and dismissed the boy. Itard felt that his efforts to help had been a total failure.

The French Academy of Science disagreed with Itard regarding the effectiveness of his treatment of Victor. They felt that Itard had made some important modifications in the behavior of the boy. Victor had learned to make relatively fine sensory discriminations between a variety of objects. He also had learned to identify the letters of the alphabet, to read with some comprehension, and to understand the meanings of a large number of words.

The work of Itard was continued by his most famous student, Edward Seguin (1812–1880). Seguin derived many of his ideas concerning the care and treatment of the retarded from one of his teachers, Jean Esquirol (1772–1840). Esquirol was best known for his pioneer work in distinguishing between emotional and intellectual exceptionality. He also realized that there were many levels of retardation.

Seguin spent some 40 years of his life as a teacher, physician, and psychologist, working with intellectual retardation. His major contribution was his development of the "physiological method" of treatment. This approach is essentially devoted to *sensory-motor* training, which will be considered in greater detail in Chapter 6. Seguin established the first successful school exclusively for intellectual retardates in Paris in 1837.

The first residential institution that provided some service for the intellectual retardate was the American Asylum for the Deaf and Dumb, which was established in Hartford, Connecticut, in 1818. The first institution established solely for intellectual retardation was a private institution founded by Dr. Hervey Wilbur in Barre, Massachusetts, in July of 1848. Today every state has at least one institution devoted to the care of intellectually retarded persons.

The education of the mentally retarded in the public schools of America started with the enactment of mandatory legislation in New Jersey in 1911. The next nine states to pass some type of legislation for the schooling of mentally retarded persons were as follows: Minnesota, 1915; New York, 1917; Illinois, 1919; Missouri, 1919; Pennsylvania, 1919; Massachusetts, 1919; Wyoming, 1919; California, 1921; and Connecticut, 1921. By 1952, all the states except Nevada and Montana had passed either mandatory or permissive legislation for the education of intellectual retardates. The pattern of financing varies greatly from state to state. In many states, special reporting of the types of services and the amount of service is required. Most of the states also provide for special training requirements for teachers of mentally retarded students.

AN INFORMATION-PROCESSING MODEL

In order to understand the child as a learner, let us imagine the child as a computer or data-processing organism. Figure 1–6 is an attempt to provide a graphic presentation of the model discussed in this book. It should be seen as an example of one type of input-output model and not as "the" model.

The child first takes in information concerning his environment through one or more of his senses (input), and the information is then processed essentially in a two-stage manner. It is first subjected to what could be called analysis. Analysis is seen as a process in which the incoming data are taken in and organized in a systematic way for retrieval (recall). An essential part of the organization process is the placing of the data in categories or sets. This process may be seen as somewhat similar to the manner in which a librarian places books in a library, so that any book may be found relatively quickly. It is essential that the child be given data, but it is equally important that the data be taken into the child's learning system in such a way that the child will have rapid access to any particular bit of data that is being stored. The second stage of processing is most appropriately seen as a *synthesis*. Synthesis is viewed as the process of taking various bits of information contained in the child's memory (storage) system and putting this variety of information into a new configuration (arrangement) to solve the current problem facing the child. Upon completion of the processing of data, the child then acts

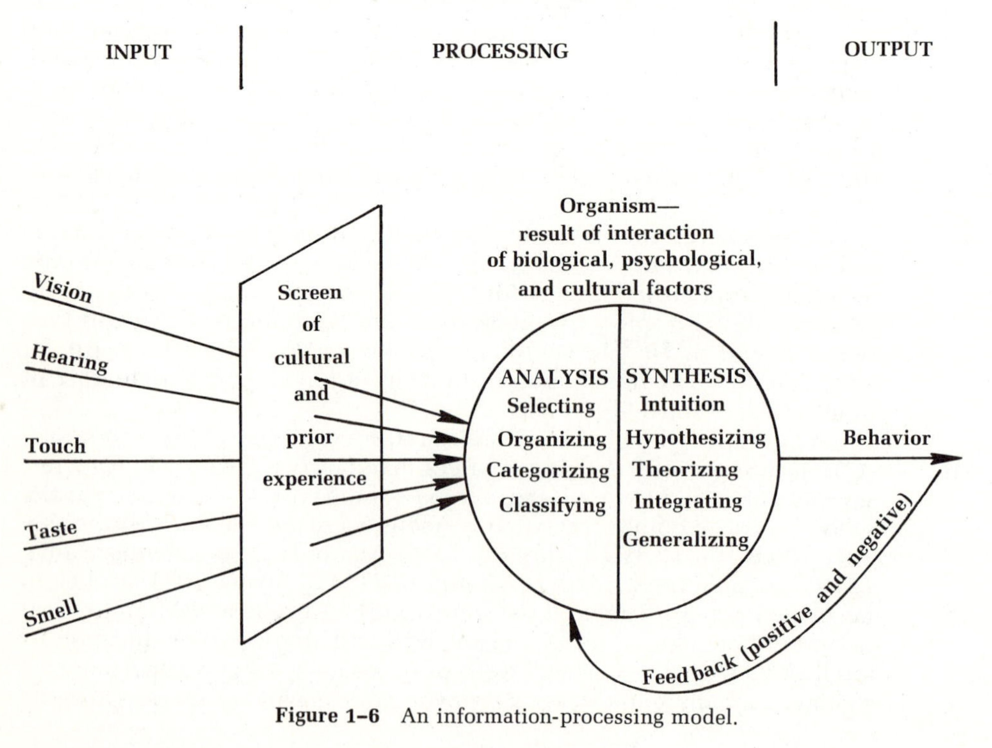

Figure 1–6 An information-processing model.

or behaves (output) in accordance with his analysis and synthesis. The next step in the learning process is for the child to observe the effects of his behavior in terms of his desires and expectations. This process is known as feedback, and, in an important way, this feedback becomes a new input channel. The feedback part of the learning process enables the child to make certain corrections that are needed to cope most adequately with his environment. The above system should be seen as a dynamic one in which all parts are in a state of change in accordance with new information and new syntheses.

An important component of the learning process is the "screen of culture and prior experiences" through which all incoming sensations (input) are filtered. Culture is seen as the broad social-psychological system in which the child lives together with all the prior experiences that have conditioned his perception of reality. In other words, the input portion of a child's learning system is changed not only by the physical component of the organism, but also by the child's equally important prior experiences and the total psychological and social system in which he lives.

The above model may be correlated with a *stimulus-response theory* as follows: (1) the *stimulus* is comparable to the input portion of the model; (2) in more advanced elaborations of the stimulus-response theory, it is now customary to put some sort of intervening variable between the stimulus and the *response*; this portion is comparable to the processing part of the input-output model; (3) the response part of the stimulus-response theory is the same as the output part of the input-output model. In other words, there is little conflict between the basic stimulus-response theoretical model and the input-output model presented here.

The total human organism is always concerned with the environment in which it operates. A child may be viewed as being located at the focus of many interacting forces. The present approach is based upon the notion that three systems (forces) act upon the child at all times and that to understand a child's behavior it is essential to have some knowledge of the effects of these interactions. The three forces are biological, psychological, and cultural. An attempt will be made to take into account the relative contribution of each force to the child's overall functioning. To understand the child, we need to know and understand the specific effect of these forces on each other, both singularly and cumulatively. The teacher must understand how these interactive forces lead to an overall effectiveness or exceptionality with respect to a child's growth and behavior. It would be folly to attempt to consider one force apart from the other two. It is also true that most of our scientific advances which have led to a better understanding of children have involved knowledge of one force acting alone. However, if one wants to understand and to assist a particular child, this book will demonstrate how to attain that goal by utilizing knowledge of the three interactive forces which affect the child.

The Freudian concept of the *id, ego,* and *superego* is somewhat comparable to our concept of the biological, psychological, and cultural forces interacting upon the individual child. A recent study (L'Abate, 1971) defines this view in terms of a three-pronged approach: (a) the *genetic*, internal environment and brain functions represent the biological forces; (b) the developmental and learning functions represent the individual psychological forces; and (c) the ecological functions represent the culture and environment. Biological functions more directly affect the ability of the child to discriminate and to understand the relationships of his sense organs to the environment. The psychological functions relate more directly to the ability of the child to select and to take on cultural reinforcements through such cognitive processes as identification and thinking. The cultural functions relate directly to the interpersonal and social *transactions* of the child with significant others in his environment.

We should always keep in mind, of course, that we are talking about an interaction between, among, and within the three forces at all levels of each force. In order to clarify the reality of the interaction of the three forces in terms of maturational factors, the reader is referred to Figure 1–7. It will be noted that in infancy the biological and cultural forces are of the greatest importance in terms of the child's development. As the child grows biologically, psychological forces become of greater importance. The degree of importance is, in turn, dependent upon the specific culture in which the child is being raised. The psychological force essentially serves as an agent of mediation between the biological and the cultural forces. The relative importance of each force will depend to a great extent on its integrity. The more effective, mature, and optimal the force is, the less dependent the child will be on that particular force. For example, in a biologically healthy child, there will be a maximal growth in both of the other forces. However, if there is any *deficit* or any *dysfunction* in any one of the forces, the other two forces will be affected. Each force has a particular and different function, and it will produce a particular kind of relationship with the other two forces. However, the specific contribution of each force to the child's overall functioning needs to be acknowledged and evaluated. Any method of evaluation that fails to realize the importance of this basic viewpoint is doomed to a fragmented approach to the individual child.

The child is an open system in that he takes in information from his environment, processes it, and behaves in terms of other components of the total system, such as the family and its members. Culture is made up of many component subsystems, the human as well as the physical and environmental factors. It is of value to break our system into its compo-

INFANCY

CHILDHOOD

ADULTHOOD

SENILITY

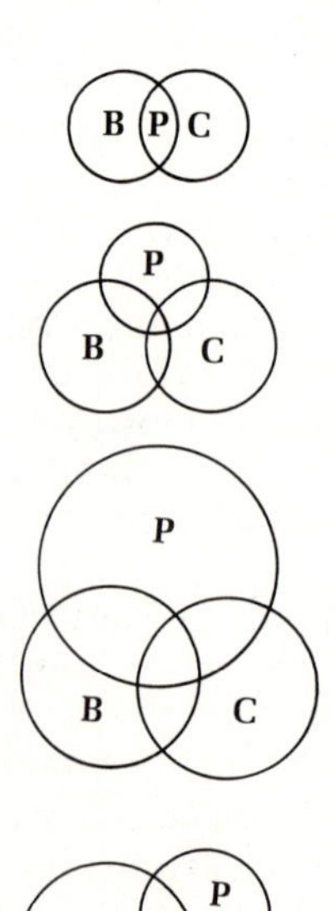

Figure 1–7 Human development as seen from the interaction of biological, *B*, psychological, *P*, and cultural, *C*, forces.

nent parts in order to allow an examination of the relationship of each component to every other component. In other words, it is important to know how each child is a product of biological, psychological, and cultural forces *and* their interactions with one another, so that a change in one force will produce changes in the other two forces. The understanding and the ability to control these specific interactions are central themes of this book. The emphasis is placed on input, processing, output, and feedback as they relate to the above three forces.

The major functions of the biological forces are to facilitate discrimination and selection of incoming information from the cultural environment. This process of input discrimination is based on sensory (visual and auditory), motor, *kinesthetic, olfactory* and *tactile* integration which permits the child to produce reactions or output that will have value in terms of his survival. The major functions of the cultural forces are both human and physical, that is, to stimulate and feed into the biological system the information that will assure survival. The major functions of the psychological forces are to integrate, link, and process the biological and cultural forces in such a way that the individual will survive and hopefully flourish.

The biological forces facilitating input are closely related to the maturation level of the child. Culture, on the other hand, is largely responsible for the intensity and type of stimulation or deprivation (lack of stimulation) that will impinge upon the child. Such influences may range from food to kisses. These, in turn, may determine the rate of a child's maturational growth, as reflected in his output. Both the biological and cultural forces are in a continuous state of interaction between themselves, affecting both the input and output sides of a child's functioning. Each side has a definite relationship to the other, through either feedback, output to input, or the influences of input to output. Any lowering of functioning in one force may produce a lowering of functioning in the other forces. For instance, if there is no dysfunction in the input channels of the eyes and ears, both organs will cooperate together to provide more information. Such information will be transmitted to the output channel, such as the hands, mouth, or legs, provided that they are not impaired.

An example of the effect of a defective channel of input might be that of the blind individual. In this case, one total input modality is blocked. In order to cope with this difficulty, one of the other input modalities needs to be utilized in such a manner as to compensate partially for the lack of vision. The lack of vision will affect the cultural and psychological forces because society tends to react in an atypical manner toward the blind, and this, in turn, causes maladaptation of the psychological component. Thus, it may be seen that at all times there is a dynamic interaction of all the forces. A summary of the interactive forces and their functions is provided in Table 1–2.

The term interaction, as used here, refers to a two-way interchange between two or among all three of the forces. Information circles back to the input side after the occurrence of output. This process is called feedback. *Positive feedback* refers to information which reinforces the organism to continue or to increase the amount of a particular type of behavior. *Negative feedback* indicates an unsatisfactory reaction to a given behavior and tends to reduce the chances of repetition of that behavior. *Feedback* is one of the most important processes of human behavior. It is very important at this stage that this term and its usage be clearly understood by the reader. It refers, in general, to the amount, type, and kind

TABLE 1–2 A SUMMARY OF THE FUNCTIONS OF EACH DEVELOPMENTAL FORCE.

Biological	*Psychological*	*Cultural*
Input	*Mediation of Input-Output*	*Output*
Sense organs	Processing and retrieval of stored memories	Movements
Discrimination	Direction and goal-setting	Actions
Selection	Self-awareness	Words
Intake of information	Self-concept	Signals
Internal stimuli	Self-assertion	Expressions
Thirst	Need to achieve	Productions
Hunger		Communications

of exchange among the three forces. Feedback, then, refers essentially to a self-corrective process which results from our behavior, our observation of the results of our behavior, and thus, our changing or modifying of it. For example, an individual might turn the steering wheel of his car too much to the left. As he notices his car moving too close to the center line, he corrects his direction by steering slightly to the right. The concept of feedback sees behavior as possessing a self-correcting potential that encourages change, process, and progress. Feedback allows for self-correction after the occurrence of output.

THE CONCEPT OF COMPENSATION

The concept of *compensation* is difficult to define. Even though it is used in everyday language and was employed by a few theorists, such as Adler, its theoretical and empirical status is weak. Although it is recognized in everyday life, it has not received the attention that is basic for an understanding of exceptionalities in children. The evidence supporting a process of compensation tends to be observational and impressionistic, and, thus, it leads to suspicion on the part of rigorous scientists. Yet, there is a need to devote some effort to clarifying this concept because its functions are important in understanding and coping with exceptionalities in children.

Essentially, compensation lies in the middle of a continuum in which *coping* and *overcompensation* are, perhaps, the two extremes. If a child does not receive input or cannot express himself through one sensory modality, another modality may take over (compensation). If a component of a developmental force is not functioning properly, other components may assume some or all of its functions. If a child cannot write with his preferred hand, he will learn to write with the other. In contrast, coping is the utilization of a dysfunctioning component in spite of its dysfunction. For example, a stuttering child may force himself to talk and to improve his speech. A child with a slight hearing deficit may strive to listen carefully in order to adjust for his handicap. Overcompensation is an attempt to excel in the very area in which one judges or feels himself to be weak or inadequate, regardless of whether such an inadequacy is real or not. An example of this extreme would be the determination of a person with a wooden leg to become a professional dancer.

An individual's means of compensation may take different forms, such as biological, physiological, anatomical, sexual, psychological, or cultural. The concept of compensation is in some ways related to such concepts as *homeostasis* or *vicariousness.* Homeostasis refers to an attempt by an organism to maintain an equilibrium. Vicariousness refers, for instance, to language being substituted for other kinds of behavior.

All the foregoing concepts relate to exceptionality in that a child may need, at times, to deal with his exceptionality through coping and compensation and, at times, even overcompensation. One of the early formulations of the concept of compensation can be found in the notion of *organic inferiority.* The importance of the concept of inferiority may be traced back to Alfred Adler's original idea that organic inferiority brings about certain defense mechanisms which serve as compensation for an individual's deficits. Dreikêrs, as quoted in Cruickshank (1963), stated that

> **the life style of each individual is not only influenced by the disability but in turn determines the final effect of any physical disability. The life style is the outcome of the experiences from the beginning of life . . . successes, failures, relationships, endowments, environment, physique . . . are all important, but most important of all is: "What does the individual do with these?"**

It is difficult to substantiate empirically and with rigorous finality the concept of compensation. However, it does appear that the preceding ideas are consistent with observations. The attitude which an individual (and society) assumes toward his disability ultimately determines whether or not it will become a handicap for him.

Lowenfield (1963), in discussing compensation as it concerns the visually impaired, stated that "the assumption that the loss of one sense is compensated by a more or less automatic improvement in the acuity of other senses is one of longstanding perseverance." Lowenfield explained this assumption, in part, according to the "wish to have nature act according to justice and thereby relieve one of feelings of guilt or responsibility to help." His survey of empirical evidence for the blind person's compensation in other modalities essentially questions whether such superiority in substituting modalities is present. Lowenfield concluded that any increased "efficiency of the blind in interpreting the sensory data perceived must be the result of attention, practice, adaptation, and increased use of the remaining faculties." He left the door open, however, since the evidence is not negative but simply unavailable. "This indicates that the last word on the problem of sensory compensation may not yet have been spoken. There may be processes in operation which so far have eluded experimentation."

Meyerson (1963) developed a theory of adjustment to handicaps within the framework of Lewin's field theory in which he outlined the concepts of compensation and overcompensation. Meyerson's assumptions were: (1) a disability is not an objective thing in a person but a social value judgment; (2) the physique is a tool, a social stimulus, which arouses expectations for behavior by influencing the person's perception of himself through comparison and other expectations; (3) developmental expectations vary according to age; and (4) a cultural point of view would also make a difference. These assumptions should help in diagnosis, treatment, education, and rehabilitation of exceptionalities in children.

In further elaboration of the input-output model, if the input is zero or near zero, the output will be zero or nearly so, unless compensation occurs. Thus, if a child cannot see to read or to recognize other persons, he must find other ways of reading or recognizing if these functions are to take place. The input must be provided through a modality other than the eyes. Consequently, the hands can compensate for the inadequacy of the eyes, as they do in providing the means of learning to read Braille. The ears can compensate for the inferiority of the eyes by developing the ability to recognize persons by the sound of their voices, and so on. Compensation in this sense is relevant to understanding and helping exceptionalities in children.

Ways and means must be found to compensate for one input deficiency through the use of another input modality. This viewpoint appears to suggest a teaching method which emphasizes a child's assets rather than his liabilities. If a child's eyes do not function, his ears and hands should be used in a learning situation. In this respect, one of the major areas of controversy concerns what steps should be implemented and what remediation procedures and types of habilitation for these children should be recommended. Should one direct his teaching to the asset or attempt to treat the liability? On general grounds, the question is meaningless. The overall functioning of a child is of the greatest importance, so that even the extreme proponents of one view will probably agree that both aspects need consideration. Each aspect is largely a matter of emphasis and personal preference selectively supported by evidence marshaled in favor of either position. In general, the major approach suggested in this book will be one which favors primarily a child's assets, within the realistic limitations of the type and extent of his assets and liabilities. Deaf children are taught in asset areas through visual or tactile information, just as blind children are taught to feel and to hear in order to compensate for their lack of vision. Of course, multisensorial approaches, those using all available channels, need to be considered, while determining the cost and efficiency of the methods. On logical, therapeutic, and empirical grounds, there are sufficient reasons to suggest that, at least initially, one pay attention to the assets of the child in order to provide a feeling of success and mastery and, thus, improve the self-concept of the child with exceptionalities. By the same token, initial emphasis on a liability may very well increase feelings of failure and frustration, resulting in damage to the child's self-concept.

Another example of evidence to support the point of view favoring rehabilitation in which the child's assets are stressed comes from studies in primate learning. All attempts to teach apes to talk have been met by failure largely because of the limits set by the chimp's biological equipment. In other words, teaching was confined to the liability area. However, as soon as teaching was transferred to the chimp's asset area, namely, visual-motor functioning through sign language (Gardner and Gardner, 1969), they learned approximately 60 words.

The placement of emphasis on one's assets does not suggest that liability areas should be ignored. Weak modalities should be considered in terms of extent and type of liability, available routes to improve them, and technological and practical means to exploit them.

Strategically, therefore, it is advisable to focus first on the assets and then to direct attention to the liabilities, as long as this approach does not interfere with the maximal utilization of the assets. Most classroom teachers are oriented toward verbal and symbolic operations. Consequently, children who are superior in visual-motor problem-solving may show consistently lower educational achievement and a great many behavioral problems (L'Abate et al., 1970). It is obvious, of course, that a child who cannot walk should be helped to walk with crutches and a wheelchair. Clearly, here, the deficit is compensated for. However, even in such an example, one should consider so-called motivational factors, such as a child's desire to be ambulatory. Emphasis can only occur within the context of the child's overall functioning and, in reality, no dichotomy of assets and liabilities can be defended. Both aspects of functioning need consideration, either at different times or in parallel and with double-barreled approaches.

THE SELF-CONCEPT

An important variable to be considered in any discussion of the exceptional child is that of the *self-concept.* The self-concept is not a unitary factor. It should be seen as multifactoral, consisting of at least four major components: as related to the physical-activity area; as related to the academic-intellectual area; as related to the interpersonal area; and as seen from the intrapersonal area (Curtis, 1964).

The self-concept is basically the way in which one perceives himself and also how he thinks others in his environment see him. The self-con-

Figure 1–8 Self-concept is the way one perceives himself and how he thinks others perceive him. ("Child Before Mirror" by S. Daynes-Grassot.) (Courtesy of The Bettmann Archive.)

cept is seen as an evolving process (Allport, 1937). The idea that the self-concept is nonexistent at birth and is differentiated out of the *phenomenal field* in the course of development seems to be generally agreed upon (Taylor, 1960). Piaget, an important Swiss psychologist to be reviewed later in this book, stated that there is no sense of self—no differentiation from the external world, no boundaries between the self and the not-self for the infant, and that the self-concept or sense of his own ego develops slowly through early childhood (Piaget, 1928, 1930, 1932).

The boundaries of the self and not-self apparently begin to be differentiated as the result of exploratory activity and experience with the body by approximately the sixth or seventh month (Murray, 1938). The remainder of the process of self-concept development is generally believed to be largely social in nature, involving identification with others, *introjection* from others, and, finally, expansion of the circle of ego involvement (Murphy, 1947). Murphy stated that the self-picture is usually fairly well integrated by the end of the third year of life.

The concern with self and its relation to motivation did not achieve academic respectability until rather recent times in the writings of William James, and more particularly with Hilgard (1949). In general, it appears that self theory centers on two basic concepts: first, in order to understand a person properly we need to know how he perceives the world around himself; second, we need to have an understanding of how he perceives himself. The following quotation provides an adequate framework in which to view the problem of self-concept as related to the exceptional child:

> **The self-concept of the self-structure may be thought of as an organized configuration of the perceptions of the self which are admissible to awareness. It is composed of such elements as the perceptions of one's characteristics and abilities; the percepts and concepts of the self in relation to others and the environment; the value qualities which are perceived as associated with experiences and objectives; and goals and ideals which are perceived as having positive or negative valence.**
>
> **As long as the *self-gestalt* is firmly organized and no contradictory material is even dimly perceived, then positive self-feelings may exist, the self may be seen as worthy and acceptable, and conscious; the conscious tension is minimal. Behavior is consistent with the organized hypotheses and concepts of the self-structure (Rogers, 1951).**

To understand the relation of the self-concept to the nature and behavior of the exceptional child, the following propositions are provided:

1. The self-concept is a learned perceptual system that is governed by the same principles of organization that govern perceptual objects.
2. The self-concept regulates behavior.
3. A person's awareness of himself may bear little relation to external reality, as in the case of psychotic individuals. Logical conflicts may exist in the self-concept for the external observer, but these are not necessarily psychological conflicts for the person observed.
4. The self-concept is a differentiated but organized system, so that even negatively valued aspects of it may be defended by the individual in order to maintain his individuality. The self-concept may be more highly valued than the physical organism, as in the case of a soldier who sacrifices himself in battle in order to preserve the positively valued aspects of his self-concept: courage and bravery.
5. The total framework of the self-concept determines how stimuli are to be perceived, and whether old stimuli are to be remembered or forgotten.

In other words, the self-concept may be seen as a factor which, to a considerable extent, governs the individual's view of himself and his relation to the world about him. The exceptional individual, owing to malperceptions of himself and of people with whom he comes in contact, frequently tends to develop a poor self-concept which, in turn, makes it difficult for him to perform adequately.

OTHER APPROACHES TO EXCEPTIONALITY BASED ON THE INFORMATION-PROCESSING THEORY

Models of psychological functioning based on the information-processing theory are numerous and will probably become increasingly popular. The ultimate fate of each model will depend on its verifiability; that is, whether it lends itself readily to experimental testing and to educational applications. The advanced and complex model of Beery (1968) offers considerable promise. The structure of intellect model of Guilford (1967) offers some interesting ideas in terms of application of the model to educational programming, as interpreted by Meeker (1969). Briefly, the Guilford model assumes three major independent dimensions—operations, content, and functioning. The components of these dimensions collectively yield 120 different elements of intellectual functioning, making this model one of the most comprehensive. This model can also be reduced to an information-processing theory framework. Meeker (1969) included three sources of input (figural, symbolic, and semantic), four channels of communication (tactile, visual, kinesthetic, and auditory), and processors (cognition, memory, evaluation, and convergent and divergent productions). As encouraging and empirical as this model may be, it should be noted that all the materials used to develop it are of the group-administered, paper and pencil type. Consequently, the visual input modality is used exclusively, while the child's hands are used to answer presumably multiple-choice questions. Meeker (1969) recognized that "the auditory and kinesthetic modes especially should receive recognition along with the visual modes." The inclusion of only the visual modality is a serious shortcoming which reduces considerably the application of this model to individual differences resulting from the interaction of sex, age, and socioeconomic considerations with certain types of behavioral and physical exceptionalities.

Other models concerned with the processing of information are those of McCarthy (undated), who developed a whole taxonomy of observable classroom behaviors and teaching techniques for groups and individuals based on information processing. McCarthy differentiated between visual-motor and auditory-verbal deficits on the receptive, associative, and expressive levels, making use of the model developed by Osgood (1953), which in turn has been utilized for the construction of the Illinois Test of Psycholinguistic Ability (ITPA) (Kirk et al., 1968). Schiller and Deigman (1969) also used Osgood's model to create a framework for an evaluation of learning disabilities and to coordinate remedial instruction. From basic dimensions of auditory and visual decoding, auditory-vocal and visual-motor association, and vocal and motor encoding with sensory, perceptual, *syntactic,* and *semantic* levels, they expanded into 24 different combinations with specific test instruments or subscales tapping each function. They attempted to match each of these 24 dysfunctions with various available approaches for remediation. The above approach is speculative and at the present time is supported by only one case study. However, their aim is the same as the authors of this text, that is, to make evident the fact that specific diagnosis leads to specific prescriptive remediation. Without the guarantee of such reciprocity between evaluation and remediation, there would not be any valid understanding and control.

Sabatino (1968) also presented a scheme relating information-processing behavior to learning disabilities. His model was tested by the Wechsler Intelligence Scale for Children (WISC), the Wide Range Achievement Test (WRAT), the Test of Auditory Perception (TAP), the Bender Visual-Motor Gestalt (BVMG), Birch's Auditory-Visual Integration Test, and the Southern California Test of Motor Accuracy. Sabatino used his results to support a view of learning disabilities that consists of heterogenous, multidimensional, etiological categories.

CONCLUSION

In summary, the purpose of this text is to provide the regular classroom teacher as well as the special education teacher with a knowledge and understanding of the basic problems involved in working with all exceptionalities. This is not expected to be a definitive treatise for the educational specialist. However, it is hoped that a teacher in reading this book will gain a greater insight into children who have a variety of problems. We feel that the regular classroom and special education teacher will be expected to cope with the majority of exceptionalities in children. The total number of these exceptionalities is simply too large for any segregated kind of educational approach to be effective. In such a situation, the attitudes of the teacher are important. It is hoped that as a result of reading this text, the teacher will gain a greater degree of understanding of the principles of human dynamics and human behavior and will become adept in a firm and practical application of them.

Section II

BIOLOGICAL AND PHYSICAL FACTORS

CHAPTER 2

BRAIN DAMAGE AND PHYSICAL DEFECTS

(Courtesy of The Devereux Foundation, Devon, Pennsylvania.)

If a child has any biological defects, he is likely to function inadequately. The impairment of a child or infant's ability to receive and utilize information from his environment is probably the major result of any defect. Such types of damage are called *endogenous,* a term which will be used throughout this chapter to refer to factors existing within the child. Endogenous biological deficits which lower the infant's ability to cope with his environment inevitably result in input reduction. Input reduction includes: (a) lower recognition; (b) restricted range of discrimination; (c) selective and shortened attention span, at times with *perseveration;* (d) decreased awareness of surrounding cues and signals; and (e) irregular or uneven sensory integration.

In this chapter, we shall discuss biologically determined deficits which result from damage to the central nervous system of the embryo or fetus. Such deficits are the effects of various conditions of infection, *toxemia, anoxemia,* metabolic disorders, dietary problems, and *traumas* which can result in a variety of organic defects and varying degrees of behavioral dysfunctioning.

Some disorders resulting from biological defects are less obvious than those previously mentioned and are somewhat difficult to understand, such as certain forms of *autism, schizophrenia,* intellectual retardation, and a variety of learning deficits. Russell (1970) indicated how various levels of biological functioning (biochemical, electrophysiological, and anatomical) affect behavior and how the external environment may influence metabolic processes, as in the case of nutrition. He observed that "behavior is very sensitive to changes induced in the body's internal chemical milieu." Biological forces do not exist in a vacuum. They continually interact with the cultural, physical, and human environments. It is the purpose of this chapter to consider extreme psychological reactions as an outcome of the biological forces.

Chess, Thomas, and Birch (1967) emphasized the "excessively maladapted temperament-environment interaction" as a decisive component in the development of behavioral problems in children. The child's temperament by itself does not produce a behavioral disturbance. The disturbance results from a particular temperament pattern interacting maladaptively with significant factors in the child's environment.

The development of behavioral problems, such as predominantly negative withdrawal from new stimuli, nonadaptability or slow adaptability to change, frequent negative mood, and predominantly intense reactions, very often results from the continuation of irregularities in biological functioning.

THE BRAIN AND BRAIN DAMAGE

The term *brain damage* is difficult to define precisely. Verville (1967) referred to "cerebral dysfunction as any damage to the central nervous system in the fetus or neonate that results in varying degrees of dysfunctioning." In order to clarify the present approach to the occurrence of biological deficits, the functioning of the central nervous system must be understood. Tapp and Simpson (1968) provided such an overview, stressing the significance of brain growth and development from the viewpoints of embryological, fetal, postnatal, cellular, biochemical, electrophysiological, and functional growth patterns. The formation of *myelin* (the covering of the nerves in the central nervous system) is a major factor contributing to the increase in brain weight from infancy to adulthood. The pattern of myelin development may be considered an index of the functional development of different parts of the brain. According to Tapp and Simpson, the brain is designed to regulate the organism's behavior in the presence of many stimuli that are continuously influencing the organism at any given moment. In order to understand fully the central nervous system, it is necessary to understand its complex aspects. For the purposes of this book, however, it is sufficient to note that various portions of the brain perform different functions with regard to taking in information, processing it, and acting upon it in terms of output.

The portion of the brain called the *neocortex* is of particular importance because it controls a number of the behaviors of the organism. Much research has indicated that considerable damage to the neocortex in early life may have no appreciable effect on the child's abilities to discriminate, see, taste, touch, and so on.

An important portion of the brain is called the *reticular formation.* It is located in the brain stem and appears to be involved primarily in the regulation and general state of awareness of the nervous system. Evidence also indicates that the reticular formation is the monitoring system for incoming and outgoing data. Other areas of the brain affect the emotions and feelings of an organism. These functions may be primarily influenced by two parts of the brain, the *rhinencephalon* and the *hypothalamus.* The *cerebral cortex* in the human being provides spatial and temporal integration of sensory and motor data.

A behavioral dysfunction may be the direct result of brain damage or may occur in conjunction with brain damage. It is important to determine the cause of the behavioral problem, so that appropriate treatment may be prescribed for each child. To know exactly what is disordered, how it is disordered, and what is the appropriate treatment are basic goals of studying brain damage. *Chromosomal anomalies,* defective genes, and *congenital* defects may cause abnormalities of function and appearance which may, in turn, directly relate to the behavioral patterns adopted by the child. Any child having an organic defect will probably encounter an uphill struggle in coping with the stresses of society.

The most typical organic defects are blindness, deafness, intellectual retardation, and cerebral dysfunctioning. The presence of an organic impairment does not automatically imply the presence of a behavioral dysfunction. Many children may show normal development and behavior regardless of their physical disabilities. This point is clearly demonstrated by the achievement of some children trained in schools for the blind and deaf and by the normal lives of epileptic children who have an appropriate home environment and whose epilepsy is controlled with medication.

Haywood (1968) distinguished nine kinds of brain disorders as follows: physical trauma, metabolic dysfunction, toxicity, degenerative brain disease, demyelinating disease, malformations, cerebral vascular disease, convulsive disorders, and *neoplasms.* Of greater significance is his statement that

> **in addition to considering the location of a particular brain lesion, it is beginning to be apparent that each of these particular etiological conditions may produce its peculiar and identifiable behavioral consequences.**

Although it is difficult to define adequately the term brain damage, it may be viewed as a dysfunction in the physical component of the child's biological forces, so that the physical component may be out of phase, partially working, or not working at all. This definition applies only to children in whom there exists a definite and identifiable brain abnormality. In reality, determining for a particular child whether or not a behavioral deficit has resulted from brain damage is the major problem.

THE RELATIONSHIP BETWEEN ORGANIC DEFECTS AND BEHAVIORAL DYSFUNCTIONS

Behavioral dysfunctions in children may be defined as consistent deviations from normally accepted patterns of behavior. They may also be described as responses to stimuli which will prevent the child from succeeding in a task that he should ordinarily be able to accomplish or as responses which are considered socially unacceptable. Bender (1949) maintained that organic injuries create situations that are conducive to psychological maladjustments. Such injuries may create tensions because they inhibit the child's ability to relate adequately to his environment. Organic impairment makes an individual vulnerable to certain environmental situations which might precipitate behavioral maladjustments. This relationship between a child's brain and his behavior will be described in this section.

An individual's biological forces are a particularly sensitive source of behavioral dysfunctioning, with the central nervous system as the focal point of the disorder. An organic impairment, such as a brain *lesion,* manifests itself externally in some characteristic form of behavioral disorder which is determined by the particular location of the cerebral lesion. Based on this idea, Broca (1861), Sherrington (1933), Halstead (1947), Reitan (1962), and Sperry (1968) developed a theory of localization of functions. According to this theory, specific areas of the brain have specific functions. Malformation, underdevelopment, disease, and gross injury to the brain are etiological conditions which often result in retardation and personality disturbances. The particular disorder depends on the area of the brain which has been damaged. Reitan demonstrated that focal lesions of the left cerebral hemisphere caused a patient to have a lower verbal IQ score than visual-motor score on the Wechsler Adult Intelligence Scale (WAIS). Patients with focal lesions of the right cerebral hemisphere scored lower on visual-motor skills than on verbal ones. Neuropsychologists assume from such evidence that verbal functioning is mediated largely by the left cerebral hemisphere and that visual-motor performance is mediated primarily by the right cerebral hemisphere. Another important distinction concerning the functions of specific brain areas was made by Netter (1962). He determined that lesions just anterior to the *fissure of Rolando* impair motor-expressive functions to a greater degree than sensory-receptive functions. The opposite is true of lesions which exist just posterior to the fissure of Rolando. To summarize, experiments have shown that organic damage to the left cerebral hemisphere may cause verbal deficits, while damage to the right cerebral hemisphere may manifest itself in motor deficits. Damage to the anterior portion of the brain might impair expressive ability (output), and damage to the posterior portion might impair sensory input functions.

Frequently, brain injuries will seriously affect the motor, perceptual, cognitive, and emotional functions of the child. Some noticeable symptoms of brain damage in a child are perseveration, distractibility, disorganization, motor incoordination, hyperactivity, emotional instability, insecurity, and mental deficiencies (Beck, 1961). Many studies of the brain-injured child present similar listings of symptoms, although different terminology may be used. Such lists have been compiled by Strauss and Lehtinen (1947), Bender (1949), Goldstein (1959), Eisenberg (1964), and Birch (1964). The characteristics of what was previously called the *Strauss syndrome,* hyperkinesis, distractibility, perseveration, perceptual disturbances, and poor impulse control, have become the stereotyped symptomology of the brain-damaged child.

The symptoms of the Strauss syndrome do seem to occur in many children; however, investigation often shows no evidence of cerebral injury. The behavioral results of brain damage are often diverse and range from no apparent behavioral disturbance to a serious disorganization of social, intellectual, and interpersonal functioning which may be almost indistinguishable from the symptoms of childhood psychosis. Such diversity has lead investigators to form a variety of opinions about the relationship between brain damage and behavioral dysfunctions. Based on the work of Penfield and Roberts (1959) and Halstead (1947) and his students, Haywood (1968) concluded that "it is now possible to make reliable generalizations regarding the effects of focal brain lesions upon specific forms of observable and measurable behavior." Haywood also acknowledged, however, that a large number of variables limit one's ability to generalize with regard to such a conclusion.

Michal-Smith and Morgenstern (1965) suggested that brain damage may affect psychological functioning in at least three ways: (1) by reducing the ability to transduce (that is, the conversion of received information from one sensory modality to another); (2) by lowering the ability to integrate information; and (3) by neural sensory overloading (that is, a breakdown in reception whenever two or more types of information are received). The last two effects may be considered associative disturbances (Osgood, 1957). These are internal, mediating disturbances that will alter any input-output relationship. Several studies support the theory of Michal-Smith and Morgenstern. Clements and Peters (1962) pointed out that symptoms other than the Strauss syndrome do occur and that their causative factors may also vary.

Goldstein (1939) stated that "the question of relationship between the symptoms and disturbances of the brain matter's function is by no means as simple as often has been thought; indeed, one can say that it has become increasingly problematical." In addition, Bayley (1955) indicated that the development of children with organic problems depends on acceptance by their families and by society rather than on the kinds or extent of organic factors. Individuals having cerebral damage often develop compensatory skills and defenses which may lessen the effects of the original damage. Organic factors may well be outweighed by the psychodynamic factors involving failure and success.

As noted in the preceding discussion, investigators vary in their ideas concerning the relationship between cerebral injury and behavioral dysfunctions. Among those finding a definite relationship are Benton (1962) and Graham (1962), who described it as a continuum. The findings of Ernhart et al. (1963) suggested that there are systematic differences in the outcomes of injuries, depending upon the individual's age at the time of injury. Darke (1944) found a continuum of brain damage resulting from the degree and duration of anoxia at birth. Pasamanick (1960) described a continuum of reproductive causality in which brain damage occurred during prenatal and perinatal periods, leading to a gradient of injuries extending from fetal and neonatal death to cerebral palsy, epilepsy, and intellectual retardation.

There are a number of reasons for the different opinions concerning the relationship between brain damage and behavioral dysfunctioning. A basic area of disagreement is the issue of specific as opposed to diffuse brain damage. There are differences in the definition of terms, and there is a tendency when conducting a study to concentrate on a specific area without relating it to the general problems at hand. There is also the inclination to consider the symptoms first and thereby assume brain damage. This procedure is somewhat unavoidable, since one can often only speculate as to the actual brain damage, as inferred indirectly from an *electroencephalogram* (EEG), until an autopsy is possible. The many variables whose affects on behavior cannot be immediately determined also contribute to the differences in opinion. They include the child's age when the damage occurred, the duration of damage, the child's age at the time of examination, the focus or amount of damage, and, as previously mentioned, such factors as the environmental conditions and temperament of the child.

Kessler (1966) stated that there should not be a dichotomy between organic and functional conditions. The intellectual retardate and the brain-damaged child have feelings and internal conflicts; they experience anxiety and employ defense mechanisms just as children without organic defects do. The emotional problems may be concurrent with the organic condition, secondary to it, or coincidental. Some functional conditions are an indirect result of an organic defect. A child with a convulsive disorder may behave asocially because of his dread of a seizure. Another child may become aggressive and antisocial because of inconsistency in parental discipline, caused by parental anxiety about the convulsions.

Some behavioral dysfunctions which are primarily psychological in nature may have an organic origin or may be influenced by genetic factors. The expression of psychological problems may be affected by an inherited constitution, which is organic in a broad sense of the word. For example, a child with a sensitive *autonomic nervous system* may develop psychosomatic complaints as a result of traumas. A child with a predisposition to allergies may develop an allergy under stress, or an individual with a mixed cerebral dominance may develop a reading handicap when psychological conflicts arise. A child with a spastic bladder may develop bedwetting, even though this condition can occur more often without an organic cause.

It is evident that the behavioral symptoms of brain damage overlap with other disorders, such as a childhood schizophrenia and intellectual retardation. It is not only difficult to separate a child's defect from his adaptation to it, but one cannot always discern which is the symptom and which is the underlying cause. Although the relationship between brain damage (an organic defect) and behavioral dysfunctions is not clear and is complicated by varying opinions, those in the field of special education must continually try to understand this relationship. In doing so, diagnosis, treatment, and special education programs may be carried out more effectively.

GENETICS AND EXCEPTIONALITIES

Any study of the problems of exceptionality should involve a consideration of genetic factors as they relate to the child's development. It is probably fruitless to attempt to arrive at any precise ratio between the effects of nature and nurture. The nature-nurture controversy presents a basic problem in that it questions how much of the variability observed in a group of individuals in a particular environment is attributable to hereditary differences. It also concerns itself with the extent to which the basic biological component can be modified by systematic changes in the environment.

Generally, it is wise to use a less rigorous approach to the nature-nurture problem by simply stating that the genetic component probably provides the framework within which the individual may evolve in a number of ways. In other words, the genes provide a limiting set of qualifications (Dobzhansky, 1972). Fuller and Thompson (1960) concisely concluded that "heredity is the capacity to utilize an environment in a particular way." It should be pointed out that the genetic baseline varies from trait to trait and from environment to environment. Some genetic traits would require a very unusual environment if their effects were not to be made evident in the child (Allen and Gibson, 1961).

A major reason for difficulty in understanding genetics and exceptionality is that most traits are determined by more than one gene. The old Mendelian model of one gene for one trait is far too simplistic to explain adequately the occurrence of various types of anomalies. Heredity refers to those traits acquired from parents as the result of the action of a single gene or a complex of genes. The genetic process becomes more complicated if the child acquires one or more genes that differ from those of his parents. These changed genes are due to spontaneous mutations or to some agent in the environment that causes a mutation. Thus, a characteristic may be genetic, but not inherited. Mutations are a common happening, and in some situations their frequencies may be increased. The term *innate* is used to denote mutations plus those factors present at birth which are the results of genetic components inherited from the parents. A common term, *congenital,* refers to any and all conditions present in the infant at birth. An additional term, *constitutional,* refers to the two preceding terms collectively plus any additions made after birth. The constitutional element is the sum total of all physiological or *somatic factors*. To clarify the prior statements, think of the terms as a sequence of additions. The base term is heredity. To this, mutations are added and this equals the innate factors. Next, factors transmitted to the child in the uterus are combined with the preceding ones to yield congenital factors. Finally, alterations added after birth yield the final, collective term, constitutional.

The basic unit of function in genetics is the *gene*. At present, the number of genes involved is unknown; however, according to Stern (1960), the number is probably in the range of 2000 to 50,000. The gene has the ability to maintain its own identity and to duplicate itself. The gene serves as a type of master blueprint and not as a direct model; that is, the genetic trait is duplicated by an indirect route (Stansfield, 1969).

The genes are closely organized into units which are called *chromosomes*. Chromosomes are in the nucleus of each cell in the body, and always come in pairs. It seems that the genes are lined up on the paired chromosomes in such a manner that the gene is across from its twin on the other chromosome. In some cases, the pairs of genes are not identical and are given the name *alleles*. The male cell contains 22 matched pairs plus the X and Y chromosomes. The female differs in that her twenty-third pair consists of two X chromosomes. The X and Y chromosomes are called sex chromosomes, while all others are termed autosomes. During the formation of egg and sperm, the pairs of chromosomes separate, so that at fertilization the new organism receives one set of chromosomes from one parent and one set from the other.

Genes are subdivided into dominant and recessive types. The dominant gene generally determines a characteristic by itself, while the recessive gene usually requires more than one gene in order to be expressed. An excellent example of a genetically determined disease is *Huntington's chorea*. In tracing the descendants of patients who had Huntington's chorea, it was found that roughly one half of them developed the disease. Offspring of the normal descendants will have normal children, but the affected descendants will produce children half of whom will eventually show the chorea. The choreic individual who marries a normal person will give his defective gene to half of his offspring and a normal gene to the other half. Children who inherit the choreic gene from one parent and a normal gene from the other parent will develop the disease because of the dominance of the choreic gene. The tragedy of this disease is that it does not manifest itself until approximately the age of 36 (Pearson and Kley, 1957; Winchester, 1966).

A large group of conditions known as inborn errors of metabolism are thought to be caused by genetic defects. An outstanding example of this type of error is *phenylketonuria* (PKU). Contrary to the case of Huntington's chorea, PKU is due to the inheritance of recessive genes. In the case of a dominant gene, it is necessary for only one defective gene to be present in order to transmit the defect. In the case of a recessive gene, however, the defective gene must be present in both parents and be transmitted to their offspring in order for the defect to be expressed (Allen, 1958; Stansfield, 1969). Some interesting facts are known about PKU. Children born with PKU, if allowed to develop without proper dietary treatment, tend to show a severe intellectual retardation and very rarely produce children. Thus, the parents of PKU children are free of the evidence of this defect. In genetic terminology, they are called *carriers*. A carrier is an individual who possesses only one recessive gene for a defect and, consequently, shows no evidence of it. According to the Mendelian ratio, if both parents possess this recessive gene they will probably produce about one in four children with evidence of PKU. Jarvis (1963) conducted a study of 266 families of PKU children and found that the incidence of PKU was approximately 25 per cent of the births. The overall incidence of PKU is about one in 25,000 births.

Microcephaly is thought to be the result of a recessive gene. A study by Book et al. (1953) indicated that parents of microcephalics seem to be moderately intellectually impaired. The authors of this study stated that it is quite probable that recessive genes in this gene pool contribute to the middle and lower grades of mental deficiency.

According to Stansfield (1969), three conditions seemingly indicate the presence of a genetic dependent disease: (1) statistical agreement with Mendelian expectancies for familial incidence and population frequencies, (2) complete concordance in identical twins, and (3) either an elevated rate of *consanguinous* marriages for rare recessive diseases or an appropriate pedigree for dominant transmission.

Simple dominant or recessive genes cannot explain the observed fact of the variability of intelligence. One explanation of this variability might be found in a multifactorial concept; that is, intelligence may be the result of a large number of randomly assorted influences working together (Stansfield, 1969; Burt, 1972). This type of phenomenon results in the famous bell-shaped curve distribution of IQ scores. The genetic hypothesis which fits the observed distribution of IQ scores is one based on *polygenic* factors. Quantitative traits are usually governed by many genes (perhaps 10 to 100 or more), each contributing such a small amount to the *phenotype* that their individual effects cannot be detected by Mendelian methods. Genes of this nature are called *polygenes* (Stansfield, 1969). We are, thus, led to believe that the factors which determine normal intelligence also determine abnormal intelligence. The polygenic concept is recognized by many authorities as a mode of explanation for the 75 per cent of all defectives who are classified as familial (Allen, 1958; Burt, 1972; Dobzhansky, 1970, 1972).

Many attempts have been made to investigate the inheritance of intelligence in man, the earliest method being that of pedigree studies. The first such study was conducted by Galton (1869). Subsequent studies by Dugdale (1877) and Goddard (1912) have erred in a manner similar to Galton's because they did not distinguish between the effects of heredity and environment. It is now generally believed that children inherit not only their parents' genes, but also their parents' culture (Burt, 1972; Dobzhansky, 1972). Many researchers have developed a distrust of the use of the pedigree method, but Kallman (1958) has shown that it is possible to use a modification of this technique to gain general insights into the probability of occurrence of some types of retardation.

The next major genetic approach to be devised was that of correlational studies, such as those conducted by Pearson (1904). Results of this method may not be reliable, since a correlation between the IQ scores of relatives does not indicate that heredity is more important than environment in determining the amount of similarity of family members.

Research has suggested that more than one genetic mechanism may operate in mental retardation. In a study by Roberts (1952), the distribution of IQ's of 562 siblings of high-grade and low-grade mental defectives was plotted. The data revealed that the mean IQ of the siblings of the low-grade individuals was about 20 points higher than that of the siblings of the high-grades. The distribution of IQ's for the siblings of the low-grade defectives was actually similar to that of the general population. These data offer strong support for the hypothesis that two different genetic mechanisms underlie mental retardation. It may be that *dominant genes* are associated with low-grade mental retardation and polygenes with high-grade mental retardation.

Studies of adopted children have been used as a mode of investigating the relationship of heredity and environment to intelligence. The earlier studies lacked the necessary scientific controls to examine properly this question (Bayley, 1955); however, the studies of Burks (1960) and Leahy (1935) produced relevant results. The basic concept of their investigations was the hypothesis that adoptive children should be less like their foster parents than natural children are like their parents. Both studies indicated a much higher correlation in intelligence scores between natural children and their parents than between adoptive children and their adoptive parents. Later findings tend to confirm these results (Winchester, 1966).

As early as 1875, Galton pointed out the value of using twins in the study of the nature-nurture problem. All twin studies before 1950 should be viewed with caution since proper controls were not employed (Price, 1950). The status of twin studies was summarized in 1950 by Price: "In all probability the net effect of most twin studies has been the understatement of the significance of heredity in the medical and behavioral sciences."

Current studies of twins make use of the Wechsler Intelligence Scale for Children (WISC) in which the analysis is based on the various subtest scores as well as the verbal and visual-motor IQ scores. The studies of Blewett (1954), Thurstone (1953), and Vandenberg (1962), seem to indicate that certain subtest scores correlate much higher than others, a result which might be interpreted as an indication that inheritance may be more involved in some traits than in others.

Allen (1957) summed up the evidence of genetic factors in mental retardation by stating the hypothesis that "recent evolutionary advances in man's nervous system have led to extreme, nonadaptive variations which will eventually stabilize by natural selection."

Because genetics has been the subject of intensive investigation during the past few years, many new findings have been disclosed. Perhaps no more startling fact was discovered than that the assumed number of chromosomes had been wrong. Tijo and Levan (1956) discovered that the true number of chromosomes is 46 rather than 48, as has been previously thought to be the case. The most recent studies of interest to students of mental retardation have been in the area of chromosomal abnormalities. Important research in this area was begun by Lejeune et al. in 1959. They established conclusively that mongolism is associated with an extra chromosome in the twenty-first pair, thus yielding 47 total chromosomes rather than the standard 46. This research has been well summarized by Ford et al. (1959) and by Lejeune and Turpin (1961).

Few other abnormalities have elicited the interest that mongolism has. First discovered by Langdon Down in 1866, it has been the subject of intense study by physicians and researchers in related fields. It was thought initially that mongolism was due to a mutant gene, but the fact that mongolism was over 100 times as common as determined by this hypothesis led to the investigation of other causes.

Statistics show that mongolism occurs about once in 700 births, and that 10 per cent of the mentally retarded are classified as mongoloid. The environment became implicated as a causative factor in mongolism when it was discovered that older women have a larger than expected proportion of mongoloid children. Something in the micro-environ-

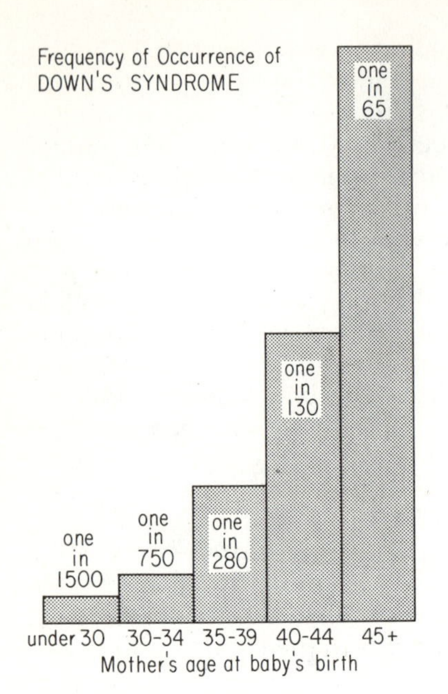

Figure 2-1 The frequency of occurrence of Down's syndrome increases with the age of the mother. (From Smith, D. W., and Wilson, A. A.: The Child With Down's Syndrome. Philadelphia, W. B. Saunders Company, 1973.)

ment of the developing egg cell (or of the sperm, but this is rarer) causes pairs of chromosomes, which usually separate, to remain in pairs, resulting in an extra chromosome in the egg. This unbalanced split can also occur after fertilization. The discovery of the extra chromosome in the mongoloid led to an intensive investigation as to the mechanism by which it caused a defective individual.

Figure 2-2 Mongoloid child enjoying play and socially structured situation (Girl Scouts). (From Smith, D. W., and Wilson, A. A.: The Child With Down's Syndrome. Philadelphia, W. B. Saunders Company, 1973.)

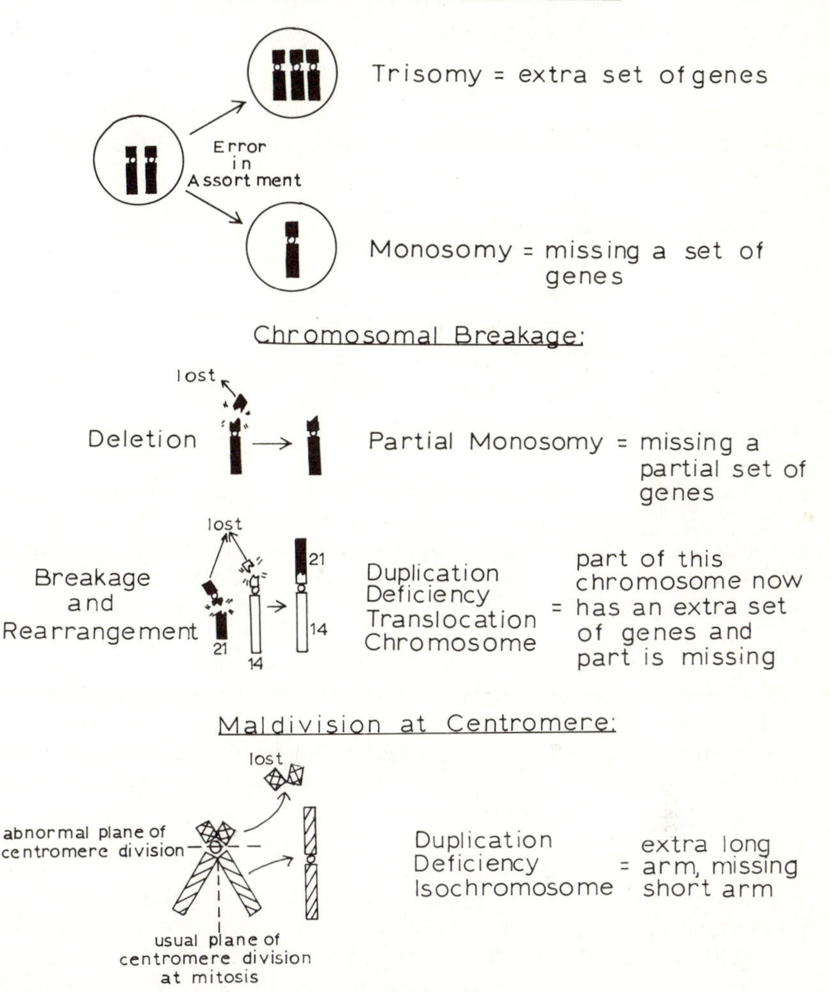

Figure 2-3 (From Smith, D. W.: Recognizable Patterns of Human Malformation. Philadelphia, W. B. Saunders Company, 1970.)

Mongolism is only one of several examples of the affect of extra chromosomes. In locations other than chromosome 21, the result of an extra chromosome has generally been found to cause mental retardation but not mongolism (Therman et al., 1961). Not only are the autosomes subject to the phenomenon of an extra chromosome, but so are the sex chromosomes. In the typical male, the sex chromosomes are of an XY combination, and in the typical female, there is an XX composition. Aberrations such as XXY, XXXY, XXXXY, and XXX have been found to date. In all the preceding cases, a lower than average intelligence may result. The work of Moorehead et al. (1961) led to the discovery of individuals having a deficiency of one chromosome. Offspring with this particular abnormality showed intellectual retardation and peculiar chromosomal composition patterns. It may be a little premature, however, to state categorically that the missing chromosome was directly responsible for the observed defect.

At present, it appears that any chromosomal deficit may lead to some lowering of intellectual function. It is not clear whether lower intelligence is a direct effect of the action of the defective chromosome or whether it is the side effect of reduced emotional tone or reduced sensory input (Gottsman, 1963).

PHYSICAL DEFECTS: PHYSICAL IMPAIRMENT NEED NOT BE A HANDICAP

Advances in medical science and public health practices have resulted in an increased life expectancy and a marked reduction in infant mortality. Consequently, an increasing number of children with physical deformities or early childhood impairments are able to survive, but continue to suffer residual limitations.

A Beginning Differentiation

Nagi (1969), in discussing the terms, *impairment*, and *handicap*, noted that impairments differ according to the following characteristics: (1) the point in the life cycle at which the disability occurs; (2) the type of onset of disability—either gradual, progressive, congenital, chronic, sudden, traumatic, or accidental; (3) the degree of pain, trauma, and threat to life and survival; (4) the nature and degree of limitations imposed upon the individual's capacities and level of functioning; (5) the degree of visability, disfigurement, or associated stigma; (6) the type of treatment and care required and received; (7) the state of underlying pathology—either eliminated or arrested, with fixed residual limitations, slowly or rapidly progressive, or with reoccurring acute episodes; and (8) the prognosis for the condition, that is, prospects for future recovery, prosthetic compensation, adaptive and restorative training, and potential for other forms of rehabilitation.

Disability differs from impairment to the extent that it is the behavior pattern evolving from the limitations imposed upon an individual's capacities and levels of functioning by the impairment. Impairment is the actual physical defect, and disability is the behavior evolving from the impairment. Handicap represents an individual's peculiar reactions to his disability and impairment. It is the extent of an individual's subjective, negative use and interpretation of his disability and impairment. Not every impairment results in disability, and not every disability results in a handicap. The most significant aspect is the individual's own interpretation of his impairment and his ability to live with it.

Varieties of Physical Defects

Amputations and Deformities

An increasing number of traumatic accidents in the home and on the highways has caused many children to suffer amputations, disfigurations, and deformities. Technology has created many advances which cannot always counteract the effects of random trauma. Advances which have been gained medically may have been lost through modern technology—automobile accidents being a classic example.

Blood Disorders

Among the many types of blood disorders, the two that are most relevant to the teacher of exceptional children are *hemophilia,* or slow coagulation of the blood, and *leukemia,* a cancer-like disorder that affects the balance of cells in the blood. The former is usually a congenital condition that may be brought under medical control. Most forms of leukemia, however, are slowly progressive in nature and usually lead to death.

Cerebral Palsy

The term "palsy" means paralysis, the inability to move or control one or more parts of the body, especially the limbs. *Cerebral palsy* is a very general term for a variety and degree of paralyses determined by organic damage in specific parts of the brain. Hewett (1970) specified six ways in which muscles can be affected by brain damage which produces palsy: (1) the *spastic* type of paralysis, in which the muscles become stiff and resistant, making it impossible for the child to move (this being the most common of palsies, affecting perhaps two-thirds of the children commonly diagnosed as cerebral palsied); (2) *athetosis,* in which the muscles are loose and limp, going usually in a direction opposite to the one intended; (3) *tremor,* or uncontrollable rhythmic movements, in which there is conflict between intention and direction of movement; (4) *ataxia,* an inability to balance one's body, usually heightened by lack of coordination in movements; (5) *rigidity,* in which the muscles become very stiff after they have been extended; and (6) *atony,* in which the muscles are very floppy and limp, so that the child is unable to govern and coordinate them. Most cases of cerebral palsy include a mixture of these six types.

The palsy can affect one or more limbs, on either one side of the body or on the upper or lower portions. The extent of the disability can range from complete immobility in all four limbs to an occasional tremor in one limb alone. In sufficiently severe cases, palsy can produce other defects of a physical or psychological nature by limiting the body's resistance to environmental stress and the child's intellectual and emotional resources which are necessary for him to learn.

Diabetes

This condition is caused by insufficient insulin production by the pancreas and results in an inefficient metabolism of carbohydrates. The disease is characterized by elevated concentrations of sugar in the blood and the urine. If not properly controlled, diabetes produces loss of weight, retarded growth in height for very young children, and complications in other parts of the body, such as the tissues and veins. If not treated, *acidosis* and resulting coma can occur. Originally, life expectancy for diabetics was lower than for the general population, but with advances in medical treatment, such as insulin injections, oral medications, and diet control, the life expectancy is increasing.

The psychosomatic aspects of diabetes have drawn much interest. Some researchers (Newman, 1970) have emphasized the role of emotional stress on the inception and management of the disease. One factor of great relevance to teachers is the medical management of the disease which requires a firm control of diet and regularity in medication. If a child is taking insulin injections, the teacher should be especially aware of insulin shock which can be counteracted with sugar intake. Because the controls of diet and medication are difficult for some children to follow, the teacher should help the child to accept and deal constructively with the realities of his condition. Its permanency and lifelong requirement for treatment are the most important aspects of this disease that will affect any child's reactions and his self-perception.

Epilepsies

The term *epilepsy* refers to the reoccurrence of seizures which are caused by an abnormal electrical discharge in the brain. These seizures are strictly organic in origin, but they can be affected either positively or negatively by the psychological condition of the individual. Folsom (1968) stated that "epilepsy is a physiological phenomenon and has little to do with psychology insofar as its basic etiology is concerned. An underlying cerebral disturbance or dysfunction is a *sine qua non* of any epileptic seizure."

For most people, including the patient, epilepsy has connotations of a disastrous illness which affects the patient both mentally and physically. Epilepsy, like any illness, is likely to have an effect on the self-perception of the child; however, it is important for children to learn to live realistically with their illnesses rather than to disregard them.

There are several different types of epilepsies, each of which differs in its characteristic pattern of seizures and electrical discharges. Specific seizure patterns are the external symptoms of the internal discharges. Folsom (1968) distinguished three main seizure patterns: the petit mal, the grand mal, and the psychomotor. Penfield (1959), a famous neurologist, classified the various epilepsies on the basis of localization in the highest level of the brain stem. Lennox (1960) a notable researcher, based his classifications, petit mal, temporal, and convulsive, on the age of the individual at the onset of the seizure and on EEG patterns. *Petit mal seizures* are characterized by approximately 15-second lapses of consciousness of which the individual has no memory. Petit mal seizures commonly begin in early childhood and persist until late adolescence. Children afflicted with this epilepsy exhibit such behaviors as daydreaming, unresponsiveness, and inability to concentrate. A three-per-second spike dome pattern as recorded by the EEG is the type of discharge which is characteristic of petit mal seizures. This fact does not imply that all individuals who exhibit this EEG pattern experience the petit mal seizure, but there is a strong correlation between the two.

The *psychomotor seizure* usually involves abnormally low electrical discharge and is sometimes called temporal overseizure. Psychomotor seizures are characterized by *automatisms* which may range from the unconscious continuation of normal activity to bizarre, inappropriate, and obsessive behaviors. Most automatisms are of brief duration, and the patient has no memory of them. Psychomotor seizures range midway between petit mal and grand mal seizures with respect to observable motor activity. They are not as devastating or disruptive as the grand mal seizures, and they involve considerably more motor activity than the relatively passive petit mal seizure.

The *grand mal seizure* involves the entire nervous system and produces considerable neural discharge. This type of seizure usually lasts about five minutes. It begins with severe contractions of the muscles and proceeds to rhythmic movements and tremors. The grand mal seizure may occur at any age. Penfield classified the grand mal seizure according to its onset. The earlier the onset, the more severe the prognosis. If only one region of the body is initially involved, then it is termed a focal cerebral seizure. If the onset is initial unconsciousness, then the

seizure probably originated in the centroencephalic region (
1968).

The various epilepsies may play a major role in the etiology o
havioral dysfunctions. They severely distort an individual's percepti
of himself and his environment and affect his ability to adjust and to
adapt. This distortion is especially serious when epilepsy occurs in
children because they have not yet had an opportunity to stabilize their
relations with the environment. Epilepsy also interferes with the learning process, and, thus, it is a source of many educational and social problems.

Heart Defects

Most heart defects in children are congenital, and many of these defects which are present at birth can be corrected or cured surgically. Another type of heart defect is produced by rheumatic fever, a disease contracted usually after age four. The *prophylaxis* for this heart defect is: (1) prevention of its epidemiological causes, such as crowded, cold, and wet conditions which might cause susceptibility to infection by the streptococcus organism which causes rheumatic fever; (2) cure of the infection through the use of proper drugs; and (3) correction of the factors adding to the exacerbation of the disease—that is, changing the internal or external factors which may make it difficult for the child to adapt to his condition.

Orthopedic Defects

In addition to cerebral palsy, which is considered a type of orthopedic defect, there are a great many types of defects directly affecting the bone structure and muscles of a child. These include *poliomyelitis* and *osteomyelitis*, as well as congenital deformities, such as *clubfoot* and *spina bifida*.

Another class of crippling defects which may produce disabilities includes *cystic fibrosis, arthritis, multiple sclerosis,* and *muscular dystrophy*. It is significant to note that all these defects, in one way or another, limit the freedom and spontaneity of the child.

Tuberculosis

Tuberculosis is no longer the public health problem of epidemic proportions that, in the past, brought about the construction of special *sanitaria*. Medical advances have greatly reduced the incidence and severity of this disease which, in essence, is an infection of tissues or organs of the body. At present, tuberculosis sanitaria are being changed into mental health facilities or treatment centers for other medically relevant defects.

The most important aspect of tuberculosis is its chronic nature. Although this disease can be arrested and rendered inactive, it does remain dormant, allowing the possibility for reactivation if it is not properly checked. The nature of the disease cannot be separated from its cultural context. Most children who are affected by it come from deprived homes of low socioeconomic status in congested and transitional neighborhoods. The most relevant outcome of this defect in children is *anxiety* (Newman, 1970). The mysterious aspect of the disease, its "invisibility," may cause children to experience fantasies and fears about themselves and to equate the disease with death (Newman, 1970).

anic Defects

gically determined defects include those caused tions in the mother, such as *syphilis, rubella,* die- ncompatibility, radioactivity, and certain toxic any of these conditions may have varying con- ding upon the type and severity of organic xemia, and traumatic birth injury may affect y decreasing his abilities to process information. Severe ectual retardation may also result from infections, such as *meningitis* and *encephalitis.*

Multiple Defects

Among the many multiple defects resulting from combinations of the defects presented thus far, birth defects have acquired an increasingly important position. The decreasing rate of mortalities at birth has produced an increasing number of children with birth defects which may range from *hydrocephaly,* an unusual enlargement of the head due to accumulation of fluids, to peculiar malformations of the cranium, such as *microcephaly.*

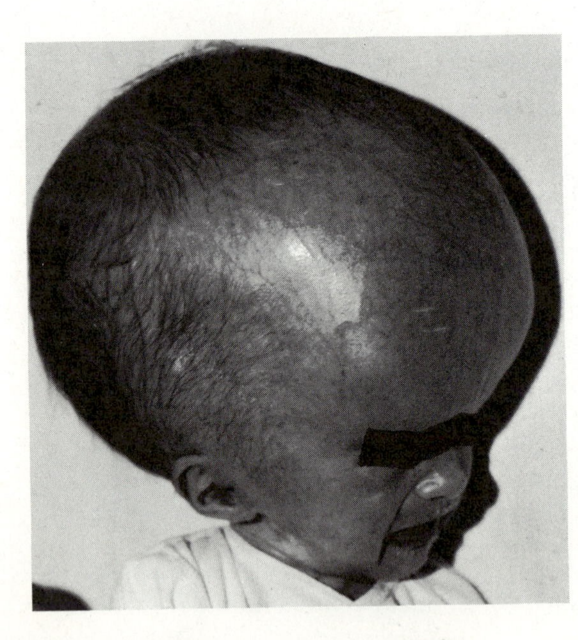

Figure 2–4 Child with hydrocephaly. (From Smith, D. W.: Recognizable Patterns of Human Malformation. Philadelphia, W. B. Saunders Company, 1970.) (Courtesy of J. M. Opitz, University of Wisconsin.)

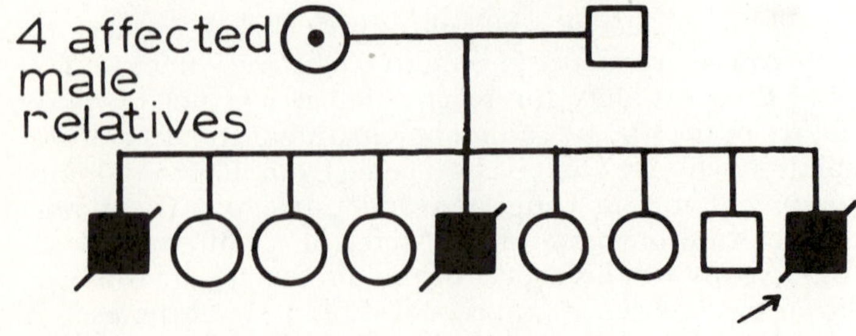

Handicapping Conditions

Each defect has a specific effect on the overall functioning of a child. While one defect might impair the mobility of a child, another defect may influence his manual dexterity. Not all defects will affect all areas of functioning. The nature and severity of the defect will determine how each part of the body will be affected.

Limitations in Perception

Brain damage, defects of the central nervous system, and systemic tissue changes affect how well a child receives information. These defects limit the range and complexity of information that a child is able to receive. The individual may not be able to respond to most relevant stimuli and cues and may select only those that are more familiar to him. If complexity is a factor, the physical defect may tend to reduce the level of perceptual complexity at which the child can respond. In other words, his perceptual differentiation may be reduced. If the stimuli are novel and complex, he may tend to perseverate with the same response that he used for a simpler question, even though the nature of the stimulus may change.

If the defect is one involving output, an individual may be able to receive and store a great deal of information. However, if he cannot express this information, as in many cases of cerebral palsy, how can the child's knowledge be determined? If the child's output is limited, it is difficult to assess how much and what kind of information he has acquired.

Limitations in Locomotion

When a child's movements and actions are impaired, his need to explore, to experience a sense of freedom, and to enhance his spontaneity may not be fulfilled. Such a limitation affects the range and variety of objects, people, and places that he can encounter in order to enlarge and enrich his store of information and experiences.

Limitations in Dexterity

The ability to produce fine hand and finger movements is one which is basic to the acquisition of various skills, ranging from tying shoelaces or a tie, to buttoning a shirt, drawing a picture, or writing. Fine hand coordination requires a great deal of conscious control and voluntary coordination between the eyes and hands. Muscle and bone defects can make fine hand coordination so difficult for an individual that frustration, anger, and regression may result. In trying to master his immediate environment, a child begins with his body. If he is successful in mastering self-help skills, such as dressing, washing, or eating, he can advance to other skills requiring fine manual dexterity. The frustration of failure, however, may cause a child to adhere to his dependency, thus, avoiding the possibility of success and advancement. By continuing to fail, the child can retain the behavior pattern that has previously brought about the greatest gains, namely, dependency. He may also withdraw from situations in which he fears failure. If he progresses to a certain degree of success, the trauma of an unexpected failure may push him into a more regressive stance of withdrawal and dependency.

Limitations in Body Image

How a child views his body depends, to some degree, on its intactness and attractiveness. If the body is incomplete or misshapen, its unattractiveness may reinforce a view of weakness and helplessness. The major dimensions of body image may be described as its weakness-strength, its completeness-incompleteness, its attractiveness or its repulsiveness, and its sex-appropriateness, masculinity for boys and femininity for girls. Many endocrine defects may distort the appearance of the body. An obese child may attract attention in a derogatory or derisive fashion just as a deformed body may produce avoidance and withdrawal. How the body looks may indeed have important consequences determined by the way in which peers and adults react to it.

Limitations in Self-Concept

The child's *self-esteem,* his sense of personal worth and importance, is affected by each of the preceding limiting factors; however, a child's self-concept may be adversely affected even in the absence of all the handicapping limitations mentioned thus far. The child can be perfectly intact physically and be severely limited in the way he sees himself. His sense of worth is also affected by the way his family and peers react to him. In spite of a strong body, the child may see himself as weak and powerless. He may view himself negatively even though he has keen perceptual, verbal, and motor skills. The child's view of himself is basic to how he will cope with his environment.

A physical defect can only challenge any possible sense of self-worth, making the self-concept a much more important consideration in children with physical defects. The self-concept is the link through which the child finds personal identification and the bridge between biological limitations and cultural factors. Psychology, to a large extent, is a study of the self-concept, the individual's interpretation of himself as a physical body and as a cultural being. A physical defect may tip the scale toward feelings of rejection, unworthiness, and inadequacy, making it crucial for the teacher to attend to the self-concept of each child, but especially the physically defective child. The experience of defeat and frustration may produce a self-concept characterized by despair, hopelessness, and helplessness. The child may tend to give up and may not try to succeed. The self is then arrested negatively and passively. It will take all the skills of any adult to help him to regain confidence in himself.

Limitations in Intellectual Functioning

Not all physical defects lower a child's intellectual functioning; however, a combination of most factors thus far considered cannot help producing such an effect. Although many exceptions may be found for any generalization about behavior and exceptionalities, all the preceding limitations will affect how well a child acquires, retains, remembers, and, consequently, acts upon information. It is impossible to separate intellectual functioning from the child's ability to acquire and retain information. Intellectual functioning is an overall ability of the total organism performing in a purposive, voluntary fashion. If there are limitations on the range and complexity of stimuli that the child can receive, he will be less able to respond to the tasks presented to him. Certain physical defects will affect intellectual functioning more than others. For instance, peripheral deformities without central nervous system impairment, may not influence the level of intellectual functioning at all. Consequently, the teacher should not expect all physical defects to impair intellectual functioning. On the contrary, some limitations on locomotion may help a person to sharpen his verbal skills and his memory to the point of distinct superiority in these areas.

A case in point is that of a child with cerebral palsy who had been diagnosed as being dull-normal to average on the basis of an intelligence test which did not differentiate between verbal and visual-motor functioning. When this differentiation was made by means of a more appropriate test, the child's verbal and cognitive assets were found to be clearly superior, even though his physical and visual-motor problem-solving were obviously retarded. Determination and a constant emphasis upon his intellectual strengths, coupled with a great deal of parental support, enabled this individual to graduate from high school, attend a college, and eventually progress to graduate school and a Ph.D. degree. The reader may guess the field of specialization chosen by this fellow.

One of the best studies, among many, concerning the intellectual functioning of children with physical defects, was performed in the state of Hawaii. It is worthwhile to cite its summary in toto:

> **This is a report of a 10-year follow-up of 1,012 children previously studied in the Kuai Pregnancy Study from early in mothers' pregnancies through a two-year pediatric and psychological assessment of physical and mental handicaps of congenital origin.**
>
> **The earlier diagnoses and predictions for the severely defective children, physical or mental or both, were largely confirmed at age 10. All had received extensive diagnostic and treatment services and three-fourths required special education or institutional care.**
>
> **IQ scores of the mentally retarded children with organic defects were very low at two years (median under 20), while those without evidence of organic involvement were higher (median 64). At age ten, the former were still low (median under 40) while the latter had improved somewhat (median 77).**
>
> **The poorest predictions involved children with eye problems. For only half of those believed to have *strabismus* by age two had any eye problem been diagnosed by age 10, and an equal number of additional eye problems had been diagnosed by that time. Among the eye cases were children whose vision problems were severe enough to affect school progress. Some of these might have been prevented by earlier diagnosis and treatment.**
>
> **Pediatric and psychological screening in early childhood, if augmented by careful vision and hearing screening, will identify most children with congenital defects and retardation who need special medical and educational services.**
>
> **In a time sample of 750 children ten years of age, 6.6 per cent were handicapped significantly as a result of physical-sensory defects or mental retardation (IQ under 70) or both. An additional 8.5 per cent had borderline IQ scores of 70–84 and were academically retarded.**
>
> **Acquired physical handicaps resulting from accidents or disease were only half as frequent as handicaps of congenital origin and mental retardation, 2.1 per cent vs. 4.5 per cent.**
>
> **Hearing and vision problems significantly interfering with school performance amounted to 1.1 per cent and 1.6 per cent, respectively.**
>
> **Over five times as many children required special educational services (39 per cent) as those who required special medical care, and almost twice as many had serious emotional problems interfering with school progress (13 per cent). The greatest need of these ten-year-olds – almost one-third of them – was for long-term educational or mental health services or both. It is clear that much greater emphasis must be placed on early identification and alleviation of deficiencies in children's environment that produce educational and emotional disabilities. These needs require as much if not more attention than has in the past been given to physical health.***

---

*From F. E. French et al., American Journal of Public Health, 1968, *58*:1388. Reprinted with permission.

PERSONAL AND SOCIAL ADJUSTMENTS OF CHILDREN WITH PHYSICAL DEFECTS

The child's physical defect will not only affect him directly, as discussed in the preceding section, but it will also affect those who come in contact with him. His parents' outlook on his defect will be largely related to their cultural and religious backgrounds. Thus, before considering physical defects in a familial context, it is important to consider the role of the larger context in which parental and familial attitudes are formed—the culture.

Cultural Attitudes Toward Physical Defects

A great many myths and misconceptions about physical defects are fostered culturally. In many ways, they are not too different from most prejudices derived from *stereotyping, scapegoating,* and *externalization,* or attribution to others of characteristics that we dislike in ourselves. After considering in detail the evidence which shows the existence of a prejudiced viewpoint, McDaniel (1969) described this evidence as being an "oversimplification." It is true that the disabled are a minority group and share an inferior status position in most cultures and especially in ours. On the other hand, as McDaniel stated, "The degree of acceptance or positive attitudes toward the disabled varies with sex, age and maturity, and possibly with level of education and sophistication as well." Safilios-Rothschild (1970) described how a "labeling process" affects one with a physical defect:

> **The process by which one arrives at defining oneself as physically disabled bears a considerable degree of similarity to the labeling process involved in the self-definitions of deviance and mental illness: social stigmatization, labels of deviance, sickness, or disability and their severity.**

Unfortunately, disability implies a much greater connotation of permanency and irreversibility than labels of deviance or of sickness.

McDaniel (1969) supported a body-concept theory concerning attitudes toward physical defects. This promising view relates the self-concept of the perceiver to his attitudes toward physical defects. He proceeded to find supporting evidence for the hypothesis that how a person perceives himself, including, of course, his own physical qualities, may determine the nature of his attitudes toward disability. The more positive the self-perception is, the more positive the perception of others will be, including those with a physical disability. Perhaps the best conclusion that can be drawn is that of Connor et al. (1971):

> **The most valid conclusion regarding attitudes seems to be that physically disabled children will experience such attitudes from time to time but because the attitudes vary from situation to situation and are applied inconsistently, to the same disabled individual, uncertainty in new situations is engendered wherever a disabled child enters unfamiliar sectors of life.**

Two investigators, Jordan (1969) and Safilios-Rothschild (1970), have studied physical handicaps and attitudes toward physical defects crossculturally. Jordan found that in societies with high standards of living (U.S.A. and Denmark) manager-executives in business regard the physically disabled person as one who limits production. In all societies, regular classroom teachers regard the disabled or handicapped child as difficult, and interfering with, or impeding the information-acquiring process. Jordan also found that people who work with those having physical disabilities tend to become interested in helping others, have less need for power over others, and are more self-sufficient and willing to work alone. Thus, they need less approval from others than people who work with "normalities."

Safilios-Rothschild stated that the direction and degree of prejudice against the sick and the disabled seems to be influenced by the following interrelated factors, among others: (1) the degree of a country's socioeconomic development and its rate of unemployment; (2) the prevailing notions about the origins of poverty and unemployment and sociopolitical beliefs concerning the proper role of government in alleviating social problems; (3) the prevailing notions about the etiology of illness and the degree of individual responsibility involved in falling ill and remaining disabled; (4) the cultural values or stigmas attached to different physical conditions or characteristics; (5) the illness or disability-connected factors, such as (a) the degree of visibility of the illness or disability, (b) whether the incapacitating illness is contagious or not, (c) part of the body afflicted, (d) nature of the illness (physical or mental) and assumed pervasiveness of the disability, and (e) severity of functional impairment and degree of predictability of its course; (6) the effectiveness of public relations groups and the dramatic-sensational image attached to a particular disability; and (7) the degree of importance of the disability to the nation's welfare, economy, and security.

The Familial Context of Physical Defects

A physical defect in a child may be a source of stress and strain for him and his parents. An inevitable reaction is for parents to look upon themselves as being responsible, in some way, for the defect. Mothers, especially, tend to feel more responsible than fathers, who may disengage themselves from the stress and focus their energies outside the home. Schopler (1970) pointed out how parents may become scapegoats for their children's real or imagined disabilities, whether they be physical or emotional. Mental health professionals have been quick to place the blame on parents, reinforcing cultural mores that make parents feel that they are criminals before the jury of public opinion. As Hewett (1968) concluded in her study of families of handicapped children:

> **There is evidence from other reports and studies that no specific kind of handicap brings unique problems to the family. Far more difficulties are shared by all families with a handicapped child than are specific to the medical category of the handicap.**

Unfortunately, most information concerning families and parents is derived mainly from one informant, the mother. The reports of handicapped people themselves (Hunt, 1966; Michaux, 1970) attest to the fact that the family as a system reacts in a variety of ways to a physical defect. It should be mentioned, however, that a far greater number of families are under stress even without the presence of a physically defective child. Consequently, the physical defect by itself is not the cause of family stress. There are other factors to be considered, such as the maturity and level of integration of the parents, the responses of siblings, and the attitudes of the community. Parents of physically defective children may not be different from other parents.

Jordan (1969) conceived of four classes of variables which determine attitudes toward physically disabled persons: (1) demographic factors, such as age, sex, and income; (2) sociopsychological factors, such as one's value orientation; (3) contact factors, such as innocence, maturity, perceived voluntariness, and enjoyment of contact with the disabled individual; and (4) knowledge factors, such as amount of factual information concerning physical disability. Jordan speculated that if

> **... the parent feels that the handicapped child was not forced upon him by some outside force (e.g., God, fate) and that having a disabled child does not denote either a weakness in himself or a rejection by society, that he will then be able to respond to the other assets of the child and consequently enjoy him more.**

Peers and Social Status

A physical defect, such as one causing decreased mobility, limits the range and depth of interpersonal and social situations which a child can experience. In most cases, the negative feelings and reactions from physically able children may produce withdrawal in a physically defective child and a tendency to group with other handicapped children. Unfortunately, this reaction is reinforced by special education groupings which are made on the basis of specific disabilities or defects. Frequent or prolonged periods of hospitalization, medical treatment, and need for special drugs may increase the child's feeling that he is different from and, at times, the opposite of physically able children. As Connor et al. (1971) concluded, "Disability is not useful in determining social rôle behavior or level of social participation."

Intellectual Level and Type of Intellectual Functioning

It is important to view physical defects as liabilities that may adversely affect certain aspects of intellectual functioning. For instance, cerebral palsy (or certain types of brain damage) may affect visual-motor problem-solving to a greater extent than verbal skills. Other physical defects may impair verbal output to a far greater extent than physical output or dexterity. In addition to these distinctions, a more basic differentiation must be made when assessing the exceptional child's intellectual functioning. Presently, most intelligence tests do not distinguish clearly between the input and output aspects of intellectual functioning. One of the few tests that recognizes this distinction and, in fact, is based on it, is the Illinois Test of Psycholinguistic Abilities (ITPA). This test is limited to children between three and nine years of age, making it difficult to test properly younger and older children; however, this limitation should not be considered as a criticism of ITPA which constitutes a considerable advance in the assessment of exceptionalities in children. More, if not all, intelligence tests should distinguish between the information a child receives and the information he expresses. Unfortunately, at present, the assessment of intellectual functioning is based on global indices that fail to show which specific assets and liabilities are affected by a physical defect. Only by finer differentiation between the receptive and expressive aspects of intellectual functioning will it be possible to be more specific about individualized courses of habilitation, rehabilitation, and teaching for children with defects. A knowledge of a child's strengths and weaknesses will allow a far more specialized program to be implemented for that child.

Early Experiences and Hospitalization

A child's separation from his parents may be one of the most traumatic events in the life of a child with a physical defect. He may develop anxieties about leaving his home for a new and possibly threatening environment and may feel a sense of loss in being separated from his parents. The extent to which he will experience these feelings depends a great deal on how the parents themselves are able to deal with separation. The age of the child as well as the reasons for the separation are other factors that will determine the extent of the trauma.

THEORIES OF IMPAIRMENT, DISABILITY, AND HANDICAP

One of the difficulties in finding a consistent theory concerning physical defects is the lack of differentiation between the terms impairment, disability, and handicap. These are distinct and separate aspects, in the sense that a child might have a physical impairment and be disabled, but not feel handicapped at all. There are many children who have no physical impairment, are not disabled, and are tremendously handicapped. It follows that any theoretical position must consider each aspect with its individual differences as it relates to the child's overall functioning. Such an approach can best deal with the three aspects as component parts of a system, since *the impairment clearly refers to the biological forces, the disability to how a culture deals with impairment, and the handicap to how the individual deals with his physical impairment.* According to this viewpoint, past theoretical positions do not deal thoroughly with this complex issue; however, it is important for the teacher to become familiar with other theories relevant to the study of physical defects.

Field Theory

Kurt Lewin's theory, as applied by Myerson (1963) to somatopsychology (the relationships between body and behavior), takes into account the *life space* of an individual. The theory defines behavior as a person's interactions with his environment. Some important concepts of this theory are *level of aspiration,* or what an individual would like to achieve, and *barrier,* whatever obstacle prevents an individual from reaching his goals.

These three concepts, life space, level of aspiration, and barrier, are relevant to an understanding of defects and disabilities. The level of aspiration of a child is clearly determined by the perception of his life space, that is, his spatial and temporal perspective of what he can or cannot do physically, and by the subjective or objective barriers that may prevent goal achievement. He will need to weigh his physical impairment in light of the personal and cultural limitations which may exist.

Organic Inferiority

As mentioned in Chapter 1, Alfred Adler developed certain concepts that are relevant to the study of physical defects in children. As McDaniel (1969) pointed out, *organic inferiority* on the individual's physical side and *inferiority feelings* on the individual's psychological side, are balanced by the desire for superiority, compensation, and overcompensation for real or imagined inadequacies. Adler's concept of life style relates to this balance. Life style is the unifying theme for the way in which an individual wants to live his life. Adler suggests that most individuals are led into choosing whether they will spend their lifetimes being inferior, unsuccessful, handicapped, dependent, helpless, or ignorant, or whether they will become superior, successful, independent, and helpful—whether or not they have a physical defect.

Body Image

The concept of *body image*, as originated by Schilder (1950), a neopsychoanalytic researcher, pertains to how one views his body in terms of size, strength or weakness, attractiveness, shape, and degree of attachment to it. This concept has attracted supporting evidence, especially as it relates to psychosomatic illness rather than to strictly physical defects. The work of Fisher and Cleveland (1958) is an example of body image research, in which responses to the *Rorschach inkblots* were used to determine the permeability or impermeability of one's body image. The Visual-Motor Bender-Gestalt Test, widely used for the diagnosis of brain damage in children, was developed from Schilder's own notions of how the body image is projected through the reproduction of geometric figures.

The use of drawings of the human figure also relates to the body-image concept. By the use of these drawings, children have a means of expressing what they are often unable to express verbally. These drawings, using a scoring system devised by Florence Goodenough (1926), give an accurate determination of a child's level of intellectual and emotional development. For children with physical defects, each of these three techniques, the Rorschach inkblots, the Visual-Motor Bender-Gestalt Test, and the human figure drawings, is useful in determining whether a physical defect has an underlying neurological basis and whether the defect has affected the child's perception of his body and his level of perceptual-motor differentiation. The body-image theory is especially applicable to the phenomenon of phantom perceptions in amputees, because it suggests that the brain still retains, for a while, an image of the entire body even after the extremity is no longer present.

Sensory-Tonic Theory

This theory, which is related to the body-image theory, was first formulated by Werner, a coworker of Strauss and Lehtinen (1947) and an original psychological theorist in his own right. One of the most important concepts of this theory is that of "differentiation" and the stages of perceptual-motor development. Perception, how a child responds to environmental stimulation through all his senses, is gross and undifferentiated at birth. An infant hears only loud or sudden noises and responds mainly to certain intensities of light and sound. As he learns to discriminate, he tends to become more specific. He breaks down the mass of sensory stimuli that affects him at any given time. He learns that certain sounds are his mother's voice and, as time goes on, that different people make different sounds. Thus, differentiation occurs from the general to the specific and from the gross to the fine. For other applicable perceptual theories, including sensory-tonic theory, the reader may consult McDaniel (1969), as well as Werner and Wapner (1955).

Miscellaneous Viewpoints

At present, most theories differ in the emphasis they place on organic, cultural, and individual factors. Some theories stress an organic view at the expense of cultural factors. Other theories (Bartel and Guskin, 1971) emphasize cultural factors, especially experience deprivation and disadvantage (Connor et al., 1971), parental attitudes, and external elements, at the expense of individual factors. In contrast, most psychodynamic and psychoanalytically derived viewpoints stress the individual by dealing with such matters as self-concept, degree of acceptance of the disability, and feelings of guilt caused by hostility. An information-processing approach, hopefully, has the potential to include all these factors as being relevant, depending, of course, on the specific case and situation.

THE NATURE OF TRAINABLE MENTAL RETARDATION

Definition

American educators usually divide the mentally retarded into two major categories, the trainable mentally retarded (TMR) and the educable mentally retarded (EMR). The term trainable is applied to those who are thought to be capable of learning (a) self-care, (b) adjustment to the home or neighborhood, and (c) economic usefulness in the home, a sheltered workshop, or an institution. The educable are those who are thought to be capable of being educated to such an extent that they will be able to function in a nearly normal manner in American society (Kirk, 1972).

The classification of the mentally retarded is complicated by the usage of other terms for this same population. The World Health Organization, the American Psychiatric Association, and the American Association for Mental Deficiency call the trainable mentally retarded the moderately retarded, while the British call this group the "*imbecile*" class. The usual practice of most groups has been to use IQ scores as a criterion for placing individuals in the trainable category, the typical range being IQ's from 25 to 50. In this text, we will use the term trainable mentally retarded and the IQ range of 25 to 50 to designate this class of individuals.

Incidence

The most thorough study of the incidence of mental retardation is that of Birch et al. (1970). According to his comparative analysis of the incidence of trainable mental retardation in a variety of populations from England, Scotland, and the United States, the number of children expected to have an IQ below 50 varied from 3.3 per thousand in Baltimore to 3.71 per thousand in England and Wales. Birch was unable to find any relation between the incidence of children with IQ scores below 50 and the social status of their parents. At the same time, Birch found that there was a relation to social class in the incidence of IQ's over 50, particularly in the range of 60 to 75. The number of educable mentally retarded was 11.1 per thousand school-age children in the highest social class and 43.3 per thousand in the lowest.

Characteristics

The fact that social class seems to correlate with the occurrence of educable retardation and not with trainable retardation may indicate that different factors are involved in the causation of each. It is thought by many authorities that the major difference between EMR and TMR is that the trainable type is largely the result of genetic factors, while the educable type probably reflects, to a great degree, socioeconomic factors (Kirk, 1972; Telford and Sawrey, 1967; Philips, 1966; Baumeister, 1967). The trainable mentally retarded tend to exhibit a definite clinical pattern and physical appearance, while the educable mentally retarded generally are normal in physical appearance (Kirk, 1972; Telford and Sawrey, 1967).

In addition to distinctions of intellectual level and physical appearance, TMR children are characterized by a general pattern of incompetence in social situations, rigid or awkward manual and motor movements, slowness in arousal and responding, and extreme dependence and helplessness in self-care activities.

THE ORIGINS OF TRAINABLE MENTAL RETARDATION

Genetic Factors

Genetic causes of mental retardation may be classified as follows: (1) chromosomal anomalies, (2) metabolic disorders, (3) endocrine disorders, and (4) cranial anomalies. Nongenetic causes are usually categorized as: (1) conditions present at birth which are not usually attributed to genetic factors; (2) brain infections which may happen before or after birth; (3) cultural and psychological factors which, in some extreme cases, may cause severe retardation; and (4) traumas of various kinds.

Down's Syndrome

The largest number of cases of trainable mental retardation are thought to result from chromosomal anomalies, and by far, the largest number of chromosomal anomalies are of the *Down's syndrome* or *mongolism* variety. As many as one-fifth of the TMR population may be classified as having Down's syndrome. Approximately 1 in every 600 to 900 live births is a mongoloid (Collmann and Stoller, 1962; McIntire et al., 1965). An interesting fact is the relationship between the age of the mother and the number of mongoloid births. One in 1,500 mongoloids are born to mothers between the ages of 15 and 24, 1 in 1,000 are born to mothers between 25 and 34, 1 in 150 for mothers over 35, 1 in 70 for mothers between 40 and 44, and 1 in 38 for mothers over 45 (Knobloch and Pasamanick, 1962; Robinson and Robinson, 1965).

It is difficult to list the basic characteristics of the mongoloid, even though the literature lists at least 50 possible distinctions, because the mongoloid does not possess these characteristics exclusively. The most exhaustive attempt to list the most common physical signs of mongolism is that of Gibson et al. (1964). They include: (1) flattened skull which is shorter than it is wide, (2) abnormally up-turned nostrils caused by undeveloped nasal bones, (3) abnormal toe spacing (increased space particularly between the first and second toes), (4) disproportionate shortness

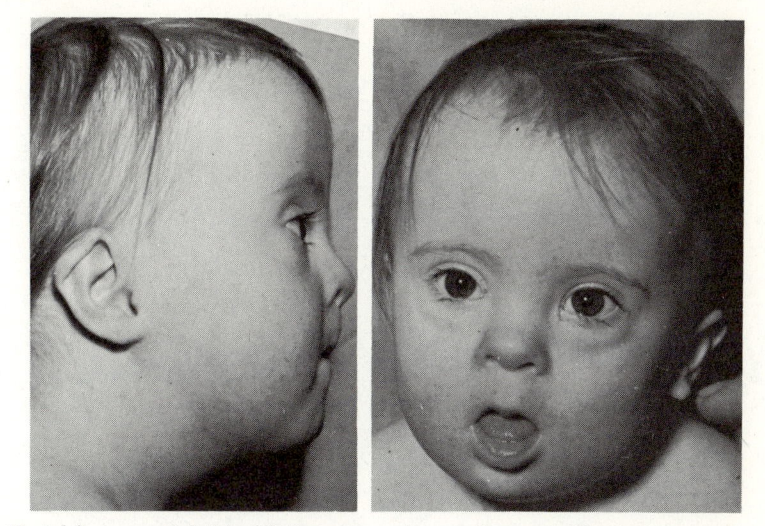

Figure 2–5 Facial features of child with Down's syndrome. (From Smith, D. W.: Recognizable Patterns of Human Malformation. Philadelphia, W. B. Saunders Company, 1970.)

of the fifth finger, (5) fifth finger which curves inward, (6) fifth finger which has only one crease instead of the usual two, (7) short, squared hands, (8) epicanthal fold at the inner corners of the eyes, (9) large, fissured tongue, (10) single crease across the palm of the hand (simian crease), (11) abnormally simplified ear, (12) adherent ear lobe, and (13) abnormal heart. Despite the problem of exclusive symptoms, Penrose (1963) felt that if four of the preceding symptoms are present, there is evidence of mongolism. The general appearance of mongoloids is of such a nature that they are frequently identified by the physician within a few days of birth. The majority of mongoloids are found to be in the IQ range of less than 50, although in some rare instances a mongoloid may approach the status of a slow learner (Wunsch, 1957).

The genetic study of mongolism began in 1959 with the discovery that a chromosomal anomaly is involved in this condition. Since that time, three types of mongolism have been identified. The most common type is called *trisomy 21* which derives its name from the number 21

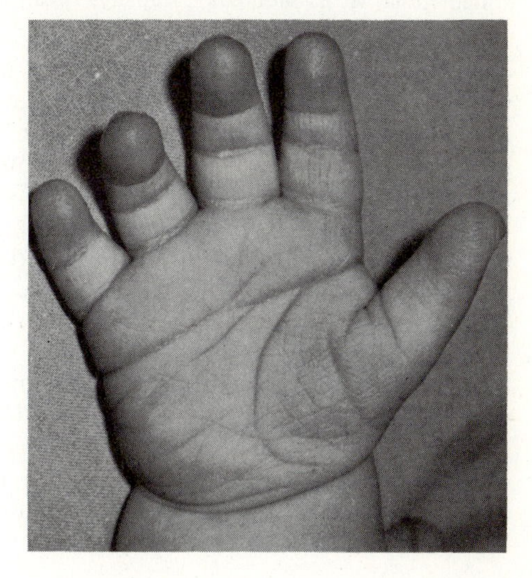

Figure 2–6 Hand characteristics of Down's syndrome. Note missing crease in fifth finger. (From Smith, D. W.: Recognizable Patterns of Human Malformation. Philadelphia, W. B. Saunders Company, 1970.)

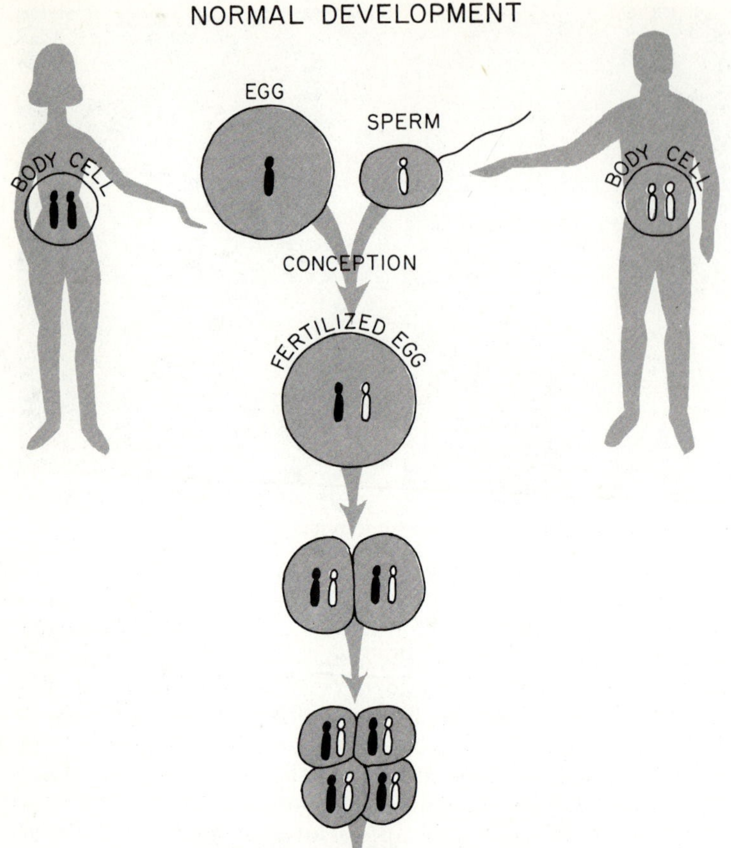

Figure 2–7 (From Smith, D. W., and Wilson, A. A.: The Child With Down's Syndrome. Philadelphia, W. B. Saunders Company, 1973.)

chromosome which is involved. The condition arises when a pair of number 21 chromosomes fails to separate at fertilization and results in an individual with three chromosomes at the number 21 position, instead of the usual two—the total chromosomal count amounting to 47 rather than the conventional 46. This extra chromosomal material is believed to be the cause of mongolism. Even though trisomy 21 is a genetic disorder, it is not inherited, and it is most frequently associated with older mothers.

A second type of chromosomal anomaly implicated in the etiology of mongolism is called *translocation.* This condition involves the attachment of an extra number 21 chromosome to another chromosome (usually located in positions 15 to 18). Translocation typically occurs with younger parents.

The third and least common mongoloid condition is called *mosaicism,* in which, adjacent cells contain different numbers of chromosomes. This form of Down's syndrome is the most variable in terms of appearance and level of intellectual functioning (Jarvick et al., 1964; Gibson and Pozsonyi, 1965).

Sex-Chromosomal Anomalies

The sex chromosomes are implicated in four types of chromosomal anomalies:

1. *Turner's syndrome:* The individual afflicted with this syndrome possesses a sex chromosomal pattern XO, that is, there is only one sex chromosome. The individual has the appearance of a female. Very short stature and dry skin are two of the common symptoms. Intellectual levels vary greatly, and cases of normal and superior intelligence are not unknown.

2. *Klinefelter's syndrome:* The individual looks male, but has the sex chromosomal pattern XXY.

3. Some females are born with extra sex chromosomes, thus their genetic sex is XXXX.

4. A fourth condition involving the sex chromosome is that of the apparent male who has a genetic sex constitution of XXXY.

The preceding chromosomal anomalies have all been implicated in mental retardation (Rundle, 1964; Haddad and Wilkins, 1959).

Metabolic Disorders

Genetic factors involved in mental retardation but unrelated to chromosomal anomalies offer a complex and difficult problem. Many conditions which are considered genetic lie in the area of metabolic disorders. These disorders are associated with the body's failure to control properly the production or usage of various substances in metabolism.

GALACTOSEMIA. Failure of the body to cope properly with carbohydrate metabolism is best exemplified by the condition known as *galactosemia.* Individuals with this condition are unable to break down galactose. An undue concentration of galactose in the blood and urine accumulates and, in some manner which is not clear at present, leads to severe mental retardation. Treatment for this condition requires a diet containing no galactose or lactose. If the treatment is started early, the child may develop normally (Rundle, 1964). Galactosemia is believed to result from a single recessive gene. It is possible to identify carriers of this recessive gene, so that appropriate preventive measures may be taken to avoid mental retardation.

PHENYLKETONURIA (PKU). The most familiar type of error in protein metabolism is that of phenylketonuria (PKU), the first type of metabolic disorder proven to induce severe mental retardation. It is probably the best known metabolic disorder causing retardation, with as many as one per cent of the institutional population falling within this category and an incidence rate of 1 case per 10,000 live births (Guthrie et al., 1963). The first test for PKU followed the discovery that the urine of children with PKU has a very particular odor (Folling, 1934). The condition is characterized by the absence of a necessary enzyme used in the first step of changing phenylalanine to tyrosine. If the condition is not corrected, severe mental retardation is the usual result; however, in rare instances, individuals with PKU have matured as normally intelligent adults (Robinson and Robinson, 1965).

Phenylketonuria is caused by recessive genes, and carriers of

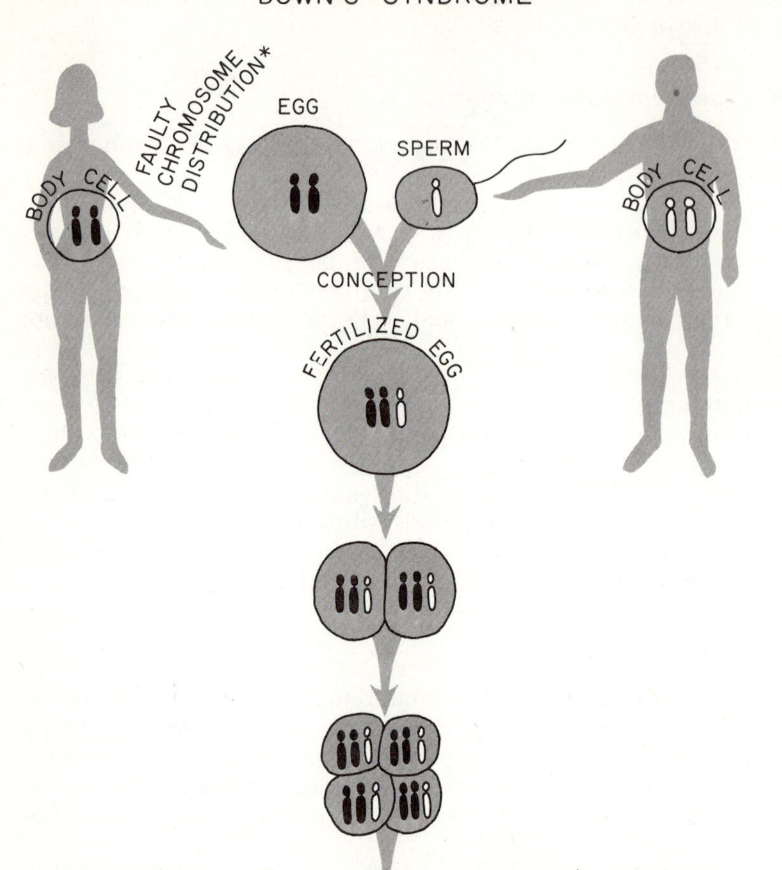

Figure 2–8 (From Smith, D. W., and Wilson, A. A.: The Child With Down's Syndrome. Philadelphia, W. B. Saunders Company, 1973.)

these genes can be identified (Hsia et al., 1957). The original test for PKU was a urine test which is still in use, but a newer approach to the identification of PKU is that of taking a small sample of blood from the infant and subjecting it to analysis. Many states now require that all infants be given this test to determine whether PKU is present or not (Telford and Sawrey, 1967).

As with a number of metabolic disorders, diet is used as the basic mode of treatment. If the diet is instituted early, it is usually possible to prevent severe mental retardation (Robinson and Robinson, 1965).

Other Protein Disorders. Other important metabolic disorders involving protein include the following diseases.

Hartnup Syndrome. This condition is somewhat similar to PKU. The particular malfunction involves tryptophan metabolism and results in oversensitivity to light and the tendency to excrete excessive amounts of amino acids and indole derivatives in the urine. The most common treatment is to add vitamins to the diet. This syndrome is rarer than PKU and

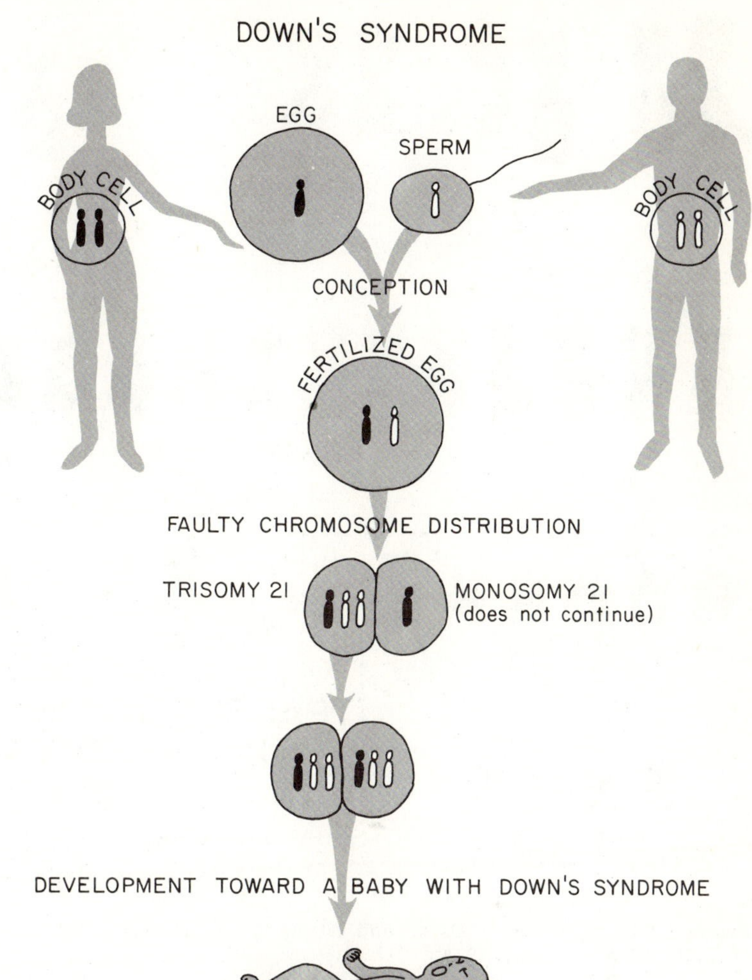

Figure 2-8 (Continued)

is thought to be due to a recessive gene. Most children with this condition are retarded (Robinson and Robinson, 1965).

Wilson's Disease. This condition, also known as hepatolenticular degeneration, is due to recessive genes (Bearn, 1957) and involves the depositing of copper in the brain, liver, and other organs, with severe retardation being the usual result. Individuals suffering from Wilson's disease exhibit tremors, muscle spasms, rigidity, and convulsions. The onset of this disease is usually slow, with death occurring within a ten-year period (Robinson and Robinson, 1965).

Lowe's Disease. This disease was first identified by Lowe et al. in 1952. Its incidence is quite rare and the symptoms are severe retardation, acidosis, excessive amino acids in the urine, glaucoma, cataracts, and spongy or porous bones which result in rickets.

Maple Syrup Urine Disease. The name of this disease is derived from the characteristic odor of the patient's urine. Severe mental retardation is the usual result. A screening method has now been developed (Moser

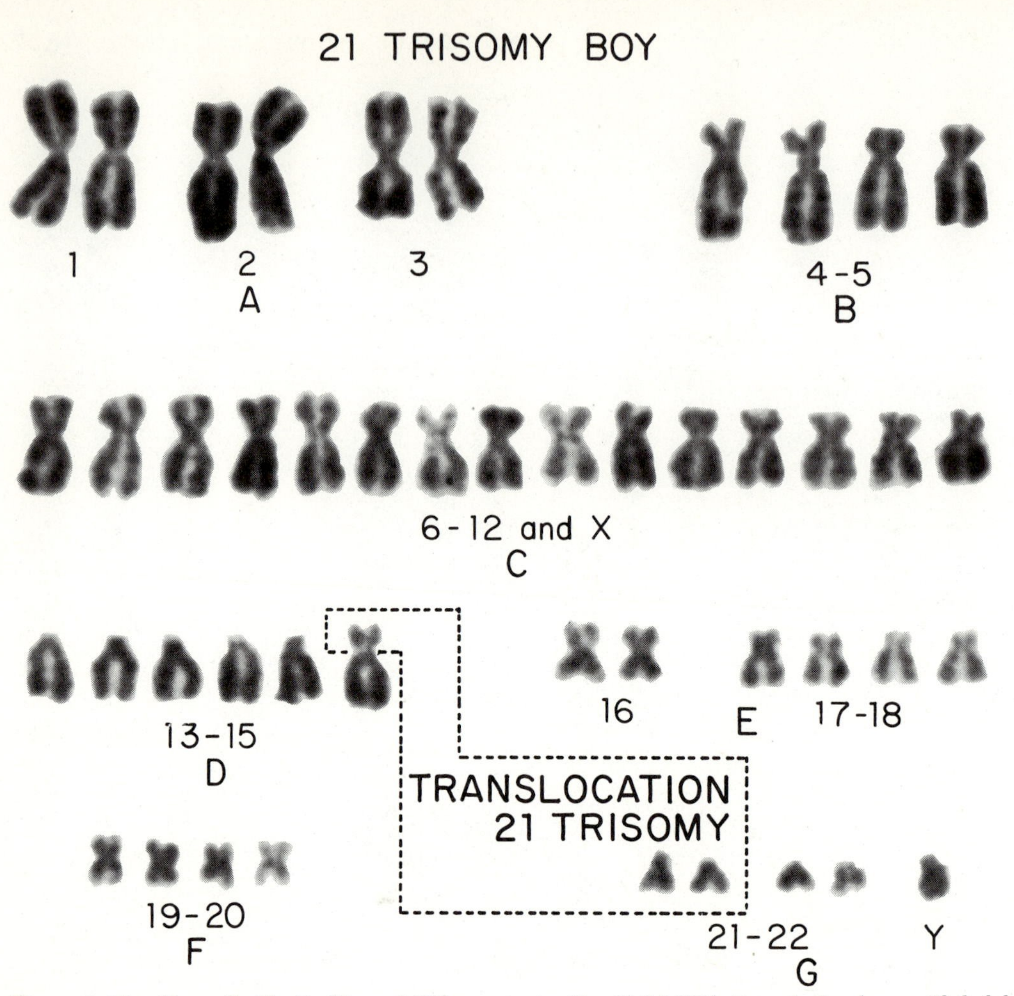

Figure 2-9A (From Smith, D. W., and Wilson, A. A.: The Child With Down's Syndrome. Philadelphia, W. B. Saunders Company, 1973.)

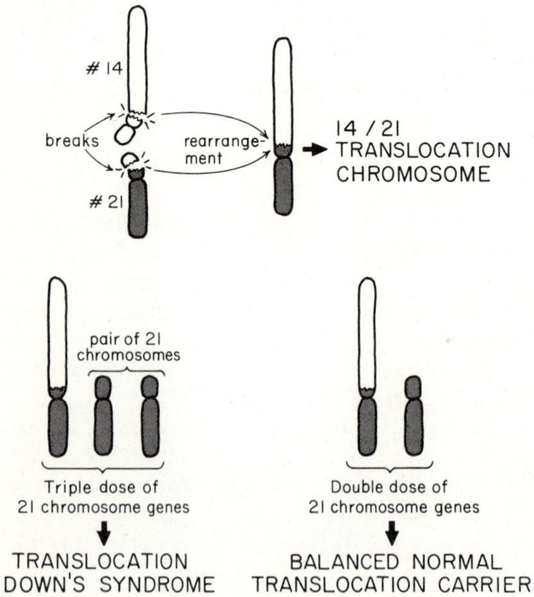

Figure 2-9B (From Smith, D. W., and Wilson, A. A.: The Child With Down's Syndrome. Philadelphia, W. B. Saunders Company, 1973.)

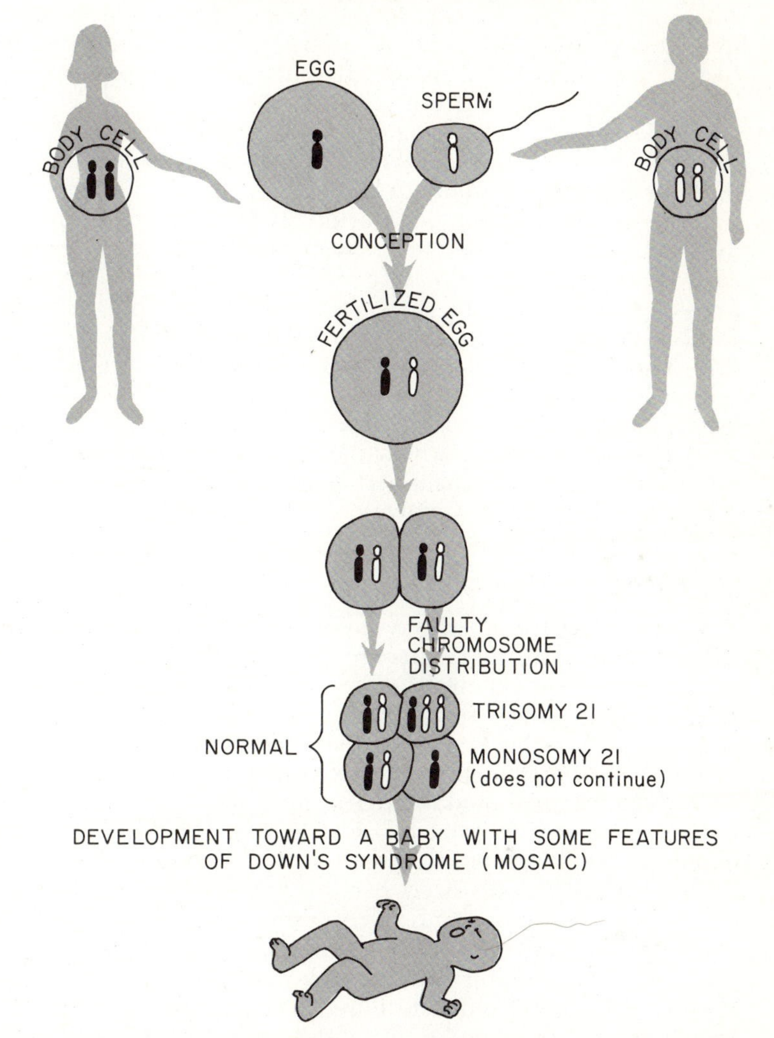

Figure 2–10 (From Smith, D. W., and Wilson, A. A.: The Child With Down's Syndrome. Philadelphia, W. B. Saunders Company, 1973.)

et al., 1964), and it is probable that the condition responds, to some extent, to dietary controls.

FAT DISORDERS. A third type of metabolic disorder concerns the failure to metabolize fats. *Amaurotic familial idiocy*, which is probably the most widely known fat disorder, is a name given to a group of related diseases which may or may not be different varieties of the same disease. *Tay-Sachs disease* is the infant form of the syndrome. It is caused by a recessive gene and occurs in the Jewish population more frequently than in any other group (Aronson et al., 1960). At birth, the infant appears to be normal, but within three to six months, the infant becomes excessively sensitive to light and sound with a generally apathetic response to other stimuli. Death usually occurs by the age of three.

Other forms of amaurotic familial idiocy are largely identified by the age at which they exhibit themselves. A late infantile type is *Bielschowsky-Jansky disease* in which onset usually occurs between the ages of two and four. *Spielmeyer-Vogt disease* is the juvenile form which occurs between 3 and 10 years of age. The late form of the disease is *Kufs's disease* with the onset taking place between the ages of 15 and 25. Older individuals uniformly exhibit a pattern of slow degeneration with severe mental retardation as a frequent result and may exhibit psychotic-like behavior (Robinson and Robinson, 1965).

A disease somewhat similar to Tay-Sachs is *Neimann-Pick disease.* The condition involves enlargement of the liver and spleen. The child with this condition may become deaf and may have visual problems.

Gaucher's disease is a disorder involving fat metabolism in which the liver and spleen are also affected. In the acute form, onset is usually early, four or five months after birth, and the child regresses to an earlier state of development. This acute form is usually fatal within the first few years of life. The chronic form is typically characterized by a delayed onset and rarely results in a malfunction of the central nervous system or in intellectual retardation.

Another fat metabolism disorder is *gargoylism (Hurler's disease).* It is an inherited disorder in which the child presents a very typical physical appearance, a peculiarly shaped head and skeletal system. Severe retardation is almost always involved in this condition.

Endocrine Disturbances

Endocrine disorders may be due to genetic or environmental factors; in either case, the results are the same. The malfunction of any part of the endocrine system leads to serious problems for the child and, frequently, to severe mental retardation.

Cretinism. This is a good example of a condition which may be caused by either genetic or environmental factors. Most cases of cretinism may be attributed to environmental factors which fail to provide enough iodine in the diet for an adequate functioning of the thyroid. There are, however, at least three distinct types of inherited cretin conditions, and all are the direct results of autosomal recessive genes. Many symptoms are common only to certain varieties of cretinism, but there is usually an enlargement of the thyroid gland in all varieties.

The physical apperance of the cretin is marked by dwarfism, muscular flaccidity, and a shuffling, waddling gait. The head tends to be large, the neck short and thick, and the skin of the cretin tends to be excessively dry and scaly. A thick tongue and protruding abdomen are also characteristic signs. The cretin is slow in movement, apathetic in behavior, and retarded in intellect.

It is essential that this condition be identified early, since treatment may eliminate many of the symptoms, although the intellectual level is usually still retarded (Smith et al., 1957).

Hypoparathyroidism. This disorder, which can be caused by environmental or genetic factors, is most commonly characterized by short stature, round face, stubby hands, cataracts, and convulsions. Mental retardation is typical, particularly with the genetically caused condition (Robinson and Robinson, 1965).

Nephrogenic Diabetes Insipidus. This disease is a type of diabetes in which the kidneys fail to respond properly. The symptoms are excessive thirst, excessive urination, vomiting, dehydration, and erratic fevers. It is probably the result of a sex-linked recessive gene. Mental retardation, which may be due in part to the prolonged dehydration which the child suffers, often occurs (Kirman et al., 1956).

Cranial Anomalies

Microcephaly may be caused genetically by recessive genes or environmentally by irradiation of the fetus or embryo or by maternal infection. The microcephalic individual is small in stature with an exceptionally small head. The genetic variety of microcephaly almost always results in severe mental retardation, while the environmentally caused variety has variable effects on intellectual ability.

In *acrocephaly (oxycephaly),* the individual has a tower or steeple-shaped skull with a high, narrow forehead that slopes to a point. The eyes are large, widely set, and tend to slant downward and toward the outside. The optic nerve is frequently atrophied. The hands and feet may be webbed and mental retardation is usual. The condition is probably hereditary, but, at present, the exact method of transmission is unknown (Crome, 1961).

Anencephaly is a cranial anomaly in which there is improper development of the cerebrum and cerebellum to the extent that the cerebrum may even be absent. This condition may result from genetic or environmental causes (Penrose, 1963). These individual live for a very short time, and no assessment of the potential intellectual level has been possible.

Combined Genetic and Environmental Factors

For a number of conditions, it is impossible to discuss genetic influences without considering certain external factors that must be present for the condition to become evident. Genetic factors may provide a basic, predisposing condition which, in certain environments, will be activated. Some of the more important conditions that fall into this category have already been mentioned in the two preceding chapters.

HYDROCEPHALY. This condition is the result of an accumulation of excessive amounts of cerebrospinal fluid either in the ventricles of the brain or on the outside of the brain in the subarachnoid space. The major external symptom is an excessive expansion of the skull, so that some infants are unable to raise their heads even slightly. If hydrocephaly is not treated, the usual outcome is extensive brain damage with severe mental retardation. If treated, however, its general effects may range from severe mental retardation to normal intelligence (Telford and Sawrey, 1967). Early intervention is now the rule in the treatment of hydrocephaly, the most common mode being surgery which involves a shunt to drain the excessive fluid from the cranium.

BRAIN INFECTIONS. A number of types of brain infections are capable of causing severe mental retardation. The more common types of infection are: syphilis, meningitis, and encephalitis. These conditions may cause mental retardation at any time during an individual's life.

EXTREME CULTURAL FACTORS. It is possible for severe mental retardation to result from cultural factors, if environmental conditions are so extreme that they deprive a developing child of the stimuli needed to make appropriate adaptations to the external world. These circumstances are exemplified in the cases of *feral* children, the most famous instance probably being that of Victor (Itard, 1932), whose case was discussed in Chapter 1.

In summary, the origins of severe mental retardation tend to be genetically determined, although some cases are caused by environmental factors. Severe mental retardation occurs in all social classes, and it is a problem requiring total care.

CHAPTER 3

BORDERLINE BIOLOGICAL FACTORS

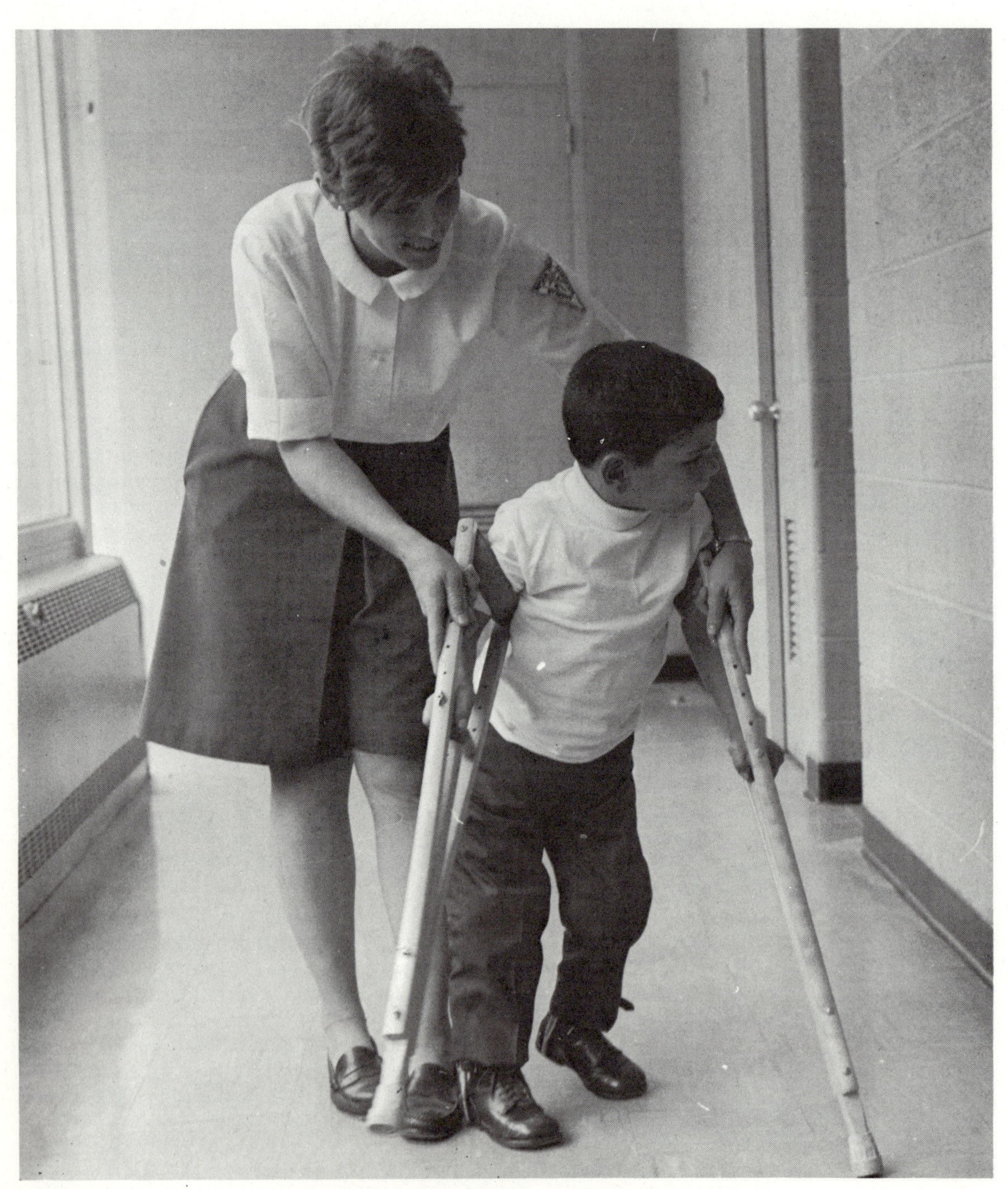

(Courtesy of The Woods Schools, Langhorne, Pennsylvania.)

Physical and biological defects take place in a cultural context. In the previous chapter, we considered physical defects whose biological origin and nature were unmistakably clear and visible. In this chapter, we shall consider behavioral deficits whose biological origin and nature are borderline, that is, unclear, questionable, and not as obviously visible. Their biological origin and nature become evident only after detailed, elaborate, and, oftentimes, difficult scrutiny. Even when such evidence is obtained, the issue of whether cultural factors add to the biological defect still remains controversial and, sometimes, arbitrary. Determining the causes of borderline deficits may become a futile, academic exercise and an indication of unresolved authority and power struggles among those who are interested in exceptionalities in children. Ultimately, regardless of the exceptionality's origin and nature, the special educator should work to cultivate the child's assets and to minimize his liabilities. To help the special education student, some further conceptual elaborations should be made to familiarize the teacher with the nature of borderline biological deficits.

CONCEPTUAL ASSUMPTIONS

Our discussion of borderline biological factors will center on four conceptual assumptions: (1) multiple etiology, (2) multidimensionality, (3) interrelatedness, and (4) continuity. The first assumption, multidetermined etiology, reflects the idea that a variety of children presenting seemingly comparable behavioral patterns (i.e., mental retardation) may present completely different historical, etiological backgrounds. As Baer (1961) indicated:

> The multiple causation principle is implicit for any kind of psychological dysfunction in which: the various combinations of organic and psychogenic components will probably affect the potency of each component. A high degree of the psychogenic component is likely to act differently in conjunction with varying strengths of the organic component and vice versa. We may, therefore, expect no simply combined or mixed causations but a more complex relationship, in which organic and psychogenic factors affect each other in producing pathology. The principle proposed here suggests that several sources are not only related temporally but also are reciprocally interactive in their effects. Interaction as used here is a term borrowed from statistics, which states that two or more independent effects have a unique joint effect.

The second assumption, multidimensionality, may be applied to the term, "biological factors," which, as any label, is a generic term comparable to such vague terms as personality or emotional maladjustment. It is necessary to specify the various dimensions that compose biological factors and make them different from other behavioral deficits.

In relation to the third assumption, the multiple etiological factors resulting in biological deficits must be viewed as always interacting with other environmental factors. This suggests that we cannot separate the biological factors from other aspects of the environment, such as the psychological functioning of the child and his family. The outlook of teachers, therefore, must shift from a view which considers biological deficits as exclusive factors to one which considers the multidetermined, multidimensional complexity of a child's overall functioning. Biological deficits cannot be separated from a child's intellectual or cognitive functioning, his reading capacity, his emotional development, and all other aspects which result from the social milieu. Often, teachers may not have considered sufficiently factors of the social environment as being related to the problem of borderline biological deficits. This interrelation indicates a need to study each exceptionality, using a variety of methods and approaches.

The fourth assumption is concerned with a continuum of biological factors. This continuum ranges from the complete absence of any biological deficits to an increasing degree of deficits. The term, "deficit," however, implies different meanings. One definition implies inadequacy in functioning due to general immaturity and developmental lag, while a second meaning refers to malfunctioning due to irregularities, such as specific brain lesions. In uncovering biological deficits, the evidence may vary from clear-cut historical, medical, and neurological signs to questionable signs and no manifestations. The type of biological deficits identified in school settings is not as clear-cut or homogeneous as the type found in hospital and clinical settings. Birch (1964) indicated that although the role of brain damage in children has been emphasized in recent years, there has been a failure to differentiate between at least two types. In one type of brain damage, the diagnosis is based on an anatomical or physiological alteration which is pathological in nature. The second type of diagnosis is based on certain patterns of behavioral disturbances. More often than not, in a school setting, the diagnosis of brain damage is made on behavioral rather than on physiological or neurological grounds. Birch emphasized that brain-damaged children do not necessarily exhibit characteristic behavior, as had been believed in the past, but, rather, they show a multiplicity of behaviors which depend a great deal on the nature of external stresses and the developmental stage at which the damage occurred.

BORDERLINE CEREBRAL DEFICITS

The continuum of brain damage has drawn much attention due to a condition called *minimal brain damage*. According to Clements and Peter (1962), minimal brain damage is characterized by at least nine different classes of behavior: (1) specific learning deficits, (2) perceptual motor deficiencies, (3) general incoordination, (4) *hyperkinesis*, (5) *impulsivity*, (6) *emotional lability*, (7) short attention span or *distractibility*, (8) soft neurological signs, and (9) borderline abnormal or abnormal EEG. Although it may be possible to identify various types and degrees of brain damage, ranging from minimal to severe, there is no agreement on the meaning of any one of these listed characteristics.

In order to explain even one of these different characteristic behaviors of minimal brain damage, such as the concept of distractibility (Zuk, 1962), we must analyze this behavior pattern. Distractible behavior, which, until recently, had been regarded as being random or undirected, actually may be goal-directed. It may allow the child to focus and to sustain an over-attention on moving stimuli, a developmental characteristic which is found in young children. Zuk differentiated between two types of distractibility: he described one type as an over-attention to moving stimuli and the other as over-responsiveness to background stimulation. In this regard, the work of Schulman and his coworkers (1965) in devising various tasks to measure distractibility is an example of how we can evaluate by *operational* means any one of these characteristics. Each class of behavior, when observed carefully, can be broken down into various subclasses.

Aside from the importance of sex differences, other developmental factors need to be considered in conjunction with borderline cerebral deficits, namely, age, *handedness*, and *neurological lag*. In considering age, one must heed the conclusion that the earlier the occurrence of a neurological involvement, the slower will be the development of the individual. In the case of traumatic dysfunctions, the person's age at the time of injury needs to be considered (Graham et al., 1962). As research with the blind (Blau, 1946) and the deaf (Birch and Belmont, 1963; Furth, 1964) suggests, the organism may tend to compensate in one modality when another modality is deficient. The extent of compensation depends on the timing and the type of injury. Handedness and its relationship to a child's eye-hand and eye-foot coordination is another important aspect to consider. Conflicts in handedness may represent a child's level of perceptual differentiation which results from the maturity or immaturity of his central nervous system. The concept of neurological lag represents the level of immaturity of central nervous system functioning in relationship to a child's chronological age and may be evidenced by body size, general clumsiness, and awkward gait or hand movements.

Intellectual Retardation and Cultural Stimulation

Mental retardation is frequently accompanied by a retarded pattern of general physical health. Studies by Kugel and Mohr (1963) have shown that there is a direct relationship between the degree of physical impairment and the severity of intellectual retardation. This relationship, although not adequately researched, seems to support the contention that a deficit in any one system may affect the functioning of any other. A biological deficit may bring about the corresponding deficits in the cultural and psychological systems, thus decreasing intellectual proficiency in other functional areas. It has been well documented that the majority of children with intellectual retardations come from families which are below the norm, intellectually, occupationally, socially, and educationally. A deficit affecting the biological, cultural, and psychological forces may result in decreased intellectual output, negative feedback from society, and, consequently, decreased psychological functioning.

As retardation becomes more severe, motor incoordination and visual-hearing deficiencies become more prevalent, producing defective attention and interest spans, limited creativity and imagination, slow reaction time, low retention power, inability to think abstractly or to visualize symbols, and difficulty in transferring ideas. These deficiencies may lead to limited initiative and self-direction, low standards of workmanship, and defective abilities in vocabulary acquisition, reasoning, defining, discriminating, and analyzing. The retarded child often develops antisocial attitudes because of his inability to think abstractly and because he is often ostracized and ridiculed by others.

Among severely and profoundly retarded children, there appears to be an especially high incidence of psychotic-like behavior (Garfield, 1963). A great many retarded children probably have experienced severe deprivation and because of their minimal resources have failed to develop any but the most primitive responses to their environment. A number of psychoanalysts interpret many instances of intellectual retardation as defective ego development resulting from anxiety and other psychogenic factors (Woodward et al., 1958, 1960).

A study by Ingram (1960) has shown that the intellectual retardate is "... frequently below average in physique and coordination and suffers from poor hearing and defective vision, but he is closer to his chronological age level in sensory discrimination than in the more definite intellectual processes." Considering this study, it is clear that decreased aural and visual input for such children produces reduced reading, intellectual, and motor abilities. Without adequate feedback in these areas, such a child would have difficulty in improving. The fact that his sensory discrimination is closer to his age level appears to result from the immediate feedback which the child receives from the physical environment. Although such feedback gives him the opportunity to adjust and improve, the level of intellectual feedback is obviously lessened with the expected result.

Children in small families receive more social, verbal, and intellectual stimulation (i.e., increased input), and thereby increased intellectual functioning is a common result. This situation leads to positive feedback which is, in turn, a means of stimulating the total input-output production. Children in larger families, on the other hand, receive more manual and less verbal and intellectual stimulation. They tend to have decreased verbal and intellectual functioning, leading to decreased output which prompts negative feedback from their families and society.

A study by Wallin (1955) indicated that dull-normal children are listless and inattentive in school and that some may completely lose interest in school studies. Relating this finding to the input-output model, one can see that the feedback that such a child would receive in a standard school setting would be essentially negative and that he would naturally react in a negative manner to it; that is, he would withdraw from the school setting. Negative feedback might also account for the tendency of many persons with a low intelligence level to become delinquent and to adopt an aggressive pattern of behavior. Consistently negative feedback from society may cause an individual to develop a negative self-image and a defensive type of behavior. The cyclical nature of such experiences is obvious.

Kessler (1966) stated that there is more evidence of emotional disturbance in retarded children than there is documented evidence in research literature. Even those retarded children with the best emotional development are not comparable to nonretarded children of the same age. Many retarded children experience unhappiness, anxiety, hostility, rejection, and feelings of unworthiness. They appear to be very vulnerable to emotional problems because of their intellectual retardation (Robinson and Robinson, 1965). They are, as a rule, deficient in judgment and have an inadequate understanding of their environment and of the results of their behavior. Such limitations increase the range of situations in which they are likely to experience failure and punishment. The environment of the retarded child (even in his home) and the responses of his parents to him are affected by the fact that he is retarded.

For children in whom central nervous system damage is a predisposition to disturbed impulse control with aversive overactivity, temper tantrums, and stubbornness, family life is likely to become a series of battles. Discrepancies between psychological levels of development, physical size, and cultural expectations combine to create further problems.

Learning Disabilities

Kirk (1972) defined a learning disability as

> **. . . a retardation disorder or delayed development in one or more of the processes of speech, language, reading, spelling, writing, or arithmetic resulting from a possible cerebral dysfunction and/or emotional or behavior disturbances and not from mental retardation, sensory deprivation, or cultural or instructional factors.**

To what extent is it possible to distinguish emotional or behavioral disturbances from cultural factors? Although the first part of Kirk's definition is acceptable, the second part deals with the difficult problem of separating, either theoretically or empirically, certain causative factors from one another. Switzer (1963) suggested that various kinds of learning problems need to be distinguished according to Werner's concept of differentiation, a factor contributing to the child's learning abilities. During the child's life, external factors (cultural forces) which have affected him would be classified as: (a) extreme environmental inconsistency, (b) intense blatant stimulation, or (c) deprivation. On the basis of this classification, Switzer recommended four remedial courses of action: (1) a routine program, (2) reduced extraneous stimulation, (3) immediate rewards, and (4) symbolic enrichment programs.

The relationships between cerebral deficits and learning disabilities are complex and are rendered even more perplexing when intellectual and emotional factors are taken into consideration (Pearson and Kley, 1957; Harris, 1961). Myklebust and Boshes (1969) suggested that there is a direct relationship between neurological dysfunctioning and learning disabilities. Among all the learning disabilities, reading deficits have received the greatest amount of attention and publicity (Money, 1966; Rabinovitch et al., 1956; Roswell and Natchez, 1964). They are the primary deficits about which there is a great deal of available literature. Some day, perhaps, it will be possible to evaluate different patterns of learning difficulties. In the meantime, a reading deficit will be considered as the best prototype of learning disabilities, since it illustrates the many problems that both researchers and teachers face.

Reading retardation has frequently been attributed to sensory and perceptual deficits (Fuller and Shaw, 1963; Smith and Carrigan, 1959). Lehtinen and Jones (1964) and Schellenberg (1962), however, found marked differences between males and females in silent and developmental reading test scores. One of the most intriguing and puzzling factors of cerebral dysfunction has been that of sex differences. Bentzen (1963) stated:

> **The human male organism matures at a slower rate than the female for chronological age, and learning behavior disorders occur three to ten times more frequently among boys than girls.**

Bentzen advanced the hypothesis that there is a characteristic disorder which is more frequently seen in boys. It is "... the stress response of an immature organism to the demands of a society that fails to make appropriate provisions for this etiological age differentiation." This hypothesis, which suggests the presence of sexual developmental lags, can potentially clarify many problems that are found more often in boys than in girls. Child-rearing practices should be evaluated in relation to the occurrence of this seeming developmental lag.

One of the most commonly utilized explanations for poor reading ability is *lateral dominance;* however, Coleman and Deutsch (1964) found no evidence indicating a correlation between these factors. Birch and Belmont (1965) supported the same negative conclusion, thus qualifying their results that retarded readers' consciousness in identification of their own body parts was associated with lower scores on sequential reading tests. Disturbances in laterality were more strongly associated with visual-motor problem-solving than with verbal IQ on the WISC. Muehl's research (1963) may further limit the generalization that laterality relates to poor reading. He administered handedness and lateral dominance tests to 62 preschool children at two age levels and found that subjects classified as left lateral dominant in eye, hand, or both made more combined left and right errors than did right hand and eye dominant subjects. These findings, considered with related research, suggest that left laterality in prereaders is associated with unique patterns of perceptual behavior. Such research, however, cannot be considered conclusive because only a three- to four-year follow-up study would disclose its validity.

Of the various kinds of cerebral defects, minimal brain damage has recently aroused the most public attention, probably because children affected by such defects are so close to being normal and have the capacity for full and satisfying lives if they receive the special education and attention that they need. Minimal brain damage presents a problem because it is difficult to detect and to manage. Early work in this field was done by Strauss and Werner (1942). They described the brain-damaged child as hyperactive, impulse-ridden, distractible, emotionally labile, and perceptually disordered and proposed four diagnostic criteria: (1) an excess of trauma, (2) slight neurological signs, (3) normally intelligent immediate family, and (4) disturbances in perceptual and conceptual thinking. Strauss and Werner felt that it was sufficient to diagnose these children as having minimal defects by utilizing behavioral data alone. However, the diagnosis is complete only if it is specific with regard to the area of dysfunction, from both physical and behavioral points of view, and it should also lead to specific suggestions for rehabilitation. It has been suggested that accurate diagnosis of minimal brain damage should include: (1) distinctive behavioral patterns, (2) performances on psychological tests, (3) history of an organic cause, (4) evidence of cerebral lesions upon neurological examinations, and (5) electroencephalographic evidence of cerebral disorder.

Kessler (1966) used the term *psychogenic* retardation to refer to the child who consistently tends to function slowly. Chronological age in a variety of circumstances is used in referring to the problems of intellectual diagnosis. Dunn (1968) points out that "... three different groups depending upon their biases could label the same child brain injured, emotionally disturbed, or mentally retarded. A dilemma, indeed!" Dunn's personal preference when dealing with minimal brain damage is to use the neutral term, "Strauss syndrome." Strauss and Lehtinen

(1947) described their subjects as having four behavioral characteristics: (1) perceptual disorders, (2) perseverations, (3) thinking and conceptual disorders, and (4) behavioral disorders, specifically including hyperactivity. They distinguished between endogenous and *exogenous* forms of intellectual retardation. In exogenous intellectual retardation, there is evidence of brain damage. In the endogenous type, there is no such evidence, and the retardation is frequently said to come from sensory deprivation or emotional maladjustment. The exogenous retardate seems to score lower on general intelligence tests and to have difficulty with abstract thinking. He also seems to have more difficulty in the perceptual areas, such as *figure ground* discrimination and *rotations.*

A child with the Strauss syndrome presents special problems to the school and to the special educator in particular, because, unlike the child with *aphasia,* he is usually well below normal in all areas of intellectual functioning. Most investigators believe that minimally brain-damaged children suffer from lesions in the cortical area, which is adjacent to those regions of the brain responsible for physical hearing and spatial or motor responses. In the classroom, a child with minimal brain damage shows signs of distractibility and hyperactivity. At home, he is restless and disorganized. His parents are often disappointed in him and feel frustrated by his inability to keep up athletically, academically, or socially with his peers (Verville, 1967).

Organic deficits not directly involving the central nervous system, such as diabetes, tuberculosis, and rheumatic fever, indirectly affect behavioral dysfunctions. In such cases, behavior is more dependent on the culture of the child. On the other hand, organic dysfunctions which directly involve the central nervous system are closely related to behavioral malfunctions. All types of organic impairments may prove to be detrimental to a child's behavior, because they may inhibit his abilities to relate, to adapt, and to adjust to his environment. In order to develop normally, a child must have a stable perception of the world, and he must have at his disposal the biological equipment necessary for normal behavior and for coping with a complex environment. An organically impaired child, especially one who suffers from brain damage, is susceptible to behavioral disturbances because the essential biological equipment is lacking or impaired. Normal organic development, however, does not by itself insure that a child's behavior will be normal. Normal organic development is a necessary but not a sufficient condition for behavioral integrity. Although the channels of input may be intact, a child's output may still be affected by adverse cultural or psychological influences.

Emotional Disturbances

Emotional factors in children with cerebral dysfunctions are compounded by temperamental characteristics, parental attitudes and practices, and the environment. These factors make the problem of differential diagnosis difficult, particularly when it is complicated by psychotic conditions or by intellectual retardation. Small (1962) found that approximately one-third of 131 children in a clinic for cerebral palsy and speech defects presented emotional problems. These results have been supported in part by the observations of other writers; the probability of emotional disturbances seems to increase with the occurrence of organic impairments. Our problem, therefore, becomes one of identifying and screening for emotional disturbances above and beyond the existence of cerebral dysfunctions.

Most children with sensory or cerebral deficits display emotional problems, and it is important to determine what place these problems occupy in the child's adjustment. The multiplicity of behaviors exhibited requires evaluation based on a variety of professional approaches. The study of the relationship between borderline brain damage and emotional disturbances in children is, at present, still exploratory. The inability of investigators to evaluate consistently emotional disturbances and to agree upon diagnostic criteria shows that there are certain characteristics that cannot readily be defined, unless a variety of approaches are used. We have, thus far, failed to furnish objective criteria for emotional disturbances that can be used by each teacher and in every classroom.

EXTREME BEHAVIORAL DEFICITS

The behavioral deficits classified as childhood psychosis are generally thought to result from psychological or cultural forces, although several authors present convincing evidence of possible genetic causation or borderline organic involvement. Among those having genetic or organic viewpoints are: Rimland (1964), who attempted to relate infantile autism to malfunctioning in the reticular formation; Bender (1947), to whom, in the words of Kessler (1966): "Behavior is primarily the result of a natural unfolding or emergence of new functions which depend upon the maturation of the central nervous system rather than on specific learning experiences"; and Kallman (1958), who researched family histories to study the incidence of schizophrenia among various degrees of kinship. This issue, of course, is still open and controversial.

Childhood Psychoses

The idea that extreme behavioral deficits result from many interactive factors has been thoroughly stated by Rutter (1969), who listed many of the pros and cons concerning the various etiological concepts of autism. His outline serves as a basis for our model of the etiology of extreme behavioral deficits (Fig. 3–1). Rutter considered eight possible etiologies of autism: (1) diffused mental subnormality, (2) genetic predisposition, (3) psychogenesis, (4) faulty environmental conditions, (5) social withdrawal, (6) brain damage, (7) abnormality of psychological arousal, and (8) linguistic and perceptual abnormality.

The American Psychiatric Association defines psychosis as "a disorder characterized by a varying degree of personality disintegration and failure to test and to evaluate, correctly, external reality. Individuals with such disorders fail in their abilities to relate themselves to other people and to their own work." The psychotic child may be identified by behavioral symptoms, such as seclusiveness and bizarre fantasy, inappropriate *affect,* abnormal reactions to stimuli, and extreme difficulty in communication. Ekstein (1966) added such additional behavioral characteristics as fearfulness, high vulnerability to both external and internal stimulation, and suspicion of ordinary objects, sounds, and comments. The child's problems in dealing with reality seem to develop from illusions and misinterpretations of stimuli, rather than from hallucinations or delusions. Bender and Helm (1953) reported that psychoses af-

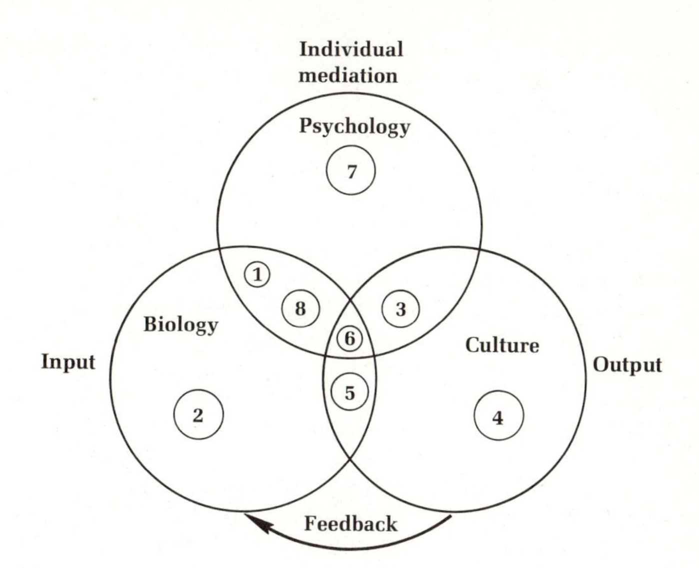

Figure 3-1 Rutter's etiologies of autism according to an information-processing model.

fect all major areas of functioning in the child and usually render him totally incapable of competent reactions.

The origin of childhood psychosis may be attributed to the interaction of constitutional, environmental, and organic factors. Pasamanick and Knoblock (1961) concluded that psychotic and autistic children show significantly more evidence of brain injury than normal children. Eickhoff (1952) found neural deficits in psychotic children which resulted in inadequate perception of touch, pain, temperature, vibrations, and sensations which are basic to the child's formation of an accurate body image.

Childhood Schizophrenia

The most severe instances of behavioral deficits in children are classified as childhood schizophrenia. This general category has been used for all forms of psychoses, or loss of reality, which originate during infancy or childhood. Bender (1947) regarded childhood schizophrenia as an organic condition. She noted abnormalities at every level of psychological functioning and in every area of integration within the central nervous system. The following is Bender's list of irregularities in six characteristic levels of functioning:

1. *Vasovegetative functions:* excessive lability of skin functions, such as perspiring or pallor; disturbances in eating, sleeping, and elimination; growth discrepancies; and delay or acceleration of puberty.

2. Motor functioning: irregular, awkward, immature, and bizarre movements, often characterized by rotating or whirling in place.

3. Perceptual malfunctioning: inability to distinguish important details from the unimportant and to utilize usual relationships of shapes and forms.

4. Emotional functions: inability to form close ties with other persons; lack of empathy; and clear states, such as panic, bewilderment, and anxiety.

5. Intellectual processes: exceptional concern for philosophical problems; excessive reactions to threatening sentences; and fragmented,

dissociated, and bizarre language. In the early years, many children are mute or continue for a long time to refer to themselves in the third person.

6. Social relationships of paradoxical nature. Some children are attractive and intriguing and some are apparently gifted because of their abstract interests and facility in symbolic expression. On the other hand, most are incapable of achieving close social relationships.

One of the more interesting studies of childhood schizophrenia is that of Goldfarb (1970), who provided the following six steps to describe the development of this condition: (1) parental inadequacy and perplexity cause the child to be deficient in positive reinforcement and to experience stimulus confusion, which, in turn, increases parental perplexity; (b) thus a deviant child may develop; (c) he may have an ego deficiency caused by the absence of normal guidelines for self-direction, action, and self-regulation with a deficit in self-identity; (d) confusions in boundaries of self and nonself may occur; (e) the child may suffer from a pronounced absence of predicted expectancy with an ultimate loss of reality; (f) this may produce catastrophic feelings of strangeness and unfamiliarity; (g) ultimately, anxiety leading to disorganized seeking or inconsistency results.

In an extensive follow-up study of 48 schizophrenic children, Goldfarb (1970) found that of the 67 per cent who were discharged to their homes, 50 per cent displayed evidence of improvement relative to status at admission, while 27 per cent showed a level of mild impairment in community adjustment and school achievements. During residential treatment, amount of improvement was related to the degree of neurological involvement. Proportionately, more children who had not become deviant till later in life showed improvement than children who were born with a deficit. Mute, unstable children showed the poorest outcome on follow-ups. Seven years after discharge, the follow-ups concerning children born with a deficit as opposed to those developing one later failed to show differential outcomes. Children who were at the lowest level of organization at admission and who manifested severe restrictions in language, self-awareness, perceptual receptivity, and educational achievement were just as impaired at follow-up. Similarly, the more organized a child was at admission, the better the chances of improvement at follow-up. Goldfarb felt that improvement after discharge occurred in response to positive parental acceptance and commitment. On the other hand, Goldfarb did not state positively the influences of either hereditary or familial factors in childhood schizophrenia, but he did recognize the need for controlled evaluation for all tentative modes of treatment of schizophrenic children. Such controlled evaluation might include residential and home treatment, with or without the treatment of the family in conjunction with the treatment of the child. This design would allow an evaluation of the affect that the family may have in the maintenance of or interference with severe behavioral dysfunctions in the child. On the basis of Ward's review (1970), such a study would seem crucial in understanding schizophrenia and other extreme deficits in children.

In a study of language skills in 24 children referred for childhood psychosis, Davis (1970) found four different subgroups composed of autistic, schizophrenic, brain-damaged, and severely retarded children. Each subgroup showed different behavior patterns related to the specific abilities left intact or those weakened by the particular deficit, suggesting that these children may share a common, basically organic etiology. Autistic children were characterized by no response to people and auditory cues and by a narrow range of inappropriate responses to some objects, visual stimuli, and adult intervention, with deterioration into more inappropriate maneuvers. Schizophrenic children were characterized by appropriate responses which deteriorated into inappropriate responses with continued contact. Brain-damaged children were characterized by the widest range of responses with a sudden decline in confidence when tasks requiring specific sensory integration, motor integrity, or verbal confidence were involved. Severely retarded children performed consistently at a level of less than half their chronological age, demonstrating also specific perceptual, perceptual-motor, or motor deficits. Davis felt that the language deficiencies of autistic and schizophrenic children were directly related to functional deficits of the learning system. Schizophrenic children had more auditory facility than autistic children, but the words they spoke were merely repeated and were not related to their current environment. Davis concluded that "not all pathological behavior of psychotic children is directly related to the organic dysfunction." She stated that psychotic children, both autistic and schizophrenic, "are totally incapable of organizing a specific response output to a specific input" (1970).

On the basis of their similarities and their failure to develop verbal skills, Davis felt that an organic deficit would be at the basis of the various behavior patterns of schizophrenic and autistic children. This study should promote a greater understanding of the role of biological factors in extreme behavioral deficits.

Early Infantile Autism

Some investigators feel that autism in children has an organic etiology with a central nervous system or neurological dysfunctioning as the cause; others feel that it is caused by environmental factors. Infantile autism and childhood schizophrenia are mysterious and extremely puzzling. There is little agreement as to whether they are equivalent disorders, two separate disorders, or whether one is a symptom of the other. Goldfarb classified these disorders as either organic or nonorganic, depending upon whether the child was born with a deficit (organic) or whether he once exhibited normal behavior and later became deviant (nonorganic). Treatment has not generally been successful in these cases, although many varieties have been tried. Schopler (1969) indicated how the extreme environmental viewpoint causes the parents of psychotic children to become scapegoats of the mental health profession. Parents often receive prejudicial discreditations based on emotional rather than on factual, empirical grounds.

In a recent review of early infantile autism, Ward (1970) defined this disorder as: (a) a lack of object relations, (b) a lack of the use of speech for communication, and (c) maintenance of the same behavioral state by way of stereotypical behavior. Both early infantile autism and childhood schizophrenia should be considered as extreme forms of retardation which are, at least in part, due to biological deficits. The major difference between these conditions is the means by which information is processed. Schizophrenic children frequently seem to take in too much data by way of the auditory channel, while the early infantile autistic child relies on visual input to facilitate movement and seems to cut off information auditorily, perhaps to the point of deafness (O'Gorman,

1967). From this viewpoint (L'Abate, 1971), we may hypothesize that both dysfunctions may represent extremes in selective maternal reinforcement of mutually exclusive modalities: early infantile autism may be the result of selective reinforcement of movement with little talking and hearing, while childhood schizophrenia may represent the reverse. The possible relation between specific biological assets or deficits and selective reinforcements or deprivations may well be the key to an understanding of both behavioral dysfunctions.

PSYCHOSOMATIC DISORDERS

In general, extreme *psychosomatic disorders* are conditions which occur as a result of continuous states of *anxiety*, stress, and emotional conflicts. All emotions and hostilities are internalized when an adequate outlet is lacking, and thus they functionally affect a particular part of a body subsystem. The deficit will most likely develop in the most inferior system and in the weakest part of that system. Some theorists claim that the part affected symbolically represents the type of strain that the person is experiencing.

Kisker (1964) explained that "every case of [psychosomatic] disorder is ultimately dependent upon a combination of factors. These are: constitutional sensitivity of the autonomic nervous system, learning in the form of conditioning, the symbolic value of a particular organ system, and the presence of a stress situation." He proceeded to explain, however, that

> ... the level of constitutional sensitivity varies, the learning situation takes different forms, the symbolic value of the symptom is frequently obscure, and the stress situation may be highly complex. For these reasons, it is often hard to understand the dynamics of a [psychosomatic] disorder and equally difficult to treat it.

Lazarus (1963) stated two fundamental ways of interpreting psychosomatic disorders:

> ... the first emphasizes the notion that particular types of conflict or emotional states (e.g., fear or anger) are associated with particular somatic mechanisms. . . . One difficulty with this hypothesis is the lack of clarity about how the particular disturbance is centered in particular organs of the body. Moreover, much of the empirical personality research in psychosomatics has not been very successful in relating specific psychological conflicts to specific psychosomatic disorders.
>
> The second notion concerning psychosomatic disturbance is that the constitutional characteristics make a person prone to express psychological tension from any source in particularly vulnerable organ systems. Thus, a patient has an ulcer not because he has a specific conflict but because he is in a chronic state of stress. This, in turn, produces biochemical changes within the stomach of a predisposed person that can produce ulcerative damage to the stomach wall.

Any biological deficit (physical or psychosomatic) will have a specific impact and influence on a family's reactions (Ross, 1964). Physical conditions produce additional stress situations which increase tensions between the parents and within the family. From this viewpoint, any biological deficit overlaps with the cultural system, and, consequently, peculiar psychological adjustments may result. Considering the cultural influence, the group of severe psychosomatic disorders could be called "somatocultural deficits"; a second group could be called "psychosomatic deprivations"; and a third could be called "psychocultural disturbances."

There is a constant search for pathological deviations in the parents of children with psychosomatic disturbances, but the results of such studies still remain unclear. In support of this theory is Bloch's study (1964) which found a significant correlation among physical, psychosomatic, and psychiatric symptomatologies in self-descriptions of maternal psychopathology, suggesting that indeed psychogenic factors in the mother are significantly associated with psychosomatic symptoms in the child.

Six of the subsystems of the body and the various psychosomatic disorders which can occur in them are: (1) the central nervous system—the resulting disorders can be headache or migraine; (2) the cardiovascular system—the possible disorders are fainting and high blood pressure; (3) the respiratory system—disorders such as breathholding, excessive yawning, hiccupping, sighing, coughing, *asthma,* allergies, and *rhinorrhea* may occur; (4) the digestive system—various gastrointestinal disorders occur, such as *ulcerative colitis, peptic ulcer, obesity, anorexia nervosa,* constipation, diarrhea, vomiting, and even belching; (5) the reproductive system—a variety of sexual problems may develop which are mostly found in adults but which have their antecedents in childhood and adolescence; and (6) the dermal system—a variety of disorders such as skin allergies and neurodermatitis may result.

Among all these disorders, those that are usually more relevant to the teacher are: (a) gastrointestinal disorders, (b) respiratory deficits, and (c) headaches.

Gastrointestinal Disorders

Chapman and Loeb (1955) considered psychosomatic *gastrointestinal* problems to be conditions such as peptic ulcer, ulcerative colitis, psychogenic vomiting, and constipation or mild stomach disturbances. However, the gastrointestinal disorders which will be considered here are those whose major source is faulty eating habits.

Eating Disorders

Feeding problems are among the first to occur, manifesting themselves in the first year of life. Feeding is the child's earliest social experience, and he learns to associate people with the relief of hunger pangs. This need for food, coupled with his helplessness, is the basis of an infant's love of mother. Gesell and Ilg (1943) described infant feeding as ". . . a growth matrix out of which other forms of adaptive, language, and social behavior emerge as though they were so many branches from a main stem." There is continuity in a child's development; his responses are modified by his history. His readiness and degree of tolerance for the frustrations which he encounters in his early years are partly determined by his attachment to his mother and by the frustration tolerance which he developed during infant feeding.

Eating problems may result from (Schwartz, 1958) finicky eating, increased tension and fighting at meals, irregular eating patterns (dessert but no main course), and arbitrary and inconsistent selection of certain foods over others. An analysis of eating problems requires a knowledge of the atmosphere surrounding meals (the time of meals, how meals are served, and attitudes established toward meals), the eating problems resulting from poverty (e.g., malnutrition), and the degree of support or interference the mother receives from the father. It must also be determined whether the eating disturbance has become a habit independent of the child's functioning in other areas (social, academic, physical) or whether it is one of the many problems in child-rearing (like sleeping problems and problems in getting up in the morning), indicating the parents' inability to manage the child.

COLIC. One of the first feeding disorders is *colic*, which is more common in the first-born. It is believed that colic is a reaction to the mother's nervous tensions. The infant's crying is fatiguing to both parent and baby, thus producing more anxiety, anger, and guilt in the parent. Such cause-effect transactions between parent and child further complicate the etiology of childhood pathology by raising such questions as: Which one is the real source of the problem?

PICA. An inadequate physical environment plays a causative role in many cases of *pica,* the eating of unnatural foods. A child who is bored, restless, confined, or unsupervised, or who has few toys, or little planned activity may develop pica; however, some children develop this behavior in the absence of these factors, which may lead one to suspect emotional disturbances or brain damage as the cause. Verville (1967) suggested that pica among older children is an attempt to punish a parent who has shown little affection toward his child.

OBESITY. One of the results of irregular and inconsistent eating patterns, together with additional biological (endocrinological), cultural, and developmental influences, is obesity. Bruch (1958) maintained that, at times, progressive obesity may be part of a poor total adjustment and, in some cases, may be caused by depressive psychosis and intense involvement with the parent. Obesity may be a child's way of overcompensating for futile, unsuccessful, or insufficient attempts to receive gratification by other means (e.g., dependency, attention, recognition, self-esteem). Bruch maintained that physically directed management, such as weight-reduction, should be undertaken only after a thorough evaluation has been made of the emotional stability of the child and his family.

Langdell (1968) listed the following factors as predisposing, precipitating, or perpetuating causes of obesity: (1) hereditary factors, such as an *endomorphic* body build or diabetes; (2) identification with an overweight parent; (3) conditioning by the mother to overeat; (4) psychological stress, such as loss of self-esteem, mourning, or depression; and (5) protection against a fear of being sexually attractive. The psychological cycle that tends to perpetuate obesity begins when one's desire ("hunger") for love and approval results in social disapproval and ridicule. This reaction leads to underactivity, depression, apathy, low self-esteem, and "hunger" for self-satisfaction which, consequently, manifests itself in overeating. This, in turn, starts the cycle all over again.

Bruch (1958) found that the obese child often had an overprotective mother who, paradoxically, was hostile toward the child and was unwilling for him to grow up. Iversen (1953) recorded that an uncertain, troubled family atmosphere indicated a correlation to obesity.

ANOREXIA NERVOSA. Another type of eating problem, which is the opposite of obesity, is *anorexia nervosa,* refusal to eat or denial of being hungry. Lesser et al. (1960), on the basis of their review and follow-up study of anorexia nervosa, which they felt was more prevalent in girls, concluded that: (a) anorexia nervosa is not an independent pattern, since it represents a constellation of symptoms stemming from diverse but severe psychopathology; (b) the younger the child, the easier it is to control this pattern, in some cases, with mild or no intervention; (c) the outcome of treatment, apparently, is related to the type of personality involved. Predominantly hysterical personality traits may make for a better prognosis than predominantly schizoid or compulsive traits. Management of the patient may, by necessity, involve more than one area of treatment since a physician may be required.

Blitzer et al. (1961) felt that failure to eat resulted from fear of eating rather than loss of appetite. Their patients denied that they were starving themselves to the point of emaciation and were greatly preoccupied by food, often serving it to the other children in the hospital ward. These investigators found that the children had a great many inappropriate fantasies and delusions concerning food and had been exposed to a great deal of open conflict between mothers and grandmothers during their infancies. Eating disturbances were found in the family backgrounds of only 50 per cent of the 15 children observed. In girls, anorexia was accompanied by lack of regular menstruation. Regression, rather than actual depression, seemed to be the major characteristic of anorexia nervosa. By not eating, the child could make himself dependent on others, obtaining, perhaps, secondary gains (e.g., attention, recognition) that he may not have received in the past.

Falstein et al. (1956) confirmed theories that anorexia nervosa is brought about by an unclear relationship among biological, familial, and individual components. Although it occurs more frequently in girls, they presented four case studies of boys, illustrating their conclusion that this disorder cannot be considered as an exclusively specific problem of girls.

Lesser et al. (1960) in their study included 15 prepubertal or adolescent girls ranging in age from 10 to 16, the median age being 14. The absolute amount of weight loss per patient varied markedly (from 10 to 40 pounds). All the patients were of at least normal intelligence according to *Stanford-Binet* IQ scores which varied from 90 to 118. Lesser et al. noted that "in about 40 per cent of the cases, the anorexia began with a self-enforced diet which the patient had undertaken because of her self-consciousness about excessive height or weight at the period of maturation of secondary sexual characteristics. In an additional 40 per cent, the anorexia developed in a competitive situation with which the patient could not cope."

The outcome of treatment was that ". . . 60 per cent of the patients became able to eat normally. One patient died. The others retained various eating disabilities. The 60 per cent who recovered from anorexia were the children who showed a significant degree of improvement in their general personality. One exception was a patient who recovered from anorexia but whose personality was not previously disturbed." The authors went on to explain that ". . . the outcome of anorexia nervosa in [these] patients was similar to that reported by other workers. . . . Favorable results were obtained in the majority [of cases]" (Lesser et al., 1960).

Ulcerative Colitis

Finch and Hess (1962), on the basis of a thorough study of physical, social-familial, and psychological factors, failed to find any direct relationships between these factors and ulcerative colitis in children, which previously had been assumed to be a psychosomatic condition. Nevertheless, they could not deny the existence of severe psychopathology in children afflicted by this disease and in their families. One aspect of this psychopathology was the inability to experience anger and hostility openly and directly and the tendency to keep a dependent, demanding position in interpersonal relationships.

Titchener et al. (1960), in studying a case of ulcerative colitis, suggested that the mutual frustration of dependency needs between the mother and father produced a rejection of their son, but left him unable to withdraw from the situation. An important aspect of this study is that such a family conflict can develop without producing ulcerative colitis, a situation which poses the question, Which biological predisposition in a child develops into a physical symptom and which does not? Other siblings in this family were not affected, indicating that "psychosomatic illness" may be the result of peculiar biological deficits, familial deprivations, and psychological predispositions.

Peptic Ulcers

Miller (1965) described five cases of peptic ulcers in children and found that these children displayed the cardinal symptom of school phobia, that is, reluctance or refusal to attend school. These children were extreme manipulators of their environments and especially of their parents. He concluded that "... the psychopathology observed is felt to result from the failure of the parent to set limits for the child and to permit the child to develop capacity for functioning in other than dependent ways." The treatment prescribed for these children and their mothers was directed at achieving mother-child separation, that is, less dependency of each on the other. The results in the first case were as follows: "Treatment was terminated after five months, at which time the boy was doing his school work, attending without protest and beginning to develop some relationships to his peers. He was without gastrointestinal symptoms and had gained 22 pounds since his hemorrhage. The mother was no longer markedly overinvolved with the child." In the second case, the symptoms of ulcer subsided spontaneously and treatment of the child and parents was undertaken in another setting, that is, out of the hospital. In the third case, the parents refused treatment. In the fourth case, the boy returned to school without resistance. He was placed in a boarding school because the diagnosis indicated that family separation was necessary. He did well there for two years and then once again became reluctant to attend. The mother, at this point, did not force the child to attend, stating that he wanted to wait awhile before returning. The fifth child was in the process of being treated.

Chapman and Loeb (1955) cited a case study of a nine-year-old boy with a peptic ulcer. His medical management consisted of dietary measures and antispasmodic and antacid medication. After three months, the ulcer crater was smaller and the child and both parents underwent psychotherapy: "The improvement in the child's ulcer was rapid and it was felt that progress had been made not only in terms of the child's gastrointestinal lesion but also in the much broader area of his emotional and interpersonal functioning."

Respiratory Deficits

The role of psychological factors in allergic disorders was reviewed by Freeman et al. (1964). They questioned the etiological importance of these factors, but they could not deny the importance of resultant or concomitant psychological distress associated with allergies in general. One of the most interesting areas of investigation pertains to determining the specific attitudes underlying specific allergies and psychosomatic illnesses (e.g., dependency in orally related disorders or power and control in anally oriented diseases). Miller and Baruch (1957) claimed improvement in a child's allergic condition after psychotherapy of his parents was undertaken. They based their treatment on the assumption (Miller and Baruch, 1957) that asthma especially is an allergic reaction with strong familial overtones. Fitzelle (1959), in comparing personality test profiles of mothers of asthmatic children with those of mothers of children suffering from bona fide physical ailments, failed to find any significant differences between profiles. Consequently, these results tend to negate a great deal of speculation, mostly psychoanalytically based, concerning the role of so-called dynamic factors in the etiology of asthma in children. If such factors are present, they may represent concomitant individual reactions of the parents and the family to the disease, rather than antecedent causative factors of the disease. The family disturbance may be the consequence and not the cause of asthma in children. This type of research may eventually provide more conclusive evidence concerning asthma and psychological factors.

Kluger (1969) conceptualized asthmatic children in terms of a systems approach which is similar, if not the same, as the one previously considered in this text. According to Kluger, the child with intractable asthma can be described physiologically as having a physical disease, psychologically as indicating a self-concept of invalidism, and socially as having a lasting pattern of constricted social functioning. Treating the child from this viewpoint may effect changes in the physiological (biological) and social (cultural) forces which will feed back positively into the self-concept (psychological) of the child.

Creak and Stephen (1958) discussed some of the psychological aspects of asthmatic children in terms of their characteristic behaviors, such as aggressiveness, overdependency, and negativism. A significant distinction between two groups of asthmatic children, those with rapidly remitting asthma and those with *steroid*-dependent asthma, was made by Purcell (1963). He hypothesized that children with rapidly remitting asthma may more often employ illness as a learned, defensive-adaptive response than the steroid-dependent group (after their separation from the home and consequent hospitalization). He found evidence for this hypothesis and also found that steroid-dependent asthmatics were more affected by extrinsic factors, like colds, allergies, and changes in the weather, than the other group. These results support the conclusion that family disturbance may be concomitant or consequent rather than antecedent to the onset of asthma in children.

Moore (1965) based her controlled study of asthmatics on Groen and Bastiaan's statement that ". . . shortness of breath occurring in oppressive life situations could become conditioned and recur whenever a similar situation was experienced." Considering this theory, she tested a method of specific deconditioning using behavior therapy with reciprocal inhibition (a method of treatment which will be described later in this book).

Bernstein and Purcell (1963) suggested that, for those with the rapidly remitting condition, asthma more often serves as a means of coping with conflict and anxiety, whereas asthma among steroid-dependent children is viewed primarily as a response to genetic, infectious, and allergic factors, rather than psychosomatic causes. Zivitz (1966) explained the success that he had in a new residential treatment center for intractable asthma in children. This is the procedure used for all patients:

> During the first two weeks the child is maintained on exactly the same dose and the same medication he had before coming to us. Only as improvement occurs are changes made, with particular emphasis on withdrawal of steroids. To date all of our patients have been able to eliminate use of the steroids, although frequent periodic courses have been required for a few patients.
>
> These children seem to lose their fear of attacks of asthma. Help is immediately available from those who have the exclusive dedication to offer this help. Professionals do not panic as their parents did – they do not evidence anxiety by repeated questioning for the presence of symptoms. Patients are not engulfed, overprotected or used to fulfill the narcissistic needs of others. The patient has found a place where wheezing is a common occurrence and all, including his peers, are united in using total treatment procedures in an effort to make him well. There is, consequently, a series of constantly occurring corrective emotional experiences.

Headaches

Headaches are often related to biological concomitants (Gold et al., 1967), such as epilepsy, tumors, traumas, infections, degenerative disease, *sinusitis*, tooth, ear, and eye disturbances, gastrointestinal disturbances and hypertension, hypertensive *encephalopathy, hypoglycemia,* and *hematologic disorders*. Most of these disturbances produce other symptoms (e.g., fever) in addition to headaches (Ostfeld, 1967; Livingston and Escala, 1967).

Headaches may assume different forms according to their various causes and components (Bille, 1967): (1) vascular headaches of the nonmigrainous type, a prototype headache without organic background, also called *cephalalgia vasomotoria;* (2) tension headaches, occurring at the vascular or muscular level; (3) severe attacks of pain with sudden onset, often at night, recurring regularly and periodically accompanied by swelling and flushing of the affected area, watering of the eye, and congestion of the nostrils, usually called *histaminic cephalalgia;* and (4) *migraines,* unilateral pains with possible nausea and *visual aura,* the kinds of headaches most often found in children. Migraines are usually found in connection with tensions resulting from schoolwork, school stress, and school conflicts. There is evidence to support this assertion because such attacks are absent during holidays.

Lulow (1967) considered nonorganic headaches to be the results of intellectual and superego conflicts between the child's desire to find gratification and the inevitable frustrations and restrictions that his immediate environment will impose on him. In early years, the need for gratification may involve dependency and aggression. In early adolescence, such conflicts may relate to sexuality and the need for independence.

Thetford et al. (1967), in considering the personality features of children with headaches, discounted the hypothesis which states that a special type of personality in children may predispose them to headaches. This hypothesis suggests that children with strong *obsessive-compulsive* inhibitions, who are unable to find discharge for their tensions in appropriate age-related and sex-related channels and are unable to ventilate anger and disappointments may be more prone to have headaches than other types of children.

CHAPTER 4

EVALUATION AND REHABILITATION OF EXTREME EXCEPTIONALITIES

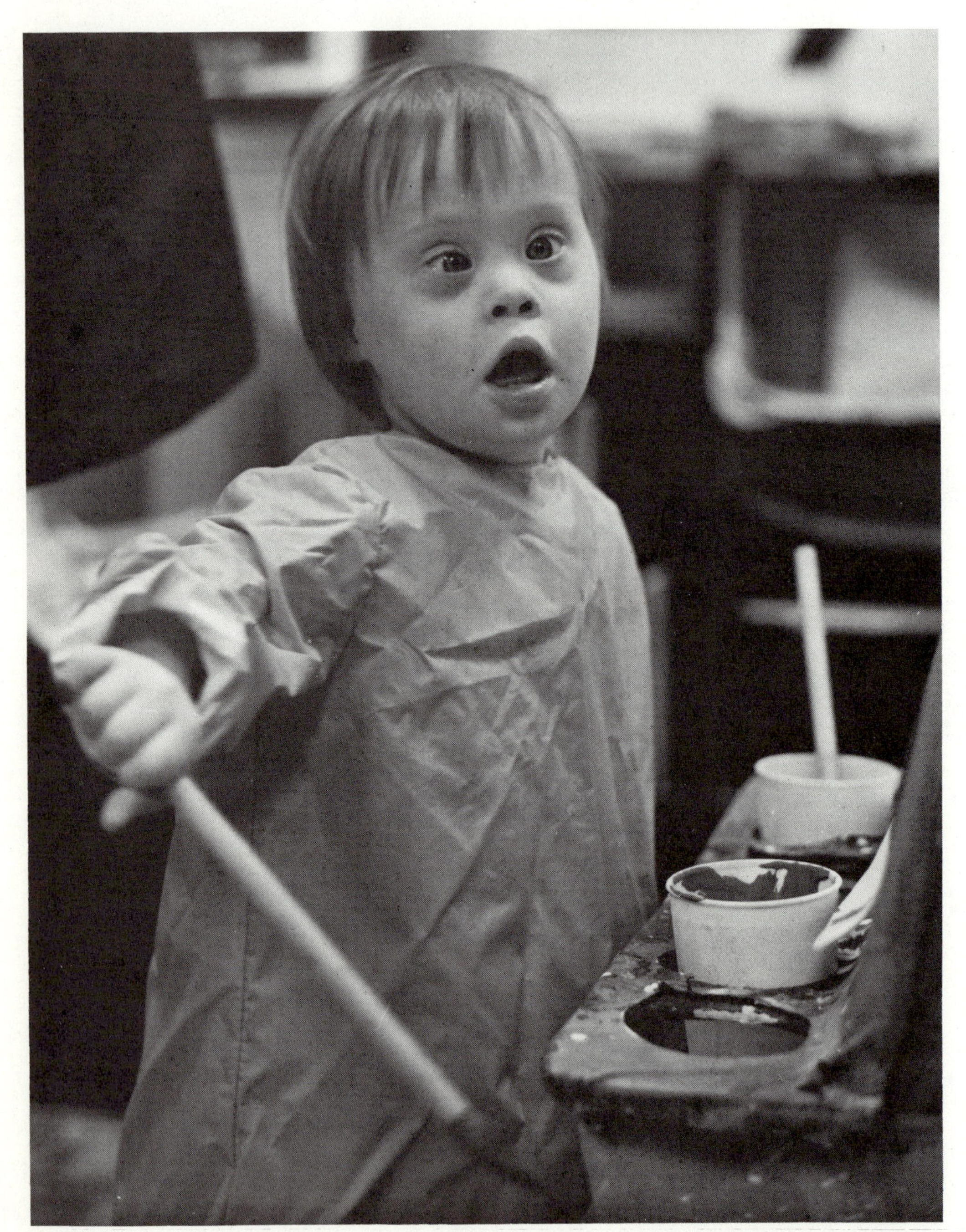

(From Smith, D. W., and Wilson, A. A.: The Child With Down's Syndrome. Philadelphia, W. B. Saunders Company, 1973.)

THE IMPORTANCE OF EARLY DETECTION

Early detection of many exceptionalities has important implications for the exceptional child and his parents. Certain exceptionalities are progressive in nature and may cause deterioration of the child's abilities. Early detection may arrest or retard such deterioration by means of adequate treatment, and, consequently, damaging effects may be lessened. Some exceptional conditions may be genetic in nature, and early detection may be of assistance in counseling parents with regard to future children. Early detection may also assist parents in making necessary adjustments concerning the care and treatment of the exceptional child.

Detection of exceptionalities in children is the responsibility of many fields including medicine, clinical psychology, social work, and education. The role of the physician is of particular importance because of his early contact with the child and his particular relationship with the family. The physician also may be able to institute medical procedures which, to some extent, may lessen the effects of the exceptionality. One condition which exemplifies the importance of early detection is phenylketonuria (PKU), as mentioned in Chapter 2. Prompt discovery of PKU enables the attending physician to institute a special diet which appears to lessen the damage to the child's brain.

Issues in Identification

Part of the problem of detection and identification of extreme exceptionalities stems from the term "diagnosis," which has been acquired from medicine. "Diagnosis" is derived from the Greek word meaning "thorough knowledge." Thorough knowledge is, of course, of great importance when it concerns the care and treatment of individuals; however, in medical diagnosis, it is usually based upon the concept of disease which has the following characteristics: (1) a common, specific etiology; (2) a common set of observable signs and symptoms; (3) a known course; and (4) a known outcome. Thus, specific courses of treatment may be instituted. In medicine, this approach has been reasonable. Unfortunately, this concept does not always apply to exceptionalities (London, 1964). We shall discuss this problem in greater detail in Chapter 12.

Evaluation

The problem of evaluation of exceptionalities is basic to all services for the exceptional child. Evaluation is essential at an early stage in order to provide effective techniques for the identification and diagnosis of problem areas. It should be a continuous process, and the final product or service should be evaluated at the termination of the treatment or training period to determine the effectiveness of the total process. In other words, evaluation is a comprehensive concept involved in all phases of working with the exceptional child.

As part of the total evaluative process, it is extremely important to consider that many exceptional children have a variety of physical difficulties. It seems reasonable, therefore, to begin the evaluation of an exceptional child with a physical examination. A thorough physical examination may help to reveal which appropriate teaching methods should be used in accordance with the child's physical condition. The importance of a physical examination is evident with the emotionally disturbed. In some cases, what appears to be a problem of emotional disturbance due to psychological factors may actually be the result of basically physical defects.

An important part of evaluation is to provide an accurate description of the exceptional child, so that it will be possible to use the most effective educational procedures. One of the most frequently employed methods of evaluation is the interview. Difficulty in effective interviewing is partially caused by the frequent inability of the person being interviewed to explain adequately his or her problems (Rosen et al., 1972). A skilled interviewer can often help to bridge this communication gap. The interviewer must remember that he should have an attitude of acceptance. It is also important to note that acceptance does not indicate approval of the behavior of the person being interviewed.

Some suggestions concerning methods to be used in interviewing might be of some assistance to the teacher. It is usually advisable to steer the questions from the general to the particular and from the less intimate to the more intimate. The teacher might first talk with the parent or child about general interests and activities before moving into specific problems involved in the child's unsatisfactory school behavior. The interviewer should always remember that each person is unique and that the individual needs of the person being interviewed must always be considered.

There is no magical list of questions or techniques by which one may be assured of conducting an effective interview. The single most important aspect of an effective interview is the attitude of the interviewer. In general, open-ended questions that call for more informal and thoughtful answers provide better information. Specific questions tend to be answered specifically and often do not provide real insight into the nature of the problem.

Whoever has dealt with small children realizes that they betray very little. They are usually resentful of having been brought to the attention of the teacher. The more normal they are, the less they like strangers probing the intimacies of their lives. The age of the child being interviewed is, of course, an important factor. It is, in general, easier to interview older children than those who are very young. One rarely gets valuable diagnostic information during the first interview. Frequently, it is difficult for a child to show hostility toward one or both of his parents or to verbalize his feelings. One device sometimes used for interviewing children is the "play interview," which is based on the idea of a somewhat unstructured situation in which a child may respond more freely, normally, and spontaneously. The play interview format is most effective with preschool children.

The interview should be considered as an initial technique and should not be expected to answer all the necessary questions. A second method of evaluation that often is fruitful is that of behavioral observations. The use of checklists and peer observations often add to the evaluative information.

When evaluating the exceptional child, the usual practice is to employ a variety of psychological devices. Teachers should not attempt to make use of advanced psychological assessment procedures, but it is important that the teacher be acquainted with the devices used by the psychologist in order to gain a better perception of psychological evaluations.

Intelligence is probably the most frequently assessed area when evaluating exceptionalities. The most commonly used intelligence tests are those of the Wechsler series, which include the Wechsler Adult Intelligence Scale (WAIS), the Wechsler Intelligence Scale for Children—R (WISC), and the Wechsler Preschool and Primary Scale of Intelligence (WPPSI). The interpretation of the profiles provided by these scales should be reserved for psychologists. Variability of test scores from subtest to subtest is probably of some importance; however, owing to the great controversy over specific meanings that can be attached to any particular profile, the reader is referred to a general text on testing. Usually, the child should be tested formally only after he has been interviewed and has become somewhat accustomed to the examiner and after a good rapport has been established. Another commonly used test is the Stanford-Binet Intelligence Test for Children. There are, of course, many other intelligence tests which may be used if the child is unable to respond verbally or in a normal manner. Such tests include the Leighter International Performance Scale and the Ravens Progressive Matrices. More informal types of intelligence assessment include the Ammons Quick Test of Intelligence, the Slosson Intelligence Test, and the Peabody Picture Vocabulary Test. These three tests may be administered by less formally trained examiners than are required for the Binet or the WISC. The overall IQ score may be of significance only in the case of extreme deviancy from the norm. However, the *inter-test scores* frequently provide clues as to some of the difficulties that may be operating within the child.

Typically, the intelligence test is followed by *projective tests*. Projective techniques are theoretically supposed to bypass overt problems and penetrate to the underlying dynamics and reasons for a child's behavior. Two of the more commonly used projective devices are the Rorschach Test and the Thematic Apperception Test (TAT). Specific projective techniques which are utilized vary with the particular psychologist, the situation, and the available data.

In attempting to assess the possibility of organic problems in visual motor areas, the psychologist may use one or more of the following tests: the Goldstein-Scheerer Test (1941), the Bender Visual-Motor Gestalt, the Minnesota Perception Diagnostic Test, the Benton Visual Retention, and Frostig's Test of Developmental Perception. The area of personality assessment will be covered in detail in Chapter 12.

A number of specific problems exist which concern the overall evaluation of extreme exceptionalities, such as: (1) the need for reliable test instruments; (2) the need for more valid assessment devices, although this may pose a problem, at times, in terms of reliability; (3) the need for objective administration is evident in order to eliminate, as much as possible, human error; and (4) the need to develop devices that take a relatively small amount of time.

In addition to these specific problems in evaluation, there is the basic problem of providing methods of testing which will prove to be valid interpretations of the "total individual." It is difficult to obtain data from a variety of sources, integrate it, and arrive at a unified picture of the individual under consideration, while also taking into account the social setting in which the individual functions.

It should be pointed out that no one test, by itself, is of any great prognostic importance, and all evaluations should be viewed as a collection of all possible data which is necessary to arrive at some idea of the child's total pattern of functioning. A complete battery of various tests that might be appropriate in light of the child's problem is the most advantageous evaluation. However, it is probably true that no single test or test battery is much better than the individual giving it. Tests are useful if properly given, scored, interpreted, and applied to a given situation. In other words, test data should be viewed as the bases of hypotheses.

Testing may be used to ascertain (on a variety of levels) the differences in a child's reactions as compared to other children, and it is also essential to make an assessment of how the child functions within his family. These evaluations may lead to a discovery of the problems which might exist in relation to a child's exceptionality. Such evidence may lead to tentative approaches to the next procedure in the child's treatment.

In summary:

1. Identification and diagnosis should be performed as early in a child's life as possible.
2. Parents and physicians should be made sensitive to and aware of the possibilities of childhood problems.
3. It should be routine to obtain neurological or psychological assessment as a child grows and develops.
4. Teachers should be involved in screening all children when they enter school. After this screening process, teachers need to make appropriate referrals and assist the child in preparing for any special procedures.
5. The complete evaluation of a child should cover most relevant dimensions of behavior.
6. Most diagnoses should involve a variety of fields, methods, and techniques.
7. Results of all assessment procedures should be conveyed in an appropriate manner to the parents and, with parental consent, should be conveyed to proper school authorities who may assist in designing more suitable procedures for working with the child.

REHABILITATION OF PHYSICAL AND PSYCHOSOMATIC DEFECTS

Rehabilitation, as a combination of medical, physical, psychological, educational, and sociological approaches, requires a realistic assessment regarding whether an individual can or cannot be rehabilitated and the extent to which the outcome will justify the energy and money involved in the rehabilitation process. Thus, it is important to consider whether a physical or psychosomatic defect can be rehabilitated and what the chances of a successful rehabilitation may be.

Safilios-Rothschild (1970) defined the goal of rehabilitation as the maximization of ability in all areas, utilizing a wide range of practitioners, for those who at termination of medical care have residual disabilities that interfere with or inhibit their return to effective or "normal" functioning.

Potential for Rehabilitation

How well and to what degree a child will respond to rehabilitative procedures depends on a great many factors, such as: (1) the extent and severity of the impairment; (2) the child's intellectual functioning and ability to learn from instructions and interactions with rehabilitative agents; (3) the child's overall motivational disposition and predisposition, that is, his personality orientation to life (e.g., is the child pessimistic or optimistic, passive or assertive, dependent or independent); (4) the child's family and his parents' level of maturity, integration, and interest in helping the child without being unduly defensive about themselves; (5) the physical, medical, and paramedical facilities available to him; and (6) community resources available to him and to his family during and after the process of rehabilitation.

One of the most crucial factors in rehabilitation is that the assessment of each child's physical, psychological, and familial strengths and weaknesses be complete and correct. Such an evaluation should not only be used to direct specific courses of rehabilitation, but it should also serve as a baseline for a subsequent re-evaluation after termination of rehabilitative efforts. Unfortunately, it is common practice to bypass such a re-evaluation, making it impossible to pinpoint which aspects of rehabilitation helped more than others. Without evaluation before and after rehabilitation, that is, without feedback from a post-therapy evaluation, it will remain difficult to improve and change the various approaches that ultimately contribute to the child's welfare.

Nagi (1969) found that educational level was proportionally related to success in vocational rehabilitation. Low intellectual functioning and severe "mental" disorders were associated with low rates of success in vocational rehabilitation. In trying to answer the question, "Who shall be rehabilitated?", Nagi (1969) considered: (1) role of physicians, (2) types of impairment, (3) stereotyping and self-fulfilling prophecies, and (4) specialization and marginality of physical and psychosomatic defects. A realistic assessment of capacities is fundamental to achieving rehabilitation. Safilios-Rothschild (1970) concluded

> **. . . that American society has a long way to go before it can meet in a systematic and comprehensive manner the social problems created by disability. At present neither rehabilitation programs nor public assistance programs reach all those who need physical and/or vocational rehabilitation or income assistance because of incurred disability. And whatever short-range predictions have been made about future medical or population trends do not suggest that the causes of disability will be soon eradicated or that fewer people will be needing rehabilitation services or income assistance.**

Corrective Surgery and Medical Care

No matter how competent, sensitive, and insightful medical personnel may be, it is difficult for many of them to consider factors beyond the physical aspects of rehabilitation. For those in the medical field, intense emotions that are related to dealing with human lives may be hidden by a variety of defensive devices (e.g., dehumanization and depersonalization) that a child with a physical defect and his parents may find difficult to cope with. When matters of life or death are the primary concern, the feelings and niceties of human relations cease to exist, at least for the time being. The success of the medical procedure becomes the concern of the surgeon or the physician, and the human context of the physical defect may become lost in the complexity of hospital routines. The child and his parents must learn to adjust to these realities. Medical care is directed toward the defect, not its emotional context. Only through the intervention of psychiatric and social work referrals will the child and his family receive extramedical care. The process of medical specialization does not allow a surgeon, for instance, to attend to the emotional needs of a hospitalized child and his parents. He is usually personally and professionally unequipped to deal with an area that he sees as abstract and different, if not opposite, from his everyday concern with physical trauma.

Occupational and Physical Therapy

Most hospitals and rehabilitation centers are well-equipped with occupational and physical therapists who will help the child regain self-confidence and use of disabled parts of his body. Unfortunately, the process of specialization has greatly affected the field of rehabilitation. For instance, speech, occupational, and physical therapists are the most commonly trained rehabilitative agents. However, if brain damage and physical defects have affected the child's self-image and his sensory-tonic discriminations and perceptions, there is a serious need for the type of visual-motor programs considered in Chapter 6. Unfortunately, formal curricula or training programs for "sensory trainers" are not yet available. Another area of specialization will be necessary.

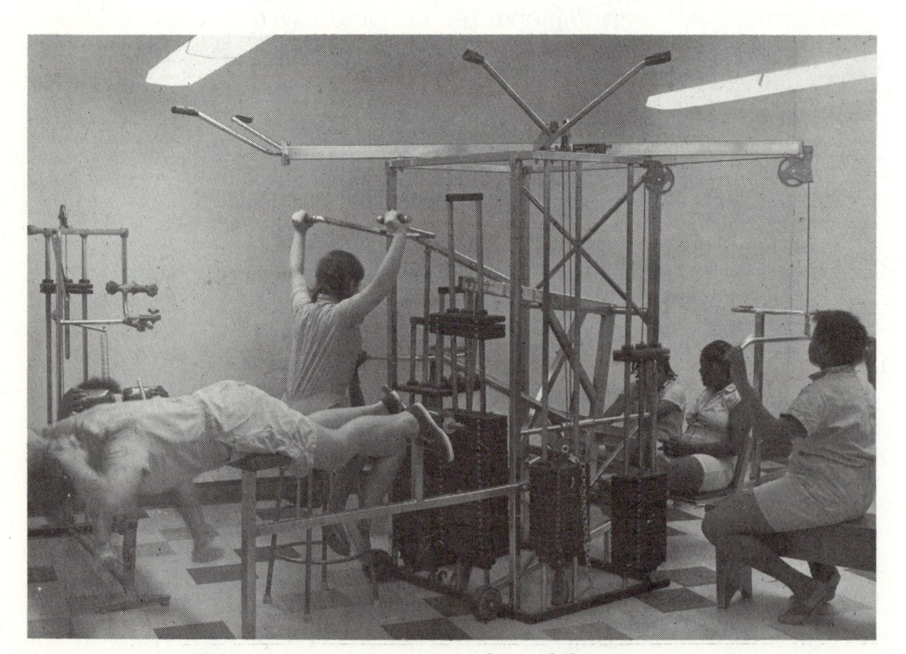

Figure 4–1 Equipment in a physical therapy room.

Personal and Familial Counseling

Techniques of play-therapy, individual psychotherapy, and group and familial counseling will be presented in greater detail in later chapters. Such techniques develop into prolonged, intimate, human relationships that treat the very aspects of human nature that many in the medical profession are unable to deal with. Rehabilitation without this additional aspect would be a cold and possibly a fruitless procedure indeed.

THE TEACHER AND PHYSICAL AND PSYCHOSOMATIC DEFECTS IN CHILDREN

Jordan (1968) found that teachers of disabled or handicapped children are more change-oriented than regular teachers. The former must experiment with new methods and work with individual differences or else they would achieve very little. Regular teachers, on the other hand, will obtain some results by adjusting teaching methods to the typical student rather than to the exceptional one. Consequently, the regular teacher may not feel compelled to experiment with new ideas as the teacher of exceptional children does.

What can the teacher do when she is faced with a child who has a physical or psychosomatic defect? Many "cookbook" rules may be available; however, four distinct courses of action need to be considered.

Awareness of Personal Reactions

If the teacher is not in touch with her feelings, it will be difficult for her to cope with a child with a physical or psychosomatic defect. *Denial, repression,* Pollyannish *reaction-formation,* and other defense mechanisms will interfere with helping and teaching the child. Fear, helplessness, hurt feelings, anxiety, sadness, or even anger may be the emotions aroused by such a child. To react by not showing any feelings would be unrealistic; however, it is necessary for a teacher to become aware of his reactions, so that he may evaluate whether they help or hinder his relationship with the child.

Avoidance of Reinforcing Secondary Gains

If the teacher is not in touch with her feelings and has not been able to deal with them successfully, there is the possibility that he or she may tend to go to extremes in reacting to the child, either rejecting the child by not giving him sufficient attention or overprotecting him by showering him with undue attention. An excessive amount of attention may enforce the child's natural tendencies to regress, withdraw, or become dependent. The teacher should recognize the child's need for attention and importance.

If the child is not learning, in spite of his intellectual potential and even when a great deal of time is spent with him, it may be necessary for the teacher to ask for help.

Strengthening the Assets

If a child's leg is broken, should the child be asked to jump on it? The other leg will be required simply to walk, and the aid of a crutch will also be necessary. This question is asked to suggest that a child's strengths should be considered first, because it is through their successful use that the child can acquire confidence in his self-worth and importance. Eventually, if and when the broken leg (or any deficit) heals, the child will need to be taught to use it again.

Bypassing the Liabilities

Bypassing the liabilities is a course of action which may need to be applied temporarily or permanently, depending on the nature and extent of the liability. A blind child will not be able to use his eyes unless some magical technological breakthrough occurs, and the child will need to use his hands to learn reading.

TEACHING THE TRAINABLE MENTALLY RETARDED

The needs of the severely mentally retarded are of such a nature as to require a lifetime planning program, because the trainable mentally retarded will, in all probability, be dependent or, at best, semidependent on others for their care and protection (Kirk, 1972; Telford and Sawrey, 1967). The general trend of any program for TMR is in the area of the development of self-help skills.

The first method of treatment for the trainable mentally retarded consisted of placement in an institution. The first institution for the mentally retarded established in the United States was founded in 1848 in Massachusetts. It is interesting to note that the first stated purpose of these institutions was to train individuals to such an extent that they could be returned to the community. For this reason, admission was restricted to those who were less seriously mentally retarded. The pattern of admission has changed over the years, and the institution for the mentally retarded today tends to encompass the entire range of mental retardation, from so-called crib cases to the educable mentally retarded. With regard to admission patterns, Goldstein (1959) reported that of those being admitted for the first time to institutions for the mentally retarded from 1922 to 1939, approximately 45 per cent were educable mentally retarded, about 30 per cent were trainable mentally retarded, and approximately 17 per cent were those usually called "idiots" (totally dependent). By 1952, Goldstein found that the admission pattern had greatly changed, with the educable mentally retarded composing some 35 per cent of the patient population, the trainable increasing to approximately 37 per cent of this population, and 20 per cent being placed in the totally dependent category.

A later study by Farber (1968) confirms the fact that the educable population continues to decline, while the trainable population increases, and the totally dependent continue to comprise some 20 per cent of the mentally retarded population in institutions. A survey of state institutions in 1965 found that there were 192,000 patients and that the population was largely of the less than 50 IQ level, with some 82 per cent of the patients so designated Telford and Sawrey, 1967).

The use of institutions to care for the mentally retarded appears to be undergoing change in both the composition of the patient population and the construction of new, large facilities. As previously mentioned, there is a trend toward using institutions primarily for mental retardates with IQ's below 50. This is partially the result of the considerable expansion of programs for the educable mentally retarded in the public schools. Many have questioned the desirability of using large institutions for care of the trainable mentally retarded (Kirk, 1972; Telford and Sawrey, 1967). It is probable that some large institutions, both public and private, will continue to exist for this purpose. However, as the public schools assume increasing responsibility for the education of the trainable mentally retarded, large institutions will probably be devoted to the care of the custodial mentally retarded and to those trainable mentally retarded individuals for whom no adequate living arrangements can be made in the home.

Changing Patterns of Care

As resistance to building new and larger institutions for the mentally retarded has grown, additional methods of treatment for the retarded have been explored. Even though many parents of the trainable retarded resisted the placement of their children in a far off institution, they felt that it was necessary to provide some type of training and educational program for them. One of the natural choices of these parents has been the public schools. There has been much disagreement concerning the use of public schools for educating such children. The best and most comprehensive argument against this issue is Cruickshank's (1971); however, in spite of such cogent arguments, parents have consistently put pressure on the public schools. As a result, in Pennsylvania, the courts have now intervened, and all public schools have been directed to accept all trainable retarded children and to abolish all waiting lists. Whether other states will accept this ruling remains to be seen.

Public education should be provided for all children who can benefit from it. Education may be considered to be more than "book learning." If the trainable retarded child can be provided with training which will result in his being able to function more adequately in self-care and in making some contribution to his economic needs, the expenditures incurred in providing such training are justified.

The current trend is to return the child to a community setting, where he may continue to have contact with his parents and natural environment. The concept of community care for all exceptionalities is growing as evidenced by the passage of the Community Health Act.

Administrative Problems of Public Schools

In designing provisions for the education of the trainable mentally retarded, public schools have faced a number of problems regarding transportation, admission, class size, and teacher qualifications. Many states have laws covering all these problems.

Transportation

The trainable retarded child is most frequently unable to transport himself to school, even when he lives within a few blocks of the school. He may need a great deal of protection and assistance to orient himself properly in terms of time and location. Usually, states provide financial assistance for local school districts for the transportation of the trainable mentally retarded child. Transportation is a major expense which may cost as much as $500 per child per year.

Admission Requirements

Admission to trainable classes is usually regulated by law with some or all of the following provisions being observed:

1. The child's age at the time of admission is usually six. This is in accordance with laws in many states which require that public education start at six years of age. There is a growing movement for early childhood education, particularly for the exceptional child.

2. The intellectual level required for admission to the trainable retarded class is usually from IQ 25 to 50. The usual requirement is that the intelligence score be verified by individual psychological examination and that there be set standards for the qualifications of the person administering the tests. The most commonly used tests are the Stanford-Binet and the scales developed by David Wechsler. Additional tests may be used, and increasing emphasis is being placed on the use of a test battery assessing a complex of skills.

3. A complete physical examination is frequently required.

4. A minimal standard of maturation may be required by the school. This is, regardless of the child's IQ scores, a common requirement, since the child must be ambulatory and able to care for some of his needs, such as feeding himself.

5. Children are typically admitted to the trainable class by means of a placement committee composed of teachers, principal, school psychologist, and any other school personnel who may contribute to the total evaluation of the child.

Size of Class

State requirements for the number of children allowed in a trainable class vary from 6 to 15. The younger the child, the more important it is to place him in a small class. Older trainable children can provide more of their own care, so the class size may be larger. It is desirable to provide an aide for each trainable class because of the great amount of individual attention needed by the trainable child.

Teacher Qualifications

At present, teachers of trainable children receive their education with teachers of the educable mentally retarded. The basic difference in training teachers for these two categories is, in general, the nature of the practicum or student teaching required. The state certification requirements for teaching mentally retarded children make no differentiation between these two categories of teaching. Some general qualifications for teachers of the trainable mentally retarded are as follows:

1. The teacher of the trainable mentally retarded needs to show great patience when the child is slow to respond to academic learning.

2. The teacher should have a full knowledge of child growth and development, especially as related to learning.

3. The teacher must be trained with regard to the characteristics of various types of trainable mental retardation, with emphasis on the relation of these characteristics to learning.

4. It is essential that the teacher master classroom management, with emphasis on *behavior modification.*

5. The teacher must possess skills in music, art, and other "how-to-do-it" activities.

6. The teacher must be familiar with appropriate curricula and materials.

7. The teacher must acquire skills in working with parents, such as interviewing and counseling.

Curriculum

Objectives

Some of the more important objectives of the curriculum for the trainable mentally retarded are as follows:

1. Self-help: It is essential that the trainable mentally retarded child be trained to care for as many of his personal needs, such as dressing and eating, as possible. Daily living skills form the core around which all other curricular skills are built.

2. Social adjustment: From the start of education for the trainable, emphasis must be placed on getting along with other children and adults.

3. Personal habits: The trainable child should be taught to control himself and to assume responsibility for his personal appearance.

4. Command of physical processes: The trainable child tends to lack coordination and time sense. An essential goal of the curriculum is to teach the trainable child to acquire a reasonable degree of coordination and a gross sense of time.

Figure 4–2 The trainable child is helped to acquire a reasonable degree of balance and coordination. (From Smith, D. W., and Wilson, A. A.: The Child With Down's Syndrome. Philadelphia, W. B. Saunders Company, 1973.)

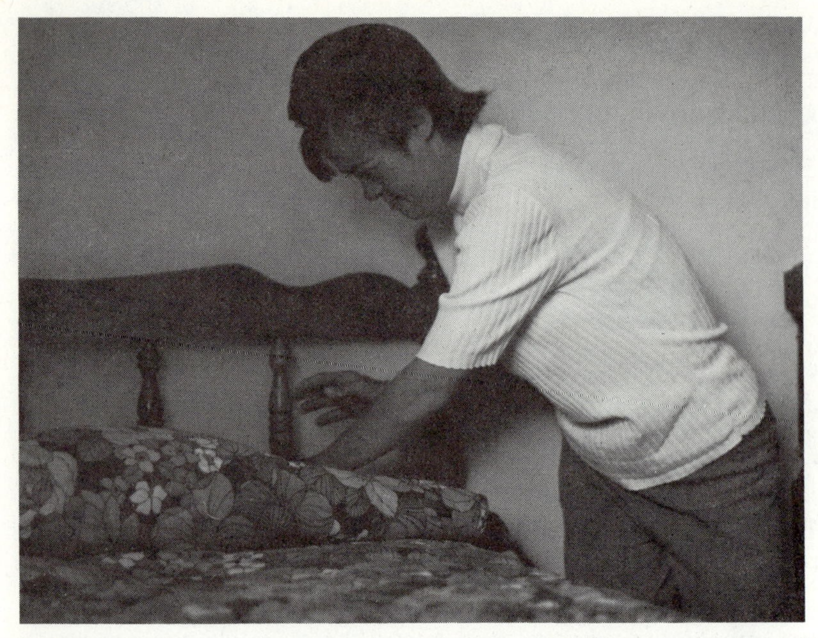

Figure 4–3A Mongoloid teenager learning domestic skills. (From Smith, D. W., and Wilson, A. A.: The Child With Down's Syndrome. Philadelphia, W. B. Saunders Company, 1973.)

5. Following directions: From the start of education for the trainable child, emphasis must be placed on teaching him to follow directions.

6. Communication skills: A major part of the curriculum is designed to assist the trainable child in learning to communicate with peers and adults.

7. Work habits: While it is true that the trainable individual will probably never be completely able to earn his own living, many can work in a sheltered workshop and thus contribute, to some extent, to their care. The trainable child can also be taught proper attitudes toward work and can be expected to learn to care for his own living quarters.

8. Academic skills: The academic skills that the trainable child can learn will be minimal, but he can often learn to read danger and information signs and thus become more independent.

Content

With all children, a major factor in the learning process is mental age. With the trainable child, the mental age varies between three and seven. This restricted range means that definite upper limits are placed on what may be expected of the child in the area of academic learning. Some skills and subjects included in the curriculum for the trainable mentally retarded are as follows:

READING. The reading level of the trainable child will rarely be sufficient for him to read newspapers and books, but there is the possibility that he may be taught a reading vocabulary of 50 to 100 words. The stress in reading is placed on the trainable mentally retarded individual's need to recognize certain important information or danger signs, such as "stop," "go," "men," and "women." Reading should be taught through the use of such techniques as the *organic approach* or the *experience method.* The trainable child does not usually respond to the controlled vocabu-

Figure 4–3B Learning simple household tasks. (From Smith, D. W., and Wilson, A. A.: The Child With Down's Syndrome. Philadelphia, W. B. Saunders Company, 1973.)

lary of the basic reading texts. Some trainable children who are said to be able to read reflect a probable misdiagnosis.

ARITHMETIC. The term "arithmetic" must be used in a very special way when applied to the curriculum of the trainable mentally retarded. Here, the teacher is not concerned with formal arithmetical processes, but rather the emphasis is placed on learning such concepts as big and small, many and few, and on learning to use a clock and a calendar. It is possible for many older trainable mentally retarded students to learn to count. Some attempts should be made to teach the child to use the telephone and to use money.

LANGUAGE. Emphasis is placed on oral communication and speech development. In this part of the curriculum, trainable children are taught to listen and to follow directions. Teachers spend a part of each day reading to the children, showing them pictures, and encouraging them to talk about what they see and hear.

ARTS AND CRAFTS. In the past, these subjects comprised almost the total curriculum; however, today, arts and crafts have been relegated a less prominent role. It is important that the trainable child be able to practice the skills of drawing, painting, and working with various media.

These activities may assist motor coordination and may help to develop an appreciation of beauty.

PSYCHOMOTOR DEVELOPMENT. An integrated physical education program is essential in order for the trainable child to acquire the ability to control his body. Both outdoor and indoor activities should be provided for the development of physical coordination.

USE OF PLAY AND DRAMA. The trainable mentally retarded child should be taught how to play and, particularly, how to behave in cooperative activities with his peers. Drama and role-playing may be used to teach social and psychological ideas. The trainable child likes to pretend to be a mother or father and can be taught many concepts by acting a variety of roles.

COGNITIVE DEVELOPMENT. The trainable child needs to develop some ability to use facts in solving everyday problems. While the concrete mode of instruction would seem to be the most useful approach to learning for him, an attempt should be made to teach some generalizations. The trainable child can use the problem-solving approach, provided that the problems are stated in very "down-to-earth" terms and that such concepts lie within the range of his experience.

SELF-HELP SKILLS. The trainable retarded child needs to be taught how to dress and undress, use the bathroom, eat, and care for personal possessions, including his clothing.

PRACTICAL SKILLS. Trainable children should be taught basic cooking, sewing, and other homemaking skills. This part of the curriculum is usually reserved for older trainable children.

WORK SKILLS. Ideally, the older trainable individual is placed in a sheltered workshop where he is taught the basic skills needed to perform certain types of work activities. The trainable retardate is usually able to earn some small part of his care by such work, and the work done by the sheltered workshop may be a real contribution to the community.

Evaluation of Trainable Education

The primary criterion for evaluation of the trainable program should be whether the goals of the program are realized. As a major result of the program, it is essential that the children be more able to cope with the problems of everyday life, including self-care and, possibly, contributing, in part, to their living costs. It is difficult, at present, to make any definitive statement concerning the effectiveness of current programs. The studies of Lyle (1959), Tisdall (1960), and Saenger (1957) all seem to show that a fairly significant percentage of trainable youngsters are destined for institutions for the retarded after completing their public school training. This outcome may be more related to lack of sheltered homes in the local communities than to any failure on the part of public school training.

The problem of helping parents of the trainable mentally retarded is complex, but there is some indication that keeping such children in public schools tends to influence the parents toward a more realistic evaluation of the final goals that their children can achieve.

It is difficult to evaluate programs for the trainable retarded based on the children's achievement, because there are so few studies conducted in this area. The studies of Hottel (1958) and Cain and Levine

Figure 4–4 The trainable child should be taught to practice skills which will help him later in life. (Courtesy of The Woods Schools, Langhorne, Pennsylvania.)

(1961) seemed to indicate that there were no significant differences between two groups of trainable individuals, one group having been exposed to special education and the other having remained in the home without any special education effort. Much more time and effort should be devoted to the concept of community education of the trainable before any realistic statement concerning effective training methods can be made.

CHAPTER 5

VISUAL DEFICITS AND VISUAL-MOTOR FUNCTIONS

(Courtesy of Overbrook School for the Blind, Philadelphia, Pennsylvania.)

PROBLEMS OF EVALUATION

Definitions

There is little consistency in definitions of blindness, and as Telford and Sawrey reported (1967), there are various types of definitions, the predominant ones being legal, occupational, and educational. The accepted legal definition is based on a 1934 decision of the American Medical Association. It recognizes a blind person as one whose vision in his better eye is correctable to no better than 20/200 and whose visual field is no greater than 20 degrees. (Vision of 20/200 refers to relative distances: the visually impaired individual has to be as close as 20 feet to see what a person with normal 20/20 vision sees at 200 feet; visual field refers to peripheral vision: a normal visual field is approximately 180 degrees.) This definition is the standard criterion for determining public assistance eligibility and income tax exemptions, occupational and educational definitions being more esoteric. Occupational blindness is defined in terms of what kind of job and tasks the individual is able to perform. Educational blindness refers to the level of educational achievement which may be reached by the individual. To define what is meant by visual impairment as it relates to educational practices, we shall adhere to somewhat pragmatic kinds of definitions. Essentially, the classical definition of a blind person is one who has a visual acuity of less than 20/200 after correction, while the partially sighted child is one having a visual acuity of less than 20/70 in the better eye after correction. These definitions are meaningless in the public school setting because of the nature of vision. The mechanical activity of the eye as measured by present techniques frequently does not correlate closely with the actual ability of the child to utilize his vision. Therefore, for educational purposes, we are most often concerned with the child's ability to utilize vision in order to acquire data from printed materials.

As a general statement on the role of visual impairment in public education, we might say that blindness tends to cause problems primarily in cognitive functioning and particularly in mobility. The classroom teacher should be aware of the visual difficulties of her pupils in order to provide optimal educational arrangements for each of them. There is generally residual, or useful, vision to some degree in most visually impaired persons.

Although visual acuity and field of vision are the two major criteria in assessing visual impairment, color sense, light, and object perception may be impaired without affecting visual field or acuity. Considering these factors, one can understand why the American Foundation for the Blind decided that the term "blindness" should be reserved for the relatively rare cases of complete loss of sight and that the term "visual impairment" should be used for all other degrees of loss, including color loss, light perception (recognition of light and dark only), object perception, and the various degrees of visual field.

The problems created by inconsistent definitions of blindness can be realized by examining the related statistics. Although 3,500,000 Americans have permanent, noncorrectable visual deficits and one million are functionally blind, only 430,000 meet the specific requirements of legal blindness; that is, they are able to demonstrate the need for financial consideration and assistance. Probably 30,000 to 35,000 of these individuals are under 21 years of age.

Compared with other disabilities, blindness comprises a relatively small percentage of the American population; however, this problem has historically received more attention, money, and public concern than any other physical impairment. There may be three reasons for this emphasis: (1) the visibility of the disability (e.g., closed, nonfocusing eyes or scars); (2) the residual "normalcy" of children who are blind but have no other malfunctions; and (3) the accomplishments and public attention garnered by people like Helen Keller—thus, the knowledge that "it can be done."

Causes

The causes of blindness or visual impairment are varied. Cruickshank and Trippe (1959) reported that 66.2 per cent of New York State's blind children were congenitally blind or became blind by or before age one. Congenital factors by far account for the largest percentage of cases. *Glaucoma* and cataracts, although the former is arrestable and the latter is correctable by surgery which is 95 per cent effective, are representative of other biological malfunctions causing blindness, each accounting for about 14 per cent of new cases of blindness in the United States. Lowenfield (1963) indicated *retrolental fibroplasia* (RLF) as the leading cause of blindness and listed other common causes, such as infectious diseases, injury, poisoning, tumor, and hereditary factors. The causes of impaired vision may be of academic interest to the special education teacher, as well as the regular classroom teacher. The following factors have been found to be the major causes of visual impairment: postnatal infections, injuries, excessive oxygen, tumors, natal and prenatal causes, such as brain damage (both central and peripheral), traumas, and toxic and hereditary factors.

Incidence

It is difficult to make an adequate estimate of the total number of children enrolled in the public education system who may be suffering from some type of visual problem. Estimates vary from as low as 1 per cent to as high as 22 per cent of the public school population. In one survey of 5000 children in California, 22 per cent of the elementary school children and 31 per cent of the high school students were found to have visual defects (Dalton, 1943). This percentage, of course, included a great many children who have visual defects which, for all practical purposes, posed no particular problem in educational performance. It is unfortunate that there are literally no dependable statistics regarding prevalence of blindness and partial sightedness. These uncertain statistics are, perhaps, due to changes in eyesight which are the results of normal maturation of the structure of the eye, by which the eye becomes increasingly capable of coping with educational practices. It has been estimated that totally blind individuals number about 385,000 out of the total population or 2.14 per 1,000 individuals (Gibbons and McCaslin, 1962).

Again, it should be noted that in public schools the concept of 20/20 vision as the primary indicator of healthy vision should not be emphasized. Visual acuity is only indirectly related to the child's ability to utilize vision in a learning situation. The traditional method of assessment of vision by use of the Snellen Chart, in which a child from some distance identifies letters on a chart, leads to many errors. The type of vision which the chart measures is not the primary mode used in the acquisition of knowledge. To measure close vision would be much more appropriate, since this indicates what a child sees when he looks at the page of a book. Such close reading may involve additional kinds of problems relating to close vision rather than to distance vision which is measured by the Snellen Chart.

The relative rarity of severe visual impairment can be seen from this data by Scott (1969), representing persons per 1,000 in the population:

Age	*Rate*
0–21	0.35
18–24	2.9
25–34	2.6
35–44	2.3
45–54	6.7
55–64	12.0
65–74	28.0
70–79	33.0

These data indicate that prevalence of blindness and visual impairment is a positive function of increasing age. These figures do not show, however, (as other statistics have) that almost 10 per cent of the blind are under 20 years of age, that an estimated one-fourth of school children have some degree of visual anomaly, or that of the 50 million children enrolled in elementary and secondary schools in the United States in 1966, about 45,000 were at that time severely visually impaired.

Between 1942 and 1959, the incidence of children born prematurely with severe visual impairment or contracting severe impairment within approximately one month increased by a large percentage. This increment was the result of RLF, a condition related to too much oxygen being absorbed by premature infants in incubators. Rates of RLF infants per 100,000 persons rose from 19.9 in 1954 to 1955 to 34.1 in 1958 to 1959. This "bumper crop" of RLF babies is now involved in the process of education and represents virtually the only significant increase in the incidence of blindness for any given cause.

Personality Factors

Blindness produces no distinctive personality pattern; however, because it causes a deficiency in a major channel of input, it may produce a tendency toward withdrawal and introversion. Because a blind child is deprived of visual input, he often shows little facial expression. Cruickshank (1964) pointed out that blind children may experience emotional disturbances resulting from parental overprotection and restrictions. Verville (1968) reported that lack of initiative is a common trait of blind children and that some may resort to overtalkativeness to hide their anxiety and loneliness. The child may also indulge in habits known as "blindisms," such as rocking, putting fingers in the eyes, whirling around rapidly, and nodding the head. Because all these symptoms may be observed in many children who have perfectly adequate vision, the concept of blindism is an oversimplification. Of course, part of the training process for all children should be to train them to avoid exhibiting behavior which calls attention to themselves in some undesirable way.

The relationship of impaired vision to other variables involved in education is frequently not clearly understood. Studies of the visually impaired indicate that blindness is not related to any particularly large incidence of emotional disturbance. The adjustment of the visually impaired child closely follows the curve of the emotional adjustment of all children of comparable ages. The emotional adjustment of children to physically handicapping conditions, in particular, is largely a reflection of parental acceptance of the deficit.

Developmental Factors

McGuire and Meyers (1971), in studying developmental problems in the congenitally blind child, found that over half of two samples of blind children exhibited a disturbed interpersonal relationship with their mothers, resulting from maternal punitiveness or verbal abuse. Parents

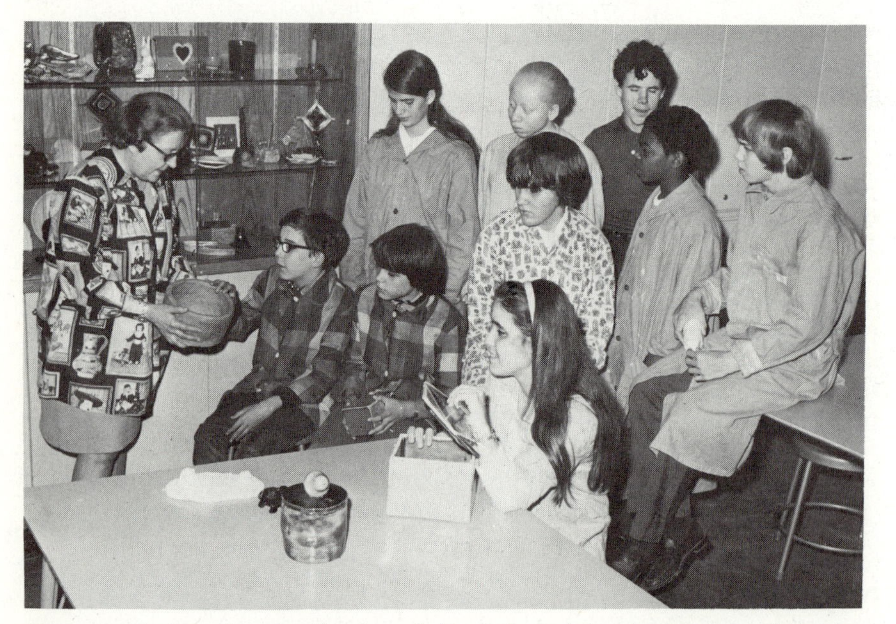

Figure 5-1A Learning identification of objects through touch. (Courtesy of Overbook School for the Blind, Philadelphia, Pennsylvania.)

reinforced their children's disturbed patterns by using arbitrary punishment methods and *negative reinforcement.* Despite learning opportunities, these children had problems in mobility which frequently were interpreted as mental retardation. Nevis (1967) suggested that visual preferences of infants are early indications of perceptual-cognitive growth. Hartlage's (1968) study demonstrated the relationship between visual deficits and the ability to deal with questions concerning space.

Chalfant and Scheffelin (1969) outlined the various steps necessary for the reception, processing, and association of visual stimuli: (1) reception of visual stimuli, (2) orienting of head and eyes to the stimulus source, (3) scanning of the stimulus objects, (4) identification of dominant visual cues, (5) integration of dominant visual cues, (6) tentative classification of the stimulus object in a visual category, (7) comparison of the resulting visual hypothesis with the actual object as it is perceived, (8) confirmation of the comparison or introduction of corrections into the previous visual hypothesis. As Chalfant and Scheffelin reported, "Children who are blind depend chiefly upon audition, while children who are deaf rely heavily upon vision."

In their review of perceptual integration in children, Pick et al. (1967) negated the notion "that visual perception is based on prior tactual, kinesthetic, or proprioceptive experience." Instead, they concluded that vision appeared to be dominant over tactual perception at all ages. This conclusion in no way negates the assumption of increasing differentiation of all other sense modalities. A sequence of visual-motor development (in space) prior to the development of auditory-verbal skills (in time) is, however, consistent with other developmental viewpoints (L'Abate, 1964). Tactual skills may tend to decrease with age, unless one

Figure 5–1B Development of tactile abilities is important for the blind. (Courtesy of Overbrook School for the Blind, Philadelphia, Pennsylvania.)

of the other modalities is defective, such as with auditory deficits or especially defective vision. In such cases, touch is more greatly emphasized as a channel of communication. Tactual discrimination is more difficult to develop than either visual or auditory discrimination, and, in general, it is used infrequently or not as frequently as the other two modalities. The more complex the task, the greater the need for integration between vision and audition, and depending on the nature of the task, the greater the need for integration among all sensory modalities at a more central level in the nervous system.

The *haptic modality*, composed of the cutaneous (touch) and kinesthetic (body movement) modalities, allows for compensation for deficits in either the visual or auditory modalities. It helps provide the organism with information about surface textures, qualities of consistency (e.g., hardness or softness), temperature, and pressure. Unfortunately, "There is little known about either the restoration or the compensation of haptic processing dysfunction in children" (Chalfant and Scheffelin, 1969), nor have we made provisions to evaluate its status in our everyday experiences. In a certain sense, this modality could be considered as manual output since it involves the hands. Kinesthetic responses usually involve one's limbs.

Development and Modality Preference

Buktenica (1968) maintained that the independence of auditory from visual perception might indicate separate neurological integrative systems for each type of perception. Unfortunately, such a conclusion was based on an inadequate assessment of children's verbal output, so that at present, the concept must be questioned, both on conceptual and empirical grounds. Rudnick et al. (1967) suggested that visual perceptual abilities decline in importance in third and fourth graders, while during these ages general intelligence, auditory skills, and cross-modal perceptual-motor skills become more important in relation to individual differences in reading ability.

Weinstein (1967) contended that there are unity and coextension between perceptual and motor development. He proposed a classification based on a theory of the interrelationship between vision and action.

Rasoff (1969) found that the order of modality preference and accuracy was visual-visual, visual-haptic, haptic-visual, and haptic-haptic, supporting the results of Gaines (1970) and Pick et al. (1967) and suggesting that the visual modality is superior to the tactual modality in shape recognition and discrimination. Kluever (1969) found that memory seems to affect visual input-output factors more directly than auditory input-output, a finding which is consistent with the developmental sequence of these modalities.

Visual Deficits, Intellectual Functioning, and Educational Achievement

Any intellectually handicapping conditions which a child may have are only indirectly related to his visual impairment. In examining the entire range of visually impaired children, a normal curve of intellectual development is found (Bateman, 1963).

The visually impaired child does not exhibit any particularly grave problem concerning the acquisition of language. However, the congenitally blind child tends to be somewhat slower in learning to speak, and his language development tends to be somewhat lacking when compared to that of a seeing child of the same age. The following have been listed as speech characteristics of the blind (Brieland, 1966; Rowe, 1958):

1. The blind speak at a slower rate than the sighted.
2. The blind speak louder, modulate their voices less, and project their voices less appropriately.
3. The blind have less vocal variety.
4. The blind use less lip movements in articulation.

These characteristics are not typically observed in all blind or visually impaired children, but many do tend to be observable in the visually impaired population.

Lehrer (1969) found that nonverbal variables contributed significantly and substantially to the prediction of achievement (especially in nonverbal intelligence) and educational efficiency. These results support the same developmental sequence of primacy in visual-motor over auditory-verbal modalities.

Telford and Sawrey (1967) concluded that

> **there are certainly no language deficits or proficiencies peculiar to the blind. Unlike the deaf, the blind acquire speech in the ordinary way and handle language in ways which are quite normal.**

This conclusion supports Lenneberg's contention of independence between the visual-motor and auditory-verbal modalities (1967). In addition, Telford and Sawrey noted that

> **the mental level of the visually handicapped, as measured by existing intelligence tests, does not differ markedly from that of children with normal vision. . . . Visual impairment produces less of a decrement in intellectual functioning as measured by conventional intelligence tests than does comparable auditory deficit. . . . Most children with visual defects have normal mental abilities.**

Their educational achievement is "on the average about two years lower than seeing children of the same grade. Their educational retardation is especially evident in arithmetic, an area specifically dependent on spatial concepts and movement" (Telford and Sawrey, 1967).

Factors in Visual-Motor Functioning

To ascertain whether the child has difficulty in receiving information visually or whether his problem is expressing information, we need to know the particular area of difficulty. Does the child have difficulty encoding visual stimuli? Does he handle auditory encoding adequately? Is his problem involved in writing language (expressive), although the information has been adequately received and can be expressed verbally? This is the specific type of information that is necessary in order to give adequate assistance to the visually handicapped child. Such information can be used to make specific educational recommendations for the child which will allow him to maximize his assets and work on his liabilities, thereby improving his overall performance and behavior. For instance, Lemmon (1968), in studying the visual perceptual characteristics of EMR children, found a moderate but positive relationship between visual memory and visual discrimination, *chronological age,* and *mental age.* He concluded that cultural-familial retardates have the ability to develop adequate *visual-closure* competencies, even though they do not learn these competencies through maturation as normal children do. These findings tend to support the present position that discrimination, defined as reception of information, is basic to development and positively related to the effectiveness and competence of the child. Ayres (1965) delineated five factors involved in visual perceptual dysfunction: (1) *apraxia,* difficulty with motor planning; (2) a deficit in perception of form and position in space; (3) difficulty in *bilaterality* in oneself, difficulty in knowing right and left, and avoidance of crossing the midline; (4) deficit in figure-ground perception; and (5) hyperactivity, distractibility, and defensive reactions.

Cross-Modality Learning Disorders

Reading and writing are complex skills based on an integration of visual and auditory input which results in verbal and manual output. A deficit in any of these four modalities may produce a lowering of efficiency in either or both skills. Arithmetical ability is closely related to: (1) general intelligence, (2) spatial ability and its subcomponents (body orientation, visualization, and kinesthetic imagery), (3) verbal ability, (4) approach-to-problem-solving, and (5) neurophysiological correlates (Chalfant and Scheffelin, 1969). Santoro (1968) suggested that both intelligence and visual perception are important to reading achievement at the first- and second-grade levels. At the third-grade level, visual and visual-motor variables were not significantly correlated with reading achievement. At the fourth-grade level, intelligence test scores were highly correlated with reading achievement. The measurement problems of reading achievement are unusually difficult. They involve a complex array of abilities, making it difficult, if not impossible, to narrow the diagnosis of a reading disability to a specific deficit in which the child needs help.

Ferguson (1967) found that children of average intelligence who showed a Frostig Perceptual Quotient score below 90, which was inconsistent with their intellectual functioning, would be expected to achieve poorly in their total academic readiness in the first grade, especially in reading and arithmetic.

Bean (1968) demonstrated that retarded reading is more related to a generalized verbal deficit than to visual-motor coordination and that sequential memory is another critical deficit in reading retardation. In contrast, Polenz's (1969) findings tend to support the relationship of specific types of reading errors to eye-motor coordination, figure-ground perception, and shape constancy. These conclusions are supported by Hafner's (1969) study of motor control and first-grade reading difficulties. All measurements of reading readiness (New York State Test), motor development (Lincoln-Oseretsky Test), intellectual functioning, (California Test of Mental Maturity), and achievement (California Test) correlated positively and significantly with a scale for evaluation of motor control activities developed and validated by Hafner herself.

This and other evidence, relating to theories upon which visual-motor training is based, emphasize the fact that providing perceptual-motor training for the child with learning problems and using the term "perceptual problems" as a catch-all excuse for a child's not achieving in school are no longer justifiable practices. Contradictory results (e.g., the studies previously discussed) caution against generalizing from a limited sample and suggest that there might be a salient relationship between the kinds of reading problems observed and appropriate teaching methods. We must not interpret coexisting defects as forming causal relationships, and we must realize that even though sensory (visual, tactual, and kinesthetic) integration affects cognitive growth, it may be part of higher level processes that are not operationally definable. It may be conceptually contradictory to speak of both integration and independent factors with regard to the same situation.

Sex and Group Membership Differences in Visual-Motor Development

Fox (1969) failed to find that sex and race were interrelated among Indian, black, and white Head Start children on the ITPA and three other tests of visual-motor functioning. He found a variety of information-processing patterns depending on the group membership of these children.

Alley and Snider (1970) found that black children were significantly superior to white children on a variety of sensory-motor tasks. They hypothesized that, perhaps, black children may be stimulated toward physical skills by their mothers in order to become physically oriented toward their environment or that they may be motivated toward sensory-motor performance as an avenue of success (i.e., sports). A third conjecture pertains to the lack of control over such variables as physical growth, previous experiential training, and attitudes toward perceptual-motor development. A fourth possibility not considered by Alley and Snider pertains to the fact that measurements of linguistic development in black children are made according to criteria of standard white English rather than criteria that would be germane to the black child's dialect and idiomatic differences.

Sapir (1966) found significant sex differences in perceptual-motor development in kindergarten children. Although boys matured more rapidly than girls during the nine-month, test-retest interval, they never reached the developmental levels of girls. Sapir felt that these findings were relevant to the reading readiness of boys and girls and the need for differentiating educational practices for boys and girls.

THE VISUALLY HANDICAPPED CHILD IN THE PUBLIC SCHOOL

Identification in the Classroom

As a rule, teachers should observe children in the classroom for the following major signs which may indicate the need for some type of visual checkup (Winebrenner, 1952):

1. Chronic eye irritations as indicated by watery eyes and red-rimmed, encrusted, or swollen eyelids.
2. Nausea, double vision, or visual blurring during or following reading.
3. Rubbing of eyes, frowning, or screwing up the face when looking at distant objects.
4. Overcautiousness in walking and running infrequently and falteringly for no apparent reason.
5. Abnormal inattentiveness during chalkboard, wall chart, or map work.
6. Complaints of visual blurring and attempts to brush away the visual impediment.
7. Excessive restlessness, irritability or nervousness following prolonged close, visual work.
8. Blinking excessively, especially while reading.

9. Habitually holding books very closely, very far away, or in other unusual positions when reading.

10. Tilting the head to one side when reading.

11. Reading only for short periods at a time.

12. Shutting or covering one eye when reading.

As with all other deficits, early identification of visual impairment may lead to corrective measures which will enable the child to perform much more adequately in the public school.

Visual Deficits and Mobility in the Classroom

Education of the visually impaired child may cause the teacher some concern particularly because of the impaired mobility of the child. It is not uncommon to observe an impression of daydreaming or apparent "not with it" kind of behavior on the part of a visually impaired child. This behavior should be viewed as being appropriate considering the fact that one of the most important factors involved in visual impairment is the limitation of mobility, particularly with totally blind individuals. Also, educational procedures center on the visual mode of input as the primary method of acquisition of learning, so that the child with a visual impairment is intrinsically handicapped in a school setting. It is essential that an alternative mode of input be devised which will help to compensate for the child's inability to acquire data in the manner of the normally seeing child.

The child with a visual impairment is, perhaps, more easily integrated into the regular classroom environment than children with other physical defects because he usually exhibits no unique physical characteristics. This is true even to the extent of no visible markings around or about the eyes. The child's limiting factor is mobility. Blind children and partially sighted children tend to score lower than normal children on physical tasks concerning gross motor performance (Buell, 1950). It is probable that this observed motor deficiency may be a direct result of impaired mobility, perhaps the single most serious obstacle in educational procedures, for the totally blind child in particular. Essentially, the partially sighted child's educational attainments tend to fall largely within the normal category. When talking about impaired mobility, we are referring primarily to the blind child, i.e., to the child whose vision is so impaired that he must have auxiliary methods provided for him in order to move freely in his environment.

An interesting phenomenon is the obstacle sense of the blind. A series of studies have been made concerning the obstacle sense, and the following are major findings concerning it:

1. There are considerable individual differences in the obstacle sense of the blind. One study found that one-fifth (7 out of 34) of the blind students studied did not possess the obstacle sense (Worchel et al., 1950).

2. Stimulation of the face or other exposed areas of the skin is neither a necessary nor a sufficient condition for obstacle perception (Supa et al., 1944).

3. Deaf-blind subjects do not possess the obstacle sense and seem to be incapable of acquiring it (Worchel and Dallenbach, 1947).

4. Under most conditions, auditory stimulation is both a necessary and a sufficient condition for the perception of obstacles (Worchel and Dallenbach, 1947).

5. Other sensory cues, such as cutaneous and olfactory are insufficient and are utilized only under certain conditions when auditory cues are not available (Ammons et al., 1953).

6. Changes in the pitch of a sound or echo are a necessary condition for the perception of obstacles. The rise in pitch of a sound as a listener moves toward the source of the sound is known as the Doppler effect.

7. At normal walking speed, sound frequencies of about 10,000 cycles per second or above are necessary for obstacle perception. Frequencies below this level are insufficient for such perception (Crotzin and Dallenbach, 1950). The higher frequencies are important in the detection of obstacles because of their better resolution of the echoes reflected from small objects. Bats and other animals who emit and perceive sounds well above the human range use the echoes from such sounds for obstacle detection. Some qualitative measurements have been made of the ability of the human blind to detect echoes (Kellog, 1962; Rice et al., 1965).

8. Blind subjects lacking the obstacle sense are able to develop it with systematic procedures (Worchel et al., 1950). Blindfolded, normally sighted subjects are, with practice, able to develop obstacle sense (Worchel and Mauney, 1951).

The preceding conclusions indicate that obstacle sense is something of an acquired characteristic and a response to ordinarily unattended cues by use of the auditory input mechanism. There is nothing unusual, mysterious, or supernatural about obstacle sense. Normally sighted individuals have and can develop this sense with a relatively small amount of training.

Educating Children with Visual Impairments

The major problem involved in educating visually impaired children is in providing either an adequate alternative method for the input of information or an adequate method for the development of the child's seeing ability, so that he is able to maximize his visual potential. The blind child, of course, will be involved in the acquisition of a very complex skill, learning to read by touch rather than by seeing. The system utilized for this purpose is called Braille, a system of six embossed dots arranged in two vertical rows of three. These dots are of a size which may be covered simultaneously by the pad of the finger tip. Grade one Braille is written with full spelling, while grade two Braille makes use of some contractions, representations of combined symbols, or whole words in some cases.

There has been a great amount of research concerning the Braille system of reading. The readability of the various dots representing the letters of the alphabet has been found not to be primarily related to the number of dots, but to the formation of the dots. Good readers use a rather uniform pressure, while poor readers are somewhat erratic in the pressure utilized in reading Braille. Touch reading is intrinsically much slower, perhaps three to four times slower, than normal reading. A good Braille reader may read as many as 90 words per minute.

Teachers having students who are legally blind are urged to contact the American Printing House for the Blind in Louisville, Kentucky, one of the major sources of Braille material, or their local state agency concerned with providing services for the visually impaired child.

The Braille method of writing may be used either with a stylus and grid or with a special Braille typewriter which provides a more uniform Braille writing. Also, teachers may wish to make use of audio input sys-

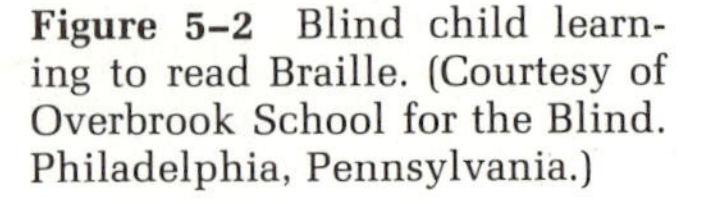

Figure 5-2 Blind child learning to read Braille. (Courtesy of Overbrook School for the Blind. Philadelphia, Pennsylvania.)

tems—tape recorders and record players have been found to be important aids in the classroom. There is much text material which may not be available in Braille, but which is provided by the audio media. Audio techniques also tend to facilitate a more rapid input of information than does the Braille method. Visually impaired children may acquire data at a rate of 150 to 170 words per minute and, under special conditions, even greater speed has been achieved. It is essential that special arithmetic aids be provided for the blind child. The Braille writer may also be used in arithmetic calculations, and special adaptations of the abacus may be used (Noland and Morris, 1965). There are additional educational aids, such as Braille maps, embossed maps, or relief globes, which may assist the teacher in providing educational facts for the visually impaired child.

Education of the partially sighted child presents fewer problems for the teacher because the child is sighted to some extent and usually tends to acquire his data in a normal manner. In the past, it was thought that children with visual impairment or partial sight should be restricted in using their eyes, and the old sight-saving classes were designed to provide this type of service. However, sight-saving classes have largely been discontinued since it has been found, in general, that the use of the eyes does not decrease their ability to be used. In fact, current studies seemingly indicate that by using and training the eyes, more effective vision may be achieved (Barrage, 1964).

The education of the partially sighted child should be viewed as being most adequately taken care of within the normal framework of public education. Teachers should be aware of certain ways of aiding the partially sighted child, such as seating him near the chalkboard, providing adequate lighting for him at his desk, and permitting him to move about so as to be as close to charts and other wall displays as possible. It may also be necessary for the teacher to provide magnifying glasses or books with large type. Two companies, The American Printing House for the Blind and Stanwix Publishing House, publish large type books for the partially sighted, and there is an increasing number of materials available with large print. The simplest way for a teacher to help the partially sighted child may be to train him to bring his eyes close enough to the material so that he can read. There is no evidence that holding a book close to the eyes will in any way harm the vision of the partially sighted child; however, magnification may be necessary for some children, so that they may be able to see the material adequately.

Educational and Administrative Procedures for the Visually Impaired Child

Many kinds of educational provisions have been made for the visually handicapped child, such as:

1. The residential school.
2. The self-contained special day school or class.
3. The special room in a regular school with some degree of integration of the visually impaired child with the rest of the school-cooperative plan.
4. The resource teacher.
5. The itinerant teacher.
6. Complete integration of visually impaired children with normally sighted children with little formal arrangement for them.
7. Home instruction.

Originally, residential institutions were the prime method for making educational services available for the blind, in particular, and for many other visually impaired children. However, it has been found that maximal integration of visually impaired children into the regular public school program is the most effective method of educating them. Little evidence exists to suggest that there is an innate or intrinsic need for these children to be segregated. It is, of course, desirable that some services be available in the school district; itinerant teachers may travel around the district and provide special training as a supplement to the regular classroom situation. The visually impaired child, with proper training, can become sufficiently mobile and capable of performing academic activities to adapt normally to the regular classroom. The regular classroom teacher should realize that the visually impaired child is essentially a normal child in terms of intelligence, personality, physical factors, and behavior and that there is usually little reason to segregate him.

The teacher must make certain minimal adaptations of classroom techniques to provide reasonably adequate procedures for the visually impaired child and should observe the children carefully, following the suggestions offered earlier in this chapter concerning signs exhibited by visually impaired children. Teachers may be surprised to learn that it is not uncommon to find a child in the first, second, or even third grade who, for some reason, has not been identified as having a visual problem. Again, we must emphasize that early identification of visual problems is essential in order that adequate provisions may be made for a full education. The visually impaired child should be expected to display normal behavior; visual impairment does not, under any circumstances, excuse misbehavior. He should be expected to take part in all classroom activities that do not involve mobility beyond his ability to participate. The child should be included in as many social activities and in as much interpersonal communication as possible.

Materials and Equipment

Aids and materials for the visually impaired are generally divided into reading-related and mobility-related areas because these represent the two major areas of handicap—communication and environmental contact. Both are problem areas when dealing with disabled children (as compared with adults). Many children are too young to be reading and too immature or unsophisticated to be taught to use mobility aids. For example, fewer than 5 per cent of guide dogs are used by individuals under 21 years of age.

For visually-impaired children, communication and mobility learning have to be accomplished slowly, with patience and with extra opportunities and stimulation being provided. While these children may be disabled in only one area, it is a very important area in our society. Audition and other sensory modalities (e.g., the cutaneous sense or smell) as well as memory can be trained to react to environmental cues and communication. With vision loss, the process is slower and requires the teacher's insight and ingenuity to help the child to arrive at the same endpoint as that of a seeing child.

For these reasons, it is advisable for parents to arrange at an early stage for a blind child's communication training, especially in the area of speech. For speech training and other communication and learning skills, play methods are being used. Music is especially effective because of the common qualities shared by speech and music (e.g., rhythm, vibration, and sound conductivity). Much extra stimulation and many perceptual cues may be learned or experienced by the child while actively playing with his family; this stimulation might be missed by the child (and never regained) if the family fears for the fragility of the blind child. Usually a combination of hard work, cultivation of a good memory, and development of latent natural faculties permits many blind people to function well.

Self-help, reading-related materials, which a blind child may use without a second person's aid, include tactile, auditory, and visual media. These aids are especially useful when the child has too little residual vision for magnification to help. Such methods as the well-known Braille system, the Morse code, and various similar tactile codes (e.g., block printing letters or the alphabet glove) open new lines of communication to blind readers and especially to blind-deaf people and other multiply handicapped persons. The Tellatouch device uses the English alphabet and Braille in a combined typewriter style machine and makes communication possible between blind-deaf people and 'nonsigning" individuals (people who are not familiar with any of the sign systems, like Braille or the deaf sign language).

For students and preschool children alike, the Talking Book series, in tapes, cassettes, and records, has proved to be a valuable aid and resource for the blind. Textbooks are not generally available in this series, but many novels and other literary forms are. This "speeded-up" form of speech reduces the listening time and, it is speculated, keeps the listener more alert. With practice and concentrated effort, the blind have found this method increasingly useful.

With the recently expanded use of computers, it should not be surprising that computer-related machines are being developed for use by blind children. These devices are primarily for students who need to "read" literature not available in Braille. Most machines are fed printed material and respond with either audio or tactile (Braille) output. Many variations of these devices exist, and they are usually quite expensive.

Figure 5-3 Blind children learning the parts of a musical instrument through touch and sound. (Courtesy of Overbrook School for the Blind, Philadelphia, Pennsylvania.)

However, price notwithstanding, self-help aids can help a blind individual to feel independent and to have the freedom to achieve and grow according to his needs. These are requirements often not fulfilled by the services of a second person.

Probably, the most familiar aid for the blind is the cane. In its many forms, the cane continues to be an important aid to the visually impaired person. Useful as it is, the cane has been improved upon with the aid of the computer. Laser-scanners and impulse-lenses currently are being used and tested as possible replacements for or supplements to the cane. The laser-scanner is commonly in the form of a cane with the addition of a device which sends light beams at ground level, waist height, and head height to detect obstacles at all three levels. When an obstacle breaks the beam, either some tactile message is transmitted to the handgrip or a significant sound is produced to indicate which area is sending the alert. The impulse-lens works essentially the same way, except that it is housed in a small box affixed to the chest of the child. It also responds with either a sound specific to the area or a tactual signal.

Another well known aid of the blind is the guide dog. Of course, sighted persons also often act as guides. As suggested earlier, neither of these means is very effective. Sighted persons acting in almost any capacity tend to thwart or at least discourage independence, which is a necessary attribute for a visually impaired person. For a child or adolescent, guide dogs seem to be more tempting as pets than as work-aids. Younger people may not have enough competence or sophistication to handle the dogs.

CHAPTER 6

VISUAL-MOTOR TRAINING PROGRAMS

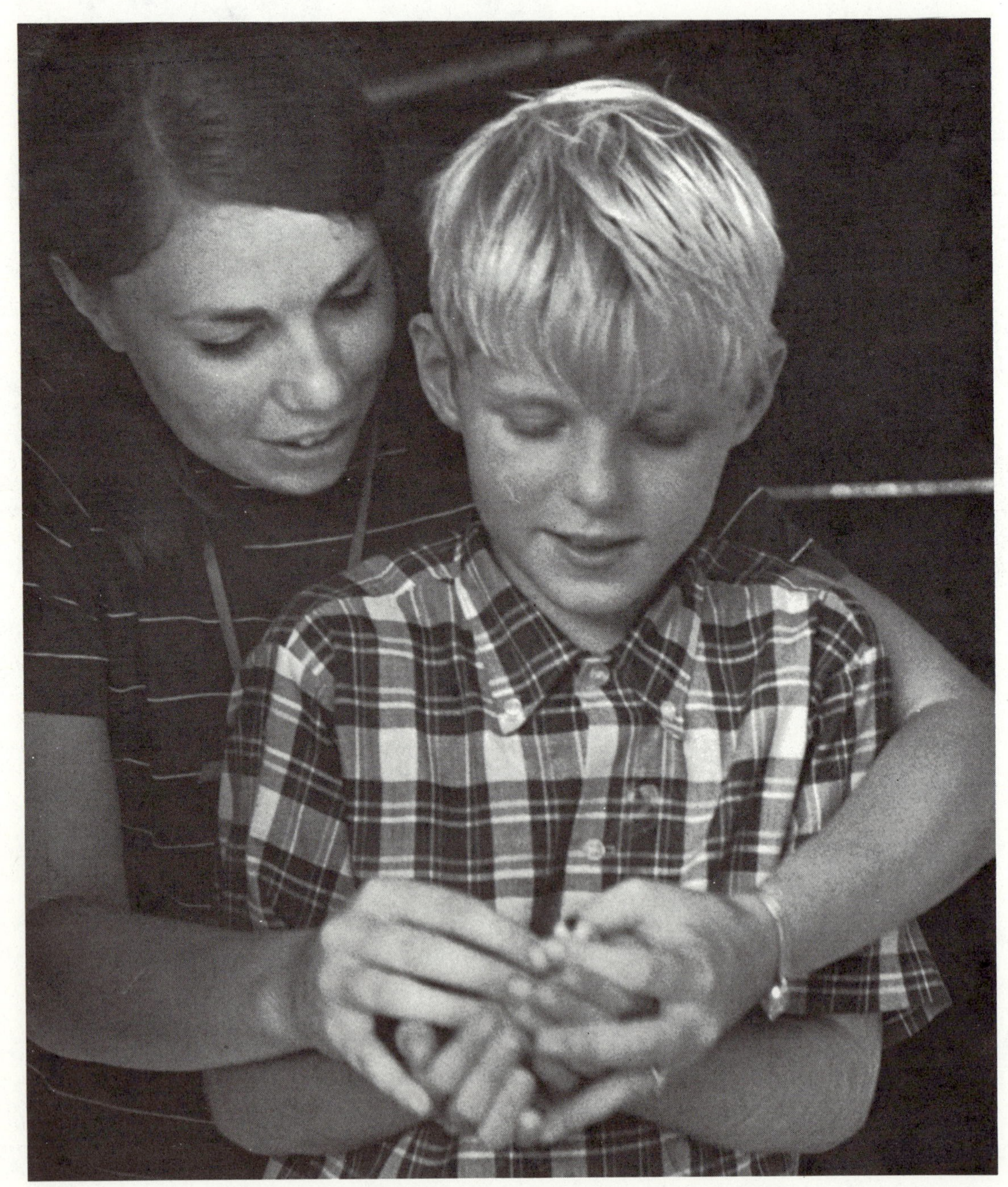

(Courtesy of The Devereux Foundation, Devon, Pennsylvania.)

There is a need for a complete rehabilitation program for children with visual handicaps. A good program will certainly require that many fields be involved in order to provide for the physical, psychological, and educational needs which are essential for adequate use of the eye. The eye is, according to most authorities, of basic importance to the acquisition of learning. An estimated 85 per cent or more of our input in learning comes by way of our visual processes (Martmer, 1959).

The purpose of this section is to evaluate critically and to integrate the available literature on visual-motor training. It is important to review this area because, in the past few years, there has been a veritable explosion of attempts to produce changes in behavior through visual-motor methods. Either theoretically or therapeutically, visual-motor training may have profound implications for the development of visual perception and knowledge of perceptual functions and dysfunctions. Of course, a definition of visual-motor training is difficult to arrive at, since there are many borderline areas that overlap greatly with such methods of training as play therapy, tutoring, educational therapy, and physical education, among possible others. For our purposes, visual-motor training is limited to physical exercises that maximally utilize kinesthetic movements to increase visual input and motor output. Usually, the general term, sensory-motor, implies any method that stimulates the child's movements. Other terms used, apparently interchangeably, are perceptual, motor, and visual discrimination.

Physical mobility or movement can be conceived of as fulfilling four different functions: (1) psychomotor development; (2) the development of body image, body consciousness, and cognition; (3) spatial development; and (4) corporal expression. It follows, therefore, that psychomotor re-education must be a specialized method of teaching movement that can be useful for the education of many children with visual-receptive difficulties. Tischer (1968) contended that psychomotor re-education can reduce reading difficulties in children who, because of motor dysfunction, are hyperactive, impulsive, or have problems of concentration, remembering, organization, or orientation. These accompanying signs of *dyslexia* tend to be noticed in children of about age 6 and can best be treated before age 10 or 11, while children are still much concerned with motion and their own physical identity, and before conditioning has inhibited their ability to respond to direct treatment. Once the child has integrated experiences at the motor levels, such as body image and space, re-education of an almost exclusively graphic nature is ready to proceed. The therapist and the special teacher should continually work together to see that graphic skills, such as forming and distinguishing letters and developing movements involving circles and lines, be incorporated into normal educational activities in conjunction with lessons taught by the teacher.

PROBLEMS OF REHABILITATION

Training Based on Input or Output?

As in any disability, there are many considerations to keep in mind in determining methods of rehabilitation for visual-motor disabilities. The first general consideration should be the degree of impairment—a blind-deaf, cerebral-palsied child would probably not be as effectively treated in a public school setting as a blind-only child. Of course, this extreme example is not the only relevant situation. The number and degree of a child's impairments as well as many other factors, including environmental considerations, will affect the child's personality and orientation. Naturally, the child—his needs and his abilities—should be the primary consideration in rehabilitation.

The question of social and emotional adjustment is a valid consideration in rehabilitative training. It must be remembered that the disability is a fact; emphasis on the disability will probably not be rewarding to the child nor will it improve productivity as will, possibly, emphasis on the child's assets. Wolman (1958) noted that a child's ability to adjust might be more a function of the acceptance level of other children and of his own expectations of himself, than of the extent of his disabilities. This conclusion was true of totally blind and severely impaired children, but children with considerable residual vision were accepted significantly less well by other children. This finding seems to cast some doubt on the degree of social acceptance as a function of the extent of disability.

The issue of whether to emphasize the input or the output in perceptual training is one aspect of the problem of whether to direct training to the asset or to the liability. The answer is that both the child's input and his output should receive attention, but this differentiation in perceptual-motor training is rarely made, so that it is difficult to determine which aspect is being considered primarily. Most training programs which we will review largely emphasize output, assuming that a positive feedback may change whatever input deficit may exist. Unfortunately, this assumption may not always be correct. The deficit may be of such a nature that no amount of output training will be sufficient. Input training is usually referred to as discrimination training; however, the reader cannot safely assume that this definition is always used consistently. Many studies deal with motor output *alone,* assuming that such training will somehow effect visual input. Two types of discrimination training were used by Bee and Walker (1968) in an attempt to improve the drawing of geometric figures by preschool children. One type of training produced a significant improvement in drawings, while the other produced a significant decrement. The results suggested that some "lag" between perceiving and performing may be due to insufficient discrimination, but part of the "lag" is apparently also caused by the child's inability or unwillingness to translate what he has perceived into his copying behavior.

Johnson (1967) examined the data from 1000 files from the Children's Physical Development Clinic to verify whether this program produced significant changes in perceptual-motor skills. Changes in perceptual skills (input) were tested with tachistoscopic presentations. Changes in motor skills (output) were tested with mirror drawings, using a 3-inch by 2-inch diamond as the figure to be traced in mirror image. Time, distance, and quality were all scored. A significant improvement was found when postclinic tests on the perceptual and motor skills were

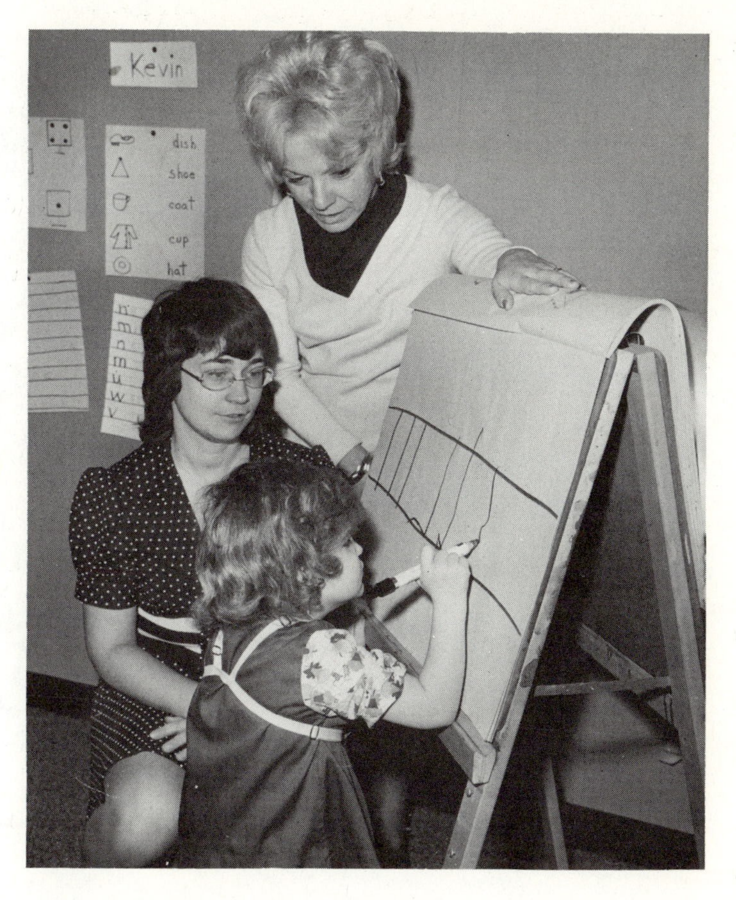

Figure 6–1 Visually impaired child learning to trace between lines. (Courtesy of Overbrook School for the Blind, Philadelphia, Pennsylvania.)

compared with the preclinic tests. Johnson concluded that the clinic program did result in significant improvement in perceptual-motor skills.

Rhythmic and Sensory-Motor Activities

Playlike, rhythmic activities based on movement presumably improve visual-motor skills. Among the many studies available, Painter's study (1966) may be considered one of the most representative. She used two groups of kindergarten children matched closely according to the Stanford-Binet IQ, Goodenough DAP-IQ, ITPA Language Age, and Beery's Geometric Form Reproduction. Training consisted of sessions three times a week for seven weeks, primarily using activities suggested by Barsch (1967) and by Kephart (1963), such as rhythmic patterns, sequencing of unilateral, bilateral, and cross-lateral movements, and changing of uncoordinated or jerky movements to large, sweeping movements. The results confirmed her expectations, since there was a significant improvement over the baseline measurements in her experimental group when it was compared with the control group. Unfortunately, as we shall see later, combination of two or more methods does not allow one to determine the specific effects obtained by each method.

Figure 6–2 Learning hands-feet coordination on a rowing machine. (Courtesy of Overbrook School for the Blind, Philadelphia, Pennsylvania.)

Sensory-Motor Training of Retardates

Intellectually retarded children have been one of the populations most frequently selected for sensory-motor programs because of their assumed deficits in the visual-motor area and their easy access and availability for study. Webb (1969), for instance, began with the assumption that defective sensory-motor integration causes (1) low levels of awareness (responsiveness), (2) impairment of body movement, (3) difficulties in manipulating the environment, and (4) difficulties in posture and locomotion—all deficits found in profoundly retarded individuals as well as the visually impaired. She selected as her experimental subjects 32 profoundly retarded children in a residential institution. Their ages ranged from 2½ to 17½, and their age in social skills ranged from 2 to 21 months with a mean of 8 months. The training period ranged from 5½ to 10½ months and included all sorts of physical activities, from sensory stimulation of each modality to active manipulations of posture and locomotion. Their progress was assessed by a rating scale, based on Piaget's work, which showed no changes at the end of training in comparison with scores obtained before training. Yet, Webb maintained that significant changes in movement patterns, reaching and grasping, and awareness were recorded by both the ward and therapy personnel.

McClanahan (1967) measured the effects of 35 hours of visual-perceptual training on the intellectual maturity, perceptual skills, and reading performances of "slow-learning," first-grade children enrolled in classes for the EMR. In addition, the study proposed to assess the differential effects of two intervening variables on perceptual learning. The intervening variables were dominance (preferred hand and eye) and body image (Draw-A-Man Test). The subjects were administered a gamut of pretests and post-tests. There was a significant difference in post-test scores of the experimental group when compared with those of the control group. This difference appeared to indicate an increase in test facility for the experimental group. The results were not related by the author to classroom performance. Subjects with unilateral dominance and adequate body image showed a significant improvement in post-test scores when compared to subjects with mixed dominance and inadequate body image.

Visual-Motor Training of Deprived Children

While perceptual training is one of the more extensively discussed problems in special education, many questions remain as to how great an effect it can produce. Having reviewed much of Piaget's work on perceptual activity, Elkind and Deblinger (1969) found it reasonable to assume that perceptual activity might help to improve children's reading skills. To test this hypothesis, a set of nonverbal exercises were devised, on the assumption that practice with materials of this type would force the children to use their perceptual abilities without using verbalization as a crutch and would not allow a situation in which teachers might talk at too abstract a level and thus lose the attention of some of the children. The study began with second-grade black children as subjects. During the experimental sessions, control groups read from The Bank Street Readers and also were taught vocabulary, reading, and comprehension on the blackboard as prescribed by the teacher's handbook. The experimental groups were involved in nonverbal exercises, such as a series of ascending and descending movements. Also, midway in the sessions, the experimenter chose children to come to the blackboard and serve as teachers. After completion of training, the subjects were retested on the individual tests of perceptual activity which had been used as pretests. They were also group-tested using the California Achievement Test. Results indicated the experimental groups to be significantly higher than the control groups on perceptual activity, word recognition, and word forms. Elkind and Deblinger concluded that nonverbal perceptual training had a greater effect upon certain aspects of reading achievement than did the more usual type of reading instruction.

SPECIFIC VISUAL-MOTOR PROGRAMS

Although at the outset some visual-motor programs were developed for specific populations, such as the brain-damaged or retardates, more often than not these programs are later applied to groups other than those originally intended. Most of these programs were not intended to be used for blind children, but have been used over the whole, broad range of visual deficits, from poorly sighted to visually normal children, that is, children with specific learning disabilities or underachievers. Even though the applicability or relevance of these programs to severe visual deficits could be questioned, their specific applications to any type of visual-motor dysfunction justifies their being considered in this chapter (Valett, 1966, 1968).

McCarthy and McCarthy (1969) classified various educational procedures for those with learning disabilities that are of value to the student as historical background. They considered perceptual-motor approaches as represented by the procedures first developed by Strauss and Lehtinen, Kephart, and Barsch. Among developmental approaches to visual perception, McCarthy and McCarthy considered those of Frostig, Fitzhugh and Fitzhugh (PLUS program), and Getman. The third neurophysiological approach developed by Delacato was also considered in detail. Among linguistic approaches, those of Orton, Bateman, and Wiseman were reviewed. The diagnostic-remedial approaches to basic school subjects were also reviewed, including those of Fernald, Otto, and McMenemy.

In this chapter, it will be impossible to review all the theorists cited by McCarthy and McCarthy (1969) or by Cratty (1972). An attempt will be made to cite selectively the prevailing programs in the area of visual-motor training.

General Characteristics

Among sensory-motor programs, the similarities are greater than the differences. Most visual-motor programs show some overlapping characteristics, namely:

1. Emphasis on some form of gross or fine discrimination, ranging from jumping from one giant alphabet letter to another to choosing one of four, small, nearly similar designs.
2. A great deal of guided, programmed, and graduated activities using eye-hand coordination, laterality exercises, and motor practices.

Major Contributors

Since the days of Itard, Seguin, and other early pioneers like Strauss and Lehtinen (1947), whose sensory-motor programs involved severely retarded or brain-damaged children, the sensory-motor form of training for all children, even those with minimal visual disorders, has gained many proponents, especially in recent years. An attempt will be made to review the work of the most significant contributors to this area.

Ray H. Barsch

Barsch (1967, 1968) provided a theoretical background for visual-motor programs rather than definite and specific exercises. He called his theory of movement as it relates to learning, "movigenics." He defined it as "... the study of the origin and development of pattern of movement in man and the relationship of those movements to his learning efficiency" (Barsch, 1967). To promote further understanding of his concept, Barsch presented 10 principles which he designated as the foundation of movigenics:

1. The fundamental principle underlying the human organism is movement efficiency—the essence of man is movement, physically, socially, psychologically, and cognitively.
2. The primary objective of movement efficiency is to promote survival of the organism economically.

3. Movement efficiency is derived from information which the organism processes from the surrounding energy.

4. The perceptocognitive system is the mechanism for processing this energy into information.

5. The terrain of movement is space.

6. Developmental momentum provides a constant thrust forward and demands equilibrium to maintain direction.

7. Movement efficiency develops under stress, whether adverse or necessary.

8. The adequacy of the feedback system is critical in the development of movement efficiency.

9. Development of movement efficiency occurs in sequential segments, i.e., increased differentiation and hierarchical integration.

10. Movement efficiency is communicated symbolically through language; "As man moves to act he symbolizes his actions to economically record his experience" (Barsch, 1967).

The study of spatial orientation occupies a major portion of Barsch's presentation. The maturing child is required to make integrated sense of a variety of relationships which confront him in space. Spatial concepts originate with the child's first encounters with his own body, and from this limited "self-space," his spatial world increases in scope and complexity as he moves out into the environment: "The behavior of the organism is always spatial in some manner" (Barsch, 1967).

Figure 6–3 Visually impaired children learning through body contact. (Courtesy of Overbrook School for the Blind, Philadelphia, Pennsylvania.)

Barsch describes three "domains of space": (1) the physical space of objects and events; (2) the milieu space or "life space"; and (3) the cognitive space of symbols, thoughts, and ideas. He discusses four "zones of space" (near, middle, far, and remote space) which imply the relativity of space as oriented around the body. In relating spatial concepts to the immediate body area, Barsch defines six "fields of space": the vertical body ordinate divides space into left and right, as well as front and back; the horizontal ordinate provides the basis for up and down. "Performance efficiency is necessary in each of these fields" (Barsch, 1967).

Movement efficiency is a product of the combination of the following factors, which, according to Barsch, are hierarchically ordered, each developing from and building upon the previous ones:

1. Muscular strength: This is the first dimension of movement efficiency. The child must progress from early random muscle movement to increased differentiation and control. Strength is necessary in first learning to hold the head erect, then in learning to walk, and finally to develop the muscular hand skills.

2. Dynamic balance: Body alignment and equilibrium are essential to bilateral balance. Balance, the ability to shift the body's center of gravity, is important in all movement. Muscular strength and dynamic balance contribute to body awareness in the individual.

3. Body awareness: As the child matures he gradually develops a stronger and more complete body image which is necessary for adequate cognitive growth. "The schema of the body is a primitive mode for development of number concepts" (Barsch, 1967). Barsch states that reading and arithmetic are directly related to body awareness.

4. Spatial awareness: As noted previously, the concepts of up-down, front-back, and left-right are critical aspects of spatial awareness.

Figure 6–4 Learning body control through the use of a balance beam. (Courtesy of The Devereux Foundation, Devon, Pennsylvania.)

5. Temporal awareness: The most complex of the movement efficiency factors is temporal awareness which, like space, has several dimensions: physiological or body time (e.g., metabolism); physical time (traditional units); milieu time (life time); and cognitive time (recognition and memory). The child must learn to organize and process time, and performance efficiency must be maintained in relation to time.

Barsch calls "perceptocognitive modes" those senses used for the processing of information and leading to conceptualization. Listed according to increasing complexity and importance, they are the gustatory, olfactory, tactual, kinesthetic, auditory, and visual modes. Each of these senses is critical to the growth and cognitive development of the child, since each provides different environmental information by which the child integrates his experiences.

Movement and performance are evaluated in terms of four "degrees of freedom," all of which, according to Barsch, are essential to the efficiency of the individual:

1. Bilaterality: Being aware of one's left and right provides a basis for orientation, but the coordination and integration of left and right are necessary for freedom of movement.
2. Rhythm: Grace and ease of movement promote movement efficiency. Rhythm is composed of biological, perceived, and performance rhythms and is especially noted in speech, gross movements, and writing.
3. Flexibility: This degree of freedom indicates the range of movement adaptability. Flexibility is both a motor and a cognitive function.
4. Motor planning: It is an essential component for growth at both the physical and cognitive levels.

Barsch also presented curriculum guidelines for the teacher using movigenics theory and techniques:

1. Have the child utilize spatial orientation and evaluate him in terms of "efficient-inefficient" rather than "successful-unsuccessful."
2. Aim for diversified development of complexity in the child; he needs to become specialized in all areas, not merely learning.
3. The child needs the opportunity to explore all muscular relationships.
4. The child needs the opportunity to explore all six perceptual modes.
5. The child requires a variety of zones of stimulation from a variety of target sources.
6. Once a task is learned, the child needs variations of the same task.
7. The child must learn his *own* range of performance ability.
8. All movement must be cognitively directed.
9. Spatial orientation must be related to reading, writing, arithmetic, and spelling.
10. The space-oriented approach is a matter of reconstructing existing procedures to emphasize spatial orientation.

Barsch's attempts to relate spatial awareness (up and down) specifically to cognitive awareness (thoughts and ideas) are theoretically interesting, but intrinsically confusing. He assumes that physical space is related to cognitive space without first explaining the relationship, as though the latter were a developmental consequence of the former. He implies that proper acquisition of all facets of physical space will automatically produce cognitive-spatial concepts in the child and provides no evidence of his own or of others to demonstrate if and how his conceptualization is valid. Consequently, it seems that he is providing guidelines for research rather than for training activities, especially because his "curriculum guidelines" seem somewhat too abstract from the viewpoint of developing a training program.

Bryan Cratty

Cratty (1968, 1969, 1972) has been among the more productive proponents of sensory-motor programs, and his extensive writings should be consulted for applications of his methods. In his introduction (Cratty, 1969) to the use of total body movement as a learning modality, he suggested that his programs could benefit retarded, hyperactive, father-absent, and immature children; however, the description and definition of these types of children are clearly qualitative. Initially considering the need to control the level of arousal and activation, Cratty begins with single-pattern recognition by having the child jump from one pattern (triangle) to another (square), either drawn or available in large size on a playground. From pattern recognition, he progresses to the second and third tasks, letter and number recognition (still on the basis of large shapes available on the playground). A fourth series of tasks consists of number games, counting, and concepts of quantity. The fifth and sixth steps include spelling and word games and concept formation.

Cratty's objective approach relies on the assumption that movement is a fundamental dimension of human behavior. If movements are interpreted properly, they allow for assessments of the intellectual processes and help to develop the human body in its totality. He believes that improvement of motor skills will help the child to function better socially. His system assumes that an effective educational program should be individually prescribed after tests are given to determine which motor skills need improvement. Therefore, it becomes necessary to provide activities that will improve specific deficits. According to this approach, motor performance is observable, voluntary, and goal-centered movement; motor learning is a somewhat permanent change in motor performance that occurs by means of constant practice; motor fitness determines the capacity to perform; and motor educability is having the capacity to learn. There is substantial evidence to indicate a close relationship between personality and athletic achievement.

Delacato (1963) agreed with Cratty's statement that some clinicians view movement experiences for the retardate and neurologically handicapped as essential tasks through which the children's intellects and various perceptual attributes may be enhanced. Staats (1968) also agreed with Cratty in his belief that some elementary sensory-motor skills are basic to other types of learning.

Cratty's Developmental Sequences of Perceptual Motor Tasks was used in formulating Daily Sensori-Motor Training Activities, which is a handbook for teachers and parents of preschool children by Braley et al. (1963). This handbook is discussed more fully later in this chapter. It contains daily lesson plans and weekly comprehensive evaluations for a 34-week training period. This program as well as Cratty's method are too new to be substantiated. Cratty does, however, refer to studies that claim success with neurologically handicapped children by using his movement activities in sequences of perceptual-motor tasks.

In his latest publication (1972), Cratty reviewed contemporary theories linking movement and cognition. He focused on three different types of theories. The first type of theory emphasizes intellectual abili-

Figure 6–5 Athletic competition for visually impaired children using guide wires. (Courtesy of Overbrook School for the Blind, Philadelphia, Pennsylvania.)

ties, as in the work of Le Boulch in France, Kiphard in Germany, and Mosston, Humphrey, Frostig, and himself in the United States. Secondly, among perceptual-motor theories, Cratty considers Kephart, Barsch, and Getman (who are all reviewed in this chapter). The third type of theory includes those based on neurological organization, like Delacato's. For the student interested in enlarging his knowledge of these training procedures, Cratty's review may prove to be invaluable.

Cratty characterizes himself as a "cognitive theorist" on the basis of "a complex four-channel theory of development," by which he rejects the assumption of many theorists "that early movement attributes are the basis of perceptual and intellectual development" (Cratty, 1972). His major guiding principles are: (1) movement is a component, not the sole basis of developing human abilities; (2) highly structured movement experiences intended to remediate motor problems should be applied only to children who show evidence of clumsiness, rather than as a cure-all for all elementary school children's problems; and (3) several areas in which movement programs may assist in the educational process include: (a) aiding the child with handwriting difficulties so he may better express his intellect, (b) aiding children to gain self-control, improve attention span, and adjust their levels of arousal to levels compatible with classroom functioning, and (c) aiding in the improvement of certain academic functions, if these functions or skills are incorporated directly into the motor activities in which children and youth are involved.

His exercises and movements generally consist of well-known physical education calisthenics and games, ranging from gross activity to more refined and specific procedures which enhance intelligence and creativity.

C. H. Delacato and R. J. Doman

The Doman-Delacato method of sensory-motor treatment is used specifically with severely brain-damaged individuals. It has received much attention in the past several years and has aroused a great deal of controversy. There are several Doman-Delacato schools in the United States. Briefly, these authors believe that brain functioning can be measured in the receptive-visual, receptive-auditory, and expressive areas of functioning. They believe that a neurological age can be computed by charting these functions and comparing the findings to those which are considered normal. This neurological age is also compared to the child's chronological age. Great emphasis is placed on the environment as being the source of sensory stimuli, and the authors stress touch, pressure, temperature, olfactory, visual, auditory, and kinesthetic sensations to which a child will react with motor responses. Doman and Delacato claim that nonsurgical methods of treatment cannot succeed if ever-increasing psychopathology is present. They perform an exhaustive examination before and after treatment. The cost of the program is great, approximately $500 for the initial evaluation alone, and there are no figures for complete treatment. The effectiveness of the program has not been proved by empirical data (McDonald, 1968).

Basic to the Doman-Delacato theory is the biological generalization that development of brain functions follows general laws of evolution. They extend this idea to levels of organization in the cental nervous system and believe that the chronological progression of neurological development is as follows:

1. Cord and medulla: The primitive reflexes, such as muscle tone, reflex movement, and cardiovascular, gastrointestinal, and breathing activities are controlled by these brain areas.
2. Pons: It functions in coordinating the vital organs.
3. Midbrain: It is the seat of binaural hearing and binocular seeing. This level of the brain is responsible for crosspatterning (rather than homolateral) mobility.
4. Cerebral cortex: It is the most important area dealing with abstract language.
5. Lateralization of hemispheres: This stage of development is unique to man and allows him to acquire such skills as reading, writing, and spelling. The left hemisphere is mainly responsible for language functions; the right hemisphere controls visual-motor functions.
6. Cortical hemispheric dominance: The two hemispheres begin to take on different functions as described above.

Proper childhood experiences (i.e., adequate stimulation) are necessary for each of these levels of organization to become developed. Delacato proposes that as a preventive measure against intellectual retardation, from birth, developmental factors, such as sleep patterns, handedness, and tonality of speech should be managed. In the case of brain damage, the natural progression of neurological organization is slowed down and sometimes never completely achieved.

Treatment using the Doman-Delacato method consists of supplying the necessary experiences for development which were missed by the child (such as crawling) or, in the case of brain damage, reliving these past experiences, so that another part of the brain can take on that particular function. Since sensory pathways develop before corresponding motor pathways, treatment consists of first supplying the necessary stimulation to activate a dormant part of the brain. When this part of the brain becomes sensorily active, it will draw a response from the corresponding motor system. Because new cells of the brain must be used, that is, cells which have previously been functionally inactive, stimulation of these cells has to be of greater intensity and duration than is normally provided by the environment.

A summary of the Doman-Delacato treatment procedure is as follows:

1. Supply basic, discrete bits of information to the brain for storage.
2. Program the brain.
3. Demand an immediate response from the brain to a basic, discrete bit of information which has just been supplied to it.
4. Permit the brain to respond to previous programming.
5. Provide an improved physiological environment in which the brain may function.

Each of these procedures is applied to visual, auditory, tactile, gustatory, and olfactory stimulation (or motor patterns which have been programmed into the brain in these sensory forms).

The major question confronting the reviewer of evidence supporting the Doman-Delacato theory is whether a program of intense sensory stimulation does, in fact, have an effect on the physical and intellectual development of retarded or brain-damaged children. There is not, as yet, sufficiently convincing evidence to support this theory of neurological organization and its relation to the preceding treatment procedure. Delacato defends his treatment methods on the grounds of unobservable changes within the central nervous system; the concepts he uses are not empirically verified or operationally defined. Delacato reports research (1963) which he claims validates his theory, but according to Wepman (1968), Delacato's proof is merely an assumption. He says that Delacato explains his theory in "charming literary terms in the face of no evidence." In a review of an earlier book by Delacato (1959), Smith (1968) stated that "although the author freely admits that data to substantiate his thesis are lacking, too frequently he obscures this lack with a smokescreen of ponderous terminology which sometimes has the aura of medicine-man salesmanship."

Does a specific program of physical activities such as that proposed by Delacato have any significance for the intellectually retarded or brain-damaged? Delacato claimed that his treatment procedure changes the rate of neurological growth from an average of 35 per cent normal to an average of 210 per cent normal. So far, the evidence to support this claim is questionable. He described (1963) a study done with 76 brain-damaged children who participated in his outpatient program. The results showed that of the 20 unable to move and 17 unable to walk, 12 were ready to walk, 8 were creeping in crosspattern, and 4 were holding onto objects. Delacato concluded: ". . . it is our opinion that the significance of the differences tends to corroborate the validity of the hypothesis set up as the theoretical basis of the program." If the program works, its success is not due to the theory behind it, but to the specific aspects of it. The question is, do the particular aspects of the program produce a significant change in the behavior of the subjects? At first, looking at the results of the study, one would say that there was a significant change; however, Wepman pointed out that the reported, empirical evidence suffers from four main problems: (1) some studies (such as the one previously described) failed to include control groups, (2) those that did have control groups showed inadequate matching between control and experimental groups, (3) there was an oversimplification of results, and (4) there was failure to refer to any of the published studies which showed contradictory results.

In a recent review of Delacato's theory, practice, and evidence, Robbins and Glass (1969) concluded:

> **1. The fundamental tenets of the theory are overwhelmingly refuted by internal inconsistencies, a lack of supporting evidence, and direct contradiction by established evidence.**
>
> **2. Studies which purportedly support the relationship between neurological organization and reading lack sophistication and proper controls consistent with current scientific procedures.**
>
> **3. There is no empirical evidence to substantiate the value of either the theory or practice of neurological organization.**

Marianne Frostig

The original Frostig program (1964) for individualized training and remediation in visual perception provides exercises in the same five areas which are covered by the Frostig Developmental Test of Visual Perception. They include: (1) eye-motor coordination, (2) figure-ground relations, (3) shape-constancy relations, (4) position in space, and (5) spatial relationships. Paper and pencil exercises are available on individual sheets or ditto masters that allow for reproduction of particular portions for classroom use.

In addition to this program, Frostig has developed two new programs. The first consists of pictures and patterns for the development of visual perception at three age levels: preschool, kindergarten, and first grade in normal children. The exercises are presented in a teacher's guide and in acetate overlays which allow children to practice tracing to develop better muscular coordination. The second program "Move-Grow-Learn" is designed to improve physical, creative, and perceptual skills in young children. It consists of 168 activities in body awareness, coordination, agility, strength, flexibility, balance, and creative movement. Color-coded activity cards make it easy to design individual programs for children with special needs or to plan programs for an entire class. The teacher's manual contains helpful suggestions for either the classroom teacher or the physical education specialist.

Because of its clarity, the structured program of visual-motor training developed by Frostig and her coworkers (Frostig and Horne, 1964) lends itself to direct testing. The program is based on the general principles of the Gestalt school of perception and Werner's organismic theory. Naville (1970) developed a program similar to Frostig's based on the European schools of Rudolf Laban and Jacques Dalcroze which teach rhythmic gymnastics. Naville stated that "only by movement and *through* movement, often animated and supported by appropriate, improvised music, the child experiences, recognizes, and learns to master his body." The Naville program consists of four main groups of exercises: (1) motor skills, (2) body image and laterality, (3) time and space organization, and (4) psychomotor education and pedagogical influence (concentration, obedience, self-control, and discipline). According to Naville, ". . . movement furthers not only the physical capabilities of the child, but also influences the development of his personality and teaches him interaction."

Figure 6–6 Swimming is an important part of any physical activity program for the visually impaired. (Courtesy of Overbrook School for the Blind, Philadelphia, Pennsylvania.)

The purpose of a study by Talkington (1968) was to apply Frostig's visual-perceptual training to retardates and to determine the practical applications of this method. Talkington's 100 subjects were given the Frostig Developmental Test of Visual Perception (DTVP) before and after the training. They were randomly divided into two groups: Group E (training) and Group C (no training). Each group contained 50 students (25 boys and 25 girls). Only Group E received three months of perceptual training with Frostig-Horne materials for one hour per day, five days per week. The retest showed that Group E made significantly greater gains on the test-retest difference scores in all areas when compared with Group C. The author concluded that "special training in visual perception can improve the severe and profound retardate's skills in discrimination, coordination, and spatial manipulations." Talkington mentioned other studies which showed a correlation between scores on the Frostig test and scores on the WISC. He suggested that the extent to which perceptual training affects performance on intelligence tests is in need of study.

N. C. Kephart

N. C. Kephart in his influential book, The Slow Learner in the Classroom (1971), presented a survey of the development of the perceptual process, how deficiencies in this area relate to slow learners, and methods of screening and retraining children with perceptual problems. Kephart discussed the various qualities which are expected in the developing child, the foremost of which is *plasticity.* He stated that ". . . plasticity of response is characteristic of organisms with more complex nervous systems." Plasticity is replaced by rigidity in the responses of children with perceptual difficulties. Two other factors which are vital to the perceptual integration and differentiation of the child are laterality and directionality. Laterality is the internal awareness of the left and right sides of the body, the ability to control both sides separately as well as simultaneously. Recognizing the difference between the two sides of the body is the essence of laterality. In relating this aspect to learning problems, Kephart provided an example: ". . . the difference between 'b' and 'd' is one of laterality only." Directionality refers to kinesthetic development, the awareness of the vertical and horizontal coordinates of space in relation to the body. The child must learn body and hand movements through space, especially in the skills of drawing and writing, in which he must be able to change direction as his hand moves and understand how and where to stop. Both laterality and directionality are important components of the child's body image, and a strong body image is necessary as a ". . . point of origin for either perceptions or motor responses" (Kephart, 1971).

The perceptual process is mediated by five separate and discrete functions that must operate together in a circular chain reaction in order to promote accurate organization of perceptions (Kephart, 1971):

1. Input—neurologically defined as activity in the sensory areas of the cortex, or "energy distribution impinging on the organism." Input refers to those incoming stimuli which are received by the individual.
2. Integration—a process of synthesis which organizes simultaneous inputs with the mediating factors of past and present.
3. Scanning—a process of translation. The organism scans and surveys the integrated inputs and translates them into "output patterns."
4. Output—patterns in the motor area of the cortex. The organism acts motorically in response to the stimulus.
5. Feedback—used as a means of control and oriented toward the input end. A method of checking the response against the original stimulus.

Disturbances in any one of these functions disrupt the entire perceptual process, producing disparities and inconsistencies in the child's behavior.

Kephart presented 10 methods by which the various stages of sensory-motor development may be differentiated:

1. Walking board—to observe balance and postural flexibility.
2. Jumping—to observe balance, including unilateral and bilateral movements for laterality.
3. Identification of body parts—to determine the child's control of body parts in response to verbal cues.
4. Imitation of movements—to observe body movement from visual cues.
5. Obstacle course—to observe body movement in relation to objects in space.
6. "Angel-in-the-snow"—to coordinate upper and lower extremities in a variety of combinations.
7. Stepping stones—to control body parts on the basis of cues received from outside stimuli.
8. Chalkboard—to determine adequacy of directionality, laterality, and symmetry of body movements.
9. Ocular pursuits—to test whether there is good eye control.
10. Visual achievement forms—to test form perception and figure-ground relationships.

In addition, Kephart recommended the use of the Kraus-Weber Tests for Muscular Fitness. Each of the preceding tasks should be satisfactorily accomplished in normally developing children at various ages, and failure in a particular area indicates the nature and extent of perceptual training which will be necessary.

Kephart described training activities for three major areas of development: sensory-motor learning, ocular control, and form perception. For sensory-motor learning, he advocated using chalkboard and finger-painting techniques and physical, whole-body exercises. Chalkboard activities seem to be the most beneficial because they allow the child a wide expanse of movement, encourage large muscle stimulation rather than fine motor control, leave a visual trace for the child to follow, and provide kinesthetic feedback through the feeling of the chalk moving across the board. The purpose of this activity is to teach a free-flowing movement, ". . . to stabilize these movement patterns in time and recognize symbolic visual patterns as permanent motor movement patterns" (Kephart, 1971). Initially, the child is encouraged simply to scribble on the board, with emphasis on large rather than small movements, in order to experience spatial movement and instantly see the trace of the chalk. Once the child has established free movement by scribbling, the teacher can then draw a simple circle shape and allow the child to trace over her circle on the board; later, the child can simply copy from a model. As the child progresses, the teacher can vary the task by altering the size of the circles, the direction of drawing, the speed of drawing, and the hand which is used. When the child satisfactorily accomplishes the circular shape, the teacher can then substitute the more difficult shapes, such as the square, rectangle, triangle, and diamond, in that order, using the same procedure which was used in learning the circle. These advanced shapes incorporate more difficult concepts of size and length, in addition to teaching the child direction—where to start, how to stop, how to turn corners. The use of templates for these tasks is helpful, allowing the child to run his finger around the shape with varying degrees of pressure and to trace from templates before tracing from a board copy. Kephart stressed three important factors in this type of training: (1) the child should never be allowed to persist in errors, and the teacher must always be ready to correct any errors; (2) drawing shapes should be accompanied by constant verbal cues, repeating the name of the shape over and over as the child draws it; (3) the idea is to begin by using a great number of visual and kinesthetic cues in chalkboard work, gradually reducing these cues as the child progresses.

Other sensory-motor training exercises are used as practice or games for developing points of reference within a strong body image. Practice on the walking board is an aid in learning laterality and directionality, since it requires the differentiation between left and right for maintaining balance. Activities on the walking board include walking forward, backward, sideways, and then turning and bouncing a ball or tossing a beanbag while maintaining balance. A trampoline is a useful device for learning balance, coordination, and rhythm. Rhythm is an important aspect of training, whether making rhythmic sounds on a drum, clapping hands, or stamping feet. Not only does it help to develop a variety of learning patterns, but it places considerable emphasis on laterality movements and provides a simple and effective means of coordinating left and right body movements. Rhythm gives the child an internal rhythmic basis for establishing laterality.

Kephart (1963) delineated more concretely the four major motor patterns on which motor skills are based: (1) balance and maintenance of posture; (2) locomotion (moving the body through space); (3) contact (manipulation of objects, such as reaching, grasping, and releasing); (4) receipt (child makes contact with moving objects) and propulsion (child imparts movement to objects). These are the four motor areas to which Kephart devotes most of his attention in the field of sensory-motor training, believing them to be the underlying processes by which academic achievement is reached and through which perceptual corrections can be made.

Ocular training consists of a combination of coordinated eye and body movements, in which kinesthetic control is matched with ocular control. One of the most efficient devices for ocular training is the Marden ball, or tetherball, a ball suspended from an upright pole by a string. The object is to hit the ball as it moves through space. Kephart often refers to the child who "lost" all awareness of the ball as soon as it went behind his head and out of his visual range, only to be angrily reminded of it when it returned to strike him on the back of the head.

Kephart advocated the use of puzzles, pegboards, and matchsticks as methods of training in form perception. He presented an interesting collection of shapes ranging from simple to complex and patterns that can be assigned to the child in increasingly advanced order.

All the preceding training procedures are presented by Kephart more as guidelines for the teacher to follow rather than as rigorously structured programs. The idea is to determine the area in which the child is deficient and to direct him to practice exercises in this area until progress is noted. It is more important for the child to gain gross skills in his problem area which will eventually allow him to return to a more academic routine of reading and writing, than to emphasize these scholastic activities over and over, hoping that they will "sink in" eventually. Kephart's program is well-designed for use in the classroom and does not require costly and intricate testing materials and scoring procedures. It can be conveniently utilized in almost any classroom setting with a minimum of effort and seems capable of attracting and holding the child's attention as he works.

Maria Montessori

Maria Montessori became interested in mental defectives in the late 1890's. After studying the work of Itard and particularly the work of Seguin, Montessori concluded that the problem of mental deficiency was primarily educational rather than medical. Through the construction and use of her own instructional materials, she taught a number of retarded pupils to read and to write well enough to be presented for examination on a level with normal children. The results, according to the reports, were miraculous. This accomplishment made her wonder why normal pupils should not also improve to a higher academic level. Her explanation of this difference was that the feeble-minded had been well-educated, while the normal children had been presented with poor educational opportunities.

"Auto-education," or self-teaching, was the keynote of the *Montessori method.* Activities and materials were so organized and designed that the children taught themselves, while the teacher withdrew into the background, merely supervising the activities. This self-teaching method was carried out by means of didactic materials that consisted of 26 different items which made provision for training all senses except those of taste and smell. To educate visual abilities, the child was given wooden cylinders to fit into holes in a solid block of wood. In the perception of dimensions, training was undertaken with larger objects which required more difficult movements and greater muscular efforts. To train the thermal sense, the hands were put into cold water, lukewarm water, and hot water, so that the child would learn to discriminate differences in temperature.

Kilpatrick (1914), one of America's foremost interpreters of Dewey's philosophy of activity and interest, was not impressed with Montessori's method. The system, according to Kilpatrick, was restrictive because of the use of didactic materials. While the practical life activities afforded excellent opportunities for self-expression, imaginative or constructive play was not promoted by the use of the didactic materials. He believed that games and fine arts were inadequately utilized and that her method was too simple because of the lack of transfer of training. In addition, Kilpatrick maintained that the best sort of self-education takes place when real problems present themselves naturally to children and that no sense can be improved by training. Experiments on the improvement of sensory discrimination have, in fact, not supported Montessori's view. According to Kilpatrick, the success of the Montessori system in the field of reading was essentially the result of the phonetic character of the Italian language.

In contrast, adherents of the Montessori method present the following points:

1. It is based on years of patient observation of children by the greatest educator since Froebel.
2. It has proved itself to be of universal application. Within a single generation, it has been tried with complete success with children of almost every civilized nation. Race, climate, nationality, social rank, and type of civilization make no difference in its successful application.
3. It has revealed the small child as a lover of intellectual work, which he spontaneously chooses and carries out with great enjoyment.
4. It is based on the child's imperious need to learn by doing. At each stage in the child's mental growth, corresponding occupations are provided by which he develops his faculties.
5. While it offers the child maximal spontaneity, it nevertheless enables him to reach the same, or an even higher level of scholastic attainment as other systems.
6. Though it does away with the necessity of coercion by means of rewards and punishments, it achieves a higher discipline than other systems. It is a discipline which originates within the child and is not imposed from without.
7. It is based on a profound respect for the child's personality and removes from him the influence of the adult, thus permitting him to grow in biological independence. Hence, the child is allowed a large measure of liberty (not license) which forms the basis of real discipline.
8. It enables the teacher to deal with each child individually in each subject, and thus to guide him according to his individual requirements.
9. Each child works at his own pace. The quick child is not held back by the slow, nor is the slower learner, in trying to keep up with one who advances more quickly, obliged to flounder along hopelessly in trying to work at another's pace. Each stone in the mental edifice is well and truly laid before the next is added.
10. It does away with the competitive spirit and its train of baneful results. More than this, it presents endless opportunities among the children for mutual help which is joyfully given and gratefully received.

11. Since the child works by his own free choice, without competition or coercion, he is freed from danger of overstrain, feelings of inferiority, and other experiences which are apt to be the unconscious causes of profound mental disturbances in later life.

12. Finally, the Montessori method develops the whole personality of the child, not merely his intellectual faculties but also his powers of deliberation, initiative, and independent choice, with their emotional complements. By living as a free member of a real social community, the child is trained in those fundamental social qualities which form the basis of good citizenship.

What is the evidence in support of these points? Our impressions can be summarized in a one-word answer: "scanty"—especially in view of the claims and costs of this method. Dreyer and Rigler (1969) measured cognitive performance in 14 pairs of children, matched in social class, age, sex, and IQ. Half of the children were selected from a Montessori school and the other half from a "traditional" nursery school. No differences were found between the parents of these children in such measurements of social and parental attitudes and behavior as: achievement orientation, traditional family ideology, dogmatism, anomie, parental control behavior, and task-oriented versus person-oriented values. The nursery school children scored significantly higher on nonverbal creativity, were more socially oriented, and were less task-oriented than the Montessori children. The child's style of approach to tests was considered to be a critical outcome of the two educational environments. The Montessori children used significantly more physical characteristics to describe commonplace objects, whereas significantly more functional terms were used by the nursery school children in their descriptions. Montessori children's drawings contained people significantly less often and geometric forms significantly more often than the nursery school children's drawings.

Use of the Montessori method in preschool is still highly controversial and must be better substantiated in order to become more widely adopted. Montessori programs seem to be less concerned with the social and emotional adaptations of the child than with the provision of disciplined opportunities in which children may acquire sensory discriminations and cognitive skills. Edmonson et al. pointed out (1965, 1967) that there are few references to comparative studies of educational approaches and that there are no follow-up findings of Montessori-trained children. His results indicated no differences between Montessori children and nursery school children in the error score on the Children's Embedded Figures Test (CEFT). Both groups were equally capable of locating the stimulus figure in the embedding context. The Montessori groups, however, did spend significantly less time on the test.

In an evaluation of the Montessori method, L'Abate et al. (1969) found significant improvement of the children only on DAP scores after eight months of Montessori training, while children of a higher intellectual level in a school (initially thought to be comparable) run according to traditional methods showed a significant improvement in a variety of verbal and conceptual skills. In considering the application of the Montessori method to culturally disadvantaged children, Kohlberg (1968) has some pertinent comments as to its usefulness and its differences from an approach derived from Piaget. He concluded:

> **As yet, however, we do not have any of the components of the Montessori approach which would be required for intelligent discussion and evaluation.**

However, the Montessori method is now primarily used for children of high social and economic status and with average to above average intelligence.

Miscellaneous Programs

Descriptions and illustrations of the following visual-motor programs can be found in the catalog of Teaching Resources (1970). Unfortunately, no comparative information is given to indicate which program should be used by which teacher for a child with particular assets and liabilities. Such a lack of specificity makes it difficult to select one program over the others and makes a comparative evaluation imperative.

AYRES PROGRAM (1963). This approach presupposes a thorough understanding of the perceptual process and an occupational therapist's training in the use of arts and crafts materials. Familiarization with the needs of the particular child or small group of children to be trained enables the therapist or special educator to devise and carry out his own program. Because of the individual nature of this approach, there are few published descriptions of actual training techniques, except for Ayres' study (1963). He recommended four phases of perceptual development for the child, emphasizing the particular areas of deficit. These phases include: (1) tactual perception, *proprioception,* and visual perception; (2) body image and motor planning; (3) visuo-spatial perception; and (4) reading, writing, number skills, and conceptualization. Within each phase, the child is trained to take in information (comprehension), to discriminate (organization), and to analyze the information (conceptualization).

BRALEY, KONICK, AND LEEDY PROGRAM (1963). This program's handbook for teachers and parents of preschool children contains suggestions for day-to-day sensory-motor activities to supplement a regular school curriculum for all types of children, normal or abnormal. Activities follow a sequence of training with regard to body image, space and direction, balance, movement, auditory discrimination, body symmetry, coordination, form, and rhythm, and evaluative procedures are provided at the end of each section. Several games are included to supplement the exercises. Although normal classroom equipment would be sufficient for most of the activities which require mechanical aids, the appendix provides instructions for building necessary equipment.

CHEVES PROGRAM (1963). This program, compiled by a teacher of special education, is primarily for the use of a teacher or a therapist with individual children, but could also be used by parents. The kit contains all necessary aids for visual-motor perception as well as an instructor's manual. Some materials which are included are fruit and animal puzzles, form puzzles, geometric shapes in different colors, association cards for reading readiness, "see and say" puzzle cards, configuration cards for arithmetic readiness, an ordinal placement board, flip and build cards for using the tactual and kinesthetic modalities to learn numbers, concept clocks, and a "show you know—then go" phonics game. All materials are presented in a way which minimizes distraction by using bright, uncluttered colors and black borders. The program is recommended to prepare children for basic academic subjects or to aid children who are already having difficulties with learning.

DUBNOFF AND CHAMBERS PROGRAM (1967). The exercises included in this program were compiled by the directors of the Dubnoff School for Educational Therapy. The main objectives of the program are to develop an orientation to reading and writing (by training which involves fine motor control), attention to starting and stopping cues, inhibition of perseveration, and orientation to the upper, left-hand corner of the page. Teachers and parents will find the materials useful for individuals or small groups.

The program has two parts. Program I consists of worksheets, crayons, and an acetate protector to permit reuse. These materials are designed to train in straight, circular, diagonal, and intersecting line concepts. Program II presents tasks in increasing levels of complexity which develop coordinated control of both hands, finger grasp, awareness of finger position, and attention to auditory cues, as well as further exercises in directionality and sequential concepts. Program II uses such materials as pattern cards, a pattern board, and rubber bands of different colors. All necessary materials are included in the kits.

HATTON, PIZZAT, AND PELKOWSKI PROGRAM (1967). This program, which is commonly known as the Erie Program of Perceptual-Motor Teaching Materials, provides training in preacademic skills with the additional help of rivalry and game success as motivational factors. Unit 1 involves practice in form discriminations, sequencing, eye-hand coordination, basic position concepts, and hand dominance. Unit 2 is presented in the form of "perceptual bingo," which can be used with several children at a time to train them to pay attention to visual cues. Unit 3 is a set of visual-motor template forms which provides further training with the addition of the tactual modality as an aid to learning.

FITZHUGH AND FITZHUGH PROGRAM (1966). This program contains a series of eight programmed workbooks designed to teach basic perceptual and academic skills to slow learners or mentally retarded or brain-damaged children. The most outstanding characteristic of the program is the instant feedback which the child receives by using "magic" scoring ink which turns green when the correct response is made, allowing any number of children to work without individual supervision. The five workbooks in the Language and Numbers series focus directly on basic academic areas. The Spatial Organization series, however, emphasizes such perceptual skills as left to right eye movement; recognition of dimensions, similarities, and differences; image movement; and spatial relationships. Workbooks for this series include Shape Matching, Figure Completion, and Shape Identification.

FAIRBANKS AND ROBINSON PROGRAM (1967). Developed by a school psychologist and an occupational therapist, this program of worksheets can be used with one or two children at a time by teachers and parents to develop visual-motor and kinesthetic skills that are necessary for academic success. Line and movement experience, shape discrimination, eye-hand coordination, form constancy, figure-ground discrimination, and spatial relations in two and three dimensions are among the perceptual abilities covered in the worksheets. The program may be used for those with a low level of academic functioning caused by minimal central nervous system impairment, mild emotional disturbance, or developmental slowness. Finger tracing, use of crayons and scissors, and feeling geometric shapes are used with the exercise sheets to employ a wide variety of modality experiences while the child learns skills.

JOLLES PROGRAM (1958). This program represents the efforts of a school psychologist to place the perceptual training suggestions of Strauss and Lehtinen in a developmental sequence which may be followed by special education teachers of retarded, brain-injured, and perceptually handicapped children. The activities, based on pegboard and block designs, are presented on nine different levels of functioning with these major objectives: recognition of basic forms, form discrimination, and perceptual organization.

KNIGHTS AND THOMPSON PROGRAM (1967). This program contains a combination of the training suggestions of Kephart, Strauss and Lehtinen, Barsch, and Delacato, which have been rewritten for individual use with children who show specific learning deficits. The use of household or classroom objects and homemade materials is required. Training focuses on tactual, kinesthetic, spatial relations, auditory, visual, auditory-visual, auditory-kinesthetic, visual-kinesthetic, and reasoning skills. The activities also involve the olfactory and gustatory senses, modalities which are often neglected in training programs dealing with academic ability. Exercises are similar to those found in Kephart's book (1971).

LEAVER, MCKINNEY, ROE, AND VERHOEKS PROGRAM (1968). Written primarily for teachers and physical educators, this manual provides suggestions for the organization of an elementary physical education program based on principles of perceptual-motor development. Normal abilities are listed for particular age levels, evaluation procedures are given, and appropriate gymnasium equipment and set-ups are described. Activities range from fine to gross motor tasks, from posture control to dancing, and from basic exercises to coordinated ball games.

GETMAN PROGRAM (1971). This program, known as the Pathway School Program for the Development of Eye-Hand Coordination, was devised by an optometrist and is to be used by therapists, teachers, or parents. The program employs a bat, ball, and target in several exercises. Because of the gamelike nature of the exercises, a child can enjoy his training by himself or in competition with another child. The exercises develop simple eye-hand coordination, postural shifts, fluidity of movement, crossing the midline, space perception, balance, rhythm, and the ability to coordinate simple skills for use in increasingly complex tasks. The activities are most helpful for children with specific perceptual deficits. Getman proposed two methods for evaluation and remediation of aphasic and brain-damaged children which are also appropriate for evaluating the "normal" child. His model focuses on the visuomotor complex. He stated that ". . . vision evolves from actions of the entire organism and is in reality a derivative of the *total action system*" (Getman, 1971).

VALETT PROGRAM (1966). This collection of materials contains a detailed, well-organized evaluation and training program for each of 53 different abilities that help a child to learn. The abilities to be developed are included under these categories: motor skills, sensory-motor integration, perceptual-motor (including auditory) skills, language skills, and conceptual skills. Also included are suggestions for the development of social skills, an area which may have more to do with perceptual development than is usually supposed. For each specific ability, a definition, illustrations, educational rationale, program ideas in three stages, a sample program, and references are given. The author suggests selection of materials according to the particular deficits and achievement level of the individual child.

VAN WITSEN PROGRAM (1967). The program booklet contains management techniques, suggestions for a structured classroom method, and training exercises based on empirical evidence of their usefulness for many special education students. Although classroom-oriented, the suggestions seem to be aimed largely at behavioral problems, such as impulsivity and distractibility, which have their bases in perceptual problems rather than in academic readiness. Games, exercises, and activities are prescribed for the purpose of developing an integration of the senses, whereby one sense can reinforce the message that another sense conveys. Training involves vision, hearing, touch, smell, taste, and kinesthesis. The appendix contains instructions for paper-folding activities.

CONCLUSION

In summary, one can say that there is some evidence to support the hypothesis that perceptual-motor training programs do increase motor proficiency, and there is some evidence that intelligence is affected by these programs; however, there are also contradictory facts. Many studies yielding results in favor of perceptual-motor training programs have been attacked on methodological grounds. Lillie (1968) stated that the trouble with some of these studies is that the training tasks are used as the measures of outcome, and this constitutes teaching for the test. Mann (1970) stated a similar argument. He said that many of the results of the training programs are not necessarily due to "perceptual" improvements and that benefits from this type of program are "superficial more often than not." These arguments have some validity, and further studies, with these arguments in mind, are required before any conclusive evidence can be obtained.

Footlik (1970) spoke in favor of visual-motor training programs, supporting the notion that some form of structured physical activity can help to develop the learning capacity of children with various learning disabilities. This notion implies that each behavior pattern has a corresponding pattern in central nervous system activity, referred to as intersensory schemata. Normal organization results from stimulation, activity, and experiences in an ordered developmental sequence. As Chalfant and Scheffelin (1969) concluded in their review of the research in this area: "There is little empirical evidence, however, supporting the hypothesis that basic perceptual-motor training leads to improvement in perceptual-motor abilities or to better academic performance." Therefore, the major factor in determining the efficacy of a program is whether it supplies appropriate sequences of exercises that will transfer to other complex skills, like reading, writing, and arithmetic.

Mann (1970), at about the same time, criticized perceptual-motor training on the following grounds:

> **Perceptual-motor training has become an education fad, based upon unwarranted extrapolations from theory and misreading of the perceptual motor difficulties manifested by handicapped children. What is of value in it can be accomplished through traditional adapted educational and therapeutic approaches directed toward functional and relevant behavioral objectives, rather than toward isolated so-called perceptual improvements.**

In our verbally oriented culture, we tend to emphasize auditory and verbal training to the point that apparently more is attempted in this field of training than in others. Formal training, speech centers, and specialists (e.g., speech therapists and audiologists) are available as a matter of course. In contrast, we lack visual-motor specialists who should be the counterparts in their field of their colleagues in the auditory-verbal field. The lack of such professional specialization denotes the lack of interest in visual-motor training that has usually existed among professionals. Yet, visual-motor training does not lack theory. Piaget, for instance, emphasized that the sequence of sensory-motor stages occurs early in the child's life and that certain organic handicaps affect the visual-motor modality most. Besides Piaget, we must remember that Werner, with his sensory-tonic theory, emphasized the importance of this modality, in that it appears at an earlier developmental stage than language. The connection between theory and practice, however, is still thin and tenuous.

CHAPTER 7

HEARING AND SPEECH IMPAIRMENTS

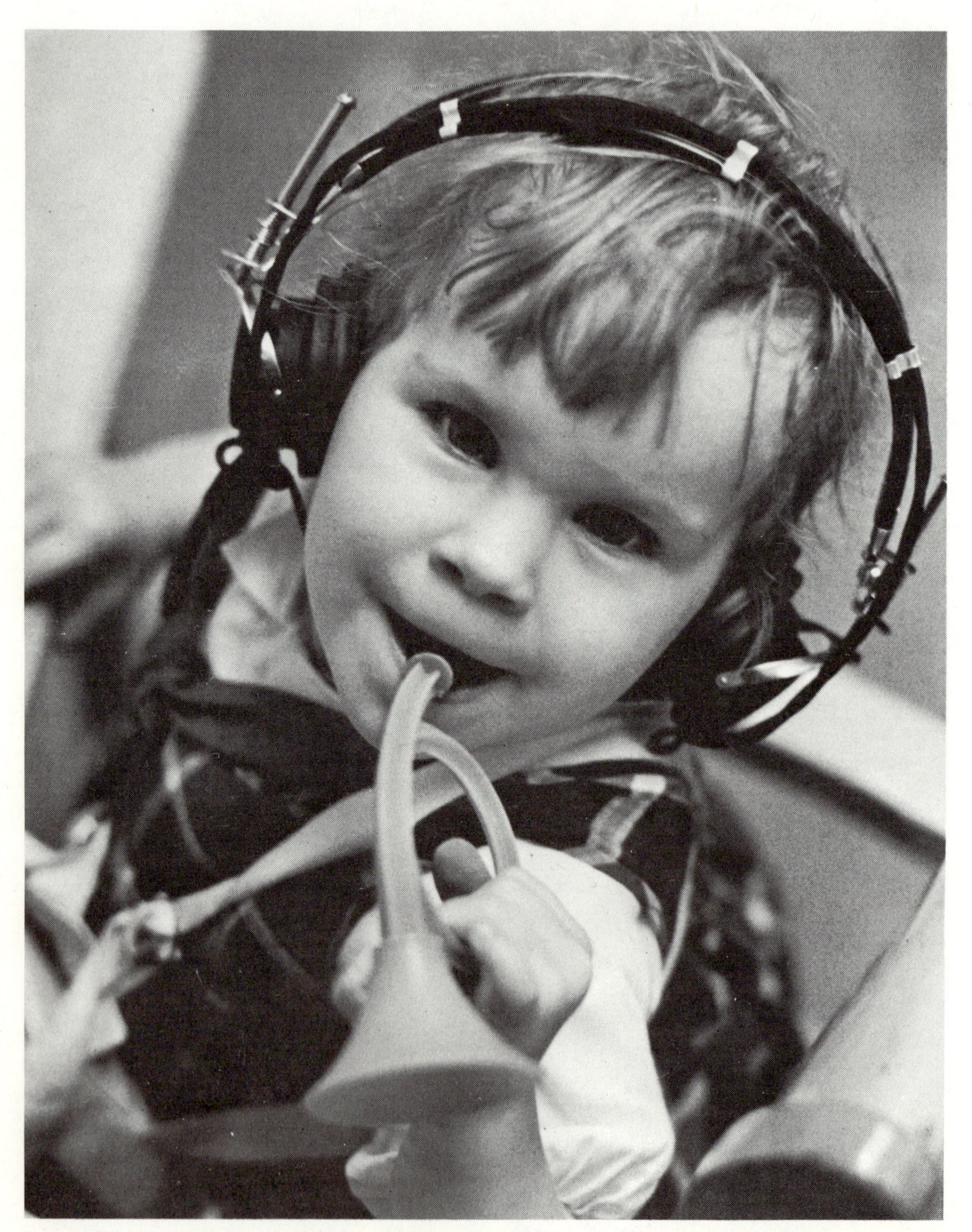

(Courtesy of Children's Hospital of Philadelphia, Pennsylvania.)

THE NATURE OF HEARING PROBLEMS RELATED TO SCHOOL ACTIVITIES

Incidence and Definition

At present, it is impossible to arrive at any accurate determination of the number of hearing- and speech-impaired children in the United States. One estimate is that there are well over 500,000 children in the United States who have significant hearing loss (McCabe, 1963). According to McCabe, the screening programs conducted by public schools indicate that between 3 and 6 per cent of children in public schools may have mild to moderate hearing impairments and that perhaps 2/10 to 4/10 of 1 per cent of the cases may be severe enough to require special auditory training. Fortunately, most children suffering from hearing impairments have sufficient hearing to be able to cope with school environments with somewhat moderate types of educational adjustment. Most of these children are receiving their educations in a regular classroom, and many are unaware of the nature of their problem. As with vision, there are technical definitions regarding the varying amounts of hearing loss as related to a continuum of hearing. The more generally agreed-upon definitions are as follows: Normal hearing involves loss of less than 15 decibels in the worst ear; both ears are presumed to be within normal limits, and there is no difficulty with speech. Near normal hearing involves more than 15 but less than 30 decibels of loss in either ear and involves some difficulty with speech. Mild hearing impairment involves a loss of 30 to 45 decibels and difficulty with normal speech, but probably no difficulty with loud speech. Serious impairment indicates a loss of 45 to 60 decibels in the better ear. An individual with such an impairment probably has some difficulty even with very loud speech. Severe impairment involves a loss of 60 to 90 decibels in the better ear and the need for electronic amplification for adequate hearing. Profound impairment implies a more than 90-decibel loss in the better ear. An individual with such an impairment is beyond the help of even a highly sophisticated hearing aid. Total loss of hearing in both ears means inability to hear any sound at all. No electronic amplification of any sort, which is available at present, would be of any assistance.

Symptoms in the Classroom

A young child with defective hearing frequently does not realize his problem, and few adults with normal hearing are aware of the hearing-impaired and the nature of their impairment. As with all other exceptional conditions, *the classroom teacher must be alerted to some of the symptoms that might possibly indicate hearing impairment.* They are, in general, as follows:

1. Tilting the head at an angle in order to receive a better sound.
2. Listless or inattentive behavior.
3. Failure to respond when questioned.
4. Defective articulation, particularly when sounding of words is important.
5. Peculiar voice quality, often high-pitched and flattish in nature.
6. Tendency to avoid association with other people.
7. Tendency to run words together.
8. Poor oral reading ability.
9. Discrepancy between academic performance and IQ scores.
10. Louder speech than would be indicated by the situation.
11. Tendency to watch the face of a speaker with considerably greater attention than is normal.

External appearance may also be indicative of hearing problems. Typical external signs are: (1) deformities of the outer ear (i.e., the part of the ear that one sees), (2) discharge from the ear, (3) undue muscular tension when listening, (4) breathing through the mouth, and (5) blank facial expression. In addition to these symptoms, children who have hearing difficulties frequently complain of the following: (1) buzzing or ringing in the head, (2) earaches, (3) nausea or dizziness, (4) inability to understand directions, and (5) headaches in the sinus areas. All the preceding symptoms should be viewed as possible indicators of hearing impairment which the teacher may consider in referring the child for assistance. It is not uncommon for a school-age child to escape detection even in the first, second, or third grades. Therefore, it is important that teachers pay particular attention to these symptoms in order that adequate care may be provided.

Classroom Screening Procedures

While it is not expected that the teacher will engage in any extensive auditory testing of students, it might be advisable for her to be aware of some less sophisticated testing approaches which may be used in addition to being alert to the symptoms previously described. The most typical test used by the less sophisticated examiner is the watch test. It consists of holding a watch to either side of the head at increasing and decreasing distances. The test should be performed, of course, so that the watch is unobserved by the student, and he may merely indicate when the watch is heard. The student may also be instructed to follow the sound of the watch by movement of the head. The whisper test is comparable to the watch test and is frequently used. The teacher stands at some distance and whispers very quietly in an attempt to ascertain whether the child has a hearing impairment. A tuning fork provides a little more objective type of auditory testing device, in that it does emit a prescribed sound wave which is stable in frequency and reasonably stable in volume. The most sophisticated device used in public schools is the pure-tone *audiometer.* The audiometer is utilized by speech specialists in the public schools. If the child is suspected of having any difficulties in hearing, he should be immediately referred by the teacher to the school district's speech therapist for further examination. Naturally, the speech therapist, upon completion of any testing, should make appropriate referrals to more specialized professionals when necessary.

Causes

The causes of hearing impairment are as varied as those for any other handicapping condition. They may be generally divided into the hereditary and the adventitious (i.e., the acquired causation). The acquired problems may vary from those involving rubella or German measles to mumps or other kinds of diseases, such as whooping cough or traumatic injuries. Verville (1967) reported that 50 per cent of hearing disturbances are inherited, 15 per cent are caused by prenatal and paranatal factors, such as rubella, and 33 per cent are the result of infantile infectious diseases, particularly meningitis.

Personality Characteristics

The relationship of personality to hearing involves considerable contradiction and is the subject of much discussion at present. Many hearing-impaired individuals seem to exhibit a greater degree of emotional instability, neuroticism, and social maladjustment than is considered to be within the normal range (Allbright, 1952; Fiedler, 1952; Levine, 1960). Of course, the deaf child does not always differ psychologically from the child who hears well. The adjustment patterns of the deaf and the hard of hearing, it is believed, are the result of environmental rather than of congenital or hereditary factors. Most problems

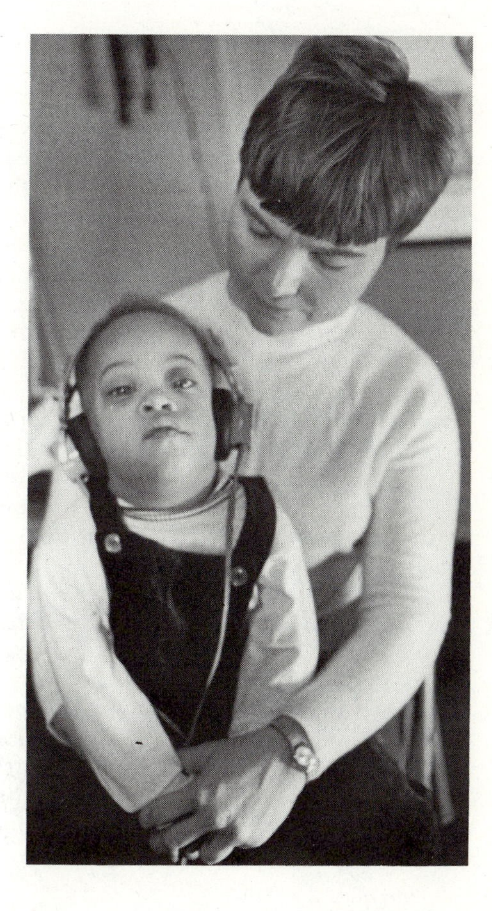

Figure 7–1 The seriousness of a child's handicapping condition often depends on his acceptance by others. (Courtesy of Children's Hospital of Philadelphia, Pennsylvania.)

do not derive directly from the hearing loss, but tend to be caused by interactive patterns. As pointed out in an earlier chapter, the seriousness of handicapping conditions tends to depend on the acceptance of these conditions by parents and by others of significance to the child.

Many personality inventories which are commonly used in examining the characteristics of children would seem to have questionable validity when applied to deaf children, since a majority of such inventories is dependent upon the acquisition of adequate language. Levine (1963), from a vocabulary analysis of many inventories used with the deaf, noted that these inventories tended to be above the reading vocabulary level of the deaf as a group and even, perhaps, further removed from their conceptual level. Considering these findings, projective techniques might be more appropriate for examining the personality of deaf children. Levine concluded that "... children with hearing defects are generally characterized by: (1) conceptual deficiencies, (2) emotional immaturity, (3) rigidity and egocentricity, (4) deficient social adaptability, and (5) constricted interest and motivation."

In spite of the preceding characteristics, one must be very careful in drawing conclusions about the relationship between hearing handicaps per se and personality development in a child. The social milieu must be examined with a great deal of care in order to provide as adequate a picture of the hearing-impaired child's background as possible.

Intellectual Functioning

There have been many studies on the intellectual level of hearing-impaired children. Over 50 years ago, Pintner and Patterson (1915) used a revision of a performance scale to test 18 deaf children and found that the mean IQ score of these children was 63. Since that time, there have been a great many studies in this area. Meyerson (1963) reviewed 25 such studies: 10 studies, using individual performance tests, found lower than normal IQ scores for deaf children, with the median being 91; in 12 studies, there were no significant differences between deaf and acoustically normal children; in 3 studies, deaf children were found to have higher IQ scores. Studies using group tests have shown slightly lower mean IQ scores for the hearing-impaired than studies using individual tests. It is interesting to note that there has been a decrease in the number of studies concerning the intelligence of the hearing -impaired. From 1930 to 1939, there were 16 studies; from 1940 to 1949, there were 12 studies; and in the period from 1950 to 1959, only 3 such studies were conducted. There is a tendency, today, toward more sophisticated selection of measurements to determine the intellectual level of an individual. In order for such measurements to be meaningful, they must be made under particular conditions, such as proper sampling and matching, and with consideration of the individual taking the test as well as with variables pertaining to the examiner. In other words, it is not a simple matter to assess the intelligence of any individual, and it becomes increasingly difficult to assess the intrinsic functioning of an individual who has a significant sensory impairment.

Also, with regard to the decrease in intelligence studies of the hearing-impaired, it should be noted that intelligence is viewed somewhat differently today. Before 1930, intelligence was generally regarded as a genetically determined, innate factor, while, today, we are very much concerned with the relationship of environment to the development of intellectual functioning. Special education, of course, assumes that there are specific methods of training and educating a typical or an exceptional child which should result in the child's being able to function socially, educationally, and, ultimately, vocationally in a reasonably adequate manner. Within this frame of reference, the relationship of intelligence to deafness becomes a much more complex issue (Reynolds, 1965).

Medical Factors

As an addition to our discussion of the public schools and the treatment of hearing-impaired persons, we might mention that there are now available a number of surgical procedures which are frequently utilized in treating the hearing-impaired child. The more common surgical procedures are as follows:

1. *Fenestration* of the *labyrinth,* in which an oval window is cut into the *semicircular canal* of the inner ear. This artificial window is then closed with a membrane which acts as a sound-sensitive surface, picking up sound waves and directly bypassing the bones of the inner ear.
2. Mobilization of the *stapes,* in which the plate of the stapes, the bone which attaches to the oval window, is loosened by breaking away the excess bone impeding its action. In other words, the bone must be able to vibrate freely if hearing is to be within reasonable limits.
3. Artificial replacement of the stapes.
4. Covering *tympanic drum* perforations with skin grafts.

Of much greater importance to the teacher is the development of increasingly sophisticated hearing aids. Modern hearing aids may be used in place of or in addition to the preceding surgical procedures. The hearing aid industry has been very active in the improvement of their products. Of course, hearing aids, which are basically sound amplifiers, do have limitations, particularly for some kinds of hearing conditions. It is important that the child be fitted with a hearing aid as early as possible, so that he may acquire language in as normal a manner as possible.

Environmental Support

The family problems presented by the hearing-impaired child and, in particular, by the profoundly deaf child are unique. If the child has any residual hearing, and, fortunately, most hearing-impaired children have some hearing, every attempt should be made by the parents and teachers to capitalize on it. After a complete otological, audiometric examination, any appropriate surgery, and installation of hearing aids, it is necessary that intensive hearing and language training be instituted at home and in the classroom. The child should be raised in a speaking environment. Special efforts should be made to see that the child receives as much practice in the use of language as possible. Van Wyck (1959) suggested to parents (and these procedures may also be followed by teachers) that they might provide the following kinds of experiences for their children:

1. Talk to the child constantly. Provide a rich speaking atmosphere. Do not use signs, and when the child uses a sign, supply the proper words.
2. Expect the child to learn speech reading and to learn to speak.

Figure 7–2 The child should be raised in a speaking environment. (Courtesy of Children's Hospital of Philadelphia, Pennsylvania.)

Start with simple phrases or meaningful words as they apply to specific situations or to concrete objects and activities.

3. Work constantly to increase his vocabulary. Systematically introduce new words and teach different words which have the same meaning to avoid the development of a stilted, limited speech pattern.

4. Insist that the child speak for himself, first to members of his family, then to friends and relatives, and later to casual acquaintances and strangers. Do not step in to speak and interpret for the child. Encourage independence and self-confidence.

5. Require and expect the child to accept responsibility to perform household duties and to participate in family life, just as the unimpaired do. Send him on errands as soon as he has sufficient vocabulary to make himself understood.

6. Discourage the use of pencil and paper or sign language in place of oral speech.

7. Provide as much pleasure and satisfaction for the child as possible when he is learning the use of language. Speech training in the house or school should never become a dull, repetitious drill.

As with other impairments, there is no precise way of indicating from physiological information the extent to which educational difficulties may be encountered by those who are hearing-impaired. Some children with a greater degree of hearing impairment, according to the decibel rate method, seemingly are able to obtain more information than others who have less intense damage to the hearing mechanisms. From an educational point of view, both at home and at school, every effort should be made to cause the child to respond by using all his available assets.

Education of the Hearing-Impaired

It is essential that all educational programs for hearing-impaired children provide adequate alternative modes of reception (input) and expression (output) of information to compensate for the inability to hear adequately. Much human interaction is verbal. Since the profoundly deaf, in particular, and the hearing-impaired, to some extent, have difficulty with verbal communication, efforts must be made by educators to provide alternative approaches to input, interpretation, and output of knowledge. We will not enter into an extended discussion of the virtues of one method of teaching the deaf over another. We do stress, however, that the profoundly deaf and the hard of hearing must, by necessity, enter into "a hearing world." Consequently, the end goal of any educational procedure for the hearing-impaired must be to prepare the student to enter into as nearly normal a life pattern as possible. This means, of course, that the hearing-impaired child must, to the best of his capabilities, be able to convey his ideas verbally (output). Additional methods, such as sign language, are not to be excluded, but this means of communication, in particular, tends to form semiexclusive societies within the larger society of American life. The proper instruction of these individuals will assist them in entering more freely into the hearing world and will lessen their need to segregate themselves.

The profoundly deaf individual will be able to monitor his own speech only by means of touch and kinesthesis. The hard of hearing child will need auditory amplification and training to make use of his residual hearing. Fortunately, since language is the cornerstone upon which all education depends, it is possible in the majority of cases to teach oral speech. Some individuals who seem to have difficulty in mastering oral speech certainly should not be neglected, nor should they be coerced into a speaking pattern which may make them feel totally inadequate. In such cases, alternative methods of communication, such as signing (sign language) may be indicated.

In summary, the profoundly deaf or hearing-impaired child needs to have the earliest possible access to intensive training. He should be fitted with a hearing aid, when the need is indicated, provided with good home training, and allowed to develop in a nearly normal environment both at home and at school. The profoundly deaf child will need specialized assistance which is usually provided by teachers of the deaf. A normal, natural nursery school program using every available assistance (e.g., hearing aids) is indicated for the hearing-impaired child.

Educational Achievement

Almost universally, the achievement testing of hearing-impaired children indicates below normal functioning. The absolute amount of educational retardation has been found to increase with age (Meyerson, 1963a). Students applying for Gallaudet College, the only national college for the deaf, have been found to have a mean age of 18 years and 9 months and a mean achievement level of ninth grade, second month on the Stanford achievement test. It should be pointed out that this achievement level is appropriate for the average 15-year-old child (Fusfield, 1954).

Reading

Lyness (1968) found that the following interrelated factors distinguished good from poor readers: memory, *form constancy,* figure-ground discrimination, temporal discrimination, and synthesis. She also found a pattern of reading success and failure with regard to auditory input. Good readers did not fail more than one auditory subtest, whereas poor readers failed at least three or four. This finding suggested that compensation for more than one specific area of deficiency becomes progressively harder as the number of defective auditory-perceptual abilities increases. Lyness concluded that on the basis of these findings, auditory perception plays an important role in learning to read. Conceptualizing dyslexia as failure to form required associations between visual forms (e.g., letters) and appropriate auditory responses, Brewer (1967) found it difficult to account for dyslexia primarily as an associative-learning deficit. This conclusion strengthens the possibility that most learning disabilities and poor reading may result from complex permutations among most input-output modalities.

Special Schools for the Deaf

In 1972, residential schools for hearing-impaired children in the United States had approximately 16,000 children enrolled. Historically, the earliest treatment of hearing-impaired and deaf children was performed in residential facilities. Presently, caring for hearing-impaired and deaf children within the framework of the community is receiving increased emphasis. It should be remembered that, with hearing impairment and all other exceptionalities, the more divergent the mode of coping with the exceptionality, the more difficult it will be for the individual to enter into the mainstream of normal, everyday life. At all times, the major goal of all educational procedures should be adequate entry into vocational, social, civic, and political activities. The disadvantages and advantages of special schools for the hearing-impaired will not be explored in this chapter. Students interested in this issue may consult Chapter 12 which discusses this topic in greater detail. At this point, it will suffice to say that to take a young child from his parents and enroll him in a school, often many miles away from his home, is not usually an emotionally reassuring method of treatment for the child.

Special Classes in a Regular School

The special class has been utilized in a number of schools, and it is not uncommon for the special class pupil to be partially integrated with regular classes. Generally, the special class is devoted to providing specialized technical skills, such as lip reading, signing, or other skills necessary for the acquisition of knowledge.

The Hearing-Impaired College Student

At present, the high school graduate who has severe hearing problems has a choice of attending regular public institutions of higher education or the only national college for the deaf, Gallaudet. Many problems of the deaf are magnified in regular institutions of higher education because there usually are no special facilities or aids for the deaf and because classroom instruction at the college level almost always involves oral kinds of presentations, largely the classical methods of lecturing and class discussion. The deaf student is only one individual among the many and, as such, often has difficulty in coping with the typical college method of instruction.

Vocational Opportunities

The following figures compare the occupational status of the deaf with that of the general population.* These figures indicate that relatively fewer deaf individuals are employed in higher professional, managerial, clerical, and sales areas than individuals in the general population. This is probably due to the greater need for high-order, verbal communication which is necessary at the professional and higher business levels. In the study which we have just cited, 85 per cent of deaf workers were rated as successful in their occupations. This percentage seemingly indicates that it is entirely feasible for educational programs for the deaf to culminate in successful placement of deaf individuals in the economic life of America.

Job Categories	*Percentage of Deaf Employed*	*Percentage of General Population Employed*
Professional, technical, and similar occupations	6.6	10.6
Managers, officials, and proprietors	3.2	15.5
Clerical, sales, and similar workers	7.2	20.7
Craftsmen, foremen, and similar workers	35.9	13.4
Operative and similar workers	35.2	20.1
Laborers and service workers	11.9	19.7

*Data from Lumbe and Vogman (1959).

Social Life

The social life of most deaf persons is very much like that of normal individuals. The average deaf person has a home, a job, is married, raises a family, and participates in the normal social and civic activities of the community. More than any other exceptional group, the deaf do seek their own kind. For example, it has been found in a study of 10,000 married, deaf adults that less than 5 per cent had married hearing people (Brill, 1961). In addition, deaf individuals have formed a larger number of adult groups which are composed exclusively of the deaf (Elstad et al., 1955). The deaf have a national association, with offices in Berkeley, California, which publishes a monthly magazine called The Silent Worker.

In summary, as far as educational procedures are concerned, if the hearing-impaired child receives very early, intensive training by skilled professionals and is raised in a home which provides optimal auditory stimulation and oral communication, it is probable that he will be able to cope with education in the regular American public schools. Usually, the more severe the impairment, the greater the need for assistance by professionals, such as the teacher of the deaf who may work with young children on a full-time basis and with intermediate, junior high, and senior high school children on an itinerant basis. However, it must be stressed that the hearing-impaired child can cope with regular American education. In addition, the majority of the hearing-impaired will be able to live reasonably adequate lives which include family life and employment.

AUDITORY DISCRIMINATION AND COMPLEX SKILLS

According to Chalfant and Scheffelin (1969), auditory discrimination on the receptive (input) side includes at least six different abilities: (1) attention to auditory stimuli, (2) differentiation of sound versus no sound, (3) sound localization, (4) discrimination of sounds varying on one acoustical dimension, (5) discrimination of sound sequences varying on several acoustical dimensions, and (6) associating sounds with sound sources. On the expressive (output) side, they noted that

> many discussions of language acquisition are confusing because little distinction has been made between (sic) the three major aspects of language performance: *Receptive auditory language, expressive auditory language,* and vocal-motor production. Few attempts have been made to identify the various central processing functions which are required in the attainment of receptive language or expressive language . . . There is little research as to how much vocal-motor behavior and receptive language is necessary for adequate expressive functioning.

Expressive auditory language is based on: (1) the child's deciding to communicate; (2) retrieving vocal-language signals; (3) executing the vocal-motor sequence; and (4) combining single vocal-language signals into more complex signals and increasing the range, rate, and accuracy of production. Reading ability (Chalfant and Scheffelin, 1969) is based on (1) attention to visual stimuli; (2) recognition of stimuli as graphic word units; (3) identification of stimuli as sequences of discrete letters; (4) retrieval of the *phoneme* for each *grapheme;* (5) recall of phonemes in temporal sequence; (6) blending phonemes into familiar auditory language signals; and finally, (7) responding by uttering a word. Writing is the final result of a developmental hierarchy of tasks starting with scribbling, then progressing to tracing, copying, completion, writing from dictation, and finally propositional language. For a thorough review of research on central processing dysfunctions in children, the reader is referred to the original, informative monograph of Chalfant and Scheffelin.

Theory Concerning Input and Output

Lenneberg (1967) presented a view which describes language as being biologically determined with little or no effect from environmental factors. Pointing out the influence of a specific anatomical localization of language components, especially with regard to the relative dominance of the left hemisphere, is a major contribution of Lenneberg. The most posterior areas of the brain tend to involve predominantly sensory aspects (input), while anterior areas affect the predominantly motor aspects of language (output).

Reception and Expression

Although Lenneberg differentiated between receptive and expressive aspects of language, he stressed the anatomical influence on both aspects and placed little emphasis on the influence of environmental factors. He contended that language development is independent of motor coordination and that *language comprehension (input) has priority over language production (output).* The evidence and arguments presented to support his position are indeed impressive and worthy of full consideration by serious language students, although the influence of socioeconomic factors is not given full and comprehensive consideration. Lenneberg's contentions "... that the understanding of language is more relevant to an estimation of language capacities" and that "... we can learn to understand a language without ability to speak it" are consistent with his statement that "by and large it is true that young children can understand more than they can say."*

> **By about 30 months, however, production soon becomes as unreliable an indicator of language capacities as is the case in the adult. Unfortunately, no studies have yet been published that have undertaken systematic research on the development of grammatical understanding of the child at this age and older. Even the best studies have relied too heavily on production.***

This conclusion, however, was made without consideration of the study of Deutsch and his associates (1967) on the language production of disadvantaged children, who (as will be discussed in greater detail in the next section of this book) are especially defective in verbal output. On the basis of the language of intellectually defective children, Lenneberg concluded that

> **... the discrepancy between speech skills and the capacity for understanding may, indeed, be observed in every child. The theoretical importance of the extreme dissociation between perceptive and productive ability lies in the demonstration that the particular ability which we may properly call *having knowledge of a language* is not identical with speaking. Since knowledge of a language may be established in the absence of speaking skills, the former must be prior, and, in a sense, simpler than the latter. Speaking appears to require additional capacities, but these are accessory rather than criterial for language development.***

Lenneberg stated that language acquisition in the congenitally deaf, which is slower and lower than in the hearing child, is "... primarily due to shortcomings in instruction and training, and not due to inherent learning incapacities of the deaf."* Regardless of this viewpoint, which Lenneberg shares with Furth (1964), the fact remains that deafness retards language skills by about four years below the child's chronological age (Telford and Sawrey, 1967). However, there is essential agreement with Lenneberg's conclusion that

> **... an individual's *knowledge* of language, as determinable by testing his comprehension, may be established in the complete absence of capacities for language- or speech-specific *responses*, that is, the ability of the learner himself to speak. This (conclusion) emphasizes the importance of Chomsky's competence-performance distinction and makes those language theories doubtful that are primarily based upon a response-shaping hypothesis (such as Skinner).***

In relating language to intellect, Lenneberg stated that "it is probably only in the areas of education proper (as opposed to the biologically given organization of the environment) that language deficits become a serious obstacle for intellectual development."*

Thus, the input-output model is essentially in agreement with Len-

---

*Biological Foundations of Language by E. H. Lenneberg. Copyright © 1967 by John Wiley & Sons, Inc. Reprinted by permission of John Wiley & Sons, Inc.

neberg and Chomsky (1967), with the exception of emphasis on different parts of the language process. Linguistic competence is more dependent on input factors and, consequently, on genetic, biological, and organismic forces; language production, as an output factor, is more dependent on environmental, cultural forces, as emphasized by Skinner. Considering the input-output model previously presented in this text, neither Lenneberg nor Skinner are wholly inclusive. They simply emphasize different aspects of language: the former viewing biological forces as mainly responsible for language, the latter viewing environmental forces as largely responsible. If we understand the specific contribution of each of these forces to different aspects of the process, one contributing to input and the other to output factors, a reconciliation of both viewpoints can and should be obtained, resulting in a better understanding of language development in children. Educational and clinical programs should incorporate both viewpoints into their procedures.

Biology and Input-Output Functions

Lenneberg maintained (1966, 1967) that language is independent from general motor development, even though language acquisition progresses through a sequence of maturationally based milestones that have neither utilitarian nor motivational bases. He indicated that language learning is related to lateralization of cerebral functions and that onset of speech is not simply related to motor control, articulatory skills, and general motor development (Lenneberg, 1966). Even though onset is "regulated by a maturational process," such a process is "independent of motor-skeletal maturation." Even though Lenneberg marshaled a great deal of evidence to support his thesis of the independence of language maturation from other processes, the interaction of the visual and auditory input systems with the motor and verbal output systems may increase with deficits in any one of these modalities. The more a child is impaired in the visual-motor or auditory-verbal modalities, the more he will need to use and become dependent upon the functioning ones. *Any decrease in functioning in a component part may well produce a reduction in efficiency in the overall functioning of the child.* One can readily argue for exceptions to this generalization (e.g., Beethoven was hard of hearing, and the deficit did not influence his musical production, even though it may have had significant effects on his social relations and overall emotional adjustment). As Chase (1966) pointed out: "The sensory receptor systems provide absolute limits on the kind and amount of information that can be received by animals and human beings." Consequently, he concluded: ". . . behavior is the result of systems of functional operation, and relatively small changes in the physical componentry of a single subsystem can radically alter the output of a system as a whole."

Competence and Performance. Lenneberg felt that the onset of language is not delayed by external conditions, such as isolation and poor linguistic environment. Nonetheless, culturally deprived children ultimately show a decrease in overall efficiency in language competence as well as in performance. Age at the time of onset may be unaffected by many cultural conditions. This conclusion is supported by evidence that vocabulary recognition is higher than expression in younger children regardless of socioeconomic background (L'Abate, 1969b). This similarity in children may well be due to biological and maturational forces. The eventual interaction, however, between biological deficits and cultural deprivation will tend to decrease vocabulary recognition. Lenneberg

(1966) conceded this point indirectly by his reference to feral children and to those severely deprived to the point that irreparable damage is produced in the input system, more often than not, irreversibly. Age, of course, is a significant factor that is related to maturation and to maturity of the central nervous system. Such an interactional view is well considered by Lenneberg. Thus, *language acquisition is closely related to biological forces, such as cerebral dominance and maturational history; however, language production depends more on cultural and psychological forces.* Apparently, Lenneberg was either unwilling or unable to make this distinction as strongly as proposed here.

Chomsky (1969) emphasized how "... we must isolate and study the system of linguistic competence that underlies behavior but that is not realized in any direct or simple way in behavior." In discussing linguistic ability, he distinguished sharply between competence, "... the knowledge of language possessed by each normal speaker," and performance, "... some of the ways in which this knowledge is put to use." He pointed out that

> **psychology conceived as 'behavioral science' has been concerned with behavior and acquisition or control of behavior. It has no concept corresponding to 'competence' [as he defined it].... The theory of learning has limited itself to a narrow and surely inadequate concept of what is learned—namely, a system of stimulus-response connections, a network of associations, a repertoire of behavioral items, a habit hierarchy, or a system of dispositions to respond in a particular way under specifiable stimulus conditions.... What is necessary, in addition to the concept of behavior and learning, is a concept of what is learned, a notion of competence—that lies beyond the conceptual limits of behavioristic psychological theory.**

In this regard, Chomsky discussed the need to include input variables when output is being considered. The exclusion of input variables plus the absence of interactional concepts (e.g., feedback) make most learning models (L'Abate, 1969a; 1969b) somewhat inapplicable to the child as an information-processing, biological, cultural, and psychological organism. Chomsky's views can also be applied to motor development, although the recognition of a lag between perceiving and performing (Olson and Pagliuso, 1968) supports the similarity between verbal and motor processes. Any future model of behavior will need to include this heretofore ignored aspect before advancing to more complex analyses.

RECOGNITION AND UTTERANCE. McNeil (1966) elaborated on Chomsky's distinction between language competence and language performance. He defined competence as the knowledge of a language that one must possess to understand extremely varied sentences. Performance, on the other hand, "... is the expression of competence in talking," a distinction that he feels must be "rigorously" maintained. The behaviorists' failure to consider this distinction has produced an oversimplification of linguistic development that has dealt "... only with the surface structure of sentences." Comprehension of linguistic features occurs earlier developmentally than the production in speech of the same features. *Competence deals with the recognition, reception, or decoding of language involving passive control. Performance deals with the production and encoding of language involving active control. Comprehension usually exceeds production.* Passive control occurs earlier than active control, and it may be affected by factors other than memory span. McNeil concluded that "... it is theoretically possible that some (factors) even constrain comprehension more than production." Constraint of receptive functions is a point about which the teacher should be informed because it is not only theoretically possible but empirically demonstrable, as in some forms of brain-damage, receptive aphasia, and intellectual retardation.

In discussing McNeil's presentation, Slobin (1966) suggested that "... one must look upon the child as engaged in an active, productive endeavor, supported by a biological *Anlage*. . . ." Most linguists, like Fodor (1966), feel that the two concepts most used by behavioral psychologists, imitation and reinforcement, are useful in the learning of language. More relevant to the purposes of this chapter is Fry's study (1966), in which he noted that hearing is not fundamental to speech production, especially in severely hard of hearing children, as is traditionally assumed. There are other modalities (vision, kinesthesis, touch) that can be used in such learning:

> **... we may say that the amount of speech a child develops depends not so much on the amount of hearing *per se* as upon the use he is able to make of his hearing for language-learning. . . . An essential part of the speech-learning process is the linking of the auditory and kinesthetic feedback systems.**

In other words, if there are deficits in any component parts of the biological system, be they auditory or visual, other component parts can take over, but the success of such a takeover depends a great deal on the methods of teaching, practice, and motivation which are employed (Hirsh, 1966). It must also be considered that deficits in language output may feed back negatively on auditory recognition and identification (Smith and Miller, 1966).

On the basis of these considerations, aspects of auditory-verbal functioning that are relevant to the teacher could be considered as two sides of the same coin. These two aspects are summarized in Table 7–1.

Figure 7–3 Other modalities, such as vision, kinesthesis, and touch, may be used in developing speech production. (Courtesy of Children's Hospital of Philadelphia, Pennsylvania.)

TABLE 7–1 ASPECTS OF AUDITORY-VERBAL FUNCTIONING.

Input	Output
Reception	Expression
Perception	Production
Decoding	Encoding
Competence	Performance
Recognition	Utterance
Comprehension and understanding	Communication
Hearing and seeing	Speaking and signing
Capacity and potential	Skill and ability
Passive knowledge	Active knowledge

COMPREHENSION AND COMMUNICATION. Sapon's study (1965) which indicated how receptive and expressive aspects of language possess different functional relationships to the environment in terms of control is relevant to the last four entries of Table 7–1. He pointed out the primacy and priority of understanding over speaking in children and adults and specified the different behaviors that stem from these two aspects. According to Sapon, understanding is the result of verbally controlled behavior; speaking, on the other hand, may be considered as controlling behavior. In addition to being functionally different, both aspects differ in antecedent learning conditions and make uniquely different demands on the organism. He criticized the theory that nonverbal behavior may be of a lower level than verbal behavior, indicating how the lack of differentiation between these two behaviors may hinder insight into retarded verbal behavior. His differentiation based on function and control is more logical and useful than the passive-active dichotomy which is functionally and descriptively useless.

Buktenica (1968), like Lenneberg, supported the concept of "... independence of auditory and visual perception (which) might indicate separate neurological input, output and integrative systems for both auditory and visual perception. ..." He also presented a model of information processing, similar to the models developed by Beery (1969), Shiffer (1968), Sabatino (1969), Osgood (1964), and others already considered in Chapter 1, based on reflex (sensory), perceptual-observational (imitation), and conceptual levels.

Environment and Input-Output Functions

Language is not sufficient for the formation of intellectual patterns of thought (Sinclair-de-Zwart, 1969). Thinking is the result of spatial-temporal operations (L'Abate, 1964) in which action, movement, and language are important aspects. Both language and action are necessary for thought, and one without the other is insufficient for cognitive development. In this regard, the contributions of Chomsky (1967) and Lenneberg (1967) need to be further acknowledged. Chomsky (Sinclair-de-Zwart, 1969) stressed that performance of individuals is far poorer than their competence. Conversely, Piaget, a theorist who will be considered in greater detail in a later chapter, apparently suggested that performance may lead to an overrating of competence. In either case, both positions indicate the necessity for the teacher to evaluate each aspect of the child's functioning rather than to infer one from the other. Both Lenneberg and Chomsky emphasized biological influence on language. Although both considered the competence-performance distinction, neither one was apparently willing to indicate that competence is relatively more affected by sociocultural forces, as we have maintained.

Lenneberg's emphasis on biological influence on language development can be contrasted with the views of Wyatt (1969), a practicing speech psychotherapist. Citing extensively from Cazden's review (1966) on language and socioeconomic factors, she stressed that the following environmental factors are related to language development and deficits: (1) the affective quality of the mother-child relationship; (2) speech development in the context of close relationships between the child and adults; (3) variety in surroundings and stimulating experiences; (4) signal-to-noise ratio—the noisier the home, the more difficult for the child to understand speech; and (5) quality and quantity of stimulation received. An input-output model can correlate Lenneberg's biological emphasis (input functions) with Wyatt's environmental emphasis. Clearly, the child's overall psychological well-being will determine how he uses both input and output and how he relates them effectively to each other. The greater the child's disturbance, the greater will be the variability, inconsistency, and instability in his functioning, as discussed in Section III.

In every bright child, both input and output channels may become increasingly integrated (multiplicatively), helping each other in the process of acquisition and expansion of information. At an average level of development, input and output channels may integrate additively. On the other side of this hypothetical, quantitative continuum, we may consider the possibility that one channel may subtract (rather than multiply or add) from another channel. For instance, even though blindness may not detract from hearing, it will restrict a child's movements (motoric and kinesthetic feedback) and limit him to certain environments, consequently, limiting the range of auditory stimuli which he may receive. There may be other disturbances of various types and degrees in any one channel that may subtract from a child's overall functioning. The notions of multiplication, addition, subtraction, and division in channel integration have some relationship to concepts like *generalization, transfer of training, spread of effect,* compensation and overcompensation, and *carryover,* as well as what Birch and his coworkers (1964, 1963) have called *intersensory integration,* which is a positive aspect of channel multiplication and addition. *Interference* is the negative result of channel subtraction and division, occurring when deficits in one modality detract and subtract from another modality.

Auditory Input and Modality Preference

Maccoby (1967), in her review of selective auditory attention in children, pointed out that the processes underlying both auditory-verbal and visual-motor modalities "are probably much the same." However, an important distinction should be made between the two modalities. Other studies (L'Abate, 1964; Hirsh, 1967) have indicated that visual-motor activities occur in the realm of space and that auditory-verbal activities occur in the realm of time. Another distinction involves the different capacities of these two modalities as channels of communication. By means of vision, we can take in a variety of objects in a visual field, while experiencing only a minimum of disturbance or interference. We can see a whole audience at one glance. However, we can hear only one source of sound at a time, since different sources of sound interfere with one another. If more than one person is speaking, the listener will hear only noise. On the basis of her review, Maccoby concluded that listening skills in childhood are related to increasing growth in vocabulary as the child grows older; that is, selective listening increases as a function of positive feedback from an increase in linguistic output.

With regard to auditory-verbal development, a few conclusions should be kept in mind. Moorehead (1968) demonstrated that young children and adults follow the same language rules and the same distinctiveness of individual phonemes in speech recognition and production. Goldman (1967) found that both adults and children preferred the auditory to the visual and haptic modalities, but that adults preferred the visual to the haptic modality, while children were equally divided in their preference between these modalities.

By comparing intrasensory and intersensory functions, Duff (1969) found that the hierarchy of difficulty progressed from visual-auditory to visual-visual, auditory-visual, and finally auditory-auditory, rated as most difficult. These findings indicate that auditory processing increases the complexity of the learning task at an input level. Auditory dysfunctions, as a whole, are more debilitating than visual dysfunctions, suggesting, according to Duff, that ". . . the mode of input and output is influential and of consequence clinically and theoretically. Consequently learning disorders need to be viewed as the results of a variety of information-processing deficits and assets."

Deficits in Auditory Input and Verbal Output

Telford and Sawrey (1967), in comparing verbalization, intellectual functioning, and educational achievement of hearing-impaired children with the functioning of normal and visually impaired children, concluded that the educational achievement of the deaf is "retarded from three to five years" and that "language and communication lag behind the motor and computational skills." In comparison with visual deficits, auditory deficits produce a much greater degree of educational and possibly cognitive retardation.

Auditory Deficits and Brain Damage

Speech and language problems are frequently associated with organic brain damage. Templin (1953) divided dysfunctional speech into four major categories: (1) voice disorders, which include deviations in loudness, pitch, quality, or flexibility of voice and intonation; (2) articulation disorders, which include distortions, omissions, or substitutions of speech; (3) delayed speech; and (4) *stuttering*.

Anatomically speaking, Haywood (1968) pointed out that mediation of language skills occurs almost entirely in the left cerebral hemisphere. "Reitan and his associates have shown repeatedly that patients who have focal lesions of the left cerebral hemisphere usually have lower verbal than performance scores on the Wechsler-Bellevue Intelligence Scale, while patients with focal right hemisphere lesions have lower performance than verbal scores." Haywood concluded that ". . . it is grossly helpful to assume that anterior lesions will result in relatively impaired receptive abilities."

Cravioto et al. (1967) attempted to determine whether early malnutrition could be related to auditory-visual integration in school-age children. The researchers selected primary school children from a rural Mexican village and assessed their degree of exposure to malnutrition on the basis of height. (Previous studies by these authors had indicated this to be a valid assessment measure.) The upper 25 per cent in height for each age and sex formed one group, and the lower 25 per cent in height for each age and sex formed the other group. All the children, a total of 296, were asked to select visual patterns of dots which corresponded to auditory patterns being tapped out on a table. Although improvement with age was shown for both groups, at each age, the tall group scored higher than the short group. Several implications of the poorer development of auditory-visual integration in the malnourished children were discussed; the most interesting of these was related to reading readiness and its possible dependence upon auditory-visual integration.

As Sabatino (1969a) suggested, an overemphasis on visual perception "may contribute to the overlooking of a very large group of children with serious auditory perceptual impairment." He (1969a; 1969b) developed a Test of Auditory Perception (TAP) which significantly discriminated normal from neurologically impaired children without hearing defects—a finding that would support the contention of lowered input functions in those having organic deficits.

Mira (1968) studied patterns of looking and listening in 12 children with hearing disabilities and 12 normal children between the ages of 6 and 11. He found individual preferences for looking and listening: 33 per cent of the children worked to look and listen simultaneously; 13 per cent demonstrated one of three types of listening deficits; 13 per cent showed differentiation deficits manifested by irregular use of these modalities; 17 per cent showed unique patterns of looking and listening. No child showed a looking deficit alone, supporting the conclusion that listening deficits are more common. It could be, therefore, that the majority of children with such listening defects may be those experiencing learning difficulties in school.

Auditory Deficits and Intellectual Retardation

O'Connor and Hermelin (1963), in their study of speech and thought in severely subnormal patients, pointed out the necessity to differentiate among (1) deficit—the lack of sufficient strength or intensity in a psychological function; (2) dysfunction—the inappropriate distortion in an otherwise adequately strong function; and (3) malfunction—the inadequate use of a function. In carrying out a series of studies on the relative impairments of input and output mechanisms, they noted that in the growing normal individual, the visual and auditory senses gradually become the main sources of information about events in the outside world and that touch and kinesthetic sensitivity may develop later. They concluded that "the restricted vocabulary of institutionalized imbeciles is at least partly due to their limited and limiting environment. The structure of the language used by them resembles that of normal children at a corresponding stage of mental development." They concurred with Lenneberg and Buktenica in supporting the independence of the verbal from the motor system. Their evidence "... points to deficits in acquisition rather than to poor perception, retention, or transfer ability. Acquisition seems to be impaired at least partly because of an inability to focus attention on the relevant stimulus features. . . . The low level of responsiveness may account for general inhibition and lack of 'output' rather than impairment in 'input' mechanism." The authors considered their main contribution to be their emphasis on deficits in acquisition and coding which they considered as more important and marked than those in retention and transfer. "The deficiency in coding consists in an inability to associate words and percepts. . . . Knowledge of the meaning of a word facilitates recognition of it in printed form."

Dansinger and Madow (1966), in applying a verbal-auditory screening test to 967 retarded children and adults, found that 11.3 per cent were untestable and 12.6 per cent of those who were testable were found to have sufficient hearing impairment to interfere with communication. *Depending on the criterion used, the relative frequency of hearing loss among retarded children was two to six times greater than among normal children.*

Auditory Deficits and Environment

Grinker et al. (1969) found that: (1) underachievement is pervasive in the deaf population; (2) rarely do families of deaf persons learn to communicate with the deaf member; (3) deaf, hospitalized patients can be treated best if grouped together; (4) psychosis in deaf patients is most frequently precipitated by physical trauma, such as surgery, or separation from family members due to death or other reasons; (5) while there is evidence of somewhat greater susceptibility to paranoid behavior among deaf patients, a significant amount of this paranoia is enforced from without by reality factors associated with deafness; (6) deaf individuals are rarely identified, nor is an effort made to meet their special needs; (7) misdiagnosis of deaf patients is common – many of them are labeled mentally retarded or schizophrenic on the basis of their linguistic disability rather than the actual presence of retardation or psychopathology; (8) the isolation, frustration, anger, and limited opportunities imposed on the deaf person by undereducation and restricted communication result in considerable depression; (9) autism is found more often in the deaf population as either part of a genetic syndrome or an interactional effect of deafness and environmental stress; (10) organic components associated with major etiologies of deafness are also contributing factors to mental illness and mental retardation; (11) the mediating process of thinking is not necessarily a verbal symbol system. Instead, language is simply one of a number of "programs" or means by which information input may occur, but its actual processing is independent of the form of input. In other words, thinking can occur with input from the eyes as well as the ears.

Neuhaus (1968) found a significant relationship between parental attitudes toward deaf children and emotional adjustment of these children in early and late childhood and adolescence, a factor that may detract from their ability to learn. Myklebust (1955) observed that because it is difficult for the deaf child to feel that he is part of his environment, he tends to withdraw, remaining socially immature and dependent upon his parents. Elstad et al. (1955) noted in deaf children a greater frequency of sleeping and feeding problems, temper tantrums, and *enuresis*, resulting in a withdrawal from social contact and deprivation of love, friends, achievement, and security.

Vance (1968), in studying the characteristics of deaf children, could not answer whether inferiority in motor abilities is a deficit inherent in congenital deafness per se, the result of limitations in the range and variety of the child's experiences, or the result of different child-raising practices and training to which deaf children are subjected. It seems that a deficit in any part of a system will affect its other components and other interacting systems. Deafness may more directly affect verbal output and more indirectly, depending perhaps on a great many external factors, affect motor output.

Auditory Deficits, Thinking, and Language

Hartung (1968), assuming that deaf children are "almost without exception" deficient readers, found that normally hearing children perform better on a task requiring them to recall alphabetical material, suggesting that memory may be the intervening variable in reading ability. As Quigley et al. (1968) indicated, linguistic skills are directly related to the "oralness" of the environment. Deaf children of deaf parents are more retarded in their speech than deaf children with normally hearing relatives. Educational achievement was highly correlated (+.87) with vocabulary, while nonverbal tests of intelligence were not good predictors of educational achievement. When deaf and hearing children were matched according to age and intelligence, the deaf made fewer errors on a part-whole task, but were significantly inferior in their ability to reason on both Piagetian tasks and a syllogistic reasoning test (Moore, 1968). Moore suggested that the influence of hearing deficits may be more pronounced in those types of conceptual behavior that do not demand the integration of immediate visual input. In fact, linguistic proficiency may be related to reasoning in which a successful performance demands the integration of several concepts.

Brannon (1968) found that significant hearing impairment reduces productivity of both *tokens* and types of words. A moderate impairment lowers the use of adverbs, pronouns, and auxiliaries; a profound impairment reduces the use of nearly all word classes. In proportion to total word output, the deaf overuse nouns and articles and underuse prepositions, qualifiers, and infinitives.

SPEECH IMPAIRMENTS

The role of language is paramount in the human being's ability to adapt. It represents the major vehicle by which we organize our world and devise a system from the infinite number of sensory impressions that are taken in during a lifetime. Difficulties in the use and comprehension of verbal symbols represent a major problem in all learning disabilities (Haywood, 1968). Of course, one standard by which auditory-verbal output may be better identified and understood is visual input and motor output. Clearly, a specific deficit is defined by the intactness in other areas of functioning, both at the receptive and expressive levels, including *cross-modal* integration. The various etiologies of delayed speech and integration indicate that the majority of these deficits may be biological in origin, supporting Lenneberg's contention (1967). Nevertheless, there are a sufficient number of unexplained speech exceptionalities that may be accounted for by emotional disturbance and social deprivation hypotheses and which should be considered seriously by the teacher.

Delayed Speech

Delayed speech may result from organic deafness, mental retardation, or *aphasia,* which Myklebust (1954) attributed to brain damage. More specifically, delayed speech output may be related (Wood, 1964) to: (1) central nervous system impairment, such as brain damage; (2) behavioral disorders associated with central nervous system impairment, such as hyperactivity, perseverations, distractibility, catastrophic behavior, visual-motor disturbances, and figure-ground confusion—all symptoms that may be included in the learning disabilities category; (3) aphasias, including the receptive and expressive types and their subvarieties; (4) *dysarthria* (defective articulation) and *dyspraxia* (severe motor problems of the jaw and tongue), either voluntary or involuntary; (5) intellectual retardation; (6) emotional disturbance; (7) hearing loss which is caused by lowering of input due to peripheral rather than central deficits, as in some types of intellectual retardation; and (8) speech deprivation and immaturity, as found in different dialectal patterns of socially deprived minorities.

Aphasias

Aphasia is another type of speech impairment which may seriously affect a child's behavior. Aphasia is a somewhat general and ambiguous term which basically suggests that the child has experienced considerable difficulty or failure in the acquisition of language or symbolic skills (Benton, 1963). The source of aphasia is said to originate with damage to relatively simple brain structures which mediate the acquisition of verbal skills (Osgood, 1953). According to the model proposed by Wepman et al. (1960), disturbances of the sensory-input potential of the child are defined as *agnosia;* disturbances of the expressive-output potential are termed apraxia; and disturbances of the central integrative function, which includes retention, retrieval, and expression of verbal symbols, are called aphasia. Thus, aphasia has serious effects on the child's capacity to think and to function on a symbolic, conceptual level. What distinguishes the aphasic child from the intellectually retarded child is that the former functions at a near normal level in the nonverbal areas of intelligence; however, it is often true that an aphasic child is also partially intellectually retarded.

Aphasia in childhood is the result of cerebral dysfunction which is either congenital or acquired, and it is characterized by both linguistic and nonverbal behavioral manifestations. There is a variety of terminologies used to describe aphasia including: *motor aphasia, expressive aphasia,* congenital word deafness, *receptive aphasia, global aphasia,* central auditory imperception, *agraphic alexia,* apraxia, developmental language retardation, and specific language disability (Horton, 1968). The child who is deficient in auditory sensitivity will show receptively and expressively significant retardation and deficits in his language ability from the earliest stages.

Aphasia is the inability to understand language *(sensory aphasia)* or to express language *(motor aphasia)* as the result of injury to the brain (Verville, 1967). Diagnosis of aphasia is difficult, and the child's verbal impairment may be interpreted as deafness, retardation, or as symptomatic of autism or psychosis. The aphasic child is characteristically tense, resistive, and withdrawn.

There are three basic premises concerning the aphasic child: (1) that there is no general deficiency in integrating sensory experiences, particularly in visual perception; (2) that the deficiency is primarily restricted to learning "symbolic handles" for naming experiences; and (3) that a deficiency in auditory memory prevents the usual association of sound with an appropriate object or action (Kessler, 1966). Although there are reports concerning treatment of the aphasic child, there is little information about the percentage of success. Some children learn to speak well enough to attend regular school; others learn only stereotyped phrases and must be told what to say. The results of treatment are similar to those achieved with emotionally disturbed children, in that there are varying degrees of cure. Cerebral lesions or lack of cortical development may be congenital causes of aphasia. Lesions affecting speech are usually located in the left hemisphere, which is dominant for speech, regardless of handedness. The nearer the lesion is to the junction of the parietal, occipital, and temporal lobes, the greater will be the disturbance of reading and writing. When the damage involves the posterior and superior temporal regions, the individual tends to show more difficulty in comprehending speech.

Behavior of the aphasic child is characterized by inability to learn to read and write, inattentiveness, and a sense of inadequacy when the individual cannot match the quick responses of others. Temper tantrums are common because of frustrated efforts to communicate. According to Myklebust (1954), the inconsistent and disintegrated behavior of aphasic children is due to their apparent difficulty in attending and integrating auditory input. There has been no research literature to contradict Myklebust's conclusion – a point that raises questions about the existence of any deficit of verbal output that is not culturally determined. A specificity of functions hypothesis, as well as Lenneberg's position, would both predict the possibility of a child's having perfect auditory input and poor verbal output. The question still remains: Can the reverse of Myklebust's conclusion be true? Can there be an organically determined deficit in verbal output without some deficit in auditory input?

Hardy et al. (1961) emphasized the importance of normal auditory functioning for the acquisition of language skills and behavioral integrity. It has been found that language-disordered children, who show more auditory impairment than visual impairment, manifest a greater lack of behavioral integrity (Blair et al., 1962; Johnson and Myklebust, 1967) than those with more visual impairment. Organic language disorders impede the child's ability to function in what is basically a symbolic world. The aphasic child is not able to compete in the classroom, because learning in such an environment is dependent upon competence in verbal skills, which is the aphasic child's principal area of deficiency.

Horton (1968) stated that "language has been described as that characteristic which makes us human, for it serves as a primary characteristic differentiating us from our predecessors along the road of evolutionary development." She expressed concern over the need for early diagnosis and remediation of speech disorders: ". . . the implication is that delay in the learning of language irrespective of etiology reduces the potential for learning." She emphasized assessment of language disorders which concerns itself with determining modality strengths and weaknesses, pointing out that ". . . all of the criteria applicable to the testing and educational and therapeutic management of brain-injured children are certainly equally applicable to the management of the aphasic child." She concluded: "Specific programs of remediation must stress modality strengths rather than devote total emphasis to work on modality weakness."

Stuttering

Orton (1928) described stuttering as basically resulting from physiological rivalry between the two cortical hemispheres of the brain. In this theory of mixed cerebral dominance, he stated that stuttering resulted when one hemisphere of the brain did not develop as well as the other, a situation resulting in poorly synchronized speech musculature. Bloodstein (1959) cited evidence to contradict Orton who, in later work, negated his earlier theory and determined stuttering to be a learned response. Other theories of constitutional predisposition have been proposed, such as West's study (1957), which regarded stuttering as the result of metabolic disorganization. The opposite extreme, complete cultural determination of stuttering, also has not found consistent support. Anderson (1968) maintained that "... the long-held position that stuttering was purely psychological in nature was no longer tenable." Furthermore, psychologically based methods of rehabilitation (life adjustment, relaxation, and parental counseling) have not had complete success. Kopp's (1968) organismic method of treatment, based on cognitive-motor dissonance, seems to be the only approach that is applicable both in theory and in practice with any significant success. In addition, it is the only therapy that can be used at all age levels without the use of technical, psychological tools or parental intervention.

W. Johnson (1953) presented the theory that undue parental criticism induces stuttering. Kessler (1966) reported that as many as 40 per cent of all children who stutter "outgrow it" and many, perhaps almost all, stuttering children can be helped by environmental manipulation. Wyatt (1969) felt that stuttering stems from a disturbance in the mother-child relationship when the child is between the ages of two and four. Verville (1967) stated that stuttering in preschool children usually can be traced to situational and emotional pressures—urgent, demanding parents and a feeling of uncertainty of parental love.

Muma (1967) found that fluent and nonfluent four-year-old children were comparable in all aspects of productivity (variability and redundancy). However, fluent children were found to have significantly longer total content and phrase-communication units. In other measurements, fluent and nonfluent children were comparable, suggesting that linguistic skill per se should not be considered as an explanatory factor for differences in the fluency of young children. It is unfortunate that Muma used no measurement of auditory input in his study.

Butler (1967) found that children with psychogenic speech defects did not differ from normally speaking children in visual-motor performance and in full IQ scores on the Wechsler Intelligence Scale for Children, although they scored significantly lower in verbal skills than children with normal speech. Information, vocabulary, arithmetic, and digit span were the subtests especially affected by severe articulatory defects. On the other hand, children with psychogenic speech problems scored higher on the Picture Completion subtest than children with normal speech. This specific superiority may indicate a heightened sensitivity to visual cues which may have resulted from their specific handicap. This finding supports the importance of this subscale as a measure of visual-input that may help in the discrimination between biological, cultural, and psychological dysfunctions (Caputo et al., 1963).

SUMMARY OUTLINES

The following lists include the different characteristics of various auditory-verbal deficits in children as summarized from the prevailing studies and literature.

A. *Hearing Loss*

1. Speech development is retarded.
2. The voice has a characteristic tonal quality. (Because the ear monitors tonal quality, the child speaks according to the way he hears.)
3. The child does not improvise sound for pleasure, but uses his voice for utilitarian purposes. (E.g., he does not sing to himself, but he will make sounds when he wants food and attention.)
4. The deaf child uses gestures to make his wants known, that is, he assumes signing behavior which is a form of language.
5. A deaf child responds consistently to those sounds which he can hear.
6. He is unusually sensitive to vibration, movement, and other visual, kinesthetic, and tactual cues.
7. The gait of the deaf child is often characteristic: he may drag his heels because he cannot hear himself walking.
8. A deaf child often makes a great deal of noise during mastication because he cannot hear himself chewing.

B. *Psychic Deafness or Selective Mutism*

1. This child has a history which reveals his problem to be primarily behavioral rather than one related to hearing impairment.
2. Most of these children have good vocal quality.
3. Frequently, the parents present good evidence for their child's ability to hear. They may state that "sometimes he seems to hear me." Often children will produce speech (e.g., "yes" or "no") under stress situations or when they are separated from their parents. We can thus conclude that they have been able to hear within normal limits.
4. Their laughter and gait are usually like those of a normally hearing child.
5. Often, paradoxically, they respond to what may be called pleasant sounds of low intensity, but show no response to high intensities, even though these may be expected to stimulate pain and fear.

C. *Mental Retardation*

1. The child is deficient in curiosity, imagination, attention, and interest.
2. There is a generalized retardation in learning to care for himself.
3. Response to sound is erratic, especially if pure tones are used.
4. Subtle responses to normal speech sounds can often be elicited.
5. Vocalizations are made in response to pleasure, and their quality is like that of children with normal hearing.
6. There are often other evidences of interference with physical development.
7. Intelligence tests, while not always conclusive, usually reveal marked retardation of a comparable nature in both verbal and nonverbal skills.

D. Aphasias (General)

1. The aphasic child is most inconsistent in his responses to sound.
2. He does not gesture if his deficit is predominantly of a receptive nature, because he lacks symbolic language.
3. He does not respond objectively to what he hears.
4. He does not respond well to vibrations, movements, or other visual, kinesthetic, or tactual cues.
5. Aphasic children are often attentional problems. They seem to be abnormally preoccupied with one activity, and they perseverate in it.
6. The aphasic child can be trained or conditioned to respond to sounds which he has learned to interpret. For example, an aphasic child can be taught to respond to the sounds involved in removing a cookie from a jar.
7. Psychological test results usually show wide discrepancies between verbal and visual-motor levels. The tests may also reveal the characteristic perceptual disturbances of the brain-damaged child.

E. Receptive or Sensory Aphasia

1. For all practical purposes, the child does not speak.
2. He lacks speech comprehension.
3. There is adequate physiological control of the articulators (tongue and jaw).
4. There is markedly inconsistent use of hearing, discrepancy between hearing behavior and listening behavior, and apparent hearing deficiency.
5. There is discrepancy between the general level of nonverbal intelligence and ability to comprehend auditory-verbal stimuli.
6. The child has normal organ and *retrocochlear* hearing.
7. Vocalization may be absent or characterized by jargon which is inflected and varies in intensity.
8. There may be *echolalia.*
9. The child may have limited use of a few words, evidenced sporadically, but which are not consistently understood.
10. He may use few or no gestures in communication.
11. He does not respond to other sensory stimulation (e.g., tactile or visual) any more than to auditory stimulation.
12. The child shows greater responsiveness to nonverbal auditory stimuli than to verbal.

F. Expressive or Motor Aphasia

1. Lack of speech but some ability to express a limited number of words is typical of a child with this aphasia.
2. There is adequate comprehension of speech.
3. Patterns of vocalization are symptomatically repetitious in intensity and inflection.
4. The child experiences partial or complete inability to imitate the actions of the tongue, lips, and mandible or sounds of words.
5. No profuse or outstanding physiological deficiency of the articulators is present.
6. The child has adequate hearing, both organ and retrocochlear.
7. There is no general reduction in overall intelligence.
8. Gestures are used for communication.

9. Hearing is used somewhat consistently.
10. Echolalia is present.

G. *Behavioral Characteristics of Aphasic Children*

1. Mixed laterality—the child is predominantly neither right- nor left-sided.

2. Delayed responses—a noticeable time lag in responding.

3. Inconsistency—erratic responses to the same stimulus.

4. Distractibility:

a. An abnormal fixation on unimportant details, while disregarding the essentials. A child may give all his attention to a page number instead of looking at the printed material or pictures on a page. This seeming difficulty in concentration or lack of attention is actually extreme attentiveness as far as the child is concerned, although he is giving his whole attention to an unimportant detail.

b. Figure-ground disturbance—a blurring or inversion of background and foreground, in which the main subject may blend with the background or the background itself may become the focus of attention.

5. Hyperactivity—a forced, undirected response to stimuli. It is a drive that compels the child to act, to flit from one thing to another, and to be unable to withstand countless stimuli which the normal child disregards.

6. Perseveration—the persistent repetition or continuance of an activity, especially if the child has experienced success or pleasure from it.

7. Difficulty in shifting from one activity to another—the inability to start or stop a series of activities.

8. Disinhibition—lack of emotional control (e.g., easy laughing or crying) which may persist beyond reasonable limits.

9. Catastrophic reaction—extreme helplessness, despair, or anxiety which is experienced when a child is confronted with a task beyond his ability, usually accompanied by intense crying.

10. Persistent repetition of questions, even though they have been carefully answered.

11. Intolerance of discipline and extreme irritability.

12. Meticulosity—exactitude demanded by the child who must have everything "just so," usually to relieve a lack of orderliness in his surroundings caused by fluctuation in his own thinking.

13. Aimless, random movements, such as pawing the air and waving the arms.

14. Abnormal clumsiness—general lack of coordination.

15. Extreme behaviors—aggressive, antisocial, or uncontrolled behavior or else quiet, daydreaming, phlegmatic behavior.

16. Short attention span.

H. *Linguistic Characteristics of Childhood Autism and Schizophrenia (As Differentiated from Aphasias)*

1. Uncommunicative behavior—no real interest in communicating with others.

a. Abnormal receptive behavior.

1. Withdrawal from sound, especially sound with communicative value.

2. Frequently more responsive to low intensity, background sound and seeming oblivion to higher intensity, foreground sound.

3. Increased attention to sound originating from inanimate sources.

b. Abnormal expressive behavior.

1. If speech is present, voice quality is "dull or wooden."

2. Inappropriate pitch, intensity, and rate changes.

3. Tendency toward high-pitched vocalizations.

4. Inappropriate gestural reinforcements accompanying speech.

5. History of acquisition of speech with gradual or sudden decrease in use.

6. Interest in singing with no history of speech use.

2. Abnormal social behavior.

a. Withdrawn.

b. Inattentive.

c. Relates poorly to people and prefers objects.

d. Does not "scan" the environment.

e. Shows much interest in mechanical objects.

f. Usually relates with people only to obtain personal desires.

g. Rejects formal testing ("untestable").

3. Abnormal motor behavior.

a. Deviant postural and *vestibular* functioning.

b. Inability to dissociate head from eye movement.

c. Minimal or absent postrotational nystagmus.

d. Primitive hand movements; preoccupation with hand movements.

e. May have good coordination with a normal developmental history for motor behavior. (This symptom is often a significant one in distinguishing these problems from severe retardation with marked brain injury.)

REHABILITATION OF AUDITORY-VERBAL DEFICITS

Among linguistic remediational approaches, the reader should consider those of pioneers like Orton, Bateman, Wiseman, and Otto. For a brief overview of these programs, the reader should consult McCarthy and McCarthy (1970).

The modern concept of rehabilitation of the hearing-handicapped is the product of the last two decades. Prior to that time, the hearing-handicapped were sent to schools for the deaf in which they were instructed in the signs of the manual alphabet and taught a trade independent of communicative needs. In 1943, aware that the war would produce thousands of hearing-impaired individuals, the U.S. Army and Navy established hearing centers in various parts of the country to provide the necessary surgical and pharmaceutical needs. Today, it is believed that any therapeutic approach for the hard-of-hearing should be aimed at one or all of the following goals:

1. Making the sound louder.
2. Making the sound more intelligible.
3. Developing communicative efficiency and awareness.
4. Developing an adequate self-concept.

It is estimated that at least 300,000 children in the United States have impaired hearing. Certain types of hearing loss can be remedied through surgery, such as an otological surgeon's changing the shape of the middle ear, constructing a new tympanic membrane, or rebuilding the *ossicular chain.* A large percentage of children with conduction deafness can successfully use a hearing aid. However, about 20 per cent of all deaf children are neurally deaf, and, at present, there is no known medical or surgical means of significantly improving neural deafness.

On the basis of findings cited earlier in this chapter, Grinker et al. (1969) recommended adoption of combined "manual-oral" educational practices rather than reliance on anachronistic restrictions to "oralism" which is the modality in which deaf individuals are least effective. Rehabilitative, psychotherapeutic, and educational programs for deaf individuals should include and involve deaf personnel at professional and decision-making levels. Parental counseling in families of deaf children is essential. It should involve: (1) instruction of parent and child in combined manual-oral communications; (2) some discussion of parental feelings involved in having a deaf child; (3) frank information about the implications of deafness; (4) counseling regarding available educational and rehabilitative programs; (5) activity-oriented therapies rather than strictly verbal ones.

The importance of integrating auditory and visual input channels is documented by Ransom (1967), who compared two groups of children, one which was trained with aural-visual supplementary first-grade materials and the other which was trained with visual materials. The children trained with aural-visual materials were superior in achievement to visually trained children and control group children. On the basis of these and other findings. Ransom recommended that boys, more than girls, need intensive training in auditory discrimination. Skinner (1968) studied the single versus the multiple modality approach in visual and auditory motor (output) training. In this case, single modality training,

Figure 7–4 Making the sound louder and more intelligible—goals of therapy for the hard-of-hearing. (Courtesy of Children's Hospital of Philadelphia, Pennsylvania.)

Figure 7–5 Integration of visual and auditory motor training in teaching the hearing-impaired child. (Courtesy of Children's Hospital of Philadelphia, Pennsylvania.)

whether visual or auditory, produced greater significant effects than multiple modality training.

Teaching Directed at Input Deficits

Because auditory deficits are usually not visible and because the hard-of-hearing are often suspected of being unmotivated, inattentive, or mentally retarded, the general public has lacked interest in and sympathy for this exceptionality. The most obvious impairment of children with auditory defects is their inability to hear the speech of others or to acquire speech in the normal way. At age five, the average hearing child has a vocabulary of over 2500 words, while the average deaf child at the same age may have almost no vocabulary.

In planning a program of aural rehabilitation, the severity of the hearing loss, rather than the type, should be emphasized. It is possible for almost any degree of residual hearing to become functional for most of the ordinary purposes of life. The first step in planning a program of rehabilitation for the hearing-impaired is to determine the nature and extent of the hearing deficit. Hearing is not a single capacity. An individual may be normal or superior in one aspect of hearing and seriously deficient in another. The aspect of most general interest is auditory acuity, also known as the *absolute threshold* of hearing. This measurement of hearing refers to the faintest sound that an individual can just barely hear. Other aspects of hearing are also important, such as, tolerance for very loud sounds and ability to recognize words amid a background of loud and confusing noise. A reported characteristic of culturally disadvantaged children is their inability to discriminate differences in auditory stimuli. It has been suggested that the limited verbal interaction in a disadvantaged home (which we will consider in greater detail in a later chapter) may interfere with a child's acquiring the ability to extract an auditory signal from competing background noise (Goldman and Sanders, 1969).

Before any aural rehabilitation program begins, a decision must be made about whether the individual will benefit from the use of a hearing aid. Although the major function of a hearing aid is to amplify sound, it is often considered to be a panacea for all hearing problems. Many people erroneously believe that a hearing loss can be corrected by simply turning up the volume of the hearing aid. They do not understand that a hearing impairment may not solely concern acuity or loudness. A greater incapacity may be caused by reduced ability to discriminate sounds. Hearing aids amplify all sounds, not just those sounds which fall within the deficient frequency range.

Guberina of Yugoslavia developed a new approach regarding hearing aids, known as the verbotonal method. He believed that deafness is seldom complete—that there are always one or more audible frequencies of sound which reach the brain's hearing centers. His technique is to find each patient's best frequency and then to filter speech through a device that removes all other frequencies: "Just as turning up the volume of a radio makes the static even more bothersome, so a hearing aid may increase the volume of interference, drowning out significant frequencies and decreasing intelligibility." Guberina invented a hearing aid that filters frequencies, making it easier for the hard-of-hearing person to understand what he hears.

After a child has been fitted with a hearing aid, he and his parents should be given some instruction in the use and care of the aid. An evaluation of 134 children with hearing aids in the Detroit metropolitan area determined that very few children or parents knew anything about the hearing aid and its care. They did not realize the limitations of the aid—that a noisy situation may be made noisier by the use of an aid, that

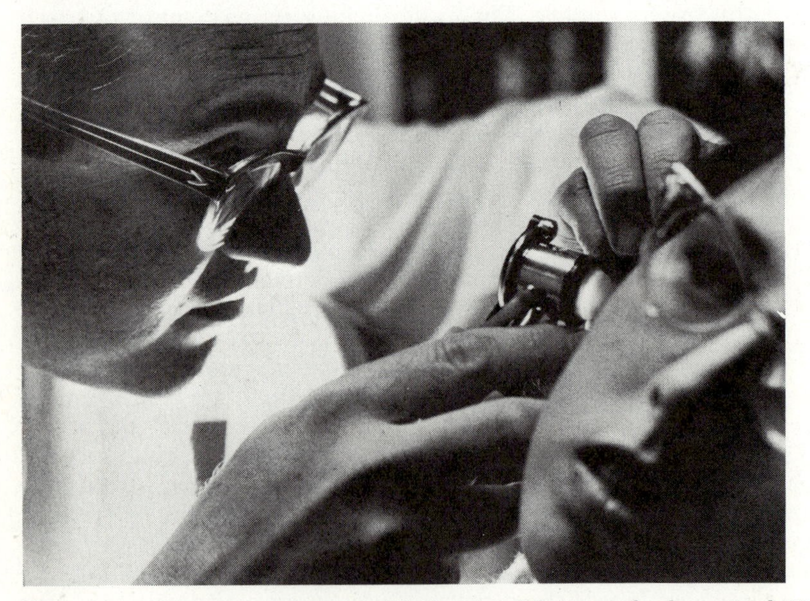

Figure 7–6 The nature and extent of the hearing deficit must be determined. (Courtesy of Children's Hospital of Philadelphia, Pennsylvania.)

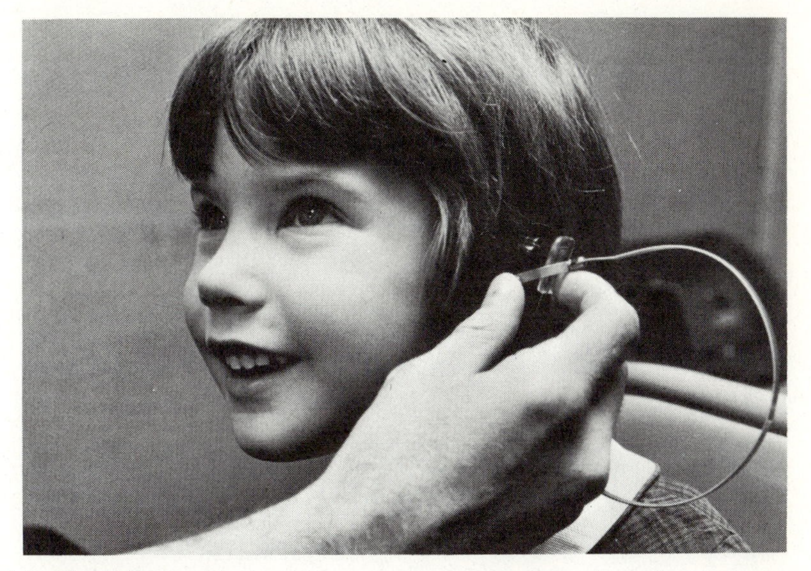

Figure 7–7 The child must be taught to recognize new patterns of sound and to associate meaning with them. (Courtesy of Children's Hospital of Philadelphia, Pennsylvania.)

no hearing aid is sensitive enough to amplify speech and reject noise, and that a hearing aid may lead to problems of sound localization and distortion. The children had received little or no instruction in how to set the aid for specific listening situations or in how often to change the batteries.

Combined with instruction in the use of the aid, there should be auditory training to help the child to deal with distorted sound, to recognize new patterns of sound, and to attach meaning to them. Hearing loss is often accompanied by *tinnitus,* intermittent or inconsistent head noises. In order to hear, an individual with tinnitus must be taught either to listen through the head noises or to disregard them.

Training with amplified sound should begin as early as possible, preferably with simple environmental sounds and music and then with slow progression to words and phrases which are associated with objects.

Rehabilitation should help the individual to take advantage of visual cues and to focus attention on those stimuli which are purely auditory. Because of the inextricable relationship between the auditory and visual modalities, instruction in speech (lip) reading should be combined with auditory training. Speech reading should be taught as a *supplement to* rather than as a *substitute for* hearing. Variables which affect lip reading, one means of visual input available to hearing-deficient individuals, include: (1) fluency, (2) flexibility, (3) space, (4) visualization, (5) reasoning, (6) memory, and (7) perceptual cognitive ability. Individuals may have a general ability to lip read for diverse stimulus material and specific lip reading abilities for specific kinds of lip reading stimulus material.

Visual communication is based upon eye training, recognition and association, and direct lip reading. Eye training for the nonhearing child corresponds to auditory training which is spontaneous in the child with normal hearing. It consists of watching and discriminating movements.

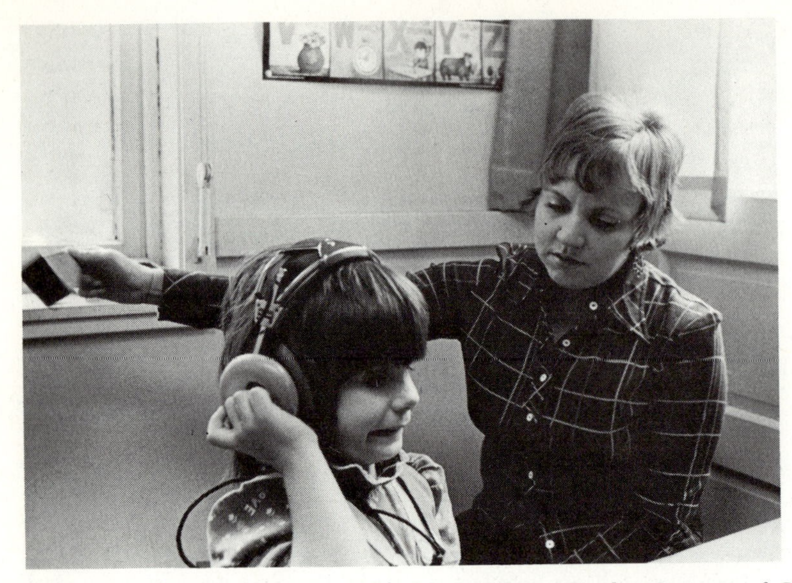

Figure 7–8 Focusing attention on purely auditory stimuli. (Courtesy of Children's Hospital of Philadelphia, Pennsylvania.)

Recognition and association require practice in recognizing and associating lip movements with meaning. Direct lip reading consists of practice in lip reading spontaneously, since any attempt to use conscious mental processes of discrimination in visual communication is impossible at the speed of speech.

There are three basic methods of visual communication. The Mueller-Walle method considers the syllable as the basic unit, while the analytical method developed by Kinzie and Kinzie emphasizes individual sounds. The synthetic approach, as suggested by Nitchie, stresses meaningful units (words and sentences). The Nitchie method is considered best for children because it is believed that no attempt should be made to teach lip reading of individual sounds to young children. Instead, lip reading should always be associated with simple words and short phrases. Daily repetition will help to develop lip reading in children, most of which will be spontaneous and without conscious effort.

The use of finger spelling as a supplement to lip reading was encouraged as early as 1878 by Westerwelt of the Rochester (New York) School for the Deaf. Because lip reading communicates only key words to the deaf, they receive only broken patterns of English and will tend to imitate this in their own language. The Rochester Method, which is said to be no more manual than writing on the chalkboard, has been used in recent years at the Louisiana School for the Deaf. A recent study has reported slightly better performances in lip reading by children who have received their instruction with the added communicative means of finger spelling than by those who have not (Hester, 1964). Hill et al. (1968) reported a technique to improve communication skills in the severely impaired child by using two response keyboards.

Programmed Materials

Several studies in recent years have attempted to determine the applicability of programmed learning to the instruction of the deaf. Typical of these studies is one which was conducted by Birch and Stuckless (1963). The subjects were 52 children with a mean IQ of 95.4 and a mean age of 10 years, 3 months. All were from schools for the deaf. A control group of 47 children, also from the same schools, was matched with the first group according to age and IQ. All the children were taught the same material, but those in the first group were taught by programmed instruction and those in the second group were taught as usual by the teacher. Those using the programmed materials mastered the material in one-half the time of the control group.

Evidence indicates that the mechanics of language, notably word order, basic vocabulary, and other elements of rote learning can be more quickly and efficiently taught by programmed instruction than by conventional methods. Programmed instruction is not a substitute for conventional instruction, but a complement to it. The supervision of a professional teacher is needed, so that the programmed instruction will not interfere with language that has already been correctly established (Brown and L'Abate, 1969).

A sample of three frames from one of the Birch and Stuckless (1963) programs follows:

Frame **Rule 5**

41) **We know that *most* words end with "ed" in the *past* tense, but some words in the *past* tense do *not* end with "ed." Some words are made differently in the past tense:**

Frame				
42)	**Past**	**Present**	**Future**	
	"went"	**"go"**	**"will go"**	**all verb tenses**
	"got"	**"get"**	**"will get"**	**all verb tenses**

Write the verbs in the *past tense:*
I (go) to the movies last night.
Mary (get) a new sweater for her birthday.

Frame			
43)	**Past**	**Present**	**Future**
	"saw"	**"see"**	**"will see"**
	"left"	**"leave"**	**"will leave"**

Write the verbs in the *past tense:*
We (see) an exciting game last night.
The boys (leave) their house each morning.

Such programmed instruction gives the child immediate feedback concerning his response to each frame, so that if his response is incorrect, he is made aware of his mistake at once and can immediately repeat the frame which is giving him difficulty.

In a study of 98 Head Start children, Brickner (1968) demonstrated how two planned and programmed techniques of auditory training methods significantly improved auditory and verbal discriminations and ability to follow directions. A programmed sequence was superior to a program of narratives read to the children. This study illustrated that this group of children could be trained to attend to individual sound input.

Frostig and Marlow (1968) suggested a testing and training program based on a model of the ITPA, in which they differentiated mainly between receptive and expressive functions and associative and sequencing abilities. This training, as they saw it, should occur within the framework of a perceptual program of motor development (Frostig and Horne, 1964), as described in the previous chapter. Whitehurst (1948) prepared supplementary materials for a course in lip reading and auditory and speech training for hearing-impaired children between 12 and 16 years of age whose language is severely impaired.

Smith and Mueller (1969), in their review of research and development concerning the Peabody Language Development Kits (programmed language stimulation materials), supported the efficacy of these materials with culturally disadvantaged children and normal children. Results with EMR and borderline retardates were "less consistent." These programs are especially effective in enhancing verbal-associative and verbal-expressive abilities (as defined by the ITPA). The usefulness of these programmed materials with deaf children must be further established.

Modifying Output Deficits: Operant Conditioning

With regard to language learning, Muma (1970) recently supported a behavioral modification approach combined with a psycholinguistic approach to grammar, especially the transformational-generative theory developed by Chomsky (1968), as discussed earlier in this chapter. Muma asked two questions which he considered basic to language learning methods: "How can an increase in the knowledge of language be effected?" and "How can an increase in the amount of verbal behavior be effected?" These two questions indicate a basic receptive-expressive distinction between "knowledge of language" (input) and "amount of verbal behavior" (output). Muma felt that "it is more efficient to utilize intervention techniques appropriate to either of the two basic questions rather than to utilize the same technique for both dimensions of intervention." According to him, "The principles of behavior modification have proved valuable in increasing, and decreasing, the amount of verbal behavior." However, most behavior-modification techniques "have typically fallen short in realizing their goal—at increasing language knowledge." This failure, according to Muma, is due to the "remarkably naive . . . conceptualizations of the nature, development, and use of language as reflected by most operant studies . . . which . . . really deal with language performance. . . ." Most of these studies have dealt with output rather than input factors. Language development and output factors (Cazden, 1966) are systematically related to contextual reinforcements (e.g., warmth, acceptance, peer language models, variety, tolerable signal-to-noise ratio, and active participation in verbal activities) and type (e.g., no excessive premium for conformity and linguistic and sequential variety) and quantity of stimulation.

Muma (1970) contended that language intervention programs would become more efficient if they were to incorporate both psycholinguistic and *operant conditioning* strategies rather than using them separately, as if they were mutually antagonistic and theoretically exclusive. The transformational-generative theory of grammar, however, ". . . provides a useful model for increasing one's knowledge of language," and it fulfills at least four remedial needs that, according to Muma, require different strategies: (1) language learning in young children; (2) language learning in children from backgrounds in which dialects or other languages are used (bilinguals, deprived children, minority groups, etc.); (3) intermodal transfer from language to reading and writing; and (4) language rehabilitation or compensation for individuals, such as aphasics, the deaf, or the retarded. From the viewpoint proposed by Muma, both transformational-generative theory and principles of operant conditioning are complementary to each other, "because they deal differentially with the dimensions of language use and knowledge." They provide a rationale and a technology for two different aspects (input and output) of language development, a distinction that is usually bypassed by most theorists.

Muma reviewed the effectiveness of most remedial techniques according to the following criteria: (1) correction—identifying faulty behaviors and their subsequent correction, usually by example; (2) expansion—rephrasing a child's utterance (usually by parents) and filling in syntactical omissions; (3) simple expatiation—expansion of a child's language in terms of semantic differentiations; (4) complex expatiation—a diffusion of semantic aspects of language in complicated syntactic structures; (5) alternatives—involving a critical confrontation of a child's utterances; (6) completion—a child's finishing a sentence started by an adult; (7) replacement—the child's changing to a more appropriate term an inappropriate word supplied by the adult; (8) alternative replacement—combining the previous two techniques; (9) combination—an exercise in exploring the syntactic alternatives of grammar; and (10) revision—changing the grammatical structure of a sentence. According to Muma, the first five of these techniques are "child-initiated" and the last five are "teacher-initiated."

Operant conditioning techniques will be considered in greater detail in a later chapter in which further distinctions than those made by Muma will be discussed. If biological forces most directly affect input, it follows that to improve language input such abilities as auditory reception, recognition, recall, attention, and discrimination must be improved. Linguistic deficits more directly related to output may usually be influenced by cultural forces and should be under the more efficient control of operant conditioning techniques. The receptive-expressive distinction has not only a theoretical and diagnostic significance but, even more importantly, also a direct application to teaching, remediation, rehabilitation, and therapy.

Johnston and Johnston (1972) have shown how children with sound articulation difficulties can be taught to monitor their own verbal utterances and to serve, at the same time, as monitors of the verbal output of peers having the same speech difficulties. This work is indicative of how operant conditioning procedures can be used to improve speech difficulties efficiently.

Berlin and Dill (1967) demonstrated that through special instruction and positive reinforcement they could improve the auditory discrimination scores of black children on the Wepman Auditory Discrimination Test. White children subjected to the same treatment did not improve, a result which shows the need for more specific reinforcements for specific subjects. What is reinforcing to a black child, i.e., positive attention from an adult, may not be reinforcing to a white child.

Torpey (1969) demonstrated the usefulness of a systematic program of verbal training, in which food and social approval were contingent on speech. However, the successful results of his study were determined by the nature of the speech deficit. The children which he treated had speech deficits "due to other than organic causes," suggesting that nonorganic dysfunctions may be more responsive to rewards and reinforcements than organically based deficits.

Brady (1968) presented a behavioral approach for the treatment of stuttering based on operant conditioning learning theory. He used a combination of (a) speech habit retraining, (b) an electronic battery-operated metronome, and (c) systematic desensitization. He downgraded the effectiveness of dynamically oriented psychotherapy, claiming a superiority of his approach over other traditional methods. Computers and other equipment resulting from operant conditioning techniques represent one of the most promising breakthroughs in this area.

Coordinating Input with Output: Verbal Remediation

In addition to the problem of hearing and understanding the speech of others, the hard-of-hearing have difficulty in acquiring speech of their own. The kind of speech a deaf child will develop depends upon:

1. The amount and type of his hearing loss.
2. The child's age at onset of the hearing loss.
3. The presence of verbal environment.
4. The method used in teaching speech.

For many years, the five-slate system, developed by Barry in 1898, was used in teaching language to the deaf. One slate represented a noun, one a verb, one the object of the verb, one the preposition, and one the object of the preposition. The deaf learned language by manipulating these slates, and it was believed that this kind of approach encouraged clear thinking. But with complex language forms, the five-slate system tends to produce stereotyping and stilted, ungrammatical language.

In the United States today, there are three general methods of teaching communication to the deaf: the oral, the manual, and the combined method. The oral method is a grammatical approach whose purpose is to provide the child with communication tools which will permit him to function in society, whereas the manual method (signing) is synthetic and informal and has a syntax and structure of its own which differ from standard English. The goal of the oral method is to make the hearing-defective individual speak. It forces the individual to talk even though his sounds may only approximate the word he wants to say. Through successive speech approximations, it is hoped that a sufficient level of verbal communication will be achieved without using any other channel of communication. Defenders of the oral method alone emphasize the need for hearing-defective individuals to function in a verbal world. They downgrade the manual methods as being restrictive and limited, since they can only be used with hearing-impaired individuals and not in the real world. Defenders of the manual method, however, emphasize that the oral method is equivalent to directing teaching to the liability rather than to the asset area. A major asset of hearing-impaired individuals is their ability to use their hands, not their voices. Only when teaching began to employ the manual method was a breakthrough achieved (Gardner and Gardner, 1969; Premack, 1971; Rumbaugh et al., 1973). In spite of these partisan arguments, most teachers of hearing-defective individuals attempt to teach communication in whatever way it is possible, using a multichannel view of assets and liabilities. Recent advances in computer technology, as shown by the work of Rumbaugh et al. (1973) with apes, have indicated that similar methodology can and will be used with hearing-impaired and language-handicapped children.

Most educators of the deaf supposedly support the oral method and 96 per cent of residential schools for the deaf include teaching speech in their curricula. But speech is usually taught on a subject matter basis, and few residential schools provide a purely oral environment for their students.

Evidence is unequivocal that signs may be learned with greater ease and less time than speech, but evidence that speech seldom develops if signs are learned first is also impressive. If children are to learn to speak, they must be given the opportunity to speak. This means that deaf children should be taught lip reading and speech from the beginning. They should be raised in an exclusively oral environment, and systematic sign language must be eliminated during the critical period of speech and language development. Deaf children have difficulty related to word order and the omission, addition, and substitution of words in written compositions. Errors typically made by the deaf are included in the following sentences: "The boys went to ride old car in village. They are named Bobby, Jim, and Rudy. Rudy told two boys come on, go the ride old car in village."

Speech correction is often a necessary part of a rehabilitation program for the hearing-impaired. In general, speech is considered defective when it deviates sufficiently from the speech of others to call attention to itself, to interfere with communication, or to cause the person speaking to become maladjusted. There are four main classes of speech disorders (output): (1) *articulation,* (2) *phonation,* (3) *rhythm disorders,* and (4) *symbolization.*

The most common speech defect is faulty articulation, characterized by the omission, substitution, or addition of speech sounds. A child with faulty articulation should be given a complete medical and dental examination. Sometimes speech defects occur as a result of organic conditions, such as misshapen mouths, misplaced teeth, or impaired hearing. The probability of a child's producing any given sound correctly is contingent upon his ability to hear the sound, and this involves the ability to distinguish one sound from another.

Disorders of phonation – voice disorders consisting of marked deviations in the loudness, pitch, quality, duration, or flexibility of sounds – have the lowest incidence of all categories of speech disorders among children. They are difficult to correct, principally because the child's speech mechanism is still developing and the voice quality is changing.

Disorders of rhythm are interruptions of normal speech flow by hesitations, repetitions, prolongations, and stoppages of speech sounds. These nonfluencies are usually grouped together under the general term, stuttering. The stutterer's difficulty varies considerably from one situation to another. For example, most stutterers can speak normally or with fewer blocks when they are alone, whispering, or singing, and when they are with people considerably younger than themselves or with someone they consider their inferior. On the other hand, their stuttering increases in both severity and frequency in situations in which they feel inferior, embarrassed, or self-conscious.

Disorders of symbolization occur as a result of injury to the brain which results in impairment of the ability to use language meaningfully.

The first stage in correcting faulty articulation in the hearing child involves ear training, during which the child learns to hear and identify the undesirable speech pattern and to recognize it as being different. There are two basic methods of teaching new sounds: the acoustic approach, which is based on imitation, and the phonetic placement approach, based on learning the mechanics of sound as determined by the position and movements of the articulatory organs. The acoustic approach is preferable if the child can hear the differences in sounds; if not, the phonetic placement approach must be used. A chief limitation of the latter approach is that there is no strictly "standard" articulatory adjustment for any of the speech sounds, because no two people make the same sound exactly the same way.

There are four basic processes involved in the alteration of faulty patterns of articulation: inhibition, facilitation, association, and stabilization. These same four processes are used in correcting articulation in both hearing and nonhearing children, but different methods of teaching sounds are used. For the hearing child, the acoustics approach is easier and quite successful. But for the nonhearing child, the phonetic placement approach, with its emphasis on visual and tactile stimuli, is necessary.

During inhibition, a new sound is substituted for an old one. The new sound is learned and practiced alone or in nonsense syllables. If a child says "wobbin" for "robin," it does no good to correct him because he does not distinguish between the two sounds. Practice must begin with a new syllable, such as "RAL" as contrasted with "WAL." Facilitation involves practice with new articulatory movement, so that it comes easily to the child. During association, the new sound is linked with other sounds. Finally, during stabilization, old pronunciation habits are unlearned and, in effect, new words are learned using the new sound (e.g., "RED" for "WED"). With increasing age, the incorporation of newly acquired articulatory patterns into spontaneous speech becomes more difficult and requires increasing conscious control.

Unlike disorders of articulation, rhythm disorders are not usually eliminated through speech correction per se. Probably less than 10 per cent of the children who stutter overcome their difficulty without assistance. Considering this view, it is important that treatment of stuttering begin early. Current treatment of stuttering is aimed primarily at the development of a feeling of adequacy in speech situations and is shifting away from emphasis on speech correction and toward emphasis on speech therapy. Generally, phonetic training is not recommended for child stutterers, because it makes them more conscious of their speech difficulties. Instead, a child's nonfluencies should be accepted, and he should be raised in a relaxed, harmonious home environment. Robbins (1964), basing his recommendations on over 1000 cases of stuttering, suggested that stutterers use the "voiced-sigh" technique—that is, that stutterers concentrate on breathing slowly through the nose, initiating a voiced sigh while the first word is spoken, and smoothly linking the first and second syllables. He further recommended that stutterers speak in short sentences which can be completed in one breath and that they not think ahead after they have formulated a complete sentence until their voices catch up with their thoughts.

In contrast, other therapists endorse speech therapy sessions with groups of child stutterers. During therapy sessions, the children are encouraged to imitate the blocks of other group members and to compete with one another to see which member can produce the best (what laymen would call the "worst") block. The theory behind such therapy sessions is that practice in stuttering helps the child to accept his blocks and eventually leads to the elimination of stuttering altogether.

An interesting approach to stuttering concerns the modification of a stutterer's blocks rather than attempts to eradicate them. In a study, representative of many, Berlin and Berlin (1964) attempted to determine the acceptability of three blocking patterns to laymen, stutterers, and speech clinicians. The three patterns of block modification considered were:

1. Pullout—dissipating the built-up pressure and making second and third attempts to utter the blocked sound, as in "th— (pause, dissipate pressure), th— (pause, dissipate pressure), this."

2. Prolongation—lengthening the blocked sound, as in "th th th th this."

3. Bounce—repetitive form of easy stuttering, as in "tha-tha-this," with no significant pause between syllables.

The pullout pattern was rated highest in acceptability, prolongation was second, and bounce was rated lowest among the three groups of subjects.

Additional Thoughts on Rehabilitation

How effective are rehabilitation programs for exceptionalities of hearing and speech? How effective are special schools, special classes, hearing aids, auditory training, and speech therapy? The general consensus seems to be that these exceptional children should not be sent to special schools unless their hearing deficit is very severe or unless they have other special problems. It is generally believed that aurally impaired children who remain with their families and attend schools with normally hearing children are superior in their adjustment to institutionalized children. The costs per child of a program in a regular school would no doubt be less than the costs of institutionalization. Speech correction for the hearing-impaired child is usually available in special classes of the public schools or from speech therapists associated with the school systems. Such instruction, therefore, would cost the child's parents little, if anything.

Ours is a largely verbal society, with language constituting the primary means of communication. Any impairment which limits an individual's ability to perceive or use language effectively severely limits that individual's ability to function as a productive member of society. Considering this fact, it is surprising and disheartening that so little empirical research concerning methods of rehabilitation for the aurally impaired and the speech-defective is being done. Most available literature, whether the theoretical or "common-sense" variety, supplies no actual data to prove or disprove the effectiveness of rehabilitative methods. There could be any number of reasons why this situation exists. First, a hearing deficit is not a visible handicap; therefore, it does not appeal to public sympathy as does a more visible one (e.g., blindness). A second reason may be that a hearing impairment is usually biological in origin. Unlike psychosomatic or emotional disorders, there is rarely a psychological basis for the impairment. Because it is usually biological, deafness seems to be a permanent disorder; no amount of psychological or behavior modification will eradicate the biological impairment which prevents a child from hearing. A third possible reason is that the modern concept of rehabilitation of the hearing-impaired developed in the 1940's when many American men were acquiring hearing impairments as a result of combat. No doubt, aural rehabilitation was of much interest to researchers then, but that interest has since faded, and the researchers' efforts have been redirected to topics of more current concern.

Speech disorders involving rhythm are an exception to the preceding discussion. They are considered to have a psychological basis, and, therefore, various kinds of speech therapy have been used in attempts to cure stuttering. The studies employing speech therapies have not been experimentally controlled, however, so little can be said of their actual value.

In conclusion, it appears that very little current empirical data are available on methods of rehabilitation of hearing and speech impairments. Instead, professional journals are filled with testimonials, subjective suggestions, recommendations, and "experiments" which employ no controls and no quantitative assessments. There is a definite need for accurate research in these areas.

Section III

ENVIRONMENTAL AND CULTURAL FACTORS

CHAPTER 8

ENVIRONMENTAL AND BEHAVIORAL DISTURBANCES

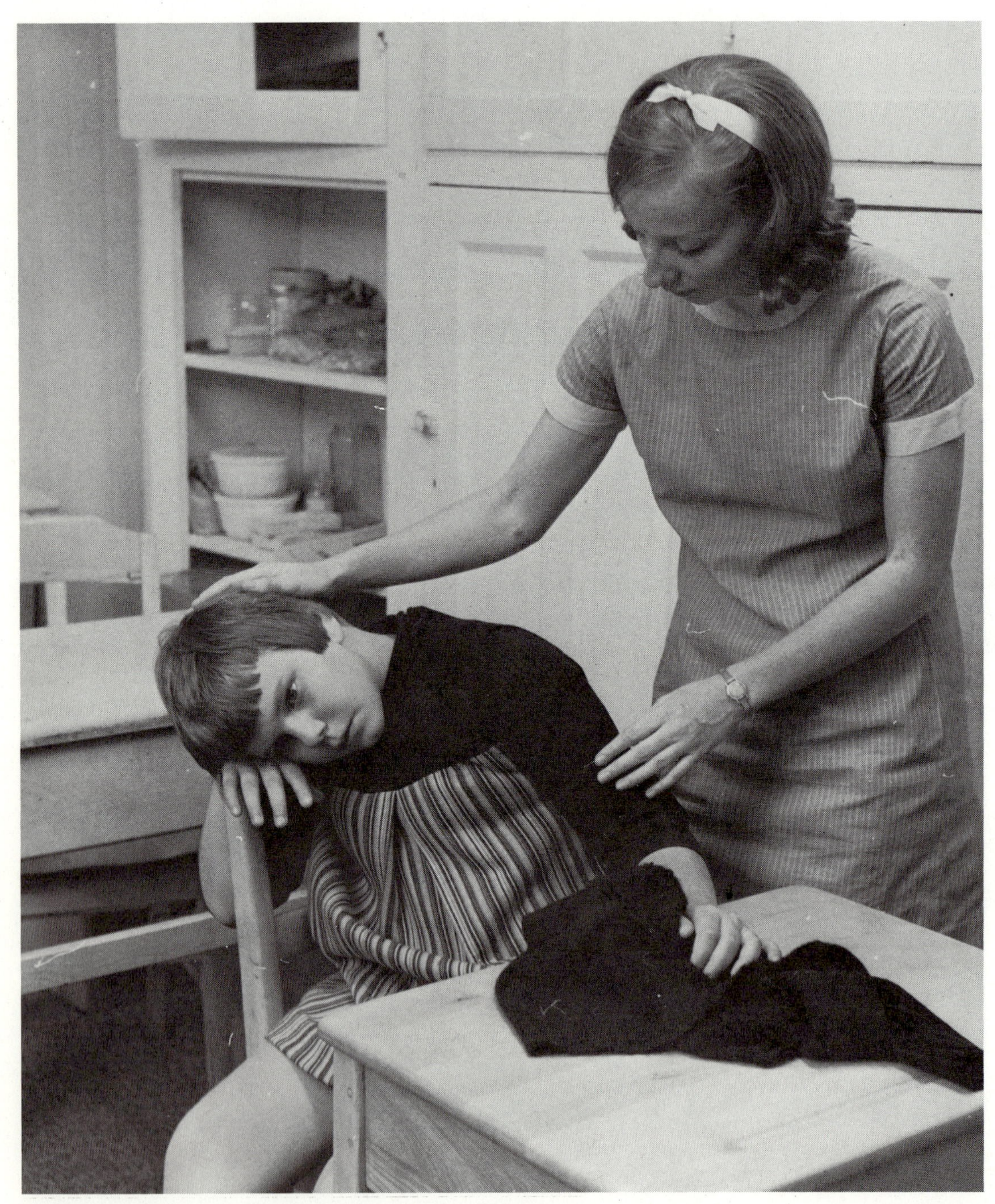

(Courtesy of The Woods Schools, Langhorne, Pennsylvania.)

The problem of disturbed and disturbing behavior has intrigued and threatened man for many years. The history of man's attitudes toward behavioral disturbance has been marked by many conflicts. People of today, in much the same way as people of the past, seem to assume that they will always behave in a rational, normal manner, so that when unreasonable kinds of behavior occur in others, they demand complete segregation of this behavior from themselves. In addition to demanding explanations for the deviant behaviors of others, many individuals frequently develop a disquietude which seems to threaten their inner selves. Disturbed and disturbing behavior was viewed as being completely separate from and opposite to normal behavior. It is only more recently, with the realization of a continuum of normality-abnormality, that we are changing our view to "them is us."

HISTORICAL BACKGROUND

Man's earliest endeavors to understand the functioning of the human mind were divided sharply between rational, scientific explanations and explanations verging on, or actually involved in, the supernatural (Alexander and Selesnick, 1966). Early man frequently prayed to the gods for relief from problems concerning deviant social behaviors. Socrates made a contribution to the early, rational concept of mental illness when he insisted that it was well within the normal, social, intellectual, and moral bounds of mankind to explain such behavior.

With the decline of the Greek and Roman empires, Europe became a morass of conflicts and disintegrating institutions. The people of this period, in trying to find relief from this situation, developed a strong belief in the supernatural. Supernatural explanations of man's overt behavior persisted for many years, and they still persist today. Indeed, not until the Renaissance period did the reawakening of rational thinking and interest in learning reoccur.

During the Renaissance, many individuals turned to more thoughtful, rational, and scientific explanations of human behavior. Exploration of the hereditary and biological bases of man (rather than supernatural and unprovable aspects) was undertaken. Biology, which was used as an explanation of man's overt behavior, was and still remains a popular hypothesis. The biological explanation relieves an individual of many inner conflicts and guilt feelings which may arise when he finds himself or others behaving in a disordered manner. All overt behavior could be explained as resulting from such factors as characterological predispositions, biological factors, and hereditary traits. The idea that every person is vulnerable to "mental illness" was prevalent during this period (although most people tried to ignore this fact), and, as always, this thought threatened man's feeling of inner stability.

In order for individuals to cope with feelings of anxiety aroused by fear of "mental illness," they placed disordered behavior in a bizarre and isolated category. Those who were deviant were called "mentally ill" (Zilboorg and Henry, 1941), and mental illness was viewed as something entirely unrelated to normal human behavior. Many individuals, both adults and children, were locked away in mental hospitals, which were little better than prisons, and were often chained and starved in an attempt to rid them of evil spirits or inappropriate overt behavior. One interesting theory concerning treatment of the mentally ill (Foucault, 1965) is that attitudes toward leprous individuals were literally transferred to the mentally ill, so that the exclusionary treatment of lepers was transferred to those whose behavior was considered extreme. Early hospitals were places in which individuals were locked away from society, and no attempts at habilitation or rehabilitation were made. The fact that such individuals were frequently exhibited in cages and chained to posts in public squares as spectacles is evidence of the ambivalent attitude toward the mentally ill during this time. Conditions maintained in the hospitals were barbaric and were often worse than those provided for wild beasts in captivity. Even the more advanced thinkers of the time, such as Pinel in the eighteenth century, were amazed at "the constancy and ease with which certain of the insane of both sexes bear the rigorous and prolonged cold" (Foucault, 1965).

It was difficult for mankind to accept the idea that disordered behavior is part of the same continuum as the behavior evidenced by so-called normal individuals. Interest in the concept of minor abnormalities and disturbances, such as neuroses, caused individuals to explore the possibility of a continuum of behavior. Typically, the most unusual cases attracted the most attention. The hysteric was ridiculed and studied because of his outlandish manifestations. Freud was one of the first individuals to postulate theoretical bases to explain neurotic behavior. Even though some of Freud's contributions are not held in good repute today, there is no doubt that some of his work in this area is of outstanding significance. Freud viewed all men as being subject to biological and cultural forces, and thus he paved the way for the readmission of those with severe mental illness into society. Freud's work brought attention to the psychotic and to the neurotic individual.

The pioneer work of Freud inspired other workers to advance many other theories to explain deviant behavior. Since Freud's work, a large range of human behaviors have become subject to treatment by mental health workers and teachers of exceptional children. Interest in neurosis has led to recognition of the effects of emotions on the physiological being and has, indeed, resulted in the development of the wholly new field of psychosomatic medicine. All these developments have brought about a growing awareness of the significance of external forces and of the effects of early childhood experiences upon later behavior.

It would be a grave error to think that all the changes in our thinking about human behavior stemmed from one person's theory. History is replete with examples of such ideas from early times to the present. It must be remembered that for ideas to take root and develop there must be a proper climate. Many early writings exhibit some of the more enlightened attitudes concerning mental illness which are now prevalent. It is difficult for man to deny the supernatural and accept rational theories. Thus, a person must be fairly secure to tolerate rational thinking when it concerns his own behavior (Lewis, 1941). As man's ability to cope with his external environment has advanced and affluence has become a way of life, at least in the United States, more and more persons have become interested in the psychological functioning of the human being (Schofield, 1964).

The work of Dorothea Dix over a hundred years ago resulted in the establishment of our early mental hospitals. Later, Isaac Ray and Clifford Beers provided impetus for the mental hygiene movement in the United States. Beers's concern for mental health stemmed from his own incarceration in a mental institution. This experience is delineated in his fascinating book, The Mind That Found Itself. Beers was the founder and director of an early institution, the National Committee for Mental Hygiene, founded in 1908, which resulted in the current National Mental Health Association. The first attempts of the committee to cope with mental health problems resulted in the establishment of many clinics for children, and, in addition, the committee worked with others to enact legislation to provide facilities for the mentally ill.

Another example of a man ahead of his time was William Healy. Healy, around the start of this century, wrote about the social and cultural origins of delinquent behavior, but not until many years later was his work resurrected and re-emphasized by current workers in the field of delinquency (Eisenberg, 1962).

Freudian psychology greatly influenced the mental health field during the early years after World War I. However, Freudian treatment of the emotionally disturbed individual was used almost exclusively for the well-to-do patient (Hollingshead and Redlich, 1958). Persons with less money and the more seriously disturbed were treated with physical methods: drugs, hospitalization, or surgery.

The increasing technological development of America and the two major world wars resulted in many changes in views toward mental health and mental illness.

DEFINITION OF NORMAL BEHAVIOR

As knowledge of mental health has been disseminated throughout the population, great concern has been expressed about what is normal behavior. Traditionally, normality has been defined in a negative fashion, that is, absence of gross pathology or defects or not being "sick" in common terminology. An individual was thought to be operating in a normal or healthy manner whenever he had a behavioral pattern that was typical of the average person or the majority of the population. Mental illness generally involved any very unusual, different, or unnatural behavior. Over the centuries, the concepts of normality and health have become synonymous. In 1865, Claude Bernard proposed that the human organism was a series of balances, and as long as balance was maintained, a healthy condition or, what we would call "normality," was maintained. This view was followed by Cannon's work (1932) on homeostasis.

There is a great need to collect new and more cumulative data on the basic characteristics that distinguish normal from abnormal individuals. It has become evident that past criteria applied to the concept of normality are faulty in a number of ways: (1) there are limitations in using a simple, statistical definition of normality; (2) normality must be considered in terms of cultural relativity; and (3) there are limitations in the use of the dichotomy of health and illness.

One of the most exhaustive attempts to define the parameters of normality was that of Levine (1942). He stated that normality is: (1) nonexistent in a complete form but existing as a relative and quantitative approximation; (2) in agreement with statistical averages of specific groups, if such norms are not contrary to standards of individual health and maturity; (3) physical normality which includes absence of physical disease, presence of good function, and maturity; (4) intellectual normality; (5) absence of neurotic and psychotic symptoms; (6) emotional maturity: (a) ability to be guided by reality rather than by fear, (b) use of long term values, (c) conscience, (d) independence, (e) capacity to love someone else but with an enlightened self-interest, (f) a reasonable dependence, (g) a reasonable aggressiveness, (h) a healthy defense mechanism, (i) good sexual adjustment with the acceptance of one's own gender, (j) good work adjustment.

At present, there are no universally accepted definitions of normality nor are there any universal theories of behavior. Redlich (1957) pointed out the unsatisfactoriness of the negative approach to determining normality that is typically used. Psychoanalysis in determining normality tends to use three criteria:

1. Normality is viewed as ideal fiction.

a. Acceptance of the universality of neurosis is one of the basic cornerstones of the Freudian theory. Freud stated that all men are at least to some degree neurotic.

b. Jones (1931) indicated the following factors as being essential to normality: (1) the normal mind must have the capacity for adaptation to reality; (2) relations with others must have a rational and affective content; (3) there must be some degree of mental efficiency; and (4) happiness must be present together with the capacity for enjoyment and self-contentment.

2. Normality may be defined, according to the Freudian paradigm, as optimal integration.

a. According to Klein (1960), in order for a person to be considered mentally healthy, he must have a well-integrated personality. Klein listed the following characteristics of the normal individual: emotional maturity, character, capacity to deal with conflicting emotions, a balance between internal life and adaptation to reality, and a successful uniting of the parts into a total personality.

b. Erikson (1950) emphasized the importance of successful mastery of various stages of development.

c. Kubie (1958) stated that the essence of normality is flexibility in all areas of development. According to him, illness represents a fixing of behavior in a rigid and alternate pattern.

d. Rank (1932) saw normality as an endless succession of separations accompanied by traumas with a continuous necessity to struggle and to create.

e. In Jung's theory (1959), the healthy person makes an attempt to gain perfection and to gain completeness within himself and within the framework of his society.

3. Normality may be considered as adaptation within a context.

a. Hartmann (1960) viewed the ego as autonomous and emphasized that each person starts life with certain basic capacities that are relatively free from conflict; throughout life, there is a continuous interaction between the relatively free and the relatively driven aspects of one's personality. A person possesses various degrees of ego strength resulting from this interaction. Thus, health is viewed as being relative to one's mental and physical environments.

b. Glover (1956) felt that a normal person is one who is not hampered by mental conflicts, who shows appropriate working capacity, and who is able to love someone in addition to himself.

c. Menninger (1945) viewed the adjustment of human beings to the world and to each other as the most effective method by which to bring about happiness in the individual. He felt that efficiency or contentment is not enough and that one must, in fact, learn to obey the rules in life cheerfully. A combination of factors leads to happiness and, to what he would call, normality.

The typical, modern-day, psychological explanation of normality is related to statistical analysis. Maslow and Mittelmann (1951) provided a list of qualities which they believed to be essential for good mental health: (a) adequate feeling of security, (b) adequate spontaneity and emotionality, (c) efficient contact with reality, (d) adequate bodily desires and ability to gratify them, (e) adequate self-knowledge, (f) integration consistency of personality, (g) adequate life goals, (h) ability to learn from experience, and (i) ability to satisfy requirements of the group.

Buhler (1959) listed four basic biological tendencies in the human being which can help one to achieve normality: (1) need for satisfaction, (2) maintenance of internal order, (3) adaptation, and (4) productivity. Engel (1960) noted four factors affecting normality that she considered crucial to psychological evaluation of children: (1) empathy, (2) control, (3) regression, and (4) time and space.

ETIOLOGICAL FACTORS IN BEHAVIORAL DISTURBANCES

During the past few decades there has been much discussion concerning the relationship between heredity and environment. The purpose of this book is not to discuss this topic in any great detail, especially since it has already been treated in the work of Jensen (1969), Shockley (1969), and others. However, it is appropriate for us to examine some of the parameters of behavior. Perhaps one of the more commonly accepted views of current psychology, relative to our discussion of behavior, is that the human organism should be viewed as a product of the interaction of its genetic and environmental components. The resultant individual is always the sum total of the interaction of these factors. Attempts to assess the individual effects of each component and their interaction with each other have been somewhat futile in the past. Research designed to identify such factors has been found to yield, at best, inconclusive and ambiguous data leading to divergent conclusions from the same research studies.

Biological Bases

The current theory of geneticists and psychologists on behavioral disturbances concerns interaction. It may be said that the nature and the extent of each factor's influence is dependent upon the other factor. It is probable that the proportional contribution of heredity to the variance of a specific trait is not constant, but that it will vary from one environment to another. Thus, it may be said that the individual is a constantly interacting organism whose behavior varies with the interaction of genetic and environmental components. Practically no studies have attempted to assess this interactive factor. Perhaps one of the problems involved in determining the effects of heredity and environment is that the wrong question has been asked in the past. The question of how much each component contributes to the total make-up of each individual is probably unanswerable and fruitless. Probably a more effective approach to the problem would be to ask how these factors interact in a given situation. Some studies are being conducted which will seemingly answer this question.

Perhaps a brief examination of some of the many mechanisms which affect the interaction of heredity and environment might be interesting to explore. Currently, geneticists and other researchers are conducting many studies concerning hereditary factors and how they influence behavior. We can only be impressed by the tremendous variety of genetic influences. One example of an extreme genetic influence is phenylketonuria (PKU). PKU is caused by specific defects (hereditarily based factors) within the genetic structure of the individual which result in intellectual malfunctioning as a result of metabolic disorders. At present, we have no environmental control factor which will completely alleviate the effect of PKU. However, the effect may be considerably lessened by appropriate diet.

Another example of the effect of hereditary, genetic factors on behavior is hereditary deafness. While it is not directly related to intellectual retardation, it may result in an intellectually deficient adult because deafness interferes with interaction between the individual and his environment, particularly the language environment. In this case, the hereditary handicap can, to a great extent, be eliminated by appropriate training procedures. In some ways, it might be said that the functioning of the hereditarily deaf person will be the direct result of proper application of appropriate instructional devices at the appropriate time.

An inherited susceptibility to certain physical kinds of diseases or conditions is a third example of a hereditary factor which can affect behavior. Such conditions lead to interference with the learning processes due to health impairment. It should be realized, of course, that circumstances determine the influences of such illnesses upon personality and learning, as evidenced by their effects which vary from minor to major depending on the individual. Widespread influences on behavior due to hereditary factors may be certain basic, individual characteristics which are hereditary, such as sex, skin pigmentation, body build, and temperament. Such factors have been utilized by various societies to discriminate between people on a social basis rather than on an intrinsic, differential basis. Differentiation on this basis tends to be shown invalid with regard to determining inherent superiority or inferiority of any individual. Modern genetics tends to indicate that there is a normal pattern of interaction which limits the range of variation that is possible for each given genetic make-up. It might be said that heredity sets norms or limits within which environmental differences will determine the actual effect on the individual. A large portion of hereditary influences are within the domain of what might be called the interactionary relationship between psychological and biological factors, as outlined by Barker and Wright (1955).

Environmental factors may have an impact upon the operating organism which may vary from strong to weak, depending upon a variety of additional factors. A more indirect type of cause mechanism may be illustrated by a severe motor disorder, such as cerebral palsy, which may or may not be accompanied by mental ability impairment. In the case of cerebral palsy, intellectual retardation may occur as an indirect result of the motor handicap if the individual has been unable to come in contact with the appropriate learning environment.

Social class (in contrast to organic factors), which is a somewhat broad and enduring environmental factor may affect the development of a child or an adult. It may influence behavior through many channels and may determine the range and nature of intellectual stimulation that is provided by the whole community through such media as books, art, and music. More far-reaching may be the effect of social class upon interest and motivation to perform abstract intellectual tasks in order to gain social approval. Social traits and the emotional adjustment of an individual may be influenced by such a factor as social economic levels.

The previous examples provide a basis upon which to examine the etiology of emotional disturbance. The etiological mechanism of any hereditary or environmental condition ultimately will lead to a behavioral characteristic. Thus, we must examine the nature and cause of hereditary and environmental conditions. Perhaps a brief examination of some promising methodological approaches to the question of how these factors occur would be appropriate at present.

During the past few years, psychologists and others interested in the etiology of emotional disturbance have begun to depart from attempting to correlate factors of mental illness with other related factors and have turned more to exploration of what might be called reactional biographies of individuals, a more descriptive approach to the problem. In addition, the tendency of the past to catalogue groups of differences into psychological traits has given way to research on changes in group characteristics following certain altered conditions.

One current methodological development has been the selective breeding investigations which have been undertaken in an attempt to identify specific hereditary conditions underlying observed behavioral differences. One such early study was conducted by Tryon (1940), who experimented with the maze-learning ability of rats. After testing a number of generations of rats to determine whether hereditary transmission of maze-learning ability had occurred, Tryon concluded that what was transmitted was not maze learning as such, but, perhaps, general intelligence. Investigators have continued to ask, with regard to these experiments, "Just what is it that makes one group of rats learn mazes more quickly than others?" Is it differences in motivation, emotionality, speed of learning, or general activity level? If so, are these behavioral characteristics, in turn, dependent upon group differences in physical development, body weight, brain size, biochemical factors, or some other organic conditions? A number of recent and ongoing investigations indicate that attempts are being made to trace, at least in part, the steps whereby certain chemical properties of genes lead ultimately to specific behavioral characteristics. Searle (1949) attempted to follow Tryon's research by working with strains of maze-competent rats and maze-incompetent rats that Tryon had developed. Searle found that the two strains differed in a number of characteristics rather than just in the maze-learning ability.

Another line of exploration regarding the relationship between behavioral characteristics and physiological variables (related to hereditary factors) concerns EEG studies and metabolic studies related to biochemical foundations of behavior. One study in this area has focused on PKU. In this particular case, the cause of PKU (defective genes), the metabolic disorder, and the subsequent cerebral malfunctioning, leading to brain damage and mental retardation, can be outlined step by step.

In addition, research concerning neurological and biochemical foundations of schizophrenia is relevant to studies on heredity and environment (Kety, 1959; Wyatt, 1971; Heston, 1970). A third approach to the problem of how heredity and environment influence the individual deals with studies of prenatal environment. Particularly of interest is the work of Pasamanick et al. (1956) which demonstrated a relationship between the socioeconomic level of the family, complications of pregnancy and childbirth, and psychological disorders of the children. In a series of studies on a large sample of white and black individuals in Baltimore, Pasamanick and his associates found that various prenatal and paranatal disorders are significantly related to the occurrences of mental defects and psychiatric disorders in children. One important finding of this study was that differences in maternal diet were evident in the low economic status group.

In line with the previous study, Harrell et al. (1955) found that pregnant women in low income groups produced children who varied greatly in incidence of deficiencies when one group of these pregnant women was fed normal, regulated diets and the control group was allowed to regulate their own diets as usual. When tested at the ages of three and four, the offspring of the experimental group obtained a significantly higher mean IQ than did the offspring of the control group.

Child-rearing practices as related to behavior have been explored by a number of investigators—Whiting and Child (1953), Davis and Havinghurst (1946), Williams and Scott (1953), and many others. The results of most of these studies, which concern child-rearing as it relates to subsequent emotional development of the offspring, have been ambiguous and defective with regard to methodology employed. Many more efforts should be devoted to this area of research to obtain more reliable data concerning the relationship of child-rearing practices to adult behavior.

The heredity-environment problem, which has aroused opposing viewpoints in popular and scientific literature, is a matter of concern for many people today. Many questions which have arisen as a result of this concern have led into blind alleys, conceptually and methodologically. Rather than asking whether certain factors are influenced by heredity or environment, it would be more appropriate to ask how both heredity and environment interact with each other specifically to produce certain constitutional or intellectual consequences. Some questions which should be pursued in the investigation of the relationship between environment and heredity would involve the following:

1. What are the hereditary conditions that influence behavioral differences between selectively bred groups of animals?
2. What are the relationships between physiological variables and individual differences in behavior, especially in the case of pathological deviations?
3. What is the role of prenatal physiological factors in behavioral development?
4. What are the influences of early experiences on behavioral characteristics?
5. What are the cultural differences in child-rearing practices, and how do they relate to intellectual and emotional development?
6. What mechanisms of psychosomatic-psychological relations are involved in development?
7. How is the psychological development of twins from infancy to maturity related to their social environment?

These questions should lead to a wide variety of approaches and hopefully to a more fruitful understanding of the interrelation between environment and heredity.

The term *temperament* might be said to refer to the basic style of a child's pattern of behavior, i.e., the manner in which he behaves, rather than why he behaves in a certain way or what his behavior consists of. Thus, temperament refers to such behavioral aspects as the child's temper, his ability to adapt, his mood range, and his basic capacity for emotional tone. It should be noted that temperament is not immutable. It is like any other characteristic; it is subject to developmental influences which are affected by environmental circumstances, and temperament is not basically different from height, weight, and bone structure of an individual. The study of temperament as related to personality is of relatively recent origin, with great emphasis being placed on this study in the 1930's and 1950's. Studies of child growth and development all seem to indicate that many behaviors found in children, which started at age six, may be said to be high predictors of adult behavior. Behavioral patterns, such as passive withdrawal from stressful situations, dependency on the family, ease of anger arousal, and social interaction, have been found to be related to behavior in children prior to their entry into school (Kagan and Moss, 1962).

Cultural and Socioeconomic Deprivations

The concepts of "disadvantage" and "deprivation" may not have been sufficiently differentiated heretofore: disadvantage refers to cultural and economic poverty; deprivation refers to either lack of stimulation or overstimulation regardless of socioeconomic status (SES).

Who are the disadvantaged? Generally, in discussing the disadvantaged, those in the poverty class are emphasized. Ausubel (1965) defined the slum child as one who

> **. . .is a child of another world. Our laws do not bind him, our standard middle class ambitions do not inspire him. . . . Teachers in first to third grades feel the child slipping away. By the fourth grade he is fallen behind. By the eighth grade his mind is closed, his behavior rebellious. By high school age he is more than likely to drop out headed for chronic unemployment, disdaining the outside middle class world that already sustains him, secretly contemptuous of himself, and a waste as a human being, a failure.**

Can we say, however, that children of middle class parents, who progress from college to professional life, are not disadvantaged in any fashion? The disadvantaged cannot be defined in terms of race, residency, job, or behavior alone. The only factor that is common to all disadvantaged groups is that they have been bypassed by the affluent stream of the current American way of life. They have not obtained the same basic goods, physical comfort, schooling, or employment as the majority of Americans.

Problems in Definition

There is a tendency to view the disadvantaged as a rather small fragment of the population, located at one extreme of the famous normal distribution curve. The very labels which are used reflect a negative connotation. For example, Reissman (1962) used the terms "culturally deprived," "educationally deprived," "deprived," "underprivileged," "disadvantaged," "lower class," and "lower social economic groups" as synonymous terms. Other terms that have been used are "culturally different," "working class," "slum culture," "inner city dwellers," "culturally impoverished," "experientially deprived," "culturally handicapped," "educationally handicapped," "disadvantaged children of the poor," and many others. All these labels are misleading, in that many of the groups to which they refer have rich and complex cultures of their own which, indeed, set them further apart from the traditionally white, middle-class, Protestant American culture. Reissman wrote: "Culture consists of the institutions, the structures and organization of the people involved." It should be noted that culture is not a moralistic or evaluative term, since it is neither good nor bad. Culture should be viewed as the sum total of the life patterns of a particular group of people. It is a positive term. Only when a dominant culture seeks to impose itself on another subculture do undesirable labels arise. "Culturally disadvantaged" is a term that is somewhat "self-conscious" in connotation. Ordinarily, it refers to the total variety of social, economic, and racial factors which block the achievement of an individual's right to learn. Literally speaking, the term "culturally deprived" is inaccurate, in that every child automatically learns his culture. If the child happens to belong to a particular subculture that is at variance with the dominant culture, an incongruity is set up which may cause some conflict. All children's experiences occur within a wide continuum, and they are not necessarily the same experiences that formal educational programs recognize as being of value.

In fact, many experiences of children of American subcultures may be considered extremely inappropriate with regard to standard school values. Failure to provide sensory stimulation experiences for the newborn and the young child is a serious factor; however, at present, it is inaccurate to state that a person born into a low socioeconomic group will

Figure 8-1 Substandard housing is part of deprivation. (From Wallace: Psychology: A Social Science. Philadelphia, W. B. Saunders Company, 1971. Courtesy of Paul Barton, Black Star.)

automatically be deprived of appropriate experiences or adequate stimulation. Such lack of stimulation can lead to malfunctioning with respect to intellectual accomplishments. Inadequate and inappropriate experiences, regardless of their origin, are detrimental with regard to verbal restrictedness and oral *intellectualization*. However, to continue to dwell upon the pathology or the deficits of the so-called culturally deprived is to confirm the inferiority of a large segment of the American population. Cultural deprivation should not be viewed as being limited only to the poor or to minority groups. The child whose major needs are ignored is culturally deprived regardless of the socioeconomic status of the group from which he comes.

One segment of the culturally disadvantaged group is composed of economically disadvantaged individuals. Poverty, economic problems, and hardships are the lot of some one-fifth to one-fourth of the American people. These individuals lack adequate funds to secure the basic essentials, food, shelter, and clothing, and may be denied the minimal, sustaining elements of physical comfort and safety. Physical hardships alone are a serious problem, but poverty is an all-pervasive phenomenon. To be poor is literally to be stigmatized, branded as a failure by mainstream Americans. In America, a person may be judged in terms of how much money he makes, what kind of house he lives in, what kind of job he has, and how much education he has acquired. Poverty and poor education tend to go hand in hand.

Cultural Influences

All groups of people have a culture of some kind. One should not, however, confuse the term "culture" with the term "environment." *Culture* can be defined as being *composed of the sum total of attitudes, traditions, and moral and ethical codes that are particular to any given society.* Within a given urban slum neighborhood, several distinct subcultures may exist; in other parts of the same city, an entire neighborhood might be composed of one culture, such as the Chinese in New York's Chinatown. Generally, distribution of culturally disadvantaged persons in the United States conforms to a geographical pattern. In the South and in most of the urban areas of the North, cultural disadvantages primarily affect the black population. Other groups, Mexican Americans in the Southwest and California, Puerto Ricans in New York, American Indians in the Southwest, West, and Northwest, and poor whites of Appalachia and the rural South, have subcultures which are associated with poverty and which have been bypassed by the mainstream of American life.

Black individuals have become increasingly concentrated in cities. One indication of this pattern is the changing percentages of blacks versus whites in cities, according to the United States Census. From 1960 to 1970, the following percentage changes occurred in some of America's largest cities: Washington, D.C., from 53.9 per cent to 71.1 per cent black; Atlanta, from 38.3 to 51.3 per cent black; and New Orleans, from 36.2 to 45.0 per cent black. Thus, we see that the black population is increasing in the urban ghettos of America's major cities. We should also note that the median age is lower for blacks in urban ghettos than for whites and that an even larger percentage of blacks is found in the urban public schools than in the general population.

Puerto Ricans who have immigrated to America in increasing

numbers have suffered some of the same problems as blacks. Handlin (1959) pointed out something of the origin of this problem: "By idling definition, some 75 per cent of the population of Puerto Rico are white, some 25 per cent are colored." Data that we have indicate that a large percentage of light- and dark-skinned Puerto Ricans found themselves in a dilemma, since color, which was of slight importance back home, was crucial in New York. The effect of this situation has been to strengthen identification with the Puerto Rican culture in the case of those who are dark-skinned and to weaken it in the case of those who are white. Many dark-skinned Puerto Ricans wished above all to avoid the stigma of identification with blacks, and they could do this only by establishing themselves as Spanish-speaking. On the other hand, whiteness became an important aspect to the remainder of Puerto Ricans in this country. As soon as some improvement in their status enabled them to "escape," there was incentive to dissolve the ties with their cultural group and to "lose" themselves in the general category of whites.

Perhaps the most excluded and deprived group in America is the American Indian (Medicine, 1971). The critical condition of some Indians was pointed out by Heline (1952): ". . .in 1948 the plight of Navahos of Arizona and New Mexico was so serious that, had it not been for trainloads of food and clothing supplied by private charity and an emergency relief appropriation later made by Congress, untold numbers would have died of starvation and exposure." Such want existed in our midst without our general knowledge, because the Indians are not generally in public view, and their depressed condition is not widely publicized.

Some of the problems involved in subculture groups' blending with the major theme of America and America's school system are pointed out by Leighten. According to Leighten (1964), Anglo-American teachers view man as master, and his major role is to master nature; however, the Indians view nature as something to live in harmony with, and the Spanish-Americans view man fatalistically, as being subjected to natural forces. In considering the concept of time, the typical Anglo-American teacher is concerned mainly with the future, while Indians view time as a current phenomenon, as do Spanish-Americans, who also view time in the present. The Anglo-American teacher views aspiration in terms of striving for success, while to the Indian it means following the old ways, and to the Spanish-American it means stereotypically to aspire to work a little and rest a little. Many other values could be explored, but these will serve to point out some of the discrepancies in value systems which are brought to the schools by various groups.

As pointed out earlier, middle-class children may have their own deprivation problems. In a special television program which was broadcast nationally in 1965, CBS attempted to examine some of the major concepts, ideals, and aspirations of the suburbs of America. The following facts were pointed out: 84 per cent of the five- to six-year-old children said that they expected to go to college; 96 per cent of the 16-year-olds indicated that they were worried about getting higher grades; 77 per cent felt that it was difficult to live with pressure to do well in class; and 54 per cent admitted that they had cheated in order to pass tests. Thus, parental pressure gives rise to a great deal of anxiety.

Any discussion of the disadvantaged would be remiss if it did not include an examination of what has been called the hidden curriculum of public schools. The hidden curriculum refers to the entire conglomerate of influences affecting a child, in addition to that which constitutes the formal educational curriculum outlined by the public school. The first and, perhaps, the most important part of the hidden curriculum is language. Language, of course, serves as the major mode of communication and of conveying cultural values and is the main channel through which a child learns in our culture. A restricted linguistic code is usually rigid in its expression; it tends to be less flexible. A linguistic code as it relates to the development of cognitive effectiveness is of great importance. An elaborate linguistic code allows for greater definition of one's awareness system and one's relationship to other subjects and people.

A second portion of the hidden curriculum is the neighborhood. From birth, a child's environment has an important effect on his development. Of course, the infant sees relatively little of his environment and is probably not aware of a great part of it. He is, however, affected by it owing to the effect that it has upon his parents and siblings. The neighborhood may affect many different segments of life. A perceptive description of the slum by Conant (1961) illustrates this point:

> **When a residential area composed of old homes formerly occupied by owners in single family groups changes economically and socially, conditions of general deterioration begin. After, the owners rent property by single rooms or small so-called apartments of two or three rooms to large families. Such conditions attract transients (who either cannot or will not qualify for supervised low income housing) the unemployed, the unskilled and unschooled, whose breadwinners have either been submitted to mental institutions or prisons or who have been recently released from such. The only possession that most of these families have is children. In such an environment, all forms of evil flourish—the peddling of drugs or dope, drunkenness, disease, accidents, truancies, physical, mental, and moral handicaps, sex perversions involving children. . . . There has not been a day since I have been at the school that there has not been one or more children in detention at the juvenile court.**

Time magazine pointed out that the environment of a slum area like central Harlem occupies only a 3.5 square-mile wedge of upper Manhattan, but 232,000 people are packed into it, 94 per cent of them being black. Under such conditions, there can be little satisfaction in one's surroundings. The black bourgeoisie live much as their white middle-class counterparts do; however, there are also the tenement-dwellers whose living conditions are abject. Half of Harlem's buildings are classified as deteriorating or dilapidated, but no classification, official or otherwise, can adequately describe the deplorable surroundings. Frequently, children play unsupervised far into the night, wearing keys on strings around their necks because there is no one at home to care for them. Half of Harlem's children under 18 live with only one parent or no parent, and the juvenile delinquency rate is more than double that of New York's as a whole. The venereal disease rate among Harlem's residents is six times higher than in the rest of the city.

These facts indicate physical deterioration of living conditions and great congestion. They point out high unemployment rates and indicate an environment of filth, disease, and violence. Lack of adequate child care is evident as a factor related to a high juvenile crime rate. The neighborhood, among other circumstances, provides a role model. A child will attempt to define himself in relationship to what he is exposed to and how he is exposed to it. The negative affect upon children living in slums cannot be overemphasized. It is not atypical to find that young children may come into contact with unemployed adults loitering at street corners, and thus these children obtain a warped concept of the role of the adult. The child may grow to identify with many adults who are unemployed. The relationship of the slum child to policemen is a particular case. The young child, free to wander the streets, learns to regard the uniformed man as a troublemaker. The child's own mother may draw on the authority of the police for disciplinary purposes. She may state: "You had better not let a cop see you do that or he'll put you in jail." Thus, hostility to authority becomes an all-pervasive factor for some children.

Another fact of life in a slum is the crowding. Hunt (1964) pointed out that crowding alone may provide a negative influence.

> **Crowding may be no handicap for a human infant during much of his first year of life. Although there is no certainty of this, it is conceivable that being a young infant among a large number of people living within a room may actually serve to provide such wide variations of visual and auditory impulses that will facilitate development more than will the conditions typical of the culturally deprived during much of the first year.**

In addition, Hunt felt that during the second year, when the infant begins to throw things and to develop his own methods of locomotion, crowded conditions could hamper his development. He is likely to find himself getting in the way of adults who are preoccupied with problems associated with their poverty and overcrowded conditions. Playthings and room to play are highly limited; circumstances of the crowded lower class offer little opportunity for the kinds of environmental encounters that are required to keep a two-year-old youngster developing at an optimal rate.

The amount of auditory stimulation in some children's environments may be detrimental according to Ausubel (1965b).

> **Psychologists will begin to discern slum children's inattention, a high skill the result of intensive training. When a child lives with 11 people in three rooms, all sharing their toilets, knowing when the man is drunk next door, and that baby is awake downstairs, a child must learn to be inattentive to survive. His ears become skilled in not hearing; his eyes in not seeing.**

In contrast to the crowded, noisy conditions of the urban ghetto, the rural poor suffer from an entirely different type of deprivation. The condition of poor migrant workers, in particular, has been elucidated by Sutton (1954).

> **The migrant child lives for short periods of time each year in several communities, sometimes 2, 4, 6, or 8 different states. Even though his family may have a well established migratory route, there is no assurance that while on the trips he will reside in the same communities year after year. To some migrant children, home is a location where they live the longest time during the winter. To others, home has no meaning whatsoever and in response to questions regarding it they answer, "Nope, ain't got no home, just any place we are at, that is my home"; or "I don't know, you see we move a lot."**

The life of the migrant worker provides little that can be called a neighborhood, that is, a unified social setting in which to mature.

The average life expectancy of the Indian is probably in the range of 41 to 46 years, depending upon the area in which he lives. Unemployment is exceptionally high. The average income has been estimated at $1500 a year. The following quotation from Haubrick (1965) illustrates the problem of the reservation neighborhood.

The general economic, social, and physical conditions on these reservations are pathetic. The traditions of fishing and minor agricultural pursuits are not sufficient to maintain any standard of living. The homes of the Indians are generally in very poor repair with inadequate facilities for sanitation, heating, and water. A state of general depression exists and has existed for a number of years. Approximately 30 per cent of the Indian families are on public welfare and this is six times the rate of a local community.

The health and welfare of the American Indian in the Pacific Northwest is extraordinarily depressed. The overriding statistic which takes precedence over all others is the average life span of the Indian. In 1960 the average life span of all Indians was 41 years, and in the Pacific Northwest, it was not more than 46 years. In essence, this means that the Indian's life span is 25 years less than that of the average American. Indians are hospitalized twice as frequently as other individuals in this country. Tuberculosis occurs at four times the rate of whites, and Indian infant mortality is triple that of whites. One is not reassured by the accurate observations that in the areas of health and welfare, conditions have improved in the past 10, 20, or 30 years. One can generally say that poverty, disease, and depression have profoundly affected the lives of these people. This hidden curriculum, which is the life style of most American Indians, provides inadequate background for the child, making it difficult for him to compete in American educational traditions. On many reservations, customs and rituals are still carried out with great determination despite the fact that living conditions which gave rise to these traditions are no longer in existence. Unlike the slum child or the migrant child, children on reservations are provided with many adult models to follow.

In contrast to the preceding discussion, suburban children have different problems with regard to deprivation. In the suburbs, the informal and formal curricula are lacking in contrast. The suburban neighborhood is very homogenous in terms of appearances, cultural characteristics, and neighborhood values. However, the fact that suburban schools and suburban children appear to have the same culture and values does not mean that the schools are geared to the reality of adult living or that the suburban setting necessarily produces the most desirable environment. The suburban community may, indeed, present a very restrictive culture for the growing child, as suggested by Wyden (1962). More and more, such children seem only to be aware of their own exclusive environment and are largely unaware of cultural diversity. These homogenous, limited surroundings are far from being representational of the world as a whole. Indeed, the very language and monotony of suburban living may serve as a limiting factor in terms of a child's experiential pattern. Life, with its different origins, values, and attitudes, may prove to be difficult for suburban dwellers to cope with. Children who have spent their formative years in such a binding culture may regard people outside this culture as remote and meaningless to them when they grow to be adults. Perhaps the major way in which upper class persons are disadvantaged is by the fact that they are removed from other cultures and do not know the ways of or the contrast in these cultures. To the poorer classes, the suburbs are often the subject of resentment. One poor mother put it this way:

They keep on telling us, those welfare ladies, to take better care of our money and save it for a rainy day and to buy food and be like them, progressive, keep the children in school, and keep our husband from leav-

> **ing us. There is nothing they don't have a sermon on. They will tell you it is bad to have your kids sleep alongside you in the bed and you are not suppose to watch television because you should be playing with your kids and it is wrong for the kids too, and it is bad for you to let them stay out after dark and they should study their lessons hard and they will get way ahead up there. Well, I will tell you they sure don't know what it is about and they can't and not if they come knocking on my door every week until the Lord takes us off. They have nice leather shoes, and their smart coats, and they pick the right order of words all right, do we know how many schools they have been to, do they have any idea what us is about. I mean if you have not got nothing for your home and you know you can't get a thing no matter what you do or how you try, well, then you die with nothing. And no one can deny that arithmetic.***

Although suburban children see adults in the neighborhood going to and from work each day, they have little or no contact with the facts of adult employment. To the suburban child, the policeman is an image of authority for good; that is, the policeman protects the child from those who might hurt him. The policeman is a "good guy," an outlook which is in sharp contrast to that of the slum child. Affected by the overall hidden curriculum of the middle class, one is likely to have misconceptions regarding the real world and may not be able to conceive of society as a multiple value, diverse, polyethnic, polycultural rule.

The family is the group with whom the child will spend most of his time. Degree of stability and communication within the family provide stimulation for the development of the child. The family structure tends to differ from subcultural groups to cultural groups. The "extended" family typically includes aunts, uncles, and grandparents, all who may play a vital role in the child's development. This is the common family structure in the black, Puerto Rican, or Indian home as contrasted with the nuclear or more restrictive family structure in middle-class cultural groups. The "extended" family is very likely to have a different effect upon the child's development than a small, restrictive family would.

The broken family has become increasingly common. At present, one out of four American marriages end in divorce, which is common to all classes. Also, divorce, separations, extramarital affairs, and other forms of family destruction are frequently preceded by violence (verbal or physical) between the parents. This involves the children, in that children often feel some guilt, some responsibility for the inability of their parents to get along. The scope of this problem, as it concerns the many children who are born out of wedlock and are reared in fatherless homes, has been delineated by Miller. Home life is another negative aspect of the poor class. Every sixth black child is born out of wedlock, and the mothers of these children must fend for themselves in a hostile world. The plight of these persons has been quite widely publicized in recent years.

Culture also refers to patterns of shared, learned behavior developed as a result of group experiences. A child's formative years are spent in the small world of his family life; therefore, the aspect of culture emphasized here will concern the intimate, interpersonal way of life which is found in the family and in peer groups. Behavioral patterns, values, expectations, and roles of each child in this smaller (family) world reflect the culture of the larger society, but in the formative years of a child's life, his family and peer relationships are his "cultural world."

Bruner (1960) views culture as an amplifier of human sensory, motor, and *ratiocinative* capacities. Yet, as he is willing to acknowledge, relatively little is known about culture as an intellectual amplifier of the

---

*From R. Coles, The New York Times Magazine. 1965, *12*:58. © 1965 by The New York Times Company. Reprinted by permission.

needs of individuals or the demands which culture makes on individuals. "We are, alas, wedded to the idea that human reality exists within the limiting boundary of the human skin." Therefore, culture may be redefined as all the environmental information that affects an individual during his existence.

Culture includes the traditional values and mores of a group, its institutions, its type of structure, and its method of organization. Culture also includes its members' efforts to cope with the surrounding environment. Often, many of these survival techniques are ineffective. The efforts may be ineffectual because of deprivations in the culture which may cause a lack of stimulation in all areas—sensory, vocal, emotional, auditory, and nutritional.

Culture also influences the biological soundness of a child, and this, in turn, affects his behavior. If there is a lack of proper nourishment and sleep, the child is more susceptible to disease, becomes easily tired, and becomes generally rundown. Such conditions prevent him from functioning at his peak.

All organized, patterned behavior results from interaction between the child and his environment. In order for a child to develop properly, the environment or cultural situation should provide sufficient stimulation, security, and permanency in relationships. Culture determines what a child's response to a stimulus will be. If culture inhibits or forbids expression, there is a reduction in feedback to the biological aspects of functioning. There will be a lack of reinforcement of expression, and, eventually, because of negative reinforcement, the child will be less aware and less alert.

The various cultural forces and systems which interact to produce behavioral dysfunctions in children can now be briefly reviewed. A child's behavior is the end result of a complex transaction between his biological system, which processes input, and his culture, from which such input is taken. The culture provides cues concerning relevant patterns of behavior which are absorbed and processed by the child. If either the input system of the individual is not equipped to evaluate information or the environment signals inappropriate information, the output of the individual will be dysfunctional, as judged by the culture. The particular type of behavioral dysfunction is determined by the psychological attributes of the child and by the unique interaction in every individual of cultural and biological forces.

Deprivation: Reception or Expression?

A major issue to be considered in presenting a hypothesis of output reduction or "response deprivation" is an alternative hypothesis, indirectly expressed by Hebb (1969) and Deutsch (1963). It concerns the lack or insufficiency and inadequacy of stimulation of the deprived child. We must distinguish clearly between input deprivation and output reduction. Is the deprived child experiencing both? How does this lack of stimulation occur? Is it possible that input deprivation may occur in the child's earliest stages of development, producing considerable and irreversible effects on his output? Input deprivation plus abuse (Zigler and Harter, 1969) may well produce many intellectual retardates. Conversely, we must consider the presence of overstimulation of an unpatterned, disordered nature. That is, some deprived children will be exposed to noise rather than clear, ordered, and patterned input. A child in this environment may be unable to distinguish figures from background, visually and auditorily. At the other extreme, we must also consider the child who has received sufficient amounts of perceptual stimulation but whose opportunities for response have been blocked, inhibited, and even punished. These circumstances might produce negative feedback to stimulus input and lowering of input levels. Thus, in considering cultural deprivation, we must hypothesize at least five possible combinations of input-output deprivation which will produce different behavioral effects which influence the development of the child, as shown in Table 8–1.

Of course, specific genetic or organic deficits and dysfunctions combined with the possibilities outlined in Table 8–1, would produce even greater stresses on the child than if he were organically intact. Thus, deprivation should be considered from both the input and output aspects of functioning.

With regard to the effects of early experiences on behavior, Denenberg (1969) stated that: (1) genetically based characteristics may be drastically modified by early experiences; (2) early experiences have long-term consequences; (3) early experiences are one major cause of individual differences; (4) early experiences have multiple effects; and (5) the age when stimulation begins is crucial.

Piaget conceived of looking and listening, both of which are viewed as means of sensory input, as existing "ready-made" at birth. Hunt (1964) stated that "Piaget ranks these attributes of key importance during early development of the intellect." The aphorism "The more a child has seen and heard, the more he wants to see and hear" seems to be applicable to Piaget's beliefs. Assuming Piaget to be correct, the disadvantaged child, therefore, comes into the world with the same sensory input channels as the advantaged child. The difference between the two individuals would stem from the kind and degree of input which the two classes of children receive in their early developmental stages. Also pertinent to this notion is the concept of feedback. The advantaged child would typically receive much positive feedback from society, whereas the disadvantaged child would ordinarily receive negative feedback, with the expected accompanying results in each instance.

A perceptual viewpoint presented by Deutsch (1963) suggested that disadvantaged children grow up in an atmosphere of "stimulus depriva-

TABLE 8–1 HYPOTHESIZED COMBINATIONS OF EARLY INPUT-OUTPUT DEPRIVATIONS

Input Opportunities	*Output Opportunities*	*Developmental Consequences*
Lacking or insufficient	Minimal or abused	Severe retardation
Present but disordered	Punished or inhibited	Severe behavioral disorders (autism, schizophrenia)
Present	Restricted	Lowering of intellectual functioning and inhibition of learning process
Present and various	Slightly rewarded	Normalcy
Pleasant and various	Extremely rewarded	Superiority in specific or all areas of functioning

tion" and that this creates for the child

> . . .few opportunities to manipulate and organize the visual properties of his environment and thus perceptually to organize and discriminate the nuances of that environment. These would include figure-ground relationships and the spatial organization of the visual field. The sparsity of manipulable objects probably also hampers the development of these functions in the tactile area. For example, while these children have broomsticks and usually a ball, possibly a doll or a discarded kitchen pot to play with, they don't have the different shapes and colors and sizes to manipulate, which the middle-class child has in the form of blocks which are bought just for him, or even in the variety of sizes and shapes of cooking utensils which might be available to him as playthings.

Morans and Lourie (1967) contended that in many instances deprived infants suffer from excessive and inconsistent stimuli which frequently force the child to retreat from his environment in order to survive. They noted that too much diffuse stimulation (e.g., noise, family quarrels, or TV) is often the problem rather than too little stimulation, although they recognized that the latter problem, too, is decidedly a factor for some children. They also held that "multiple mothering," a situation in which the child is alternately cared for by the mother, big sister, aunt, grandmother, and neighbor, can negatively affect the child's ability to maintain meaningful relationships, an ability which he needs in order to attain intellectual and emotional maturity. Examples from Morans and Lourie could be extensively expanded, but their findings are cited here merely to illustrate some early environmental influences which negatively affect the disadvantaged child.

Deprivation or Disadvantage?

Morans and Lourie (1967) tended to believe that the disadvantaged child frequently must devote all his energy to the performance of a few functions which are essential to his survival and that "these techniques constitute a premature consolidation of reaction patterns that tend to preclude modification by later experience." They proceeded to hypothesize that typical life patterns of the disadvantaged child must be interrupted early enough by the kind of environmental stimulation which will succeed in breaking the cycle. They suggested that this intervention must begin in the child's prenatal period with adequate medical care, nutritional balance, and a reasonable degree of emotional stability in the home. To accomplish any widespread change in life patterns of disadvantaged persons will admittedly take generations.

Frost and Hawkes (1966) stated:

> In an educational context, 'disadvantaged' refers to children with a particular set of educationally associated problems arising from and residing extensively within the culture of the poor. This is not to say that other cultural groups within society escape similar problems, but that the ills restricting the intellectual, social, and physical growth of children tend to be concentrated here. We may change the name, but the problems remain, passing from generation to generation and sustained by discrimination, lack of opportunity, and an exploding population.

By this definition, cultural deprivation or disadvantage is inherently linked with poverty, wherever it may exist. It must be noted, however, that being poor does not necessitate being culturally deprived, whereas cultural deprivation almost always occurs in association with poverty.

Morans and Lourie (Hellmuth, 1968a) described the disadvantaged child as one who is "deprived of the same opportunity for healthy growth and development which is available to the vast majority of the other members of the larger society in which he lives." Telford and Sawrey (1967) stated that "individuals may function inadequately either because they lack the potentiality for learning or because of inadequate or inappropriate experiential backgrounds. The latter are the culturally disadvantaged." Thus, the disadvantaged may be said to be all those persons who are born into a culture of poverty which affords little opportunity for advancement and which is essentially out of touch with the mainstream of middle-class American culture.

Relationships Between Biological and Environmental Factors

In a series of studies in a North African, underdeveloped country, Boutourline-Young et al. (1968) found that height, weight, skeletal development, and other fine indices of physical and intellectual growth are directly related to socioeconomic background. The middle-class child of the North African country is lower in all these measurements than an American child of comparable chronological age. The lower class child in that and other underprivileged countries is lower in all these measurements than his counterpart in the higher socioeconomic classes. These findings are supported by work with Mexican children done by Birch and Gassow (1970). These studies clearly indicate the effect that nutrition and diet, both resultants of the physical environment, may have on the biological and psychological growth of the child. Lower social class typically correlates with smaller children of lower intellectual functioning who have greater susceptibility to infection and disease. Longevity and mortality rates may well be affected by socioeconomic class. According to the data of Redlich (1957), there is also evidence to indicate that the lower the socioeconomic level, the greater the incidence of psychiatric breakdown. Pasamanick and Knoblock (1960) also found a greater incidence of neurological defects in lower class children. Thus, at birth, even though body weight may be the same for children of different socioeconomic levels, we cannot presume that these children are the same. Even if they were, early feeding histories are convincing evidence that the diet of lower class children may be inadequate.

Kosa et al. (1969) found that in our society, the poor receive different care for physical as well as for psychiatric disorders than the higher socioeconomic classes do. Children of lower socioeconomic status are systematically rejected from traditional child guidance clinics which are not equipped, conceptually and emotionally, to deal with the problems of the deprived child (L'Abate, 1969d).

Brain Damage and Environmental Deprivations

Predictions regarding whether patterns of functioning are the result of brain damage or cultural deprivation may differ. Any diffuse neurological defect will result in decreased visual discrimination (Reitan, 1962; Parsons, 1970), unless, of course, the damage is specifically in the left hemisphere. In this case, language functions will be more directly decreased. Damage to the right hemisphere, however, will produce a different pattern; manual performance (visual-motor problem solving will be more directly affected. Cultural deprivation will primarily affect verbal output. Thus, if these two output functions (verbal and motor) were to be assessed by the same test, such as the Wechsler scale, two different patterns would result: diffuse brain damage would be indicated by a higher verbal I.Q. than performance I.Q.; cultural deprivations would be indicated by a lower verbal I.Q. than performance I.Q.

When damage is specifically localized in the left hemisphere, verbal I.Q. is lower than performance I.Q. At this point, a differential diagnosis could be made to determine whether the problem is a communication disorder due to organic brain damage or a communication disorder due to cultural deprivation. Input in the verbal area would become the most differentiating pattern. Left hemisphere brain damage would be indicated by low input and low output. In cultural deprivation, the auditory input would be near average (depending on age), and the verbal output would be low.

In a group of 80 children with neurological learning disability syndromes (minimal brain damage), Silver (1970) found that four times as many were adopted as compared with a population of normal children. The reason for such an incidence can only be speculative, since adoption agencies do not allow any retrospective analysis of their records. Can these learning disabilities be attributed to less than adequate prenatal care and diet, increased stress on the mother, her socioeconomic level, and her state of health? The answers to such questions involve the consistent overlap among biological, cultural, and psychological forces.

McDermott et al. (1967) failed to find any differences in the incidence of psychosis among five social class groups (professional-executive, upper white-collar, skilled labor, and unskilled labor). They discounted the role of social class as being an important factor in the diagnosis of psychosis in children at their clinic. However, they felt that the expression—the modality through which the psychotic illness appeared—correlated with social class. Severe withdrawal and autism occurred significantly more often in the professional-executive group. Disturbances of thinking occurred significantly more often in both professional-executive and skilled labor groups. They suggested that these findings could be attributed to family styles and customs of child-rearing that may influence the expression of psychosis.

McDermott et al. (1967) discovered that occupation was related to the frequency with which they diagnosed chronic brain damage and mental retardation, despite the fact that no correlations were found between the frequencies of these diagnoses and other historical and clinical data which are usually related to such diagnoses. Secondly, they found the lowest incidence of diagnosed chronic brain syndrome and retardation in the lowest occupational class, where it is usually anticipated that one would find the highest incidence of both diagnoses. Most serious defects of intellectual, organic functioning were somewhat evenly distributed among the various social classes.

Connally (1969) found that the home of the brain-damaged child had a less relaxed atmosphere and that there were greater differences between the mother and the father than in the homes of normal children. The home of the brain-damaged child was less democratic, with the parents expressing omnipotent control over the child. Unfortunately, this and other studies cannot answer the question of whether it is the presence of the brain-damaged child that produces such reactions in parents, as any kind of prolonged and intense stress eventually could.

Sex Differences and Cultural Emphases

Repucci (1969) found that performance on cognitive tasks by two-year-old girls was related to parental education; however, the same relationship did not apply to boys. Two possible interpretations were considered by Repucci. One concerned the interaction between biological and environmental contingencies, and the other considered no biological and environmental assumptions. The latter interpretation is based on the fact that mothers treat their daughters (offspring of the same sex) differently from the way they treat their sons. Using either interpretation, Repucci concluded that his results, together with those of other investigators, "strengthen the conviction that girls are more susceptible to environmental influence than boys and (are) affected by it earlier."

Bell's review (1969) indicated that there are sexual differences in the child-mother relationship which may well explain, in part, the significantly higher frequency of problem behaviors in boys than in girls.

Cultural Deprivations and Behavioral Disturbances

Society refers to the network of interrelated roles which exists among people in an organized group, such as a family. Culture refers to the particular patterns of behavior prescribed and proscribed by the various roles which make up society. *Culture is concerned with values and society with relationships among people.* If a child is biologically sound, he will absorb the values of his culture through socialization, and these values will be reflected in his behavior. Thus, culture shapes the personality of a child. The most effective social institution for the transmission of culture is the family, in which the child's personality is molded through numerous interactions with parents and siblings. The child's intelligence, perceptions, *affects,* and abilities are, to a great degree, a function of his family's social class. The behavioral dysfunctions of a disadvantaged child can often be improved by eliminating the inadequacies of his environment. These behavioral dysfunctions are not genuine emotional disturbances, but rather they are the results of cultural deprivation. Behavioral dysfunctions in children are the results of cultural and biological deficiencies.

The Influence of the Family on the Child

For many years, many theorists believed that the basis of a child's pathology stemmed from the family setting. Contemporary theory attributes much psychopathology in children to the behavior of parents, especially the mother. Although in many cases, parental deviations contribute to problem behavior in their children, these parental behaviors should be judged on an equivalent basis—as being caused, in part, by the child's behavior. We can no longer assume, as it has been assumed for a long time, that parents are responsible, guilty, and to be "blamed" for their child's behavior (Tulkin, 1968). Such assumptions derive from psychoanalytical or psychodynamic inferences which are independent of empirical evidence. When, in addition to Bell (1969) and Thomas et al. (1968), one considers Frank's (1965) skeptical review of any possible connection between parental pathology and the child's behavior, much caution and suspension of judgment seems to be needed in dealing with this matter.

Ferster (1958) stated that "... most of the behavior of an organism exists because of its effect on the environment," that is, a given instance of behavior causes a particular event to occur. Most human behavior is social because it has its effect on other people, who, in turn, arrange contingent reinforcements. Thus, through differential reinforcements, an individual's behavior is shaped or can be modified. Such interactional processes influence feeding disorders, speech disorders, language development, intellectual dysfunctions, learning disorders, and juvenile delinquency.

Stressing the importance of familial relations, Verville (1967) listed individual differences, such as sex, intelligence, and physical health, as important behavioral determinants. Size of family, the child's ordinal position, whether he is an only child, a twin, a stepchild, adopted, or illegitimate are also factors of importance. Whether there are other relatives in the home, the values and customs of the family, and its race and ethnicity must also be considered. Other social factors affecting behavior are socioeconomic status, neighbors, and permanency of the home, school, and church.

Under the heading of interpersonal determinants of behavioral dysfunctions, Verville listed:

1. Fixation of immaturity. Immaturity is fixated in a child by prolonged, unnecessary care, by immediate availability of the parent to assist and comfort, and by restriction of the child's associations and freedom of action. Overprotective parents fail to understand the effect of stress on the child's growth. They are motivated by a desire to mold the child into a perfect testimonial of their excellence as parents, by long-standing habits of domination, or by a need to bind the child in a too close relationship of affection, appreciation, and companionship.

2. Neglect. A parent's neglect is motivated by fatigue, self-concern, or feelings of inadequacy as a parent or as a spouse.

3. Unbalanced social experience. A child, whose association with his peers is rare; warped by constant contact with children who are younger, older, or of the opposite sex; or subject to the interference of siblings or parents, fails to acquire social behavior appropriate for his age and sex.

4. Fatigue. The fatigued child achieves at an inferior level, and his actions are imitative, rather than spontaneous or original. He reacts to pressure with avoidance and negativism, and he may regress to earlier forms of behavior.

5. Rejection of responsibility. Irresponsibility occurs in the child who remains inexperienced in working at home, studying at school, and earning and spending money appropriately.

6. Distortion of parental role. Distortions may occur in any one of five forms: (a) reversal of mother-father roles, (b) absence of a parent, (c) reversal of parent-child roles, (d) identification of the spouse with a child, and (e) parental assumption of peer status with the child.

7. Damaged self-respect. A child's opinion of himself is based on his parents' opinions of him, and he must have parental confirmation of his worth in order to achieve self-respect. Parents who damage their child's self-respect are usually those who do not respect themselves.

8. Excessive punishment. When punishment serves to intimidate the child or to provide an outlet for adult aggression, it fails in its intended purposes, and the child develops personality and behavioral problems as a direct result of the punishment.

9. Freedom to defy and attack. The child learns self-control only if he first learns to accede to the control of adults who are responsible for

him. Aggressive and self-centered behavior which is not curtailed becomes habitual and is retained as the individual's sole mode of reaction.

Senn and Hartford (1968) believed that there are six distinct aspects of family life that operate as "catalytic forces" upon the child: (1) parental expectations for the child and their feelings concerning expectations fulfilled by the child; (2) communication, regularity and flexibility of scheduling, techniques of management, relation of expectation to behavior, and paternal behavior; (3) socioeconomic status and extended family and spatial arrangements; (4) marital and familial relationships and personality characteristics involved in coping with anxiety and hostility, dependency and sense of security, feelings of adequacy, planning and impulsiveness, and self assertion; (5) emergence of family integration patterns, such as family structure, division of labor and balance of power, and developmental achievement; and (6) social behavior of the child, prospect of possible siblings, and family status in the community.

The Influence of Deprivation on the Family

Families in a disadvantaged community usually: (1) are large, with other relatives living in the home; (2) are missing one parent, usually the father due to death, desertion, illegitimacy, or divorce, thus leaving a female as head of the house; (3) are in a very low economic status; (4) are lacking in close interpersonal relationships; (5) cannot provide consistent care for the children; (6) are lacking in adequate models for the children to imitate; (7) use poor language patterns; (8) are subject to frequent moving; (9) suffer from poor nutrition; (10) are economically insecure; (11) are disadvantaged by parents who (if present) work long hours; (12) experience less sibling rivalry than higher classes do; (13) are more vocationally than academically oriented; (14) employ inconsistent discipline; (15) use physical punishment; and (16) have inadequate facilities. Any combination of these factors will have effects on the behavior of the family members.

The effects of poverty become evident early and accumulate throughout life. In the deprived home, the mother has little time or energy to talk or play with the baby. Thus, early in his life, the child is deprived of auditory, tactual, or visual stimulation. Hebb (1969) believed that the deprived child experiences insufficient stimulation in his early development and that this deficiency accounts for his lower intellectual functioning when he grows older. Lack of stimulation may lead to inferior auditory and visual discrimination, as well as general perceptual difficulties.

There seems to be a characteristic pattern of interaction in a disadvantaged family. The environment of this type of family is usually noisy and disorganized. Although the quantity of input is generally not deficient, the quality and variety of it is. The environment in such homes is often so haphazard and distracting that selection of stimuli which are relevant to cognitive development is inhibited (Ellis, 1963b).

Most of the mother's energy is spent in coping with her children, rather than in giving positive reinforcement and encouragement to them. The mother, because of her unfortunate situation, also has fewer opportunities to relate to her children than her middle-class counterpart. The disadvantaged child probably receives greater reinforcement from peers and siblings than from his parents, who are engrossed in other activities. Reinforcement which these children receive is more often conducive to inhibitory rather than exploratory behavior; that is, behavior conducive to cognitive growth is inhibited, and behavior that makes coping easier for the mother is rewarded. These patterns of interaction in disadvantaged families are, perhaps, the real source of cultural deprivation and the behavioral problems associated with it.

Another factor contributing to deprivation of the disadvantaged child is family disorganization (e.g., mother-headed families, divorce, desertion, separation, and illegitimacy). How does this situation affect male members of these families? Confused masculine identity and a subsequent drive toward exaggerated masculinity are often the results of family disorganization. Several writers, including Moynihan (1966) and Grier and Cobb (1968), have discussed the use of sexual prowess as the one recourse by which the disadvantaged male may assert his masculine identity. Overemphasis on pseudomasculinity may also result from self-hatred and low self-esteem which have been shown to exist (Deutsch et al., 1967) in disadvantaged children early in life.

A striking similarity in the way of life of disadvantaged people is evident when comparing Oscar Lewis' portrayal (1961) of life and people in the slums of Mexico City with the life of urban black Americans. The overcrowded homes, the transiency of marital bonds, and the precocity of sexual interests and activity among the children are variables that may affect all poverty cultures. Pavenstedt (1965) gave this description of a disorganized family:

> **The outstanding characteristic in these homes was that activities were impulse-determined; consistency was totally absent. The mother might stay in bed until around noon while the children were also kept in bed or ran around unsupervised. Although families sometimes ate breakfast or dinner together, there was no pattern for anything. The parent, incensed by the behavior of one child, was seen dealing a blow to another child who was closer. Communication by means of words hardly existed. Directions were indefinite or hung unfinished in mid-air. Reprimands were often high-pitched and angry. . . . As the children outgrew babyhood, the parents differentiated very little between parent and child roles. The parents' needs were as pressing and as often indulged as were those of the children. There was strong competition for the attention of helpful adults.**

Malone (1963) discussed the behavior of preschool children from disorganized, slum families. These children showed low frustration tolerance, impulsivity, and unreliable controls; dominant use of motor action for discharge; language retardation; a tendency to employ concrete thinking; need-satisfying object relations; and little evidence of constructive play or use of imitation. Malone also noted other factors typical of these children, such as their poor concept of time, magical thinking, lack of "object constancy" in the home, and restriction of motor activity in the crowded homes.

The disadvantaged child often develops anxiety because he does not know how to behave in order to please all those who care for him. He seeks to force others to pay attention to him by various methods of misbehavior. Often, he may be lonely, withdrawn, and depressed. The anxiety he feels will impede his intellectual development, and his verbal and manual skills will suffer. Because he feels rejected and unwanted, he will avoid being hurt further.

In the disadvantaged home, parents or adults often fail to require the child to meet any responsibilities. When the child is not required to accept responsibility, he feels that nothing is expected of him, and he ceases to try. He sees little value in working in school, so he becomes an underachiever. He refuses to try new things because he is afraid of failing and limits himself to only those things that he knows he can do.

Because of crowding in the home, a child at age two is likely to find himself in the way of older people, and his activities become severely restricted (Deutsch et al., 1967). The mobility of the deprived family also increases his insecurity. If moves are made because of adult instability, the child suffers from impermanency and uncertainty.

Adolescent gangs are created by a need for union of peers who suffer frustrations and loss of self-esteem in the home and school. Gangs give the adolescent a degree of status and acceptance which allows him to acquire a feeling of superiority when he engages in antisocial behavior. Assault is practiced because the child is accustomed to that form of behavior as it has been used against him. Adolescent gangs and their activities are the result of deprivation in all areas. Thus, culture and all that it entails has a great effect on the child from birth throughout his lifetime. The effects are compounded as the child grows older, and they will influence all areas of his functioning.

Adults who neglect to commend a child for his worth as a person will soon damage the child's self-respect. Often in deprived families, there is little time spent commending each child. The parents do not express acceptance or approval of the child and do not let him take on responsibilities because they do not think he has adequate ability or judgment. Feelings of inferiority may lead to withdrawal or aggression in the child. He may grow to hate his parents and may take revenge on others, or he may take the role assigned to him, that of being useless—"no good." This type of parent often fosters delinquency in his children.

Excessive punishment, which is often practiced among the underprivileged, leads the child to believe that adults disapprove of him and consider him worthless. If a child is punished for every act, he will soon lose the ability to know what is simply an error in correct behavior and what is truly incorrect behavior. He will relinquish his self-control and behave in unpredictable and uninhibited ways when his parents are not present to control him.

Often in disadvantaged homes, discipline is absent or, at best, inconsistent. Lack of consistent discipline leaves the child free to be aggressive and self-centered. A child learns self-control from adults who care about him and take responsibility for him. If adults permit, reward, defend, or encourage misconduct, it will continue. When a child exhibits antisocial behavior, it may be that it is the only kind of behavior that he knows; he may be unaware of many moral concepts of behavior. He may feel anxiety because he is his own "boss" and is solely responsible for his behavior.

THE MOTHER-CHILD RELATIONSHIP. Ecological research, of the type performed by Cravioto et al. (1967), describes early transactions that occur between mother and child at the biological and cultural levels. Size of the infant at birth is not only related to the size of the mother, which in itself is related to socioeconomic factors, but also to her personal hygiene. These authors summarized their research with underprivileged Mexican mothers and children by stating:

> **Since the biological characteristics of the mother vary in accordance with her social status, both the biological condition of the mother and the environmental circumstances associated with it are inevitably related to fetal and neonatal growth.**

This type of research clearly indicates that no child can be considered as a biological system independent of cultural forces. The peculiar combination and integration of both biological and cultural forces produce a unique outcome which is the individual's psychological system.

Escalona (1968) showed how biological and cultural forces interact in a unique manner. Physiologically, even normal infants differ from one another in excitability, which is a biological property of the organism. Maturational advances are dependent on the infant's self-generated activities, that is, his responsiveness to sensory-motor stimulation in the immediate environment. He seeks out stimulation from the environment, and if he does not receive it from outside sources, he will probably attempt to obtain it from self-generated activities (e.g., rocking or mannerisms):

> **. . . it is the interaction between various aspects of a particular social milieu and such intrinsic factors as age, endowment, previous experience, and inborn reaction tendencies that accounts for the variable consequences for development of any one aspect of experience (Escalona, 1968).**

Escalona noted how infants vary in modality preference (e.g., auditory versus visual, kinesthetic versus auditory) and how mothers also show preferences for certain modalities (talking to a child rather than moving him, singing rather than touching). In some cases, there is congruence between the modalities used by both mother and child; however, in other cases, such congruence is not present, and there may well be conflict between modality preference in the child and in the mother:

> **. . . babies who . . . used their eyes and ears more often and more intensely than others also tended to be the ones whose test performances were superior for their age. . . . The prominence of the visual and auditory spheres in the infant's day-by-day experiences is only partly dictated by the richness of stimulation in these modalities (Escalona, 1968).**

Thus, the mother can stimulate, overstimulate, neglect, or deprive one modality more than others, reinforcing receptive, expressive, or auditory-verbal functions at the expense of visual-motor or other functions.

Situations within the family which lead to deviant behavior in children usually focus on the mother. Because of a child's extreme dependence on his mother from the time of his birth, any inadequacies or deficiencies in her behavior are reflected, to some degree, in the child's personality. An inadequate mother usually exhibits one of two behavioral patterns: she is either oversolicitous for the child's needs or cold and rejecting toward the child (Mahler, 1968). Either type of mother tends to promote a relationship which inhibits normal personality development in the child. Maternal rejection or overprotection may lead to defects in social relationships (autism), in perception of reality (psychosis), in cognitive development (intellectual retardation), or in conscience (psychopathic personality).

Maternal rejection has been associated with childhood behavioral problems involving feeding, toilet training, and aggression. The latter behavior may result from either extreme punishment or overpermissiveness, as emphasized in a study on child-rearing practices (Sears et al., 1957). Radke (1946) stressed the important fact that children tend to identify with authoritarian parents. Children in such families responded to the rigidity and excessive punishment of their parents by displaying aggression and insensitive behavior toward their peers. Kanner (1944) described the mothers of some autistic children as being cold, rigid, and overly intellectual. Because of these defects in the mother's character structure, the child is unable to develop an emotional relationship with her, and, consequently, the child is incapable of relating to other people.

Bowlby (1951) stressed the severe intellectual and emotional impairment which results from disruption or distortion of the mother-child relationship during the child's infancy. Endogenous retardation, psychogenic retardation, and pseudoretardation are some of the terms used to describe retardation which stems from deprivation of maternal care in the child's first year of life. It is just as debilitating as organic retardation, yet it is attributable to a cultural situation arising within the family. Spitz's (1963) views regarding the deleterious effects of institutionalization and maternal deprivation corroborate Bowlby's thesis, as does the work of Provence and Lipton (1962).

The findings of Lewis (1954) and Goldfarb (1955) support the findings of both Bowlby and Spitz that prolonged separation of the mother from the infant promotes behavioral dysfunctioning and intellectual retardation in the child. Goshen (1963) hypothesized that severe maternal depression during the child's first year of life is a functional cause of intellectual retardation. Gerard (1953) stressed the role of a hostile, rejecting mother in the etiology of psychosomatic disorders. Rank (1949a) developed the concept of the schizophrenogenic mother; her immature, narcissistic personality is viewed as the primary cause of childhood disturbances. Levy (1943) described two basic patterns of maternal overprotectiveness: overindulgence, which leads to a submissive, dependent, and passive child; and domination, which is associated with an imma-

Figure 8–2 Children at a foundling home in Iran. All are above three years of age and mentally normal, yet only a few can stand or walk. (Courtesy of Professor Wayne Dennis, Brooklyn College, Brooklyn, N.Y.) (From Whittaker, J. O.: Introduction to Psychology. Philadelphia, W. B. Saunders Company, 1970.)

Figure 8–3 The role of the mother in the development of the dysfunctioning child is crucial. (From Smith and Wilson: The Child with Down's Syndrome. Philadelphia, W. B. Saunders Company, 1973.)

ture, disobedient, and temperamental child. The anxious mother tends to develop an excessively close relationship with the infant which prolongs his dependence and helplessness. Mahler (1955) stated that maternal *psychopathology* is the major cause of *symbiotic psychoses.* Although this view was later modified to include a child's constitutional predisposition as a causative factor, Mahler still emphasized the role of the psychopathogenic, overprotective mother. Bruch (1958) associated excessive solicitude and overprotectiveness in the mother with childhood obesity. She theorized that an obese child tries to compensate for his feelings of inferiority and dependence by excessive eating. Johnson (1941) suggested that an anxious mother communicates her own feelings of dependence to her child. Such feelings produce anxiety in the child over separation from his mother which, in turn, causes school phobia. The role of a dominating, controlling mother in the etiology of learning disturbances has also been emphasized. Such behavior supposedly leads to an irresponsible, dependent child, who lacks the initiative and motivation to achieve in the classroom. An overly close relationship with the mother has also been hypothesized as a source of psychosomatic disorders (Arthur, 1963). All this evidence, taken together, supports the theory that the overprotective mother, just like the rejecting mother, precipitates a variety of behavioral dysfunctions in children.

The mother's role in the development of a dysfunctioning child is greatly stressed because of the frequency and intensity of mother-child interactions. However, various patterns of parental interaction with siblings, which include both mother and father, have been related to childhood disorders. For instance, with regard to the etiology of schizophrenia, Bateson et al. (1956) indicated isolation of the child, which arises from the ambivalence and uncertainty of his relationship with his parents, as a probable cause of the illness. The feeling of isolation arises from contradictory parental directives, which involve sanctions whether the child obeys or disobeys the directive. This type of situation is referred to as the "double-bind" hypothesis. Other researchers have noted the deleterious effect of inconsistent patterns of parent-child interaction. Glueck and Glueck (1950) reported that consistency of parental discipline is a more important factor in conscience formation than relative amount of leniency or strictness. Contradiction in communication, changing moods, dual standards of treatment, and marital disagreements are all ways in which parents are inconsistent in their relationships with their children. Frequent, pronounced inconsistencies in parental behavior make it difficult for children to form any stable image of the environment and what to expect from it. This confusion leads to anxiety and withdrawal reactions whenever such children are presented with novel situations (Sandler, 1957). The role of the mother and the family unit, especially among the middle and upper classes, is perhaps the principal cultural factor in the etiology of childhood behavioral dysfunctions. Of course, a woman's inadequacy as a mother is largely dependent on her relationship with her husband.

THE FATHER-CHILD RELATIONSHIP. The role of the father in the formation and functioning of the family is much greater than present theories imply. As the work of Robins (1966) and Barry's review (1970) have attested, the father's position is crucial to the well-being of the whole family.

Most past literature has emphasized the mother-child relationship, to the point of nearly excluding the father (Nash, 1965). However, a recent integrative review by Biller (1968) indicated the father's importance in the child's development. The family is as strong and as adequate as the father. He determines the quality of interaction with his wife which decidedly influences the quality of interaction that she, in turn, will have with the child. Similarly, the mother has an effect on the father's relationship with the child. These relationships involving both parents suggest the sobering thought that from a systems viewpoint a great deal of research focusing strictly and narrowly on the mother-child relationship is inadequate if the father is not taken into consideration. As long as the father and his crucial role are omitted, our understanding of child development will remain incomplete. Any future research or rehabilitative efforts may need to consider the family as a whole if any adequate understanding of the father-child relationship is to be revealed.

Often, in the disadvantaged family, the male adult figure is missing. His absence has a greater impact on the male children of the family than on the females, since the principal means by which a child learns how to act is by imitation of the parent of the same sex. Strong psychosexual identification is a basic index of personal adequacy and emotional stability.

At times, the father of a disadvantaged family remains unimportant to his wife and children because the mother is the one who is able to keep a job and provide for the family. Often, she, rather than the father, is the power figure, and, consequently, the male child does not have an adequate male model, thus perpetuating the system of maternal power and male irresponsibility. The burden of the underprivileged male may cause severe psychological effects. His self-esteem will tend to be quite precarious, if he cannot support his family, be an effective parent, or even challenge the matriarchal power in the family structure.

Also, if there is no father image, the boy's view of achievement, competition, and masculinity becomes distorted. If the life of a grown man appears not to be appealing to the child, why should he work in school or want to grow up to be a man? The fatherless child may also develop traits that are not masculine because of the lack of a male model. This inadequacy may isolate him from his peers, and he may react to the isolation by easily resorting to aggressive acts.

An inadequate father-daughter relationship may eventually be the cause of the daughter's inability to choose adequate male partners or to achieve prolonged heterosexual relationships. She may tend to perpetuate with males the same type of interpersonal patterns learned from her father. The absence of the father-daughter relationship may exacerbate future male-female relationships in the life of the female child.

CHAPTER 9

EDUCABLE MENTAL RETARDATION

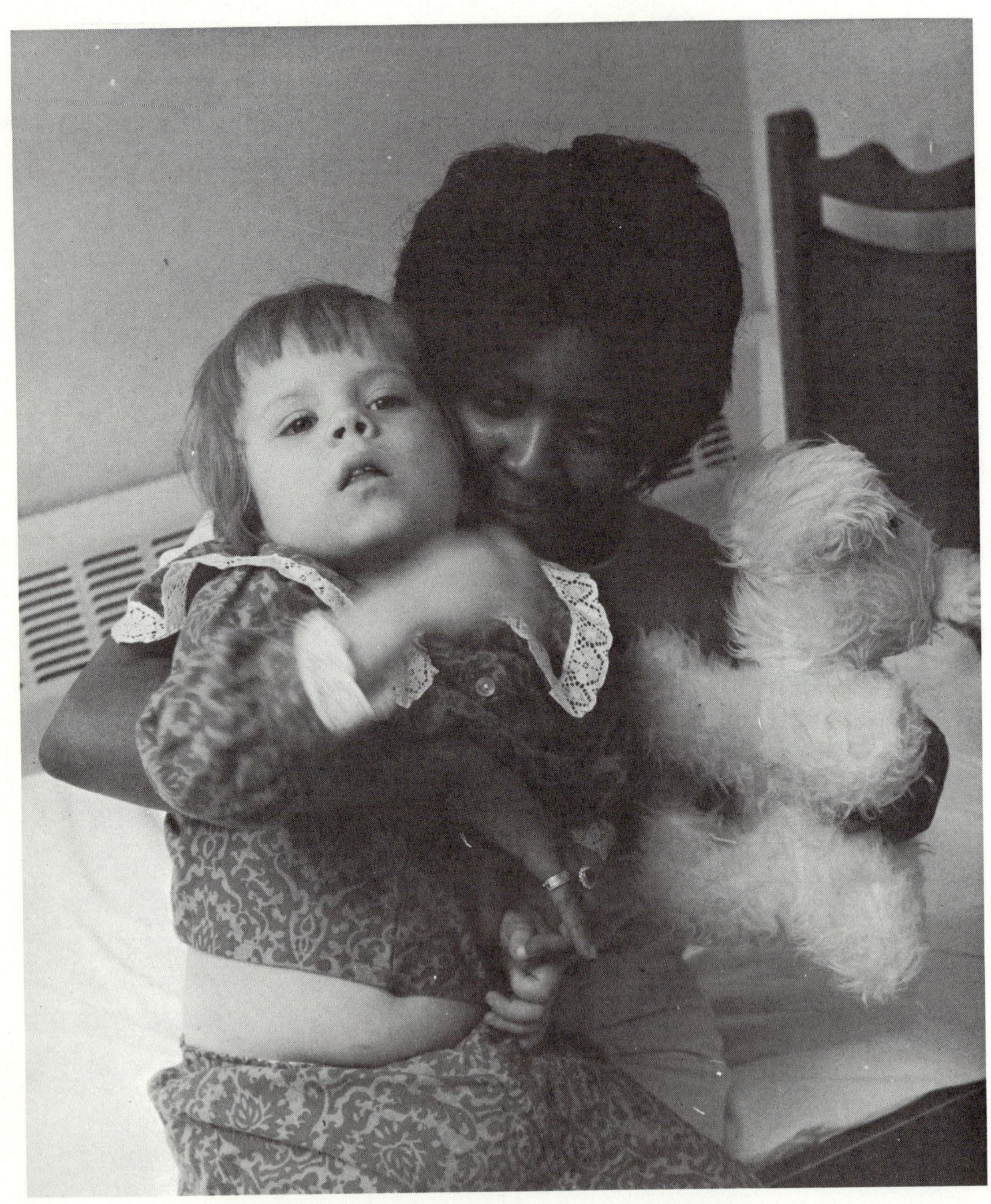

(Courtesy of The Woods Schools, Langhorne, Pennsylvania.)

In this chapter we shall focus on the segment of the retarded population designated as the educable mentally retarded (EMR), by far the largest group of retardates. Dingman and Tarjan (1960) estimated that there are at least five million individuals in our population at this level of intellectual retardation. Cultural-familial or educable mental retardation (IQ 50 to 75) has long been a subject of controversy. Most definitions exclude the presence of physiological impairment. The two major aspects in dispute are genetics and unknown environmental factors. While heredity is definitely thought to play a major role in determining a person's intellectual capacity – a capacity no one ever fully utilizes – diagnostic procedures (IQ testing) constitute a bias for a particular cultural background, therefore making it difficult to determine those specific social or cultural factors which might have an influence on intellect.

FAMILIAL MENTAL RETARDATION: RETARDATION OR DIFFERENTNESS?

Intelligence and achievement tests are biased toward an analytical, *conceptual style* of testing which predominantly suits the middle- and upper-class western cultures. The educational establishment and society as a whole view the *analytical mode* as the most desirable and, therefore, the correct mode of testing. Perhaps this is a culturally biased value judgment. In the same way that gifted children are often not superior in IQ but perform outstandingly in specific areas (Chapter 15), familial retardates, especially borderline cases, may not be determined to be average by IQ tests (analytical measurement) but might be average in other areas.

Most *familial retardation* occurs in low socioeconomic and culturally poor environments. Since most retardates fall into the familial category (Harper, 1962), there is an urgent need to investigate further the correlations between economic level and IQ. Heredity, according to Jensen (1973), may be the main factor influencing IQ. His study indicated a high rate of family members in the upper ranges of the mental retardation classification. He neglected, however, to consider the possible cultural, ethnic, or social background which these same family members had in common. Zigler (1967) proposed that possibly a motivational or emotional component in different cultural and social groups may influence IQ test results. Considerable research has been conducted to attempt to substantiate the hypothesis that there are cultural and social influences which might influence IQ test results. However, correlation of these factors does not mean that the causes of the problem have been found. To assume that it does is a major methodological shortcoming which must be taken into account.

Several studies have been carried out by Cohen and her coworkers to determine cultural and social influences on skills measured by IQ tests (which are the primary evaluative tools for categorizing the mentally retarded). Although she did not specifically use mental retardates in her studies, Cohen reported a possible correlation between socioeconomic level, primary group characteristics which dominate at this level, and skills necessary for success in taking IQ tests (Cohen, 1968a; 1968b).

Cohen analyzed the "ten most widely used" intelligence and achievement tests to determine their generic requirements for success. The three characteristics typically necessary for success in the tests were found to be: (a) breadth and depth of information, (b) analytic abstraction, and (c) field articulation. The latter two requirements can be obscured by the informational context in which they are being measured and can require a specific approach to selecting and organizing information. Although individuals differ in their methods of selecting and organizing information or in their conceptual styles, these tests and public schools require one specific approach to organization—the analytical. Those who tend to use a different approach may become underachievers and, eventually, dropouts.

A different conceptual style has been described as "relational" or "self-centered" as opposed to the "stimulus-centered" characteristic of the analytical style (Kagan, 1965). Other distinctions of both styles were summarized by Cohen (1968a). She postulated that the preponderance of certain social characteristics, associated with organizational characteristics which reflect the relational style, are the "result of different social environments that stimulate, reinforce and make functional the development of one style of conceptual organization and constrain and inhibit others" (1968b). Primary group structures and other environmental factors which seem to be characteristic of those employing the relational and analytical styles are also summarized by Cohen.

One of the main problems encountered in the definition of familial mental retardation has been the lack of studies using comparable tests to relate familial mental retardation to cognitive style. Considering the controversy over the validity of intelligence measurement as indicative of actual cognitive capacity, further study is needed to determine what these tests measure and if there are cultural and social biases inherent in them, as Cohen found. The possible correlation between cognitive or conceptual style and variables, such as socioeconomic status, age, and sex, should also be further investigated. No test has yet been devised to measure the functional efficiency of cognitive styles differing from the analytical mode. Besides these relatively new areas of inquiry, a duplication of the Cohen study might prove to be helpful. With further study in these areas, perhaps the relationships (if any) between socioeconomic level and IQ score, socioeconomic level and mental retardation, mental retardation and IQ scores, and different conceptual styles can be better understood.

THE EFFECTS OF LOW SOCIOECONOMIC STATUS

The phrase, "culture of poverty," was coined by Harrington (1962), who wrote: "Poverty in the United States is a culture, an institution, a way of life." Despair, apathy, hopelessness, and no identification with middle-class values are characteristics of the disadvantaged. In a study by Tulkin (1968), correlations were found between race (black, white), class, family background, and school achievement. He found that when social class was the control, racial differences were found in both achievement scores and family characteristics. However, when family differences were also statistically controlled, there were no significant racial differences on achievement scores in the upper socioeconomic group, although differences remained significant in the lower socioeconomic group. One reason for this difference was proposed in a study by Pettigrew (1964), which maintained that the economic "floor" of lower-class blacks is distinctively below that of whites. In other words, regardless of the impoverished socioeconomic level, blacks are always at a distinct disadvantage because of their generally depreciated status in the culture. Some characteristics of the disadvantaged father-mother *dyad* follow:

1. Lack of communication which may develop into a couple's "losing each other" for weeks or even years after a relationship which may have produced several children.
2. Depreciation of each other as discussed by Grier and Cobb in Black Rage, in which the man and woman view themselves as devalued objects and promote the self-depreciation of one another in their interpersonal relationship.
3. A concept of children as objects or commodities, with little feeling of involvement or genuine concern, especially on the part of the father.
4. Uncertain delineation of parents' and children's roles and a type of involvement similar to a peer relationship.
5. Escape to a fantasy life that seems to stem from a sense of impotence regarding the ability to control their own lives.
6. Much involvement by neighbors and relatives which diffuses the parent-child relationship but provides protection for the individual.
7. A life style requiring immediate gratification of needs, a pattern which is associated with much acting-out.
8. Lack of interpersonal involvement beyond the sexual level.

Jensen (1968) summarized the effects of cultural disadvantage on learning as follows:

> **The culturally disadvantaged are seen as not lacking in the basic learning abilities but only in the appropriate environmental inputs which go to make up what we call intelligence. . . . Middle class children, on the other hand, have had the necessary input, and the extent to which they have applied intelligence from this experience is a function of their basic learning ability.**

Other factors affecting the output of culturally disadvantaged children are: dependency upon motor facility for learning rather than aural stimulation, limited ability to comprehend what is heard because of failure to learn to listen, difficulty with symbolic learning, and a strong sense of immediacy in approaching any situation. Consequently, there is an obvious need for immediate positive feedback if their patterns of life are to be changed. This positive feedback has often been ignored or neglected as an instrument of change in schools.

Resnick (1969), in comparing two groups of children differing in socioeconomic status, suggested that "the disadvantaged child's visual-perceptual abilities are primitive, poorly articulated and diffused when compared to his counterpart from an average cultural environment." He indicated that perceptual, integrative abilities can be improved with training (as discussed in Chapter 6), but that training is relatively more effective when children come from an average socioeconomic level. The lower the socioeconomic level of a child, the greater the frequency and intensity of stimulation needed to bring him up to the level of adequacy of a child from an average or above average background. Depending on the type and specificity of treatment, presence of biological deficits, and socioeconomic status, frequency of stimulation may not only need to be many times greater than for the average child, but may need to be coupled with additional rewards and satisfactory consequences which will motivate the child to become involved in the treatment. The child from a higher socioeconomic level may not need the same rewards or frequency of stimulation and may find the activity rewarding for its own sake.

Bartel (1968) found that by the fourth grade, middle-class children become significantly more internally controlled than lower-class children. Focus of control and control factors showed significant correlations with standardized achievement test scores, reading readiness scores, and teachers' ratings of achievement of middle-class children. The same correlations for lower-class children were substantially lower, although positive. Bartel explained these differences in terms of differential reward systems on the part of teachers, a process that remains open to further investigation.

On the basis of four subtests of the ITPA and the Personal Social Responsiveness of the Preschool Inventory, Howard et al. (1970) concluded that children from higher socioeconomic groups are more adept at: (a) relating to their personal world, (b) responding to instructions and demands of adults, and (c) establishing rapport with another person, than are lower-class children. Higher-class and lower-class children do not differ in their abilities to understand or comprehend the spoken word or to interpret sentences. It is only with age and lowered verbal output that comprehension of words and sentences may tend to decrease. Higher-class children respond with greater grammatical complexity and verbal facility than lower-class children; however, lower-class children may be superior to higher-class children in some aspects of visual-motor problem-solving.

Intellectual retardation and cultural stimulation studies show that the child with an IQ between 70 and 89 usually comes from a larger family than the child with a normal or superior IQ. Normally, such children have parents with similar intellectual abilities. To relate these findings to an input-output model, the input which the child receives might be considered as being reduced because of the size of the family. When there are many children in the family, the parents do not generally have sufficient time to spend in verbal stimulation of each child. Therefore, exposure to language would be sufficiently reduced for these children, and experiential input might also be reduced because of increased noise and confusion. With low verbal and experiential input, the child's output would be correspondingly lowered. Feedback in such an environment would also be inadequate because of the limited ability of the parents to react and respond to each individual child.

The influence of cultural factors can be illustrated in the special case of the institutionalized child. Quite often, children who have been institutionalized at a very young age (orphans, semiorphans, and foundlings) are found to be retarded. Investigation indicates that their retardation is due to limited handling and few learning opportunities. Dennis (1960) compared an orphanage in which children received frequent handling and care with two orphanages in Iran in which understaffing greatly reduced the amount of handling and attention which infants received. In the institution that was able to give infants a great deal of handling and attention, the children's mental development resembled that of home-reared children, while children in the other orphanages were often retarded in mental development. Institutionalized children are a special case of cultural disadvantage and serve as direct evidence of the effects of deprivation in early childhood.

Wolins (1970) contrasted 25 adolescent children who were under age 7 when they entered group-care settings in either Austria or Yugoslavia with 77 later admissions and with 139 family-reared children. He found no significant differences among the three groups or between early and later admissions on measurements of intellectual functioning, personality development, value acquisition, and problem behavior. He explained the lack of differences as being due to the structure of the settings in which these children were cared for and particularly the availability of affective ties to adults and older children. In other words, institutionalization in and by itself does not necessarily deprive, as may be assumed on the basis of Skeels's work (1965). In Dennis's opinion (1960), the primary importance of his observations of institutionalized children is that they challenge the theory set forth by Spitz (1946) that infant development depends largely on stimulation of a motor sequence which is little affected by learning.

Skeels's (1965) prolonged follow-up studies of adults who were adopted children showed that they achieved consistently higher than would be expected from the intellectual, socioeconomic, and educational levels of their biological parents. Even mentally retarded children, raised in a noninstitutional environment, have shown decided increases in rate of intellectual growth, have become self-supporting, and have achieved at least the equivalent of a high school education. A comparable group of children who remained wards of an institution showed a consistent decline based on most of the criteria used. Children of mentally retarded parents who were separated from their parents before age two and were placed in adoptive homes also showed an increase in intellectual functioning.

Race as a Cultural Factor

From a biological standpoint, racial differences would affect development genetically, somatically, and temperamentally, mainly influencing input factors. Considered as cultural factors, however, racial differences would mainly influence output because of the effects of economic deprivation, cultural isolation, and parental inadequacy. There is some evidence (L'Abate, 1971) which supports the second rather than the first interpretation, making race or ethnic origin synonymous with socioeconomic status.

Psychologically, racial factors have more direct effects on the child's self-concept, his psychosexual identification, and his defensive maneuvers. On these grounds, this construct of race is more relevant to cultural deprivation than to biological deficits. The lowered output of the deprived child feeds back negatively into his input, thus lowering his overall functioning and producing what Deutsch (1967) called the "cumulative deficit" with increasing age.

Kennedy's studies (1969) suggested a wide discrepancy between black and white children in intellectual functioning. This discrepancy, magnified by Jensen's incendiary review (1969), created a national controversy (Whitten and Kagan, 1969) over genetic differences as related to intellectual functioning and the dubious effectiveness of compensatory educational programs like Head Start. Many logical and empirical weaknesses are present in studies like Kennedy's; for example, intellectual functioning was assessed globally through the Stanford-Binet Intelligence Test for Children. This test is a less than systematic array of items which fails to acknowledge the importance and presence of the receptive-expressive distinction which is basic to intellectual functioning. As long as this distinction is not considered, many results from similar studies are either invalid or irrelevant. The basic question is not whether underprivileged children, regardless of race, are intellectually more retarded but, as Lesser et al. (1965) pointed out, which modality of functioning is most affected by socioeconomic factors, and how it is affected. Of course, in the lowest socioeconomic groups, the degree of deprivation may be such that most modalities of functioning, intellectual as well as motivational and interpersonal (Deutsch, 1967), will be affected.

To distinguish assets and liabilities that are related to *cultural* factors from assets and liabilities in each child that are related to his own peculiar *biological* background and *individual psychological* functioning is the major issue. Although the constant interaction of all three systems has been acknowledged from the beginning, this term—interaction—does not mean that it is impossible and infeasible to distinguish the specific effects that each system has on the overall functioning of the child.

We maintain that socioeconomic factors mostly influence the rate, frequency, and quality of output. The lower the socioeconomic level, the more inadequate the output (especially verbal output). The poorer the output, the greater the negative feedback into input functions. The lower the output, the lower the input will eventually become. Even with a biologically healthy organism, which a lower-class child is not likely to be, such a vicious circle would reduce the threshold for discrimination and intake of information. This conclusion is corroborated by Burnes's (1969) findings which are in support of intellectual functioning (WISC) as being more related to a child's socioeconomic level than to his race. Guthrie and Jacobs (1966), in their study of child-rearing and personality development in the Philippines, showed how a culture can shape distinct patterns with minimal influence from biological factors.

Auditory-Verbal Functioning and Socioeconomic Status

It is quite possible that children from deprived homes may acquire perceptual deficiencies. Since experience and practice are influential in perceptual development, and these children have few toys, picture books, or household objects to stimulate them, their visual-perceptual development may be deficient. This also applies to the auditory modality because of lack of directed interchange combined with continual undifferentiated racket made by many occupants who are cramped into small living quarters. These factors, combined with teaching materials and focus in schools on subjects that are often entirely unrelated to the child's background and experience, clearly encumber these children from the outset with an extensive handicap in trying to learn the expected academic work.

Telford and Sawrey (1972) called attention to the fact that the culturally deprived child may live in a world that is predominantly physically rather than ideationally and verbally controlled. In accordance with the feedback concept, citing Deutsch, they stated that

> **there is evidence that social class differences in the general environment orientation and in the perceptual abilities of school children *decrease* with chronological age, whereas social *language differences tend to increase*.**
>
> **Early linguistic patterns are more resistant to change by ordinary educational experiences than are general perceptual and orientational processes. . . . Many lines of evidence indicate that language is the area most sensitive to the impact of the multiplicity of problems associated with experiential deprivation and cultural disadvantage.**

Auditory discrimination has been found to affect a child's reading ability. With deprivation in this area, the child will have reading difficulties which will cause problems in school. Bruner (1960) found that children who are victims of sensory deprivation are handicapped not only in constructing models of the environment but also in developing strategies for evaluating information.

Children first learn to talk by babbling and by having the proper sounds reinforced by praise and repetition from an adult model. If they do not receive reinforcement from the environment, they will soon stop "playing" with sound. This avoidance will lead to delayed speech which is usually found in children in disadvantaged areas. Disadvantaged parents consider the child's verbal development less important than his ability to take care of himself physically.

Other aspects of the environment influence development. The foundations of a child's verbal development are formed in the home and are influenced by his initial experiences in loving, depending, and belonging. Language patterns of the disadvantaged are different from those of other groups in the culture, and the child naturally learns this different pattern. In the disadvantaged home, there is minimal verbal exchange among all members of the family, and the sentences which are used are of the most basic construction. Language is developed, but it deviates from so-called standard English and contains a profusion of slang and regionalism. Because of deprivation, there are few experiences about which such children may verbalize and form concepts. This limited experience will cause a deficit in the child's ability to conceptualize and will prevent proper language development. Usually, the child has had little opportunity to ask or answer questions which will satisfy and increase his curiosity.

Ours is a verbal society, and the ability to manipulate verbal symbols is at a premium. Lack of stimulation in the home, lack of reinforcement or reward for verbal abilities, and poor modes of communication further handicap the child in his ability to perform scholastically, an ability which is dependent on development of language, verbal, and conceptual skills. Also, according to Minuchin et al. (1967):

> **Other stylistic features which may clash with the culture of the school are their [disadvantaged children's] action and excitement orientation and motoric patterns; aggression and physicalness in relating to others; reliance on paraverbal rather than verbal channels of communication; deficiencies in introspective as well as empathic skills; inattention and memory difficulties; poor time orientation; and lack of expectation of rewards for successful performance.**

Language is important because it represents a major vehicle through which we organize our world and form a system to organize all sensory impressions. Language assists in man's capacity to think and in his ability to act freely; if acquisition of language is interfered with, then one's total development is altered. With proper control of language, the child has more control over his behavior because he can substitute words for actions.

Cazden (1966), in her review of subcultural differences in children's language, found that black-white differences in receptive verbal skills were "virtually absent." However, ethnic background may affect the pattern of mental abilities, and social class status may affect the level of scores on mental ability scales. Deficiency in expressive patterns seems to be the greatest effect of social class: lower-class children speak in short sentences or connect simple strings of words with "and"; upper-status children utilize more complex syntactical patterns. The most important factor related to language expression and complexity is the amount and richness of language stimulation which is available in the context of face-to-face interaction. Cazden, relating retardation to the development of substandard language, concluded that "evidence of retardation among lower class children is extensive. . . ."

Hertzig et al. (1968) indicated that cultural deprivation affects language output more than any other modality. They found that Puerto Rican children did not respond as well verbally as a comparable sample of white children. Their responses were inadequate and/or inappropriate to the task demands. Their usage of language and stylistic differences in responsiveness to cognitive demands were explained in terms of child-rearing practices. White, middle-class mothers emphasize task orientation and task completion. Puerto Rican families, in contrast, usually encourage social interaction and enjoyment without emphasis on time, business, and schedules. Middle-class families stress task-mastery and independence; Puerto Rican families often discourage efforts of children to become independent and masterful. In the former, verbalizations were task-oriented, and task-oriented verbal instructions were carried out by the child. In the latter, verbalizations were social and affective without insistence that verbal instructions be followed by action on the part of the child.

Frazier's study (1964) suggested that there are three kinds of underdeveloped language to be found among disadvantaged children with learning disabilities: (1) actually less language; (2) language which is highly developed but deviates sufficiently from standard English to require further language development; and (3) language which is well-developed, but in certain aspects of experience which are valued by schools there may have been no occasion to verbalize meanings.

Grotberg's review (1969) included the experiments of Deutsch (1963) which found that disadvantaged children have inferior auditory and visual discrimination, time concepts, and number concepts. He found no physical defects of the eyes, ears, or brain. The deficiencies were attributed to inadequate habits of hearing, seeing, and thinking. He postulated that these children were deprived of a sufficient variety of stimuli to which they were motivationally capable of responding and were therefore less prepared for school learning. Deutsch and Brown (1964) found that being a member of a lower class is a greater determinant of low achievement and low IQ scores than race, but that race increasingly becomes a determinant as class level goes up. Evidence of continued decline in aptitude and achievement test scores of disadvantaged children over the years, regardless of race, is consistent (Sarason and Doris, 1969).

One of our students (Conn, 1967) attempted a simple test of the hypothesis that socioeconomic status will influence total verbal output more directly than input. He attempted to replicate Loban's findings (1961) that the number of words per communication unit was always higher among upper-status children. Conn constructed a standard interview consisting of 10 questions dealing with neutral, common topics that would not allow a yes or no answer. He used 8 first-graders (age 6), 12 third-graders (age 9), and 8 seventh-graders (age 12). Fourteen of these children came from a low socioeconomic background, and 14 came from a middle-class background. They were classified according to the father's occupation, income, and place of residence. The major shortcoming of this study, of course; is that the interviewer knew the subjects' backgrounds beforehand. Their answers were tape-recorded and coded according to (a) total number of words for each answer and (b) total duration per answer in seconds. Since the correlation between these two measurements was sufficiently high, the mean total number of words was used to report the findings, as shown in the following chart:

Grade Level	***Mean Total Number of Words***	
	Lower-Class Group	*Middle-Class Group*
1st	38	47
3rd	47	75
7th	46	114

While with age the lower-class children did not increase in total number of words spoken, middle-class children showed a significant and consistent increase. The mean disparity of 9 words between socioeconomic levels in the first grade increased to 27 words in the third grade and to 68 words in the seventh grade. These disparities were greater for boys than for girls, a factor that may be related to the sex of the interviewer.

These findings suggest that with age increased verbal output that is further increased by social class may feed back into the amount and rate of information which is received, recognized, selected, and stored by the child. Increased output will stimulate further growth in input reception, a growth that would not or could not occur in the lower-class children. Conn reported that the middle-class children showed a greater sense of feeling important, greater assertiveness, and a quicker willingness to enter into an unfamiliar situation and to express themselves verbally than lower-class children. On the other hand, disadvantaged children acquire language in a more passive, receptive manner. Consequently, their use of language in verbal mediation is deficient in comparison with that of middle-class children. This deficiency results in disadvantaged children's lower overall levels of performance in the classroom. Deutsch and his coworkers (1967) conducted research which supports the hypothesis that verbal ability is a function of social class. This study also provided evidence that an early enrichment program offsets verbal disability and a high rate of school dropouts.

Heiner (1968) found that inner city black, nine-year-old children spoke fewer sentences than white nine-year-olds during conversational periods, using verbs and nouns in a nonstandard manner in approximately 15 per cent of the sentences. The white children made similar errors in 3 per cent of the sentences spoken. The black children produced fewer sentences using clauses or complements than did the white group (9 per cent versus 15 per cent). Heiner interpreted his results in terms of Bernstein's *restricted* versus *enlarged* speech patterns of different class groups.

Entwisle (1968), on the basis of word associations data, maintained that inner city children are more advanced in certain areas of language, as shown by such measurements as word associations, than suburban children at the time of school entrance. She interpreted her results as being consistent with evidence that lower-class children of both races do as well as middle-class children on comprehension of paragraphs spoken by other children (an input function). Apparently, she attempted to explain the lack of differences in input measurements. Her results deserve careful consideration and replication because, as she acknowledged, they raise "... important questions about cultural deprivation and also about the role of cultural factors in early linguistic development." Furthermore, these results provide evidence which seems to discount the possible validity of other data and would necessitate a reorganization of theoretical and empirical paradigms.

Stephenson (1969), in studying the effects of sex and race on the psycholinguistic abilities of lower-class, first-grade children, found that white children surpassed black children of comparable socioeconomic status in the ability to express ideas vocally, in the ability to anticipate future linguistic events from past experiences, in total language age, and in mental age, all seemingly verbal output factors. Black children surpassed white children in the ability to repeat a sequence of symbols previously learned (rote memory?). Race and sex, a cultural variable and an organismic variable, from our present point of view, significantly influenced psycholinguistic abilities, total language age, and mental age (measured by the Peabody Picture Vocabulary Test).

Webb (1969), using the ITPA and Wepman's Auditory Discrimination Test, found that lower-class Anglo-American, black, and Latin-American children were deficient in psycholinguistic abilities in comparison with the normative sample and that they were lower in auditory-vocal functions than in visual-motor processing. White and black children surpassed Latin-American children in individual language aspects and in auditory discrimination. These findings support the position that socioeconomic status affects psycholinguistic abilities and perhaps output linguistic functions to a greater extent than the visual-motor input-output modality.

Kline and Lee's study (1970) compared Chinese children in British Columbia with the general school population. They concluded that: (1) socioeconomic status is not important to school learning; (2) incidence of learning disability appeared to be related to difficulty with language and patterns of association needed for learning the language; (3) visual perception, as emphasized by Frostig, is not a significant factor in learning to read; (4) body image is not related to reading disability; (5) functional neurological factors may play a role in some cases of reading disability; (6) teaching methods appear to be important to reading ability, and a multisensory approach is favorable; and (7) above a baseline, reading disability is not related to intelligence. These conclusions, of course, disagree with many already accepted assumptions that have been propagated in special education. The reader must not forget, however, that these conclusions are based on one study involving a seldom used minortiy group whose backgrounds may not be fully understood.

Irwin (1960) reported that talking to one-year-old children increases their vocabularies. The child typically imitates his mother and talks if she talks. In the case of an overprotective, overindulgent parent, the child's every need is provided, so that he has little desire or need to communicate. Kessler (1966) reported that regression caused by separations, birth of a new baby, hospitalization, or other traumatic experiences may cause speech problems. Freeberg and Payne (1967) reviewed the role of parental influence on cognitive development in early childhood and suggested that verbal deficits may relate to social class levels; however, at the time of their review, findings were still unsystematic and unsatisfactory. Siegel and Perry (1968) showed how the concept of cultural deprivation includes a variety of patterns, as measured by the ITPA profiles of 25 black children.

In summary, disadvantaged children enter school with a different language system than middle-class children. The language they use is characterized by a smaller vocabulary, fewer descriptive terms, simpler syntax, and nonstandard terms which are not acceptable in the academic situation. Verbal activity is limited to brief sentences and commands, with much communication being achieved gesturally. With a deficit in verbal skills upon beginning school, these children experience great difficulty in expressing themselves and in learning to read. With poor expressive and reading skills, the child is doomed to repetitive failure experiences in school.

Educational Achievement

There are other factors found in the cultural setting of deprived individuals that foster behavioral dysfunctions which contribute to poor achievement in school. Social class influences parental attitude and behavior that the child learns and relates to school and educational achievement.

There are three assumptions which are generally made about the learning process: (1) The social milieu in which the child grows up is highly influential in determining the kind and degree of his experience. (2) The ease of acquisition of new knowledge and skills—learning—is based largely on prior experience and knowledge of the child. (3) The nature of the stimulus—its organization, speed, manner of presentation, and the like—is influential in acquiring new knowledge (Deutsch, 1967). Because of nonstandard langauge development, the disadvantaged child has difficulty in meeting educational standards and falls progressively further behind his classmates in academic achievement and learning. This process eventually results in the school dropout who quits school because he feels that he is accomplishing nothing and is wasting his time at something he hates. The poor reader has a 50 per cent chance of not finishing high school. When a child experiences only failure in school, it is not surprising that he drops out without graduating. The next step in the life an an individual who has quit school is to go to work and begin to earn money. His next failure experience involves discovering that he cannot get a decent job, perhaps not any job at all, because he is unskilled and unprepared to perform any type of service in the labor market. As a result, hopelessness and violence leading to criminality are common in such an individual's life.

Verbal ineptness in both vocal and written communication may contribute to the child's negative attitude toward school. The basic concerns and value systems of the home, neighborhood, and community also influence the child's degree of acceptance or rejection of the importance of school. Usually, disadvantaged parents have ambivalent attitudes toward school. Generally, they have had little education themselves and thus place little emphasis on education. At home, the child has no satisfactory place to study because of crowded quarters, noise, and distractions. He has no one whom he can ask for help if he cannot do his homework.

Parental attitude regarding the importance of school has a major influence on the child's attitude and on his attendance. Often, the disadvantaged consider school as a "prissy" place dominated by females and feminine ideas. The disadvantaged child often drops out of school in order to escape from a crowded, noisy home. Yet, he cannot escape until he secures a job which, in turn, may require that he finish school. To achieve this end, the child is interested only in the educational fundamentals which will help him get a job; he has little interest in the fine arts and other seemingly impractical courses offered by the school.

Teachers and schools often foster low achievement and dissatisfaction with education. Discrimination exists in the classroom, PTA, guidance office, etc., which alienates the child and his family and which leads to anger and aggression. The culture of the school is primarily middle-class, and it tends to overlook and underestimate the abilities of the disadvantaged child.

Some teachers have biases that work against the disadvantaged child, and they may use materials and methods that are unsuited and uninteresting to the child because of their unfamiliarity. Materials may be presented too fast for comprehension, since the child has limited abilities, and his slow understanding may irritate the teacher who has not been properly prepared to cope with this situation. Teachers sometimes favor the middle-class child over the disadvantaged child even when his achievement is satisfactory. Deprived children accurately perceive the teacher's rejection of them.

The teacher's negative image of such a child causes a depreciation of the child's self-perception or self-image which will affect his behavior in school. Classroom rebellion is more the result of rejection and a feeling of alienation from the school routine than a rebellion against authority. Deprived children may be among the least popular children in school, less often permitted into cliques and often perceived as being unattractive.

Drews (1957) found that parents of poor achievers demand less from their children and make demands later in their children's lives than other parents. The best educational insurance which a child can have is a family that places a high value on education. If a child identifies with an uneducated, unemployed parent, he is more likely to copy this model than one of higher achievement and thus not fully develop his educational potential. Deutsch (1967) found that the following environmental factors relate to learning: (1) housing dilapidation, (2) educational aspiration, (3) number of children under 18 years of age, (4) dinner conversation, (5) cultural experiences, and (6) attendance in kindergarten.

Makita (1968), noting the absence of reading disability in Japanese children, questioned ". . . theories which ascribed the etiology of reading disability to local cerebral abnormalities, to local conflict, or to emotional pressure . . .," which he felt might be valid in some instances. He indicated that ". . . the specificity of the used language, the very object of reading behavior, is the most potent contributing factor in prevention of reading disability. Reading disability, then, is more a philological than a sensoripsychiatric problem." Thus, Makita's results and observations support the view that reading efficiency is influenced not only by the child's biological status but also by the symbols used by the specific culture of which he is a member.

EDUCABLE MENTAL RETARDATION AND ITS ENVIRONMENTAL CONTEXT

The disadvantaged child usually scores low on IQ tests because of various factors. His low verbal ability and the attitudes and responses that he has learned from his culture are handicaps. He also lacks test-taking skills and the motivation to do well. Many tests are not culture-free, a shortcoming which handicaps the disadvantaged child. The child may not be able to function on a higher level owing to intellectual retardation, especially in the EMR range (IQ 50 to 75), which is quite prevalent in disadvantaged populations. The retardation may derive not only from his immediate deprivation but also from the effects on his parents of past, cumulative deprivations which occurred before the child was born. The disadvantaged pregnant mother may not receive proper medical care; she may be undernourished or have an improper diet. Prematurity is more prevalent in low socioeconomic and deprived communities, and it increases the probability of neurological disorders.

The inability of lower-class children to perform in the classroom was, in the past, typically assumed to be caused by an inherent mental deficiency generally considered characteristic of such persons. Rarely has it been concluded, therefore, that the school can significantly increase the intellectual or social functioning of such children. In most instances, disadvantaged children are assigned by the school (as the representative of society) to a perpetual state of limbo in which they are to be pitied or tolerated but are seldom really helped.

A culturally disadvantaged child who appears stupid or retarded to school personnel because his output (lack of verbal facility, etc.) is extremely limited, in reality, may or may not be intellectually retarded. If he were to be evaluated solely on the basis of his output, it could not be reasonably determined whether or not he is retarded. It is only when his output is measured in comparison with his input that such a categorization can be validated. In most instances, poor environmental conditions are the cause of his limited output rather than an inherent mental deficiency (input). It has been widely demonstrated that a large proportion of the intellectually retarded come from families who can be labeled as disadvantaged.

Zigler (1969) contended that a great deal of nonorganically based retardation is essentially related to lack of adequate stimulation, a basis of deprivation, and to inadequate positive reinforcements rather than to anything intrinsically related to the state of the child. He believed that this assumption holds especially for mild and moderate degrees of retardation in which no organic deficit is present or demonstrable. He believed (1967) educable intellectual retardation to be the outcome of various types and degrees of deprivations, abuses, and neglects that lower the child's motivational needs to learn as most normal children do.

Benda's review (1963) showed that 78 per cent of all retarded children with an IQ below 75 are classified as having a familial or subcultural abnormality. Most of this group come from lower-class families in culturally deprived, poverty-stricken environments which tend to be characterized by inadequate nutrition and medical care, interrupted schooling, limited intellectual stimulation, and poor adult supervision. Verville (1967) attributed mental subnormality to the same cultural influences as those described by Benda by stating that the child who is deprived emotionally and environmentally during infancy and preschool years performs poorly in school and earns low scores on intelligence tests. Children from homes of low socioeconomic status or from isolated rural areas or children who have been residents of institutions most of their lives give minimal responses to stimulation and exhibit low motivation to learn, to experiment, and to create. Pasamanick (1963) attributed the higher rate of mental deficiency among blacks to socioeconomic segregation and to lack of care during pregnancy. Verville cited studies of culturally deprived children who accelerated in intellectual activity and responsiveness when exposed to kindergarten and increased personal contacts.

Stodolsky and Lesser (1967) reviewed the literature on learning patterns among disadvantaged children and concluded that different cognitive, personal, intellectual, motivational, and other attributes are related consistently to ethnic group membership. Since each ethnic group reinforces or suppresses different aspects of behavior, certain assets and liabilities are produced that form a conglomeration which is peculiar to the particular ethnic group. Lesser's data (1965) indicated that the intellectual abilities of Chinese and black children from two different socioeconomic levels differed not only as a function of ethnic group membership but also as a function of socioeconomic level.

Flory (1969) obtained a positive correlation of .57 between Stanford-Binet IQ scores and a combined measurement of the child's extent of verbal interaction with adults and the form of his play activities. Size of family greatly affected the degree of this correlation. In small families, the correlation was .81 before preschool and .65 after kindergarten, whereas in large families the respective correlations were .35 and .51. Form of play activities was strongly linked with social class; it correlated .66 with socioeconomic status. Among lower-class subjects, family size was not related to preschool IQ, but its correlation with kindergarten IQ was −.59; the correlation between family size and IQ gain between preschool and kindergarten was −.57.

Educable Mental Retardation or Environmental Deprivation?

In considering educable retardation, Zigler (1967) demonstrated that a great many retardates without any evidence of brain damage (a category in itself) come from the lowest socioeconomic level and evidence the greatest amount of abuse and gross physical punishment. Thus, many of these children with intelligence between the moderately retarded and dull-normal levels may be retardates as a result of social neglect and abuse and not because of any mysterious, intrinsic reason. In addition, a host of social, nutritional, experiential (Haywood, 1967), and cultural factors should be taken into account before considering retardation as being a separate entity from deprivation. As the literature indicates, lack of early stimulation (Hellmuth, 1967; 1968; 1970) can produce significant reductions in cognitive responsiveness and in overall perceptual attention to external stimuli. As Escalona (1968) suggested, gross deprivation of external input may increase attention to internal stimulation (hunger, thirst, discomfort, etc.). Clarke and Clarke (1967) stated that "... complexity is a major determinant of transfer," indicating that lack of stimulation makes it difficult for many deprived children to deal with complex situations because of insufficient prior learning.

Clausen (1967), in an assessment of behavioral characteristics of retardates through the use of a large battery of physiological, sensory, motor, perceptual, and complex intellectual tests, concluded that neurologically impaired retardates had lower scores on finger dexterity, gross body coordination, grip, and eye dominance. Differences in scores were obtained only when extreme categories of subjects were compared, supporting Zigler's thesis that any comparison of retardates with normal subjects is inappropriate, especially if socioeconomic status and degree of abuse and deprivation are not considered. Clausen's study indicated lower scores in motor and complex motor functions rather than in sensory and perceptual functions, supporting the position previously presented that a great deal of educable retardation may be due to output deprivation rather than to any internal condition. Syndrome analysis produced three groups of subjects: (1) a relatively high-level group with little variability; (2) a group characterized by a specific impairment in pure tone threshold and somewhat additional impairment of simple motor functions, a finding which supports the work of Birch concerning the importance of intersensory integration; and (3) the third group, in addition to the impairments of the second group, showed impairment in complex motor functions. Clausen concluded that retardates are not as homogeneous as normal children; they differ from each other in many little ways which prevent the formation of identifiable subgroups. Perhaps an approach based on input-output differentiation may be one means of surmounting this difficulty.

Although Clausen eschewed etiological subgrouping in favor of behavioral characteristics, he speculatively suggested an arousal mechanism or a central internal function, which is obviously an oversimplification in need of refinement and modification. Some of the data which he collected were not consistent with the concept of arousal. Instead of hypothetical control mechanisms which, in many cases, may turn out to be elusive either logically or empirically, the approach suggested by Zigler (1967) may be logically more consistent and empirically more fruitful. Major refinement of Zigler's concepts would involve looking for evidence to support or weaken the thesis (input-output) presented in this text.

Havighurst (1970) further differentiated the general proposition that "human learning is influenced by a variety of rewards, which are themselves arranged in a culturally based reward-punishment system." Between birth and age four, a child is particulary sensitive to the gratification or deprivation of physical-physiological needs (e.g., food, relief from pain, toys) by parents. In the early school years (ages 5 to 10), he becomes especially sensitive to praise or approval from outside persons (teachers and parental substitutes, peers and peer groups) as well as from himself. In puberty and early adolescence (ages 10 to 15), he becomes particularly sensitive to approval-disapproval from the community in general and to how it affects his own self-perception (ego in Havighurst's terminology). Each stage of development possesses its specific action area that is particularly reinforced. These action areas cover a wide range from motor and verbal skills at the outset to work and family roles in adulthood.

Havighurst added six major propositions that have educational implications for most children and especially for educable retardates:

1. Different cultures guide their children along an evolutionary pathway at different rates and in different ways.

2. There are differences between ethnic subcultures and among disadvantaged groups in the reward systems that they teach their children.

3. In general, external rewards (concrete or intangible) have positive values for children who are disadvantaged or failing in their school work.

4. An effective reward system in a complex, changing society must be based upon a strong ego (conceived as a source of reward-punishment as well as the executive and planning function of personality).

5. A strongly developed ego provides a sense of personal control and personal responsibility for important events in one's life.

6. People learn to operate at all the several levels of reward by the time they reach adolescence, and the level at which they operate varies with the action area.

Essentially, Havighurst helps us to make the point that cultural-behavioral transactions shape, in part, how the child perceives himself. One of the important aspects of internal control systems is what Rotter (1966) has called internal-external locus of control. Self-concept, self-esteem, and other so-called intrapsychic hypothetical constructs (to be considered in greater detail in the next chapter) cannot be considered developmentally as being separate from both biological and cultural antecedents. Deviations and extremes in biological-cultural transactions will produce behavioral dysfunctions in children.

Educable Mental Retardation and Cultural Background

Learning

McCandless (1964) felt that the most serious social problem associated with intellectual retardation is that which concerns the educable mentally retarded. He further suggested that this group of children is most seriously affected by the forces of our culture and that, at least for practical reasons, this is the group to which we should devote our attention.

Environment as it relates to educable mental retardates is of great importance because most of these individuals come from somewhat undesirable backgrounds with regard to current social values. The environments of educable mentally retarded children are probably malignant in a number of ways. They may be financially and culturally deficient, lacking in respect for these children as individuals, devoid of what is ordinarily considered intellectual stimulation, and often ethnically discriminatory against them (McCandless, 1964).

The British study of Spencer et al. (1954) presented much evidence of the effects of deprivation on child development. Clarke and Clarke (1960) considered the following to be the factors which most adversely influence the mentally retarded child in a deprived culture: (1) social isolation, (2) cruelty and neglect, (3) institutional upbringing, (4) adverse child-rearing practices, and (5) severe separation experiences. According to McCandless (1964), our most pressing concern with the environment should be to find an answer to the question: "What are the learning experiences through which the child goes, how can these be quantified, and what relations do they have to his development, intellectual and otherwise?"

McCandless (1952) proposed two learning hypotheses which are applicable to how educable intellectual retardation develops. First, an environment which fosters educable retardation is one which provides minimal opportunity for learning skills subsumed under the term intelligence; and second, it is one in which the child has had maximal opportunity to learn "self-defeating" techniques, expectations of failure, absolute as opposed to relative thinking, concrete as opposed to abstract thinking, and belief in his essential worthlessness.

Sarason (1953) showed the hopelessness of the environments from which these children come. Often, there is total poverty, parental abandonment, social humiliation, rejection and defeat, and frequently, one or both parents are retarded or psychotic.

Lantz (1945) indicated that even relatively minor limitations in experience may cause a child to miss those types of experiences that would help him attain a higher score on an IQ test. Failure tends to become an increasingly common experience, and each failure tends to make the retarded child less willing to try again.

Home Environment

The longer the time that a child spends in a disadvantaged home, the lower his IQ scores tend to be (Kephart, 1940). Transfer to a more appropriate home causes a definite rise in the IQ of such children. It is apparent that the earlier a child is placed in a better learning environment, the less likely he is to show severe damage with regard to academic learning.

Charles (1953) conducted an interesting study on EMR children which concerned their functioning when they reached adulthood. The study was conducted with 127 children who had all been enrolled in an opportunity room. The children had an average IQ of 60, and all had scored below 70 on IQ tests.

In the follow-up study when the subjects were in their thirties and forties, Charles found that a larger proportion had died than would be expected from national norms. Almost one-third of those who had died, mostly males, had had violent deaths. More than one-third had been entirely economically self-sufficient during their adult lives. Fewer than one-half of the subjects had been on relief rolls, and fewer married than one would expect from national statistics. About 18 per cent of the subjects had been institutionalized for at least a period of time. Those who had married had 2.03 children, which is just slightly below the national average. The subjects' children who could be located during the follow-up study (73 in number) ranged in IQ from 50 to 138 with a mean IQ of 95. About the same percentage of subjects had been divorced as one would expect from national norms. About one-half of the subjects lived in their own homes, which is in accordance with national standards. Most of the men worked as laborers, and the women were largely housekeepers. About 40 per cent of the subjects had been involved in some form of lawbreaking. Twenty of the 127 were retested for IQ. The average IQ score was 58, approximately the same average as that determined by the original testing. A more modern test gave an average IQ score of 81 for the same subjects.

Mean scores made on verbal subtests, as compared to performance subtests, indicated a typical depressed score on the verbal test. (Respective IQ's were 72 and 88.)

Social Class

The effects of social class on intelligence were fully reviewed by Jones (1954). He contended that social class clearly influences intelligence. It is also evident that environment substantially affects social and intellectual development. Studies such as Jones's do not negate studies on heredity, but they do provide some hope for the educable retarded, in that while little, at present, can be done to control hereditary factors, as a society we can make substantial changes in the environment.

Regardless of social class, level of parental education, or parental intelligence, the correlation between measurements of parental social status and children's intelligence is about 0.50. One conclusion that seems to be warranted by these studies is that the higher the socioeconomic class of the parent, the brighter, on the average, his child will be. A large study involving 45,000 children (McGehee and Lewis, 1942) which investigated the relationship between social class and intelligence indicated some interesting results. The study concerned children from 455 schools and in 310 different communities in 36 states. Their fathers' occupations were classified from I to V, with I signifying the highest social class occupations and V the lowest. Class I produced 2.4 times more superior children than would normally be expected, and Class V produced only 0.3 as many as would be statistically expected.

In general, children from cities score higher on intelligence tests than children from rural settings do (McCandless, 1952; Jones, 1954). Wheeler (1942) studied children from the Tennessee mountains and concluded that a barren environment had significantly affected the children's intelligence. An interesting study of black children in Louisiana (Klineberg, 1935) indicated that the nearer the children lived to New Orleans, the higher their IQ scores were. Knobloch and Pasamanick (1960) found no difference in intelligence test scores of black and white infants up to 40 weeks of age. They did find that by age three language intelligence scores differed by some 16 points in favor of the white children. They attributed this difference to socioeconomic factors.

Adoption

Children of mothers classified as intellectually retarded who are placed for adoption in more advantaged circumstances show that the predicted intellectual retardation of offspring does not hold true (Charles, 1953; Snygg, 1938). The Charles study found that the average IQ of those children who could be located approached normal levels, and in one case an IQ of 138 was found. The Snygg study of 312 children separated from their mothers before age four found that the children had average IQ's of 91, even though the average IQ of the mothers was 70.

Speer (1940) studied a group of children whose mothers had an average IQ of 49. IQ's of the children who were separated from their mothers before age two averaged normal. The average IQ of some 16 children who stayed with their mothers until they were from 12 to 15 years of age was 53.

The well-known study of Skodak and Skeels (1949) concerning a group of 100 adopted children showed them to have an average IQ of 117, whereas the national average is 100. Skeels and Harms (1948) conducted a study on children of parents who were thought to have inferior social backgrounds and found that the average IQ of the adopted children was 105.

The most important study in this area is Skeels's follow-up study (1965) of three groups of adopted children. Mothers of the 87 children in the first group all had intelligence tests scores of less than 75; fathers of the 111 children of the second group came from the lowest vocational class; and mothers of a third group of 35 children scored below 75, and the fathers were at the lowest levels of occupation. About 80 per cent of the children in this study were illegitimate. The average IQ's of these three groups of children were 105.5, 110.3, and 104.0 respectively. All three groups of children scored above the national mean IQ. The correlations between the IQ's of the true mothers and the IQ's of their children were 0.23, 0.22, and 0.12. In no case did the intelligence of the true mother account for more than about 5 per cent of the child's variability in his intelligence.

McCandless (1964) suggested three reasons for the above average IQ's of adopted children: (1) all obviously retarded children are screened out before adoption, so that there are few or no retarded children in the adopted population; (2) adopted children are genuinely wanted by the adoptive parents, and thus, they probably receive more than the average amount of attention and love; and (3) since most adoption procedures are conducted by social agencies, adoption is generally restricted to the "better" homes.

Institutionalization

The effects of environment with regard to intellectual retardation appear to be related to the type of child involved. In 1940, Kephart and Strauss studied children who were enrolled in the Wayne County Training School. Brain-damaged children were separated from the neurologically normal children. Growth patterns before and after admission to the school were checked. The findings of the study indicated that those children who were listed as neurologically normal appeared to have suffered more damage from early deprivation than the children with definite brain damage did.

In another British study, Mundy (1957) investigated a matched group of 28 women with intellectual retardation (between the ages of 18 and 50) who differed only by the fact that some of the women left the institution and lived in the community while others remained in the institution. The study found that the group living in the community gained about 11 points in IQ and that the subjects remaining in the institution gained only 2 points.

In studies by Goldfarb (1945), Levy (1947), and Hsu (1946), it was found that the longer an infant was retained in a depressed environment, the lower his developmental quotient was likely to be. Spitz (1963) stated that the effects of such deprivation may well be irreversible, and the evidence of Goldfarb and Levy tended to support this contention.

A 1960 study by Dennis in Teheran, Iran, indicated that children living in a public institution were greatly retarded in their motor development. They received little environmental stimulation, and thus, crawling, standing, and walking were considerably delayed in these children. None of the institutionalized children walked before age 2, and only 8 per cent walked between the ages of 2 and 2 years, 11 months. These findings are in contrast to children reared in private institutions where 15 per cent walked by age 2 and 94 per cent walked between 2 years and 2 years, 11 months. Dennis felt that these differences could be ascribed to the lack of learning opportunity for children reared in public institutions. However, it is possible that most of the retardation in motor development may not have been permanent in nature. He observed that many children between 6 and 15 years of age who had been reared in such an environment exhibited little or no evidence of its effect.

Not all institutions have an adverse effect on children, as has been indicated in a study by Harms (1953). The study showed that much affection and attention were given to the children by the nursing staff, with the result that the children approached normal intelligence, even though their parents were retarded.

Early Stimulation

An interesting study by Scott et al. (1959) demonstrated the importance of environmental deprivation on intellectual functioning. The study was conducted in Canada with a group of white male college undergraduates. For relatively short periods of time, up to four days, the students were placed in a highly restricted visual and tactual environment with the result that their performance on intelligence test items definitely declined.

Owing to the general resistance to human experimentation, many controlled studies on the effects of early stimulation have used animals as subjects. It is, of course, risky to translate directly findings on animals to human beings; but perhaps it may be acceptable simply to point out some studies and some possible implications for the human being.

Hebb's work (1949; 1955) served as the basis for much of the research in the animal world. Thompson and Heron (1954) made a very extensive study of the effects of isolation on problem-solving behavior. The subjects in this case were 26 Scottish terriers, which were all descendants of one litter and hence would be expected to present similar genetic backgrounds. Thirteen of the dogs were reared as pets in private homes or laboratories from about 4 weeks of age until about 8 months of age. In contrast, the other 13 dogs were reared under very different circumstances. Three isolation conditions were imposed upon the experimental dogs: (1) Two dogs experienced severe isolation, spending all their time, up to seven months of age, in one of two types of small cages. Each day they changed cages through a sliding door. One cage was kept in darkness, whereas light entered the other, so that the dogs spent every other day in darkness. (2) Eight pups experienced moderate restriction, 2 to 3 of them per group living for 8 to 10 months in standard dog cages whose cardboard covered walls kept out most visual stimulation. Light entered only through the tops of the cages. These dogs were in contact with humans for about 10 minutes each day while their cages were being cleaned. (3) Three pups were slightly restricted and lived for about seven months in cages similar to those of the moderately restricted dogs, except that their cages were open at the front to allow the dogs to see. Thus, they were able to have some perceptual experience, but only in their immediate environment.

After the experimental period, all the dogs were treated like normally reared dogs. The restricted dogs exhibited poor coordination; they bumped into things, had trouble with stairs, and were somewhat hyperactive. A year after the end of the experiment, the dogs were given a series of intelligence tests appropriate for dogs, and the experimental dogs were found to be somewhat retarded in a number of areas.

The early effect of stimulation on the young was demonstrated by Gibson and Walk (1956). In this study, rats were reared in two types of cages, one in which the rats were exposed to pieces of metal cut in the forms of triangles and circles and another which was normal in every respect. No effort was made to provide the rats with any information concerning the additional stimulus. The rats all came from the same litter and were divided in a random fashion. After 90 days, all the rats were provided with training in shape discrimination involving the triangle and the circle. The rats that had previously been exposed to the extra stimulus were superior to the control rats in learning the discrimination. Other similar experiments on rats found essentially the same conclusions.

Research reported in previous sections of the text concerning the effect of environment on growth and development of the human being suggests that heredity does not have full control over intelligence and that a systematic attempt to modify the environment may alter the performance of a human being in adulthood. Much research in this area concerning types of stimuli and time of alteration of the environment is needed. The general indication of early deprivation research is that children may be seriously harmed by lack of opportunities.

Mental Retardation in a Complex Industrial-Technical Society

As a society grows in complexity, it tends to place increasing emphasis on the higher intellectual processes. Educable intellectual retardation has probably always existed but has received little attention until recently. This lack of attention may be due to the EMR population's ability to blend into society when it makes no undue demands on them. It should be remembered that the bulk of populations of the past did not read or write and that most jobs demanded little in the way of school-like skills.

A technological society demands a more educated population, and it is precisely in this academic climate that the intellectually retarded fail to perform. The abilities of reading and using arithmetical processes are of great importance in acquiring the data necessary to profit from new knowledge. Current society is growing at an increasingly rapid rate with regard to learning and scientific knowledge; however, the intellectually retarded individual frequently learns at a slower rate and, perhaps, is more rigidly restricted in what he can learn, so that adaptation to the changing environment is of increasing difficulty for him. In addition to the retardate's having a less efficient intellectual system, he also tends to have parents of lower socioeconomic status and, thus, suffers from lack of opportunity to acquire necessary intellectual concepts. Much evidence exists to indicate that EMR individuals can be trained to assume responsible, self-sufficient roles even in today's society, if they are provided with the type of education they need and if they are then placed in a vocational setting suited to their limited intellectual abilities. Later portions of this text will fully explore all these factors, and evidence will be presented to show that educable intellectually retarded persons can be useful citizens in today's world.

JEAN PIAGET AND EDUCABLE MENTAL RETARDATION

Any study of the exceptional child would be remiss if the work of Jean Piaget were not included. According to Piaget, the development of intellectual functions is the story of personality formation (Flavell, 1963), and imitation is an intellectual function with no affective connotations. Piaget makes a point of stressing the importance of play in the evolution of intelligence. Language is a product of cognitive activity, and is viewed as a natural development in the evolution of the intellect. Piaget does not stress perception, but rather he considers perceptions to be momentary in nature and not as a part of the mainline of intellectual development. Affect is seen as a natural process following the same basic developmental rules as intelligence, but there is an ambivalence with regard to the equality of affect and intellect in Piaget's theory (Flavell, 1963).

Piaget views the total human personality as a composite of interactions between intellectual and affective processes, with the intellect as the integrative force in the development of personality. He stresses cognitive equilibrium as the major goal of human functioning which helps one to make a proper adjustment to a constantly changing environment. Piaget defined equilibrium as a state of balance between opposing forces, such as the resolution of conflict between the personal desires of an individual and the demands imposed on him by his environment. Striving is a constant state (Flavell, 1963).

According to Piaget there are three basic inborn, genetically determined drives: (1) the hunger drive, including the capacity to seek and utilize food; (2) the drive toward a sense of balance; and (3) a drive for independence from and adaptation to the environment plus a certain hereditary capacity to gain such independence.

According to the views of Piaget, development is fixed, unalterable, and evolutionary. His developmental concept is divided into a series of subunits, and this philosophy might be summarized as follows:

1. There is an absolute continuity of all developmental processes.

2. Development proceeds through a continuous process of generalization and differentiation.

3. This continuity is achieved by a continuous unfolding of new phases. Each level which is achieved is based on the preceding level and will form a continuous link with the future ones.

4. Each phase involves a repetition of processes of the previous level in a different form of organization. Previous behavioral patterns become inadequate and develop into parts of a new and superior level.

5. The difference in organizational patterns creates a hierarchy of experience and actions.

6. Individuals achieve different levels within a hierarchy. Although there is in the brain of each individual the possibility for all these developmental levels, they are not all realized.

Piaget divided the developmental sequence into three major divisions: (1) the sensorimotor phase from birth to age 2, (2) the period of preparation for conceptual thought from ages 2 to 11 or 12, and (3) the phase of cognitive thought from age 11 or 12 on up.

The sensorimotor phase is primarily devoted to sensory and body-motor experiences. It is an exceptionally dependent stage with the bulk of all communication being restricted to the use of the body for self-expression. The young child's interest centers on primary gratification of bodily needs, with little or no knowledge of a larger area of social awareness than himself. The major developmental tasks of this phase focus on the need for the young individual to gain control of his coordination and motor activities. The newborn child must attain some sort of an accommodation with his environment and must relate his needs to his immediate experiences.

According to Piaget, the sensorimotor phase is a very important period, and as a matter of course, he elaborates more on this stage than on any other stage of development. This first stage is divided into six major parts: (1) use of reflex, (2) development of primary circular reactions, (3) development of secondary circular reactions, (4) coordination of secondary schemata and its application to new situations, (5) development of tertiary circular reactions, and (6) invention of new means of coping with the environment through mental combinations. Piaget's major ideas concerning this period may be summarized as follows: (1) The child in this first stage is still basically unaware of distant and near objects as being different phenomena, with little or no awareness of cause and effect. (2) Qualitative and quantitative differentiation begins to take place. (3) All the large variety of response patterns are finally unified into a single, action sequence. (4) This coordination of the separate experiences of the newly born child leads to the creation of perception within the child that he too is a part of the total sphere of action. (5) A primitive time sense begins during this period with a dim perception of a before and after sort of action sequence; a sense of the future in a very elemental form may develop in this stage. (6) The gradual differentiation of particular stimuli as parts of a total action sequence introduces the use of symbols as a kind of shorthand to facilitate comprehension and eventually communication. (7) There is increasing variety of available patterns of action, initial recognition of some sort of a symbol system, increased tolerance of stress, and an increase in the intentional be havior of the child.

After the sensorimotor developmental stage has been achieved, the child starts to use three additional processes: (a) imitation, (b) play, and (c) affect. Imitation is dependent upon the capacity to differentiate among several events and then to select and to react to them. Repetition is merely the use of what Piaget calls self-imitation. Play is an important concept to Piaget, and affect becomes increasingly evident in the first two years of life, with some being evidenced during the first six months. Ability to imitate is dependent upon the abilities to accommodate systematically and to discern differences between perceived objects. This latter ability tends to emerge toward the end of the child's second year. Play serves an increasingly important role as an expressive function.

As the child nears age two, he enters the stage of invention, and the ability to do mental combinations becomes a part of the repertory of the child. The early part of a child's life is based on a limited knowledge of his environment with concern being focused on his own action sequences. Toward the end of his second year, the child becomes aware of objects as being independent and autonomous, with properties beyond his intent and action. Piaget was very concerned with the question of a child's discovery of the permanence of external objects, and it is between ages 1½ and 2 that the child first indicates this awareness.

Piaget's second stage of preconception which lasts from ages two to four is less clear. Little research and writing exist concerning this phase. It is viewed as a transitional phase serving as a sort of bridge between the child who is totally preoccupied with himself and the child who is rapidly becoming a socialized being. This period appears to be one of great activity in which the child is constantly investigating his environment. Play is the central theme, and language increases in importance. The child displays an increasing ability to relate words to visible objects but evidences little or no ability to use quantitative and qualitative modes at the same time, nor does he appear to be aware of the relationship between them.

The third phase of intuitive thought is primarily concerned with an increasing social interest. Constant interaction with other persons forces a lessening of egocentricity. This phase, which lasts until about age seven, is actually a continuation of the prior stage. It is preoperational in nature and in many ways serves as a bridge between the child's passive acceptance of his environment and his ability to manipulate his environment in a more realistic manner. During this stage the child begins to use words to express thoughts, and his struggle is concerned with the resolution between *accommodation* and *assimilation.*

Language serves a threefold purpose during the third stage: (1) It is an important tool of intuitive thought and is used to reflect upon an event and to project into the future. Self-conversation is very common. (2) Speech remains focused on egocentric concerns, with assimilation being the most important adaptive process, and it is limited to a few expressions, since the child assumes that everyone thinks as he does. (3) Speech is used as a means of social communication in order to understand the external environment fragmentarily.

Play appears to become more social during this period. It still seems to be somewhat egocentric, but now the child is able to extend his thought process to a broader area than himself.

The phase of concrete operations lasts from ages 7 to 11. Operational thought is separated into two distinct phases, the concrete and the formal operational thought processes. The concrete phase is based on the assumption that mental experimentation depends on perception.

Assimilation and accommodation become less an experience of opposing forces than one of dynamic equilibrium. Two levels of cognitive thought may be described as follows: (1) As any whole becomes known for its parts, the child studies the "parts" and classifies them in relation to each other. This eventually leads to an understanding of the "whole." (2) In this stage of development, the child becomes concerned with establishing for himself a system of classification. He will constantly seek to classify each object as a part of a larger one, and will tend to organize his parts into hierarchical systems.

Piaget introduces two terms at this point that are necessary in order to understand this stage of development: (a) nesting, and (b) lattices. Nesting is a descriptive term for classifying an internal relationship between smaller parts and their all-inclusive whole. This term is used similarly to the term nesting blocks, which are a series of blocks fitting one within another. Lattices refer to a special form of classification which focuses on connective links and the parts which they link together. Ordering conceptually by means of a hierarchy of lattices stresses the creation of subclasses of related objects. Related subclasses are consequently linked together in order to create a coordinated whole.

At this stage of development, the child's use of language is somewhat restricted in that he tends to use word definitions without an awareness of all the connotations. Language is primarily used as a tool of communication but is increasingly employed as a tool of thinking. The child now has the ability to use thought concepts and language rather than only his physical being.

Piaget stated that intellectual advancement finds expression in involuntary behavior. The child is now aware that his dreams are a private happening and are perceived only by him. He understands that dreams are in his own mind and that they become available in sleep.

The last phase of formal operations occupies the period from ages 11 to 15, the end of childhood and the beginning of the period properly called youth. Piaget thought that much of this period is the result of cerebral maturation. The youth, unlike the child, thinks beyond the present and creates hypotheses concerning everything. He becomes able to perceive beyond current reality, and the world of ideas takes precedence over the "concrete" world. Cognition makes greater use of symbolism, and propositions are used in setting up theoretical systems for exploration. Assimilation and accommodation have little importance in this period. They are relegated to an unconscious process and are used spontaneously in processing data.

A major tool of this period is the hypothesis, and the youth frequently uses it in exploring his environment. Another tool which he utilizes is logical deduction. Deduction introduces a possible way in which contradictory and apparently unrelated wholes may be logically related.

Piaget's basic ideas concerning the stages of development may be summarized as follows:

1. All development tends to proceed in a unitary direction.
2. Developmental processes are in consistent order and can readily be described by criteria which indicate five distinctive developmental phases.
3. There are distinct organizational differences between childhood and adulthood in all levels of human functionings.
4. All mature aspects of behavior have their beginnings in infancy and evolve through all subsequent patterns of development.
5. All developmental trends are interrelated and interdependent; developmental maturity means the final and total integration of all developmental trends.

Piaget does not make any direct references to intellectual retardation, but his theory has been viewed as a system dealing with the process of intellectual development. Thus, we may well examine the relationship between Piaget's theory and intellectual retardation.

A major hypothesis which Piaget proposed is a sequence of definite stages of development. An assumption is made that these stages occur in the same basic order in most children. However, there is no assumption that each stage is linked to a specific age or that social and cultural influences have no relevance.

In order to examine properly the relevance of evidence either for or against Piaget's theory, we should examine the following hypotheses: (1) that children's responses to problems devised by Piaget can be classified in the categories of thinking which he devised; (2) that the order he suggests for the succession of different types of thinking is the same in the development of most children; and (3) that different types of thinking constitute certain stages of development (Woodward, 1963; Ellis, 1963a).

In considering the relation between Piaget's findings and intellectual retardation, we will primarily use his later work (Piaget, 1953b). McCarthy (1954) found a high consistency among different scorers who classified children's spontaneous speech in the categories described by Piaget. Piaget's concern with egocentric and socialized speech development has been subjected to criticism (Nass, 1956), but McCarthy (1954) made a full review of studies concerning this topic and stated that discrepancies in the proportion of egocentric speech reported by various investigators can be accounted for by differences in the definition and interpretation of Piaget's terms. Also, differences in the situations in which speech was recorded and differences in children's personalities may have been important factors.

To examine the application of Piaget's concepts to subnormal persons is pertinent to our study of intellectual retardation. Woodward (1959) observed a group of 147 idiots and young imbeciles from the viewpoint of Piaget's stages of sensorimotor development. All subjects failed to reach the lower limit of the Revised Stanford-Binet Scale. They were classified according to the problems of the stages of sensorimotor intelligence which they solved. All the problems of all the stages were administered to 65 of the subjects, and 60 subjects solved all the problems of stages lower than that in which they were classified. This suggests that the sequence of sensorimotor development which Piaget observed in normal infants also occurs in low-grade intellectual defectives. When the child's stage of sensorimotor intelligence (based on problem-solving) was compared with his stage of development of a concept of permanent objects, 87 per cent of the 147 subjects were at the same stage for both aspects. Hand movements and manipulations of toys were readily classifiable as primary, secondary, derived secondary, or tertiary circular reactions, which should occur at stages 2, 3, 4, and 5 respectively. Only 43 per cent of the subjects in stages 1 to 5 showed this correspondence. In all but six of the noncorresponding cases, the discrepancy was due to the manipulation scores being lower than the problem-solving scores. Behavioral disturbance was significantly more common among subjects with discrepant results.

Woodward (1962) found that in a group of 90 child and adult subjects intellectual retardation tended to produce lower-stage responses for copying geometrical figures by drawing than for number concepts and for other problems involving spatial concepts.

Inhelder (1944) suggested that Piaget's stages could be used as a new means of classifying different levels of intellectual retardation: those who do not advance beyond the sensorimotor stage would form the group with the most severe degree of retardation; those who develop as far as the stage of concrete operations would constitute a mildly subnormal group, corresponding to the present feeble-minded or moron category; and those who reach the intuitive and preconceptual stages would constitute two intermediate levels of educable mental retardation. This classification might be appropriate for adults who have completed their growth; however, application of this scheme to children would require some conjecture as to the final development of the child.

EDUCATING EDUCABLE MENTAL RETARDATES

A number of techniques, methods, and procedures have been utilized in the past in providing education for intellectual retardates. The first mode of treatment was to place the child in a regular classroom with all other children, without any regard for individual differences. It must be remembered that, in general, early American education seemingly assumed that all children were able to perform at grade level. Use of the regular classroom for all children initially resulted in a general rejection of the child with intellectual exceptionalities because of his inability to maintain academic performance in accordance with his peers. The retarded child also frequently exhibited immature social and behavioral manifestations which made him an object of ridicule and again caused him to be rejected by his peers and frequently by his teachers.

As a result of the failure of the regular classroom to provide adequate treatment for intellectual retardation, early in this century several school districts began to establish special classes designed to cope with the special needs of children with intellectual exceptionalities. In practically all cases, these classes were what we now term self-contained segregated classes. Each child was identified as intellectually retarded by some type of procedure and was placed in a classroom for the entire day with others of similar intellectual levels under the care of a teacher. The theory behind this type of treatment was that it would improve the children's social image, or self-concept, because they would be with others like themselves and would not feel constantly threatened by their inability to perform like normal children. The regular classroom made no allowances for intellectual differences with regard to the child's performance, whereas in the self-contained classroom for intellectual retardates, individualized programs could be devised in accordance with each child's ability. The result of institutionalization of special education classes has been phenomenal. Classes have grown from few in number to many thousands throughout the United States. Every state now provides special education classes for intellectually retarded youngsters.

Current research, such as the effectiveness studies conducted by Dunn (1968b) and G. O. Johnson (1962), seemingly indicates that special education classes have not always provided the expected results. Evidence indicates a general tendency for children in special education classes to perform less well academically than comparable children who remain in regular classrooms. Johnson (1962) pointed out in Special Education, A Paradox that even social adjustment cannot be said to be substantially greater in special education classes than in regular classes.

Failure of the self-contained classroom to provide adequate care for intellectual retardates has caused much soul-searching on the part of professionals involved in training and special education. Philosophically, there have long been objections to the use of segregated treatment of the atypical child. The very concept of labeling a child "mentally retarded" and placing him in a setting apart from his peers tends to set up psychological and sociological barriers which make it difficult for him to cope with, or to adjust to, a regular society at a later date. There is also a tendency, it appears, on the part of many teachers in self-contained classrooms to set too low a goal of expectancy for the child's performance. Many studies, such as that of Rosenthal and Jacobson (1968), Pygmalion in the Classroom, indicate that a teacher's expectancy is very closely related to a student's performance. As a result of these considerations, changing circumstances in our society, and concern for minority groups, other modes of treatment for intellectual retardation have been proposed.

Methods of Educating the Intellectually Retarded Child

During the last decade, ineffectiveness of educational services for the intellectually handicapped child has caused much concern. The result of this concern has been a widespread movement aimed at providing special services for these children. Federal and state legislation has been passed which provides, and in some cases requires, special services and specially trained personnel for the intellectually handicapped.

The following review describes some of the methods of educating such children that have grown out of this special education movement.

Methods Used in the Special Classroom

The Engineered Classroom. Hewett (1968) developed the educational model which is now known as the Engineered Classroom. Hewett's model was designed for the inattentive, failure-prone, hyperactive child who cannot be contained within the usual classroom structure. These children have been labeled as "educationally handicapped."

Hewett's model is based on the concept of the developmental sequence of educational goals. These goals or behavioral categories range from attention, response, order, exploration, and socialization to mastery. The implication is that we must hold a child's attention and make contact with him, encourage him to participate in and respond to learning, aid him in adapting to routines and direction-following, and help him to explore his environment accurately and thoroughly through multisensory experience, to gain the approval of others and avoid their disapproval, and finally to master academic skills of reading and arithmetic and to gain knowledge in curriculum content areas (Hewett, 1968). Although the ultimate goal of the teacher is to help the student to attain the mastery level, in helping the educationally handicapped child the teacher can profitably use the behavior modification principle of shaping rather than simply waiting for the ultimate goal to be achieved.

The physical environment of the Engineered Classroom can be described according to four major centers: the mastery center, the exploratory center, the communication center, and the order center. The mastery center consists of the student desk area where academic assignments are undertaken and study booths where the student can continue academic progress in a more individualized setting. The exploratory center should be located near windows and where there are sinks; it is used for simple science experiments, arts, and crafts. The communication center is for the purpose of improving social skills, and it contains record players, tape recorders, and games which require communication skills. The order center consists of tables where there are games, puzzles, exercises, and activities emphasizing attention, orderly response, and routine.

Instruction is based on a fixed daily schedule which includes activities for the group and time for individual instruction. At the beginning of each day, each student is given an assignment card. He should work on the assignment during the individual instruction periods when the teacher is working with other students. At the end of the day there is an activity period during which the student may choose an activity card from any of the four centers and may work on his own. (The following chart shows a sample daily schedule for the Engineered Classroom).

Daily Schedule (Engineered Classroom)

8:45	Order: Order task
8:55	Reading Individual reading Word study Skill reading
9:55	Recess
10:05	Arithmetic Practice in basic facts Individual arithmetic
11:05	Lunch
11:35	Listening time
11:50	Physical education
12:05	Activity period
1:00	Student checkout

(Adapted from Hewett, F. M. In N. Haring and A. H. Hayden (Eds.), Proceedings of Workshop in Instructional Improvement: Behavior Modification. Seattle: Special Child Publications, 1968.)

In every area of the curriculum, a task is selected for its "interest value" rather than because it falls within a certain grade level curriculum. For example, science experiments are chosen for their multisensory rather than their intellectual value. Another element of this program is that it attempts to provide rewards on a concrete, immediate basis. The reward, at first, may be candy and later, check marks are given. Each child has a work record card on which he collects check marks that can be traded in on candy rewards, choice of free activity, or a report card-complimentary note which is sent home to parents.

During the 1967 and 1968 school year, an extensive evaluation supported by a United States Office of Education grant was conducted to determine the effectiveness of the Engineered Classroom method. Three groups of students were compared: educationally handicapped (EH) children in the Engineered Classroom; students identified as educationally handicapped in regular classrooms; and "normal or average" students in regular classrooms. The EH students in the Engineered Classroom outdistanced their EH counterparts in regular classrooms and approached or exceeded the normal students both academically and behaviorally (Hewett, 1968).

SOCIAL LEARNING CURRICULUM. The Social Learning Curriculum has been found to be an effective guide for teaching educable mentally handicapped children.

Reduced to essentials, the two main characteristics which are requisite to social competence in a society such as ours are the abilities to think critically and to act independently (Goldstein, 1964). The goal of the Social Learning Curriculum is to help educable mentally handicapped students to acquire these abilities.

The Social Learning Curriculum represents a departure from traditional concepts of curricula for the retarded only in the sense that it gives priority to concepts and facts that lead to knowledge and behaviors which are necessary for assimilation into society when one reaches maturity (Goldstein and Seigel, 1958). The Social Learning Curriculum recognizes that while mentally retarded children require daily sessions in language arts and arithmetic, they also need sessions that will build skills which have important applications as problem-solving tools in socio-occupational events.

This curriculum recognizes five environments through and within which ordinary growth progresses. These five environments are designated chronologically as follows: (1) self, (2) home and family, (3) neighborhood, (4) community, and (5) extracommunity. The curriculum is designed to equip the student with the knowledge, skills, and behaviors that will assure him of a better than chance achievement of success in each environment (Goldstein and Seigel, 1958).

According to Smith (1968), the Social Learning Curriculum should be very effective in preparing students for eventual job placement. It provides learning experiences and preparation for employment throughout the child's education, whereas earlier programs for the retarded offered a watered-down academic curriculum on the elementary level and a "cram course" on vocational adjustment at the secondary level.

The Social Learning Curriculum has progressed through the conceptualization phase and is now being field-tested in classroom settings throughout the country (Goldstein et al., 1965).

THE SOME SYSTEM APPROACH. The SOME System is a logical sequence of activities that the special education teacher can use in planning her instructional program. It begins with a survey of what are called "S" variables. "S" variables include societal goals for education, school laws and regulations, and a survey of specific student needs, strengths, and weaknesses. The societal and school laws are included only to point out their indirect influence. The basic elements of the system are diagnosis and assessment of students' strengths and weaknesses. An individual profile is made for each child, and these are converted into a class matrix which can be used to predict the range of variance in different kinds of abilities.

The "O" in the SOME System signifies objectives. Data from the student profiles are used to plan highly individualized instruction. Sequencing and organizing objectives are key steps in designing this type of instructional program. The objectives can be related to one of three major areas—cognitive, affective, or motor—and they must be expressed in behavioral terms.

The third major part of this system includes the particular modality that the student demonstrates for learning. This can be determined in formal assessment with the ITPA, the Frostig test, or other instruments. Grouping children according to needs in modality training can be of great value, in that the teacher can select materials which are to be used based on appropriateness, mode of presentation, and rate of learning required.

The final component deals with evaluation. The critical evaluative criteria are how well the objective was achieved and if it satisfied expectations. If the objective is met, new ones may be undertaken. If the objective is not achieved, the problem area must be found before moving forward.

The SOME System is considered to be a model which provides the teacher with a unified and systematic way of developing a curriculum. Gage (1964) pointed out that models derive their usefulness from their generality. In this respect, the SOME System provides the special education teacher with a simple and adaptable method for educational planning and remediation.

Integrating the Retarded Child into the Regular Classroom

INDIVIDUALLY PRESCRIBED INSTRUCTION (IPI). IPI is an instructional system which is based on specific objectives combined with diagnostic tools and teaching materials (Scanlon, 1971). It stresses assessment of pupil abilities and continuous monitoring of pupil progress. The teacher diagnoses the student's abilities through a placement and achievement pretest that represents objectives within a learning unit. Based on this assessment, the teacher writes a learning prescription using the set of objectives and complementary instructional materials. The teacher's role in IPI becomes that of progress analyzer, tutor, and instructional manager.

The child in an IPI classroom acts as his own instructional agent by working toward mastery of objectives that have been prescribed for him. As he finishes a work assignment to his satisfaction, he turns it in to a teacher's aide who scores it and informs the teacher of the student's progress.

IPI is based on reinforcement theory principles and is geared to facilitate learning in the regular classroom through careful specification of objectives, pacing of instruction, and reward for mastery. Since this system does not depend on any prerequisite achievement level, it is not contingent upon homogeneous grouping. With the IPI program, retarded children might work at their own pace in the same classroom with normal peers without revealing their inadequacies in learning, which are often amplified in group instructional settings.

RESOURCE CENTERS. The resource center is a relatively new concept which is rapidly taking hold throughout the country. It is another example of a program which emphasizes pupil assessment as an approach to planning instruction (Rynders, 1972).

Resource centers are usually set up within a school system or in the area of several counties. The centers receive referrals from a classroom teacher, and some preliminary tests are then administered to the child to see if he is in need of the center's services. If the child is found to need special help, then (depending on how the center is set up) the child either goes to the center or is visited in his school by a resource teacher for evaluation and assessment.

After evaluation of a student, it is the job of resource personnel to prescribe steps for the classroom teacher to take. The center instructs the teacher in the use of materials if they are not available in her school.

In some cases, only when absolutely necessary, the student may receive some out-of-class help from resource personnel at the center or in his school. However, the resource and regular classroom teachers try to reduce out-of-class time by designing instructional material that will permit the student to progress without requiring too much extra attention from his regular teacher.

DIFFERENTIAL STAFFING. Other organizational and administrative procedures have been proposed by many authorities in the field of special education as appropriate methods of providing for individual needs. One method which has been proposed is differential staffing. The philosophy of differential staffing is much more important than the technical, organizational, or schematic design of the system. Its procedure is philosophically based on a completely individualized, flexible programming approach to the education of all children. The second part of the procedure is the concept of collective judgment, evaluation, and instruction of all children. Differential staffing raises many fears within existing faculties. It calls for drastic reformulation of attitudes, methods, and behaviors and especially for a new way of perceiving the teacher's role in the educative process.

Briefly, the differential staffing approach is one in which the total school is divided into units, which may be chronologically defined (e.g., primary, intermediate) or may be based on a combination of age and size of class. It is probably unwise to attempt to cope with too many children in a given unit. Each unit is ideally composed of children and staff in a setting in which a child may be provided with a variety of educational experiences. The staff of each unit is composed of a master teacher, who serves as coordinator and supervising administrator of the unit, together with associate teachers, assistant teachers, aides, clerical assistants, and volunteers. Each unit is responsible for providing the curriculum and activities for all their students. Each student is evaluated and planned for by the entire team and has a program which is unique for him. The programs may vary from day to day in accordance with the needs of the child.

Instructional procedures may vary from instruction en masse, to tutoring, individual research assignments, and field experiences. Thus, theoretically, differential staffing would allow the entire community to be utilized, if necessary, to provide for the needs of a child or a group of children. The differential staffing concept also allows for children to function at different levels in different subjects and for programming of curriculum in such a manner that each child may proceed at his own speed in each subject area.

EDUCATIONAL PARKS. For the future, it has been proposed by many that educational parks be set up in our cities and rural areas to provide a more fruitful environment for learning. Each educational park would be large in terms of physical area and also in scope of operation. The parks would be designed to cross racial and economic lines, thus eliminating any objections from minority groups regarding discriminatory educational facilities. All children living at sufficient distances from the parks would have to be transported to them. Such facilities would be available to individuals from earliest infancy to adulthood. The educational park would serve as a community cultural and educational center where activities would be provided for all ages and all types of individuals. The day care center would be an integral part of the educational park, since many parents must work and, therefore, are in need of adequate daytime care for their children. All children would have the physical and psychological environments which are essential for maximal realization of their potential.

Conclusion

All the methods which have been reviewed have one factor in common: their ultimate goal is to help the handicapped to adjust in society. Special education is a growing field and, hopefully, will continue to grow and change as needed to meet its goals. Special educators must invest greater resources in efforts to make general education more capable of accommodating the educational and social needs of handicapped children.

All the plans which we have discussed are contingent upon many social and economic factors. Possibly, some alternative methods may be developed during the next few years to cope with not only intellectual retardates but with all children. Teachers in training must constantly be alert to the need for change and for evaluating what they are doing to provide educational opportunities for their pupils. It is essential that schooling always be facilitating and never limiting.

The Teacher of Educable Mental Retardates

Characteristics

It is, of course, impossible to discuss in general the role and functions of the teacher. Teachers of EMR children should have all the skills, competencies, knowledge, and understanding of a regular classroom teacher plus specific types of knowledge, understanding, and skills required in the field of special education.

Many studies and articles have been written concerning good teachers and their roles, such as those of Charters (1963), Havighurst and Neugarten (1962), and Stiles (1957). All the studies have sought to arrive at some perception of the basic roles of a teacher during a teaching career. Perhaps one of the most difficult problems involved in teaching is to realize the proper role at a certain time, under particular conditions, and for specific purposes. Stephens (1965) viewed the roles of the teacher as being generally representative of the adult world. The teacher acts as a specialized director of learning, as a symbol of cultural values, as a symbol of morality and character, and as a friend and confidant of children and youths. In other words, teachers translate the needs, desires, and hopes of adult society to the oncoming generation.

Most studies (Allen, 1960; Foster, 1933; Taylor, 1962) have indicated that first-, second-, and third-graders, in particular, view their teachers as persons who should be patient, cheerful, friendly, and humorous. In all cases, children exhibited a dislike of the cranky, bossy, and "difficult-to-get-along-with" individual. It is interesting to note that even as children progress through the school system, they still show an intense resentment of the teacher who is unpredictable, erratic, and indisposed to treat students with concern.

Attitudes of children toward their teachers vary according to chronological age level, with younger children placing more emphasis upon parental type roles of the teacher. The teacher offers emotional as well as intellectual support for these students.

The most traditional role of the teacher is that of specialized director of learning, that is, the person who is responsible for providing the opportunity and methods by which students should be able to acquire knowledge and understanding of the world in which they live. This role has been thoroughly investigated by Fleming (1958), Smith (1960), and Woodruff (1962). A discussion of some of the components of this role follows.

1. The role of imparting knowledge, the traditional role of the teacher, involves informing students of what things are like, who did what, where, when, and why. It might be called an informing and explaining role. In conjunction with this, the teacher is often expected to be able to show how specific tasks may be performed. This role is particularly important for specific skills such as teaching a language.

2. An often neglected role, which is involved in directing the student's education, is that of providing additional or supplemental materials for the standard curriculum. In no case do textbooks or regular curricular materials encompass even an appreciable portion of the available material for students' usage. A crucial function of the teacher is to explore all available sources and to attempt to provide those which are most relevant to learning in her classroom.

3. The functions of a diagnostician and remediator are included in the teacher's role as a facilitator of learning. As the child progresses in school, gaps in his knowledge appear. A skilled teacher should be aware of these gaps in order to provide corrective procedures when they are indicated. Therefore, all teachers should acquire the basic knowledge of how and when to diagnose students' learning difficulties. An important part of this function is the knowledge of human growth, development, and psychological health, so that the teacher may know when to make appropriate referrals to other agencies.

4. In a changing and complex industrial society, symbols and cultural values have vital roles. They become roles of conflict in many cases because in a world in which values are constantly changing, it is difficult for a teacher to know what values children should be taught. Teachers are expected to guide their students' development of values, and inevitably, all teachers impart their own value systems, since all perception is governed by one's own experiences and understanding. Teachers should examine their value systems carefully and should study the value systems of their society, so that they will not impose misconceptions on their students.

An important subrole of the teacher is to create a climate in the classroom which is conducive to learning and to mental health. The teacher can, without a doubt, promote an atmosphere of good mental health for students. Implicit in any value system, and particularly in ours, is the teacher's role of creating opportunities for each child to earn status and respect from his peers as well as from his superiors.

The teacher of educable retardates should be able to function in all the roles we have discussed and, ideally, should possess detailed knowledge and understanding of the nature of intellectual retardation. The problems of EMR children impose certain limits on their functioning in certain academic circumstances. It is also essential that teachers be provided with the experience of working with intellectually exceptional children. The vicarious exposure of many teachers in an academic, collegiate classroom fails to provide practical insight into the nature of children with whom they will actually be working. Therefore, it is necessary that, as early and as much as possible, all future teachers of intellectual retardates be provided with many opportunities to work directly with youngsters having various degrees of intellectual retardation. The teacher must necessarily possess patience, tolerance, and flexibility, in addition to having keen insight into matters concerning parents. Parents of intellectually retarded children often exhibit anxiety, guilt, and frustration. Therefore, the teacher must be able to explain to parents their children's work in the public school and also must help parents to accept the limitations of their children.

Another function of the teacher who deals with intellectual retardation is to impart knowledge of this exceptionality to other members of her faculty. Most teachers and administrators fail to understand the potential of children with intellectual retardation.

Training

At present, teacher-training programs throughout the United States provide a traditional pattern of education during the first two years of college, that is, a liberal arts curriculum. In the junior year, the traditional college program for training teachers of intellectual retardates provides beginning specialization and work with such children. Increasingly, states are requiring all teachers to have advanced graduate studies, so that many institutions which provide training for teachers of intellectual retardates offer master degrees in this area of education. The emphasis, in all cases, is on both the practical and the theoretical aspects of teaching. In the past, teaching in a self-contained classroom (i.e., a classroom in which all students are intellectually retarded and are segregated from the remainder of the student population) was stressed. As pointed out in earlier sections of this text, the current trend is toward the integration of intellectually retarded students into the regular school routine. Development of this approach necessarily calls for changes in certain training procedures.

In addition to the generally accepted roles and skills discussed in this chapter, it is essential that resource teachers be provided with intensive training and experience in working with other members of the faculty, since one of their key functions will be to help students to integrate into a regular classroom setting. In addition, resource teachers need to have intensive training in teaching basic skills, so that they will be able to provide assistance to all their students. It is not uncommon for a resource teacher to teach children from grades one through seven. Resource teachers are expected to assist the school administrator in providing the best possible program for the child with intellectual retardation and also to provide the principal with information concerning the nature of retardation and what might be expected from a child with this exceptionality in a regular classroom setting.

In-service Training

The United States Office of Education is currently preparing a program for in-service training of teachers which has been called a "teacher renewal project." It has been proposed that a number of settings be provided throughout the states where teachers may come to receive appropriate retraining which will help them to function more effectively in teaching exceptional children and, indeed, in teaching all children. Public education's part in in-service training has mainly involved calling outside experts into school districts to lecture to the faculties on a variety of subjects. In-service programs, in general, throughout the United States have been largely a product of tradition, and little emphasis has been placed upon providing the kinds of experiences necessary for teachers to improve their attitudes and performances. In-service training should be intensified and every effort must be made to upgrade the attitudes and skills of all teachers to make them more capable of working with students in the regular or special classroom.

Training of Teachers and Parental Education

Failure of the teacher in public relations may be indicated by the failure of many tax and bond referendums. Teachers and administrators in the past have not been provided with adequate training in working with parents. It is essential that parents be involved in the decision-making process in education. Too frequently in the past, public schools have assumed that teachers automatically know how to work with parents and that parents should only be involved minimally in the actual instructional process. The current trend in America toward involvement of all persons in all walks of life would indicate that the school should be made aware of the importance of involving parents from the beginning in decisions concerning the education of their children. A parent who is involved in his child's education and who assists in making basic decisions concerning the educative process is far less likely to oppose the school with regard to acquisition of necessary facilities and necessary salaries for personnel. Teachers should have not only academic knowledge concerning parents and problems of child-rearing, but also simulated opportunities to improve their abilities to work with parents by means of a practicum in which they would spend some time interviewing parents under close supervision of their university faculty.

Relationships of Teachers with Other School Personnel

In the past, many teachers of intellectual retardates have felt downgraded by other members of the faculty. These teachers need to develop specific competencies, knowledge, and understanding of how to explain intellectual retardation to regular classroom teachers. Perhaps the most effective method by which this may be accomplished is by properly teaching all children with exceptionalities. If regular classroom teachers see that children with intellectual exceptionalities behave as adequately as (or better than) the regular classroom child, then they are likely to develop favorable attitudes toward exceptional children and subsequently toward their teachers. Teachers of intellectual retardates must constantly be mindful of the fact that mental retardation is no excuse for misbehavior. Intellectually retarded children can and should perform in a socially acceptable manner.

CHAPTER 10

MODERATE AND MILD EMOTIONAL DISTURBANCES

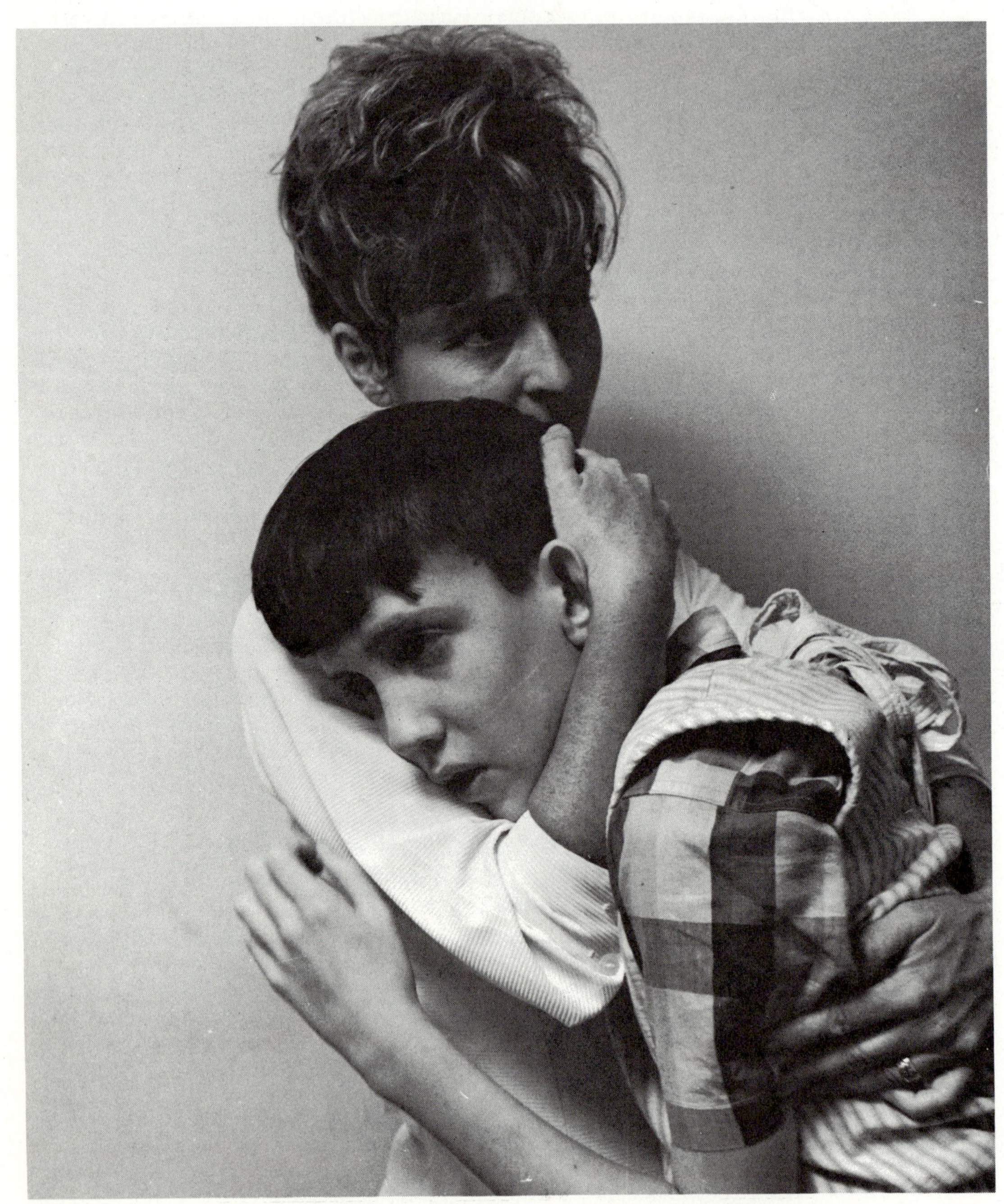

(Courtesy of The Woods Schools, Langhorne, Pennsylvania.)

A natural concomitant of a child's growth and development is his relation to the external environment. As the newborn encounters his total environment, he begins to utilize all his sensory and intellectual receptors. The relationship between a child's development and his emotional state has been the subject of a variety of theories and hypotheses. Many theories have been adduced to support a variety of hypotheses concerning emotional state as it is linked to environmental influences. We will examine major theoretical systems to ascertain their contributions to an understanding of these relationships.

Freudian concepts account for many of the current attitudes toward mental health, development of personality, and emotional development.

CHILD DEVELOPMENT AND FREUDIAN THEORY

The theory developed by Sigmund Freud (1856 to 1939) and all its elaborations by his many followers are far too complex to summarize properly in this text. Readers are referred to the voluminous literature for a full explanation. We should remember that Freudian theory as it is viewed today is the product of a long evolution. For our purposes, the later findings of the psychoanalytic school are suitable for examining the relationship between development and emotional functioning.

One of Freud's basic concepts is the idea of energy which he viewed as the basic driving force behind all mental processes (Freud, 1949). Freud was concerned with opposing forces, as is much of psychoanalytic literature. In the case of energy, Freud felt that there are two basic forces. He called the creative, liberating force Eros. Eros involves the instincts for life, love, and creativeness. The opposing force or energy is termed Thanatos, a destructive force known as the death wish. The essence of Eros as a basic driving force is explained by the portion of Freud's theory involving the *libido*.

One of Freud's basic constructs is the three-part system of consciousness. The id and libido are thought to be the oldest parts of this system; they represent all the basically inherited factors that are present at birth. An outgrowth of the id which develops as the id makes contact with the external environment is the ego, whose basic task is to mediate between the id and the external world. The most important task of the ego is self-preservation. Development of the ego is most closely related to Freudian belief in the development of emotional maturity. According to Freudian theory, environmental stress on the maturing child causes him to learn the basic principles of his culture. During this period of ego development, the third part of the system of consciousness, the superego, evolves. The superego may be most closely related to the concept of conscience. It is an internalization of external control factors, such as a mother's admonitions concerning socially unacceptable behavior. The superego processes ideas before they are implemented by actual behavior.

Mental processes, according to Freud, may be viewed as having three components—conscious, preconscious, or unconscious. The conscious refers to current awareness of one's environment, and the preconscious exists at the lower threshold of the conscious. Information in the preconscious is available for use at the conscious level. The preconscious is a sort of link between the conscious and the unconscious. The Freudian concept of the unconscious is of great importance and has become a popular concept in contemporary metapsychology. According to Freud, the unconscious composes the largest portion of the mental system and provides the basic "motive power" for much of man's behavior.

A central feature of Freud's concept of the developmental process is the stages of development. According to Freud, these stages are: (1) the oral stage of dependency which lasts until age 2, (2) the anal stage of retention or expulsion from ages 2 to 4, (3) the phallic stage during the oedipal rivalry with the parent of the same sex from ages 5 to 7, (4) a latency stage from ages 8 to 12, and (5) adolescence which ends with the teen years.

The defense mechanism is one of the most popularly accepted concepts developed by Freud. He believed that defense mechanisms come about because of a three-way struggle between the id, ego, and superego. The id makes certain demands for gratification of physical or psychological needs, and the superego vetoes many of these demands. As a result, the individual develops what Freud called anxiety. In a sort of stand-off between the id and the superego, the ego must turn to some sort of protective devices, and these are called defense mechanisms.

Defense mechanisms which are most commonly used follow:

1. *Repression* involves forgetting certain feelings, needs, or even actual happenings because their remembrance is too painful to bear. Such painful memories are supposedly buried in the unconscious.

2. *Reaction formation* involves denial of a disapproved motive by giving expression to its opposite. As a result of this mechanism, if a person fears his desire to drink, he may react by becoming a temperance worker. It has been suggested by some that this mechanism might underlie many social reform movements.

3. *Introjection* is a common mechanism that is concerned with the internalization of external social requirements. This mechanism is most important in the development of the superego, as in the case of taboos and restrictions that we assume to be part of our personality make-up.

4. *Isolation of affect* suggests that in some cases a person may be capable of separating an act from the emotional reactions usually associated with that act. In other words, a person may be able to talk about very brutal behavior without the emotions normally aroused by such behavior.

5. *Denial* is a defense mechanism by which intolerable actions, impulses, or wishes are negated. This defense may sometimes be coupled with a subsidiary defense called *suppression.*

6. By *displacement* the emotional charge related to one set of ideas is transferred to other, initially unrelated, ideas; that is, kicking one's dog instead of kicking one's spouse.

7. *Projection* is a defense mechanism by which one's own undesirable

behavior or thoughts are attributed to another. An example of this might be the person who sees hostility and aggression in others or often imagines them to be enemies.

8. *Regression* is a common form of behavior in which a person returns to an earlier form or stage of behavior in order to cope with a currently existing problem.

9. *Sublimation* is, in reality, a very mature defense mechanism by which an individual is able to substitute an acceptable form of behavior for an antisocial or unacceptable one.

This brief review is not representative of Freud's tremendous impact on contemporary thought concerning child development, emotional adjustment, family relations, sexual mores, and mental health in general.

THE ROLE OF THE FAMILY AND PARENTS

The findings of LaPray and Downing (1968) support current conclusions about the role of parents in the development and maintenance of emotional disturbances in children. Using the Parental Attitude Research Inventory (PARI), they found that "mothers of emotionally disturbed children differed significantly from the mothers of normals in their feelings toward their husbands," whom they saw as "inconsiderate of their feelings, actions, and ideas." LaPray and Downing considered the fact that these mothers might be attempting to compensate for inadequate marriages by fostering dependency in their children. Of course, size of family was also related to the child's psychopathology: the larger the family, the greater the incidence of emotional disturbance, suggesting also the importance of a child's ordinal position in the etiology of emotional disturbance. Another finding of this study was the greater incidence of emotional disturbances in children whose parents were professionals (teachers, social workers, lawyers, physicians, etc.), with the least incidence of emotional disturbance occurring in children whose parents were employed in labor occupations. This finding is incongruent with the usually reported relationship between emotional disturbance in children and social class. On the basis of these findings, LaPray and Downing formulated these questions:

> **Is the child's pathology due in part to the attitudes of the parents toward the child and toward each other, with the mother having definite feelings of hostility toward the father, not being able to accept these feelings at the conscious level, and not being able to communicate well with either the children or the father? Could it be that the mother compensates for the lack of attention given her by a husband who is "chained to his work," by attempting to obtain more love and dependency from her children and by the production of more children to obtain more compensated love?**

Rosenzweig (1969) found that mothers (of children in the latency stage postulated by Freud) who were able to establish mutuality of needs between themselves and their children had children who achieved higher academic adjustment than those mothers who were not able to establish such mutuality. Children of the former group of mothers showed higher internalized aspirations for achievement than children of the other mothers.

Birth Order as a Variable

Birth order as a behavioral determinant has been the subject of many different studies, although these studies have not always resulted in similar findings (Schooler, 1972). Sharder and Leventhal (1968) found that parents reported more positive attitudes for their last-born children when they were asked to "write a general description of the kind of person your child is." Also, parents who sought help for a last-born child mentioned fewer problems than parents who sought help for an only, first-born, or middle child. This study included 599 consecutive child guidance cases. The general results indicated that later-borns, especially last-borns, were reported to have had fewer problems than first-born children. Rosenow and Whyte (1931) also reported that more first-born children from two- and three-child families were referred to child guidance centers than later-borns.

Sampson and Hancock (1967), in an attempt to find relationships between birth order and specific personality and psychological factors, such as delinquency, conformity, alcoholism, interpersonal manipulation, sociability, and intellectual achievement, reported that problems in these areas were less likely to be found at either end of the birth order. First-borns, only children, and last-borns are likely to express overt aggression and are more likely to seek companions when they are anxious.

Schachter (1964) found that first-borns were more influenced and manipulated in their sociometric choices by social expectations and other persons' ways of thinking than later-borns. He reported that first-borns are more dependent, are more apt to conform, and have a tendency to evaluate their friends according to what other people think of their choices. From these findings, Schachter anticipated more interpersonal conflicts for first-borns than for later-borns. Later-born children were reported to be more independent, less suggestible, and less influenced by social expectation and authority figures. Later-borns were more social, outgoing, and popular among their peers; first-borns were more adult-oriented, more serious, less popular among their peers, and had lower self-esteem than later-borns. Some studies support the idea that first-borns have higher achievement levels than later-borns. Rosen (1961) found that first-borns are reared to be more adult-oriented and more concerned with adult approval and attention, both being characteristics which might contribute to higher achievement levels and which might help the child to gain teacher and parental approval.

Staffieri (1970), in analyzing birth order and creativity, found that first-borns are more suggestible, more conforming, and more dependent with regard to need for social approval and support than later-borns. Similarly, MacDonald (1969) found first-borns to be more socialized than later-borns in conforming to social standards.

Adams (1967) also found that first-borns, in contrast to later-borns, were more highly motivated in academic endeavors. He used teachers' ratings of students in specified classroom behavior to measure the children's motivation. His research also indicated:

1. Overrepresentation of first-borns among college and university students.

2. Overrepresentation of first-borns among men of great accomplishment.

3. Higher academic achievement scores of first-borns as compared to later-borns.

4. Differences in early achievement training of first- and later-borns.

This study also indicated that first-borns tend to consider the positive and to ignore the negative aspects of school-related feelings and behavior.

Blustein's (1968) study on first-born and second-born children from two-child families measured the differences between these children in school performance and behavior and indicated that first- and second-borns did not differ in scholastic aptitude. First-borns had higher achievement levels according to teachers' evaluations and most standardized tests. First-born boys were more apt to conform to classroom expectation of behavior than second-born boys. First- and second-born boys and girls did not differ in self-rating of their school abilities.

Newbert (1967) found that teachers rated middle (in birth order) children as being significantly more vulnerable to maladjustment. The middle children appeared to be more excitable (demanding, impatient, attention-getting, jealous, egotistical, and undependable) and more energetic (zestful and given to action) on a variety of ratings from personality questionnaires.

As Bradley (1968) concluded in his review, first-borns are more inclined to attend college than their later-born peers. By the time students reach graduate and professional school levels, the proportion of first-borns tends to be even greater. They fulfill their teachers' expectations, show more susceptibility to social pressure than later-borns, exhibit greater information-seeking behavior, and are more sensitive to tension-producing situations. First-borns are usually judged by others to be more serious and to display less aggression than later-borns, thus strengthening their motivation for achievement and helping to enhance their academic performances. Their competition with less successful siblings is bound to leave some scars on those who are unable to compete with them. Later-borns, consequently, may be more susceptible to conflicts and stress and more prone to fail than their older siblings. Later-born school beginners indicated lower self-esteem than first-borns, in contradiction to Schachter's findings (1964). Other measurements of complexity and self-centeredness showed relationships that indicate a promising area for future research and theoretical interest.

Essentially, birth order becomes a psychological factor because it influences how a child functions interpersonally and intrapsychically at various levels and how he views himself. His prolonged interaction with more dominant or submissive siblings will determine a long chain of competitive or noncompetitive attitudes that will shape his reactions in the future when he is separated from his brothers and sisters. Within this context and the context of his relationship with his parents, the child develops the way in which he views himself and the means to use successful or self-defeating patterns. In the daily, continuous interaction with his siblings, a child comes to see himself as a winner, a loser, a failure, a competitor, or a rival. His status position in the family will determine how others react to him and how he learns to react to others. By the peculiar overlap of status, power, roles, rivalries, liaisons, and cliques existing in the family, he will learn a degree of "give and take" that some day he will transfer to the external world. A child's ordinal position and status (Adler 1964; 1969) will become lifelong components of his psychosexual identification and self-esteem, determining his relationships with his spouse, his friends, his coworkers, and eventually his own children.

SYMPTOM-ORIENTED APPROACHES TO EMOTIONAL DISTURBANCES

Behavior may be viewed as a continuum which ranges from extreme withdrawal at one end to normality in the center to extreme hyperactivity and aggression at the other end. According to this outlook, behavior can deviate from the center (norm) in varying degrees. Small degrees of deviation in either direction would indicate transitory behavioral disorders; moderate deviation would signify neurotic anxiety or a character disorder; and extreme deviation would be manifested in psychosis. When we are dealing with behaviors within a continuum, it is often difficult to assign labels, because of the complexity involved in pinpointing exactly where an individual's behavior lies on the continuum. The following suggested criteria (Kessler, 1966) may be used in considering childhood behavioral disorders: (1) age discrepancy—dealing with outgrown behavior, (2) frequency of appearance of a symptom, (3) number of symptoms, (4) degree of social disadvantage suffered by the child because of his symptoms, (5) intractableness of behavior, and (6) general personality appraisal. However, the main problem involves the extent to which the child deviates from the norm before he needs treatment.

At times, during a period of stress, a child may regress in his behavior and exhibit symptoms of behavioral disturbance, but when the period of stress is over, the child returns to normal behavior. Such regression could be associated with the illness of a parent, a new baby in the family, or the family's moving to a new city. Such a behavioral disorder is transitory, not very serious, and does not require treatment. In many cases, it would be somewhat surprising if the child did not respond in some way to the additional stress of the situation. However, if the child were to continue to become more disturbed and if spontaneous remission of his symptoms did not occur, treatment might be in order.

In addition to degree of severity, age is also a factor in symptom selection in children. Preschool-age children may exhibit eating problems (not eating or eating too much), sleeping problems (usually not sleeping, wandering about the house, or having bad dreams), problems of elimination (enuresis, encopresis, and constipation), temper tantrums, and awkward motor habits. School-age children may experience insomnia, nightmares, fears, depression, nail-biting, nervousness, sibling jealousy, poor relationships with peers, psychosomatic illnesses, speech disorders, and academic problems. Adolescents may display symptoms of psychosomatic illness, poor peer relations, academic problems, and sexual problems, and they may exhibit the more classic adult disorders as well. All these symptoms are subject to varying degrees of severity, and most of them are related to either passive-withdrawal or active-aggressive reactions. The root of every symptom is found in everyday "normal" behavior, but as a symptom the behavior is distorted from its original state. Degree of distortion from normal behavior may be an index of the severity of the behavioral problem (Anthony, 1970).

Apparently, differences in family background can be found between children who display inhibited behavior and those who are aggressive. Jenkins (1966) found that behavioral symptoms of inhibition were exhibited by the child who had a close bond with a somewhat neurotic mother, who was rarely openly hostile and who seemed to have an overdeveloped conscience. Conversely, the aggressive child had an openly hostile mother with an underdeveloped conscience and general instability. The aggressive children had experienced rejection and neglect. The general differences between children having passive-withdrawal and active-aggressive reactions seem to be somewhat stable factors from childhood to adulthood. This fact raises the question of whether the reactions are based on family background (environment) or temperament (biology). A predominant response pattern of either passive-withdrawal or active-aggression is probably based on interaction between the child's temperamental make-up and environmental factors present in the family (Thomas et al., 1968).

The term, "neurosis," has been traditionally used to describe moderately severe behavioral disturbances, including character disorders (which will be considered in the following chapter), academic learning disturbances, and the more "classic" neuroses such as phobias, hysteria, and obsessive-compulsive reactions.

Anxiety Neuroses

One type of neurosis is overanxiety. If a child experiences constant anxiety, or anxiety for which no stimulus can be found, then the child is usually considered to be neurotic. Small repeated stresses can build up anxiety, or a single traumatic experience may be the cause. Anxiety may develop without the child's being aware of the circumstances under which his neurosis developed.

Phobias

Phobias are anxiety states in which the focus on anxiety-producing stimuli is sharpened. The child knows which stimuli give rise to his feelings of anxiety, but he does not know why he fears them, and his fear is out of proportion to the real danger. Most people withdraw if they have a phobia, and withdrawal is usually followed by a reduction of fear, but the phobia does not become extinguished. Eysenck (1960) found that younger children more frequently have phobias than older children. These fears lessen as the child gets older, but around age 11 the fears reappear.

SCHOOL PHOBIA. Most children experience school phobia at some time. School phobia may be caused by fear of doing poorly in school or by the child's anxiety over leaving his mother, or more rarely, his father. Lapouse and Monk (1959) found that 38 per cent of 482 normal children experienced worry and fear about school marks, and 20 per cent worried about exams. They found that fear of exams was more common in older than in younger children.

School phobia is a learning disturbance only in that if the child cannot go to school, he will have difficulty in keeping up with his academic work. Some feel that school phobia is a specific form of separation anxiety, interacting between the mother and child, both of whom are anxious about the separation that school requires. Others feel that it is a typical phobic reaction directed at school. As in most phobic reactions, fear of aggression or aggressive impulses leads to the child's withdrawal. When treatment is instituted at an early stage, therapy produces encouraging results; however, if the beginning of treatment is delayed for a semester or more, the phobia can persist for months or even years. Children sometimes experience animal phobias or phobias of certain objects, but they are quite similar to school phobia in that misdirected aggression is their underlying cause. The child is unable to cope either as a result of what he perceives as aggression in the outside world or as a result of his inability to express his own fears and underlying anger and frustration.

FEARS. The inclusion of fears and phobias among psychological disturbances results from lack of knowledge concerning the influence of cultural factors on their origin and maintenance. As Berecz (1968) concluded in his review of the literature concerning cultural influences on fears and phobias: "Socioeconomic class seems to be an important consideration which has been given short shrift by psychologists studying fears in children." Although few persons would deny that cultural factors influence the kinds of phobias that children experience, the relationship is poorly understood; that is, what may be called "truancy" in the ghetto may be called "school phobia" in a middle-class neighborhood.

For the purposes of the symptom-oriented approach, fears and phobias will be distinguished according to how they are related to personality functioning and how they effect the overall psychological functioning of the child. Some phobias may be viewed as encapsulated habits that may have been reinforced independently of the overall functioning of the child. Thus, the distinction between fears and phobias is based on degree of intensity and the relative degree of interference with personality functioning.

Hysteria

Hysteria in children is not too common, but when it occurs it is quite similar to the symptom pattern in adults. When repression of threatening instinctual urges does not hold up, the symptoms appear as: (1) isolated emotional outbursts, (2) disturbance of sensation, (3) alterations in consciousness, or (4) temporary loss of sense of reality (Kessler, 1966). At times, hallucinations, which are midway between the normal person's "voice of conscience" and the psychotic hallucination, may be present. Treatment, as with the adult hysteric, is fairly easy because such children are quite suggestible; however, insight therapy may be necessary to relieve the child of the underlying conflict.

Conclusion

For a thorough review of research on symptoms of emotional disturbance in children, the reader should consult Anthony (1970). One of Anthony's conclusions, which is in accordance with the symptom-oriented approach, is that it is difficult to separate functioning from dysfunctioning in children:

> **In summary, these longitudinal, cross-sectional and retrospective studies all point to the fact that there is a fairly sizable pool of disturbance in the general children's population, varying in amount with such factors as class and culture. Certain ages make a larger contribution to the pool and boys in general add more than their share. The pool is in a constant state of flux, with symptoms coming and going, and certain stages of development seem more prone to certain constellations of symptoms. Apart from intensity and persistence, there are certain types of symptoms that are far more likely to be found in clinical subjects. Although symptom tolerance is undoubtedly a factor affecting the referral, the making of a child patient is not actively a function of the complaining parent. Certain transformations take place in the child—internalizations, identifications, defense organiza-**

tion—and render him diagnosably different from children undergoing a transient developmental stress with the manifestation of transient symptoms.

SUICIDE IN CHILDHOOD AND ADOLESCENCE

Suicide has been increasing among children and adolescents at a rate which is higher than that of any other group. In 1970, suicide ranked as the fourth leading cause of death in the 15 to 19 age group. It is estimated that 12 per cent of all suicide attempts in the nation are made by adolescents, and 90 per cent of these may be attributed to females. Despite the predominant number of females who attempt suicide, male deaths by suicide outnumber female deaths by a ratio of three to one. From a racial standpoint, Puerto Rican youths have the highest suicide rate of any other group, followed by the white population. Blacks have the lowest percentage of suicidal deaths of any major ethnic group, although the rate has begun to increase in recent years (Ellis and Allen, 1961; Gould, 1965; Toolan, 1968).

A study by Toolan (1968) revealed a predominance of first-borns among young suicide attemptors. Another significant variable is time of year, with the highest incidence of suicide occurring in the spring months. One study indicated that the most likely time for adolescent suicide is between 3:00 P.M. and midnight, which differs from the adult peak, occurring between midnight and 6:00 A.M. (Tuckman and Connon, 1962).

Most reports conclude that suicide in children under age 12 is very rare, usually impulsive, and not particularly associated with depression and suicidal preoccupation (Balser, 1966). Shaw and Schelkun (1965), however, considered reports of childhood suicide incidence to be misleading for three reasons. First, since children have less access to tools of self-destruction, their deaths are often classified mistakenly as accidents. Second, they are much less likely to leave notes or other signs of intent. Finally, there is a cultural tendency to underestimate the strength of a child's emotions and motivations.

Most studies agree that the dynamics of suicide might be better understood if the individual's background could be reconstructed, with emphasis on early development, rearing, emotional climate of the home, and traumatic life experiences. However, since the persons who know most about the child's life may be unreliable, owing to defensiveness stemming from guilt feelings, this task is particularly difficult. Even so, certain similarities have emerged from studies in recent years. Perhaps the most significant factor is the unstable or broken home. Family disorganization and the factors usually associated with family breakdown characterize the life experience of suicide attemptors. One study revealed that of the attemptors being studied, 40 per cent had stepparents, usually stepfathers, and in every case the stepparent was viewed by the child as being unwanted. Parental neglect, cruelty, and even abandonment were not uncommon (Toolan, 1968).

Illnesses, operations, and accidents were also found to be frequent occurrences in the life histories of suicide attemptors. Chronic physical diseases, prolonged periods of pain, and poorly controlled or debilitating disease, such as diabetes, seem to *decrease* the child's willingness to endure the problems of living. This conclusion is contrary to the folk belief that prolonged illness makes a child stronger and less susceptible to stress (Finch and Poznanski, 1971).

Suicide attemptors become increasingly socially alienated from community organizations and are unable to maintain satisfying peer relationships. One study indicated that although intelligence of attemptors was in the normal range, 75 per cent were one to four years behind in school because of sporadic or chronic academic failure (Rosenberg and Latimer, 1966).

Jacobs' book (1971) which deals exclusively with adolescent suicide includes an analysis of the progressive steps leading to adolescent isolation which precedes suicide. He found that suicide attemptors typically had long-standing histories of social and personal problems, intensified by a sudden escalation of problems. In addition, he noted that such individuals displayed progressive failure of available adaptive techniques for coping with old and increasing new problems. The final step was characterized by a chain reaction of dissolution of any remaining meaningful social relationships in the weeks or days preceding the attempt.

The psychodynamics of suicide are different in the child, adolescent, and adult. There is no universally accepted etiology, since suicide is a symptomatic act which may have varying multiple causes. Some authors clearly distinguish between suicide attempting and suicide committing, citing a probable psychodynamic difference between the two. Others accept Schrut's conclusion (1964) that the attempt is a phase in the continuum of self-destructive behavior, which may or may not end in death. This is an important consideration since inferences in the literature are usually based on unsuccessful attempts, while most data concerning actual suicide are provided by coroners. Also, a large number of adolescent suicides are unreported because of social, religious, and legal taboos. Application of conclusions drawn from studies on unsuccessful attempts may not be valid in predicting risk factors of successful suicides.

Whereas depressive behavior is almost always associated with suicidal ideation in the adult, this is not the case with children. Schrut found that only 4 out of 19 cases of suicidal children that he studied were chronically depressed, schizoid children, while 15 were "hostile and aggressive, acting out, or openly delinquent" (Glaser, 1965). Toolan (1968) noted that in the young child, behavioral problems such as temper tantrums, disobedience, truancy, running away, accident proneness, masochistic actions, and self-destructive behavior often indicate depressive feelings. Other authors, already cited, include boredom, restlessness, preoccupation with trivia, sadism, and magical thinking in this symptomatology.

Most young people who attempt suicide consider death to be the only rational solution to their problems. A study on attitudes toward death found that suicidal adolescents feared death less than nonsuicidal peers and were more aware of and concerned with the manipulative aspects of death. They viewed death not as an adventure but as a cure for their problems (Lester, 1971). Most parents included in this study did not have a clear image of their children's problems. Mutual frustration had developed between parent and child and had led to uneasy resignation, until both had stopped trying to understand and to communicate with each other (Teicher and Jacobs, 1966).

Toolan (1968) indicated five categories of suicide attempts: (1) anger at another which is internalized in the form of guilt and depression, (2) attempts to manipulate another to gain love and affection or to punish, (3) signal of distress, (4) reactions to feelings of inner disintegration, and (5) a wish to join a dead relative.

Since discussion of death is a social taboo, a realistic understanding of death is inhibited in our society. Suicidal children may have no concept of the finality of death. They often feel that they will somehow witness the suffering and grief of those who are objects of their anger. The culture strengthens this ideation by maintaining notions which testify to the unreality of death under the guise of "protecting the child," such as the use of euphemisms ("Grandpa went away"). The media, also, treat death casually and present characters who are virtually invulnerable. Horror comic books have been blamed repeatedly for being the cause of both deliberate and accidental child suicides. Psychoanalytic theorists believe that adolescent suicide represents an active attempt to overcome, by magic and omnipotence, passively endured trauma in the preoedipal and oedipal periods.

Tuckman and Connon (1962) contended that suicidal behavior does not represent a form of mental illness, but rather *acting-out* behavior in an attempt to control the environment. The motivating emotions of acting-out may be anger and hostility toward controlling parents, feelings of worthlessness and guilt, and frustration in attempting to find solutions without resorting to dramatic actions (Glaser, 1965).

Glaser (1965) distinguished six groups having different major motivational factors behind their suicide attempts. The first group is motivated by loss (real or imagined) of a love object followed by acute or prolonged grief. Secondly, there are those who view themselves as "the bad me." Such a markedly self-depreciating opinion of oneself demands self-punishment and blame. Low self-esteem is reinforced by parental comments and actions. The suicide attempt represents an effort to obtain restitution for "wrongdoings." Children in the third group are those expressing a final cry for help from beyond the immediate family, usually when family disorganization and crises reach a peak. The fourth group includes the revengeful teenager who seeks to punish another, usually a parent, and the fifth group includes the psychotic adolescent having a history of extremely unstable behavior. Finally, there are adolescents engaging in suicidal games, relatively rare phenomena which include Russian roulette, racing at high speeds, and accepting dangerous dares from peers.

Shaw and Schelkun (1965) discovered certain constitutional correlations associated with suicide in children. They observed that hypersensitivity, characterized by intense reaction to emotional stimuli and low tolerance for frustration, is typical of these children. They are also quite suggestible, easily absorbing a conscious or unconscious death wish from parents. Grieving parents have recalled unintentional "suggestions" that proved fatal, such as "go hang yourself." The second constitutional correlation relates psychological or physical pathology, including schizophrenia, psychoneurosis (especially with internalization), and impulsive hyperactivity associated with brain damage, to childhood suicide. The final factor, developmental disturbance, was manifested in difficult adjustment problems, especially in adolescence.

Because of the possibility of death or permanent injury, any expressed intent concerning self-destruction constitutes a psychiatric emergency, which requires special therapeutic approaches and preventive techniques (Glaser, 1965). The teacher should be alert to obvious warning signals which must be seriously heeded and evaluated according to the child's mood changes, increased temper outbursts, change in school performance, and withdrawal from friends. Usually, the first place the child's difficulties are noted outside the home is in the school setting. Early identification of those in the high-risk group is essential for prevention of suicide attempts. An intensive after-care program for all such individuals should be mandatory. This is indicated by the fact that 42 per cent of adolescents who repeated suicide attempts after hospitalization had a significantly higher rate of contacts with social agencies such as welfare agencies, mental health clinics, or hospitals than those who did not reattempt suicide (Jacobziner, 1965; Barter et al., 1968).

Toolan (1968) theorized that it is always preferable to have a period of observation in a hospital setting where the child can be prevented from hurting himself. The hospital stay also provides immediate release from the pressures and frustrations of the home situation. Further supportive measures are provided by the constant availability of a therapist to care for and listen to the patient. The patient must be assured that he and his problems are being taken seriously, and any procedure which further diminishes the patient's self-esteem must be avoided. Hospitalization allows the therapist time to understand the child's situation without offering empty reassurances (Gould, 1965).

The therapist constructs an appraisal of the seriousness of the suicide attempt by analyzing the depth of conflict, the child's inner resources, and available outer resources and by assessing the stressful situation. The next step is to stimulate the patient to undertake constructive action and to control destructive impulses.

The prognosis for young suicide attemptors is dependent on the reactions of those with whom the child comes in contact and the overall supportiveness of his environment, including the school. The patient's ability to verbalize his difficulties and his willingness to communicate his distress in less destructive ways are also significant factors. The most hopeful prognosis is definitely for first-attempt adolescent females. The outlook is less favorable for adolescents who have made a series of attempts and who continue to engage in fantasies of suicide.

The literature stresses the need for awareness among parents and educators of the signs of adolescent and childhood depression leading to suicide. Constructive action by means of counseling (personal and family), environmental changes, and an atmosphere of general supportiveness before the actual attempt is the most effective and efficient form of prevention.

THE RESULTS OF SEPARATION AND DIVORCE

Temporary neglect of a child by his parents because of a separation or divorce may cause the child to feel guilt and resentment. Often, trying situations, such as the child's being forced to divide his loyalties between his parents, the social stigma attached to divorce, the custodian parent's dating or remarrying, or the presence of an unfit parent, such as an alcoholic, may cause this to be a critical period in the child's life. Some, all, or none of these problems may arise when there is a divorce, but in most instances of divorce or separation, the child's position may be viewed as that of a hostage, an extremely destructive circumstance for the parents and the child. A hostage, or person kept as a pledge pending the fulfillment of an agreement, rarely has faith in his captors. While this situation can exist in an intact home, in a broken home the child may be "hostaged" for four reasons. He may be used: (1) as a means of depriving a parent of affection in retaliation for deprivation of affection that the other parent experienced; (2) as a means of insuring attention; (3) to insure total allegiance to one parent; and (4) as a means of obtaining payment of money. When a child is subjected to this kind of treatment, he too may learn to take advantage of others as a lifelong pattern in dealing with people. The child may submit to the role of a hostage because of guilt arousal, or he may bargain his allegiance to one of his parents. He may comply with both parents' wishes as a method of calming anxiety, or he may fight for self-survival in an aggressive way (Harris, 1961). Divorce or separation need not foster these destructive patterns, but awareness of their harmful effects on the child is necessary.

Divorce is prevalent in American society. In 1966, 10 per cent of all children were in female-headed homes, with 27 per cent of all nonwhite children, 30 per cent of poor white children, and 44 per cent of poor nonwhite children being in this category. It is estimated that 20 per cent of all adults have had single parent families for part of their formative years. This trend appears to be growing, and unless the nuclear family is superseded altogether, children of divorce will be more and more typical of our society, producing at least a temporary type of exceptionality.

COGNITIVE FUNCTIONING

Emotional disturbances may be viewed as representing different levels of cognitive structure. It is difficult, if not impossible, to separate cognitive from emotional functioning. Even though "emotional behavior" is defined as that which is not rational and hence not related to cognitive development, most evidence necessitates consideration of both types of development as being inseparable from each other.

Cognitively, there is a convergence of viewpoints among conceptual systems (Harvey, 1967), ego functioning (Loevinger, 1969), and moral development (Kohlberg, 1969). These are "stage" formulations which see behavior as ranging from an instinctive, presocial, and amoral stage to the fearful, dependent, opportunistic, conforming, conscientious, and autonomous stages. Sullivan et al. (1970) found low to moderate correlations among measurements developed from each viewpoint (after age was partialed out from the correlation coefficients), suggesting that each viewpoint is related to certain common developmental dimensions of behavior which are considered here under the rubric of cognition. Consequently, psychological disturbance could be viewed as representing various developmental levels and different types of cognitive functioning.

A promising feature of this approach is the matching of different conceptual styles with different instructional and, perhaps, therapeutic methods (Hunt, 1965). Harvey and Felknor (1970) indicated how different familial antecedents determine four different types of conceptual systems, which he distinguished as the conforming, rebellious, dependent, and articulated systems. They represent the various aspects of the concrete-abstract dimension that appears to be basic to psychological growth. Harvey's conceptual systems are similar to Loevinger's milestones of ego development and Kohlberg's levels of moral development.

Psychological Identification and Self-Concept

Most self-concept theorists (e.g., Rogers, 1959; Kohlberg, 1969) consider self-esteem to be an important component of one's cognitive structure. How one views himself tends to influence how he views the world. The relationship between negative self-concept and adjustment has been best illustrated by Kaplan and Pokorny's research (1969). On the basis of interviews with a random sample of 500 adults, they found significant relationships between self-derogatory, negative attitudes and reports of anxiety, depression, and utilization of medical and psychiatric resources.

In measuring children's self-concepts as they are related to race, Stabler and Johnson (1970) concluded that the colors black and white in and by themselves have meanings that are substantially similar to meanings which are, unfortunately, commonly associated with racial membership: white is "good," and black is "bad." Using black and white boxes and self-concept statements, they found that statements like "I am good," "I like myself," and "I'm glad I'm here" were significantly associated with a white box, whereas statements such as "I am stupid" and "I am the loser" were significantly related to a black box. White boys as a group were more differentiated in this respect than white girls and black children in general.

Posner (1969) found that children of low socioeconomic status (SES) displayed significantly more negative self-images than their counterparts from upper-middle SES, and that black children significantly more often had negative self-images than white children. The self-images of Puerto Rican children did not differ significantly from those of either white or black children. Children with below average IQ scores more often had negative self-images than their counterparts with superior IQ scores. Finally, low SES children showed significantly more pronounced self-ideal discrepancy than children from the upper-middle SES level. These and other findings, according to Posner, fail to support a developmental approach that views self-ideal disparity as being positively related to social and cognitive maturity. Instead, she interpreted her findings as supporting a relationship between positive self-evaluation and healthy personality development. How a child views himself is determined by biological, cultural, and intrapsychic factors.

Ziller (1969), in an extensive series of studies on self-other orientation, measured the components of such orientation in terms of: (1) self-esteem, (2) social interest, (3) self-centrality, (4) identification, (5) majority identification, (6) complexity, (7) power, (8) openness, (9) inclusion, and (10) marginality. In children, he found that preschoolers categorized as less mature for school entrance showed lower self-esteem. Black school beginners showed lower self-esteem than white school beginners in two rural southern schools.

Many of the inconsistent results of studies on selected aspects of self-concept and external behavior may well be attributed to the doubtful validity of the instruments used to measure these variables. The self-concept, as a genotype, is so far removed from self-presentational and phenotypical levels of functioning that any objective and direct method of assessing it may be distorted by the child's need to behave favorably, according to socially acceptable norms. Therefore, what the child reports may have little, if anything, to do with how he truly feels about himself.

LEARNING DISABILITIES

Definitions

Defining learning disabilities, as they are related to the exceptional child, is a difficult and somewhat confusing task. It would be impossible to include all the definitions of learning disabilities in this text; however, some of the major definitions that have been advanced follow:

> **Learning disabilities refer to retardation disorders or delayed development in one or more of the processes of speech, language, reading, spelling, writing, or arithmetic resulting from a possible cerebral dysfunction and/or emotional or behavior disorder and not from mental retardation, sensory deprivation, or cultural or instructional factors (Kirk, 1962).**
>
> **A child with learning disabilities is one with significant intradevelopmental discrepancies in central motor, central perception, or central cognitive processes which lead to failure in behavioral reactions in language, reading, writing, spelling, arithmetic, and/or content subjects (Kass, 1966).**

In essence, all definitions of the general area of malfunctioning in learning refer primarily to the inability of a child to perform adequately in academic subject areas supposedly because of conditions other than instructional factors or mental retardation. Even in terms of brain damage, minimal or otherwise, the biological deficit develops within a social context (the family) which may *deal* with the deficit in constructive or destructive ways. There is a whole class of learning disabilities without any evidence of the slightest perceptual or cerebral deficit.

Characteristics of Behavioral Disorders and Learning Disabilities

Regardless of the definition applied to learning disabilities, certain symptoms, which are viewed collectively as a syndrome, are sometimes used to identify this exceptionality:

1. Perhaps the most commonly noted symptom in the literature is hyperactivity or distractability. This particular symptom has been reported since the time of Strauss and Werner (1942). Parents typically describe the child with this symptom as not being able to stay still or as being habitually in motion. Included in the problem of distractability or hyperactivity is short attention span. At times, distractable children have been referred to as "grasshopper" children, that is, children who "light" for only a moment and then proceed to some other kind of behavior or drift into *dissociation.* Many children with this symptom seem to be unable to select the appropriate stimuli from the total number that are available to them in their environments. This particular condition has also been associated with other exceptionalities such as cerebral palsy, epilepsy, and other central nervous system disorders.

2. A second typical symptom of learning disability is lack of appropriate muscle coordination, either gross or fine. Parents and teachers frequently report that a child seems to be a little more clumsy than most children or a little less able to perform adequately. As an infant the child might have spilled his milk or managed to knock things off surfaces more frequently than is normal. Often, this symptom is somewhat difficult for parents to describe, although in some cases the incoordination may be evident. For example, the child may be unable to catch a ball or hit a ball with a bat.

3. A problem frequently occurring in children with learning disabilities has been called "dissociation," that is, the inability of a child to respond to a totality (a *gestalt* or a whole). The child tends to respond to only a portion of a total pattern or total configuration.

4. Figure-background disturbance (confusion of a figure with its background) is another common symptom (Cruickshank et al., 1957).

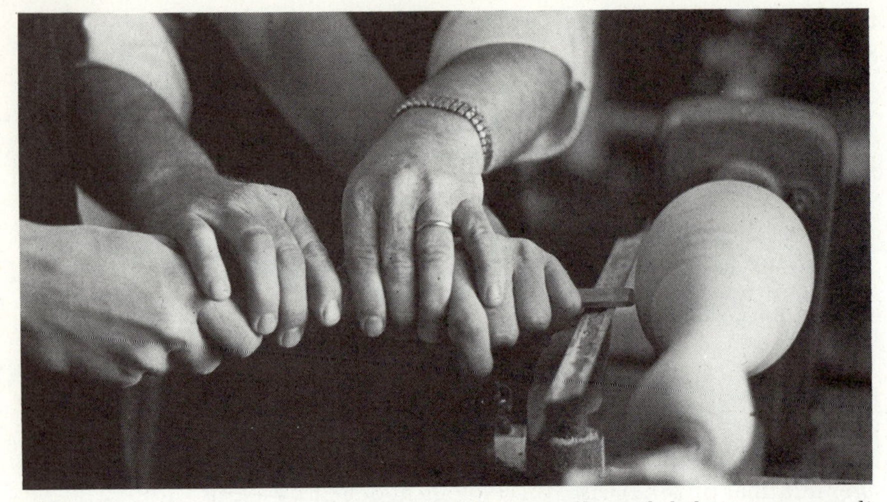

Figure 10–1 The child with a learning disability typically needs help in motor coordination. (Courtesy of The Woods Schools, Langhorne, Pennsylvania.)

Apparently, there are two varieties of figure-background disturbance. One variety is visual; the child fails to recognize or to differentiate appropriate stimuli from their backgrounds. The second type is auditory; the child is unable to select appropriate auditory signals and thus responds inappropriately or fails to respond at all. These factors appear to be somewhat related to dissociation and *disinhibition.*

5. Perseveration is a common symptom of children with learning disabilities which is compounded by the fact that it is also a problem of deaf, mentally retarded, and emotionally disturbed children. Perseveration refers to the child's inability to shift from one activity to another or to his giving the same response to a series of different stimuli.

6. The self-concepts of these children tend to be somewhat depressed; they tend to indicate feelings of inadequacy and incompetency.

Perhaps more serious than the problems of defining learning disabilities and listing symptoms is the problem of school placement of these children. School placement should always be the result of an intensive examination, and the ultimate decision should be the responsibility of a multidisciplinary placement committee. All significant individuals who will be or who have been involved with the child should be included in the placement committee. Decisions involving school placement should always be geared toward minimal intervention; that is, placement of each child should result in as little change in normal education as possible, but should provide for optimal attention to his particular needs, as reported by the various individuals who work with the child. The basic goal of the child's placement should always be that of transition from current difficulties to a fully functioning role in the regular classroom.

ACADEMIC UNDERACHIEVEMENT

Academic underachievement can be caused by biological deficits, cultural deprivations, or psychological disturbances. In the absence of biological deficits or cultural disadvantage, we may consider the cause of the disturbance to be emotional. Academic learning disabilities with psychological etiologies quite often involve the concept of achievement. Adequate academic achievement is defined as equality between intellectual functioning and rate of learning. Underachievement represents a slower rate of learning than would be otherwise predicted by the level of intellectual functioning. Some children tend to be overachievers, and others tend to be underachievers, who present serious problems both to society and to themselves. The adequately achieving child copes with his anxiety, places a high value on his own worth, accepts authority, has positive relationships with his peers, has little conflict over independence-dependence decisions, engages in activities centered on academic interests, and has realistic goals. The opposite is true for the underachiever. Furthermore, the gifted underachiever tends to be self-sufficient and unsociable toward his peers, identifies little with his parents, and has few surrogate parent models among his teachers, because they usually tend to be overachievers.

Underachievers may be classified in two general groups: the first group includes the more withdrawn, passive individuals who never reach their potentials; the second group includes hyperactive and aggressive children who disrupt classes and annoy their teachers. The aggressive, hyperactive child can usually be helped by his parents. By determining what is upsetting the child, they may be able to help him by changing their behavior toward him and reassuring him. Most children who have a reading disability have some sort of biological deficit or cultural disadvantage, but some do not. The latter group are dependent children who are accustomed to relying on others. They should be given remedial reading instruction, and their parents should allow them to practice more self-reliance and independence.

Reading should be considered as a complex act that is based on the integration of most input-output functions. However, as Gibson (1970) found, it is based mostly on the ability to discriminate properly. For instance, she found how differentiation between scribbling and writing at the kindergarten level is strongly related to socioeconomic level. In the kindergarten having children with the highest SES, 75 per cent of the students were able to make this distinction, while only a few children in a lower class cooperative school could distinguish scribbling from writing. Without the initial ability to discriminate—an input function—it becomes difficult, if not impossible, for the child to learn to read and write. Gibson emphasized the fact that

> **motivation and reinforcement for cognitive learning such as speech and reading are internal. Reinforcement is not reduction of a drive, but reduction of uncertainty, specifically the discovery of structure that reduces the information processing and increases cognitive economy. This is perceptual learning, not just remembering something.**

Thus, the child's underachievement represents a failure to integrate various subcomponents of his biological, cultural, and psychological forces. In some instances, it may be based on subtle, minimal dysfunctions in input. In other cases, underachievement may result from a failure to integrate output and input in terms of cognitive and affective components.

Theories of Underachievement

Brower (1967) defined academic underachievement as a "...significant and sustained disparity between capacity and performance, which defies rehabilitation through stimulation, tutoring and exhortation." According to Brower, there is a developmental sequence that is really unrelated to psychopathology (when underachievement is not related to acting-out). The steps in this sequence are as follows: (1) *assimilation-recall disparity*—a gulf between what the child actually understands and what he is capable of recalling (an information-processing discrepancy?); (2) test anxiety produced by low test grades and parental and teacher pressures; (3) intellectualization of failure through rationalization and projection of blame upon others; (4) breakdown of intellectualization and eventual regression; (5) goal-defection—the child feels stupid and helpless; (6) utilization of a shortened ego parameter, that is, by now the child has lowered his aspiration level and has received satisfaction from a lower level of output (increased attention from parents, teachers, etc.)—his behavior (lower output) has been rewarded; (7) reduction of test anxiety—by decreasing his expectations, the child can decrease the gulf between his expectations and his achievement; (8) reduction of assimilation-recall disparity by a lowered reception of information that, in turn, lowers his output.

Halpern and Halpern (1966) chose to use the term "antiachievement" rather than underachievement because they viewed this pattern as a defect in the child's attitude toward accomplishment, production, and mastery, and as the child's rejection of competence as a goal. In short, it is a disturbance in output that is not related to cultural causes but rather to individual psychological causes. Antiachievement is related to masochistic character formation that keeps the child in an orally dependent state. The antiachiever ignores social and educational requirements, upsets his parents and other adults, and at times becomes involved in aggressive behavior. He underestimates his self-defeating actions and grandiosely overestimates his ability to cope. In so doing, he hurts and defeats adults (parents, teachers, therapists) without being overcome by guilt, and he hurts and defeats himself without being deterred by injury to himself.

Kotkov (1965) distinguished seven different syndromes of underachievement: (1) passive-receptive parasitism—a process of magical thinking about laborless achievements, the product of maternal overprotection; (2) perfectionism—constant dread of failure in academic performance; (3) sublimation of hostility—masking anger with underachievement; (4) school phobic somatization; (5) chronic invalidism—inability to meet the demands of academic pressures; (6) acting-out sociopathic behavior—denial of anger and guilt and displacement to external targets; and (7) self-encapsulation—characterized by emotion-laden oscillation.

Rosen (1965) researched achievement motivation as related to cultures and concluded that achievement motivation is more characteristic of Greeks, Jews, and white Protestants than of Italians, French-Canadians, and blacks. Social class and ethnic origin interact to influence motivation, values, and aspirations, as shown also by Lesser et al. (1965).

Daniels (1964; 1967) believed that "morbid envy" plays an important role in underachievement, in that nothing can satisfy the morbidly envious person because a crippling belief in his relative inferiority is at the core of his self-esteem. Daniels supported Harry Stack Sullivan's contention that there are two underlying antecedent conditions for chronic envy: (a) either the child's parents subjected him to excessive direct criticism, or (b) they expected too much from him, so that he came to believe that he could never prove his worth or live up to their expectations. A third possibility, suggested by Farber (1959), is that envy flourishes in a domestic atmosphere of envy in which both parents are habitually envious. Under these conditions, the child learns to avoid success out of fear of provoking invidious comparisons. The harmful effects of such envy are directly proportional to the shrunken self-esteem on which it thrives.

Speery et al. (1958) explained underachievement as a response to a family pattern in which the children become the scapegoats of unsuccessful parents by presenting themselves as unaggressive, compliant, and in need of help. By failing, they can maintain dependence on their parents, whereas the parents hide their hostilities, deny their resentments, and conceal painful feelings.

Negative attitudes toward school and toward teachers are far more common among underachievers (Wilson and Robeck, 1965). However, such attitudes seem to stem from the individual's underestimation of his own intellectual capacities. He often views academic achievement as being incompatible with being "a regular guy" or "good Joe." His level of aspiration is lower than that of the high achiever.

Empirical Findings on Underachievement

Parental Practices

Chance (1965) found that children whose mothers favored earlier independence training made more school progress in both reading and arithmetic relative to their intellectual abilities than children whose mothers favored later independence training. Drews and Teachan (1965) found that mothers of high-achieving junior high school students were more authoritarian and restrictive in their treatment of their children than mothers of low achievers. This finding implies that a child's ability to achieve may develop within a familial context which provides a structured environment (clarity of rules) in the home that may help the child to become familiar with a firm and clearly defined environment like the one he will encounter in school.

Gill and Spilka (1965) found that, among Mexican-American secondary school students, high achievers consistently manifested less hostility and more social maturity, intellectual efficiency, and conformity to rules than low achievers. Achieving girls and underachieving boys appeared to come from mother-dominated homes. It is unfortunate that a different subculture group was not used to check the generality of these findings.

Grunebaum et al. (1962) suggested that fathers who display inadequate self-images and resignation, despite objective indications of educational and occupational adequacy, may foster "neurotic" learning inhibitions in their children. Mothers of these children typically maintained an image of masculinity that made it difficult for their sons to incorporate a masculine image into their achievement strivings.

Wilson and Morrow (1965) found that the parents of bright, high achievers (high school boys) shared in more activities, ideas, and confidences with their children, were more approving, trusting, affectionate, and encouraging (but not pressuring) with respect to achievement, and were less severe and restrictive, while experiencing greater acceptance of their standards by their children than parents of low achievers. Wilson and Morrow felt that family morale promoted academic achievement among bright high school boys by favoring interest in school and positive attitudes toward teachers and school.

Giuliani (1968) found that reading readiness in kindergarten children was directly related to "verbal-mental" ability as assessed by the Van Alstyne Picture Vocabulary Test (an assessment of mainly receptive intellectual functions). Children in the superior and high-normal reading readiness groups showed significantly higher self-concept test scores than children rated low-normal or poor-risk in reading readiness. Reading readiness was positively and significantly correlated with self-concept scores. No sex difference in scores among these groups was found.

Dudek and Lester (1968) commented on how adolescents with chronic learning problems tend to demonstrate a pattern of intellectual functioning characterized by unevenness and deficits in attention and concentration. They found that the children employed "good child" facades to cover up unsuccessful coping with underlying aggression and anxiety.

Ussery (1968) differentiated between those children having difficulty in performance (academic grades being significantly lower than the level predicted from achievement test scores; i.e., nonperformers), and children having difficulty in learning (academic grades and achievement test scores being considerably below average; i.e., nonlearners). Two conditions, competitive-success and competitive-failure, lent some support to his differentiation, suggesting differences in motivational and informational processing in nonperformers and nonlearners.

Silverman (1968) found that children rated as apathetic and withdrawn in nursery school achieved a lower academic level in grade school than children who were rated as interested and outgoing in nursery school. He failed to confirm the same relationship for children in nursery school who were rated as angry and defiant.

Hicks (1969) found that among introverts in an institution for disturbed children and adolescents there was a very strong correlation between school achievement and measurements of ability, while for extroverts such a correlation was not found. Higher achievers were less neurotic, suggesting that they may be better adjusted than lower achievers.

Berenbaum's (1968) data support the view that the nonachievement syndrome represents a consistent pattern of personality characteristics, differentiating this particular syndrome from others and thus indicating a significant type of behavioral disorder that appears to be independent from either biological deficits or cultural deprivations.

Santostefano (1969) found reading disability to be associated with constricted cognitive styles, a finding which supports the concept of cognitive styles as a means of further investigating reading disability.

Sex Differences. Carpenter (1968) found that internal-external control factors related only to girls' academic skills, whereas achievement, hope of success, and fear of failure were more effective in predicting the school performance of boys than of girls. Blustein (1968) found definite differences in academic achievement and classroom behavior between first- and second-borns. The child's ordinal position in the family and his sex significantly affected grade point averages.

Almeida's (1969) study indicated significant correlations between ratings of paternal love by average achieving and overachieving third-grade boys and their academic grades. Underachieving boys rated their fathers lower on paternal love than average achievers and overachievers. Underachieving boys also scored the lowest on intellectual traits, self-control, and emotional stability and the highest on traits of dominance and seriousness. Shaw (1967) also found significant sex differences in patterns of underachievement. Underachieving boys started to receive low grades in the first grade; however, underachieving girls did not start to receive lower grades until the sixth grade.

CHAPTER 11

ANTISOCIAL DISORDERS

(Courtesy of The Woods Schools, Langhorne, Pennsylvania.)

Acting-out against society is a natural outcome of the destructive cultural factors discussed in Chapter 8. It has been estimated that only one fourth of youthful lawbreakers are actually "emotionally disturbed" and that the other three fourths are psychologically normal youngsters from the lower classes or disadvantaged groups.

Three types of adolescents labeled "juvenile delinquents" are sometimes distinguished: (1) the social delinquent, (2) the emotionally disturbed delinquent, and (3) the unsocialized aggressive (psychopathic or sociopathic personality) delinquent.

Environmental deprivation is usually related to antisocial behavior. This relationship between environment and behavior may apply to the unsocialized aggressive delinquent, although psychological factors are also involved. For the deprived youth, delinquency may be a reflection of the society in which he lives, and the expression of his frustration in delinquency may be fostered by his magical thinking. He may have needs that he feels can be fulfilled only by stealing and may feel that he will not get caught if he is "cool."

In contrast, the unsocialized aggressive individual or young sociopath is antisocial and unable to exhibit the guilt or remorse expected of a normal adolescent. Such individuals present a psychological problem, which according to some researchers has an organic basis; however, since they usually come from lower-class families in which backgrounds of desertion, alcoholism, drug addiction, neglect, cruelty, or criminality are typical, their problem may be closely related to cultural factors. Although all juvenile delinquents are not members of disadvantaged families, most of them are, and obviously, widespread juvenile delinquency is closely related to the deprivation experienced by children of the lower classes.

GENERAL CHARACTERISTICS

The delinquency-prone child often lives in a home in which violence, arguing, screaming, and fighting frequently prevail. Instead of receiving favorable attention from his parents, the child is more often fought over, beaten, or punished. The child's own cruelty results from imitation and aggression, which he uses as means of revenge against the deprivation he has experienced.

There are, however, many overlapping biological, cultural, and psychological factors which are related to delinquency. Aichorn, in his book Wayward Youth (1935), approached the concept of delinquency from a psychoanalytic point of view. He described delinquency as "... a consequence of an inhibition of development or of a regression, which takes place somewhere along the path from primitive reality adaptation to social adaptation." He suggested that every child is born with a combination of hereditary factors and the need to express his own congenital character; however, the child's environment is a decisive factor in how he develops. Bandura and Walters (1959), in contrast, suggested that sociological factors which are conducive to the development of antisocial behavior may more readily operate. The seeming imbalance of cultural and psychological factors accounts for delinquency and acting-out children who do not come from the disadvantaged group.

Definitions

To define "juvenile delinquency" is exceedingly difficult. The definitions may cover a wide range; they may suggest a psychological phenomenon or a purely legal term. Perhaps the most exhaustive definition of delinquency is that of Carr (1950). He listed the following types of delinquents: legal delinquents—all deviants committing antisocial acts as defined by law; detected delinquents—all detected antisocial deviants; agency delinquents—all detected antisocial deviants receiving assistance from any agency; alleged delinquents—all apprehended antisocial delinquents brought to court; judged delinquents—all court antisocial deviants legally found delinquent; and committed delinquents—judged delinquents committed to institutions. The incidence figures on delinquency vary according to which of the preceding definitions is employed.

Stone and Church (1968) differentiated five types of delinquency based on psychological origin. First, there is normal or casual delinquent behavior. This type of behavior is typical of small children who experimentally steal from their mother's purse, shoplift from a store, or indulge in peer group prankishness or street fights. These incidents are not serious and most of these children develop their own inhibitions and controls without any action by authorities.

Second, there is subcultural or socialized delinquency which is characteristic of the lower-class child who grows up in a "ready-made" delinquent subculture or who turns to delinquency when frustrated. Such delinquency is typical gang delinquency and may eventually lead to individual adult criminality. It is important to recognize that this is not psychological delinquency; rather it is delinquent behavior according to middle-class norms. A gang member behaves in a manner which is acceptable to his culture and need not feel guilty. In fact, he would be more likely to feel guilty if he questioned the mores of his gang.

Third, there is the *neurotic* type of delinquency which often takes the form of symbolic stealing or is an indirect expression of unfulfilled needs. The individual actually has no interest in the stolen object; he is, in effect, stealing love which has been withheld from him or stealing to punish those who withhold love. He may steal in a way that insures his being caught in order to satisfy a need for punishment caused by unconscious guilt. So-called neurotic delinquents do not require punishment: they require treatment.

The fourth type is *acting-out* delinquency. This form of delinquency involves the free, deliberate, and often malicious indulgence of impulse. It is basically a form of revolt which is often directed against middle-class

Figure 11–1 Use of graffiti as a mode of expressing frustration. (From Wallace, J.: Psychology: A Social Science. Philadelphia, W. B. Saunders Company, 1971. Photo by Gordon Cole.)

morality. Acting-out delinquency is essentially an individual matter and does not involve peer group sanctions as subcultural delinquency does; like neurotic delinquency, however, it may express unfulfilled needs. The acting-out delinquent is often a member of the middle or upper class, and he may be motivated by hostility toward the adult world or by simple boredom which he expresses as aggressive, cruel, and destructive behavior. He needs help in order to channel his behavior in socially constructive ways.

The fifth type is psychopathic delinquency, which begins early in life and is thought to represent failure of the basic identification process, so that the individual is incapable of true feelings for others. The psychopathic personality may appear normal in other respects, but lacks strong emotional ties to reality. Unlike the acting-out delinquent who can be deliberately cruel and vicious, the psychopathic delinquent is genuinely unconcerned about the effect of his actions on others. Punishment does not alter his behavior, and the probability of therapeutic success is not very high.

A child with a character disorder, or psychopathic personality, is often classified as an unsocialized juvenile delinquent. He knows what social expectations are and can comply if he wants to, but instead he misbehaves and breaks the law without remorse or guilt. One might say that his superego is undeveloped. Such a child appears to be both aggressive, because he certainly exhibits aggressive behavior, and withdrawn from society, because of his nonacceptance of social values and rules. Sometimes this disorder is related to an organic deficit, but quite often the child with character disorder comes from a deprived environment. In a large percentage of cases, the parents of a character-disordered child are alcoholic, psychotic, criminal, or otherwise disturbed.

Incidence

The major source of data concerning the number of juvenile delinquents in the United States is the Uniform Crime Report (Kelley, 1974) published annually by the FBI. According to the 1974 crime report, there were 1,717,366 persons under age 18 who were arrested. Nationally, persons under age 15 made up 9 per cent of the total police arrests, while those under 18 composed 26 per cent; those under 21, 41 per cent; and those under 25, 55 per cent.

Not all arrested persons are turned over to the court system. There are many reasons for this, such as failure of the victim to cooperate or to appear for the prosecution. For example, about one-half of the juveniles who are arrested are handled by the individual law enforcement agencies without being formally charged or without being referred directly to juvenile court.

Forty-two per cent of the persons processed for Crime Index offenses were young persons under juvenile court jurisdiction. As in previous years, juvenile referrals for auto theft were significant: 62 per cent of those charged with auto theft were juveniles. The following percentages represent the juvenile referrals out of the total number of persons charged with each crime: burglary, 55 per cent; larceny, 39 per cent; robbery, 35 per cent; forcible rape, 22 per cent; aggravated assault, 17 per cent; and murder, 11 per cent.

Related Factors

A number of related factors should be taken into account in discussing the foregoing figures on juvenile delinquency:

1. Age: Statutory age limits varied from 16 to 18. The average age of juvenile offenders was 14.3.

2. Geographical Distribution: Both the FBI and Children's Bureau reported juvenile delinquency rates in urban areas as being three times higher than those of rural areas.

3. Sex: In keeping with statistics on other social problems, there were more boys referred to juvenile courts than girls, and the types of charges brought against boys and girls differed. Almost half of the boys were apprehended for property offenses, while more than half of the girls were charged with specific juvenile crimes such as running away or sexual delinquency.

4. Family Stability: The rates of delinquent behavior have been found to vary greatly with stability of the home. Research has indicated that children from broken homes, as compared with those from intact homes, frequently display more than their share of delinquent behavior (Eaton and Polk, 1961).

5. Socioeconomic Factors: Delinquency appeared to be a predominantly lower class problem. Reiss and Rhodes (1961) found that out of 9238 white boys registered in a junior-senior high school of Davidson County, Tennessee, the greatest portion of delinquencies were in the lower status areas.

Despite the preceding data, some workers are convinced that delinquency is not a lower-class phenomenon. They contend that the higher rate of delinquency among the lower classes was found only in large cities. Studies conducted in small cities and towns have not reported greater rates of juvenile delinquency among lower classes (Empey and

Erickson, 1966). Clark and Wenninger (1962), using a total of 1154 public school students from four different types of communities, found that social class differentiation is unrelated to the incidence of delinquent behavior within small communities. These investigators have theorized that there are community controls within small towns which are related to delinquent behavior irrespective of social class. There are other studies concerning undetected delinquents which have also failed to substantiate the fact that there are greater numbers of juvenile delinquents in lower socioeconomic groups. Some investigators are concerned about the inadequacies in official court records and in the criteria for illegal behavior. They have attempted to bridge the gap between official and unofficial delinquency rates by studying the extent of unreported delinquencies. Short and Nye (1958), using a questionnaire on a 25 per cent sample of all boys and girls in grades 9 to 12 in three medium-sized towns having populations ranging from 10,000 to 30,000, found no significant differences in delinquent behavior of boys and girls in the different economic social strata. The data indicated a greater amount of delinquent behavior within the highest economic status category than expected.

6. Racial and Ethnic Factors: There are often considerable variations among reports of delinquency rates of various racial and ethnic groups. For instance, Jewish children are reported to contribute far less than their proportionate expectation of delinquency (Robinson, 1957). In 1952, Jewish children comprised 15 per cent of the general population in New York City, but accounted only for some 3 per cent of juvenile court cases. Japanese-Americans also are reported to have a very low rate of delinquency, perhaps because of their traditions and family structure. The contention that delinquency is related to cultural factors is supported by Sollenberger's analysis (1968) of Chinese-American child-rearing practices which showed how these practices may relate to the relative absence of delinquency among Chinese-Americans.

7. Body Build: Much interest has also centered on physical build as it is related to delinquency. A classic study comparing delinquents and nondelinquents (Glueck and Glueck, 1956) reported a much larger proportion of muscular, big-boned, broad-shouldered boys among delinquents. Conversely, chunky, stocky boys and tall, thin boys were less apt to become delinquent. The significance of this relationship according to most authorities is that physique most likely plays a predisposing role in delinquency rather than a causative one.

Psychological Characteristics

Despite the fact that delinquents and nondelinquents are frequently found to have comparable socioeconomic backgrounds, they often differ in personality characteristics. Studies using the Minnesota Multiphasic Personality Inventory (MMPI) indicate that characteristics such as impulsivity, aggressiveness, and irresponsibility are commonly found among those who engage in delinquent activity. On the other hand, people who score high on scales measuring social introversion, depression, and masculinity-femininity tend to have a lower than average rate of delinquency (Quay, 1965b).

A number of investigators (Reiss, 1952; Quay, 1964; 1966) have identified three personality types among delinquents: the psychopathic delinquent, the subcultural delinquent, and the neurotic delinquent.

The psychopathic delinquent is defective in the socialization process, and boys and girls manifesting this defect have been given a variety of labels (e.g., psychopath, sociopath, nonsocialized aggressive, and defective superego delinquent). The problems of these youths are usually the results of rejection in the home. Professional workers generally regard this type of delinquency as the most severe and as having the poorest prognosis. Consequently, some form of residential treatment is required to cope with the psychopathic delinquent. As a rule, psychologists are somewhat reluctant to classify a youngster as a psychopath or sociopath, since this tends to denote that he is incorrigible and incurable. From the clinical viewpoint, psychopathic individuals exhibit at least some of the following behavioral characteristics:

1. Inadequate moral behavior is perhaps the most outstanding problem. While unsocialized aggressive children are able intellectually to distinguish between right and wrong, they frequently fail to observe such distinctions in their everyday behavior. Stealing, lying, drinking, and sexual misbehaviors are their typical norm-violating activities.

2. Associated with the psychopathic delinquent's defective conscience is the superficiality of his anxiety and guilt. Though these individuals often verbalize such feelings in difficult situations, they seem incapable of experiencing these emotions to the degree typical of normal youth.

3. Rebelliousness and impulsivity are also common characteristics. Typically, these adolescents are "in trouble" in both the home and the school.

4. Their egocentricity is also readily apparent. Although they appear to be outgoing, gregarious, and optimistic, they tend not to form close personal ties with others. In general, their emotional ties and loyalties are extremely shallow, even with their own family, and they tend to have a poor sense of responsibility.

5. They are inclined to be extremely punitive and are unable to postpone activities for future satisfaction.

6. They often make favorable impressions on others and have frequently been called "con artists", since they are able to persuade people to act according to their wishes (Clarizio and McCoy, 1970).

Subcultural delinquency is the result of what might be called deviant socialization with regard to the larger society and not to the child's subculture. In this case the subculture tends to be at variance with larger cultures. Delinquent children scoring high on this dimension are typically referred to as subcultural delinquents, socialized aggressive delinquents, or delinquents. They usually come from stable lower-class homes in a poor section of their community. From an early age, they tend to have encounters with law enforcement agencies. It should be noted that these children are not emotionally disturbed. Aside from their delinquent activities, they are normal children. The prognosis for this type of delinquent is usually favorable in that the majority become reasonably law-abiding citizens.

Unlike the subcultural and particularly the psychopathic delinquent, for whom guilt tends not to be a factor, the neurotic delinquent often experiences pangs of conscience and remorse caused by his transgressions. The motivations underlying his antisocial behavior are presumed to be essentially unconsciously based, in contrast to those of the subcultural delinquent, who often consciously opposes a larger social order. Clinical observation suggests that much of the individual's delinquent behavior is unconsciously fostered by defects in his parents' consciences. Hence, the child adopts the antisocial attitudes which his parents convey to him in subtle ways. The neurotic delinquent tends to come from a middle-class neighborhood and home which may, at times, have an atmosphere characterized by hostility and lack of love. The neurotic delinquent is more inclined to engage in criminal activity by himself, in contrast to the cultural delinquent who seems to prefer group delinquent activity (Clarizio and McCoy, 1970). Neurotic delinquents often engage in behavior apparently hoping that they will be caught.

Other psychological characteristics of the juvenile delinquent are below average intelligence, which is generally in the high 80's or low 90's (Louttit, 1957), and academic retardation. Peck (1958) indicated that delinquent children usually do not value academic achievement and that the so-called acting-out is a direct expression of a need for achievement of, what are to them, socially feasible goals. The child of low socioeconomic status, according to Peck, is handicapped by several factors in his effort to learn to read. "He is deficient in preschool readiness experience. Attitudinally he is unprepared for school living and learning. His use of oral English is poor and in view of subcultural de-emphasis of verbal communication, his interest in language skills is minimal." A number of authorities have found the child of low socioeconomic status to be deficient in language skills (Stranahan et al., 1957).

Self-Concept and Acting-Out

Fitts and Hammer (1969), using the Tennessee Self-Concept Scale with delinquents, employed assumptions which are, perhaps, basic to any view of intrapsychic determination of behavior, whether it be cognitive, affective, conative, or otherwise. They assumed that: (1) the way in which an individual views and interacts with the world around him is partly a function of the way he views himself (his self-concept); (2) an individual's behavior is a reflection or expression of his self-concept; (3) his self-concept is influenced by his behavior, by the reactions he elicits from the external world, and by his own reactions to himself; that is, an individual's self-concept is continuously interacting with the environment, and it is sensitive to feedback from the environment. On the basis of these assumptions and the scale, which applied to various types of delinquents and other deviant and handicapped groups, Fitts and Hammer found that the self-concept of public offenders is: (a) negative, (b) uncertain, (c) vague, (d) conflictual and confused, (e) variable and internally inconsistent, and (f) weak. It seems that the delinquent views himself as bad and worthless, and he acts accordingly.

Fitts and Hammer reported that factors such as age, sex, intelligence, education, race, geographical area, and nature of crime were not sufficient to explain these unique features of the delinquent's self-concept, which differed substantially from that of other handicapped groups, such as psychiatric patients, the physically handicapped, and the culturally deprived. These findings were confirmed by responsiveness to treatment and improvements in condition, since those delinquents who responded best to treatment had different self-concepts than those who did not respond. Recidivists had the poorest self-concepts and displayed the least change in self-concepts during treatment, whereas nonrecidivists showed marked self-concept improvement during treatment.

Aggression and Delinquent Behavior

Aggression is the most prominent way in which the delinquent expresses himself and his inner thoughts. On the Thematic Apperception Test (TAT), delinquents showed a pathological lack of distance between aggressive antisocial phantasies and their expression (Wattenberg, 1955), meaning that they commonly carried out their pathological phantasies. Also, half of the males in another study depicted their image of a hero as engaged in asocial, physical aggression (Young, 1956).

Aggression, as an attribute of the hero-heroine character, was predominantly emotional and verbal in delinquent girls. More female delinquents are found to have an intraaggression-dejection syndrome; that is, their aggression is turned inward more so than that of boys, who take out their grievances on outside targets. The school is less influential than the home setting, but it does affect social behavior. There is a significant relationship between the number of school grades that the offender completes and the type of community in which he is living at time of the offense. For delinquent girls who must repeat grades, school seems to be a tension-producing situation. These girls show an inability for sustained effort, especially in simple, relatively monotonous tasks to which they freely verbalize resistance (Vane, 1954).

At times, it has been hypothesized that delinquency is guilt-motivated as a result of the individual's need for punishment; yet, there is no basis in research to support this claim. Rather, it has been found that the defenses of the nondelinquent are guilt-motivated (Lyle, 1958).

Sexual Acting-Out

Sexual activity typically has been one avenue of acting-out for girls. Many atypical sexual patterns, however, including heavy masturbation, heavy petting, promiscuity, homosexuality, rape, and incest are found in children and adolescents, regardless of their sex.

One important aspect of sexual behavior is that some children and adolescents become victims of adults' acting-out (e.g., rape, homosexuality, or incest) (De Francis, 1969). It is important for the teacher to become aware of victims of sexual abuse as well as perpetrators of sexual acting-out. Girls, especially, may become willing or unwilling victims of parental irresponsibility and permissiveness.

In dealing with sexual behavior, the teacher should first distinguish sexual behavior with no social consequences (dating, kissing, heavy petting) from sexual acting-out with social consequences, which may reach the level of sexual criminality (De Francis, 1969). Among the latter are abductions, lewd acts against a minor, carnal abuse of a child, sodomy, incest, indecent exposure, and first and second degree rape. First degree rape is determined by the female's incapability to give consent because of mental retardation, mental disturbance, or immaturity or by the fact that force and threats of bodily harm are involved. In second degree rape, also termed statutory rape, the female's consent is not considered a defense if she is not of legal age (above age 16 or 18 depending on the state). Most children involved in sexual crimes come from families characterized by instability (broken homes, minority groups, economically and socially deprived families and families with many children) (De Francis, 1969). Behavior indicative of psychosocial disturbance was identified in 41 per cent of the parents of victims of sexual crimes and in 18 per cent of their siblings. The greater the family pathology, the greater the tendency for the offender to be more closely related to the family. Conversely, in families with lower pathology, the offender tended to be a stranger. A majority of the sexual offenses occurred directly or indirectly as a consequence of parental neglect (either emotional, physical, medical, or educational) or inadequate controls, supervision, or protection of the victim. The factor most profoundly affecting the victim was parental failure to provide necessary after-care and emotional safeguards. Parents exacerbated the emotional climate by taking punitive measures against the offender and the victim, but failed to acknowledge their personal responsibility for the situation.

Denial of these patterns and refusal to recognize their existence (or their potential existence) in any school is tantamount to shutting one's eyes and ears. The question of prevalence and incidence of such behaviors is not as relevant to the teacher as the fact that they indicate self-defeating and destructive behavior in children. Sexual offenses involving children concern the teacher when they are related to disruptive and disturbing behavior in the classroom and to lowering of academic achievement.

There are different rates of sexual maturity in boys and girls and different standards for sexual behavior in the various socioeconomic, ethnic, and religious groups. Regardless of the sexual and socioeconomic background of children, the teacher should recognize that sexual acting-out denotes a problem within the individual and within his family (Friedman, 1969). Likewise, with drug usage and other forms of unacceptable behavior, the teacher must recognize the self-destructive motive of such behavior in order to help the individual and his family to assume responsibility for it by accepting referral to appropriate treatment facilities. Sexual acting-out and drug abuse, as well as any other forms of acting-out and disturbing behavior, may be signals of family disharmony and disorganization that often are not recognized or openly acknowledged by the parents. Under these conditions, the child is the *scapegoat* of unsatisfactory parental relationships and the product of his parent's projection and denial of personal responsibility. It is easier for parents to make their child a scapegoat than to recognize personal and parental inadequacies.

As Schofield (1965) concluded at the end of his extensive study of sexual behavior of young people in England:

> Those who are worried about the extent of premarital sexual intercourse among teenagers must accept that these activities cannot be eliminated altogether in the foreseeable future.... Several differences between those who do and those who do not have sexual intercourse... do not reveal serious anti-social tendencies in those teenagers with experience of sexual intercourse. The experienced boys were gregarious and outgoing, even hedonistic, but they were not misfits.
>
> Sexual experience among teenage girls is closely associated with a desire for freedom and independence from the family, but they were not debauched.... Nor is there any evidence that premarital sexual intercourse leads to or encourages adulterous relations after marriage.... This research has found an association between sex experience and lack of parental discipline.

This latter finding, however, was not the most important part of the report. As the author commented:

> There is a danger that some people will seize upon this as if it is the most important finding in the report because it fits in with their preconceived

ideas and because it appears to be easy to remedy. . . . In the face of much of the uninformed criticism about teenage sexual activities, it is tempting to spend too much time in pointing out that many of the generalizations are without factual foundation, that there are no signs of moral collapse, that more thought should be given to adult immorality, that many teenage attitudes are refreshing and stimulating, that there are as many serious young people with great intellectual achievement and high aspirations.

Before judging and castigating sexual behavior, the teacher should assess his own moral and personal biases and the extent to which the sexual activity is related to other self-destructive activities in the individual. If sexual acting-out is blatant, flaunted, and coupled with other self-destructive activities, such as classroom disturbance, use of drugs, and academic underachievement and failure, the teacher must intervene forcefully, not with regard to the sexual behavior but with regard to the academic situation. The teacher cannot be a judge of morality, except as it directly affects the behavior of students in the classroom. When such a situation has been recognized, the next step is to bring it to the attention of the principal or superior and those directly responsible for the individual's welfare. Such a referral should be made without judgment as to who is at "fault" but rather with an attitude toward helping parents to realize (a) that something can be done to help their child and (b) that it can be done quicker and more directly if they assist in the treatment. Finger-pointing and fault-finding should be avoided and if they occur between parents or between parents and children, their destructive and self-defeating nature should be pointed out.

Acting-out and Types of Drugs

A brief description of types of drugs should give the teacher an idea of their general nature and specific effects. Drug effects vary widely, depending on the quantity consumed, the purity of the drug, the presence of other drugs in the user's system, and most importantly his personality and the setting in which the drug is taken (Leavitt, 1974). Even though alcohol, caffeine, and nicotine are not legally considered drugs, some restrictions as to their use apply to legal minors. Possession and sale of inhalants are generally unrestricted, although amyl nitrite and nitrous oxide require prescriptions. Possession of barbiturates, tranquilizers, amphetamines, antidepressants, and some narcotics is legal only if prescribed medically. All hallucinogens (except nutmeg!) are illegal, as are cocaine and all cannabis drugs.

STIMULANTS. Among these drugs are amphetamines (e.g., Benzedrine and Dexedrine), antidepressants (e.g., Tofranil), caffeine (e.g., in coffee, cola, and tea), cocaine (as in coca leaves), and nicotine (e.g., in cigarettes, cigars, pipes, and snuff). These drugs increase alertness and excitation, produce a feeling of self-confidence and euphoria, and relieve anxiety and depression. Their excessive use may bring about insomnia, irritability, restlessness, and stomach and lung disorders.

PSYCHODELICS. Drugs in this category include the products of the cannabis plant (e.g., hashish or marijuana), the hallucinogens that may be synthetically derived (e.g., LSD), or products of the nutmeg tree, psilocybe mushrooms, or the beubane plant. They produce alterations in perception, leading to hallucinations, delusions, panic, or eventually psychosis.

DEPRESSANTS. Among these drugs are alcohol, barbiturates (e.g., Nembutal, phenobarbital, and Seconal), inhalants (e.g., glue), narcotics (e.g., codeine, heroin, and opium), and tranquilizers (e.g., Librium, Miltown, and Thorazine). Alcohol is classified as a depressant, although it may initially have a stimulating effect. Eventually, after the high has passed, a more depressing response (or a hangover!) is the most common reaction. These drugs are used to attain relaxation and breakdown of inhibitions, but they decrease alertness and may produce excessive sleepiness, incoordination, and damage to either the kidneys, the bone marrow, or the brain.

One of the most dangerous inhalants which has reached the level of a fad among adolescents is the glue which is typically used to build plastic models. Among the dangers of glue inhalation are brain damage and even death. Since glue inhalation is achieved through the use of paper or plastic bags, the teacher should recognize telltale signs and should alert students to the dangers of this practice.

Teachers cannot play either judge or detective, but they must not be ignorant or unaware of the potential danger of drugs and should question students with regard to the presence of drugs whenever necessary. To do otherwise would be blatant irresponsibility.

THE FAMILY AND ANTISOCIAL BEHAVIOR

Parental Influence Before Adolescence

Parental influence upon the child prior to adolescence is of great importance. Although the particular disciplinary pattern of the parents is, in part, determined by sociological factors, the influence on their children is totally psychological and is great enough to merit considerable mention in any discussion of delinquency. Parents of lower-class status tend to use the more severe types of physical punishment, while middle-class parents are more apt to try to reason with their children. Studies in this field show a high positive correlation between severe and inconsistent punishment and inclination toward delinquency (Conger and Miller, 1961).

Parental rejection or acceptance of a child is also of major significance, because a child who is rejected by his parents often exhibits aggressive behavior outside the home. Conversely, if parents are overindulgent, their child may react by displaying both demanding behavior and withdrawal (Rogers, 1962).

The absence of one parent during the child's early years due to death, a broken home, or the mother's having to work may seriously affect him, although these effects may not manifest themselves until years later. A child requires continual love, understanding, and patience and demands a great deal of time and attention from his parents (Young, 1956). The importance of the parents in a child's preadolescent period cannot be overemphasized.

Parental Influence During Adolescence

In one study of parental relationships with adolescents, a group of delinquent boys taking the Thematic Apperception Test yielded these findings: One fourth of the boys referred to the father as being absent from the home. The boys admired their fathers more than their mothers, and they saw more "good than bad" in both parents. There seemed to be more animosity toward the mother figure, because the delinquent boys viewed their mothers in a punitive role. The mother, not the father, required the child to work and study (Young, 1956).

For girls, relationships with their parents were somewhat different. Delinquent girls are referred for treatment because of behaviors that are unacceptable to the mother or not in keeping with the mother's wishes, i.e., staying out late on dates, dating undesirable boys, or going to disreputable places or parties. Other mother-daughter maladjustments were evidenced by the finding that runaway girls are usually attempting to escape from their mothers (Young, 1956), and a high correlation was found between stealing and bad mother-daughter relations. The only delinquency factor that seemed to be directly related to the father-daughter relationship was sex (Kelley, 1956).

Absence of the father during adolescence is of special significance for boys. Many tests have demonstrated the male child's need for masculine *identification,* and this need is well evidenced by the fact that almost all delinquent boys have had inadequate or no identification with a hero-type male. Since the early years of a child are often almost entirely dominated by females, male children need male figures at least for the purpose of role identification. The child may be able to identify adequately with an older boy in the family, *if* he represents a positive model. Of course, if the older brother's behavior is also questionable, the younger brother's chances for a favorable adjustment become almost nil (Parsons, 1966).

PEER GROUP INFLUENCE

The peer group is probably the second most important influence on the juvenile delinquent, since peer association is a critical factor during adolescence. Because adolescents typically undergo anxiety, they tend to affiliate for mutual support. As would be expected, those who are crime repeaters have poorer peer group relations than those who are not (Wattenberg, 1955). The peer group satisfies many needs of male and female adolescents, such as expression, belonging, and social identity. Much of the adolescent's sex education and appropriate conduct expected when in contact with the opposite sex is learned from the peer group and in accordance with the rules and values of peers.

The Criminal Gang

The criminal gang arouses public interest, since its crimes are more readily reported and publicized. This situation is not due to the fact that gang members commit more crimes or even more serious crimes than non-gang members, but rather because their parents are unable to make retribution for damages or to remedy matters at the police station before the offenses are recorded against the adolescent. As the foregoing discussion indicates, criminal gangs are largely composed of individuals from lower socioeconomic groups (Cloward and Ohlin, 1960).

Lower classes have a higher ratio of *matriarchal* homes, a family structure which often leads to problems for the children. One result is that male adolescents from such homes frequently attempt to prove their masculinity. Joining a gang affords male companionship and, quite often, a leader or "hero-type" with whom male adolescents can identify.

Their need for an adult masculine figure is imperative, and if a male adolescent is not provided with a good model, he will find his own (usually a model not acceptable to most of society) (Conger et al., 1965).

For many lower-class individuals, life fluctuates between periods of relatively routine or repetitive activity and situations of great emotional stimulation. The search for excitement or thrills is a most characteristic feature of their life style. Activities including alcohol, gambling, music, and sex frequently lead to lowering of inhibition and to violence.

Gangs value highly the ability to outsmart, "outfox," outwit, dupe, "take," and "con" others and the capacity to avoid being outwitted. "Trouble," a situation which involves officials or agencies representing the middle-class culture, is always a major concern. For the boys, trouble usually results from fighting or sexual adventures which often occur while drinking. The girls usually consider the worst situations to be sexual adventures with disadvantageous consequences.

Gangs take part in delinquent acts which result in monetary gain, since the economic status of their families is such that their material wants are not satisfied. Unless something can be sold for cash or unless cash can be paid for their services, they are not likely to participate. Gang members are loyal to their gang, and protecting the members is of primary importance to them. The gang provides members with a sense of belonging, defines the roles of its members, and offers understanding and, in some cases, a solution to their immediate problems. When gang members are together they can talk about their problems and freely express themselves without fear of reprisal, because the problems are usually common throughout the group. When such a gang can be penetrated, and the leader convinced of the importance of constructive mores and values, many worthwhile activities for the members and the community may be undertaken.

The members of a criminal gang, however, seldom receive the help they need and continue their deviant path until they become involved in bigger crimes by association with the criminal faction of their community or by being sent to an institution which is notorious for recidivism. There is little hope that a correctional institution will have anything but an adverse effect on such an individual (Shaw and McKay, 1942).

The only hope these young people have for success is the one big "score" which will supposedly establish them for life. Since they have no accurate idea of money management or the amount of money required to support themselves, they may expect that a few thousand dollars will solve their problems. The image of the big score remains the symbol of success throughout their lives (Kvaraceus and Miller, 1959).

The Conflictual Gang

The conflictual gang includes boys from the upper lower, lower middle, and middle income families. Both parents and teachers urge the adolescent to be a joiner and to become group oriented. The adolescent is in constant competition for status and recognition and often is led to delinquent acts in order to gain attention. The group-oriented adolescent is less likely to think of delinquency as being serious than the parent-oriented adolescent. Within the group, delinquent acts become "the thing to do" and are accepted as normal acts rather than delinquent ones. This group probably steals as much as lower-class gangs, but for a different reason, namely, to see what they can get away with. The monetary value of the stolen object is not as important as the *way* the crime is committed, and if the object is large or difficult to obtain, the crime is considered even more successful.

The conflictual gang influences the style of clothing that its members wear and the slang that they use, since they have their own terms for describing people and events.

The activities of this type of gang center on a car, and drive-ins often become their meeting places. Quite often the car is used as the gang's means of committing a crime, including offenses such as speeding, playing chicken, or blocking traffic. On many occasions, the privacy of a car facilitates the gang's indulgence in alcohol, drugs, or sexual experimentation.

The crime that is almost exclusively a trait of the conflictual gang is car theft. The excuse usually given by adolescents for having committed such a crime is that they had nothing else to do or that they were just borrowing the car and would return it later. Many of these cases never go to court nor do the adolescents involved incur police records because their parents have enough influence to keep them from being punished. The current increase in this type of crime may be due, in part, to the mobility of neighborhoods. As working class families have moved into what were once exclusively middle-class areas, the differing values of the two groups have caused the middle-class adolescent to re-examine his own values. An office worker's son who cannot afford to have a car might become jealous of a welder's son who has one (Conger and Miller, 1961).

The Escapist Gang

The escapist gang includes individuals from families of all incomes and social categories. These adolescents attempt to withdraw from soci-

Figure 11–2 Withdrawal and escape —frequent adolescent methods of coping with reality, (Courtesy of The Woods Schools, Langhorne, Pennsylvania.)

ety by using drugs and narcotics which help them to escape from reality. Escapism arises from continued failure to attain goals by legitimate means and from an inability to use illegitimate routes because of internalized prohibitions. The conflict is resolved by abandoning both opposing elements, the goals and the norms, so that escape is complete, the conflict is eliminated, and the individual is asocialized (Merton, 1956). Such persons are usually motivated to obtain higher status, have accepted the middle-class mores and values, and want to improve their life styles. They cannot, however, meet the requirements for advancement, and the result is frustration. They eventually attempt to cover up their shortcomings by using drugs. The gang structure is formed when drug users join together in order to insure a source of drug supply and sometimes for the purpose of group parties in which drugs play a major role. Since the needs of these young people require money, many middle-class and upper-class adolescents are likely to be members of the escapist gang (Becker, 1955).

The Neurotic Gang

The neurotic gang is composed of middle- to upper-class adolescents who participate in antisocial acts as a result of weak and inconsistent controls in their families. They are differentiated from the conflictual and escapist gangs by the following characteristics:

1. Unlike the subcultural and unsocialized delinquent, in particular, in whom guilt tends not to be an influencing factor, the neurotic delinquent often experiences pangs of conscience and remorse over his transgressions.
2. The motivations which prompt the neurotic gang member's antisocial behavior are presumed to be more unconsciously based in contrast to those of the subcultural delinquent who often consciously opposes a larger social order. Clinical observations suggest that much of the individual's delinquent behavior is unconsciously fostered by defects in his parents' consciences. Hence, the child comes to adopt the antisocial attitudes which his parents convey to him in subtle ways.
3. The neurotic delinquent tends to come from a middle-class neighborhood and home which is sometimes characterized by an atmosphere of hostility and lack of love.
4. This delinquent is more inclined to engage in criminal acts by himself than the subcultural delinquent who seems to prefer delinquent activity which includes other members of his gang (Clarizio and McCoy, 1970).

Members of a neurotic gang often engage in criminal behavior that will almost insure their being caught. Although a great deal of the motivation for antisocial behavior is individual, such adolescents may tend to associate with those of similar backgrounds and may, at times, join with members of other types of gangs.

THE ETIOLOGY OF ANTISOCIAL BEHAVIOR

Delinquency, a complex, multidimensional problem, may be approached from many points of view. To investigate all aspects of the problem simultaneously or to discuss the etiology of delinquency in terms of biological, psychological, and cultural forces would be a difficult task. Most theories concerning the etiology of juvenile delinquency may be classified in one of two broad categories. One category includes those theories which emphasize the importance of the attitudes and emotions of the individual delinquent. This theoretical position is predicated on the assumption that delinquency results from emotional problems. The other major approach treats delinquency as a sociological problem, and advocates of this viewpoint stress the importance of the broader social environment as a source of delinquent conduct. Sociologists, therefore, are seeking to find positive factors in the social problems involving the delinquent's environment. Our discussion will concern sociological factors as they are related to juvenile delinquency, since so many of the delinquent's problems have social origins.

Status deprivation is related to the lower-class child's being exposed to middle-class pressures to achieve success. A lower-class child may be sensitive to the pressures of the middle class but is experientially hindered in his ability to conform to middle-class standards. He is, for example, unable to postpone gratification of immediate wants and has less of a working ethic in his background. A loss of status results in social devaluation which, in turn, leads to rebellion. The lower-class child, therefore, achieves status by his antisocial behavior which becomes a mark of prestige rather than a mark of failure.

Gang delinquency may be seen as the result of obstacles to the attainment of highly valued middle-class success. Cloward and Ohlin (1960) studied the "opportunity structure," stressing the lower-class child's inability to measure up to middle-class standards. They emphasized the unjust unavailability of opportunity among the lower class. Lower-class children, in response to the limited opportunities offered to them, blame the social order.

Miller (1958) suggested an alternate theory which is at variance with the preceding theories on status and attainment. Objecting to the reactive theory, Miller explained the *life style* of gang delinquents as a manifestation of lower-class culture. He contended that gang delinquency among lower-class adolescents is an expression of the values and thoughts pervading the lower-class culture rather than a reaction against middle-class values. According to Miller, the focal concerns of lower-class cultures are trouble, abruptness, smartness, excitement, faith, and autonomy. Lower-class delinquents thus become acculturated to a way of life that is consistent with these concerns but is at odds or inconsistent with dominant norms and values.

Bloch and Niederhoffer (1958) described a gang as a group which satisfies a deep-seated need experienced by adolescents in all cultures and, thus, emphasized the problems of adjustment which are common to all adolescents. Shaw and McKay (1942) attributed delinquency to the cultural conflict between immigrants and their children, to the presence of adult criminal groups, and to slum conditions which make it difficult for parents to control their children.

The preceding theories tend to ignore the psychological element in delinquency and fail to account for many types of delinquency which may be described as idiosyncratic of a family or an individual. Jenkins and Glickman (1947) label such delinquent individuals as emotionally disturbed.

Bandura and Walters (1959) suggested that sociological factors may not by themselves be the causative agents of delinquency. Their primary importance may be that they provide conditions under which the psychological factors conducive to development of antisocial behavior may readily operate. According to this theory, the delinquent adolescent who has had no obvious environmental disadvantages may have a psychology similar to that which is so greatly magnified by poor social conditions.

There are, however, some characteristics of delinquency which distinguish it from the broad category of emotional disturbances. Most delinquency committed by an individual rather than by a gang is of a neurotic variety, but the reverse does not necessarily follow. The unconscious is said to be a major influence on the actions of the emotionally disturbed delinquent. Advocates of the psychological approach assume that antisocial acts have a meaning to the individual delinquent, in that his conduct is either a reaction to frustration within the family or peer group or is an effort to meet some unfilled need. Although the majority of delinquents are probably not emotionally disturbed, there are a significant number of delinquents who may be considered in this category. The psychological approach to delinquency is thoroughly discussed in the study of Healy and Bronner (1936), which is based on data on 105 delinquents who had nondelinquent siblings near their own age. In spite of similar backgrounds, the delinquents differed largely from their nondelinquent siblings in personality traits, attitudes, and interpersonal relationships. The most noticeable differences between the two groups were found in the areas of family attitudes and emotional experience. Almost 90 per cent of the delinquents were very unhappy with their life circumstances or extremely disturbed because of their experiences. In contrast, inner stress was found in only 15 per cent of the nondelinquent siblings.

Ausubel (1965b) presented the view that the basic causative factor of juvenile delinquency is not a pathological personality structure but rather the developmental cultural phenomenon of youth-adult alienation, which many adolescents experience. According to Ausubel, adolescents who are alienated from adult society become involved in a peer culture which provides them with norms for status-giving activities or behaviors and a distinctive training institution of their own. At the same time, however, participation in a peer culture reinforces their feelings of alienation from adult society and promotes compensatory antisocial modes of behavior which may take the form of juvenile delinquency. Alienation from adult society is greater among boys than girls and more pronounced among adolescents in majority groups and in middle-class groups. Middle-class delinquency is usually the result of a serious deterioration in the moral values of middle-class adults which has occurred since the end of World War II.

As indicated by our discussion, the etiology of juvenile delinquency is related to many factors. In fact, there are enough theories so that one may be chosen to suit any personal prejudice or any conception of society. Regardless of the etiology, emphasis should be placed on recognition of delinquent tendencies and solutions to the causative problems.

THEORIES OF AGGRESSION AND ANTISOCIAL BEHAVIOR

Whether juvenile delinquency is defined in a legalistic manner (behavior on the part of a child between ages 7 and 17 which violates existing law) or simply as a child's engaging in antisocial aggressive behavior which is condemned by the community, the common element, which we will focus on, is that antisocial behavior involves the acting-out of aggression and hostility. We shall consider aggression as the entire range of assertive, intrusive, and attacking behaviors. Aggression thus includes both overt and covert attacks, such as defamatory acts (sarcasm), self-directed hostility, and overly dominant behavior. Violence, which often accompanies aggression, is destructive aggression and involves physical damage to persons or property. Violence may be collective or individual, intentional or unintentional, and apparently, justified or unjustified. Violence, or what we shall refer to as acting-out behavior, can best be understood in the context of adaptation, because it has a role in man's struggle to adapt. By adaptation we mean a behavioral and biological fit between a person and his environment (Gilula and Daniels, 1969).

Every culture prescribes the range of coping behaviors available to its members, but within this range individual adaptive behavior is forged and tested in terms of stress. Coping is a continual and usually successful struggle to accomplish tasks and goals with adaptive consequences. An individual is coping when his behavior increases the likelihood that a task will be accomplished within the range of behaviors and values that are acceptable to both the individual and the group in which he lives. Stress can lead to disappointments and failure as well as the opportunity for learning, since a number of stressful situations may challenge and develop coping skills. These crises are associated with transitions in life, including adolescence, separation from parents, and marriage. The transitional periods provide the opportunity for learning and developing more sophisticated ways of coping with problems. By living in society we obtain satisfactions, develop identity, and find meaning in life, and basic social values take on special importance for they determine the limits of acceptable behavior as we adjust to life.

Stress can be dangerous when it overwhelms an individual or a group. Either the situation itself or anxiety created by the situation may block our usual resources and problem-solving behavior; as a result aggressive reactions occur. These reactions are primitive forms of behavior including passive adjustment, withdrawal, blaming others, rage, violence, and confusion. By understanding that these behaviors are a reaction to overpowering stress and failure of the coping mechanisms, the public offender is seen in a different role. Instead of being viewed as the inhumane, primitive animal (a viewpoint which is inferred by the action society has taken against him in the past), he can be considered as another human being who is a victim of circumstances which he could not control or effectively cope with. This knowledge suggests that society should assume *some* of the responsibility for his actions, because the stress originated in society. The implication is that society has failed to define or to teach acceptable behavior which is needed to cope with stressful situations.

The professional literature seems to support the viewpoint that delinquency involves multiple and complex causes. In order to facilitate comprehension and organization, the studies which we will review are classified according to the three current categories: biology, culture, and psychology.

Of the three schools of thought on the causes of delinquency, the oldest is the biological and constitutional approach, often referred to as criminal biology. In accordance with this approach, the "mainsprings" of deviancy are sought in inherited physical and mental characteristics, that is, those qualities which constitute tendencies toward criminality. Research has centered on studies of criminal twins (Lange, 1931), body-mind types (Kretschmer, 1955; 1956), proneness (Schneider, 1959), habitual versus occasional offenders (Fry, 1946), constitutional body types most frequently related to delinquency (i.e., mesomorphic, athletic body types [Sheldon]), specific patterns of brain waves, and unusual patterns of chromosomes.

Biological Theories

Even those in the field of criminal biology find it difficult to specify exactly what proneness to delinquency is, although it appears to be a sort of weakness of character. Evidence of the inheritance of such proneness is scant and unimpressive and takes the form of unreliable family tree assessments. The theory was first widely supported by Cesare Lombroso at the beginning of this century. He believed in the hereditary transmission of acquired traits and classified biological traits that are frequently found among criminals. His theory has since been disregarded by criminal biologists. Sheldon (1949) was able to specify different kinds of *somatotypes* much more definitely than Kretschmer was able to describe specific body-mind types. A group of 200 problem youths in a Boston hostel, according to Sheldon, tended to have mesomorphic (athletic) builds as well as several forms of mental deficiency (Feshbach, 1970).

The Gluecks (1956) discovered that of 500 delinquent and 500 nondelinquent boys, the delinquents proved to be much more mesomorphic than the nondelinquents. The characteristics associated with mesomorphy were physical strength, social assertiveness, uninhibited motor responses, and less submissiveness to authority. These studies are based only on high positive correlations and do not imply that mesomorphy is the causative factor of the characteristics. Such studies only suggest that the same factors that produce mesomorphy also produce certain other qualities. Moreover, Sheldon's theory cannot explain why so many mesomorphs do not become delinquent.

The Gluecks (1959), who are outstanding authorities on delinquency, have amassed much data on delinquency and crime. Based on their studies, they have developed a prediction scale for potential delinquents which was derived from a comparison of 500 persistent delinquents and 500 nondelinquents, matched by age, intelligence, ethnic origin, and residence in a depressed area of Boston. The Social Prediction Table is one of four derived from the study. The scale is based on five factors of family background: (1) affection of mother for boy, (2) affection of father for boy, (3) discipline of boy by father, (4) supervision of boy by mother, and (5) family cohesiveness.

Their report revealed that 50 per cent of the delinquents studied displayed the first overt signs of antisocial behavior before age 8 and that 90 per cent displayed these signs before age 10. A study was made in retrospect by applying the Social Prediction Table to available records of children who were persistent delinquents when they were younger than age 10. In 9 out of 10 cases, offenders would have been identified at age 6 as persistent delinquents. The Gluecks cited numerous studies involving hundreds of young people of varied backgrounds who had committed all types of offenses. The studies were performed by many different researchers, and most supported the validity and reliability of the scale. Results of correctly identified delinquents range from 53.5 per cent to 91.3 per cent of the cases studied. Studies in Japan (87 to 92 per cent correctly identified) and in France (approximately 90 per cent correctly identified) support the widespread applicability of the table.

A long-term study involved 244 boys in high delinquency areas of New York (Glueck, 1960). In 1960, seven years after the study began, of the boys who were predicted seven years earlier to remain nondelinquents, 94.6 per cent were still nondelinquents. Thirty-seven were predicted to become delinquents and at the time of the report, 17 or 46 per cent were already delinquents. In 1963, when the boys had reached age 16, of those predicted to remain nondelinquent, 96.4 per cent were still nondelinquent; of the 27 predicted at age 6 to become delinquents, 23 or 85.2 per cent were delinquents at age 16 (Craig and Glick, 1963).

In another study involving 1000 delinquents, intensive research was undertaken by the Gluecks on the way in which these individuals reacted to their environments (1965). They found the following factors to be dominant characteristics of the subjects and their backgrounds:

1. Native-born sons of foreign parents.
2. Parents having little education.
3. Large families.
4. Poverty.
5. Parents divorced or separated.
6. Unruly, quarrelsome families.
7. Inadequate care and discipline.
8. Families having little regard for money management.
9. Lack of temperance and morality.
10. Frequent criminality in the family.

They concluded that the degree to which these handicaps and weaknesses are present could determine an individual's chance of becoming a delinquent. The more numerous the handicaps, the more difficult for the child to adapt in a socially acceptable way.

Psychological Theories

Psychogenic theory stresses as the cause of delinquency the formation of an antisocial character which can be traced to faulty relationships within the family during the child's first few years of life. This school of thought developed directly from the work of August Aichorn and indirectly from Freudian analytic theory. Aichorn (1935) stated that faulty development during infancy and early childhood makes it impossible for the child to control his impulses. The child remains a psychological infant, living in accordance with the pleasure principle and failing to develop the reality principle in his life. Friedlander (1947) indicated that this defective development leads to an antisocial character structure which is incapable of coping with reality.

Redl (1951), a disciple of Aichorn, viewed the delinquent child as one who has failed to develop a management system over his impulsivity (i.e., one who has failed to develop an adequate ego and superego). Psychogenic theory only partially explains the personality of the delinquent. Admittedly, there are some individuals whose ego and superego are too weak to control impulses and to handle ordinary expectations, but which children have experienced faulty socialization early in life is not clear. Nor does the theory explain why some children who have poor impulse control do not become delinquent.

Originally, Freud, in Civilization and Its Discontents (1930), spoke of aggression as one of the two basic instincts of man. He contended that "... men are not gentle, friendly creatures wishing for love, who simply defend themselves if they are attacked, but that a powerful measure of desire for aggression has to be reckoned as a part of their instinctual endowment." Freud attempted to relate his theory to a biological process, and the idea of aggression as a basic instinct came from the discovery of decaying processes that are continually at work in the cells of the body. The formation of conscience and the experience of guilt are explained by this basic aggressive drive *(death wish)*. Any outward-directed aggression which is not actualized is directed inward against the ego in the form of the superego (conscience). According to analytic theory, the source of guilt feelings and of the conscience and the most effective means of controlling aggression is dread of authority. This includes, first, the dread of external authority (e.g., fear of punishment, loss of love) and, finally, the dread of guilt imposed by the superego.

The child who has failed to accept his parents' values (i.e., the values have not been internalized and incorporated into the superego) has no internal controls to counteract his instinctual aggressive tendencies. He experiences no feelings of guilt for harmful acts; that is, he has no conscience. We say that such an individual is undersocialized, and he is termed a sociopath. This biological-instinctual theory suggests that aggression is inevitable because it is part of human nature. Most individuals repress and control their aggressive impulses or find socially acceptable ways of expressing them. The individual who fails to develop internal controls for his aggressive impulses is immature and has not adopted the values of society as his own. He, therefore, expresses his aggressive nature at will.

The analytic position is exemplified by Abt and Weisman's view (1965) that aggressive behavior is a form of acting-out. He emphasized past experiences as they relate to current behavior and actions and described two types of acting-out: (1) aggressive-destructive acting-out, characterized by verbal and nonverbal destructive acts, such as hitting, kicking, failure to pay fees, late arrivals, direct verbal assaults (criticisms or contempt), and indirect verbal assaults (sarcasm and ridicule); and (2) aggressive-controlling acting-out, characterized by verbal behavior that seeks to maintain aloofness, enhance status, or manipulate others.

Most children are able to curb socially unacceptable drives by age three, because object relationships (love bonds) have begun to be more important than drive gratifications. The child who continues to act-out has become fixated at a more primitive stage of development. Abt concluded that the major causes of aggression are concern and anxiety over the loss of a love object, usually the parent.

Analytic theory is predominantly supported by studies which are in the form of case histories. We shall, however, present some of the current research which focuses on specific variables but lends support to the overall theory.

Allen and Sandhu (1967) investigated the variables of alienation, *hedonism*, and life vision of delinquents. The hypothesis investigated was that delinquents exhibit more alienation and hedonism and have a poorer perspective of the future than nondelinquents. By testing 175 institutionalized boys, aged 16 to 18, by means of a 14-item questionnaire which had been standardized on nondelinquents, the hypothesis was confirmed at a significant level.

Reckless et al. (1957) investigated the self-concept as a factor in relation to delinquency. Thirty sixth-grade teachers nominated 192 boys whom they expected would not experience contact with police or juvenile authorities in the future. After eliminations for past offenses, 125 boys remained. Through testing, interviews, and rating scales, the boys

Figure 11–3 Cooperation is a natural developmental process. (Courtesy of The Woods Schools, Langhorne, Pennsylvania.)

were determined to have positive self-concepts. One year later teachers nominated 101 boys who would probably experience police contact in the future. These boys were assumed to have negative self-concepts, and 70 of the boys with negative self-concepts were located. In the year that had passed, four boys in the positive self-concept group had had contact with the juvenile court an average of one time. Twenty-seven of the boys in the negative self-concept group had had contact with the juvenile court an average of one time, and 27 had had contact with the juvenile court an average of 3 times each. The researchers concluded that a positive self-concept is a deterrent to involvement in antisocial behavior.

In an intensive long-range study by the Gluecks (1950), 1000 juvenile delinquents were followed throughout adolescence into adulthood, and some interesting conclusions were reached. The results lend support to the biological theory of delinquency but also to the analytic interpretation that delinquents are fixated at a primitive stage of development.

The researchers found that by the time most delinquents had reached age 29 almost 40 per cent had "burned out," that is, ceased to be criminals. Even those who continued criminal activities showed improvement. At the beginning of the study 75.6 per cent of the group were serious offenders, and after 15 years only 47.8 per cent could still be classified as serious offenders. The researchers attributed the improvement to physical and mental changes that are part of the natural process of maturation. A comparative study of those who continued to be serious offenders and those who became minor offenders revealed that the serious offenders had inferior congenital endowment and were reared under less favorable conditions than those who ultimately committed petty offenses only.

They concluded that, normally, when a person reaches adulthood, the development and integration of his physical and mental powers make it easier for him to achieve a capacity for self-control, foresight, and resourcefulness. He can postpone immediate desires, profit by experience, and develop self-respect and regard for the opinions of law-abiding persons. These characteristics enable the person to adapt successfully to the demands of society and to avoid drifting into or persisting in crime. The results of Glueck and Glueck's study were supported by Robins (1966).

Dollard and Miller (1950) incorporated Hullian learning theory into their frustration theory and defined aggression as "that response which follows frustration which reduces only the secondary frustration-produced instigation and leaves the strength of the original instigation unaffected" and as "an act whose goal response is injury to an organism." The two critical issues are that aggression is instigated by frustration and that aggression is goal-directed behavior. Their theory states that aggressive behavior results from interference with ongoing purposeful activity. A person feels frustrated when a violation of his hopes or expectations occurs, and consequently, he tries to solve the problem by behaving aggressively. Frustrations can take various forms, such as threats to life, thwarting of basic needs, and personal insults. Aggression, as a response to frustration, is viewed as a learned rather than an innate behavior. Frustration-evoked aggression is an attempt to remove obstacles to goals, hence, the frustration theory also relates to adaptation. The aggressive response to frustration is often a form of coping behavior that may have not only adjustive but also long-range consequences.

Inhibition of aggressive acts—whether or not overt aggressive responses occur—is a function of inhibitory forces. Inhibition of an act varies according to the amount of punishment anticipated to be a consequence of that act. If instigation is strong enough, inhibition due to fear of punishment will be overcome. Punishments typically inhibit (delay) aggressive acts, but if the punishment is too extreme, it may further frustrate and increase the instigation of aggression.

Another concept related to learning theory is that aggressive behavior is learned by children through identification with the parents and modeling of parents' behavior. If a parent becomes aggressive and thereby gets something he wants, the child is quick to perceive that this is an effective means of dealing with thwarting situations. Parental permissiveness may lead to either direct or indirect aggression (i.e., fantasy). If a child's aggressive efforts to "get his way" are continually reinforced by compliance with his wishes, the frequency of overt acting-out will increase, and the imagined acts, as a result, will become even more extreme. Parental restrictiveness may lead to either low direct or high indirect (fantasy or displacement) aggressive behavior. Fear of punishment inhibits overt acts, but the instigation remains unaffected and must find outward expression to relieve accumulated tension and anxiety. The result is a high incidence of aggressive acts committed in daydreaming and fantasy. Sometimes the energy of the drive is displaced and finds expression in subtle ways of attack, such as slander, sarcasm, blaming others, or rough play in sports. Aggression may even be displaced by watching violent movies or TV (Feshbach and Singer, 1971).

These postulates of the frustration theory have created a vast amount of research aimed at testing their validity. Yates (1966) cited over 50 studies dealing with aggression in the learning theory context. Dollard and Miller's theory has, thus, initiated much research; but unfortunately, many of these studies utilized animals, and the results constitute sweeping generalizations when applied to humans.

Basically, the learning theory position on aggression is that the child, in his efforts to get what he wants (goal), discovers that "he can secure compliance with his wishes, *i.e.,* rewards from the social environment, by hurting.... The devices he learns are a function of what the parents and others respond to, and the extent or degree to which he develops such a motive is a function of their rewarding responsiveness when he behaves injuriously, *i.e.,* aggressively" (Sears et al., 1953). Thus, a child observes aggressive behavior in others, and on being frustrated, he imitates that behavior. If he subsequently achieves his goal, reinforcement occurs. If he is thwarted, his frustration increases, and therefore instigation of aggression increases. If he is severely punished, his anger (frustration) is aroused and, once again, instigation of aggression occurs.

Another category of theories which might be more representative of an eclectic view is social learning theory. This position emphasizes aggressive behavior as the result of child-rearing practices and other forms of socialization. The American culture places relatively high emphasis on military glory, incidence of crime, and aggressive-defensive behavior. From the social learning theory, it can be inferred that as long as a nation values and accepts violence as an effective coping strategy, violent behavior will continue. Bandura and Walters (1959), who support this viewpoint, based their theory on an extensive study which evaluated the influences of child-rearing practices and family relationships. Analytic observations provided their data and learning theory provided the process by which these data were interpreted. Their study of delinquent boys, who were *not* deprived or handicapped, demonstrated that conditions conducive to the development of aggressive behavior are related to parents' child-rearing techniques.

In order for socialization to be effective, the primary condition is the development of a dependency motive, whereby the child learns to want the interest, attention, and approval of others. Demands must also be made on the child to conform to society rather than to expect immediate unconditional gratifications. A child's frustration arises from a lack of affectional attention and a punitive attitude by the parents and from inconsistency of parental disciplinary practices. The values which the child internalizes from his parents are also important. Bandura and Walters suggested the crying and kicking of a hungry child as evidence that frustration elicits aggressive-like actions from the time of birth. Aggression during the first years of life is a means of obtaining something which is desired or ridding oneself of something unpleasant. It may reduce tensions brought on by frustration (even if the goal is not achieved) and may be learned as a response to tension-producing situations. If attempts at satisfying dependency motives (securing affectional rewards) are frustrated or punished, the child will learn to be fearful and to avoid close attachments and dependency, thus compounding an asocial pattern. Disadvantage or sociological factors contribute to aggressive behavior, but they are not necessarily the causative factors. They are only conditions under which psychological factors conducive to aggression may readily operate.

Scott (1956) presented a somewhat novel view by theorizing that frustration in personal attachments generates the mechanisms of attack, removal, and avoidance. Once it becomes apparent that an affectional relationship cannot be established, the offending person is converted from a loved one to an enemy: "The desire for love is so crucial and intensive that it cannot be assuaged merely by turning to another love object: it has first to be destroyed by substituting hate." Hostility seems most directly related to family insecurity, but individual vulnerability to stress must also be considered.

Maslow (1962), a pioneer of the humanistic viewpoint in psychology, saw man's inner nature not as instinctively evil, but rather as either neutral or good. What we call "evil" behavior appears most often to be a secondary reaction to disparagement of an individual's intrinsic worth. Psychopathy generally results from the denial or distortion of man's essential value. Thus, aggression and destruction are not inherent in man, but rather are caused by such denial. As soon as the frustration is removed, aggression disappears. Maslow postulated two basic tendencies in man. The first is man's tendency to satisfy physical and psychological needs, and the second is the actualization of his potentials. He stated that a theory that is formulated from studying "sick" people will result in a sick theory. Therefore, he based his theory on an intensive and far-reaching investigation of people who were self-actualized (e.g., Thomas Jefferson, Thoreau, Eleanor Roosevelt, and Einstein).

Cultural Theories

Sociologists have continuously called attention to inadequate environmental conditions. Around 1940, a basic American sociological theory of delinquency, differential association, was formulated by Sutherland (1947). According to his theory, delinquent behavior is learned by association with other individuals and is affected by frequency, intensity, priority, and duration of contact with these persons. Glaser (1956) proposed "differential identification" as a substitute for differential association. He theorized that individuals adopt models of behavior from those reference groups that they identify with, and this identification does not necessarily result from face to face encounters. One can identify with an individual or group without having actual contact with them. Cohen (1955) contended that working-class boys, who abandon middle-class values, find the solution to their status problems in the delinquent subculture of the gang.

Differential association theory is a general theory which applies to the total spectrum of delinquency, so that it includes all class structures and all types of personalities. The major shortcoming of this theory is that it does not account for those who do not become delinquents, nor does it explain which individuals are and which are not apt to internalize delinquent modes of behavior. In addition, Cohen did not specify which individuals abandon middle-class values or why only some gang members become involved in delinquency.

Institutional Influences on Antisocial Behavior

The delinquent who is sent to a correctional institution, in most cases, merely "graduates" to a higher level of crime upon his release from the institution. For male adolescents, there is not a high correlation between successful institutional adjustment and success on parole, meaning that good behavior may be a means of obtaining freedom in order to try out new criminal acts (Kosofsky, 1955).

Institutionalization produces great anxiety, and unfortunately, it seems that the higher a boy's anxiety rating is, the more difficult are his institutional and postrelease adjustments. States of dependency, depression, guilt, and religious involvement play a part in the institutional effect. For instance, a boy with a high dependency rating will experience a more negative postrelease adjustment; whereas an individual with depressive tendencies will have a more positive adjustment after release, as will a boy with high guilt ratings. A large degree of religious involvement within the institution may be indicative of positive adjustment within the system and more negative adjustment upon release.

IDENTIFICATION AND PREDICTION OF ANTISOCIAL BEHAVIOR

Identification of children likely to become delinquent has been attempted by many reasearchers in this field. The Gluecks recommended that delinquency prediction be made when the child enters school (approximately age six). There has been one major study involved in testing a group of children at age six and following up on these results to determine the predictive validity of the Glueck and Glueck instrument. Between 1952 and 1953, the New York City Youth Club selected a sample of 224 first-grade boys from high delinquency neighborhoods. Ratings on social factors were obtained by interviews conducted by social workers in the child's home setting. The investigators, in an effort to refine the social factor table, devised a scale to measure three factors: (1) supervision of the boy by the mother, (2) supervision of the boy by the father, (3) and family cohesiveness. There was also a two-factor scale which was to determine: (1) supervision of the boy by the mother and (2) family cohesiveness. After nine years, a comprehensive follow-up study (Glueck and Glueck, 1964) concluded that the scale was a good differentiator between serious, persistent delinquent behavior and nondelinquent behavior. The results indicated that the three-factor scale had predicted accurately 70 per cent of the delinquents and 85 per cent of the nondelinquents.

While these findings are encouraging, objections have been raised by critics (Kvaraceus, 1966). His objections center on the subjectivity of the social workers' ratings, questionable statistical analysis, and nonapplicability of certain areas. In addition, the cost (in terms of time and money) of administering these scales and analyzing their results would be high for the general population.

The Minnesota Multiphasic Personality Inventory (MMPI) is perhaps the most widely used and well-known structured personality test. It consists of 655 true-false statements and yields scores on a variety of clinical scales. A sample of more than 15,000 ninth-grade students in Minnesota was tested by means of this inventory in an effort to predict who would become juvenile delinquents. A follow-up study involving research into police and juvenile court records was conducted two years after the initial test. From these data, Hathaway and Monachesi (1953; 1957) found that elevations in certain scales were more closely related to the prediction of delinquency than elevations in others. Peaks on the psychopathic and mania scales seemed to be predictive of antisocial forms of behavior, thus providing a combination of characteristics associated with the psychopathic personality (e.g., impulsivity, rebelliousness, minimal guilt, inability to learn from experience) and characteristics associated with mania (e.g., expansiveness and restlessness) to delinquency. Certain neurotic indicators, however, such as tendencies to worry and to be anxious are thought to be favorable signs in that they seem to have an inhibiting effect on potentially delinquent behavior.

Wirt and Briggs (1959) found that delinquency can be more accurately predicted by the frequency of an individual's contact with social agencies combined with personality profiles than by either indicator used singly. These findings indicate the desirability of combining social factors with personality inventories in the prediction of delinquent behavior.

Kvaraceus (1953; 1955) devised a scale called the KD Proneness Scale which is composed of 75 multiple-choice items designed to differentiate delinquents from nondelinquents. It explores differences in personality make-up, home and family backgrounds, and school experiences. There is also a nonverbal scale which has received the most extensive validation of all the KD prediction scales. Kvaraceus (1966) scales consist of 62 separate items which contain pictures designed to differentiate delinquent from nondelinquent behavior; the child is simply asked to select the picture he likes most. Kvaraceus conducted a three-year study involving 1600 junior high school students which indicated that there is a positive relationship between delinquency and nonviolent behavior. This result is inconsistent with the original hypothesis (i.e., delinquency and nonviolent behavior "should" be negatively correlated) and raises questions about the scale and the hypothesis. The correlation may be attributed to the fact that delinquents are more defensive and admit to nonviolent behavior more readily than "normal" adolescents. In any case, this inconsistency suggested that the scale should not be used for predictive purposes on a routine basis.

In spite of all the attempts to devise predictive scales for delinquency, a really effective instrument has not as yet been produced. Kvaraceus (1966) noted that we might well have to accept separate scales to identify lower-class and middle-class delinquent children. He also pointed out that predictive scales might be more effective in identifying subcultural delinquents than emotionally disturbed delinquents. The need for a reliable scale is emphasized by the cost of errors in prediction, including (a) the cost of professional treatment for a child who would probably not have become delinquent anyway, (b) the cost and availability of total facilities, and (c) the cost of obtaining predictive information. Also, in order to develop a satisfactory scale, we must specify what we consider acceptable rates of predictable success. Until we have dealt with such situations, the real worth of any predictor cannot be realized. In addition, two major issues must be considered. The first issue concerns the moral and professional implications of treating a misdiagnosed individual for behavior which he is unlikely to be guilty of. The second issue involves the stigma which results from labeling any individual, correctly or incorrectly, as a juvenile delinquent.

ALLEVIATING AGGRESSIVE AND ANTISOCIAL BEHAVIOR

The Department of Justice estimates America's annual crime bill to be billions of dollars, and there is ample evidence that the less tangible human cost is much greater. Many authorities in the field believe that crime and juvenile delinquency are the most serious cultural problems of this age. Existing correctional institutions are plagued with high personnel turnover, low salaries, poor working conditions, and a scarcity of well-trained professional staff members. These conditions have resulted in poor rehabilitation and treatment programs, inadequate attention to physical and mental handicaps, idleness, and periodic riots and disturbances. Past experience has proven that buildings and laws by themselves change few people from offenders to nonoffenders.

Unfortunately, public *apathy* toward correctional institutions has resulted in inadequate financing and poor staffing and has minimized the development of sound treatment and rehabilitation services for public offenders. A recent study of a juvenile correctional institution in Georgia indicated that approximately 60 per cent of those at the institution had disabilities that would qualify them for vocational rehabilitation services (Prigmore, 1965). The results of our past policies indicate that although we have "quarantined" public offenders, we have utterly failed to rehabilitate them in any meaningful way. If the offender is to be rehabilitated, it is necessary to determine why children are driven to acts of destruction. We must examine these acts and strive to understand the contexts in which they occur, how they are initiated and developed, how they are conceived and perceived, and how they fit into the lives of the public offender. Delinquency, like aggressive behavior in general, can be understood as the expression of underlying hostilities or as an acquired way of life. Delinquency is an ill-defined research area, and much research is needed to clarify its etiology and to develop means of prevention and treatment. It is evident, however, that theory and therapy are far more advanced than the institutions on which society still relies to solve this problem.

Shortcomings of the behavioral sciences and our correctional institutions have been their resistance to change and the lack of communication between the two areas. Both have failed to ask which methods are the most efficient. Often, when a delinquent child greatly deviates from social norms, he is referred to a psychologist or psychiatrist, but in the majority of cases, the professional is requested *only* to assess the child's behavior. If severe personality disturbances are present, the child may be placed in psychotherapy; otherwise, he is returned to the courts with a report which may state that he shows deviant behavior patterns and possibly is a psychopath. No further action is taken, except to repeat the same correctional procedures used in the past, which have failed to obtain significant results. The courts and correctional systems, of course, do not have the financial resources to afford individual treatment for each offender.

With the increasing rates of crime and delinquency, it is imperative that we reject the attitude that nothing significant can be done for the public offender and that, therefore, the best alternative is to lock him away from society where he can do no harm. Available research has consistently supported the fact that offenders can be helped to become nonoffenders, and it remains the task of our correctional systems and educational institutions to employ methods whereby this goal can be accomplished.

Schwitzgebel (1967) conducted a study in which he attempted "short-term operant conditioning of adolescent offenders on socially relevant variables." There were 35 in the experimental group and 14 in the control group. The procedure was to reward consistently the experimental group for promptness, favorable verbal behavior, and favorable nonverbal social behavior, whereas the control group members received no praise and were punished frequently. The praised group exhibited significantly more favorable behavior. The punishment group showed no improvement, although there was no significant decrease in previously established base line behavior.

Gottesfeld (1965), in an interesting study which investigated motivation for therapy, presented a list of 65 treatment methods to be evaluated by 235 professionals and 332 gang members. The professionals were asked to rate the methods for usefulness; the delinquents rated them by preference. Analysis of their preferences revealed that the professionals preferred a nonjudgmental, nonauthoritarian role and avoidance of personal relationships with the client. The delinquents preferred a therapist in the role of a parental surrogate and rejected the professional in the role of "pal." They wanted, instead, a mature adult, who would be concerned about them, teach them to relate better socially, and help them to take their place in the world. The author concluded that the discrepancies suggest new strategies for the professional (i.e., surrogate parental relationships, group therapy, and even direct attempts to socialize the delinquent).

Persons (1967) reported that a one-year follow-up study on 41 delinquent boys who had participated in 40 group therapy sessions and 20 individual therapy sessions showed these boys to be better adjusted than 41 matched control delinquents who received no therapy while they were incarcerated. The therapy group had a lower recidivism rate when compared to the control group and to the insitutional base rates. The therapy group committed fewer offenses, broke parole less frequently, and had a greater percentage of boys employed for a longer period of time. The therapy group demonstrated more favorable adjustment at a significant statistical level than the control group.

Pierson et al. (1966) reported a significant study on structured group living. A group of 123 male delinquents, aged 14 to 18, lived in cottages for eight months, receiving therapy in a group setting. Another group of 43 matched control delinquents were confined in a maximum security cottage for eight months and received no therapy. Both groups were administered the High School Personality Questionnaire (HSPQ) before and after the eight-month period. In a follow-up study one year after release, the recidivism rate dropped from 20 per cent among the therapy group to 16 per cent—an all-time low for the institution base rate. The control group showed no positive change, and they did experience increased tension and anxiety as measured by the HSPQ. This study provided the first substantial evidence, on a sizeable sample, that guided group interaction, structured group therapy, and academic and vocational training significantly improve delinquents' personalities.

Weeks (1963) reported on a study in which 229 16- and 17-year-old offenders, while incarcerated, received short-term group interaction treatment. A matched group from a traditional reformatory received no treatment. Results showed that after being discharged the therapy group adjusted more successfully than the reformatory group.

On the basis of their research on self-concepts of delinquents, Fitts and Hammer (1969) stated that rehabilitative, correctional, and educational institutions must first understand delinquents and public offenders in order to help them and that this understanding is incomplete without an evaluation of how the delinquent individual sees himself. Demanding, degrading, and overly punitive treatment tends to reinforce the delinquent's already negative self-concept and to perpetuate his antisocial behavior. Delinquents require firm but fair external controls but need to be treated as worthwhile and useful human beings. To find new and better ways of modifying behavior and the self-concept and to discover positive behaviors which will allow delinquents to obtain positive reactions from others and especially from themselves are major goals still to be attained. Advances in this regard include the use of *programmed instruction* (Brown and L'Abate, 1969), recommended by Fitts and Hammer, and the active participation and involvement of the delinquents (essential factors) in the planning and operation of treatment programs. Such programs should take into consideration the nature of the delinquent's self-concept.

In the Draper (Alabama) study of John McGhee, delinquents were trained to learn anything from how to comb their hair to college level courses using teaching machines administered to them by individuals representing authority figures. The recidivism rate in this population was reduced from 80 per cent to 20 per cent. McGhee and his associates are currently offering their consulting services and techniques to state institutions for offenders at no cost. Payment is deferred until a former offender has been out of jail for a year without any further offense (Brown and L'Abate, 1969).

Prevention and Treatment

How can juvenile delinquency be prevented? An individual who views delinquency as involving basically sociological problems might make an attempt to manipulate the environment of the delinquent in order to prevent delinquency, and rehabilitation within the child's existing environment might be implemented. Those in support of a psychological approach, however, usually see delinquent behavior as a symptom of some underlying problem (i.e., poor self-concept). In this case, the child would be treated by psychological methods. Since the sociological approach attempts to improve the individual through a community or group program, sociological intervention generally is more comprehensive than psychological intervention.

One of the better known projects utilizing a community approach is the Chicago Area Project instituted by Shaw and his associates (Kobrin, 1959). The first project was developed in 1932, and by 1959 similar projects had arisen in 12 Chicago neighborhoods. These projects were predicated on the philosophy that adults living in these slum areas must become motivated to accept greater responsibility in promoting socially acceptable behavior among children in the area. The central aim was to involve local children in various activities, so that they would adopt conventional rather than delinquent modes of behavior. The program was initiated by having a staff member identify leaders in the community and enlist their support for a strong local movement to combat delinquency. These "natural" leaders then formed organizations, directed the community in establishing a program, and raised the funds necessary to support the program. Thus, the primary responsibility for the maintenance and effectiveness of the program was assumed by indigenous members of the low income community. Outside professional assistance, although given a definite role, was secondary. The area projects differed with respect to the specific contents of their programs, but all contained three common components: (1) establishment of recreational programs, (2) strengthening of community bonds, and (3) direct work with gangs and individuals. The roles of prestigious community leaders served the dual purpose of attracting both adults and youth members and offering models worthy of copying.

Another method, started in the 1920's and given impetus by Thrasher's work (1927) with gangs, is the detached worker approach. It has been noted that most delinquency takes place where delinquency has previously occurred. Considering this fact, caseworkers developed methods which reached the child's family and were extended to predelinquent or delinquent peer groups. One of the most ambitious work programs is Miller's juvenile delinquency project (1962). This project was designed to counteract delinquency in the lower-class Boston area and was continued for a period of three years, 1954 to 1957. Unlike some group projects which simply encouraged the child to become a member of an organized group, such as a baseball team, this program attempted to influence the value systems of lower-class street gangs, because their values often led them into conflict with law enforcement agencies. The project furnished 205 children (7 corner groups) with extensive services. (By extensive, we mean approximately 18 to 21 hours of actual contact per week.) The treatment ranged over a period of 10 to 34 months. Of the 7 groups, 4 were composed of white males, mostly Irish, 1 of black males, 1 of black females, and 1 of white females. The control subjects consisted of 7 groups which had received only supervisory assistance. The ages of the subjects ranged from 8 to 12 at the start of the program. There were three major phases of the project: (1) to establish personal relationships; (2) to modify antisocial behavior through organized group activities and to serve as intermediaries between the youth and adult institutions; and (3) to terminate the relationship in a therapeutic manner. Unfortunately, no follow-up report is available to check the effectiveness or outcomes of this project.

Psychotherapy for the Child, Guidelines for the Teacher

There are many techniques and methods which attempt to deal with aggressive behavior. Abt and Weisman (1965) pointed out that the acting-out child is considered to be the most difficult of all child patients to treat. Bandura and Walters (1959) stated that most methods apply to oversocialized rather than undersocialized individuals. By the time constructive intervention for the acting-out child is attempted, the pattern of aggression is thoroughly learned and the conditions that make possible the socialization of aggression are difficult to reproduce. Completely effective and economical methods of treating the acting-out delinquent child are not available. Since a lifetime of experience is needed to establish delinquent patterns in the aggressive child, a considerable amount of time may be required to change these response patterns.

Dollard and Miller (1950), basing their method of therapy on learning theory combined with analytical techniques, considered the goal of behavioral change to be the extinguishing of undesirable response patterns. Suppose that, in the past, a child has been rewarded for aggressive behavior by getting what he wants. Simply stated, if these responses are not rewarded, they will eventually cease to exist. If anxiety and frustration build up in a child, he will react without thinking to the drive for release of tension. Dollard and Miller believed that anxiety causes us to think irrationally and to respond to feelings rather than to employ problem-solving behavior. In conjunction with the extinction of aggression, reinforcements are systematically applied to any desired responses that the child may make.

Behavioral change may occur by establishing a permissive relationship with the child, so that existing frustrations can be reduced by verbal or motoric expression which is neither rewarded nor punished. The teacher then encourages constructive behavior (usually acts that are incompatible with aggressive) to replace aggressive acts. These incompatible acts are reinforced and tend to inhibit aggressive responses. When this method is systematically applied, the aggression will eventually become extinguished. Any underlying problem which may have initially instigated the aggressive behavior (e.g., poor or negative self-concept) will require discussion and consideration.

Psychoanalytically oriented management basically attempts to reduce aggression by means of providing constructive channels for its expression. This goal is accomplished when the child is systematically socialized, that is, when he incorporates the values of society into his life style. Analytical therapy relies on the technique of transference, a process through which the child transfers or projects his attitudes and feelings from his parents to the teacher. The child will then act out his feelings toward the teacher who has the opportunity to interpret the behavior to the child. The interpretation consists of explaining why he is acting aggressively and helping him to realize the self-defeating nature of the behavior. Transference also permits identification with the teacher which subsequently leads to the child's incorporation of the teacher's values.

Abt and Weisman (1965) listed the following methods for treating aggressively acting-out children on the basis of short-term therapy:

1. Remove the child from the situation which precipitates the aggressive behavior.

2. Employ cathartic interpretation, dealing directly with the drive expressed in acting-out. This may have limited usefulness in view of the child's defensive reactions which may result from interpretation.

3. Attempt to make the behavior ego-alien. By utilizing this most useful method, one may point out the repetitive and harmful nature of the behavioral patterns and may explain to the child that he is a victim of his unconscious distortions. By making apparent the passive role that the child plays in relation to his impulses, much of the feeling of omnipotence and "magic," which is inherent in acting-out, can be removed.

4. Since immediate action is a factor in aggressive behavior, any delay (e.g., physical restraint, holding operations) tends to interfere with the behavior.

5. Become familiar with the part of the child's personality that wishes to control the impulses. The superego can be strengthened by appealing to the person's conscience.

Long-range therapeutic measures for the acting-out child include: prohibition, interpretation, and strengthening of the ego; the systematic use of prediction; routinely reviewing and relating disassociated events by means of interpretative statements; explaining that every act of aggression fortifies the wrong response; and employing the classroom as a unique opportunity for learning and "unlearning" in actual social situations.

The social learning theory of aggression (Bandura and Walters, 1959) suggests that the control and reduction of violence require changes in cultural traditions, child-rearing practices, and parental behavior. Parents who violently punish their children for violent acts are teaching them how and under what circumstances violence can be performed. Other changes in cultural traditions which are advocated by this theory place emphasis on prevention rather than punishment of violent acts and, equally important, promote human rights and group effort rather than excessive and isolated self-reliance. The first step is examination of values, so that those values which foster aggressive acts may be recognized and altered. Especially critical in the treatment of delinquency is the struggle to elicit feelings of affection, confidence, and love. One's capacity to feel strength in these emotions is the greatest safeguard against callousness,which often results in violence against a seemingly impersonal world and impersonal people.

Bandura and Walters (1959) stated that the goal of behavioral change in antisocial persons is the development of internal restraints.

The establishment of a close dependency relationship between the child and the teacher, similar to that of a child and his parents, is a necessary condition for the development of internalized controls. Establishing such dependency may be difficult because of generally negative responses from the child, who views the teacher as just another authority figure to fear and distrust. The child has developed a pattern of negative expectation, and his dependency anxiety leads him to anticipate rejection. The teacher must, therefore, adopt a nonpunitive attitude and must allow the hostile, provocative responses to become extinguished. This process will probably be a prolonged one but must occur before the tentative bids for dependency gratifications are made. As soon as these take place, the teacher may actively attempt to produce a sharp distinction between his own attitudes and those of punitive authority figures (e.g., creating deliberate situations in which to demonstrate himself as a source of help and support).

The second phase of management of the acting-out child is the establishment of internal controls by behavioral change resulting from the child's fondness for the teacher and his adoption of the teacher's values. The third phase consists of involving the parents in the child's treatment. Ways should be found to break patterns of parental rejection of the child.

In Scott's study (1956), children were treated by welfare workers who were available to them at school and were on call at their homes. Scott's program for treatment of aggressive children and prevention of delinquency includes the following practical measures: (1) involvement of school welfare service, (2) employment of facilities for diagnosis, with (3) tutorial provisions, (4) residential schooling (where needed), (5) residential industrial training, and (6) leisure time provisions and facilities.

Although this program may appear to be a simple prescription, it was shown to produce average results (i.e., 66 per cent success); 21 of the 33 subjects in the study showed no further legal offenses. Scott pointed out that the chief method of therapeutic intervention with regard to the temperamental child who is vulnerable to stress involves a holding operation—waiting until the child's processes of maturation develop.

Another example of an innovative combination of approaches is illustrated by the work of Massimo and Shore (1967), who attempted a controlled study which utilized vocationally oriented psychotherapy with emphasis on teaching social skills and coping behavior. The multiple services approach included vocational placement, remedial education, and psychotherapy, which utilized a single therapist for all services. The subjects were 20 white male delinquents, aged 15 to 17, who had been suspended from school. They were divided into two groups of 10 each. One group received treatment over a 10-month period, and the controls received no treatment. The therapist established contact with each boy in his community, often at locations frequented by the boy. No attempts were made to have the boys return to school, and the therapist adopted a nonauthoritarian role and made himself available to them at any time, day or night. The first phase considered vocational aspects, including activities such as field trips to different job settings or instruction in filling out job applications. The therapist accompanied each boy to his first job interview. When a full-time job was obtained by the individual, the focus shifted to his job performance. Remedial education included any necessary skills and academic training, and therapy focused on general attitudes, problems at home, and personal problems.

Section IV

DEALING WITH ENVIRONMENTAL AND CULTURAL EXCEPTIONALITIES IN THE CLASSROOM

CHAPTER 12

IDENTIFICATION, EVALUATION, AND PLACEMENT

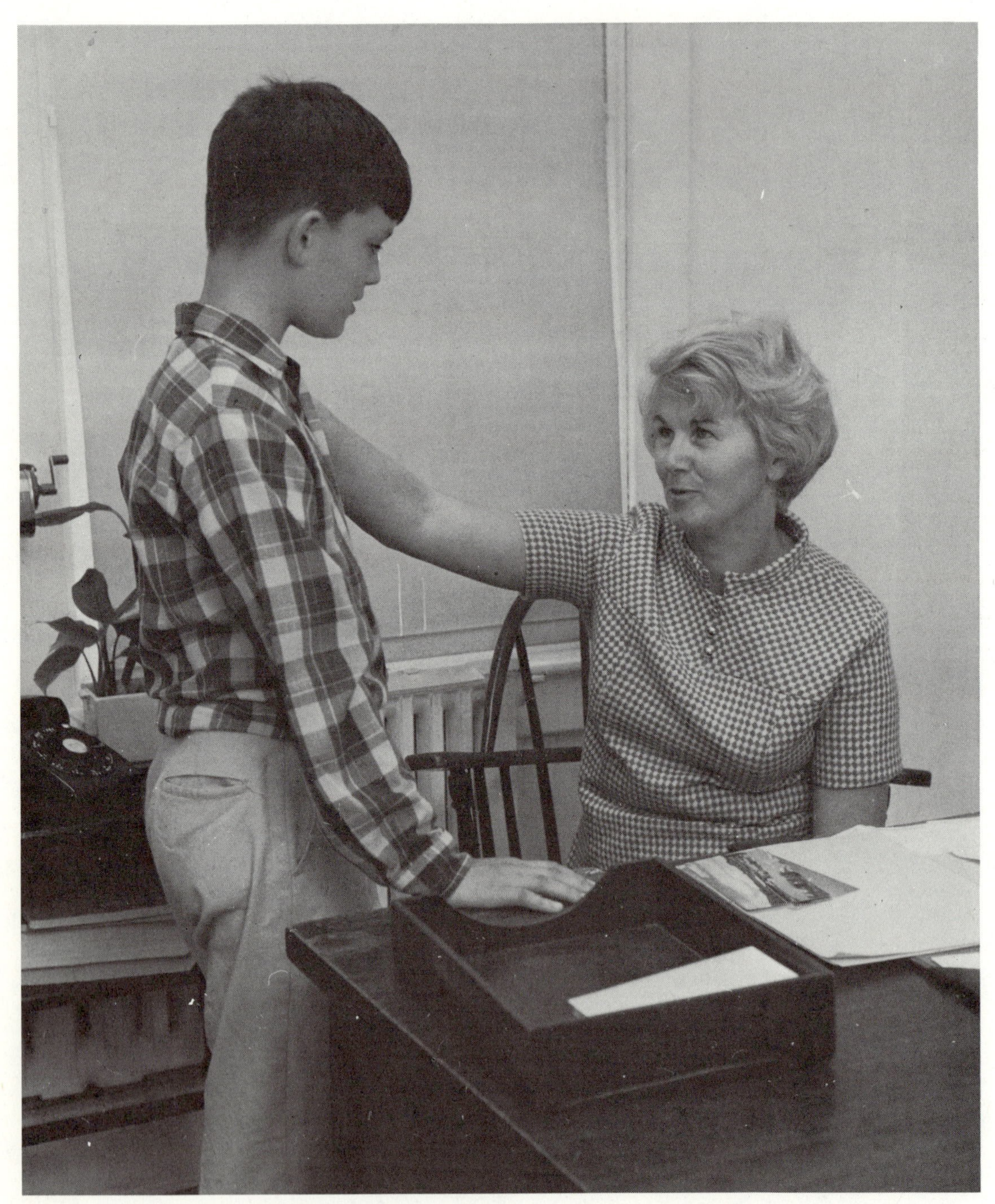

(Courtesy of The Woods Schools, Langhorne, Pennsylvania.)

DEALING WITH THE EDUCABLE MENTALLY RETARDED

Identification of the child with a severe exceptionality poses few problems. He tends to exhibit pronounced symptoms, such as an extremely enlarged head, an unusually small head, inability to focus the eyes, exceptional physical immaturity, or poor control of muscles. The proportion of the population included in this category is very small in comparison with the number of individuals who will, at some time, be categorized as exceptional in some modality. The majority of children with borderline retarded intellectual functioning remain undetected and unidentified until they reach school age. This lag is probably due to the fact that the developmental divergence (the borderline manifestations) of this exceptionality from the norm does not exhibit itself so as to come to the attention of parents, in general, and of physicians, in particular. The deficiencies of the educable mentally retarded tend to be most noticeable in their school performance (Kirk, 1972). In the past, the teacher has played a key role in identifying borderline intellectual retardation, because such a child's deficit does not become evident until he experiences a situation in which particular abilities are required of him, mainly the ability to acquire skills in reading and other academic subjects. A parent's shock at discovering that his child has such a condition, when the child is of school age, is severe in many cases. Early identification could ameliorate the situation, and in addition, many steps could be taken to decrease the later detrimental effects of retardation upon the individual.

Describing the symptomatology of the educable mentally retarded (EMR) is a difficult task. In general, these children present few, if any, extremely divergent types of physical symptoms which might separate them from their peers. There are, however, some developmental lags which may be indicative of later difficulties. Such developmental lags include delayed speech or excessively immature or poorly articulated speech. We hasten to add that these conditions are only indicative of a possibility of intellectual retardation. In addition, the EMR child is frequently less well coordinated than the normal child and tends to be less able to cope with interpersonal relationships at the same level as the normal child; that is, the EMR child tends to prolong the *parallel play period.* It should also be remembered that EMR children have a greater incidence of concomitant disabilities, such as visual, hearing, and general health problems (e.g., heart conditions) than normal children. Early identification of educable mental retardation requires the assistance of many specialties. Without the observation of many skilled individuals, the EMR child will probably escape detection until he has experienced failure in his first year of school.

The School Nurse and Screening of EMR Children

In her function as a representative of the health field, the school nurse often sees children in her clinic. In working with children, the nurse should be alert to developmental anomalies and should call to the attention of school personnel the importance of observing all such factors. In case of need, the school nurse can often assist the school in working with parents. Another function of the school nurse is to keep medical records and to become familiar with various medical specialties needed in certain school systems.

The Teacher's Role in Assessment and Evaluation

At the present stage of educational organization, the bulk of all assessment and evaluation of intellectual retardation falls to the lot of public schools, and the key figure in this evaluation procedure is the teacher. Many training programs for teachers do not provide adequate preparation in this area. It is essential that all teachers be provided with a minimum of skills, knowledge, and understanding which will enable them to perform a screening function. Usually, there are many more children requiring the attention of the school psychologist than his time will allow. A thorough screening examination, performed by a competent teacher, can facilitate and implement the work of the evaluation team, which should be involved in planning programs for exceptionalities in public schools.

All teachers should be taught skills in observation. It is very probable that skilled observation is still the key talent needed by teachers in order to make good evaluations of their children. Observation involves paying close attention to all behaviors of the children, in many settings, and while they are performing many activities. In order to systematize their work, it is suggested that teachers make use of a checklist. Many checklists have been devised, but it has been our experience that they need to be kept simple and concise if they are to be properly utilized by teachers.

A much neglected skill in teacher training is the ability to work with parents. A parent interview needs to be conducted with tact, sympathy, understanding, insight, and a willingness to perceive the world through others' eyes. Parental interviews, ideally, should be conducted in the parents' home, where they have a natural advantage and perhaps will be inclined to feel less defensive. Teachers should arrange parental interviews at a time when it is possible to talk to both parents, even though it is sometimes difficult to persuade fathers to participate in parent interviews. Many children with exceptionalities involving the intellect suffer from inadequate male influence. Therefore, it is important to observe those who are being interviewed, their attitudes, the environmental conditions, and to attempt to draw objective conclusions from the interview. During parental interviews, teachers should be especially aware of their own attitudes which may be conveyed by nonverbal means. A raised eyebrow, a hunched shoulder, or neglecting to shake hands may be indicative to the parents that they are not well regarded by the teacher. The teacher should attempt to establish a business-like, but friendly, tone. Above all, the teacher should not create an inquisitorial environment! Parents are not subject to inquisition, and teachers should remember that it *is* possible that parents might know something about their own child. The teacher should engage in intensive self-monitoring behavior during interview sessions in order to observe himself as accurately and objectively as possible.

Appropriate Tests for Teachers' Usage

The teacher's task of assessing children in order to identify possible retardation may be greatly facilitated by the use of a number of psychometric devices that are appropriate for relatively untrained and unsophisticated examiners. The most commonly used testing procedures in public schools today are those which center on group testing of children for achievement and intelligence. Both the group achievement and group intelligence tests provide a beginning point for screening for possible retardation. The teacher should remember, however, that group intelligence tests are frequently invalid because of the lack of reading ability of some children who are examined.

A general rule to follow when using group intelligence and achievement tests as preliminary devices is that any child scoring one or more standard deviations below the mean of the test should be provided with additional evaluation. Three intelligence tests have been developed for individual administration, and little advanced training in psychology is required in order to administer them. In many cases, the following devices aid the teacher by furnishing additional insight into the possible retardation of children: (1) the Quick Test (the Q.T. Test), published by Psychological Test Specialists, Missoula, Montana; (2) the Slosson Intelligence Tests; and (3) the Peabody Picture Vocabulary Test. These tests are short and have been proved effective by a considerable number of validation studies. In addition to the administration of one or two of the preceding tests, it is suggested that an individual achievement test, such as the Wide Range Achievement Test, be administered.

After the preceding tests have been utilized, the teacher should carefully examine the results. If the child scores below 80 on at least two of the intelligence tests or if he scores two or more grade levels below his actual grade on any one of the achievement tests, he should be referred to the school psychologist or psychometrist for further evaluation.

The principal aim of the teacher in the screening process is to remove children from referral lists, thus decreasing the demanding load on the psychological staff of the school district.

Alerting Parents and Professionals to Identification of EMR Children

All pertinent individuals involved in child growth and development and child-rearing should be made aware of the problems of educating and treating EMR children. Owing to the difficulty of early detection, it is important that all persons involved, including parents, be aware of the possibility of intellectual retardation, so that proper treatment procedures may be instituted as early as possible. The medical professional, in particular, should be observant of minor developmental lags that may be indicative of future difficulties in intellectual functioning.

Parental education has a major role in the identification process. Children are entitled to knowledgeable parents, and parents should be informed of those facts which will assist them in providing adequate environments for their children. Parental education, properly conducted, will help parents to observe their children and to call to their physicians' and to other professionals' attention behavior which may be indicative of future difficulties.

SCHOOL PLACEMENT

There is a great need for all school districts to use a placement committee to insure that each child will receive appropriate consideration before any program is prescribed for his intellectual, emotional, and academic needs. Every effort should be made to conduct intensive and extensive observational procedures with systematic recording of behavior to provide an appropriate baseline from which to prescribe remedial activities.

The Role of Teachers' Observations in the Placement Process

Observations may be divided into two major aspects: direct and indirect. Direct observations involve an observer's being present with the person being observed. Preferably, direct observation should occur under a variety of conditions and in a variety of settings in order to ascertain the full range of behaviors of the child. Indirect observations involve a number of techniques, for example, the use of questionnaires, records, or documents pertaining to the child. It is essential that individuals involved in observation undergo a period of training to improve their skills in observing and in reliable recording and that they attend to the relevant data, that is, data relevant in light of the desired goals and outcomes of the observation. Many studies seem to indicate that the very presence of an observer tends to change behavior. This fact should be considered in interpreting one's observations. It would be ideal if one could devise techniques and methods by which observation might be conducted so that the person being observed would be totally unaware of the process.

Perhaps the most commonly utilized method of observation is the anecdotal record, which has been used by teachers for many years. The anecdotal record usually involves the recording by the teacher of some particular behavior that she has observed. The record is usually filed in the child's cumulative folder. In the past, the anecdotal method has left much to be desired, largely because of the fact that observations tend to be made as a result of a crisis situation or interpersonal conflict. Also, teachers have tended to utilize terminology in anecdotal reports which may be not only noncommunicative but also damaging to the child. For example, teachers may record that one child is lazy or that another lies or steals. Teachers should be careful when recording such information on permanent records. Observations of transient kinds of activities should be made very carefully. Another disadvantage of the anecdotal record is that such notes tend to be inserted in an unsystematic fashion and thus are likely to be unrepresentative of the total behavior of a child. Anecdotal records also tend to emphasize negative aspects of behavior. It is rare to find a positive note regarding a child's behavior. Teachers should consider the fact that all behavior has both negative and positive aspects and that knowledge of the total pattern of behavior is important in devising appropriate procedures for the education of any child. Some basic rules should be observed when using the anecdotal record as an observational device:

1. Notes should be inserted regularly into the child's cumulative folder.

2. Anecdotal records should be kept on all children, not just troublesome children, and systematic notes on their behavior should be placed in their files.

3. All behavior, both negative and positive, should be noted in order that an adequate sampling of the child's behavior can be obtained.

4. Teachers should use purely factual and specific terms in recording their observations rather than judgmental labels.

5. The teacher should record observations briefly, since lengthy notes tend to obscure communication rather than to enhance it.

6. Teachers should avoid subjective judgments.

7. A standardized format should be used in recording observations (Woody, 1969).

Anecdotal records may be of considerable importance if careful, systematic, periodic notes are kept. It is important that nonjudgmental terms be used. Such terms as lazy, immature, or belligerent are of little use in evaluating a child's problem. Teachers should remember that it is important to use words that are descriptive of actually observed behavior. For example, "Billy hit Margaret three times"; or "Billy threw his book on the floor"; or "Billy went to sleep in class"; or "Billy refused to participate in baseball." In other words, all behaviors should be recorded first, and then later, attempts should be made to evaluate the meaning of such behaviors. It is crucial to report the environmental situation in which the behaviors occurred. Behaviors never occur in a vacuum, but always under highly dynamic circumstances.

An interesting device which may be used for observation is the adjective checklist, which consists of a long list of both negative and positive adjectives concerning all types of behavior. The teacher simply makes a check or tally beside the adjective that most adequately describes a child's behavior at the moment that he is being observed. Of course, an adjective checklist would have to be restricted, since some studies indicate that there may be as many as 18,000 adjectives which could be used. Ideally, teachers utilizing a checklist should have received some training in their use.

A third device which may be used for observation is a rating scale. One example of such a device is the Rutter scale, which was specifically designed to be used by teachers. The teacher reads a statement and then responds as to whether the particular behavior occurs frequently, infrequently, or not at all. Examples of items on the Rutter scale are: "often restless," or "runs about a lot." One disadvantage of the Rutter scale and other scales of a comparable nature is that they tend to be unreliable in that each teacher interprets the items according to personal experience. Such scales provide little interobserver reliability unless teachers have been specially trained to use them. One of the more reliable scales is that of Bower (1969); it attempts to divide positive and negative types of information. In addition to the use of published scales, it is possible for a teacher to devise small scales of her own.

The Placement Committee

It is recommended that a placement committee be formed for each referred child for the purpose of planning for possible further referral and placement of the child in a specialized program. The placement committee should consider all available evidence in order to arrive at the most appropriate educational procedures for each child. At a minimum, the placement committee should consist of all teachers involved with the child and those who might become involved with him if he is placed in a special class. The principal of the school should always be a member of the placement team, although it is frequently inadvisable for him to serve as chairman of the committee because of his position of authority. The school psychologist can always offer valuable assistance to the committee, since generally speaking, he has conducted the most intensive investigation, in terms of objective assessment procedures, to discover the needs of the child. The school psychologist frequently serves as chairman of the placement committee. If he does assume this role, under no circumstances should his conclusions be automatically approved by the rest of the placement committee. In systems where there are school counselors and school social workers, these individuals should be included in the placement committee so that their specialized skills may contribute to the total assessment procedure.

Special Education Placement and the Law

In this section we will discuss briefly the major trends concerning all testing and especially the testing of such factors as intelligence, which may result in the placement of a child in some sort of special education program. Teachers and other school personnel must be concerned with and aware of the problems involved in assessing children in order to assist and not to hinder children's education. Ross et al. (1971) discussed some of the major concerns of parents and other groups with regard to current practices in evaluation and placement of children:

1. Testing does not accurately measure the learning ability of many children. Many of the current devices were standardized on white, middle-class populations, and such tests may discriminate against children of different backgrounds.
2. The administration of tests is often performed incompetently. The person administering the test must understand the variables that may affect test-taking.
3. Parents are not given an adequate opportunity to participate in the placement decision.
4. Special education programming is inadequate.
5. The harm created by improper placement may be irreparable.

A number of cases involving the preceding concerns have been decided in court, and some are now pending. A few of the more important cases follow:

In Hobson vs. Hansen (1967), Judge Skelly Wright held that the "tracking" system used in the Washington, D.C. public schools was illegal since it was in violation of the equal protection clause of the United States Constitution. He ordered the abolition of the entire tracking system which had been based on standardized group intelligence and achievement testing.

In Diana vs. State Board of Education, filed in the District Court for the Northern District of California in February, 1970, 9 Mexican-American public school students of ages 8 through 13 claimed that they had been improperly placed in classes for the mentally retarded on the basis of inaccurate tests. As a result of this suit the following practices were mandated:

1. All children whose primary home language is not English must be tested in both their primary language and English.

2. Such children must be tested only with tests or sections of tests that do not depend on such factors as vocabulary, general information, and other such unfair verbal questions.

3. Mexican-American and Chinese-American children already in classes for the mentally retarded must be retested in their primary language and must be reevaluated only as to their achievement on nonverbal tests or sections of tests.

4. Each school district must submit to the state, in time for the next school year, a summary of retesting and reevaluation and a plan listing special supplemental training which will be provided to help each child return to the regular class.

5. State psychologists are to work on norms for a new or revised IQ test to reflect the abilities of Mexican-Americans, so that in the future Mexican-American children will be judged only by how they compare to the performance of their peers, not to the population as a whole.

6. Any school district which has a significant disparity between the percentage of Mexican-American students in its regular classes and in its classes for the retarded must submit an explanation which states reasons for this disparity.

A most important case involving special education placement is Covarrubias vs. San Diego School District, filed in February, 1971. This case made school personnel involved in evaluation and special education placement liable for payment of damages and also attempted to ban all testing for placement in special education classes until appropriate tests were developed.

In October, 1970, the case of Stewart vs. Phillips in Boston included the poor in the classes of children who are to be specially considered.

We have briefly summarized some of the implications of the preceding decisions: (1) many schools may appear to be using special education to further racism; (2) educators must fully examine all current attitudes and methods of evaluating all children; (3) the consumer (of public school education) must be included in decisions involving universities and colleges which train school personnel; (4) in all probability, there will be accountability legislation in many states; and (5) it will be very costly to maintain the status quo.

Our brief summary of current problems involving special education further emphasizes the need for evaluative functions above and beyond placing a label on a child. All evaluation should be for the purpose of better instruction. This is the major reason that the teacher is considered as being of prime importance in evaluation. It is hoped that the teacher will use any test only as a means of obtaining information which will assist her in providing a more appropriate curriculum for each child. *Under no circumstances is the teacher to use testing as a method of limiting alter-*

natives for children. At the very most, the teacher might use test results to make a needed referral to the school psychologist.

Social History and School Records

Schools should practice comprehensive, complete, and thorough maintenance of records of all their children, including social and developmental histories. This kind of data would make it much easier to arrive at appropriate educational procedures. Attention should be given to the confidential nature of these records; they should not be released without written parental consent.

The Role of the Principal in the Process of Evaluation and Placement

The school principal is frequently overlooked in the processes of identification, evaluation, and placement of EMR children. The principal, in essence, is the key individual in any school; the building and all its activities are his responsibility. Good administrative procedures demand that the principal be involved at every level and in an intensive fashion in the identification, treatment, and placement of EMR children. The principal must have some knowledge of this area of exceptionality and should serve as the source of approval for all referrals being made from classroom to central office staff. Thus, he will be in a position to examine referrals and will be able to determine the need for specialized assistance in his particular school. It is also suggested that the prinicipal assume the responsibility for assisting his teachers in their evaluation of children by providing them with all the necessary tools and, if need be, by providing release time, so that the teachers may more adequately evaluate their children.

The Role of the School Psychologist

The role of the school psychologist has been studied since the work of Bardon (1964; 1965). At present, the role of the school psychologist varies from school district to school district (Herron and Psaila, 1970). Magary (1966) found some 13 separate descriptions of the school psychologist's function; he supplied the following definition: "The school psychologist is one who brings a psychological frame of reference to bear upon a set of school related observations or behaviors, with the end in view of facilitating learning, creativity and self-actualization for as many school children as possible." The problem of overlapping functions with other school personnel, such as the school social worker, is discussed by Shaw (1967). Many school personnel tend to see the school psychologist as somewhat threatening (Bower, 1955).

The public appears to believe many myths concerning the school psychologist. The most common of these myths have been listed by Michael (1965): (1) that all school psychologists have the same training; (2) that all psychologists have the same type of job and do the same thing; (3) that all expectations of administrators with regard to school psychologists are the same; and (4) that all school psychologists can make themselves understood and can make sense to those with whom they talk. Michael continued with his discussion of myths concerning the role of the school psychologist by noting three myths that he feels the profession believes about itself: (1) that school psychologists agree on what they should be doing in the schools; (2) that all universities agree on what the training program for school psychologists should be; (3) that all school psychologists should be trained to function alike.

Mullen (1967) listed the following duties as the major functions of a school psychologist: (1) He should serve in the capacity of a consultant and coworker with all teachers and educational services in the public school system. (2) His major interest should be the mental health of all the children. Considering the preceding functions, his responsibilities lie generally in the following areas: (a) He deals with psychological problems which involve the diagnosis, treatment, and prevention of learning and behavioral problems and personality disorders. (b) He conducts psychological examinations which include gathering case history data by personal interview and the use of psychological testing. (c) Following analysis of the results revealed in the examination, he recommends a corrective program, including prescriptions for various corrective techniques and for educational adjustment. (d) He collaborates with parents, teachers, visiting teachers, and other school personnel in the study and treatment of pupils who are maladjusted. (e) He participates in an active program of research on psychological problems as they are manifested in the school setting.

The Role of the School Social Worker

The profession of school social worker is one that is rapidly growing and one that may be of great assistance to teachers and parents alike. A crucial problem of retarded children is parental acceptance of the condition. School social workers, functioning as trained persons in a social setting with parents, can be key figures in helping the school to explain to parents the nature, extent, and probable outcomes of treatment of educable mental retardation. The social worker can also promote liaison with other agencies in the community in order to assist parents in obtaining any additional help which may be needed.

THE TEACHER AND THE BEHAVIORALLY DISTURBED CHILD

Some signs that may help the teacher to identify behaviorally disturbed children are: restlessness, short attention span, impulsivity, and irritability. These signs call for a program designed by the teacher which will provide a fairly large amount of physical movement under controlled, structured conditions. In some cases, speech problems will be part of the child's behavioral disturbance. This problem, of course, requires the skills of the speech specialist in the district; however, the regular classroom teacher may be able to provide some kind of language development assistance. A child's inability to listen comprehensively would call for special training in how to listen, which might partially be accomplished by tape recordings with earphones for the child. Poor motivation and poor work habits are frequently characteristic of the behaviorally disturbed child. Therefore, it is essential that training in study skills be provided by the regular classroom teacher. Such children may exhibit poor ability to participate in peer activities. The teacher should take this into account in devising activity programs which will pair such children with other children who are more congenial. Some behaviorally disturbed children exhibit a great deal of aggressiveness. This behavior may be partially compensated for by providing appropriate outlets. Special supervised activities on the playground should eliminate some of these behaviors. The withdrawn, shy child should receive as much attention as the acting-out child and should be encouraged to participate in as many activities as possible.

Identification of Emotional Disturbances

Cruickshank (1971) reported that informed estimates reveal that there are 2.5 to 4.5 million children with emotional disturbances. Stennet (1966) found that 5 to 10 per cent of the children in elementary schools need professional attention because of adjustment problems. These statistics indicate that identification of emotionally disturbed children is of great importance.

Zax et al. (1967) demonstrated how it is possible to identify emotionally disturbed children early in the first grade. In a follow-up study, after six years, these identified children scored significantly more negatively on measurements of achievement, classroom behavior, peer perceptions, attendance, and school nurse referral.

In measuring the prevalence of behavioral symptoms of emotional disturbance in kindergarten, first, and second grade children, Werry (1968) found a decrease of symptoms after age five. After a sharp drop, however, between ages 5 and 6, there was a beginning increment in symptoms at age 8. Boys tended to show higher indications of acting-out and disruptive symptoms, while girls showed a slight excess of neurotic-type symptoms. Thus, boys seemed to show a higher rate of emotional disturbance and to be more "at risk" in our society than girls. It could be that girls may show a higher incidence of psychopathology as women later in life.

Lapouse and Monk (1964) found the same fluctuations in the number of symptoms with age as reported by Werry, supporting the hypothesis that such deviant behavior may occur in school-age children as a transient developmental phenomenon. Maladjustment in younger children was related to speech difficulties and physical inactivity. In older children, maladjustment was related to thumb-sucking, nail-biting, compulsivity, behavioral control, and body habits.

Burdock and Hardesty (1967) were able to differentiate mentally retarded from emotionally disturbed children on the basis of an observational technique, the Children's Behavior Inventory. Hospitalized retardates seemed to adapt as effectively to their surroundings as physically ill children. On the whole, emotionally disturbed children showed greater anger and hostility, conceptual dysfunction, incongruous behavior, lethargy, and dejection than either retardates or physically ill children.

There is increasing evidence to indicate that there is little or no validity to the time-honored notion that children outgrow behavioral problems which are detected during their early years of life (Balsur, 1965; Cowen, 1966; and Stennett, 1966). It has been observed that children who have adjustment problems as early as during the nursery school years tend to have problems in their later life, usually of the same nature (Westman et al., 1967). This evidence suggests the importance of the development of screening devices which could be used to detect psychological disturbance in young children.

The report of Stringer and Glidewell (1967) is more than a technical analysis of the Academic Progress Chart (APC) as a screening device. It offers to those individuals who are interested in the educational and emotional adjustment of children an informative description of the healthy versus the less healthy child. An account of their screening device accompanied by an effective description of the differences between the two groups of children will be helpful.

By using matched pairs of first-graders, who were alike in age, sex, IQ, and classroom behavior, but unlike in APC patterns, Stringer and Glidewell developed a simple and effective design for controlling extraneous variables. Caseworkers interviewed the children's mothers in order to collect social history information that would enable the researchers to discover other (social, familial, medical, psychological) determinants of APC patterns, past, current, and future. Neither the mother nor the interviewer was aware of the APC patterns of the child. The information from the interview was then assessed in light of the child's APC patterns at three specific periods: the year of the child's selection for the study, the year of the interview with his mother, and the year following the interview. This information also was accompanied by additional ratings on two symptoms and on the Mental Resources Inventories.

This experimental plan could then test three areas: (1) the predictive efficiency of the APC, (2) the congruence of professional judgments and concurrent APC performance, and (3) the possible "postdictive" value of the APC. The interview material pointed out the particular disturbances that the APC screening might not pick up and noted those children who produced low APC's but seemed to be healthy to some degree. This project did substantiate earlier studies which linked poor academic progress with children who have emotional problems (Stennett, 1966; Westman et al., 1967). Emotional disturbances were also related to a high number of symptoms as shown by the Symptom Inventory. At the same time, there was an inverse relationship between the Mental Resources Inventory and symptoms in relation to the mental health of the children.

Both inventories were tested as screening devices and were found to have valid decision rates of between 84 and 88 per cent as compared to 66 per cent for the APC. They do, however, require a great deal of sophistication on the part of the screener and are considered impractical for detecting emotional disturbance in children in the early elementary school years. The APC is believed to be more efficient and effective in this respect.

Descriptions of the two groups of children (healthy and disturbed) derive from the developmental histories and the personality patterns of the children whose mothers were interviewed. These descriptions can easily be related to their classroom behavior.

The healthy child appears to enter school already having learned good interpersonal relationships and has self-esteem, which gives him a capacity for competence, productivity, responsibility, and enjoyment:

> **... the healthy child enters school with an adequate supply of coping strengths derived from his experiences with his parents and others in his**

> **home. . . . In his first year in school he moves early into the upper half of his class, academically, and establishes himself. . . . By the end of the first grade, his self-esteem will probably have taken on an aura of cocksureness . . . (Stringer and Glidewell, 1967).**

Of particular interest is the tendency of healthy children to do well in their first year of school and then to show alternating slower and faster rates of progress in the succeeding years and to tend to alternate together as a group. The pattern is a relatively mild year-to-year zig-zag which terminates somewhere between the fourth and sixth grades, at which time these children surpass those who are less healthy:

> **It is difficult to imagine that educators would deliberately so plan that children would learn more rapidly in one year, less rapidly in the next, more rapidly again the year following, and so forth. It is more reasonable to assume that the children themselves set this particular norm. If this is true, [one] may mean by 'mental health' not so much conformity to group norms as the capacity to establish group norms on a consensual basis amongst the healthy youngsters (Stringer and Glidewell, 1967).**

The most noticeable characteristic of the less healthy group is that, as a group, they show great diversity. They can, however, be divided into two categories: nonstrugglers and strugglers. The nonstrugglers seem normal except for their low academic progress. Their behavior is usually described as gentle and well behaved, and they exhibit few symptoms. They are usually peripheral members of the class. If given external persuasion their school work will improve, but in the absence of such persuasion they appear to "let things ride." In contrast are the strugglers who look and act disturbed, showing a great number of symptoms of

Figure 12–1 The daydream is a typical method of meeting a currently unsatisfactory situation. (Courtesy of The Devereux Foundation, Devon, Pennsylvania.)

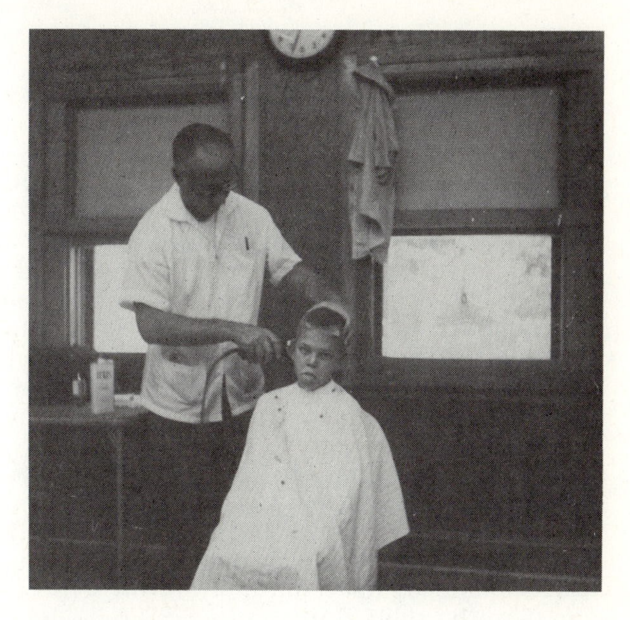

Figure 12–2 Exposure to social situations strengthens coping abilities. (Courtesy of The Woods Schools, Langhorne, Pennsylvania.)

emotional disturbance (anorexia, enuresis, lying, daydreaming, etc.) and difficulties in interpersonal relationships. There are four subgroups:

1. Troublemakers: They constantly struggle for social power with classmates, teachers, and authority figures. They can do well academically but usually have little desire to do so.
2. Very high achievers: They make the grade academically but are never satisfied with what they accomplish.
3. Quiet strugglers: They take school so seriously that they sacrifice everything to make the grade. School usually becomes harder every year, probably because they cannot keep up with their peer group.
4. Deliberate failures: They choose to fail as a means of maintaining their personal integrity against adult pressures.

The implications of the Stringer and Glidewell report should be viewed in light of the following conclusions:

1. A higher percentage of children than would be expected when compared with adult percentages were judged to have emotional difficulties of sufficient severity to warrant professional attention. This is probably due to the fact that during his formative years a child must learn to cope with his world.
2. Of these children with emotional difficulties, a significant number will be unable to resolve their problems without help.
3. As the child with adjustment problems progresses through school, he tends to fall further behind his peers.
4. The APC is an effective device which is readily usable in the schools and will identify, sometimes as early as first grade, those children who need special attention to enable them to benefit from the educational process.

Thus, it seems that the APC can help greatly in identifying adjustment difficulties of the young. Meanwhile, the results of this study may help researchers to determine which characteristics differentiate children who often appear to "heal" themselves from those whose problems can only be solved with professional help. We are inclined to agree with Stringer and Glidewell's view that it is the social education which the child receives, either at home or in school, that strengthens his coping facilities and psychological resources.

Today's schools have a formidable task before them if they are to produce psychologically healthy and educated children. The APC screening device (and others similar to it) is now available and is adequate for the identification of psychological disturbances.

Stennett (1966) determined a number of elementary school children to be emotionally handicapped and then undertook a follow-up study through a "phase" to determine who would improve without treatment and how many children really required treatment. He found that these children fell further and further behind their peers in their academic work. About 10 per cent of the children classified as emotionally handicapped in the beginning were still classified as such three years later, leading him to conclude that a significant number of children require treatment to recover.

The teacher serves a major role in the process of labeling a child as "emotionally disturbed." Certain consistencies are observable with regard to the concerns evidenced by teachers in their referral processes. Teachers consistently report children who are apparently of normal intelligence and are not suffering from any sensory or biological malfunction, but who still fail to acquire academic knowledge at the expected rate. These children also, as reported by teachers, tend to exhibit hyperactivity, difficulty in concentrating for any length of time, and mild to moderate incoordination.

Identifying Emotional Disturbance in the Classroom

On the basis of past research, how can the teacher identify emotional disturbance and differentiate it from biological deficits and cultural deprivations? The following discussion may serve to simplify this problem.

Inconsistent Variability Between Reception and Expression

Can all behavior and behavioral dysfunctions in children be accounted for in terms of biological and cultural forces? In the absence of biological deficits and cultural deprivations, there are certain behavioral dysfunctions that are dependent on individual psychological forces (i.e., how the individual child integrates, or fails to integrate, his biological make-up with cultural influences). Another way to answer the same question would be that even though a child may have a sound and healthy biological make-up and a relatively stimulating culture, a great deal of variability in behavior may occur. It is inevitable that a certain child in a peculiar set of circumstances may show some degree of emotional disturbance. When neither biological nor cultural factors can account for the child's behaving in a disturbed or, more often than not, disturbing manner, we can consider the presence of an emotional disturbance. There is still sufficient variability in behavior for the individual child to be able to create a disturbance in his environment from the very moment he is born. He may affect his most immediate culture as much as that culture may affect him.

How can one differentiate between what is cultural—or culture-bound—and what is psychological? This is not only a logical but also an empirical question that awaits solution. In some cases, the terms are used synonymously, so that no real conflict is acknowledged. Here, however, it is preferable to differentiate clearly between the two forces in the way that they affect the child. Culture influences mainly the output of a child, how he expresses himself, whereas the child's peculiarly individual integration of his biological and cultural forces is his "psychology." How does the child integrate the input, how does he select from it, and how does he process it? His unique processing is the developmental resultant of all three forces interacting together. The child's psychological adjustment is his personalized bridge between his organismic state and cultural demands.

Inconsistent Discrepancies and Psychological Functioning

Although variability, both intraindividual and interindividual, is a mainstay of psychological functioning, we may not assume that such variability is either random or erratic, and hence unpredictable and unidentifiable. If testing for intraindividual variability is lawful (i.e., IQ testing), some of its sources can be partialed out. The most direct and available source of variability is discrepancy of scores among similar and disparate measurements of educational and psychological functioning. "Normal" variability is noted as limited discrepancies among various scores. Each source of variation possesses its own specific emphasis and type of variability. In general, the larger the discrepancy in scores, especially between similar measurements of one modality, the greater its significance. One might say that malfunctioning or dysfunctioning is essentially related to score discrepancy, which in and by itself is an important index to be considered in each of the various areas of functioning.

Discrepancies in Intellectual Functioning. Within the area of intellectual functioning, there are various score discrepancies that should be considered: verbal versus performance scores, receptive versus expressive scores, and within various indexes of verbal functioning or of performance, both receptive and expressive aspects should be considered. As obvious as such a statement may appear to the reader, it is important to stress that the consistency of such discrepancies should be evaluated, for if the discrepancy is valid and reliable, it will reappear in other tests measuring similar functions. Thus, regardless of the method of evaluation, a child should show the same pattern of assets and liabilities.

Discrepancies Between Intellectual Functioning and Educational Achievement. As the report of Stringer and Glidewell (1967) suggests, one important index of emotional disturbance is the child's academic achievement level in relation to the level predicted for his chronological age and intellectual functioning.

Parental Role in Identification

Parental failure to recognize emotional disturbance in a child stems from lack of knowledge of normal child growth and development and lack of adequate models with which to compare their own child. Some of the following criteria may be used for possible identification of emotional difficulties in children:

1. Age discrepancy, i.e., comparison of a child's development with maturational norms provided by authorities in the field of child growth and development.

2. A frequent symptom exhibited by the child that may cause concern to either the physician or the parent.

3. Presence of a number of symptoms which interfere with the child's adequate functioning.

4. Presence of behaviors, such as bedwetting, which tend to separate the child from his peers.

5. Reactions of the child to his environment which may exhibit themselves in such overt behavior as nightmares.

6. Unusual, bizarre behavior such as starting fires, self-inflicted injuries, or extreme fantasies.

Identification and Evaluation After Entrance into Public School

The bulk of identification of behavioral disorders will, of course, occur after the child has entered school. To provide for appropriate early identification and treatment of the school-age child, it is first necessary to destroy the myth of teacher incompetence in identifying emotional problems. Unfortunately, in the past, only psychiatrists or psychologists were thought to be competent to identify emotional disturbance. The extensive work of Bower (1969) and others seems to indicate that this belief is simply untrue and that under proper conditions, the regular classroom teacher can acquire reasonable competencies in the identification of emotional problems. Once the basic concept of the teacher as a screener of potential emotional problems has been accepted, we may concentrate on the development of appropriate methods to help teachers to perform in such a role.

One such attempt has been made, namely, the development of a test by Educational Testing Service, revised by Bower and Lambert (1961). It is interesting to note that these researchers pointed out the necessity of a three-pronged approach, including teacher perceptions, peer perceptions, and personality tests. All three of the screening approaches are essential if there is to be proper identification of the emotionally disturbed child. The first step in this process is to clarify the definition of the term "emotionally handicapped," as it is used in this study. Bower and Lambert listed five criteria for identification of the emotionally handicapped:

1. An inability to learn that cannot be explained by intellectual, sensory, or physical factors.

2. An inability to establish satisfactory interpersonal relationships with peers and teachers.

3. Displaying inappropriate behavior under normal conditions.

4. A tendency to express a pervasive feeling of unhappiness and depression.

5. A tendency to develop physical symptoms, such as speech problems.

Bower and Lambert emphasized the fact that "screening" is devoted exclusively to identifying children who are not functioning adequately in a school situation. The screening process makes no attempt to determine the cause of the difficulty or whether it is a transitory or a long-lasting condition. The purpose of screening for emotional difficulties should be comparable to the purpose of screening for visual or hearing conditions: to identify needs and to provide appropriate kinds of educational procedures as a result of the identification.

Objectives of the screening process are:

1. To insure the early identification of children with emotional defects.

Figure 12–3 Gaining information through the child's perception of himself—what he feels that he is and what he would like to be. (Courtesy of The Woods Schools, Langhorne, Pennsylvania.)

2. To insure the institution of appropriate corrective, remedial procedures.

3. To assist teachers in becoming aware of emotional defects and of appropriate methodology to cope with them.

4. To provide the appropriate type of educational procedures to insure adequate care for the child suffering from emotional deficits.

In addition, Bower and Lambert pointed out that any screening device should be relatively simple and as objective as possible. It should be efficient in terms of the time required for its administration and interpretation:

1. The teacher should be able to complete the screening with the information available to her and without any outside authorities.

2. The device must be usable by the teacher without the need for long periods of intensive training in its usage.

3. The procedure should result in a tentative type of diagnosis which may lead to a referral to an appropriate authority.

4. The process outlined above is not meant to imply that the teacher should become "an amateur psychologist" or that the teacher should attempt to make a complete diagnosis and to prescribe for an emotionally disturbed child. Rather, it is a simple screening device, leading to appropriate referral.

5. The process should not violate the principles of privacy or good taste.

6. The process should be inexpensive to use.

7. It should not pose a threat to any child.

The concept of teacher screening is based on the belief that teachers, due to their prolonged contact with children, are in an ideal position to conduct preliminary screening for the detection of emotional disturbances.

The Bower instrument includes the administration of a peer-rating device. The peer-rating device, to be administered to kindergarten and primary school aged children, is called Classroom Pictures and is composed of 12 pictures with a total of 20 scoring items. Five of the 20 items are related to boys behaving in a maladjusted manner, and 5 are related to girls behaving in a maladjusted manner; five items are associated with boys behaving in a neutral manner, and five of the items are related to girls exhibiting neutral or positive behavioral patterns. Bower and Lambert indicated that they believe that the Classroom Pictures provide an opportunity for children in a class to systematically give observations of their peers.

A third device utilized by Bower and Lambert is the Class Play, which is usually administered to children in grades 3 through 7 and is most appropriate for grades 4, 5, and 6. The Class Play is also a peer-rating device to be administered to the class and should take between 35 and 45 minutes. The first section of the play is devoted to the presentation of 20 hypothetical roles in a play. The second section of the Class Play focuses on the student's selecting those roles that he feels he would like to play or that he feels others would select for him to play.

For grades 7 through 12, a survey type of peer rating is employed by Bower and Lambert. In order for this device to be most effective and most valid, it is essential that the students within the class have ample opportunity to interact socially as well as academically with their peers.

Still another device used in the Bower-Lambert identification process for kindergarten and primary school children is called Picture Game. The Picture Game is composed of 66 pictures. The child is instructed to select those pictures which are happy or unhappy. For grades 3 through 7, there is a device called "Thinking about One's Self." This instrument furnishes data concerning a child's perception of himself, his relationship with his environment, and what he thinks these should be. This device yields a discrepancy score between what a child feels that he is and what he would like to be (i.e., between the real self and the ideal self).

There is also a Bower-Lambert test for junior-senior high school students called the "Self-Test." This instrument also elicits a discrepancy score between the real self and the ideal self. It is possible that some students who are seriously disturbed will be unable to respond adequately to these last two tests in terms of presenting a difference between the ideal self and the real self.

The Bower and Lambert scale is an example of rating devices by which an assessment may be made of the emotional state of children. The teacher interested in additional devices is referred to the bibliography at the end of this text.

Werry and Quay (1969) developed a rating scale for the direct observation of pupil behavior, based on a classification system which includes three categories: deviant behavior, attending or work-oriented behavior, and teacher-pupil interaction. Using these categories, they were able to differentiate between emotionally disturbed and normal elementary school children. In addition to the Werry and Quay scale, there is a variety of behavioral and adjective checklists available to teachers, such as those developed by Walker (1962). Leary (1957), and Zuckerman et al. (1965), and many others, like the Devereux School Rating Scale.

One of the most promising, nonverbal, objective personality tests, which is used for screening for emotional disturbance, is the Missouri Children's Pictures Series developed by Sines and Pauker (Register and L'Abate, 1972). It can be administered to large classes in about 10 minutes and yields scores on 8 personality dimensions.

The process of identification and diagnosis of the behaviorally disturbed child consists of a number of stages. The first stage might center on the use of a simple device such as a behavioral checklist, and the second stage might include the use of behavioral rating scales. The final stage, before contacting the parents, might focus on careful noting of the child's behavior by direct observation.

The Process of Referral

Perhaps more serious than labeling, classifying, or listing symptoms is the process of referral of emotionally disturbed children. Referral should always be the result of a rather intensive examination of the child. As previously discussed in this chapter, we recommend a referral committee whose members represent many disciplines. All significant individuals who will be or have been involved with the child should be included in the referral committee. Referral should always be made in light of minimal intervention; that is, each child should have those procedures prescribed for him which will result in the least amount of displacement from the normal educational system but which will provide the optimum attention to his particular needs, as determined by the various individuals who work with him. Always, the basic goal of referral should be the child's transition from his current difficulties to a fully functioning role in the regular classroom in the public schools.

After all observations have been made, collated, and studied, a decision must be reached as to whether or not a referral is in order. Kessler (1966) listed seven criteria by which one may determine if a referral should be recommended:

1. Age discrepancy: Is there a discrepancy between the child's actual observed behavior and his chronological age?
2. Frequency of occurrence: What symptom is involved and how often does it occur?
3. Number of symptoms prevalent: Is the problem an isolated one or are a number of problems present?
4. Amount of disadvantage: How much does the child's misbehavior affect his interpersonal relationships?
5. Intractability of behavior: Does the problem persist even after many attempts to alleviate it?
6. Self-satisfaction: Does the child still show dissatisfaction with his current situation and his current status?
7. General personality factors: Is there disruption of the child's general psychosocial adjustment pattern?

The regular classroom teacher is usually the initiator of a referral process which may result in eventual placement of the child in a special education setting. Often, the person who next deals with the referral process within a school setting is *the school counselor.* Many elementary schools are currently adding school counselors to their staffs, and it is logical that the counselor serve as the second advisor in the referral process. Next in line is the school psychologist, who traditionally has been assigned the role of providing diagnostic service for the rest of the public school staff. It should be pointed out that an equally important function of the school district psychologist is the role of consultant. He may serve as a consultant to the school staff, the teacher, the principal, the counselor, and also to the families of children involved in the referral process. The school psychologist may also promote good relations with other agencies in the community which deal with emotionally or behaviorally disturbed children (Gray, 1963; Magary, 1967). As a consultant, the psychologist may assist the teacher in gaining insight into the nature of human behavior and learning. He may also serve as coordinator of procedures for the child in the school and in the home.

The task of complete differential diagnosis requires that the school psychologist consult with all other appropriate school personnel before arriving at a final evaluation of a child. It is important that the school psychologist work closely with the teacher, so that he may obtain an accurate picture of the child's total classroom behavior. When the diagnostic work-up is completed by the school psychologist, in conjunction with other school personnel, the school principal usually insures that the appropriate referral process is continued at the next level. The principal generally becomes involved in the referral process after all other studies are completed, since he frequently lacks direct sustained contact with individual pupils within the school setting, except in cases of disciplinary situations. The principal should be involved in most levels of referral for the children within his school and, in addition, should promote liaison with the school community. The principal often has many valuable contacts which he might use in order to bring appropriate individuals into the school to provide services for the faculty and children.

Referring Emotionally Disturbed Children

The process of referral is complex and must take into account many factors, such as the type of assistance available, the needs of the child, and his family background. Referral probably should be undertaken in three stages, the first being a discussion with the parents concerning the possibility of referral. Such an interview must be conducted with care to be sure that the parents have a full understanding of the implications. Secondly, the teacher must describe to the parents his perceptions of the child and of the child's possible needs. The teacher should be aware of the fact that he may encounter considerable resistance from parents when discussing the possibility of a referral. For example, the teacher may be confronted with resentment, antagonism, or fear (on the part of parents) of psychiatrists or psychologists. Many parents jump to the conclusion that the teacher believes that their child is "crazy" whenever a referral to a psychologist or psychiatrist is suggested. In addition, consideration of referral for psychological problems tends to arouse anxiety and guilt in many parents who may assume that they are totally at fault for their child's difficulties. In other words, they view the suggestion as a reflection upon themselves or upon the child's upbringing.

The third and final stage of referral should involve helping the parents to make a realistic decision.

Clinical Resources

Parents should be given some indication of the likely outcomes of referral and the progress that their child is likely to make if such a referral is completed. The teacher must be careful not to make any undue promises, since there is a tendency on the part of many lay people to regard psychiatrists and psychologists as miracle workers, and thus false hopes may be aroused in many parents.

Another important factor in making the referral is to prepare the child. The child has a right to be informed as to where and why he is being referred. He should be reassured and realistically acquainted with the process in accordance with his age and maturity. It is worthwhile to let the child have some idea of what is likely to happen, in terms of actual procedures that will be used in working with him. Parents and teachers should avoid conveying to the child any negative ideas concerning the referral process.

After both the parents and child have been prepared for referral, the appropriate agency, such as a mental health clinic or child guidance center, must be selected. Most reputable agencies maintain on their staffs a variety of professional personnel, including psychiatrists, clinical psychologists, and social workers. It is essential that each discipline involved make as thorough an evaluation of the child as possible. Typically, such a process begins with an intensive interview (lasting one to two hours) of the parents by the psychiatric social worker. The information usually sought in such an interview concerns one or more of five categories:

1. The present problem of the child.
2. The current functioning of the child.
3. History and attitudes.
4. Family relationships.
5. History of the parents.

The assessment is concerned with all phases of the child's current functioning, and the goal is to acquire a picture of the child's personality as the parents see it and as the school sees it. Such information as toilet training procedures or developmental milestones (e.g., when the child first talked, or when he first walked) is ascertained. Also, any problems concerning the actual birth process or the period of pregnancy are thoroughly investigated.

Much current research data indicates that a considerable portion of the information which is amassed may be irrelevant in providing adequate treatment for the child. Of course, it is essential to determine parental attitudes in order to learn some of the dynamics that may be operating within the family, although it is somewhat difficult to detect the real attitudes of parents. Every effort should be made to ascertain the stresses, strains, and other influencing factors of family life. If it is difficult to obtain data from parents, it is even more difficult to gain appropriate knowledge and understanding of a child's behavior by conducting a child interview. In most clinics, different functions are handled by the members of the various mental health disciplines (psychologists, psychiatrists, and social workers). When such facilities are not available, however, individual professionals handle most of the responsibilities for further evaluation and treatment.

CHAPTER 13

TECHNIQUES OF REMEDIATION AND REHABILITATION

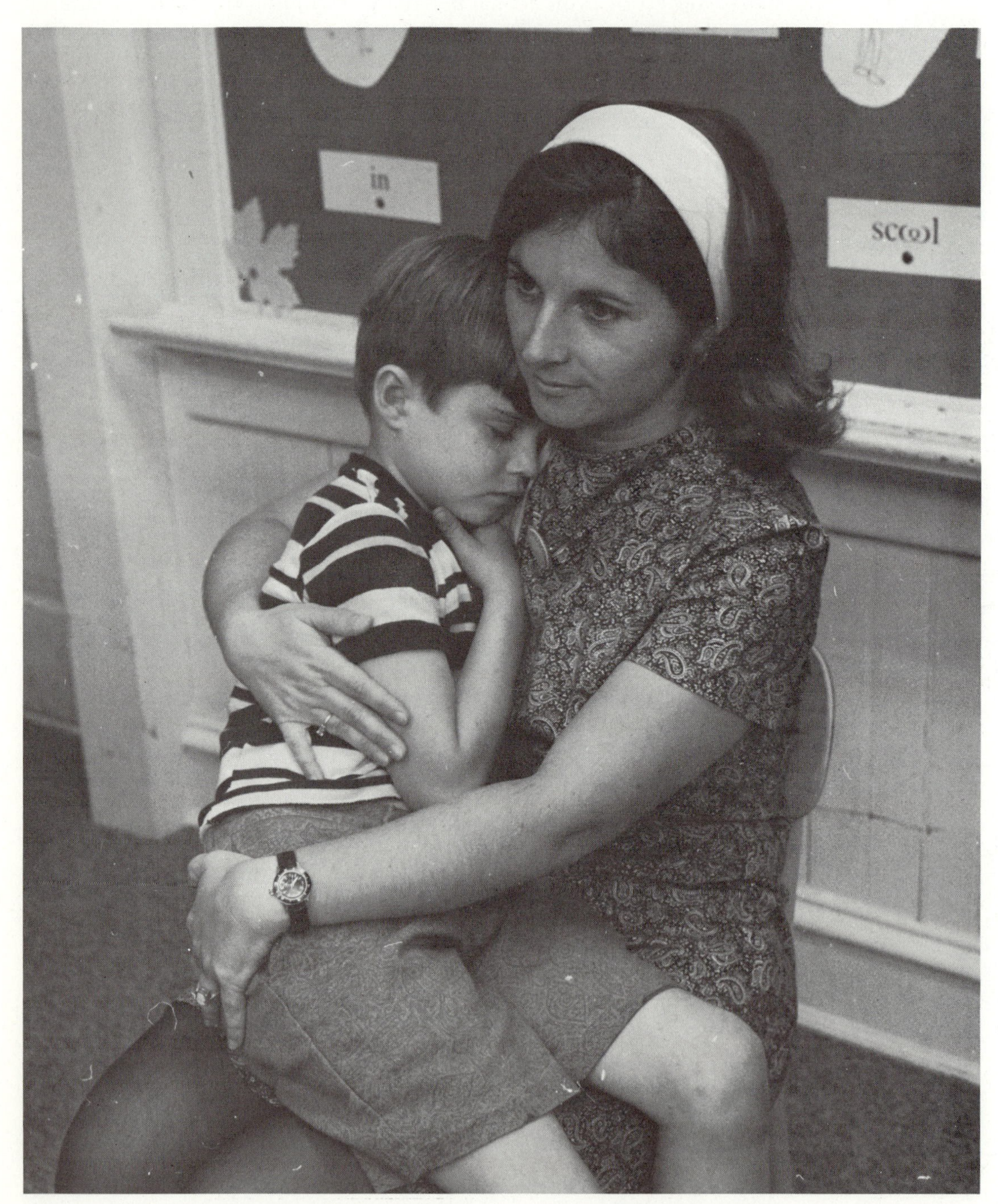

(Courtesy of The Woods Schools, Langhorne, Pennsylvania.)

In this chapter we will survey techniques that seem promising in helping disturbed or disturbing children. There are many techniques to choose from, but on which criteria should we base their adoption? Ideally, the selection of the most appropriate method of correction for a child's dysfunction should be empirical, or at least based on rationale and experiential grounds. Unfortunately, this ideal "match" has not, as yet, been achieved. Many of our selections of specific treatment procedures are based on informed biases, certain theoretical viewpoints, and information obtained through research. Although a technique should be chosen on the basis of a child's individual needs, there are other realistic factors that must be considered: (a) financial factors—cost of treatment per unit of time; (b) time—frequency of visits and length of treatment period; (c) feasibility—it would be useless to arrange a weekly meeting with a child whose family must travel 200 miles or more; (d) need—a child's needs may not necessarily coincide with those of his parents.

In this chapter we will emphasize the categorizing of rehabilitative techniques according to the nature and complexity of the behavioral problem. This continuum of techniques ranges from the most elementary level of the education process to the more complex levels of group processes. Remediational and rehabilitative techniques can be classified in five major groupings: (1) remedial-educational, (2) symptomatic-behavioral, (3) individual-holistic, (4) groups, and (5) institutions and schools.

Although there are medical means (e.g., *electroshock,* drugs) and paramedical therapies (e.g., occupational, physical, and recreational therapies) for changing behavior, these methods will not be considered here, since they are tangential to the aims of this chapter.

RECOMMENDATIONS FOR REMEDIATION AND REHABILITATION

After we have screened, identified, evaluated, and attempted to educate children with exceptionalities, what procedures should then be employed? What is the teacher to do with an unmanageable and uneducable child? The child may be referred to a pediatrician, or pharmacological treatment might be recommended if hyperactivity stemming from neurological causes is a problem. If parents need help in dealing with the situation, group discussions with other parents could be attempted. Rehabilitation must follow multiple, concurrent, or alternate routes based on a variety of procedures. The more research evidence that is available, the more appropriate will be the recommendations.

A multiple rehabilitation approach is suggested by the research of Abrams and Belmont (1965), who applied three different remedial approaches to the problem of severe reading disability. They divided children into four groups: those individuals who received reading instruction and psychotherapy; those who received reading instruction and group therapy; those who received individual psychotherapy but no reading instruction; and a fourth group who received no instruction but did attend group psychotherapy sessions. The treatment lasted two years, and the number of treatment sessions for the four groups was consistent. As one would expect, the combined approaches used for the first and second groups produced a greater improvement in reading than the single treatment approaches used for the third and fourth groups. The first group showed the greatest amount of improvement.

In addition to the more traditional remedial methods presently in use, innovative concepts and programs, based mostly on sensory stimulation, are appearing. Experimental results suggest the superiority of auditory or combined auditory-visual modalities over just visual modes of remediation. It is important, however, to determine which sensory input channels are assets to the child as they relate to output channels. The controversy concerning whether an asset or liability should be chosen could be resolved by advocating a gradual program of rehabilitation, by which the child feels that he is achieving mastery by experiencing success in major asset areas, with concomitant rewards for every improvement in a liability area. Some aspects of this principle have been advocated by Kirk (1962), Frostig, (1963), Frostig and her coworkers (1961), and Silver and Hagin (1965).

It is important for the teacher to distinguish which modality is of more importance in order to use the appropriate remedial methods. On the basis of this distinction, a teacher should be sufficiently flexible, so that initially phonetic methods may be used to train children with assets in the auditory-vocal area, while visual methods of training could be introduced later to children with liabilities in this area. Special remedial programs should match the child's specific disabilities.

Teachers should be cautious in the premature use of unvalidated methods of treatment that have become well known as a result of weekend supplements or popular magazines. If definite conclusions cannot be reached, the opinions of experienced psychologists should be considered.

There are many procedures that are promising as aids for various types of biological and intellectual deficits. In the following sections we will discuss the necessary skills for adequate functioning in our culture, the changing concepts with regard to development, some hypotheses about the effects of deprivation on dependency, and some common assumptions about preschool remediation.

THEORETICAL BACKGROUND

Necessary Skills

The following list describes skills which are necessary for functioning in society as a whole, as proposed by Rae-Grant et al. (1966):

1. Orientation toward the future and the ability to plan effectively.
2. Belief that one can sufficiently control one's own destiny, so that planning is worthwhile.
3. An ability to delay gratification in order to attain a future goal.
4. Perception of how one relates to the large social system of which one is a part.

5. An ability to formulate problems in a relatively abstract and generalizable form.

6. Flexibility to perceive alternative solutions to most important problems.

7. Acceptance of the fact that hard and often dull work is necessary and even perhaps desirable in attaining goals.

To what extent and by what means disadvantaged children can be helped to acquire these skills is difficult to say. Any program of treatment for the disadvantaged should probably focus on prevention of the situation and re-education of parents. The program should include an attempt to modify the communication, behavioral, and cognitive styles of these families before other changes occur.

Changing Concepts

Hunt (1961) presented some interesting theoretical concepts of remediation as well as some concrete suggestions for applications. He listed five areas of changing beliefs:

1. The belief in fixed intelligence: Tracing this idea from Galton through Terman, who believed that improving the lot of man lies not in *euthenics* but in *eugenics,* Hunt concluded that ". . . any law concerning the rate of intellectual growth must take into account the series of environmental encounters which constitute the conditions of that growth."

2. The belief in predetermined development: An individual's development is predetermined by his species and is nothing more than a function of maturation. Learning has little effect on development.

3. Brain function conceived as a static switchboard: Hunt stressed the importance of abandoning the "telephone model" (input-output without brain mediation) in favor of the computer model which includes: (a) memories and information which are stored in the brain; (b) logical operations that deal with the information in memories; and (c) hierarchical arrangements of these operations and memories in programs. Hunt suggested that "the function of early experience can be conceived as one of programming these intrinsic portions of the cerebrum so they can later function effectively in learning and problem solving."

4. Preverbal experience regarded as unimportant: Hunt stated that "the general notion that the emotional characteristics of persons are most influenced by early experience while the intellectual characteristics are not influenced is also quite wrong." Based upon his own experiments with rats, he concluded that ". . . it looks now as though early experience may be even more important for the perceptual, cognitive, and intellective functions than it is for the emotional and temperamental functions."

5. The belief that all behavior and all learning are motivated by powerful stimulation or homeostatic need: Hunt hypothesized that rather than a powerful intrinsic motivation that induces behavior, action is stimulated by an "incongruity" or discrepancy between what is expected on the basis of past experience and what is observed.

Citing the need for practical application of his theory, Hunt defined cultural deprivation as "a failure to provide an opportunity for infants and young children to have the experiences required for adequate development of those semi-autonomous central processes." He cautioned educators to take into account the "problem of the match," that is, providing a proper match with what the child already has learned and accomplished. Recommending the Montessori method because of its appeal to the child's intrinsic motivation, Hunt concluded, "It gives the individual child an opportunity to find the circumstances which match his own particular interests and stage of development. This carries with it the corollary advantage of making working fun."

If the prenatal environment can be improved through medicine and nutrition, the child will be born without the biological deficits which presently occur in many disadvantaged children. Environmental improvements would include concern for the prenatal condition of the child through care for the mother. Secondly, if the postnatal environment can be improved enough to afford greater emotional stability than is typical at present in the disadvantaged home, then the cultural deficit which is so frequently found will also be reduced. In addition, with improved biological inheritance and adequate cultural conditioning, the child should be able to grow psychologically through transactions resulting in positive feedback.

Hypotheses of Dependency

Palmer's summary (1969) includes a variety of hypotheses which are relevant to our discussion. They basically concern one of the results of deprivation, increased dependency at the preschool level.

Hypothesis 1: High dependency drive is a function of the frequency and intensity of previous auditory, visual, kinesthetic, and tactile contact with the mother. Hypothesis 2: The child with high dependency drive, upon initial separation from the mother, will manifest withdrawal, hyperexcitability, and anxiety responses. The duration of these will be a function of the extent to which behavioral patterns appropriate to the situation surrounding separation have been previously fixed. Hypothesis 3: The child with low dependency drive will not evidence the maladaptive responses of the highly dependent child upon initial separation from the mother, regardless of the level to which behavioral patterns appropriate to the situation have been fixed. Hypothesis 4: The child with high dependency drive and a low level of fixed behavioral patterns appropriate for preschool situations will persist in maladaptive responses to school situations and is a candidate for subsequent behavioral problems. Hypothesis 5: The child with low dependency drive and low fixed patterns of behavior appropriate for preschool situations will become a low achiever in subsequent schooling at the preschool and primary levels. Hypothesis 6: Behavioral change, which is associated with frustration resulting from the initial separation, will be influenced by: (a) the extent to which the mother-child relationship is altered by the conditions surrounding separation, (b) the remedial action taken by the mother or new caretaker to meet problems associated with the separation, and (c) the extent to which the new situation is related to already existing behavioral patterns and is reinforcing for their continued use and development. Hypothesis 7: The human infant has a drive for stimulation which increases with exposure to stimuli. Hypothesis 8: When a deficit from lack of stimulation occurs, it more frequently results from the lack of increasingly complex stimulation related to subsequent demands by the child's environment than from the withdrawal of stimulation per se. Hypothesis 9: The child requires and can develop responses to increasingly complex stimuli from the time of his birth onward. Hypothesis 10: The longer the child is without increasingly complex situations, the more severe the deficit in intellectual and emotional behavior will be. Hypothesis 11: The success of remedial treatment will be a function of: (a) the duration and intensity of deprivation, (b) the level of development at the time of deprivation, and (c) the extent to which treatment begins in the modality and at the level of complexity where deprivation occurred.

Common Assumptions

On the basis of his hypotheses, Palmer re-examined the four major assumptions concerning the present-day preschool movement in relation to deprived children:

1. "Early intervention is superior to later intervention." This assumption holds true, provided that the stimulation is specific for the modalities concerned and for the level of development when deprivation occurred.
2. "Any intervention is better than none." This assumption cannot be supported because of its lack of specificity. Intervention that is not carefully programmed to the needs of the child could be detrimental.
3. "A rich program for a limited period of time will ignite growth which until then was dormant." This assumption is still questionable because continued growth requires increasingly complex stimulation.
4. "Diverse compensatory stimulation is required when the child's environment has been limited." This assumption is also too vague and generic because stimulation must be specific for the deficit.

PREVENTIVE SPECIAL EDUCATION

Based on the foregoing theoretical premises, what are the current principal methods of preventive treatment for preschool disadvantaged children? Weikart (1967) classified preschool programs in three categories. The first includes those programs which employ nursery school methods. Under this first heading he included Strodtbeck's reading readiness program and Operation Head Start. The second category is comprised of those programs which provide structured nursery school environments. Under this heading, he placed Deutsch's Institute for Developmental Studies. The third category includes those with task-oriented environments, including Bereiter's program.

Cowles et al. (1970) found that the experience of kindergarten in and by itself may improve performance on the ITPA, especially in the areas of verbal expression, auditory memory, visual reception, visual association, manual expression, and visual closure. They concluded that "poor, rural children profited enormously from kindergarten when compared to counterparts who had not had a similar opportunity." These findings support those of Zigler and Butterfield (1968) on the positive influence of nursery school on IQ scores.

Nursery School Programs

Strodtbeck (1965) dealt with the issue of the hidden curriculum of the middle-class home. Based on the idea that middle-class children are subtly prepared from birth to enter middle-class schools, he geared his reading readiness program to compensate for the absence of this curriculum in the lower-class home. His program consisted mainly of giving more individual attention to each child, while maintaining the conventional nursery school approach. Students are allowed a fair amount of motoric and special freedom.

Operation Head Start has been a massive program, involving more than 500,000 children at its inception in 1965. The atmosphere is like that of a conventional nursery school. The main differences between Head Start classes and conventional nurseries are in two areas. The Head Start program operates as a child development center (Miller, 1967) in which the goal is involvement of the parents in the education of the children. The services of professionals and nonprofessionals are united at the center of activity, the classroom. Parents are to attend meetings and consult with professionals. Pseudoretardation, resulting from medical and dental problems, is treated. The second major difference involves the size of the classes: the pupil-teacher ratio in the Head Start classes is supposedly significantly lower than in most nursery schools.

Thus, the program largely focuses on the preschool child, aiming at enrichment of the child's environment in the early stages of development. These programs generally offer enrichment in language development, perceptual development, cognitive skills, self-image, and nutritional improvement. Quite often there is additional contact between the workers and the parents to encourage continuation of the stimulation and development of the child at home. The problem is that many dedicated people are attempting to rectify the situation by implementing these programs but have not maintained adequate controls for reportable evaluation. It is necessary not only to put programs into action, but also to find out what is effective and efficient in achieving the desired goals. The only way to achieve this goal is to use controls and to report on the comparative results achieved by these many programs.

Structured Environments

The prevalence of preventive programs results largely from the development of the theory of cumulative deficit by Deutsch et al. (1967). According to these researchers the discontinuity between the lower-class home and the expectations of a middle-class–oriented educational system causes the lower-class child to experience early failure in school. To Deutsch, this sense of failure acts as a negative reinforcement, causing the disadvantaged child to dislike school and to lose interest in it completely. This theory, on which so much of the work with disadvantaged children of preschool age is based, stems from these assumptions: (1) the environment plays a crucial role in the development of the child; (2) it is through the child's experience that much development is stimulated; and (3) appropriate stimuli are necessary for the development of certain functions.

Deutsch's Institute for Developmental Studies represents a structured type of environment. Based on Deutsch's concept of the effect of input on output, the Institute concentrates on many areas to encourage language development. Children are frequently asked questions to which they gradually learn to respond. The Institute stresses four areas: language and conceptual abilities, reading, self-concept, and social interaction. The children are called upon to weigh, estimate, measure, and learn discriminations and comparisons, such as long-short and big-small. They are encouraged to discover concepts such as texture, weight, and color. They sort objects to build concepts of discrimination gradually. To develop each child's self-concept, the students' names are placed prominently in the classroom beside their pictures. The classroom itself is structured, as is the curriculum. Objects are arranged by areas.

Deutsch et al. (1967) stated that the orientation of the lower-class child is in the present rather than in the future. Consequently, these children have difficulty in conceptualizing future time. In the classroom emphasis is placed on developing a concept of future time through the use of calendars.

A great variety of materials are utilized to speed the learning process. These include the Bell and Howell Language Master, a tape recorder built to play back and to record from a strip of tape to which is fastened a special card on which words, sentences, and pictures can be attached. The tape has two tracks—one prerecorded by the teacher, and one used to record and play back student responses. The controls are designed so that a four-year-old child can operate them.

Another aid frequently utilized is the record player. Children are encouraged to move rhythmically and to respond to music. Special listening centers are available, so that the child can listen to records without disturbing the rest of the class. Some teachers use the listening center in conjunction with filmstrips.

Each classroom has a library corner where children are encouraged to familiarize themselves with books. To aid in exercises of perceptual discrimination, a variety of devices are employed which may utilize such items as blocks of varying colors to teach size and color discrimination. The study of Silver et al. (1967) substantiated the idea that this type of perceptual training can improve reading ability. The Institute also uses a letter formboard as an aid in reading development. The board is a device for matching letters with forms which teaches discrimination and is used at the kindergarten level (Powledge, 1967).

Task-Oriented Environments

Bereiter's program is classified by Weikart (1967) as task-oriented. Children meet for only two hours a day and are mobilized in 20-minute sessions of intensive instruction, with separate teachers for each subject. Language is approached almost like a foreign language, and the emphasis is on drill. The reading program stresses phonics. Bereiter likens his programs to an athletic drill (Miller, 1967) in which there is a great deal of praise for trying hard, improving, and thinking.

Autotelic Responsive Environments

Meier et al. (Hellmuth, 1968a) suggested a "New Nursery School" for deprived children, located within walking distance of all the children who attend the school. It is called "new" because it is not similar to other nurseries. The inventors of the program admitted that the basic principles of the school activities are, in some ways, based on Maria Montessori's ideas. In the first New Nursery School established, most of the children were Spanish or Indian. Rooms were L-shaped with an art area, a block corner, a reading corner, a listening area, and a manipulative toy area. There were cubicles for each child's coat.

One of the basic underlying principles of this school is that "education must begin before the child enters the first grade." As Deutsch et al.

(1967) reported, failure generally begins in the first grade and increases year by year (cumulative deficit). Minority and deprived pupils' scores are as much as one standard deviation below the majority pupils' scores in the first grade. At the twelfth grade level, results of tests in the same verbal and nonverbal skills show that, in every case, the minority groups' scores are further below the majority than in the first grade. Schools do not provide opportunities for most minority groups to overcome their initial deficiency; in fact, the children fall further behind.

The New Nursery School offers practical ways of solving the problems that Deutsch (1967) found as a result of research with disadvantaged children. The objectives of this program are: (1) to develop a positive self-image, (2) to increase sensory perceptual acuity, (3) to improve language skills, and (4) to improve problem-solving and concept formation abilities.

The general principles followed in the New Nursery School are:

1. Experiencing some success in this school and noncompetitive activities help the child to gain a positive self-image.

2. Early cognitive training is important, especially for environmentally deprived children.

3. Maturation is essential in learning. Pushing the child beyond his abilities causes frustration and, possibly, dislike of school in the future. This is not a problem in the New Nursery School because the child works in a self-pacing environment.

4. In conversation, the teachers do not correct the child's wrong sentences but repeat them in the correct way without any comment.

By closely observing the children in this school as they work, one may discover what a child can do and will learn or what a child cannot do and will not learn. Such information can be a valuable source of research on early childhood curriculum planning. The materials in the New Nursery School help children in the following areas of learning: (1) search and match; (2) word construction; (3) reading and writing; (4) concept formation and problem solving: (a) the concepts of "same" and "not the same" and (b) the concepts of relative size, such as longer, longest, shorter, shortest; (5) shape and patterns; and (6) colors and shades of the same color.

The New Nursery School is an example of what Moore (1964) called "autotelic responsive environments." He listed five important characteristics of responsive environments:

1. They permit the child to explore freely.

2. The child is immediately informed of the consequences of his actions.

3. The environment is self-pacing; that is, the child is allowed to work at a rate determined by himself.

4. The child is likely to make a series of interconnected discoveries about the physical, cultural, or social world.

In the responsive environment, there is no formal step-by-step teaching. The child's activities are controlled by the choices of educators regarding what to include or exclude from the classroom. No task is forced on the child by adults. There are group activities, but the child is not required to take part unless he wants to; after two or three weeks, however, almost all the children join the group activities. The teacher is part of the responsive environment. As the child spontaneously manipulates his surroundings, the teacher responds not by teaching but by assisting the child's learning. The teacher waits till the child initiates conversation or starts any other activity. In all activities, the teacher waits until the child finds the right way of performing tasks, solving problems, and discovering relations.

SPECIAL EDUCATION PROGRAMS

Our educational objective for the deprived child should not be to demand immediate increased output of which he is incapable, but rather to concentrate on raising the level of aural-visual stimulation, which, in turn, will tend to waken the "sleeping" input ability and make increased output feasible for the first time for most deprived children.

It has been pointed out by Riessman (1962), however, that lower-class children possess several positive aspects that are usually ignored, such as slowness and hidden verbal ability. Slowness is not necessarily a detriment to learning, and in fact, may serve to reduce careless, hurried errors. Emphasis on speed is clearly of little value in teaching these children and should be avoided. Riessman ended his review of the literature on disadvantaged groups optimistically. Emphasizing the distinction between slow and dull, he asserted that "a pupil may be slow because he is extremely careful, meticulous, or cautious. He may be slow because he refuses to generalize easily." Riessman was concerned that schools traditionally impart skills, techniques, and knowledge rather than training the disadvantaged to acquire useful problem-solving skills. He listed several reasons why the positive aspects of disadvantaged children should be emphasized. Such action will: (1) encourage the school to develop approaches and techniques appropriate for the cognitive style of deprived children; (2) enable children of low income background to be educated without middle-classifying them; (3) stimulate teachers to aim high and to expect more from these children; (4) discourage the current tendency of overemphasizing both vocational and nonacademic education for children of low income background; (5) provide an exciting challenge for teachers if they realize that they need not simply aim to "bring these children up to grade level," but rather can actually develop new kinds of creativity; and (6) lead to real appreciation of slowness, one-track learning, and physical learning as potential strengths which require careful nurturing.

In addition to the more traditional forms of classroom teaching and the establishment of special classes and courses for emotionally handicapped and retarded children, substantial technological advances in the application of audiovisual aids to the rehabilitation of deviant behavior have occurred in the last few years. Among these advances the most notable ones have been: (a) recordings and television, (b) programmed instruction and teaching machines, and (c) tutorial-remedial approaches to special sensory and physical handicaps.

Audiovisual Aids

It is difficult to distinguish between hardware (tape recorders, projectors, films, video tape, television) and software (books, programs, manuals, paper and pencil materials) aids. However, the following discussion points out this difference with respect to the need to motivate disturbed or disturbing children. Such motivation may result from an appropriate matching of techniques with the specific needs of the child.

Television, of course, will be a powerful tool not only in formal teaching but also in remediation (Moore et al., 1965).

Programmed Instruction. According to Skinner (1953), the present school method of learning by aversive control produces such problems as truancy, vandalism, early dropouts, apathy, and inattention. He stated that, contrary to popular opinion, the trial and error method does not always strengthen learning. With the use of teaching machines, however, "the student remains active, proceeds at his own rate, follows a coherent sequence, and is immediately reinforced." He stressed the "active" part of this approach, stating that "to acquire behavior a student must engage in behavior." Skinner believed that teaching machines "generate sensitivity to the environment—discrimination" and that thinking is a form of "self-management" by reacting to the environment in different ways.

Programmed learning can be presented in one of two forms:

1. Linear programming presents lessons in small steps, provides immediate reward or reinforcement, and requires overt responses. The steps are a sequence of discriminative stimuli that insure the probability of answering the next question correctly. This type of programming fosters the ability to compare and to choose.

2. Adaptive programming is found only in machines. The machine changes the kind of question to match the error rate of the student. The level of difficulty of the questions is raised if the student is making too few errors, and vice versa, assuming that a certain number of errors is necessary to learning. One of the most direct applications of this method is computer-assisted instruction.

Teaching machines come in many forms, from programmed books to language labs, reading pacers, and listening and viewing devices. The advent of the computer has also produced a variety of machines. One, in particular, named "Mentor," is capable of receiving not only written responses, but also multiple-choice answers or audio responses by microphone.

Most studies support the value and efficacy of teaching machines. The concept of immediate feedback and reinforcement seems especially applicable to the field of teaching. Filep (1963) contended, however, that these studies provide little conclusive information. He felt that human learning may be intrinsically reinforcing.

Breakthroughs in the application of programmed instruction (software programs) to interpersonal relations (Brown and L'Abate, 1969) suggest the usefulness of this approach beyond its immediately educative limits. In using programmed instruction and teaching machines, one should consider certain advantages: First, these machines may relieve the interpersonal anxieties and resistance which are present in responding to a teacher. Secondly, programmed instruction employs a step-by-step approach which is adaptable to the individual needs of each child. Some children, however, benefit by this type of learning more than others. The question is, Which children will indeed learn by programmed instruction and which will not? For instance, it could be that a withdrawn child may need an interested adult to help him learn within a context of programmed therapeutic efforts. Thus, a withdrawn child faced with a teaching machine may increase his withdrawal from interpersonal contact. On the other hand, certain children whose major problem is acting-out against society may indeed receive much greater control from teaching machines, since the interpersonal threat of authority figures is decreased. A danger in the use of these machines in treating disturbed children might be mismatching—the wrong pupil may be matched with the wrong machine or program. Again, this mismatching should not occur once we recognize under which conditions learning may best occur. Again, this is a problem of individual evaluation.

We must add that criteria for selection and matching are lacking, even in this area. As McKee's work (Brown and L'Abate, 1969) suggested, these techniques may work best in institutions and perhaps with children who have characterological difficulties that make them overreact to personal or prolonged interaction with authority figures. This type of individual (e.g., juvenile delinquents, drug addicts) may be best habilitated when help, even through a machine, is offered to him by those whom he sees as equals.

Brown and L'Abate (1969) reviewed the role of programmed instruction in rehabilitation and concluded that it provides: (1) a source of factual knowledge about the learning process, (2) an adjunct to behavior modification and to psychological rehabilitation, and (3) a unique source of positive reinforcements which frees the subject from fear of punishment which is usually found in interpersonal situations. Recent applications of programmed instruction to the modification of deviant behavior range from its use with defective, brain-damaged, autistic, exceptional, and handicapped children to its application to adult psychopaths, criminals, and normal individuals. Of course, its role in rehabilitation is still ambiguous. Much research must still be conducted regarding the motivational process and the specific application of programs, usually created for the majority of "normals," to the rehabilitation of deviates.

As Morrill (1961), in his review of programmed instruction and teaching machines, noted:

> **The use of automated teaching devices may be optimized, perhaps, if there is a proper balance between this technique and other compatible teaching methods. What percentage of a course should be machine taught? What subject matter is best suited to automated devices?**

The answers to these questions are still unknown. Determining the role of each teaching method, *in conjunction with other methods,* will be a "wide-open" area for future research.

Tutorial Remediation

Among the tutorial approaches, we will distinguish between those involving the direct confrontation of pupil and tutor and those involving the use of hardware. The latter approach seems to be the most promising development, since only through technological advances will we be able to reach the many children in need of help. In this case a one-to-one (tutor to student) approach is seldom practical except, perhaps, in the case of older pupils helping younger ones.

Remedial therapies have focused on different modalities of input (auditory and visual) or output (kinesthetic, verbal, and manual), and the rash of new programs has made their specific selection difficult even for the expert. As in programmed instruction, application has exceeded evaluation, and chaos and confusion have resulted. Remedial training will require specialists trained in specific programs involving such areas as directional orientation, visual memory, auditory discrimination and phonic recognitions, and sound blending, as well as extra-remedial applications of behavior modification and group techniques. The area of learning disabilities in children will be the testing ground for the application of new techniques, because in this area the needs are the greatest. Unfortunately, as in psychotherapy, research will lag behind application, and the ever-present schism between service and research will retard progress. This separation, however, may be prevented if evaluation closely follows remediation. Unless this unification occurs, progress will be hindered. Progress may be inevitable, but the cost and effort expended on inadequate or even faulty and insufficiently evaluated programs will be great.

The tutorial methods illustrated by Levi (1965) stress the importance of dealing with the specific problem at hand and the necessity of combining various approaches. Her conclusion supports emphasis on evaluation and detailed diagnostic study of the individual, so that appropriate treatment can be provided.

Perhaps one of the best studies comparing different approaches is that of Romano (1957) with juvenile delinquents. He compared a remedial reading group geared to the specific correction of the disability, an interview therapy group geared to the improvement of mental health through interaction among all the members, including the therapist, and a tutorial therapy group geared to the simultaneous correction of reading disabilities and the improvement of mental health through the integration of remedial reading and group therapy techniques. He found that the third group affected a greater improvement in psychosocial adjustment than either of the other groups. He concluded that either method, remedial reading or psychotherapy, may be necessary but that in and by themselves they are insufficient. Special educators may well profit by learning group therapy techniques; likewise, group therapists may need training in remedial teaching. This study also illustrated the point that no one method of treatment can claim complete therapeutic effectiveness. Behavior is too complex and multidetermined to be changed by just one method. Even when only one method (e.g., psychotherapy) is used over a prolonged period, time is the adjuvant.

BEHAVIOR MODIFICATION IN CLASSROOM MANAGEMENT

One of the most popular and current methods being used in the public school classroom belongs to the area loosely defined as behavior modification. Behavior modification is popular because it is effective in controlling certain types of behavior.

We will first point out some of the historical bases of behavior modification prior to a discussion of specific techniques involved in behavior modification as a whole. The current development stems from the work of B. F. Skinner and his associates, though its historical origins date earlier. In 1953 these gentlemen were under contract with the Office of Naval Research and were requested to conduct a study to ascertain the effectiveness of operant conditioning with regard to working with extremely disturbed patients (Skinner, 1953). Wolpe (1969) defined behavior therapy as "the use of experimentally established principles of learning for the purpose of changing unadaptive behavior." The objectives and purposes of behavior therapy or modification are as follows:

1. Behavior therapy is based on properly formulated premises leading to deductions.

2. Behavior therapy is derived from experimental studies specifically designed to test basic theories and the deductions resulting from them.

3. It considers symptoms as unadaptive conditioned responses.

4. It regards symptoms as evidence of faulty learning.

5. It considers symptomatology to be determined by individual differences in conditionalability and autonomic reactivity as well as by accidental and environmental circumstances.

6. All treatment of neurotic disorders is concerned with the symptoms existing at present. The historical development is largely irrelevant.

7. Cures are achieved by treating the symptoms themselves; that is, by extinguishing unadaptive conditioned responses (CR's) and establishing desirable CR's.

8. Interpretation, even if not completely subjective and erroneous, is irrelevant.

9. Symptomatic treatment leads to permanent recovery, provided that autonomic as well as skeletal CR's are extinguished.

10. Personal relations are not essential in curing neurotic disorder, although they may be useful in certain circumstances.

The direct application of behavior modification procedures to the public school classroom has been described by Frank Hewett et al. (1969):

1. Select a terminal goal and ideas, such as reducing "out-of-seat" behavior or improving self-care or academic skills.

2. Prepare a series of tasks involving reasonable increments which lead up to such a goal.

3. Through careful selection and presentation of stimuli and consequences, modify the child's behavior, so that the resulting behavior will fulfill the goal.

Behavior therapy operates on the basic assumption that all behavioral problems are the result of simple maladaptive habits and that if we change the behavior the problems will be eliminated. Behavior therapy or behavior modification has been used successfully with a wide variety of behavioral disorders. In order to provide more insight into the nature of behavior modification, it may be advisable to explore the behavior modification system of treatment as compared with other approaches.

London (1964) proposed that all psychotherapy can be divided into two categories: insights and actions. London maintained that this division denotes the role of observable behavior in relationship to the goals of counseling and psychotherapy. Insight theories apply to those treatment approaches in which the primary focus is on providing help for the individual, or rather on providing assistance so that he may help himself. These theories emphasize the concept of the individual's gaining insight into his own behavior and an understanding of the psychological bases and unconscious motivations which are involved and stress helping the individual to accept his behavior. Insight therapists contend that if change in behavior is to result, gaining insight or self-understanding must be the primary goal. Insight therapies include Carl Rogers' client-centered approach, Freud's psychoanalytic theory, and Alfred Adler's concepts. London (1964) felt that these systems do not differ essentially and pointed out that each utilizes verbal communication as the major component of therapeutic treatment and that the success or failure of the treatment in all the preceding systems depends on the client. In other words, the techniques and procedures utilized by insight therapists are very similar.

The behavior modifiers, or action therapists or behaviorists as they are sometimes known, feel that behavior is essentially a reflection of prior learning and that it does not necessarily relate to underlying motivations. They feel that neurotic behavior or emotional problems are the result of inadequate or inappropriate learning. Behavior modifiers are likely to view psychological disorders as being only casually related to behavioral problems and usually regard insight as only an incidental factor in the therapeutic situation. The action therapist tends to treat behavior problems by manipulating learning opportunities. One of the major differences between insight and action therapists concerns the use of symptomatology. Both agree on the definition of symptoms, but they disagree on the importance of the relationship between symptoms and treatment. Action therapists are generally consistently indifferent to the etiology of symptoms and primarily devote their efforts to eliminating or at least reducing the amount of discomfort resulting from the symptoms. Certain criteria for assessing the clinical status or usefulness of their method should be related directly to the welfare of the client. Secondarily, additional criteria should be concerned with the amount of effort required by the therapist or the cost of the treatment to the client (London, 1964).

Symptomatic improvement (i.e., the relief of symptoms in relationship to the client) is the sole concern of the behavior modifier (Wolpé, 1969). The insight therapist is not primarily concerned with the elimination or severe modification of symptoms but is primarily concerned with whether or not the client understands why he behaves the way he does and with helping him to accept his behavior. Also, they are not concerned with economy or the amount of time involved in the treatment procedures. Psychotherapy has been discussed in terms of insight and action theories in order to promote an understanding of the treatment procedures for behaviorally disordered individuals. Whenever the term client or patient is used, educators should realize that we could equally well substitute the term student. Regardless of which approach is utilized, an effort must be made to substantiate its values.

Much criticism has been leveled against the insight approach. Perhaps the most devastating statement concerning its value is that of Eysenck (1965): "Children suffering from emotional disorders and treated by psychotherapy recover and improve to approximately the same extent as children not receiving psychotherapy." He added, "Neurotic patients treated by means of psychotherapeutic procedures based on learning improve significantly more quickly than do patients treated by means of psychoanalytic or eclectic psychotherapy or not treated by psychotherapy at all."

To understand behavior modification properly, it is essential that some of the more common terms utilized in the field be clearly defined. *Positive reinforcement* refers to any kind of reinforcement that increases behavior. It may be called reward reinforcement; that is, when a student behaves in a certain manner he is rewarded by verbal or by concrete methods for his behavior. The opposite of positive reinforcement is *negative reinforcement,* which has been called aversive conditioning or aversive reinforcement. Negative reinforcement decreases behavior. Both are reinforcing; that is, both are designed to control a certain behavior. The entire reinforcement concept centers on the idea that whenever a certain behavior occurs, the conditioner or person wishing to change behavior institutes either positive or negative reinforcement to regulate the emitted behavior. Therefore, if there is no emitted behavior, there can be no reinforcement and no conditioning. A common term for this method of reinforcement is operant conditioning.

To understand thoroughly positive and negative reinforcement, it is necessary to introduce other related terms which involve schedules of reinforcement. *Continuous reinforcement* is that type of reinforcement which is rewarded every time that a given behavior is emitted. In other words, there is a 1:1 relationship between behavior and reinforcement. From a practical standpoint, however, an intermittent schedule of reinforcement is usually used. Partial or *intermittent reinforcement* means reinforcing a given response only some portion of the times that it occurs. It is probable that intermittent reinforcement, once established, tends to be more effective and more consistent than continuous reinforcement. A teacher should remember that initially, when attempting to control a given form of behavior, continuous reinforcement may be essential. The intermittent schedule, however, is probably more effective for maintaining behavior over a long period of time. *Selective reinforcement* refers to the selection of appropriate kinds of emitted behavior and to the reinforcement of only those particular types of behavior. Reinforcement cannot be applied to one's total behavior but must be applied to given specifics. Thus, all reinforcement that is effective will be selective in nature. The process of selection is very complex and involves the wishes of those instituting the procedures.

An extremely important concept in the area of reinforcement is that of *successive approximation.* Successive approximation refers to the idea that in order to assist an individual in changing his behavior it is frequently essential that rewards be instituted for minor "movements" in the direction of the desired goal. For example, it is frequently too great a distance to go from point A to point X in one jump. Therefore, it may be essential to go from point A to point A_1, point A_2, and point A_3, step by step toward the desired point or desired form of behavior. The assumption underlying this approach is that success is essential on the part of the student if he is to reach the ultimate desired behavior. Therefore, it is wise for the teacher to select a small behavioral change and to reward the student when the change is accomplished. Preceding this, of course, the teacher should make a careful analysis of the kinds of behavior which he will consider as being successive approximations or steps toward the desired goal. The basic rule when employing positive reinforcement can be simply stated: Those behaviors which the teacher desires the student to engage in should be attended to; that is, the teacher should reward these behaviors in some way. On the other hand, those behaviors that are considered to be undesirable should be ignored. We hasten to add that these behaviors must be within the realm of reason, since it is understood that all behavior cannot be tolerated in a public classroom. It should be remembered, however, that the more exceptions that are made, the more difficult it is to institute behavior modification in an effective manner.

In general, two types of rewards or positive reinforcement may be utilized. One might be called an object reward, and the other is social recognition. The object reward perhaps is more familiar to teachers in that it has been given a considerable amount of attention in the press as the M & M approach to behavior modification. However, teachers should be aware that social reinforcement is equally rewarding and perhaps has always been engaged in by teachers. Problems in effectiveness may be due to the fact that most social recognition as used by teachers has not been employed on a systematic basis toward desired goals of behavior but rather on a random or even on an emotional basis.

The teacher should decide ahead of time which reinforcement schedule to use. If the reinforcement is to be continuous, that is, if the student is to be rewarded for every behavior, much difficulty may ensue with regard to keeping track of the types of behavior that are to be rewarded. The schedule which is adopted should be decided upon prior to the institution of behavior modification for a given student. In addition, the reward, whether it is social or tangible, should be provided specifically for the particular desired behavior. There is the danger of rewarding undesired behavior rather than desired behavior. Therefore, the teacher should be extremely observant in order to reward immediately those actions which he is trying to elicit from his students. The basic concept in the institution of behavior modification is consistency. The teacher must be able to perform in a consistent manner if behavior modification is to be successful.

Wolpe (1958) introduced the term reciprocal inhibition, which is of interest to the classroom teacher. Frequently, the teacher will observe undesirable behavior in a child. A child may avoid participating on the playground or may exhibit undue fear of certain objects, or he may experience school phobia, fear or dislike of school. Reciprocal inhibition has been used in treating these kinds of problems. With assertive responses (i.e., anxiety inhibition responses), the teacher might encourage acting-out behavior on the part of the child. Every teacher is familiar with the child who is too shy, too reserved, too retiring, and too unassertive. Such a child might be well suited for the reciprocal inhibition approach. The teacher might start by asking the child to imagine a situation and then gradually to institute closer and closer approximations to the actuality of participating in a "rough and tumble" situation on the playground. The general procedures of reciprocal inhibition involve setting up a hierarchy of situations. It is necessary, at times, to establish behaviors that are considerably removed from the desired behavior. For example, the teacher might provide the unassertive child with an opportunity to talk about what it would be like if he were assertive, and then gradually the child might be able to attempt this behavior. The child may talk about it in the classroom and then may move out to the playground but still continue just to sit on the side lines and talk about the behavior. Next, the child might be asked to interact with one other child. Each situation in the hierarchy will be carefully sponsored by the teacher. The basic procedure has been called desensitization, and frequently relaxation is used as a component part of the reciprocal inhibition treatment, since it has been asserted that relaxation reduces the amount of anxiety induced by given forms of behavior.

An important form of behavior modification is verbal conditioning. Teachers have always engaged in verbal reinforcement without realizing that this is a form of conditioning. Verbal conditioning may be used in any setting, and it has been shown to be a very effective technique in modifying behavior. The basis of verbal conditioning is what was previously referred to as social reinforcement. Social or verbal reinforcement from a person that the student esteems tends to cause behavior to improve. It should be remembered that verbal reinforcement, as with all reinforcement, should be employed systematically and must be directed toward highly specific types of behavior.

Many experiments have been performed to test the effectiveness of verbal conditioning. Greenspoon (1951; 1955) conducted studies that confirmed the belief that stimuli can be used to reinforce classes of verbal responses.

The second major method of conditioning in behavior modification is the use of aversive control, which has two main categories: negative reinforcement and punishment. According to Hilgard and Bower (1966), negative reinforcement increases a behavior by *removing* something undesirable or by the threat of something aversive. For example, a child learns to avoid touching a hot stove, so that his avoidance behavior is increased. Punishment may have the same effect as negative reinforcement but is defined differently by Skinner: it is the *addition* of a negative stimulus or the removal of something positive. For our purposes, the definition is more applicable to an experimental situation than to a classroom environment, and we may consider punishment simply as a means of aversive control. The use of aversive stimuli such as drugs, electric shock, noise, fatigue, or any other kind of stimuli which induces discomfort or pain may be effective under some circumstances. Aversive stimuli should always be applied in direct conjunction with unacceptable behavior; it is essential that the two be closely associated. If the aversive conditioning is maintained for a long enough period, it is likely that the undesirable behavior will be extinguished. Aversive stimuli, in serious applications, are generally administered under controlled conditions and for more difficult problems. For example, emetics have been utilized in the treatment of alcoholics. The person is required to take an emetic drug in conjunction with the intake of alcohol, which produces an unpleasant reaction which results in vomiting.

There are drawbacks to the aversive approach. It is, of course, not a pleasant experience for the client or for the therapist who administers the aversive stimuli. There are philosophical and moralistic reasons which preclude the extensive use of aversive stimuli. With regard to its use within the classroom, the teacher should realize that the use of aversive forms of stimuli is likely to produce unpredictable results and that this mode of conditioning students should be engaged in only after positive approaches have failed.

The second use of aversive stimuli (i.e., the withholding or withdrawal of positive reinforcement) is considered to be a reasonable application for the control of behavior. This method may be equally effective with the more diverse practices. In the typical public school classroom, it is not unrealistic to use a combined technique, that is, to combine positive and negative reinforcement to obtain appropriate behavior from students who are behaving in an unacceptable manner. There are, of course, certain practices in the application of negative and positive reinforcement that must be followed closely and systematically. The goals and methods to be utilized in obtaining desirable behavior should be thought out clearly by the teacher. Essentially, behavior modification may be effective by using a variety of techniques which do not contradict one another. In fact, some evidence indicates that the combination of positive and negative reinforcement may be the most effective of all means for modifying children's behavior in a public setting (Woody, 1969).

As a general rule for teachers and one which we highly advocate, accentuate the positive. Reward students when they do something right, and associate it as closely with the behavior as possible. Do not pay attention to the negative unless it becomes necessary to do so. It might be noted that by paying attention to the negative you may, in fact, be reinforcing it. Even in dealing with the troublemaker, the teacher can usually find something to reinforce positively, and if this good behavior increases, the undesirable behavior will probably decrease.

The following list includes the basic principles and concepts that teachers should keep in mind when employing behavior modification:

1. Behavior modification is based on the idea that all behavior is caused or learned, not inherited.

2. Since behavior is learned, it may be unlearned, or other learning may be substituted for it.

3. Learning takes place whenever there are conditions which are responsive to the stimuli being received. Such learning tends to occur repeatedly when it is combined with desirable circumstances or, technically, when it is stimulated by the presence of a reinforcement.

4. The basic principle of behavior modification can be summed up as follows: we pay attention to those behaviors which we want a person to engage in, and we ignore or apply aversive stimuli to those behaviors which we do not want a person to engage in.

5. An essential part of the behavior modification program is determining which rewards should be utilized. The teacher should know the student well enough to have some idea of what kind of rewards the student prefers. It is hoped that teacher and student can proceed from tangible rewards to social reinforcement procedures in a relatively short period of time.

6. Simple attention is a reinforcing phenomenon. Teachers should remember that any behavior which is noticed is reinforced, and conversely, failing to pay attention to behavior tends to cause that behavior to decrease or to become extinguished. It is easy for the teacher to confirm a student's belief that the best way to gain attention is by misbehaving. Teachers must simply remember which students tend to get the most attention in each classroom.

7. The teacher must be aware of the need for appropriate timing in reinforcement. In order for reinforcement to be effective, it should be related as closely to the occurrence of the behavior as possible. Since any intervening behavior may be unintentionally reinforced, the desired behavior should be followed by reinforcement. This is evident by the fact that while correct performance of problems or exercises assigned by the teacher should be reinforced, reinforcement of an intervening failure to perform may be counterindicative and may cause maladaptive behavior.

8. In order for teachers to make the transition from tangible rewards to social reinforcement rewards, the behavior modification program from the start should involve a procedure called pairing; that is, at the time that a tangible reward is given, the teacher should provide a verbal reward, such as, "Very good Johnny." Pairing the tangible reward with the nontangible will make it possible for the nontangible reward system to be instituted.

9. Scheduling rewards is an important part of behavior modification. We previously discussed two basic kinds of scheduling, continuous and partial. Generally, it is most effective to start with a continuous reinforcement schedule (i.e., each occurrence of the desired behavior is attended to). On the other hand, partial scheduling is a more effective method of promoting persistent behavioral patterns. Thus, after the basic pattern has been fairly well established, the teacher should use a partial reinforcement schedule (e.g., reinforcing every third response or

every fifth response), while always observing the student and his reaction to the scheduling procedures. When a teacher shifts from a continuous schedule to a partial schedule, it is reasonably safe to decrease the reinforcement schedule by one-fifth. Again, each student's behavior should indicate to the teacher whether or not the decrease in the reward schedule is too great and whether an adjustment should be made in accordance with the observed behavior.

10. In behavior modification, the process of shaping is often employed. Shaping is a method by which a person systematically learns a complex response by successively acquiring and extinguishing prerequisite responses which become increasingly comparable to the goal response (Browning and Stover, 1971).

11. When using behavior modification, the teacher should institute careful observational procedures. The teacher must understand what kinds of behavior are occurring and with what frequency they are occurring.

12. In establishing a behavior modification program, the teacher should define or outline the particular behavior that is to be modified.

13. After the behavior modification program has been instituted, the teacher should conduct "before and after" observations. Behavior prior to the institution of behavior modification procedures is compared with behavior following the procedures, and the frequency of emission of undesired or desired behavior is noted.

14. It is essential that the teacher record all behavior in an objective fashion in order to illustrate or document clearly the progress of the child. The application of behavior modification techniques to the public school classroom has been well outlined in an article by Long and Newman (1971), who indicated that there are four alternative methods of coping with behavior: (a) permit behavior, (b) tolerate behavior, (c) interfere with behavior, and (d) formulate a preventive plan.

Critique

Behavior modification and its various subtypes (Franks, 1969) has presently reached the stage of success that seems to characterize a great many aspects of American culture. This success was long in the making and certainly overdue, especially in a society where physical punishment and blame on a verbal level reach destructive proportions. The emphasis on rewards and on positive rather than aversive methods is not only overdue but welcome. It is time that we offer children more than a kick and a shove in an irresponsible fashion. The behavior modification movement seems to have brought relief from the irrational and impulsive use and abuse of aversive disciplinary methods that have characterized some child-rearing practices in the United States. The success of this movement and its clearly beneficial effects should not blind us, however, to some of its shortcomings as far as the practice of applied child psychology and special education are concerned.

The lack of specificity in behavior management (L'Abate, 1969d) is due, in part, to individual differences in reactions to different reinforcements. What is reinforcing for one child may not be reinforcing for another. Understanding the interaction between individual characteristics and reinforcements requires a knowledge of both aspects (i.e., the child and the reinforcement) of this complex relationship. An upper-class or middle-class child may be completely unmoved by candy, which he has previously always received, but may well be motivated by verbal reinforcement, which may be completely irrelevant to a deprived lower-class child (Wright and L'Abate, research in progress). Emphasis on the behavior to be modified with attention to the individual and contextual characteristics of the behavior makes it difficult to generalize the findings of behavior modification to various classes of problems, children, families, and cultures. Specifying the child's individual characteristics allows for a more adequate evaluation of procedures. Behavior modification is a powerful, but by no means the only, way to change behavior.

A practical limitation of behavior modification pertains to the nature of the problems to be handled. Although it is effective against many heretofore unsolvable problems, there are certain disorders, especially those dealing with input processing and self-concept or self-esteem variables, that must be dealt with by other psychotherapeutic approaches. Even though there are still many behavioral dysfunctions, yet to be identified, that could be dealt with by behavior modification techniques, the variability of human processing is too great to hope that all behavioral problems could be alleviated by any single technique, no matter how effective. Once its therapeutic limitations are discovered, it will assume its specific place among the many tools of the applied psychologist and special educator. In combination with other techniques, it almost certainly will become an important device.

Another major drawback is of practical importance where children are concerned. The more independent the child is from biological deficits and cultural deprivations, the freer he is to learn appropriate behavior. Given the opportunity, most children learn without deliberate manipulation of reinforcements and situations (as in the learning of language; Chomsky, 1969). In the majority of cases, children learn what the direct consequences of their behavior are and internalize them as part of their growth. Clearly, behavior modification would be limited and less relevant to children who show evident failure to internalize standards, for whatever reasons (family disorganization, poor management, poverty, etc.). Thus, this method is specifically applicable where a system (social or personal) or an individual is unable to organize his reactions systematically to assure the maximum benefits and growth. It must be recognized that for many persons reinforcement is internal and not external. Consequently, this method applies to some, but not all, the dysfunctions found in children. Unfortunately, some behavior modifiers may wish to apply this technique to all their cases. However, if one were to examine their practices in detail, one would discover that their excellent results apply to a selective range of problems and individuals.

CLASSROOM MANAGEMENT TECHNIQUES: PSYCHOANALYTIC APPROACH

In previous sections of this book we have discussed the psychoanalytic approach to personality. It might be wise at this point, however, to review briefly some of the underlying therapeutic principles involved in psychoanalysis, which, of course, was originated by Sigmund Freud. Freud maintained that the unconscious is largely responsible for the apparent behavior of individuals and that some information is placed in the unconscious, where it is not readily available to the individual, as a result of a variety of differences in the ego structure. Freud proposed that behavior may be viewed along a psychosexual continuum ranging from oral to genital and that people develop problems in thinking about those things which make them feel anxious or guilty or about which they have feelings which are unpleasant. The inherent nature of a child's sexual feelings greatly affects much of his adjustment to his environment. Many thoughts and behaviors according to Freud are repressed and can only be exhibited in dreams or fantasies. Freud felt that many neurotic problems stem from guilt over fantasies about unusual sexual concerns or activities which the individual could not readily admit in his conscious state. Many attempts have been made to relate learning theories to psychoanalytic therapeutic approaches, such as those of Dollard and Miller (1950), Mowrer (1950), and Breger and McGaugh (1965). All psychodynamic or psychoanalytic therapies involve a relationship between the psychotherapist and the patient which is considered to be the focus of the treatment procedures. The emphasis in psychoanalytic therapy involves release of emotions, relief through play, and efforts to re-educate the child.

There are many variations within the psychodynamic approach, one of the more interesting being relationship therapy. Relationship therapy was derived from the psychoanalytic philosophy of Otto Rank, a follower of Freud who later formed his own psychoanalytic school of treatment. Another approach to relationship therapy is that of Melanie Kline and Anna Freud, which was derived directly from Freud's psychoanalytic philosophy. Rank felt that therapy should be concerned with the understanding and constructive use of a patient's reaction to the therapeutic situation and that this should be the starting point of therapy. He believed the relationship between client and therapist to be the essence of the therapy, and from this standpoint the therapeutic program might be planned. This concept indicates "playing down" the traditional Freudian emphasis upon unconscious motivation as a primary source of information during treatment. A basic characteristic of relationship therapy is the time limit that is placed on the therapy. From the start, the therapy is limited by a timetable or calendar to which the therapist and client adhere. It is felt that the patient's acceptance of this type of timetable is a step toward acceptance of reality and is essential if good therapeutic results are to be obtained. Therapy is said to begin when the relationship between the therapist and the client solidifies and becomes clear to the client. This supportive relationship allows the client to explore his problems with some amount of security. A warm and friendly relationship is achieved, with the time limit always being kept in mind.

Another form of psychotherapy related somewhat to the psychoanalytic or psychodynamic approach is called release therapy, which has best been described by Levy (1938; 1939). The major concept of release therapy is derived from Freud's idea of *abreaction*, that is, acting-out or talking about some emotion that has been suppressed. In essence, Levy used a cathartic approach as a method of assisting children in developing a release from symptoms of maladaptive behavior. Release therapy originally was thought to be related to a diagnostic concept and was limited to somewhat severe kinds of behavioral dysfunctions. Unfortunately, less serious problems were often not brought to the attention of guidance personnel, and at present, release therapy is utilized for many childhood problems.

Another variation of the psychodynamic approach is play therapy.

The best known experiment employing this therapy is that of Axline (1947). Her eight basic principles of play therapy follow. The therapist must: (1) develop a warm, friendly relationship with the child; (2) accept the child exactly as he is; (3) establish the feeling of permissiveness in the relationship; (4) be alert in order to recognize the feelings of the child and reflect them back to him, so that he gains insight into his behavior; (5) maintain a deep respect for the child's ability to solve his own problems; (6) allow the child to lead the way; (7) not attempt to hurry the process; and (8) establish only those limitations that are necessary to activate realistic relationships and to make the child aware of his responsibility in the relationship.

The play therapy suggested by Axline is a natural, spontaneous, and somewhat free-form approach. She believed that nondirective play therapy should focus on complete acceptance of the child, and of course, the child must also like and accept the therapist.

All forms of psychoanalytically oriented therapy are most usually used in child guidance clinics (Anna Freud, 1946a), although they certainly are not restricted to these conditions. Anna Freud described the beginning phase of treatment as a period of time in which one attempts to induce in the child a willingness to cooperate. This important initial step is often overlooked. A variety of techniques, which depend partly on the situation and partly on the therapist or teacher, are used for the purpose of gaining insight into the problems of the child and helping the child to understand the therapeutic processes. The teacher or therapist should attempt to promote a close relationship with the child, so that he will look forward to contact on a regular basis. Even with psychoanalytic approaches the techniques must vary with the age and ability of the child, the nature of the symptoms, and the general characteristics of the situation. Children are, of course, more likely to provide daydreams rather than night dreams for analysis by a therapist in the classic situation; but the social milieu of the teaching situation can provide additional information for analysis and remediation.

In the learning theory variation of psychoanalytic therapy, the idea has been advanced that the basic cause of all neurotic behavior is learned and that, consequently, all behavior does conform to the laws of learning and what has been learned may be unlearned (Mowrer, 1939). Mowrer stated that fear and anxiety can serve as drives that motivate undesirable behavior and that reduction of fear can serve as a reinforcement. He felt that neurotic symptoms are self-perpetuating because they tend to reinforce one's own behavior patterns. Learning theorists tend to regard anxiety as external; that is, anxiety results largely from fear of being punished by external authorities.

It is probable that most current theories of psychotherapy derive some of their bases from the psychoanalytic approach, perhaps because it was historically first. The psychoanalytic approach, however, is rarely followed today in its pure form.

METHODS OF REHABILITATION BEYOND TEACHING

Art Therapy

One of the oldest and most often utilized forms of therapy involves the use of art in its many forms, ranging from finger painting to sculpturing. The use of art as a therapeutic device has been studied by psychi-

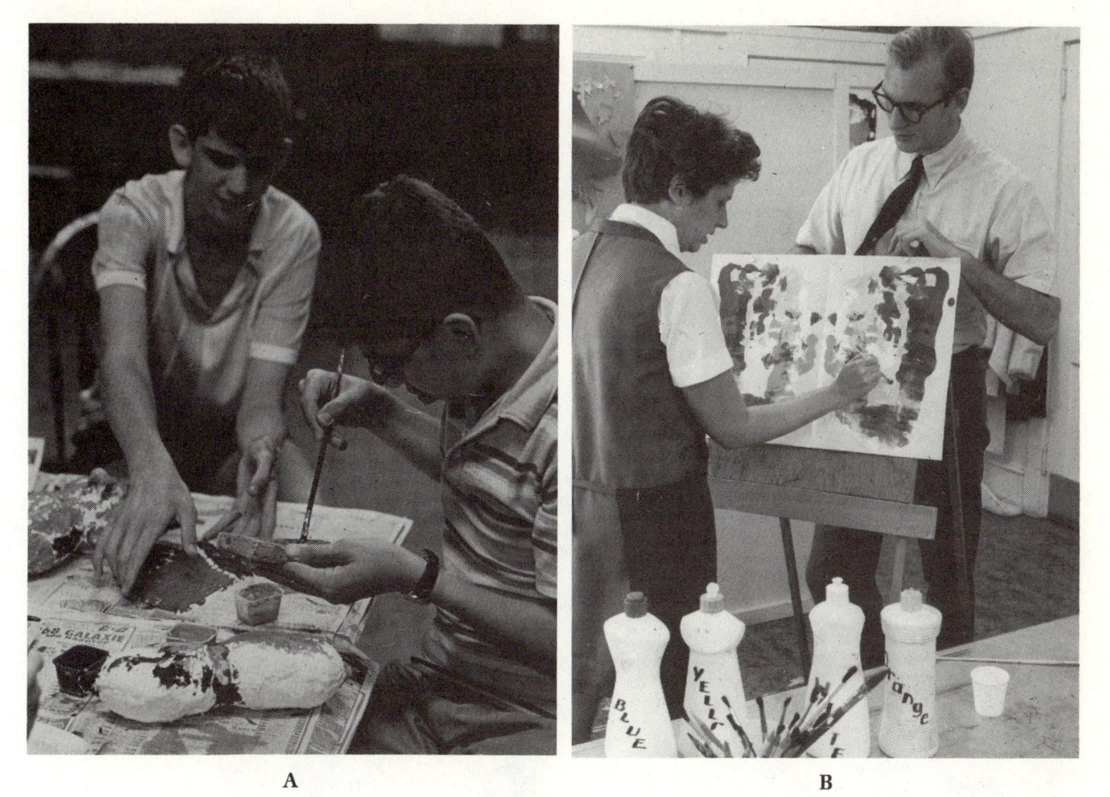

A B

Figure 13–1 *A* and *B*, Art therapy. (*A* and *B*, Courtesy of The Woods Schools, Langhorne, Pennsylvania.)

atrists and psychological researchers for many years. Art therapy has many advantages in that it may be instituted by relatively untrained individuals and in a variety of ways without fear of harming the individual being treated. In some cases, the individuals participating in art therapy exhibit more interest in art than in therapy, but the reverse may also be true. Art therapy provides outlets by which the behaviorally disordered individual may express himself through nonverbal means and in a manner which enables him to feel secure; that is, he is not exposing himself. Although it facilitates insight into the inner dynamics of the individual through his work, one should be careful when employing art as a device to interpret behavior. As with all therapy, considerable caution should be engaged in by all personnel involved. Art therapy as a medium of expression for the behaviorally disordered, however, may be used without any undue fear. Individuals displaying violent behavior should obviously not be allowed to use instruments by which they may inflict harm on themselves or others.

Music Therapy

Music has long been used as a supplementary method of treatment for the behaviorally disordered individual. Music therapy may involve performing, listening, or a combination of the two. It may involve basic rhythms or other musical expressions as therapeutic devices. The disturbed child may be able to respond or relate to music by using musical instruments to express his inner feelings. The child who exhibits an extremely outgoing kind of behavior may use an instrument, such as the drum, to relieve pent-up emotions. Music has been employed in both active and passive procedures. Teachers utilizing music in the classroom should observe very carefully the effects of different types of music on the atmosphere of the classroom and should be governed by the reaction pattern of the students involved. It is perfectly legitimate for music to be

Figure 13–2 *A* and *B*, Music therapy. (*A* and *B*, Courtesy of The Woods Schools, Langhorne, Pennsylvania.)

Figure 13–3 Music and dance therapy. (Courtesy of The Woods Schools, Langhorne, Pennsylvania.)

used as a pacification device in order to induce a reflective or tranquil mood in a classroom setting, so that more productive work can be undertaken by the students. It is also permissible for the teacher to utilize march music under some circumstances and to have the children march around the room. Music should be used in light of the desired goals of the teacher.

Music as a therapeutic device is often accompanied by dance as a method of treating behaviorally disordered individuals. Children, by using this nonverbal mode of behavior, may release many of their inner tensions. Release of tension is exhibited by many of the modern dances as performed by the youth of America. In addition, dance is an excellent means of training for coordination and for the development of more effective interpersonal relations. It may be used to reduce the inhibitions of students in a school setting. Dancing should be conducted in an informal atmosphere and without stress or strain with regard to ability to perform.

Bibliotherapy

Reading may serve as an avenue of treatment for certain students in our public schools. If the student reads well and tends to respond more effectively to a pattern of behavior involving just himself without interaction with others, book therapy may be indicated. The individual may be guided to read books, essays, poems, or plays which discuss ideas, situations, or behaviors that the teacher wants the student to engage in. Careful selection of reading material will insure that it is within the reading ability of the child and that it does not contain material which is too stringent or too emotionally related for the individual to cope with at the time it is presented. As with all other therapy, it must be closely supervised in terms of the reactions of those taking part in it. Bibliotherapy offers the advantage of not conflicting with other methods of treatment and may be highly individualized in that each student in a classroom may be reading something particularly designed for him and his specific problems. Many materials are available, including relevant stories of individuals who have had problems comparable to those of children in any classroom.

Puppetry

Many children exhibiting emotional problems respond to the use of puppets. For cases in which a child is unable to communicate verbally with adults, the use of puppets may prove to be a rewarding technique. Puppets offer the child the opportunity to express himself without directly exposing himself and also help the child to employ his imagination and creativeness. The child should be provided with a variety of puppets to choose from when he is creating a story. Ideally, these stories should be recorded for later listening, since puppets may used for diagnosis as well as for treatment. They offer relief from the regular tedium of classroom procedures and thus may be utilized to create interest. In addition, they may be used as a reward for desirable behavior or to assist a student in expressing aggressive feelings which would be difficult for him to exhibit under normal circumstances. Because the puppet may be treated in any manner and does not feel any pain, it may symbolically assist the student in releasing his pent-up emotions. The make-believe characteristics of the puppet allow the child to freely explore many forms of behavior. The teacher may propose situations for children to act out to obtain insight into the current status of a child's thinking under certain circumstances. Puppets may also be used along with various art forms as projects to stimulate children's interest. Puppets offer many approaches to working with the behaviorally disordered child, and teachers are encouraged to explore puppetry as a method of communication with such children.

Play and Recreational Therapy

Play therapy has been employed as a treatment procedure for many years, and it can be utilized in a standard school setting by the regular classroom teacher. Alexander (1971) stated that play therapy in the school is somewhat different in its application than that which is actually used in a psychotherapeutic environment, but in both instances it can be used for problems in interpersonal relationships. The teacher may find that some children exhibit hostile, withdrawn, or aggressive kinds of behaviors. Play therapy as used in a school setting may create an attitude which may help the student to release some of these aggressive feelings. The teacher must be sensitive to the child, must listen very carefully to him when he is engaging in play therapy, and must exhibit complete faith and confidence in him in order to assist him in ridding himself of feelings of suspicion. The teacher might start with some general statements concerning the nature of the material available and the "boundaries" for the behavior of the student. The teacher may employ play therapy by designing play situations, such as role playing, in which children may exhibit their feelings or attitudes in a variety of situations. Teachers must realize that children will frequently test the limits; that is, they will attempt to use words or behaviors which often are condemned outside of the play therapy situation. If the teacher hopes to use role play or play therapy in its broader applications, he must be prepared to accept as much deviant behavior as possible, in light of the currently existing situations in the community.

Group Play Therapy with Children

Group play therapy is not a specific type of therapy, but a medium in which almost any type of therapy may be employed, such as psychoanalysis, nondirective therapy, or behavior modification. It includes many devices, such as symbolic interpretation (a form of communication with the child), abreaction and catharsis (means by which the child can express himself), and social modeling. Group play therapy has become popular because it keeps the child interested (often a major problem in child therapy), allows the child to be spontaneous, and probably most important of all, does not restrict the therapist to a particular theoretical basis.

Clement (1967) showed that tangible reinforcement can be used in group play therapy to increase social approach behavior and to decrease discrete problem behavior. He assigned 11 third-graders to three groups: Group I had a therapist who was to reward the children with tokens for social approach behavior; Group II also had a therapist, but the subjects were given only verbal reinforcement for social approach behavior; and Group III had no therapist and therefore neither token nor verbal reinforcement. All three groups met for one hour a week for 14 weeks. None of the children in the study had a history of psychosis or perceptual motor problems. They had been described by their teachers as being socially withdrawn or lacking in spontaneity. None of the children had behavior problems great enough to keep them from attending public school regularly. The mean IQ for the group was 100. As would be expected, the greatest change was seen in Group I and the least change in Group III. This change was indicated by measurements of social approach behavior. There was no change in measurements of "productivity" (grades), anxiety (Children's Manifest Anxiety Scale), or "general psychologic adjustment" (Q sort).

In 1950, Bills reported on an interesting study with retarded readers. His subjects were eight third-graders who were classified by their school as slow learners. Seven of these eight children were also described as emotionally maladjusted. The study was divided into three periods of 30 school days each. The first period served as the control; usual classroom procedure was used. The second period was the therapy period; nondirective group and individual play therapies were employed, following Rogerian technique. The third period was used for ascertaining the lasting and cumulative effects. Three tests were administered to determine the results: the Gates Test of Paragraph Meaning, the Gates Oral Reading Paragraphs, and the Revised Stanford-Binet, Form L. These tests were given at the beginning of the control period and at the end of each of the three periods. The subjects did show improvement during the control phase (probably due to factors such as practice effect, etc.). However, improvement in the second and third periods was significantly greater (at .01 level) than that in the first period. Later, Bills did a similar study with eight third-graders who were classified as slow learners but who had no signs of emotional maladjustment (as tested by the California Test of Personality, the Rorschach test, and the TAT). The same three periods were used, along with the same tests and retests. The results indicated that the subjects showed no significant gains in reading ability. Bills, therefore, concluded that significant increases in reading ability will not occur in retarded readers who exhibit adequate emotional adjustment when nondirective group play therapy is used. This means that the results in the previous study can be attributed to the treatment of emotional maladjustment.

One of the first studies utilizing group play therapy with psychotic children was reported by Rose et al. (1954). The subjects consisted of seven hospitalized psychotic girls (aged 16 to 20). Therapy was given for 1 hour each day, 5 days a week, for 3 months. By manipulating the games used by the subjects, the therapists moved from aggressive games to nonaggressive games to games requiring the cooperation of two or more people. As a result of the therapy, Rose reported that: (1) social interplay shifted from nonverbal to verbal and (2) destructive and solitary play was replaced by competitive games. It is presumed that the group acted as its own control, and the results were taken from before and after measurements.

In a well-organized study, Leland (1959) investigated the possibility of using group play therapy techniques to rehabilitate postnursery school retarded children when other therapy techniques had failed. The subjects were four aggressive, hostile, and destructive boys and four withdrawn boys. Their ages ranged from 4½ to 9½ years. A test-retest method of evaluation was used, and therapy consisted of 90 hours of group play therapy over a one-month period. All but two of the boys improved on the Vineland Social Maturity Scale, but not to a statistically significant degree. The WISC showed definite intellectual growth on the Verbal Scale, but no significant change in the Full Scale. Ratings by teachers and therapists showed that six of the eight boys were better adjusted and were no longer considered disciplinary problems. A follow-up study which rated the boys seven months later showed that they had improved even more.

Leland's conclusions from this study were that: (1) group play therapy does not create a major change in the level of social maturation for mental retardates, but there does seem to be an improvement in discipline; and (2) there is a slight change in IQ due to group play therapy.

The effectiveness of group play therapy was evaluated by Schiffer (1965). Thirty-three boys, 9 to 11 years old, who were selected from a Child Guidance Center waiting list were divided into five groups. Two groups received play therapy, while their parents participated in parents' therapy; one group received play therapy, and their parents were not treated; one group met with a recreation leader, and their parents met in "leaderless" groups; and one group remained on the treatment list. None of the groups showed improvement on measurements of likeability, impulsivity, social isolation, pure aggression, aggressive dependency, immature dependency, depression, rejection, or total aggression. The group that met with the recreation leader did just as well as those receiving group play therapy with a therapist; the peer relations of each group stabilized. The untreated group exhibited increased maladjustment on all socially deviant scales except pure aggression. The recreation leader was just as effective as the therapist, and treatment of parents showed no significant therapeutic effects.

In summarizing the more conclusive results of the previously described studies, one can say that: (1) behavior modification can be profitably introduced into a group play therapy situation (Clement, 1967); (2) there have been positive results in the treatment of emotional disturbance by utilizing group play therapy; and (3) group play therapy does not seem to have any *direct* effect on intelligence (Bills, 1950).

In spite of scant supportive evidence, group play therapy is growing in popularity. Ginott (1961), one of the foremost researchers of group play therapy, justified its use on the grounds that: (1) it can be tested scientifically; (2) it is better suited to meet the growing demands for treatment; (3) the experience of being accepted and understood by several people is more rewarding than being understood by one therapist; (4) the adult therapist becomes less threatening to the child when the child is in the company of children his own age; (5) group play therapy provides a new medium for catharsis (besides that of verbalization), which is play itself; and (6) a group allows for a greater range of reality testing.

Ginott did not feel that group play therapy is the only method of treating behaviorally disordered children, but rather that it is helpful only when the child's disorder centers on social adjustment problems, such as withdrawal, immaturity, phobic reactions, habit disorders, and conduct disorders. Group play therapy would not be indicated in cases involving intense sibling rivalries, sociopathic children, or children exposed to severe trauma, for which family therapy may be a more appropriate method.

Working with Families

Family therapy refers to working with parents and children together. When only a husband and wife are involved, even though they legally constitute a family, such therapy is generally referred to as "couples therapy" or "marital therapy." The concept of family therapy may include more than parents and children; grandparents, aunts, uncles, maids, or any other members of the nuclear family may be involved, either all the time or occasionally (Ackerman, 1958). Jackson and Satir (1961) pointed out four possible combinations in family therapy:

1. Members of a biological or nuclear family attend sessions conjointly, meaning that all family members are seen together at the same time by the same therapist. (*Note:* Many times two therapists work simultaneously with the family; see Warkentin and Whitaker, 1967.)

2. Members of a family are seen together for diagnostic purposes, and they are then assigned on an individual basis to different therapists who work collaboratively. (Such a practice is fairly common in clinics.)

3. Family members are seen individually from the outset by a single person who then pieces together the picture of family interaction and continues to treat the family members individually. Family members may also be seen individually from the outset, each by a different person. The therapists then pool their findings to try to arrive at a picture of family interaction, which is followed by subsequent individual treatment.

4. The identified "patient" is seen in individual therapy, and family members are seen occasionally to determine how their aid may best be enlisted, or simply to urge them not to interfere with the patient's progress (Jackson and Satir, 1961).

The fourth method has considerable limitations, since it is based on the theoretical concept that the patient alone is sick and that the other family members are well. The first three approaches are based on an assumption which views the symptoms of the identified patient within the total family situation, assuming that there is a relationship between the symptoms of the child and the interaction of the family.

A considerably large amount of the available literature on family therapy is concerned with the adolescent or adult schizophrenic and his family. Relatively little information is available concerning family therapy involving children.

Parent-Child Groups in Schools

L'Abate attempted group therapy of parents and their children on the school grounds (privately in the library or on the stage of the auditorium). Although this was clearly a demonstrational approach, it was possible to screen children and their parents with quick intellectual measurements obtained from school records, or at the time of interview, or from teachers' ratings. The group sessions took place for such a short period of time (2½ months) and at such intervals (once every two weeks) that it was impossible to produce significant changes. The teachers of the children participating in group therapy were also included in this demonstration. Most impressionistic reactions to the feasibility of the project were favorable, at least demonstrating the potential usefulness of this approach.

Group Therapy and Rewarded Activities

In the same rural county L'Abate attempted for one summer to help a group of acting-out children, who were selected as being "the worst" in the county. Most of the children were intellectually or academically retarded or both. Sessions were held in a classroom once every two weeks for two hours. Their problems ranged from extreme withdrawal to extreme acting-out. They sat together for one hour of discussion and then painted, wove, and listened to records for another hour.

They received money for painting and weaving (mostly potholders) and were served refreshments at the end of the two hours, regardless of whether they participated in the group discussion or in the activity. This experience demonstrated the feasibility of group therapeutic procedures with such children, provided that: (1) procedures are made contingent upon concrete activities for which the child is rewarded, and (2) the children's verbal interactions occur within a framework of control over their tendencies to act out and to abuse the motoric rather than the verbal modality.

In some cases a combination of methods may be more advantageous, especially if it has been demonstrated that each method in and by itself does produce beneficial results.

Role-Playing and Dramatic Group Procedures

Halpern (1965) studied the therapeutic and educative applications of role-playing to the black ghetto child in a number of sessions (from November through June) with 28 children in grades six to eight. She suggested that role-playing may be a tool by which to achieve: (1) relaxation of tension among children from contrasting backgrounds, (2) projection of differing needs that may be harmonized in a more appropriate context for the child, and (3) a sense of self-awareness, identity, and human dignity.

Harth (1966) studied role-playing to verify that when children use play therapy they undergo a positive reaction to frustration and attitudes toward school. There were 2 girls and 3 boys in the experimental group and 1 girl and 4 boys in the control group. The experimental group was trained in role-playing techniques. The Peabody Inventory Rating Scale on Emotional Disturbance was used to measure classroom behavior change. Within the training period of five weeks, the classroom behavior of the experimental group changed significantly in a positive direction, while the behavior of the control group did not change. Of course, extra variables such as added attention toward the children were not checked for or discussed in the article.

Thompson (1969) found that older children (aged 10 to 12) were better role-players than younger children (aged 7 to 9). There was a strong suggestion that the better adjusted children were better role-players than poorly adjusted children.

Conclusions

The results of many therapeutic methods are discouraging. Furthermore, many of the treatments were not specifically described but were defined in general terms, with a combination of several techniques being used and labeled as "intensive," "moderate," or "no treatment." The cost has not been evaluated in terms of the effectiveness of the treatment.

Comparisons of therapies and follow-up studies have not shown that one type of treatment is significantly better than any other. Rutter et al. (1967) conducted a follow-up study and concluded that: (1) only a minority of autistic children reached good social adjustment (as indicated by employment, marriage, etc.), while one-half remained incapable of living independently and were being cared for in institutions; (2) the amount of schooling received correlated positively with later adjustment; and (3) failure to develop language by age five correlated with failure to adjust in later years.

In a follow-up comparison of three types of therapies by Eaton and Menolascino (1967), the results were equally discouraging. Twenty-nine children were classified according to type of psychosis and treatment. The psychoses were classified as autism, schizophrenia, and brain damage with psychosis. The three types of treatment were defined as: (1) intensive, in-patient therapy, including play, milieu, and individual therapies, medical management, and parental therapy; (2) moderate, weekly outpatient therapy which often included the parents or brief intensive therapy followed by less frequent outpatient treatment; and (3) controls—no treatment except for the initial evaluation. The following results were reported: (1) specific diagnoses beyond "psychosis" were not conclusive (children originally diagnosed as autistic later had to be classified as brain damaged); (2) speech development was again found to be important in later adjustment; and (3) no correlation between treatment and later adjustment was found.

Phillips (1960) compared short-term, nondepth therapy (2 months) with traditional therapy at a community child guidance clinic. Groups were matched according to number of members, IQ, age, and diagnosis. The nondepth therapy yielded significantly better results as judged by the parents. The success ratio for the nondepth therapy was 92 per cent, while the traditional therapy yielded only a 60 per cent success ratio. A five-year follow-up study of cases treated at a child guidance clinic compared a treatment group (having received at least 10 hours of therapy) with a no-treatment group (Levitt, 1963). Follow-up data included objective psychological test results, objective facts, such as completion of school, marital status, institutionalization, and parental opinions and evaluations. The results showed no significant differences between the treatment and no-treatment groups.

MILIEU THERAPY IN RESIDENTIAL INSTITUTIONS

The oldest plan for the education of dysfunctional children is the residential school. This method of meeting a community need was undertaken as early as 1829 with blind children in Massachusetts. In 1837, the Ohio School for the Blind became entirely state supported. Today, residential schools are found in every state.

Residential institutions are of various types and provide for physically handicapped, intellectually retarded, mentally ill, blind, deaf, or delinquent children, and lately, for the epileptic and orthopedically handicapped. Until recently, similar types of arrangements were frequently developed for crippled children only as treatment centers in parts of hospitals and medical centers. Residential institutions are both publicly and privately supported and may be administered at the national, state, regional, county, or municipal level. Some of these are multipurpose institutions, serving all ages, both sexes, and all degrees of disabilities. Others are special purpose institutions which accept only children with one type of exceptionality and also have restrictions on age, sex, and extent of disability.

Short-term residential facilities are usually small and close to local communities. These provide short-term diagnosis, care, treatment, and training or rehabilitation. They may serve as half-way houses during transitional periods of long-term patients about to be discharged, as facilities for those to be admitted to a long-term residence, and as trial facilities for children whose parents are uncertain about institutionalization. Children are referred by social agencies, other children's institutions, outpatient clinics, boards of education, private therapists, physicians, juvenile courts, and families.

In 1965, there were approximately 192,000 people in this country who were residents of public institutions for the mentally retarded. The 1965 directory of the American Association on Mental Deficiency (A.A.M.D.) lists 134 public, residential institutions for the mentally retarded. In a recent doctoral dissertation, Anderson (1965) reported that there were 80 residential institutions for the deaf in the United States, their major admission criterion being that deafness be the child's "primary disability." The majority of the children in residential treatment facilities are white, nearly 25 per cent are nonwhite. Although ages range from 5 to 21, the mean age is 12 years old.

Thirty per cent of the residential schools included in a study by Hulton (1964) indicated that they sent their children to local public schools. In such cases, the student returns to the residential center for his meals and lodging and any course work not taught at the public school, the assumption being that the best preparation for living a normal life is maximum participation during the school years in the normal community. The emotional problems of many children in residential treatment schools and therapeutic day schools, however, frequently make it difficult for the children to adjust to a structured school setting or for a public school to tolerate the behavior that they may sometimes exhibit. Thus, many residential facilities have established their own educational programs.

A factor which has served to separate the residential school from public school programs has been the method of instruction which is employed. For instance, in reference to the deaf, the two methods are manualism (often a combined method) and oralism. The proponents of manualism have almost exclusively been residential school personnel. Manualism is a system of communication between deaf individuals. Thus, it facilitates adjustment within this homogenous grouping of residential schools. The combined method includes speech development. Oralism almost always typifies the day school program. As the name implies, this method stresses speech and lip reading in order to provide a means of communication between the deaf child and his peers with normal hearing. In this way, he is not segregated socially or emotionally because of communication failure.

In many cases, an institution provides relief from the tension of a hostile home and community and often provides access to physical facilities not available at home. Together, these conditions create an opportunity to gain self-confidence. In order to avoid an institution-like atmosphere, frequent weekend trips are encouraged. In addition to providing a therapeutically sound environment and private psychotherapy if it is needed, the institution must fulfill the functions of parents, school, and family physician, as well as offering the cultural and recreational opportunities of a middle-class suburb. All this must be done with salaried personnel working in three shifts.

Several studies which were undertaken to establish and evaluate the effects of institutionalization (Stevenson, 1961; Lyle, 1959; Kaufman, 1963; and Zigler, 1963) have concluded that a prolonged institutional experience produces deleterious effects on the psychological functions studied. Masland et al. (1958) observed loss of personal spontaneity and expression, excessive fantasizing, avoidance and fear of new situations, and excessive dependence as the results of institutionalization. Elonen and her associates (1967) maintained that residential institutions reinforce the original developmental lag.

Kaufman and Levitt (1965) evaluated the differences between institutionalized and noninstitutionalized children by measuring the frequency of: (1) self-stimulating behaviors—body rocking, head banging, arm flapping, pacing, etc.; (2) social behaviors—attention given to others, social play, aggression, talking and crying in response to others, etc.; and (3) manipulation of the environment—playing with hooks, latches, closed doors, etc. The noninstitutionalized control group was chosen from the institution's waiting list. Medical records of the institutionalized children were screened to rule out emergency admissions, since none of the waiting list children were determined by the admissions committee to require immediate emergency placement. Equal numbers of children (i.e., 23) were matched according to mean chronological age (group differences were not significant), and all were either moderately, severely, or profoundly retarded. Results showed that the institutionalized group consistently exhibited more self-stimulating behaviors than the home group. Moreover, the home group exhibited significantly more social behaviors than the institutionalized group and tended to use more speech for communicative purposes. Group differences were not significant, however, on manipulation of the environment. This study seems to support the idea that once committed to an institution, children remain at their low functioning level or sink even lower—probably due to insufficient stimulation or neglect.

In general, because of the characteristic geographical isolation of residential institutions, they do not have all the professional services which are available to public school children, nor can they afford such services. In a survey by Baumeister (1967), it was shown that out of

120 institutions which were questioned, 53 failed to meet the most nominal and minimal psychologist-to-patients ratio (1:400, as proposed by the A.A.M.D.) for profoundly retarded patients. Psychodiagnostic testing in these institutions was consistently most highly regarded by the superintendents. Psychotherapeutic functions were rated second in importance, followed by training responsibilities. Research was rated as the least important activity. In public institutions, there were approximately 10 times as many medical personnel, 3 times as many special activities personnel, and 2 times as many social workers as psychologists. The psychologists' traditional role in residential facilities has clearly been that of psychometrician.

Today, the residential institution is beginning to play a new role in the treatment of its patients. Families are demanding that training and rehabilitation replace custodial maintenance. The nature of the institutionalized population is also changing. Patients are younger and more severely retarded. Such individuals are not well suited to traditional psychometric evaluation procedures. The majority of institutionalized patients are not physically ill, and hence, do not require hospitalization; thus, custodial care and hospitalization are no longer the primary purposes of the institution. We are seeing a movement away from the former medical model of the institution. The appropriate goal of institutionalization is currently centered on rehabilitation through behavior modification rather than custodial care. Professionals are abandoning their traditional roles in favor of training and supervising subprofessionals who may implement treatment and training programs. Psychologists are becoming behavioral engineers who are getting involved more directly and actively with behavior itself. Since operant conditioning has been successful with nonverbal children, it is believed that this procedure is best for initiating behavior modification of the retardate.

The great range of abilities among institutionalized children, especially the mentally retarded, favors decentralization of the large institution and establishment of varied community facilities. An innovation toward this goal is the cottage plan, in which small groups of children live with a married couple in cottages on a campus in simulated family situations. These cottages are secure, homelike, work-centered, self-sufficient units grouped in villages where there are schools for vocational rehabilitation. Regular cottage personnel are being trained to use behavioral management techniques. Consequently, temporary placement is replacing indefinite institutionalization. Rickard and Dinoff (1971) illustrated how a broad range of maladaptive behaviors can be improved at an eight-week therapeutic summer camp. Many institutions have rapidly evolved multiple programs aimed at supplementing community resources, facilitating transactions between the institution and the community, and minimizing institutionalization itself by providing such programs as day care centers, trial placements, day work, and foster home programs.

In the study by Hulton (1964) on the costs of residential centers, several characteristics of these centers were pointed out: a high ratio of staff to children, required services of a clinical staff, self-sufficiency, a therapeutic milieu, inclusion of many treatment modalities in the programs, therapy programs for parents, continued therapy after discharge. Out of the children seeking admission to these institutions, only one out of six was admitted. There was a preponderance of boys among the residents (75 per cent), and an average length of stay was found to be 972 days. Of the children admitted, 53 per cent had received some prior therapy. The costs per child-year of services ranged from $6244 to $19,055, an average of $9685. Ninety-two per cent of this amount was for institutional care. These costs were also broken down by type of child. The average fee which was charged to the families of the children was $3600 per year, although most centers had a sliding scale fee, ranging from no charge to over $9000. The costs of the medically directed center were significantly higher than the nonmedically directed programs; the costs of public residential centers were higher than the costs of private centers. One must question whether the cost of residential care is out of line with the effectiveness of its services.

CHAPTER 14

CURRICULA FOR ENVIRONMENTAL EXCEPTIONALITIES

(Courtesy of The Woods Schools, Langhorne, Pennsylvania.)

A curriculum is basically concerned with the specific program of an educational institution and should include all the activities that are planned for the students of the school. In the field of special education, great emphasis is placed on designing a curriculum that is tailored to the specific needs of various exceptional students. The first part of this chapter is concerned with general factors that relate to curriculum planning, regardless of the type of exceptional student that is being educated. It explores the common factors affecting all exceptional children. The remainder of the chapter is devoted to specific exceptionalities. The deficits and needs of many exceptional children tend to be difficult to isolate in specific categories; therefore, the teacher may need to "blend" suggestions from various parts of the chapter.

BASIC CONSIDERATIONS IN CURRICULAR DEVELOPMENT

1. All professional personnel involved in the public school should assist in developing the curriculum for the exceptional child.

2. The purpose of a curriculum is to serve as a translating agent for the school program. Thus, it is essential that the curriculum provide for practical application of procedures by turning general goals into specific practices in the classroom. These practices should be as applicable to everyday life as possible.

3. The curriculum for exceptional children must be designed realistically with regard to academic goals. It must be closely related to the intellectual and social functioning of the children and must be based on the readiness of the student and on his abilities to acquire knowledge.

4. Programs for EMR, and to some extent for all exceptional children, should provide an experience-centered curriculum which provides many real life experiences.

An essential concern in designing a curriculum is to arrange for grouping children according to their various levels of intellectual functioning. The general procedure for grouping educable mentally retarded children is to divide them into four groups: the primary, the intermediate elementary, the junior high, and the senior high school levels. Chronological age, of course, is only a minor concern. The intellectual ages associated with each of the preceding groups are of greater relevance: primary level—ages 3 to 7, intermediate level—ages 5 to 9, junior high level—age 7 and above, and high school level—age 9 and above.

In order to relate the curriculum to practical objectives, four areas might be considered in setting up the program: (1) health, physical development, and safety; (2) social and emotional competency; (3) vocational competency; and (4) general knowledge of basic school subjects. The class work should be organized according to these major areas. The area of health, physical development, and safety, for example, might include a course on personal grooming. Each of the areas should be interrelated. A spelling course should not be isolated from the oral and written uses of language. Spelling words should be selected from everyday language, in order to adhere to the ultimate goals of the program.

Patterns for Curricular Development

In developing a curriculum, one should keep in mind at least some of the following factors: (1) the teacher's skill, training, experience, and resources; (2) the school and the community environments; (3) the nature and degree of intellectual functioning of the children who are to be taught; and (4) the philosophy of the person or persons responsible for developing the program. All programs in special education should focus on the individual child and must take into account the nature of the child, his needs, the goals of the program for the child's development, the activities involved in achieving these goals, a means of evaluating the program, and of course, a means of reevaluating and reprogramming in light of the results of the evaluation. The evaluation should always involve information gathered from all possible sources.

ADMINISTRATIVE FACTORS IN CURRICULUM

Use of Adjunctive Personnel

It is important that the modern school district provide teaching staffs with increasing numbers of adjunctive personnel, including school psychologists, school social workers, school counselors, and in some cases, school physicians and nurses. Such individuals have significant roles in the total educational process in the areas of diagnosis and treatment and of involvement with the teaching staff and with parents. It is the job of adjunctive personnel to be fully aware of suitable management procedures, learning patterns, and interpersonal dynamics if they are to give appropriate assistance to teachers and other educational personnel.

Consultative Assistance for School Personnel

In working with exceptional children, all school personnel must be assured of having consultative services made available to them. In particular, teachers of exceptional children should be provided with technical and supportive consultation on a regular basis. The teacher should expect to spend some time working with the consultant to solve those problems which are encountered in teaching exceptional children. Such consultation may help the teacher to become aware of what might be called "the limits of the system." Every school, neighborhood, and community operates within certain restraints. As a part of teaching exceptional children, the teacher must be fully conscious of these factors in order to provide as realistic an educational program as possible. The teacher must be able to distinguish between that which is optimal and that which is possible. One of the major roles of the consultant is to assist teachers in maintaining a realistic outlook. The consultant can help teachers to cope with and to interpret cues from their students. The teacher must be aware of the fact that children communicate verbally and nonverbally. Much of our society tends to emphasize the verbal factors to the exclusion of the nonverbal. Teachers must be sensitive to those children who are unable to communicate verbally but who communicate volumes by means of their nonverbal behavior.

One problem that arises in consultation is the issue over when consultation becomes therapy. Let us say simply that the consultant should provide the kinds of assistance which will enable the teacher or other personnel to be as effective as possible. Which person engages in the consultant role should be left to the discretion of the school district authorities, who will consider availability of time and money and the particular skills needed. Remember that the professional title does not necessarily imply competence to carry out certain functions within an actual school setting.

IMPORTANCE OF APPROPRIATE ATTITUDES FOR THE TEACHER

Let us re-emphasize the significance of the teacher as the pivotal factor in classroom mangement and in the classroom mental health climate. We will not belabor the point by a lengthy discussion of the teacher's role in providing a milieu in which children may learn and grow, both mentally and emotionally. A brief examination of current school practices, however, will quickly point out the fact that the idea is often more honored in the breech than in the observance. Those who train teachers must keep in mind the importance of helping teachers to develop feelings of value and of worth and to understand personality deviations, disorders, and conflicts, so that they may be able to cope with them without feeling threatened. Perhaps the most important factor as far as the teacher's mental health is concerned is his confidence in himself and in his ability to do what must be done. This presupposes that the teacher will bring to the students factual knowledge concerning the subject matter, but in addition, the teacher must be aware of personality dynamics, communication, child growth and development, and emotional factors as they relate to good classroom procedures. The teacher must develop self-monitoring processes by which he may observe his own behavior in relationship to children's reactions in the classroom. If the children react in an inappropriate manner, the teacher's first question should be, What should I do to obtain a more effective type of behavior, so that the child may learn in a more effective manner? Teachers must be objective about each situation and not feel that they are on trial. Above all, teachers must realize their own fallibility. Every teacher makes errors; the point is not to dwell on these mistakes but rather to learn from them. If teachers view the classroom as an interesting challenge to which they may apply all their abilities and knowledge in an attempt to devise learning situations, they will become less defensive, feel more secure, and thus be able to exhibit a better mental health pattern in the classroom.

GENERAL OBJECTIVES OF PROGRAMS

In order to design appropriate curricula for exceptional children, the goals of such programs must be clearly stated. The general goals and objectives should include, as a minimum, the following features:

1. The program should develop emotional security and independence in the school and in the home through a climate conducive to good mental health.

2. The educational program should teach children to enjoy their leisure time by the proper use of recreational activities.

3. It should help children to become adequate members of the community by emphasizing community participation.

4. The students may become adequate members of their families through an educational program that stresses home membership and function as a part of the curriculum.

5. The program should provide for basic school subjects to the extent that the students' intellectual abilities permit. Even though these abilities may have limitations, each student's potential should be maximized.

6. It should help students to develop good relationships with others by providing for opportunities in which students may cooperate and work with their peers in the classroom.

7. The students are entitled to work experience which will prepare them to support themselves and to take their normal place in the community as economically self-sufficient individuals. This opportunity may be realized by a work-study program.

8. The school curriculum should teach the students good health and sanitation habits through appropriate health procedures.

These general goals should allow all exceptional children to achieve economic, social, and civic competencies. There is little available evidence that exceptional individuals cannot function adequately in this

Figure 14–1 The curriculum should satisfy children's needs. (Courtesy of The Woods Schools, Langhorne, Pennsylvania.)

Figure 14–2 Learning good health habits.

regard. Indeed, the bulk of evidence indicates that proper sequential curricula can, in most instances, graduate individuals who can function adequately with respect to furnishing their own economic, social, and civic needs.

Integration of Exceptional Children with Other Children

A frequently unstated goal of all programs is the integration of the exceptional child with the regular school population. In order for some integration to take place, the following points should be considered:

1. The principal's role includes creating a climate within the school which will enable the integration of exceptional students with regular students. Therefore, administrators should be required to take special courses which will equip them with a working knowledge of exceptional children.
2. As part of the training program, special education teachers should be taught how to work with their peers in the public schools in order to inform them of the nature and functions of exceptional children and thus promote a climate in the school which is conducive to integration of special and regular school children.
3. Increasingly, regular classroom teachers should be provided with training during the course of their teaching education or in-service education which will assist them in accepting and working with exceptionalities within their classrooms.
4. Schools with both regular and exceptional children should have some sort of training program for regular students to familiarize them with the nature of exceptional children, so that they may more readily accept them within the school setting.
5. It is essential that an exceptional child in a regular public school be equipped with the basic skills, knowledge, and behaviors which will make him more acceptable to the regular school population.

Evaluation

A basic part of any school program is the evaluative procedure as a means of gaining feedback. More and more, authorities are requiring that evaluations be built into all programs from the beginning (Kirk, 1972). In designing curricula for exceptional children, one should consider the evaluative procedure in light of the following questions:

1. Upon completion of the program, what will be expected of those individuals who have participated in it? What skills, attitudes, and knowledge should they have acquired as a result of the program?
2. Are the expectations of the program appropriate and are they obtainable, considering the nature of the particular learner who will be involved in the program?
3. Do the methods outlined in the program best meet the needs of the learner and do they form consistent patterns with the goals outlined for the program?
4. What types of materials and equipment will be needed to achieve in full the desired results outlined in the program?
5. What provisions are made in the program for evaluating the student's progress? How will the progress be reported to parents, and how will it be recorded in the student's permanent record?
6. Does the program provide for starting at the child's level and progressing according to his abilities?
7. Are the goals of the program for intellectual exceptionalities in concurrence with the generally approved goals outlined by society for its normally functioning members?
8. Does the program allow for supervision and specialized assistance for the teacher of intellectual exceptionalities in order that the program be fully implemented?
9. Are auxiliary services available to assist classroom personnel in developing appropriate methods for achieving the program's goals?

One of the greater deficiencies of modern education is failure to evaluate its programs. All procedures should be subjected to consistent scrutiny in order to ascertain what kinds of problems exist and how successful we are in doing what we have set out to do. It is unfortunate that many in public school education appear to be reluctant to assess the system's effectiveness.

Other Aspects of Program Design

An essential component of all programs designed for exceptional children is the school-community relationship. The education of exceptional students is, in reality, a problem of the community. The community and the school should cooperatively design programs that will assist these students in assuming relatively normal roles in the community. Some administrative concerns in designing special programs, of necessity, center on financial problems. There are many ways of financing programs for intellectual exceptionalities throughout the United States. In general, financial aid for school programs is furnished by the following sources: district funds which are raised from local taxes, basic school aid funds, specialized equalization funds designed to assist the excess cost factor of educating exceptionalities, and federal funds, which are being utilized for many programs (Kirk, 1972).

Many aspects must be considered in setting up special programs in the public schools. In the past, a major consideration has been whether or not to design separate classes for EMR children. Dunn (1963) summarized the research on regular vs. special class placement for EMR children as follows:

> **The data suggest that retarded pupils who remain in the regular grades slip further and further behind, until finally their gains and achievements are only about one third of expectancy. In the meantime, the brighter pupils have been neglected and the mental health of the teacher and retarded pupils is badly strained.**

Special class placement for the educable mentally retarded child may be justified on four major counts: (1) to provide a more adequate curriculum which stresses the development of social and vocational skills as well as the acquisition of skills in the basic school subjects; (2) to allow for more individualized instruction; (3) to remove the pressure on the child by reducing failure and providing a sound mental health approach; and (4) to enable the regular teacher to give more attention to average and bright students when the range of individual differences in regular classes is reduced.

Special classrooms should be located so that education of exceptional children may be undertaken in normally functioning elementary and secondary schools. In other words, children with exceptionalities need to attend the same schools as their relatives and friends do. This point of view is supported by Kirk (1972): "... special classes for mentally retarded children should be organized within regular elementary and secondary schools. In school systems, one elementary school from among three or four can be selected to house one or two special classes. It is preferable to have the children go to a neighborhood school rather than to one central school." The rationale behind the above statement is based on the concept that it is essential for any special program to offer services which do not set the individual child apart from his peers any more than is necessary to achieve the goals of the program.

The number of special classrooms will, of course, vary in different school districts in accordance with the need. The incidence of intellectual retardation and other exceptionalities in school districts varies, since functional intellectual retardation appears to be related to sociological factors. The number of special classrooms should never oversaturate a given elementary school. The classrooms should be large enough to provide adequate space for an activity-centered type of program.

The minimal requirements of special classrooms include: adequate lighting and ventilation; adequate temperature control; effective sound control; sufficient floor space for program activities; maximal flexibility of the classroom arrangement; adequate bulletin board and chalkboard space; hot and cold water and access to a sink and drinking fountain; adequate storage space for clothing, supplies, files, and the like; tables and chairs for work stations and additional work tables; room darkening equipment for the use of audiovisual materials; a teacher's desk; a locked file cabinet; attractive decorations; and a large number of electrical outlets. The special classroom should be designed to facilitate activities in the following categories: personal hygiene and grooming, physical development and coordination, manual skills and dexterity through arts and crafts, social development and interaction, communication skills, and pre-readiness and readiness for the basic school subjects of reading, writing, and arithmetic.

MANAGEMENT PROCEDURES FOR EXCEPTIONAL CHILDREN

The exceptional child should, in general, be expected to behave in school in a manner comparable to other children of his or her age. There is no evidence from the research literature that exceptionality is an excuse for misbehavior. The same basic procedures utilized in coping with other children are appropriate for children with exceptionalities. There are no specific management procedures for exceptional children, with the possible exception that these children are more susceptible to intervention by authority figures than are children of the same age in the normal population.

Good instructional procedure is a basic part of the classroom organization; it should be adapted for the individual in a prescriptive mode. Perhaps the most exhaustive and clear-cut directions for coping with the behavior of children in the classroom are those procedures outlined by Long and Newman (1971). The four major alternatives which they suggested are: (1) permitting behavior, (2) tolerating behavior, (3) interfering with behavior, and (4) preventive planning.

Some practical ways of influencing behavior include: (1) Planned ignoring: Sometimes it is wise for the teacher to ignore a child's behavior, assuming that it will not be imitated by others and that the child will soon discontinue it and turn his attention to learning activities. (2) Signal interference: These are nonverbal techniques, such as eye contact, hand gestures, facial expressions, and body posture, that communicate to the children the teacher's disapproval and thus re-establish control. (3) Proximity control: The teacher places himself in close proximity to the child and gently places his hand on the child's shoulder, thus helping the child to control his impulses. (4) Interest boosting: If a child's interest in an activity is waning, it is sometimes helpful for the teacher to show genuine interest in the child's assignment or in one of his personal interests. This often results in helping the child to mobilize his efforts in an attempt to please the teacher. (5) Tension decontamination: A humorous comment by the teacher often helps to relieve a tense and anxiety-producing situation, so that everyone will feel more comfortable. (6) Successful lessons: The teacher should help the child when he is frustrated by a classroom assignment that he does not understand or that is too complicated for him. In this way, he will not transfer his frustration into nonattentive or disruptive motor behavior. (7) Restructuring the classroom program: Sometimes it is necessary for the teacher to deviate from his regular scheduled program when it appears that the class is not fully prepared for the planned activity, since learning will not be likely to occur under these conditions. (8) Supportiveness of routine: A daily schedule or program will help some children to feel more secure, less anxious, and therefore more able to channel their energies into learning activities. (9) Direct appeal to value areas: It is sometimes possible to appeal to students by way of internalized values rather than to make an issue of some behavior in an attempt to prove that you are in control. (10) Removing seductive objects: The teacher can often quietly remove objects which are distracting the child without interrupting the teaching process. (11) Antiseptic measures: When a child's behavior reaches a point at which the teacher questions whether the child will respond to verbal controls, a short trip around the room or to the drinking fountain or an "important" errand will give the child a chance to regain his self-control. (12) Physical restraint: If a child loses complete control so that he may injure himself or others, it will be necessary to restrain him physically (Long et al., 1971).

Good management methods for all children will facilitate careful planning and the use of structured classroom procedures, interesting material, and individualized instructional materials in a class actively involved in the learning process.

Curricular Modifications as a Management Procedure

School personnel often fail to realize that much of the observed maladaptive (or apparently maladaptive) behavior of children in a school setting is derived from the environment and not primarily from the student or the teacher. One of the least explored ways of working with children who fail to conform to proper school behavior is that of curricular adjustment. A basic rule regarding behavior should always be remembered: people who are doing things in which they are seriously interested rarely tend to exhibit maladaptive behavior. In other words, children who sleep in the classroom, talk out of turn, or misbehave frequently use these behaviors to protest to what they are required to learn. It is difficult for the average child to see the relevance of much of the material that is presented to him, and indeed, it is true that many of the current curricula are essentially irrelevant to the majority of students. Is it not illogical to expect conforming behavior of children who are faced with irrelevant curricula? A most rewarding area of behavioral management would involve teachers' examining what they are accomplishing in terms of their teaching goals. They might consider whether or not the subject matter is being taught in a manner which is interesting or whether the material is relevant to the child and to his experiences. All individuals understand best those things which they are able to relate to. The curriculum should be devised primarily to meet the needs of the child. Thus, material should be presented on a sequential basis—that is, taught to the student at the most appropriate moment for him to learn the particular subject matter.

Teachers should keep in mind that all curricula are selective with regard to subject matter. Since it is impossible to study all the current knowledge in even a small segment of any field, only the most relevant subject matter should be presented. Unfortunately, most currently existing curricula derive their status largely from historical practices rather than from an analysis of current society and current needs. We suggest that each curriculum be explored in light of the question, Does it meet social reality? The result of all education should be that a child will be more able to cope with a constantly changing environment. A curriculum which is presented in a rigid manner by a rigid instructor seems unlikely to be able to fulfill this goal.

Parental Counseling and Classroom Management

One of the least explored avenues of classroom management is parental involvement. We are not referring to the practice of complaining to parents about the misbehavior of their child in the hopes that they will punish him for his maladaptive behavior. We are suggesting that the parent-teacher combination provides a powerful instrument by which to obtain desired behavior. After the teacher has become adept at interviewing parents, it is quite possible that they may develop a rapport and be able to plan programs jointly which will eventuate in the child's developing behavior conducive to learning. If teachers and parents are genuinely concerned about the well-being of their children, they should work cooperatively to determine what steps should be taken in order to help them. These might include revisions in the curriculum or in the length of the school day or any other alterations that may help the child to benefit from his learning situation. Teachers should develop skills and competency in interviewing parents. Together, schools and parents can create policies, ideas, and procedures which will, hopefully, produce a more effective education program for all children.

Organizational and Environmental Considerations

When coping with children who exhibit emotional problems, attention must be given to the organization and environment of the classroom. The teacher should keep in mind that factors such as the physical arrangement of the classroom and the scheduling of activities within the school affect the management of children. The following basic techniques have been found to be effective in helping teachers to manage classroom behavior:

1. The teacher should have the daily schedule well planned and, preferably, written down so that the school day will proceed in a logical, orderly, and systematic fashion.

2. Since the teacher has many individuals in his classroom, his program should be devised to provide the maximal amount of individual instruction in accordance with such factors as availability of time and materials.

3. The daily routine should be well established to furnish structure and consistency for the students in the classroom. In general, students dislike ambiguity, uncertainty, and whimsical behavior in the learning environment.

4. The teacher should observe the behavior of students at all times. This will frequently enable intervention before misbehavior disturbs the class or is engaged in by other students.

5. The teacher should maintain a positive frame of reference in reacting to student behavior and should realize that the behavior of children is usually not directed at the teacher but rather at the frustrations involved in a given situation.

6. The teacher should reward and pay attention to desirable behavior and should ignore undesirable behavior as much as possible, remembering that attending to behavior is reinforcing and rewarding. If maladaptive behavior is noticed, it tends to occur in ever-increasing amounts and thus brings about the use of aversive procedures which may, in many cases, become self-defeating.

7. Lessons should be planned by the teacher in increments according to the developmental stage and attention span of the children. If the children have a 15-minute attention span, no assignment should require more than 15 minutes to complete.

8. Peer teaching frequently offers the teacher a considerable amount of assistance. Students who have accomplished a certain task may assist others who are still working on the assignment and may be of great value in helping other students to learn.

9. All directions should be specific, short, and consistent. The

student must know exactly what is required of him in order to meet the teacher's expectations.

10. All assignments should be as realistic as possible, even in light of many districts' curriculum requirements.

11. An important fact to remember is that a student's self-concept is improved when he is successful in doing things which he considers important.

12. Much behavior in the classroom stems from home conditions. Therefore, within reasonable limits, the teacher must maintain good home-school relations and should work with all parents as much as possible.

13. Students must be kept constantly informed as to their progress in their school work and usually want information with regard to two areas: their performance in relationship to their peers and in relationship to themselves. It is suggested that the latter be more frequently discussed than the former.

CURRICULUM AND LEARNING DISABILITIES

Educational Prescriptions and Recommendations for Remediation

A few comments may be helpful to the regular classroom teacher concerning education of learning disabled children in the public school.

At all costs, the teacher should avoid significantly differentiating her teaching procedures for the learning disabled child from those utilized for other children; no child likes to gain attention by being made an example. One of the more appropriate methods of approaching the problem is by way of task analysis. Task analysis involves analyzing the method or mode by which an individual behaves in a learning environment. The first task might be to make an analysis of intrasensory factors, such as auditory discrimination. The next task might include an examination of which modalities are utilized by certain children and the ways in which they are utilized. The ability of the child to use verbal or nonverbal modalities should be investigated as well as the level of functioning for a given task. Since many tasks can be assigned at a number of levels, the appropriate level must be utilized for a given treatment. The teacher must also decide what kind of response will be expected of the student. There are three possible responses that a teacher may require: a "picking up" kind of response, such as gesturing, pointing, or moving; a verbal or oral response; or a written response. These suggestions are more fully outlined by Bateman (1964).

Bateman lists three approaches for the selection and planning of educational procedures for children with learning disabilities:

1. The Etiological Approach. The etiological approach centers on the goal of eventually eliminating the learning problem by prevention or scientific treatment of the condition. Because of the limited knowledge of this approach and of its relationship to specific learning problems, this particular plan is not the most frequently employed method in the classroom.

2. The Diagnostic or Remediation Approach. The use of assessment instruments precedes the application of this approach. Deficits are discovered, and then procedures are instituted to remediate or, at least, modify the effects of the deficits in relationship to learning.

3. The Task Analysis Approach. This method is somewhat similar to the remediation approach. It is concerned largely with the development of behavior and focuses on the behavioristic approach to education, with a minimization of the importance of the child's teleological development. Behavior modification has been employed with children having learning problems as reported by Ullmann and Krasner (1965). (See Chapter 13). Valett (1967) presents a comprehensive approach to task analysis with the learning disabled child. He compiled some 229 test items, selected from a variety of other tests, which theoretically are related to educational recommendations or treatment. They concern factors such as motor integration, physical development, tactual discrimination, auditory discrimination, language development, verbal fluency, visual-motor coordination, and conceptual development. The Valett test items are divided into the following general categories: gross motor development—rolling, sitting, crawling, jumping, and dancing; sensory-motor integration—balance and rhythm, tactile discrimination, and laterality; perceptual-motor skills—auditory acuity, auditory memory, auditory sequencing, visual-form discrimination, visual memory, and visual-motor fine muscle coordination; language development—vocabulary, spelling, word attack skills, and articulation; conceptual skills—number concepts, arithmetic processes, general information, and classification; social skills—social acceptance, anticipatory response, value judgments, and social maturity. The test items which the child fails are examined, and treatment follows from the particular deficits which are found.

Another approach to task analysis is that of Bereiter and Englemann (1966). Their method is a systematic analysis of a task in order of difficulty from most simple to most difficult. The Bereiter technique (1966) includes the following 18 procedures:

"1. Work at different levels of difficulty at different times.
2. Adhere to a rigid, repetitive presentation pattern.
3. Use unison responses whenever possible.
4. Never work with a child individually in a study group for more than about 30 seconds.
5. Phrase statements rhythmically.
6. Require children to speak in a loud, clear voice.
7. Do not hurry children or encourage them to talk fast.
8. Clap to accent basic language patterns and conventions.
9. Use questions liberally.
10. Use repetition.
11. Be aware of the cues the child is receiving.
12. Use short explanations.
13. Tailor the explanations and rules to what the child knows.
14. Use lots of examples.
15. Prevent incorrect responses whenever possible.
16. Be completely unambiguous in letting the child know when his response is correct and when it is incorrect.
17. Dramatize the use value of learning whenever possible.
18. Encourage thinking behavior."

Bereiter and Englemann's approach is not concerned with whether or not normal children exhibit certain performance levels of behavior, but rather it is related to the specific needs of the particular child which must be met in order for him to perform certain kinds of educational tasks. For example, if the goal is the ability to succeed in the first grade, then certain tasks (in the case of Bereiter and Englemann, 15 tasks) must necessarily be taught to the preschooler. They developed specific approaches or techniques for teaching those tasks which are essential for the child to learn, according to their theoretical system. They stress the teacher's role in education and have frankly stated that if the child does not learn, it is the fault of the teacher and not of the child. In such cases, they would conclude that the child had not been properly taught.

All three approaches may be used singly or conjointly. At present, each of the methods should be further explored in order to determine clearly the effects of each. The etiological approach can probably best be utilized by psychologists, medical doctors, or other specialists, whereas teachers should be more concerned with either the remediation or the task analysis approach to provide optimal learning opportunities for their students.

Teachers should be particularly aware of students who have short attention spans. Tasks should be devised that are suited to the amount of attention that a child is able to exhibit. Of course, the teacher should seek to expand the attention span by every possible method. Tasks should be highly specific and structured and should be assigned in a very direct, matter-of-fact way. As the child learns the tasks, he should be rewarded by being provided with success experiences, which include having his accomplishments noticed by the teacher and the class. Tasks should be assigned in small increments, since presentations which are too lengthy may be confusing. For example, a whole page of arithmetic problems may be more than the child can cope with, and it may be necessary for the teacher to present the problems singly or, at most, with two or three widely spaced on a page.

Classroom Instruction for the Learning Disabled Child

Many approaches are possible in treating or educating children with behavior disorders or learning disabilities. The three basic theoretical approaches, however, are the psychodynamic, psychoneurological, and psychoeducational methods.

The psychoneurological model has been accurately described by Struther (1963):

Psychoneurological Model

1. General personality characteristics
   a. hyperactivity, restlessness, aimlessness, random movement
   b. distractability—uncontrollably drawn to all new stimuli
   c. impulsivity—spontaneous and compelling inclination to respond
   d. emotional instability—sudden mood changes, exaggerated and inappropriate emotional responses
2. Specific disabilities
   a. perceptual disorders—errors in form discrimination, form consistency, and spatial orientation
   b. motor disorders—incoordination, awkwardness, clumsiness
   c. language disorders—errors in processing auditory components of speech, inability to associate words with objects, confusion as to time and sequential patterns
   d. concept formation and reasoning disorders—inability to grasp concepts or to make associations between ideas, faulty judgment of relevance of associations

Struther's list is comprehensive and attempts to fit a number of conditions into a comprehensive organizational system. This approach tends to lean toward medical psychological treatment procedures. The basic underlying cause of the disability according to this theory is injury or damage to the central nervous system either during or after the pregnancy. Many well-known authors have advocated this type of approach. The major supporters of it for the treatment and understanding of learning disabilities are Bender and Strauss. The treatment is outlined by the medical etiological model which includes the application of drug therapy, physical therapy, and physical training processes. Some of the more popular terms utilized in this approach are alexia, aphasia, dyslexia, minimal brain damage, autism, hyperkinesis, and word blindness.

Psychodynamic Model

According to the psychodynamic school of thought, the child's behavior is largely a result of environmental forces; the parents are often thought to be the cause of the child's maladjustment through the use of improper child-rearing practices. As a result, the child's social values may be in conflict. For example, a child from a slum area who attends a middle-class school may exhibit a poor self-concept. The diagnostic procedures which are employed for such problems necessarily involve psychological devices, such as projective techniques, case histories, observations, and other intensive assessment and evaluative procedures. A major supporter of this approach has been Bettelheim. As with most psychodynamic theories, the proposed method of treatment is psychotherapy involving the parents, the child, or with increasing frequency, both parents and child. With this method, attempts have been made to improve environmental situations in order to solve behavior problems. Remediation through educational intervention is often proposed. Some psychodynamic terms which describe the behaviorally disordered child are: passive-aggressive, emotional blocking, insecurity, immaturity, motor incoordination, and poor social or emotional adjustment.

Psychoeducational Model

The psychoeducational model calls for diagnostic procedures involving carefully composed case histories, observations, and careful assessment of all learning components. Well-known advocates of this model have been Bateman, Frierson, Frostig. Hewett, Barsch, Kirk, and McCarthy. The basic treatment model focuses on compensatory training and correctional remediation. Children treated according to the psychoeducational approach are often labeled as perceptually damaged, educationally disabled, or disabled in auditory or visual perception; they may have figure-ground confusion, short- or long-term memory deficits, or laterality problems. The best and perhaps most comprehensive outline of the psychoeducational approach is that of Bateman (1965). Four major categories are included in the psychoeducational approach:

1. Sensory skills
   a. auditory and visual perception
   b. visual and auditory discrimination
   c. auditory and visual functioning

   d. visual and auditory memory
   e. kinesthetic sensitivity
2. Motor skills
   a. eye-hand coordination
   b. laterality
   c. perceptual speed
3. Language skills
   a. temporal sequencing
   b. verbal facility
   c. language comprehension
4. Association skills
   a. selective capacity for attending
   b. auditory-visual association
   c. speech orientation

In this particular approach, the etiology is of minor importance and is not as concerned with medical models as the two preceding theories. From the viewpoint of psychoeducational theorists, diagnosis is primarily devoted to matching a specific prescription with a particular disability. After the specific disability has been pinpointed, every effort is made to provide remedial activities to eliminate or at least to modify the effects of the deficits. It might be found, for example, that a reading disability is related to memory deficits; this condition would be treated by attempting to eliminate the memory deficit. The approach employs practical methods by which to treat the specific difficulties involved. Training may be said to be the key word in educating the learning disabled child. It is tacitly, even explicitly, accepted by theorists in this field that damage may be repaired. Inadequacies in this theory center on the tendency to use labels merely to discuss the nature of the problem, that is, to determine all the problems that a child may have but to make no specific provisions for treatment. Most programs in public schools are tailored for the central two-thirds of the school population. The psychoeducational model proposes a diversification of formal academic methods in order to include such areas as motor development, perceptual training, concept formation, impulse control, and self-concept improvement. Problems may stem from a lack of trained personnel in the school district who may serve to organize the programs and provide adequate treatment. Effective application of the psychoeducational approach demands that supportive personnel be available in the school district. School psychologists, physicians, nurses, social workers, and guidance counselors all may contribute to the educational needs of each child. The lack of a properly trained staff makes it difficult for adequate provisions to be made under the psychoeducational model, or indeed under any of the models.

Intensive diagnosis followed by highly individualized instructional procedures to remediate or to modify problems found during the diagnostic process is the basis of the psychoeducational approach. The most fruitful course of action involves the resource teacher in conjunction with the regular classroom teacher. There are literally millions of learning disabled children in the public schools of the United States. Therefore, it is highly unrealistic to propose that these children be provided with special classrooms. Indeed a general rule for the treatment of all exceptionalities should be that no child receive intervention procedures that are more drastic or extensive than those which are needed to accomplish the goals. The further a child is removed from the mainstream of education, the more difficult it is for him to return. The resource room model allows for some specialized instruction of the child and in addition provides assistance for the classroom teacher in obtaining appropriate materials. We hope that such a model may lead to increased awareness on the part of classroom teachers, so that all students may be viewed as highly individual and worthy of specific programs designed for their particular needs.

Intervention Strategies

Intervention may take many forms. The key factor in working with all exceptional children is the attitude of the classroom teacher, for it determines many of the subtle environmental factors which influence the child's learning. Teachers must be aware of how their own behavior affects the learning environment of their students. Intervention should be the result of carefully planned procedures stemming from extensive diagnostic processes and consultation with associate personnel. It must be based on all available knowledge, with emphasis on what seems most likely to work, and should allow for a means of evaluating whether the procedure does work. Intervention strategies may include mild remedial procedures, such as exercises of various types, or more extensive procedures, such as the use of cubicles in the classroom, removal of the child from the classroom, or instituting a limited day for the child. Intervention procedures should be utilized only after all factors have been considered. The child's ability to progress when a particular means of intervention is used should be the ultimate criterion by which all procedures are judged.

SCHOOLS AND CURRICULA FOR THE DISADVANTAGED

In the past, school programs have concentrated on the common aspirations of the middle class; they have been oriented toward a life style in which "getting ahead" is the major theme. The lower socioeconomic groups, however, tend to have other values.

Teachers and other school personnel often assume that everyone has the same basic value system as they have. Careful consideration shows this to be a false assumption. The United States is composed of many cultures which have many different value systems.

Current school curricula are extremely rigid in their construction. It is assumed that all children must fit the curriculum rather than that the curriculum should fit the child. Schools assume that there are certain basic kinds of knowledge that are necessary for all children. We suggest that this tendency toward rigid curricula must be thoroughly explored.

The American society still tends to be intolerant of that which is different. For years, teachers have given lip service to the ideals of individual differences and a democratic way of life. Yet, all one must do is examine the current school systems to become aware that these ideals are not put into practice. That which is different is frowned upon. For example, the first-grade child who discovers an alternate answer to an arithmetic problem is told that he is wrong or made to feel stupid because he failed to conform to the teacher's preconceived idea of "what is correct."

The current school curriculum must be carefully examined in light of its effect on a child's development. As we have previously pointed out, each child enters school with a hidden cirriculum. The disadvantaged child is frequently a casualty of our current educational system, as noted in the following quotation: "The dropouts, by and large, don't like middle class culture. . . . Dropping out is one way of telling us, and it is about time that we turned our attention to the things about the school that are 'bugging them'" (Friedenberg, 1965).

Criticism of the current approach to general education applies to several areas. Many current curriculum practices are indicative of a life style in which all members of the family are happy, have plenty to eat, and live in secure and pleasant surroundings. How can we expect children, who are subjected to such distortion of reality during their early years, to become mature and enlightened adults? The middle-class values of many curricula are communicated to children, not only by reading materials but in many ways throughout the school day, such as the way teachers dress, eat, or teach. The school demands that children act according to their own experiences and sense of judgment and at the same time expects them to accept the school's version of reality. Today's generally accepted curriculum ignores reality and will probably have long-term detrimental effects on many children, not just those of lower-class backgrounds.

The second problem concerning current school curricula involves the nonessential school curriculum. Do you remember the many "objective facts" that you have been required to learn throughout your education? And yet, would you feel comfortable about taking a standard high school algebra examination or a test on Silas Marner? There is a great amount of useless subject matter in the formal cirriculum. The absence of any content dealing with how people feel and how they behave has been pointed out by Havighurst (1970). It seems that schools have found it more sensible to instruct students in geography, grammar, and the multiplication tables than to spend some time each day helping children to understand their behavior and the behavior of others. Because most children's needs are ignored in the curriculum, they must acquire much of their knowledge through informal educational means. A child's major concerns involve understanding his own emotions and how to get along with others, both of which require the child to have a good reference system.

Still another problem is the limited curriculum. How frequently do teachers respond to student's questions with such answers as: "when you grow up you will have to know this"; "studying colonial times will help you to understand our life today"; "we are studying nutrition, so that when you have a family you can help keep them healthy"; "pay attention in class now at the beginning of the term and you will be promoted"; "study in school and you will be able to comprehend these reasons in terms of 'living for tomorrow'." With regard to disadvantaged children, at least three facts are evident:

1. Their learning style is different from the teaching style of the school.
2. What they already know is not utilized by the school.
3. The school manages to avoid helping these students with those matters which they are really concerned about.

In order for education to improve, our society must change many of its basic attitudes and must accept a multivalue system. Schools must provide curricula which are relevant to all students. The problems of environment, population, war and peace, employment, technology, human relations, and above all, how to become increasingly more human are relevant to all individuals. Curricula should be devoted to evolving a society that will be free to become more human and humane.

Providing Basic Tools of Learning

Public schools should no longer accept the failure of any of its students. It is not the child that fails, but rather the teacher, the school, and the family. It is foolish to prescribe unrealistic and remote learning tasks in an aseptic environment and then expect children to be responsive, interested, and curious. However, to provide every child with the means for acquiring knowledge of his environment is essential. Reading, listening, and the use of mathematics to solve everyday mathematical problems are the basic tools in our current society. These three tools are necessary if the child is to learn to function adequately. At present, reading is still the most efficient way of acquiring knowledge. In the future, perhaps other methods will be developed, but currently reading is one of the most effective methods of learning. Therefore, all children should be taught to read well, and all the current reading research clearly indicates that there is no reason why every child cannot learn to read at least at his mental age level.

Nutritional Factors

It is important that our society provide adequate nutrition for all its citizens. A poorly fed population tends to be unresponsive, irrational, erratic, and poorly behaved. (Hungry people are not usually very reasonable.) Moreover, early malnutrition may lead to permanent brain damage, and thus individuals who might have made vital contributions to our society will not reach their full potentials.

The Need for Early Assistance

All current research indicates that the earlier the child receives assistance, the more effective it will be. Children up to about 18 months of age appear to be very similar in cognitive development, but after this age, a rapid divergence takes place which is dependent on many variables, such as the family, the home, and the community environments.

Language and Nonverbal Communication

The importance of language and of nonverbal communication cannot be overstressed. All teachers should be aware of the implications of the new studies in linguistics and semantics. Incongruity between the spoken word and behavior can profoundly influence a child. Too frequently teachers and parents say one thing to a child, while conveying a different meaning by body stance, tone of voice, or their own actions. It is essential that language be presented in a way which increases the scope of a child's cognitive and affective domains.

Amelioration of Poor Language (Usage). Since one of the most prevalent problems of disadvantaged and deprived children is poor language usage, investigators in the area of language have provided some specific suggestions for enhancing language development. Newton (1964) stated that "proficiency in both vocal and written language is fundamental to a citizen's social, intellectual, and economic well being," and added that "the line that separates the intellectually advantaged from the intellectually disadvantaged is the language line." She listed the following premises: (1) vocal (or oral) language is the most important of the communicative arts; (2) visual (or written) language is a conventionalized, coded representation of vocal language; (3) there is a universal sequence in developing the use of language; (4) speaking and writing perform the same function in the communicative cycle; (5) listening, speaking, reading, and writing vocabularies vary markedly; (6) the structural arrangement of one's native language is learned automatically in infancy and early childhood through auditory perception and vocal imitation; and (7) the structure of American English poses formidable problems in the acquisition of its written form. Newton stated that "the verbal environment of the first years of life occupies a crucial place in the language development of the individual."

Based on the foregoing premises, Newton suggested a language arts program for disadvantaged children and youth which focuses on the following principles: (1) the language arts program should be a continuum of linguistic experience from nursery school through grade 12; (2) development of proficiency in reading should be the dominant concern; (3) the thinking process should be an integral part of language activities; (4) many varied audiovisual materials should be utilized to reinforce multisensory learning; (5) teachers of the verbally handicapped must avoid alienating the pupil from the teaching-learning experience; (6) the language teacher must function as a prototype in all communicative situations; and (7) promising instructional innovations, such as the use of learning machines, books reflecting the culture, peer teaching, and provisions for learning standard language patterns, as one would a second language, should be experimented with. Developing good language skills will not guarantee these children success, but without these skills they do not stand a chance.

Normally, language develops from listening to speaking and then from reading to writing. All people have different vocabularies for each of these four modes of communication. Children from disadvantaged homes have vocabularies that vary markedly from the standard in all four modes. Basic language patterns are learned automatically, and thus it has been suggested that it might be helpful, at first, to teach disadvantaged children standard English as a foreign language, with emphasis on listening and speaking. In this manner, they could learn the basic patterns of standard language in order to form a basis for reading and writing skills. With increased and appropriate auditory-visual input, the child's output capability should be enhanced as he enters the middle-class–oriented educational world. With improved initial output as the result of increased input, the child should receive immediate positive feedback, which will serve to increase input further. Thus, the negative cycle could perhaps be broken, and a more positive one might be initiated.

EDUCATING THE ORGANICALLY AND PHYSICALLY HANDICAPPED

Role of the Public Schools

The role of public schools in educating the organically and physically handicapped is in a state of flux at present. The most common mode of treatment in the past has been to educate these children in special facilities operated by a variety of social and public agencies, such as the Crippled Children's Society or the state division on crippled children. As with other exceptionalities, it is possible to see a movement toward a more integrated approach. Little research has been conducted to validate the superiority of educating such children in the regular classrooms of public schools rather than in special facilities (Kirk, 1972). We contend, however, that unless there are special circumstances, it is generally preferable to educate these children in as nearly normal a setting as possible. This viewpoint is consistent with the previously stated principle that it is best to intervene in any educational system only when necessary to obtain the desired results and with the conceptual input-output model presented in Chapter 1. Cultural factors are important influences in the development of any individual, and thus a drastic variation in the culture is certain to affect the input and, consequently, the output with regard to social adaptation and blending with the total culture.

Educational Treatment

In general, the physically impaired child does not have the intellectual limitations which are characteristic of other exceptionalities (Kirk, 1972). The major concern of regular schools is to make the special adaptations to the physical environment that may be needed.

In addition to educating physically impaired children in regular classrooms, there is often a need to make special provisions for acute or chronic cases. Many states make these provisions in the education code for homebound and hospital teaching. The majority of physically impaired children participate in these two programs on a temporary basis, and thus these are essentially adjunctive educational programs, designed to help students keep up with their classmates.

Many innovative and unique programs have been developed, so that education might be provided for those children who, because of physical or psychological problems, have been unable to attend regular schools. Modern communication technology has made it possible for a child in his home to have full communication with his class in a two-way exchange. The trauma of hospitalization has, to some extent, been lessened by the hospital teacher who provides continuity of lessons and a structured program by which the hospitalized child may continue to learn. Homebound teachers educate many chronically ill as well as temporarily ill children in the home. It is customary for hospital and homebound teachers to keep in contact with the child's regular teacher in order to assign similar types of educational experiences. An important part of the hospital and homebound instructional programs is the necessity for individual instruction; the diversity of the children forces a flexible approach to education.

Providing education for the physically handicapped child has prompted public authorities to examine the nature of the physical environment. Many of the older school buildings with their long, narrow flights of stairs present nearly impossible barriers for physically impaired students. The need for special bathroom facilities for children in wheel chairs has caused planners of new school buildings to design appropriate structures for all children. In some states, laws have been passed making it mandatory that all public buildings have ramps and other accommodations for the physically handicapped. The total physical environment must be carefully examined in order that appropriate adaptations may be made. Classroom procedures may remain relatively the same if the furniture and equipment in the classroom are adapted to the needs of the physically handicapped. Special equipment, such as electric page turners, may be required so that these children may function independently in the classroom.

An essential part of the program for public school education of the physically handicapped child is the provision for transportation. Many states furnish excess cost financing so that special buses may be used to transport the students to school.

Many physically impaired children must be under careful medical supervision. The school and the child's doctor should examine the special problems involved, and together they must devise the best available adaptation for a given child. In addition to homebound and hospital teachers, some school districts provide special schools and special classes for very severely handicapped children. This is probably the most commonly used method of education for such children at present (Kirk, 1972).

In line with the basic concepts presented earlier in this text, we believe that there is a need for public school officials to re-examine the total educational system with the aim of placing as many of these children in the regular classroom as possible. In general, they are of normal intelligence and do not need special curricular provisions with regard to academics. Moreover, both the physically handicapped student and the regular student would benefit by attending classes together. It has been the habit of many individuals to support the concept of individual differences in the school, but not to help put the idea into practice. It is time to create an educational system in which flexibility and individualized educational procedures are the rule rather than the exception.

School Programs

In order for the physically handicapped child to obtain a complete education, his educational program must begin during the preschool years. The preschool curriculum should center on the development of motor and perceptual skills, language skills (including special speech assistance for those children who need it), and interpersonal skills, as well as special assistance for the physically handicapped child in developing an adequate psychological system to cope with his disability.

The elementary school program will, in general, be similar to that of the regular student. In special cases in which a physically handicapped child is mentally retarded, he should be educated in special classes for the mentally retarded, or in some extreme cases, there may be a need for special school placement for a period of time.

By the time physically handicapped children enter secondary school, they should have acquired most of the basic skills and knowledge required in the regular classroom. Many colleges and universities are now providing special ramps and elevators for students in wheel chairs. Again, the major emphasis regarding adequate education for the physically handicapped student at the secondary and college levels is basically on making external changes in the environment which will enable these students to benefit from regular public schooling.

TREATMENT PROCEDURES IN THE SCHOOL FOR THE BEHAVIORALLY DISTURBED CHILD

Owing to the many individuals involved, it is inappropriate to leave the care and treatment of behaviorally disturbed children to the special education teacher. It is estimated that at least 10 per cent of any school population is likely to need some assistance with behavioral problems. A regular classroom teacher may expect a minimum of one disturbed child in a class, but frequently, there are more if we include mildly and moderately disturbed children. As much as 15 to 20 per cent of the class may be involved. This obviously makes it inappropriate to assume that only the special education teacher can cope with behavioral disturbance. To illustrate the extent of this problem, using the 10 per cent figure for a school-age population, we would probably be including a minimum of five million boys and girls who need some type of specialized approach in order to profit from the traditional school programs.

It is imperative that teacher training institutions adequately prepare regular classroom teachers to cope with the problems involved in planning appropriate educational procedures for behaviorally disordered children. It might be of assistance to teachers to note the range of behaviors of these children which is likely to be encountered. The regular classroom teacher is expected to cope with these behaviors either by himself or in conjunction with other appropriate school personnel, such as resource teachers, school psychologists, or school counselors. The behaviors may range from extremely passive, withdrawn types to extreme acting-out hyperactivity. Some children may behave in an overly dependent manner, while others may act in a hostile, aggressive fashion. It should be noted that the mere removal of overt classroom symptoms does not automatically insure that the child will be able to perform academically at an appropriate level. It is essential that the teacher be assisted by the appropriate school personnel and that the school administrator be sensitive to all problems in this area and to the teacher's need for supportive assistance. One factor that regular classroom teachers should consider in dealing with behaviorally disordered children is that such students tend to respond well to a highly structured environment; that is, the school day must be clearly delineated, and educational procedures must be sequenced, structured, and concrete. Many behaviorally disordered children lack the ability to exert inner control. Thus, it is essential that outer control procedures be carefully organized by means of classroom design and programming. Many of these children are impulse ridden (i.e., unable to cope with their own inner drives). Teachers must, therefore, assist them in gaining control of their responses. The physical arrangement of the classroom may require reorganization, so that the behaviorally disordered child may be placed in certain positions in the room to help him to function reasonably well.

The teacher should be especially aware of reinforcing appropriate behaviors and should not allow inappropriate behaviors to be reinforced by the student's peers. The behaviorally disordered child often has a gross misconception of his environment. This frequently involves confusion of signals entering his perceptual system. The teacher must attempt to ascertain what the world is like in terms of the child's perception. The very young behaviorally disordered child may have some difficulty in proper space and time orientation and may not have an adequate awareness of size, shape, form, and color. The teacher should convey to the child her role within the classroom, so that the child can have an appropriate response to the classroom situation. The anxiety induced by a typical classroom situation should be reduced as much as possible especially for the behaviorally disordered child, since undue anxiety tends to impede learning. The child's educational program should be devised specifically in light of the child's deficits and assets and in accordance with his interests and observed needs. The academic process itself may be somewhat therapeutic in that it provides the child with a structured environment and with skills and knowledge which may help him to develop more adequate interpersonal and intrapersonal concepts.

The teacher must realize that teaching involves the whole self and that it is important that there be congruity between his verbal and nonverbal behaviors. Teachers frequently convey erroneous messages to the behaviorally disordered child when there is inconsistency between what they say and what they do. It is important that the child learn to identify with the teacher and that he be able to derive satisfaction from performing the tasks of a regular public school classroom. Teachers must constantly improve their understanding of the relationship between behavior and learning. This may be accomplished by formally attending classes or professional meetings concerned with this topic or by reading professional publications on the subject. As the teacher becomes more able to apply knowledge of human behavior to behaviorally disordered children, the total problem of providing adequate education for them will decrease. Teachers must master instructional procedures and must always be aware of the significance of their own behavior as it affects their teaching. The teacher is the single most important factor in setting the emotional climate of the classroom.

METHODS AND PROGRAMS IN THE SPECIAL CLASSROOM

The most traditional approach for the care and treatment of the behaviorally disordered child has been segregation, placement within the confines of highly structured self-contained classes taught by specialists in educating the behaviorally disordered. It will probably always be necessary for the extremely deviant child (one who is so difficult to cope with that he cannot be handled within the confines of the regular school setting) to be placed in a self-contained environment. It is preferable that the special classroom for the behaviorally disordered child be located within the regular public school in order to facilitate the child's return to the regular classroom. Generally, the further he is removed from a normal setting, the more difficult it is for him to return to normal functioning within the regular classroom. Teachers in self-contained classrooms for behaviorally disordered children must be fully certified and trained if they are to present appropriate educational programs to their students. The classroom must be large enough to allow for a number of learning settings within the room. Every self-contained classroom for severely emotionally disturbed or behaviorally disordered children must have, in addition to the teacher, a teacher's aide, and usually no more than 6 to 8 children should be in the classroom at a time.

An important role of the special education teacher is working with the parent. Parents often exhibit feelings of anxiety and guilt concerning their children. Thus, it is important that the teacher be trained in skills which facilitate the necessary therapeutic processes for working with such children and their parents. The special education teacher must also work closely with the faculty of the school in order that a full understanding of the behavior of these children may be conveyed. The school principal must be fully informed of the nature of the behavioral problems in order to provide appropriate programs for behaviorally disturbed children.

The Resource Classroom Concept

One of the most popular means of care and treatment for exceptional children is the concept of the resource room. The resource room is a kind of interclassroom treatment. It is an attempt to assist the regular teacher in coping with the needs of atypical children. The resource teacher provides intensive, specific instruction as needed for certain children, and at the same time, assists the regular teacher with most of the daily instruction for specific students. A typical procedure is for the behaviorally disordered child to attend the resource room for one to three hours a day. For cases in which the child simply cannot function for any prolonged period in either the resource room or the regular classroom, it may be necessary to place him on a limited day schedule. In this way, he can attend school but is not required to stay a full day, as are regular students. The major role of the resource teacher may be viewed as a facilitator of learning. Resource teachers must have a broad understanding of learning and of behavior and must have stable personalities. They must have a dynamic and flexible approach in order to meet the needs of their students and should be secure in their knowledge of how a child learns and of educational procedures.

Basic rules must be instituted when behaviorally disordered children are placed in resource rooms. The length of time that they are to remain in the resource room and the expectations of such placement must be determined. The entire staff of the school should be fully aware of the resource teacher's role and what they may reasonably expect from his services. Unrealistic expectations lead to disappointment on the part of regular teachers and may lead to total rejection of the procedure. The resource teacher must work in cooperation with regular teachers in order to gain greater insight into the behavior of their students.

The Concept of the Crisis or Helping Teacher

The crisis or helping teacher concept of Morse (1971a) has given rise to many fruitful ideas by mental health professionals. Basically, the concept centers on a skilled practitioner being made available within a local school to cope with any emotional crisis. Morse pointed out that one of the major problems in schools is that they are usually unable or unready to cope with children during crisis situations. Essentially, the crisis teacher is one who is ready to intervene, to help control the situation, or to relieve the regular teacher whenever a child becomes uncontrollable or exhibits patterns of behavior which are deemed extreme in a normal school environment. There is little doubt that children often do exhibit "crisis behavior."

The Morse system for teacher training and for the use of the crisis model offers valuable assistance to teachers and schools. We suggest, however, that the crisis model could be effectively coordinated with the concept of the resource teacher. The crisis model exhibits one major defect: intervention takes place only at moments of extreme behavior. We maintain that most behavior can be predicted prior to its "explosion" and that a resource teacher might offer some preventive assistance to teachers. In this way crises will be alleviated (more on a preventive basis) and the child will benefit more than if he were helped only at moments of stress.

The Life-Space Interview Approach

In terms of classroom management, the psychoanalytic approach is based largely on the assumption that the teacher comprehends the developmental and psychodynamic nature of behavior. Tolerance and understanding of children's behavior will help the teacher to cope more ably with the classroom situation. The life-space interviewing technique (LSI) was developed to help teachers become skilled in talking effectively to children and to help them use this skill as a specific management tool. The main goal of this technique is to assist the child in conforming to and developing certain behavioral standards. It should be pointed out that this is not a moralistic but rather a dynamic approach, based, as was the psychoanalytic approach, on the teacher's ability to improvise and to establish effective relationships with the child.

In contrast to psychotherapy, which is usually conducted in a highly clinical setting, such as a child guidance clinic, the life-space interview takes place in the child's normal environment. As far as the teacher is concerned, LSI fulfills a primary need in that it provides on-the-spot therapy when maladaptive behavior occurs. LSI can be employed when the child is in a state of stress and enables the teacher to re-establish equilibrium. In addition, the technique is applicable because when people are under stress they are more apt to ask for and to accept assistance. LSI is suited for the classroom situation because the teacher has many opportunities to apply "instant therapy." The objectives of LSI are to explore life events clinically and to provide emotional first aid (Redl, 1959).

The teacher is concerned with two kinds of goals: the immediate and the long-range. On occasion, the teacher may need to deal with a crisis situation, while at other times, he may wish to assist the child in achieving long-term goals. Accomplishing long-range goals may involve: (1) presenting a reality orientation to the child who frequently misinterprets his interpersonal relations or who fails to understand existing social circumstances; (2) showing him that his behavior is neither functional nor fruitful; (3) pointing out to the child areas which are unfamiliar to him or to which he is not sensitive, as well as the dominant values at present; (4) helping the child to see by the teacher's own behavior that there are other ways of acting which may be more satisfying for him; and (5) expanding the child's psychological scope, so that he may become aware of and may accept other adults and teachers in order to develop more effective types of behavior.

"Instant therapy" may: (1) help the child rid himself of pent-up hostility, frustration, or aggression; (2) provide the child with support and encouragement, while helping him not to become overwhelmed by feelings of panic or guilt; (3) help him to maintain relationships, so that he will not choose to retreat as a method of coping with a crisis; (4) allow the teacher to supervise social interaction in a way which will assist maladaptive pupils to conform to the rules of the group; and (5) assist the teacher in settling complex situations.

Bernstein (1963) provided the best guidelines for the use of life-space interviewing:

1. Be polite. Offer the child a chair, and produce a tissue if it is

needed. Although teachers and other adults demand good manners from children, they themselves are often guilty of rudeness toward children.

2. Do not tower above a child; bend down to him. Have a chair in the office for very young children and another one for yourself. Be wary of lifting a kindergarten or first-grade child onto a desk or table. Although the action is well-meant, it may cause a frightened child to panic because he feels trapped in midair and cannot get down.

3. Being sure of yourself is a great advantage when using this approach. Confront the child with your knowledge of his misdeed and be firm. This can greatly relieve a child who otherwise might make an effort to deny the facts. Confrontation, however, is not likely to be successful with the child who feels that everyone is his enemy.

4. Be sparing with your use of "why." It is difficult to explore the reasons for a child's actions and all but impossible for a child to explain his motivations. It is much easier to say: "We cannot have this art on the laboratory walls. I will not let you continue. We have to talk about this a little."

5. Encourage conversation about the actual situation. Obtain a description of what happened, and listen to what the child says.

6. If you think a child is overwhelmed with guilt or shame, begin by minimizing the weightiness of the problem at hand by saying, for example: "This action does not bother me too much, but we had better look into it, for it can cause you trouble."

7. Say what you know the child wants to say but cannot put into words: "You were very disappointed, weren't you? You had been counting on this talk for a long time and could not stand to wait any longer."

8. Be aware of the kind of thinking demanded by the particular situation. Bright children frequently become involved in relationships which are beyond their understanding in terms of emotions, personality, and maturity.

Figure 14–3 Winning the confidence of a child (Courtesy of The Woods Schools, Langhorne, Pennsylvania.)

9. Make specific plans with the child to improve the situation.

10. At some point in the interview give the child an opportunity to ask you questions, or say: "Is there anything you want to tell me, or is there something you would like me to try to do for you?" Be prepared for some remarkable questions and disclosures. After having followed this procedure a few times, you will be moved by the depth and intensity of each child's desire to behave well.

While there is little doubt that the life-space interview may be an effective device for management of behavior under certain circumstances, there are at least three limitations of this technique that should be pointed out:

1. LSI does require the teacher to have a considerable degree of sophistication, since this particular procedure relies on a somewhat in-depth knowledge of human behavior. The method requires sensitivity and awareness of individual and group dynamics. The teacher should know how to select appropriate issues for exploration during life-space interviews and, in addition, should know when to institute the particular procedures. It is essential that the teacher be adequately familiar with reality interviewing, since it involves more of an art form than a science form.

2. In a standard classroom with 30 or more children, it is difficult, if not impossible, for the regular teacher to conduct many life-space interviews. The problem may be partially alleviated by providing resource or crisis teachers to carry out this particular function.

3. Life-space interviews could, of course, be most effectively implemented in a totally therapeutic milieu. The approach does demand good cooperation among all members of the school staff and, in particular, requires that the principal understand all procedures, so that the teacher may feel free to do what is needed to provide a good therapeutic environment. Many teachers may be unfamiliar with LSI and may be opposed to its use in the school. Therefore, teachers utilizing this approach should be aware of and be able to cope with faculty resistance.

TEACHING STRATEGIES WITH REGARD TO BASIC LEARNING STYLES

Curriculum and Methods

In teaching all children, and especially children with exceptionalities, appropriate methods, strategies, and materials are required. The teacher must ascertain the learning avenues which are used by his students, so that these particular modalities may be utilized to instruct the students in the most efficient manner possible. Knowledge of which teaching strategies to employ is acquired by completely assessing the student's abilities.

Learning Academic Subjects

Behaviorally disordered children typically fail to achieve success in academic subjects. Whether the emotionally disturbed child is placed in a special class or remains in a regular classroom, however, the curriculum should center on success experiences. Essential to this process are materials which will elicit the student's interest. Materials and techniques that are intrinsically interesting will help the child to acquire academic knowledge through a series of success experiences.

Comparability of Basic Curricular Techniques with Behavioral Disorders in the Regular Classroom

In our discussion of education for emotionally disturbed children, psychological or therapeutic treatment may have appeared to be emphasized above all other factors; yet, this is not the case. Our viewpoint is that all procedures should be basically educational in nature, since the school is an educational and not a psychiatric institution. The basic goal of each program is learning.

Because learning is directly related to the problems of control and motivation, it is the school's job to devise suitable, dynamic, and interesting programs which will help behaviorally disordered children to acquire appropriate academic knowledge. Curricula for these children are comparable in all major aspects to those provided for regular students. However, most programs for behaviorally disordered children usually center on remedial approaches, at least in the beginning stages. If the need for remediation is typical of all behaviorally disordered students, then it is essential that they be taught reading and mathematical skills, as well as social competencies, such as developing self-control and effective interpersonal relationships. Teachers should keep in mind that frequently one indication of a child's improvement is his increasing interest in academic areas.

Ordinary approaches, lacking in creativity, can provide an adequate curriculum for the emotionally disturbed child. As in all educational procedures, however, the teacher's skills are the deciding factors. The teacher must be particularly aware of the social and learning environment of the classroom. Procedures which are instituted in the classroom

Figure 14–4 Subject matter should interest the child. (Courtesy of The Woods Schools, Langhorne, Pennsylvania.)

must be clearly outlined, so that all students may know the behavioral limits and what is expected of them academically. All teachers must realize that in working with the behaviorally disordered, progress is likely to be different for each student. At times, students will react aggressively, boisterously, sullenly, or in a withdrawn manner; these are usual reactions of behaviorally disordered children. The teacher must be sensitive to the overall moods of the class and aware of external conditions that may affect the classroom environment.

Under all conditions, the teacher must be able to rely on the judgment and support of the administrative staff in order to cope adequately with the students. Such support should be extended to removing a child from the class for a period of time if this action is felt to be appropriate. Each child requires a different type treatment. The label, behaviorally disordered, tends to lump children into a uniform group, which is far from an accurate representation of behavioral disorder. Such children may exhibit behaviors ranging from extreme acting-out to extremely withdrawn reactions. The problem is that both types of behavior are likely to occur within the same classroom. Good teaching requires that each child be provided with the particular kind of educational and psychological approaches which will enable him to function most effectively.

The teacher must be conscious of motivational problems in working with behaviorally disordered children. Motivation is determined partially by the developmental stage at which the child is functioning. This may pose problems within the classroom. For example, it is possible for a student of high school age to be motivationally operating at a nursery school or kindergarten level. Obviously, it would be unwise to place older and younger children in the same class; therefore, it is essential for the teacher, in such a case, to promote appropriate motivation in accordance with the chronological and emotional ages of the child.

Individualization of curricula must be stressed, for it is just as important to select procedures as it is to select materials. Some individuals may think better on a concrete level than on an abstract level or may react more positively to an active approach than to a passive one. All applications must be specific. In presenting materials to behaviorally disordered children, the level of difficulty may be reduced, but the interest level must always be maximized. Teaching methods will be effective only if the teacher takes the time to prepare individual materials suitable for each child at the stage at which he is currently functioning.

Children differ widely in their abilities to cope with group and individual situations; however, every attempt should be made to encourage group participation as much as possible.

In the beginning stages of working with behaviorally disordered children, the most common cause of difficulty in academic subjects is inadequate reading ability. Thus, all education programs must include reading remediation. In order to determine an effective approach to the problem, the child's history of reading failure must be explored. It may have stemmed from original maturational lag or from perceptual difficulties. Whatever the problem, it is essential to promote success experiences in a nonthreatening atmosphere, after which the child may begin to show progress in academic subjects.

One essential and often neglected facet of working with emotionally disturbed children in public schools is the inclusion of play in the curriculum (not to be confused with the children's recess period). Many of these children may be uncomfortable in a play situation, but it should be remembered that play provides a powerful means of promoting motiva-

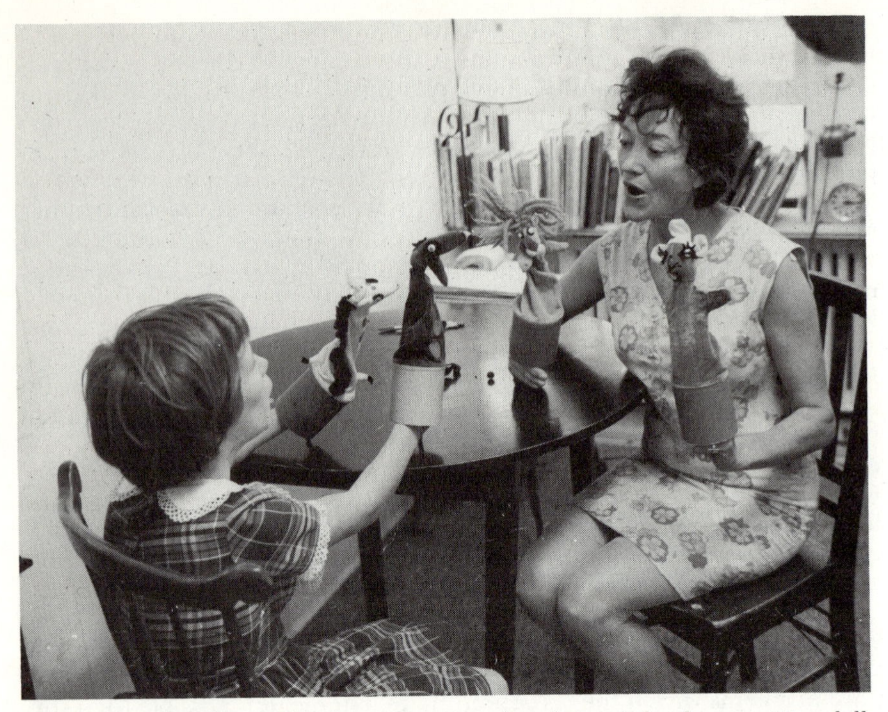

Figure 14–5 Puppets provide an opportunity for play and develop cognitive skills. (Courtesy of The Woods Schools, Langhorne, Pennsylvania.)

tion and change. Craft work is actually an extension of play and may be used psychotherapeutically as well as educationally. Puppets and drama offer other opportunities for play, as do painting, drawing, and modeling with clay.

Behaviorally disturbed children usually tend to place a strain on the educational program, and as a result, they are excluded from extracurricular activities. This very exclusion may prevent the school from coping with the needs of the child. Often, providing extracurricular activities for these students may help them to gain needed skills and competencies.

Education is concerned with evolving the capacities of individuals. We can assume that all children have a desire to learn and to explore, that they have curiosity about the world, and that these feelings are just as real for behaviorally disordered children as they are for normal children. Frequently, the behaviorally disordered child exhibits problems which are related to the social structure (i.e., to the community, home, church, or school). It is necessary for the school to determine the nature of these problems.

DEVELOPMENT OF A UNIT

The unit approach to teaching is considered to be the ideal method of instruction. The unit is defined by the Dictionary of Education (Good, 1945) as "an organization of various activities, experiences, and types of learning around a central problem or purpose developed cooperatively

Figure 14-6 A learning experience should have satisfying and immediate consequences.

by a group of pupils under teacher leadership, involving planning, execution of plans, and evaluation of results." Thus, the unit method may be said to be a portion of everyday life, including many kinds of knowledge and skills. Its relation to everyday life makes the unit particularly valuable.

A unit of study begins with recognition and motivation of pupil interest. The teacher identifies certain interests that pupils want to explore in a given area of study. The project should always be initiated in a natural manner, because natural situations form an interesting and motivating basis for study. Selection of a topic may be prompted by many situations: (1) A child may bring an object to class that interests him, and his classmates may also indicate interest which could lead to a unit of study. The object that might arouse such interest could be an insect, a pet, a picture, a toy, or a seashell. (2) The teacher may show an object of interest to the pupils, such as a souvenir, pictures taken while visiting a place of interest, or costumes from other countries. (3) A local, state, or national event may occur, for example, a circus coming to town, the state's reserving a nearby area as a park site, or the observance of national fire prevention week. (4) Interesting incidents may occur in which worthwhile learning situations are involved, for example, a national election or severe weather, such as a flood, a hurricane, or a snowstorm.

Goals of the unit approach should always be formulated in accordance with the abilities of the group with whom the teacher is working and with an understanding of the overall possibilities of the unit. Both long-term and short-term goals should be definitely determined before the class proceeds with the project.

The Unit of Study in Action

The following kinds of activities may evolve as the unit of study progresses:

1. Rearranging classroom furniture to facilitate work on the project.

2. Demonstrating and exhibiting materials which have been contributed by the teacher and pupils.

3. Making booklets containing information, pictures, and sketches concerning the various aspects of the topic being studied.
4. Listening to reports given by members of the class.
5. Using reading materials which suit the level of the individual child's potential.
6. Locating and selecting information from a variety of sources, such as textbook materials, pictures, and television.
7. Solving mathematical problems of a practical nature which are connected with the unit of study.
8. Developing skills in language arts through daily reporting, listening, writing, and speaking.
9. Accepting responsibilities for individual and group work, according to one's abilities, interests, and age.
10. Participating in a variety of appropriate activities related to the purposes and goals of the study.
11. Participating in suitable field trips.
12. Contributing to the study through crafts or the use of tools.
13. Gaining knowledge in the area of natural science.
14. Learning information in the social sciences, such as history and geography.
15. Changing or modifying the original plans of the unit being studied (almost a universal procedure). As the study progresses, there will be interesting deviations from the original outline of the project, with such additions and deletions as the study content indicates.

Evaluating the Unit of Study

Evaluation of the activities should occur daily and also at intervals. The procedure should probably include evaluation of achievement through conferences with each child, so that he may have the opportunity to explain what he is doing and why he is proceeding in a certain way. Assessment should be directed toward each portion of the project to determine what the most worthwhile activity was and why, which activities were not successfully performed and why, some suggestions for improvements, and which activities should be included that were not originally planned for.

Criteria for an Effective Unit

Some of the following questions may be helpful in determining the effectiveness of a unit plan (Ingram, 1960): (1) Does the unit stem from real life situations? (2) Is the unit suited to a child's social, physical, and intellectual levels of development? (3) Does it further both individual and group goals? (4) Does it provide for the development of desirable habits and attitudes of social living and for an acquisition of knowledge and skills? (5) Has it been planned to develop interest, skill, habits, and attitudes that will carry over into life outside the school? (6) Does it allow for practical use of school subjects? (7) Does it give opportunities for many kinds of experiences, such as writing letters, reading, keeping records, figuring, and measuring?

Some suggested topics for units of study are: neighborhood stores, such as the food, department, or drug stores; the community school; people who help us; how to make people happy; the home and family living; pets; the post office; the police department; airplanes; farm life; and clothing.

Figure 14-7 An invited speaker in the classroom explaining his work.

All units should involve all children in the classroom in activities which will provide interesting and valuable information concerning important aspects about everyday life. Generally, units should be initiated by a normal classroom situation and should evolve rather than being presented to the child in a completely developed form.

WORK EXPERIENCE EDUCATION

The work experience program is most applicable to the EMR child, but to some extent, it is relevant to all exceptional children. Completion of the curriculum culminates in work experience education. One of the major goals of all instruction is successful placement of the individual in a gainful occupation, so that he may assume a fully functioning role as a participant in all phases of life. The following essentials of the work experience program are outlined in the Handbook of Work Experience Education, published by the California State Department of Education in 1953: (1) The school adopts a specific plan of operation, based on a written outline that shows the prospective role of the school, the student, and the employer. (2) The school assigns qualified personnel to direct the program and to coordinate jobs for students with the subject matter taught by the school. (3) The school makes certain that students' jobs are of a useful, worthwhile nature and that federal, state, and local laws are followed. (4) The school, with the help of the employer, evaluates the work of students, awards credit for work successfully accomplished, and enters pertinent facts concerning the student's work on his permanent record. Thus, work education is a part of the school curriculum, as much as history, English, mathematics, business, and mechanics.

Because a successful program depends on close coordination between the classwork and the work experience situation, the teacher is best suited for developing the total plan for the education and work experience of secondary aged pupils. Another important factor is the development and location of work training positions. A close, cooperative relationship must be maintained by the teacher with potential employ-

Figure 14-8 Work experience can take a variety of forms. (Courtesy of The Woods Schools, Langhorne, Pennsylvania.)

ers, and a list of vocational areas for on-campus and off-campus work should be supplied. The administrator must provide an atmosphere and the "machinery" by which the work experience program can flourish.

The work experience program generally starts in the tenth grade, with provisions being made for the student to work within the school itself. In order to provide more normal work experiences, the program can be expanded to the community, on a rotating basis during the junior year and on a long-term basis during the senior year.

Selection of students is of key importance. Students who wish to participate in on-campus or off-campus work experience programs must be carefully selected, because the success of the program depends on placing only those students who are ready for job placement; that is, those students who have a reasonable chance for success on the job. Every student enrolled in the high school special education program may need a sheltered work environment. Some students may be able to proceed rapidly through their work experience, while others may need to postpone their assignment until later. Therefore, an adequate student evaluation should be made before the student is assigned to exploratory work experiences.

A conference with parents should be held, and written permission for the student to participate in a work experience program should be obtained before the student enters the program. The approach to work experience for exceptional children must be different from the approach for regular students. Only a small number of the more mature students with intellectual exceptionalities are able to survive general work experience which is designed for regular high school students. Most students in special education programs may be unable to locate jobs for themselves, and those who do find jobs independently may have difficulty in maintaining them, unless they have had previous experience or specific guidance in doing the work. Therefore, their work experience program must be closely coordinated with classwork and must be under the supervision of the special education teacher. The teacher should be able to evaluate each student's social and vocational development and his ability to undertake assignments. Job placement should probably occur only after the teacher has recommended it; the teacher usually knows the student best.

CONCLUSION

All the methods which we have reviewed have an ultimate goal in common—to help the exceptional child adjust to society. Special educators must devote more time and effort toward improving general education, so that it may better accommodate the educational and social needs of *all* children. Special education must continue to grow and change in order to meet this goal.

Section V

SPECIAL AREA

CHAPTER 15

TEACHING THE GIFTED CHILD

(Courtesy of R. R. Kersey)

An exceptionality which is frequently overlooked in public schools is giftedness. Concern about a condition which might be called a "plus" type of phenomenon may seem somewhat odd. However, an examination of the current educational scene indicates that of all the children in public education, the needs of the gifted are probably the most poorly met (Hildreth, 1966). The gifted child has long puzzled public education and has been assumed by many to be capable of coping with any learning environment and to present no particular problems to public education. A careful examination of current educational practices indicates the inadequacy of the majority of public school programs in meeting the needs of the gifted child. The gifted child has been viewed by many as a threat or as an odd or undesirable kind of individual. Giftedness is a national resource, and every effort should be made by public schools and by society in general to capitalize upon it (Hildreth, 1966).

DEFINITION OF GIFTEDNESS IN CHILDREN

Many definitions have been used to describe gifted individuals. It was popular at one time to describe an exceptionally brilliant individual as a "genius." However, in current usage, the term genius is restricted to those individuals who have actually performed, that is, to individuals who have achieved. Therefore, it would be correct to state, "Thomas Jefferson was a genius"; however, it would be incorrect to describe an unaccomplished youngster with an IQ of 180 in the same way. The term gifted has also been confused with other expressions, such as child prodigy, precocious, highly talented, creative, bright, brilliant, *ad infinitum.*

The term gifted became popular during World War I when it was used in a number of reports. Further exploration of the literature indicates that Whipple (1924) used the term "supernormal" in much of his early writings and that Hollingsworth (1926) used the expression "prodigious child." Lewis M. Terman, who is famous for his extensive investigation of giftedness in children and adults, originally used the term "bright" to indicate mentally superior children. Later, he used the term "genius" which is now outdated when describing children who exceed the norm in academic potential.

A further complication of defining a term such as gifted is the tendency for words to become confused through usage, as in the case of the word "talented." Originally, "talented" referred to individuals who possessed some particularly outstanding individual trait, such as ability in music, art, or poetry. Today, there is a tendency to make very little distinction between "talented" and "gifted," so that in popular usage the terms tend to become somewhat synonymous. Thus, according to some, giftedness in young people refers basically to specialized talent; the gifted child is one who exhibits outstanding abilities in one area such as music. An example of this in the past is the work of Mozart.

Any definition of giftedness will have to be arbitrary to some extent. Those who are gifted cover a wide variety of kinds of individuals; that is, a gifted person is not any one particular type of individual. It is popular today in our psychometric age to assess all traits in terms of the normal curve. According to the normal curve, the gifted child is one who is signified by the upper limits of this curve, but the exact point showing giftedness on the normal curve is not clear. One of the earlier definitions of giftedness was that of Witty (1951) in which he defined a gifted person as "one whose performance is consistently remarkable in any potentially valuable area."

Sumption and Lueckins (1960) defined giftedness by means of an intellectual continuum. "The gifted are defined as those who possess a superior nervous system characterized by the potential to perform tasks requiring a comparatively high degree of intellectual abstraction or creative imagination." Some authorities have included creativity in the definition of giftedness (Lucito, 1963).

We could continue to list many other definitions; however, it is sufficient to say that the gifted, generally speaking, are individuals who deviate from the norm by having superior abilities which are typically viewed as intellectual in nature. Abraham reported (1958) finding some 113 different definitions of giftedness (Hildreth, 1966). Hildreth listed five distinguishing criteria of the gifted person:

1. He is superior to his age-mates in traits other than those capabilities that are purely physical, physiological, or dependent primarily on muscular development.
2. He possesses intellectual powers and qualities which are essential for success in advanced education and training in general or in his speciality.
3. His superior developmental maturation is reasonably consistent from the early years of life to maturity.
4. His unusual ability may be general or specialized; his superior trait single or multiple.
5. The traits and abilities in which he shows superiority are those required for unusual achievement or productivity in areas of high social value.

Current practices tend to restrict the term gifted, with regard to individual IQ assessment, to children with IQ's of 130 or above. This restriction should not be viewed by readers of this text as an absolute or even a desirable cutoff point. Giftedness should be viewed as a relative kind of behavior in which a child exhibits unusual competencies, abilities, knowledge, or skills by which he performs other specialized or generalized kinds of tasks requiring abilities beyond those of the average person.

IDENTIFICATION OF GIFTEDNESS IN CHILDREN

The identification process should involve the entire range of school personnel. As has been frequently emphasized in this text, the teacher should have an integral part in identification of all kinds of exceptionalities. Laycock (1956) suggested the following 20-item checklist which may be utilized by a teacher to assist him in possible identification of a gifted child.

1. Possesses superior powers of reasoning, of dealing with abstractions in order to generalize from specific facts, of understanding meanings, and of perceiving relationships.
2. Has great intellectual curiosity.

3. Learns easily and readily.
4. Has a wide range of interests.
5. Has a broad attention span that enables him to concentrate on and to persevere in solving problems and pursuing interests.
6. Is superior in quality and quantity of vocabulary as compared with other children of his own age.
7. Has ability to do effective work independently.
8. Has learned to read early, often well before school age.
9. Exhibits keen powers of observation.
10. Shows initiative and originality in intellectual work.
11. Shows alertness and quick response to new ideas.
12. Is able to memorize quickly.
13. Has great interest in the nature of man and the universe, problems of origin and destiny, and the like.
14. Possesses an unusual imagination.
15. Follows complex directions easily.
16. Is a rapid reader.
17. Has several hobbies.
18. Has reading interests which cover a wide range of subjects.
19. Makes frequent and effective use of the library.
20. Is superior in arithmetic, particularly in problem-solving.

More refined measuring instruments have been developed over the last few decades, and consequently, definitions of giftedness in children have changed. At one time giftedness was measured solely by achievement, but now it has come to mean high aptitude and creativity as well. Gallagher (1964), in his attempt to identify the gifted child as being distinct from the academically talented, found a few factors that the gifted have in common. They have the ability to absorb abstract concepts, to organize them better, and to apply them more effectively than the child with only high IQ.

No one method of identifying gifted children is in itself sufficient. Therefore, a combination of methods and personnel must be employed. The process of identification includes teacher observation, individual intelligence tests, group intelligence tests, achievement test batteries, and creativity tests. In order for an individual to utilize any checklist with reasonable competence, it is essential that he possess an understanding of developmental norms, so that he may have a relatively reliable standard by which to use the checklist for aid in identifying a gifted child. Readers interested in a more extensive review of possible checklists are referred to Abraham (1958) and Brumbaugh and Roshco (1959).

Flanagan et al. (1962) proposed what might be called a situational approach to identification of gifted children and was concerned with a critical value concept for the observation of pupil behavior; that is, how does the individual behave in certain kinds of critical situations? For example, suppose that something is upsetting the class. The teacher might ask the child, "What do you suggest?" in order to test his reaction to the situation. If an accident occurs on the playground, the circumstances may cause a gifted child to make suggestions as to what might be done. As with the identification of many exceptionalities, the teacher must utilize his skill in observation. He should observe how the child behaves in everyday life and particularly in situations which require behavior of a superior nature.

It is essential that a continuous record be kept of all children. Such a procedure, as proposed in earlier chapters of this book, would enable the identification of any exceptionality to be made more easily. Consistent usage of anecdotal records furnishes a basis upon which decisions may be made at a later date. Identification of giftedness requires several steps, the first being a preliminary kind of screening in which the teacher, utilizing the preceding approaches, makes a tentative identification. It should be pointed out, of course, that standardized tests of achievement do not always indicate the ability of a child who is gifted. Group tests of intelligence, in contrast to individually administered tests, have been utilized to a large extent in preliminary investigations of children's intellectual functioning. There are a number of problems in this procedure that have been outlined by Martinson and Lessinger (1960) and Pegnato and Birch (1959).

Martinson and Lessinger (1960) found in their studies that less than half of a group of 332 pupils who scored over 130 on the Stanford-Binet test made a score as high as 130 on the group intelligence test. Pegnato and Birch reported comparable kinds of data. The problems in group testing include the following: (1) most standardized group tests do not have a fully stratified sample of the total population, and there tends to be a lack of appropriate representation of those children scoring over three standard deviations above the mean; (2) time and other testing procedures are designed for the average child and thus fail to take into account the more rapid response time of the gifted child; and (3) the cognitive and symbolic levels of the content are designed to meet the needs of the average student and tend to bore the gifted child.

Individual intelligence tests administered by highly skilled individuals are certainly not a routine matter in public schools, but it is essential that such examinations be conducted as a major part of the identification of gifted children. During the preliminary screening procedures, school grades are frequently employed. It is, of course, reasonable to assume that a child making A and B grades is more likely to score higher with regard to giftedness than a child who makes a grade of D or C, although we should hasten to point out that this is not always so. Thus, the preliminary process should be viewed as tentative in nature. We feel that it is better to refer more children for investigation than to miss a child who might have been assisted if he had been properly identified at an earlier time.

Subsequent to the initial screening and referral processes by the teacher, the child should be referred to the school psychologist for intensive psychological examination. The school psychologist should utilize such standard devices as the Stanford-Binet Scale and/or the Wechsler Intelligence Scale. In addition, it is advisable for the school psychologist to employ other tests which explore such areas as creativity, personality, achievement, and functioning level in a variety of activities. Upon the child's completion of the examination, it is highly recommended that appropriate placement committees be organized which are composed of, at the minimum, a school psychologist, the principal of the school, the teachers who are involved, and any other school personnel who have significant data to contribute to the discussion and who may aid in considering appropriate methods of coping with the individual identified as gifted. The whole battery of creativity tests designed by Torrance (1966) could be used in answering many questions concerning giftedness. The Torrance tests of creativity center on the elicitation of responses that call for maximal openness and lack of structure. A sample question might be: "In one minute list all the uses one can make of a brick, a pencil, or a newspaper."

REASONS FOR DIFFERENTIAL EDUCATION OF GIFTED CHILDREN

1. Gifted children learn at a faster pace and solve problems at a more mature level than their age-mates do.

2. Undifferentiated programs of schooling waste the time and talent of many persons (and the parents' and taxpayers' money).

3. Uniformity would leave many children improperly and inadequately educated.

4. Well-educated, gifted persons set the pace for a higher standard of living, better recreational facilities, more hospitals and social service agencies, and better schools and child care services in communities. If what they want does not exist, they invent it.

Conversely, reasons for opposition to programs for gifted children are often listed as follows: (1) the programs are undemocratic; (2) they are unpopular with parents of those children who are not identified as being gifted, and these children always compose the majority of the school population; (3) there is fear that special provision for the gifted will hamper improvement of general education for all; (4) the gifted already have many advantages, and this will enable them to outdistance the average child further and to obtain a number of exclusive opportunities; (5) some feel that any extra effort and money should be used for the benefit of those who are handicapped; and (6) the gifted are able to take care of themselves without any extra assistance.

Counterarguments to the preceding points might be stated as follows: (a) Most opposition to special sectioning of bright children occurs during the early elementary years when mothers have close contact with schools. By the time children reach grades six or seven, parents achieve a more realistic attitude, since their children's aptitudes have been tested over a period of time. There is, however, some rivalry of parents even in secondary schools. (b) The test of any school in a democracy is how well it provides for the individual talents and capacities of *all* its children. (c) There need be no conflict between providing the best for all and making special provisions for the most promising.

Opposition to programs for the gifted may be reduced by:

1. Not calling attention to elite groups in school.

2. Stressing excellent features of the school which are shared by all pupils.

3. Publicizing efforts which help the disadvantaged and which tailor school programs for every individual need.

4. Making it known that the extra expense of educating the gifted is fully justified because these young people will repay society in the largest measure.

5. Helping others to realize that the cost of education for the gifted is only a fraction of the cost of remedial work for slow learners and of teaching and counseling problem children.

6. Showing others that provisions for the gifted raise the level of the whole school system. Special facilities and services tend to sift downward throughout the whole system.

CURRICULUM FOR GIFTED CHILDREN

Curricular patterns that may be utilized in designing educational programs for the gifted child tend to vary depending upon the philosophical basis upon which the school district operates. As a rule, three separate approaches are used throughout the country for educating the gifted child, that is, in addition to the fact that the majority of school districts simply ignore the facts concerning giftedness.

1. The segregated approach to the education of gifted children may be established by providing a special classroom (i.e., a self-contained classroom) where gifted children are presented with specialized programs in much the same manner that classrooms are designed for special programs for the mentally retarded. An alternate to this approach is the institution by the school district of a total school devoted to the needs of the gifted. The Bronx High School of Science is an example of this type of approach.

2. A second approach to educating the gifted is acceleration. Acceleration has been utilized for years as a method of assisting children who are capable of progressing at a more rapid rate than the average child. One outstanding example of extreme acceleration is the case of Dr. Norbert Wiener in which acceleration was the primary mode of coping with his giftedness. Dr. Wiener was awarded the Ph.D. at age 18.

3. A third method that is utilized in coping with the gifted child is "enrichment." Enrichment is concerned with curricular provisions for greater depth and breadth of academic work.

All the preceding methods have their proponents. It seems advisable that none of these methods should be excluded from education of the gifted and that any school district might operate effectively by using a combination of these methods.

Briefly, the argument against segregation of children is that it provides a program which tends to separate children from the mainstream of public education. Although this may be true, it should be pointed out that gifted children tend to segregate themselves in some way. A properly designed specialized program for the gifted need not emphasize its exclusive nature. A resource room concept would probably apply to the gifted with great advantage. Thus, the gifted child could be provided with such educational procedures in particular subjects in which he needs extra opportunity to advance. This situation would not set him apart to the extent that a self-contained type of classroom would. In general, a combination of acceleration and enrichment in educating the gifted child should be advocated. However, each child needs to have a program designed to meet his own particular needs, and no general rules are actually applicable.

Acceleration must be in accordance with many other factors. For example, does the child possess physical and social characteristics which will enable him to function reasonably adequately at the level to which he has been promoted? Will the promotion tend to isolate the child from his peers? How will his parents cope with the problem of acceleration? On the positive side, acceleration plus enrichment can possibly provide a highly tailored program for each child.

The word "enrichment" has been much abused in the way that it has been applied to the education of gifted children. Enrichment does not mean "more of the same." Enrichment means providing opportunities for children to engage in activities which will provide increased depth and breadth in their quest for knowledge and understanding of their world and the universe. Gifted children are quite capable of perceiving more subtle relationships and more abstract kinds of phenomena than average children of the same age, and they should be encouraged to use their creative capacities in order to solve problems. Enrichment pro-

Figure 15–1 Enriching the curriculum of gifted children through the use of teaching machines (programmed instruction). (From Hicks, B. L., and Hunka, S.: The Teacher and the Computer. Philadelphia, W. B. Saunders Company, 1972.)

grams should be highly individualized, so that each child may pursue those interests which are most pertinent to him. School personnel often have the idea that all children must progress through every subject at the same pace. This erroneous concept can only lead to utter frustration of the gifted individual. In considering curricula for gifted children in elementary school, we might examine some methods by which we may best teach such children.

1. *Special projects and reports.* Within the regular classroom it is possible to provide special projects and reports (in depth) for the gifted child. He will thus be able to maintain socialization and interaction with his peers, and such assignments will give him an opportunity to become a leader. Special help from the librarian and other persons with resources in areas such as foreign languages, music, art, and science may be utilized. Training in library resources and the use of reference materials may be of great assistance. This regular classroom treatment works best with a moderately sized class in which there are other children who are capable learners or in which there are several bright children who may form a subgroup within the class.

2. *Laboratory method of study.* The laboratory method of study provides for small groups or for individual work in areas where children may perform simple experiments. Gifted children tend to need less time for some assignments or to want more time in some cases than the ordinary child in order to engage in certain kinds of activities.

3. *Release time.* The concept of release time is gaining recognition throughout the country. The program is simply one in which the child is allowed a certain portion of the day to engage in activities which are relevant to his particular education. One of the authors of this text had the experience of allowing a gifted child in the sixth grade to spend half of his day in the high school library to do independent research and study. This particular approach with this particular child was found to be most effective, and the child was able to progress in accordance with his capacity for unit learning. Many teachers tend to regard the unit approach as unsuitable for the gifted child. However, it might be pointed out that the unit approach is probably one of the more effective devices that may be utilized by the elementary school teacher in order to provide differential opportunities for all children. In the designing and execution of any unit, it is possible and probable that there will be many types of tasks. The gifted child may be asked to help to design, to evaluate, or to theorize about some of the factors involved in unit construction.

5. *Team learning.* Children may be grouped in small teams, given assignments, and allowed to work together, teaching and checking up on one another. This type of learning may be carried on in departmentalized classes, in special classes, or in regular self-contained classes.

CURRICULUM FOR GIFTED SECONDARY SCHOOL CHILDREN

A number of approaches may be utilized in providing curricular adaptations for the gifted secondary school pupil.

1. Ability grouping or sectioning of basic required courses is of value in teaching gifted children. For example, a course or a section of a course in English might be designed as a "Creative Writing" class. In a more traditional curriculum, we might utilize a course called "Senior English," which has traditionally been devoted to English literature, for a more intensive study of the subject matter by the gifted than is typically engaged in by the average student in high school.

2. The advanced placement program has been utilized by many high schools to allow progress for its more able pupils. The advanced placement program allows high school students to take college work at a neighboring college at the same time that they are enrolled in a high school and to receive credit for the college course. In some cases, high schools are authorized to offer college level courses which may later be used as transferable credits at accredited institutions.

3. The honors program has been utilized by many high schools as a method of assisting the gifted child. The honors program allows for special kinds of sections or programs in which a student may design a particular kind of approach to a problem and may present it after he has completed the project.

4. The utilization of special seminar courses in high school is becoming increasingly popular. The seminar approach will allow the gifted child not only to present and to prepare material but also to interact with students who are on his own academic level.

5. Small workshops and laboratory classes may be used to provide specialized assistance for gifted children. The gifted child, contrary to popular concepts, likes to tinker with gadgets, materials, and tools. Indeed, research indicates that the gifted child frequently is superior in practical applications as well as in theoretical applications of knowledge.

6. Cluster groups within the regular classroom may be used. The teacher may give a general assignment and may allow small cluster groups to attack the general problem by way of many different approaches.

7. The use of extracurricular or extraschool activities (e.g., after-school clubs and special classes) is a great help in providing individual assistance for the gifted child. Gifted children have formed small business concerns during their high school years through which they have earned money that will be of assistance in paying for their college educations. Other gifted children have undertaken special projects in working with local law enforcement agencies. The limits for such projects are only those imposed by the individual who provides this kind of activity for the gifted child.

8. Television may be utilized to afford specialized assistance. Many good programs are shown in schools today which are specially devised to benefit the extra-talented individual.

9. Independent study on an individual basis furnishes a helpful type of program for the gifted child in that it is generally agreeable with the make-up of gifted persons. They tend to like to do things individually, and this will allow an opportunity for them to question and to pursue knowledge to its logical limits.

10. Cooperation of community resources, libraries, and museums in offering programs for the gifted can be a great asset. Every community has a great many natural resources within its structure which may be utilized in the education of the gifted child.

Hildreth (1966) listed the following goals for the gifted:

1. Creative thinking: (a) recognizing problems, (b) formulating hypotheses, (c) discovering and organizing data, and (d) arriving at tentative conclusions and acting on them.
2. Developing independence of thought and action.
3. Acquiring scholarly habits.
4. Setting high achievement standards.
5. Educating the whole child.
6. Building good character.
7. Learning about physical fitness.

MOTIVATING GIFTED CHILDREN

Many of the problems in devising curricula for gifted individuals arise from misconceptions about these persons. One erroneous conception of the gifted child is that he is a bookworm who is odd or is a social outcast. These beliefs have been refuted by many studies, the most well-known being that of Terman (1925). As a general trend, children who score high on IQ tests also seem more likely to have other favorable characteristics, such as social popularity and emotional stability. These characteristics cannot necessarily be attributed to high IQ but may be the result of an enriched family environment or other such factors.

Because there are gifted children among the underachievers, or low producers, Gallagher (1964) paid particular attention to their problems. A child with a high IQ is more conventional than the creative person who will take calculated risks, some of which are most annoying to a teacher. A gifted child who is a low producer is the outgrowth of many forces, such as family disturbance, lack of outgoing family goals, and unfavorable culture. More boys than girls are found in this group.

Low-producing gifted children may be classified in one of two groups. One group includes those coming from a good cultural environment whose difficulties seem to center on the personality of the student and his family relationship. Research evidence shows that these individuals have poor relationships with their fathers and often have negative self-attitudes. The second group of underachievers includes those coming from lower-class backgrounds in which the cultural environment is generally unfavorable. These children exist in a climate in which achievement is not the desired norm.

It is a known fact that gifted children do not thrive under any and all circumstances. Appropriate educational programs must be adopted, so that these children may fully realize their potentials. It was once believed that enrichment within the regular school program was the answer, but because of the range of abilities within a given class and the limitations of teachers in content background, this method may require a considerable amount of reevaluation and amending.

There are alternate plans which we have discussed, such as grouping or acceleration. The problems presented by such plans include teachers' lack of knowledge of advanced subject matter.

New approaches in curriculum are now being developed in the schools. These approaches are moving away from a functional approach, toward a content approach, and toward teaching the basic structure and theory of the content field. Instead of focusing a study on an airplane engine, kinetic energy might be the subject which is studied. Instead of concentrating on the dance and clothing of the American Indian in the Southwest, a minority group might be studied in relation to its dominant culture. Teaching arithmetic to gifted children may involve the introduction of set theory, probability, geometry, and logic at an elementary school level. The basic limitation of this approach is that teachers must be specially trained in order to present these difficult mathematical concepts to bright but immature minds. In the field of science education, as in the field of mathematics, there is now a tendency for those in the educational field to move away from the functional and toward the theoretical in teaching gifted children. Scientific concepts are presented to the child at an early age, and an attempt is made to encourage the gifted student to participate in all kinds of thinking processes that the scientist utilizes in solving problems and in making scientific discoveries.

In order that the gifted child will be able to develop as a complete, integrated individual, emphasis should be placed on the proper emotional atmosphere in all classrooms. The atmosphere for gifted children must be permissive and must allow for freedom to diverge from the general line of study that is employed in teaching average children.

A great deal of evidence indicates that there is a reasonable sequence of stages which a creative person tends to follow in his intellectual processes. They include:

1. Preparation—problem-identification and fact gathering.
2. Incubation—thinking about the problem, association of new information with old.
3. Illumination—creator suddenly sees the idea, concept, or solution to the problem.
4. Verification—ideas obtained are put to the test to see if they are valid.

Educational programming has been weak with regard to the middle stages of incubation and illumination, and much school curriculum can be identified as stage one activity. The student should then be taught how to evaluate an idea, that is, a stage four type of operation.

The method of discovery and inquiry has been especially productive in teaching the gifted child. Gallagher (1964) suggested that children need to be problem solvers and that teaching the method of discovery and inquiry calls for training on the part of the teacher. According to him, teachers must substitute guidance and supervision for "lazy" thinking.

If progress is to be made in educating the gifted child, additional trained personnel must be added to the school staff. Different types of personnel are needed to handle different gifted groups, such as the high aptitude, high performance group and the high aptitude, low performance group.

In addition, training programs are needed to prepare the necessary skilled personnel for programs being initiated through increased state and federal financial assistance. When educational and civic leaders plead for support for programs which will educate teachers of gifted children or for appropriate programs for gifted children, many legislators oppose their cause, arguing that not even the experts know how to identify those who are gifted. If they cannot identify these children, why do they educate teachers for the gifted and provide special educational opportunities for gifted children?

One problem is that the concept of giftedness has broadened to include more different types and varieties of gifted children. Another problem is the fixed notion that giftedness usually means high IQ. Only recently has Hildreth (1966) been supported in defining giftedness as "consistently superior performances in any social [useful] endeavor." If a level of giftedness is based on a single criterion, many children gifted in other areas will be overlooked. With gifted persons, intelligence may vary, depending on a variety of physical and psychological factors, both within the individual child and within his environment. The child might respond quite creatively and originally to one task, and to another he may barely respond at all. Congressional legislation of the early seventies stated that children differ more in quality of ability than in amount. This legislation recommended a tripartite classification of secondary schools based on the idea that there are three main types of giftedness:

1. Literary or college type.
2. Mechanical or technical type.
3. Concrete or practical type.

Getzels and Jackson (1962) showed in a study that highly creative or divergent-thinking adolescents achieved as well as their highly intelligent peers in spite of the fact that their average IQ was 23 points lower. It is important that teachers not show disapproval when children answer questions or offer solutions to problems in a different way or ask unusual and penetrating questions.

In another study conducted by Getzels and Jackson (1962) dealing with two kinds of psychosocial excellence or giftedness, high social adjustment and high moral courage, it was found that just as a highly intelligent student is not always highly creative, a highly adjusted student is not always highly moral. Furthermore, it was found that although highly moral students achieved at a higher level than highly adjusted students, teachers perceived highly adjusted students as the leaders rather than the highly moral individuals.

Longstanding beliefs in predetermined development have been frequently used to support the concept of fixed intelligence. Much evidence, however, indicates that deprivations of experience make a difference in rates of various kinds of growth. Theories concerning inherited patterns of mental growth have been placed in doubt by the work of Hunt (1961), Ojeman (1959), and others. Evidence seems to indicate that intellectual development is affected when children are exposed to guided, planned learning experiences rather than encountering only what the environment happens to provide. This finding has led to the suggestion that educational programs should be based upon guided, planned experiences which, in turn, are based upon an analysis of the requirements of learning tasks and the condition of the child. Educational concern should focus on potentiality rather than norms and single measures of giftedness. The gifted child can potentially help or hinder civilization. Thus, it is important that the teacher ask himself, "What kind of person can I help the child become?"

Since most classroom time is devoted to average students, the problem of motivating and guiding the learning and thinking of those who are above average still remains; however, recognition programs have been found to exercise powerful motivating influences on gifted children. It is difficult to tell whether a child is learning at the level of which he is capable, because it is almost impossible to determine what the potentiality of a child is if he is not motivated to perform well on tests or on other indicators that are utilized in assessing his potential. It is important that teachers be alert to all indications of a child's potential. Without knowledge of a child's potential, a teacher may place too much pressure on a child who is already too strongly motivated and is unable to learn because he is overanxious or, a teacher may be unconcerned about a potentially bright student whose achievement is only mediocre. Actually, it is sometimes difficult to distinguish a gifted child who is not motivated to perform well from an average or slow learning child.

The following reasons may explain why some gifted children are poorly motivated (Torrance, 1965):

1. No chance to use what is learned – children should have inner stimulation or intrinsic motivation. Children need to be able to use what they are learning as tools for thinking.

2. Interest in what is learned rather than in grades – students would be more strongly motivated to learn if teachers and parents were more interested in what children are actually learning and achieving rather than in how well they do on a particular test.

3. Learning tasks are either too easy or too difficult – children will become unmotivated if tasks are consistently too easy or too difficult.

4. No chance to learn in preferred ways – man fundamentally prefers to learn in creative ways but needs authority too.

5. No chance to use test abilities – children respond to the method of the teacher, and some do better on certain types of tests than others.

6. Lacking in purposefulness – some children are not motivated to achieve high grades. For example, they do not want their writing to be corrected but would rather that it be a means of communication.

A pattern for educating gifted children should be initiated in kindergarten. There are times when the kindergarten teacher should resign herself to the fact that children prefer to learn creatively and should postpone learning by authority until the necessary experimentation can take place. It is important to keep fantasy alive in kindergarten children until they have achieved the kind of intellectual development that makes problem-solving and decision-making possible.

The teacher of gifted children should be "fully alive," well-educated, curious, excited about learning, and free of hostility and psychological need to punish.

The curriculum for gifted children must be flexible, idiosyncratic, and designed to stimulate, encourage, and assist. The gifted child should be provided with a curriculum and with administrative organizational systems which will enable him to unfold, to flower. A simile which might be applicable is that the gifted child is like a plant in a garden that simply needs to be cultivated in order to bear beautiful blossoms.

TEACHING THE CREATIVE CHILD

To define the term creativeness in such a way that it is clearly separate from other components of human behavior is a difficult task. There are a number of factors that may be associated with creativity. Taylor (1960) maintained that there are five major components that should be considered in studying the characteristics of creativeness. They are (1) personal characteristics of creative persons, (2) the products they create, (3) the creativity processes, (4) the relation of environment to creative performance, and (5) the influence of types of tasks on creative behaviors. Taylor maintained that if all five of these areas are considered as elements in describing creativity, it will be possible to design a framework by which a total mass of data concerning creativity may be organized.

One of the major points of emphasis in most studies of creativity is the product that results from creative activities. Such products are usually original, novel, nontraditional or infrequently associated with commonplace elements. Creative products may possess these characteristics relative to the environment or conditions under which they are being studied. Torrance (1966) maintains that the creative process should result in products which reflect the following: (1) its degree of novelty and worth either to persons or to society; (2) its degree of deviation from conventional traits and ideas; and (3) its degree of truth and usefulness in generalization.

Jackson and Messick (1967) felt that the difference between intelligence and creativity could be briefly stated: intelligence represents an objective, observable type of response to logic and reality, and creativity represents a response to a subjective kind of reality. According to Jackson and Messick, persons with a creative bent have a different but positive side. Their personality traits and accomplishments are somewhat different from those of other persons.

Guilford (1967; 1968) discussed creativeness at great length as being related to his structure of intellect and generic model for problem-solving in creativity. By using the model of structure of intellect, Guilford attempts to specify the particular abilities that are involved in all types of mental activity. The major dimensions of certain mental processes are represented by his model; operations are performed on certain types of tasks which are called contents. In turn, the resultants of this interaction are labeled as products. Guilford (1967) stresses the situational variable in relation to creativeness. He maintains that creative behavior may involve different configurations than those represented in his model of intellect depending on the type of creative activity and the person. For example, he calls attention to a variety of roles in which creativeness is displayed, such roles as inventor, writer, mathematician, artist, and others. Guilford also discusses the idea that success in different academic areas may demand different approaches. Thus, the creativeness involved may present a different configuration.

A study by Wallach and Kogan (1965) concerned the differences in behavior of a group of girls who were classified as having either high creativity-high IQ, high creativity-low IQ, low creativity-low IQ, or low creativity-high IQ. In confidence and appearance, the high creativity-high IQ group were found to be, more than all other groups, the least likely to have doubts, to hesitate, or to downgrade themselves or their accomplishments. The high creativity-low IQ group were, more than any other group, likely to be cautious, to hesitate, and to downgrade themselves and their accomplishments. Those in the low creativity-low IQ group were found to have these feelings less than the high creativity-low IQ group but more than the high creativity-high IQ group. The low creativity-high IQ group was found to be similar to the high-high group. In terms of disruptive, attention-seeking types of behavior, the high creativity-high IQ and high creativity-low IQ groups were found to be high, whereas the low creativity-low IQ group was low, and the low-creativity-high IQ group was lowest of all. In terms of orientation, the high-creativity-high IQ group was found to have the highest level of attention span with the greatest amount of concentration and broadest range of interest in academic tasks. The high creativity-low IQ group had the lowest level of attention and very poor concentration; they reacted to academic failure by withdrawal. Those in the low creativity-low IQ group compensated for poor academic achievement by involving themselves in some type of social activity. The low-high group demonstrated a high level of attention span and concentration and were strongly motivated to achieve academically. In terms of peer acceptance and seeking peer acceptance, those in the high-high group frequently were sought as companions and frequently sought the companionship of their peers. The high-low group was the least chosen and frequently avoided interpersonal relationships as much as possible. Those in the low-high group often were sought as companions, but they tended to remain aloof and cool.

Presently, one area of concern is the ability to assess creativeness, and many formal tests for this purpose have been developed during the past few years. The Torrance Test of Creative Thinking (1967) was used in an evaluation of some 300 studies that had employed this test. Other tests have been developed by Wallach and Kogan (1965), Wallach and Wing (1969), and Ginsberg and Hood (1970), who made use of the Remote Associates Test to identify creative types of tasks. Schaefer (1970) discussed the uses of a similes test as a measurement of creativeness. The Guilford Test of Creativeness has been widely utilized, and Holland and Baird (1968) described a test to measure creativity. At present, all tests of creativity should be viewed as being in the experimental realm and subject to revision.

The teacher who seeks to identify and to teach the creative child might find one or more of the following suggestions helpful: (1) The teacher may ask experts from the outside to judge the creativeness of students' accomplishments, such as stories, poems, or paintings. (2) Teachers may become familiar with various items used in tests which are designed to measure creativeness and may select those items which she feels will help her to identify creative students. (3) Teachers may become familiar with characteristics that are typically associated with creative students and their activities and may observe their students for this type of behavior. Rendulli, Hartman, and Callahan (1971) constructed a rating scale that teachers might use for identifying creativity. This study recommended that teachers observe the frequency of displays of certain behaviors in order to make some type of assessment of the creative levels of their children. For example, gifted children frequently read reference books for enjoyment, and they may do this in preference to other behaviors which the teacher may deem more appropriate. Discretion should be used by the teacher concerning activities that the gifted child prefers to choose after his essential work has been completed. Generally, the behaviors of gifted children differ from those of normal children with regard to speed of response and breadth and depth of response.

GLOSSARY

Abreaction: Release of emotional tension caused by conflict and frustration.

Absolute threshold: The intensity or frequency at which a stimulus becomes effective or ceases to become effective, as measured under experimental conditions.

Accommodation: (1) Adjustment in order to make something suitable or congruous. (2) Change in the shape of the eye lens as an individual focuses for a different distance.

Acidosis: A pathological condition resulting from accumulation of acid or loss of base in the body and characterized by an increase in hydrogen ion concentration.

Acrocephaly (oxycephaly): A congenital condition in which the top of the head is pointed. The eyes are large, widely set, and tend to slant downward and toward the outside, and the optic nerve is frequently atrophied. The hands and feet may be webbed and mental retardation is typical.

Acting-out: Behavioral discharge of tension in response to a present situation or stimulus, as if it were the situation or stimulus which was originally associated with the tension. Often a chronic and habitual pattern of response to frustration and conflict.

Affect: Emotional feeling tone or mood.

Affective disorder: Disorder of mood or feeling with resulting thought and behavioral disturbances. The chief forms are manic-depressive psychosis and psychotic depressive reactions.

Affective processes: Involving emotion, feeling, or mood; the feelings accompanying a thought—pleasant or unpleasant, intense or mild.

Agnosia: Loss of the power to recognize the import of sensory stimuli.

Agraphia: Inability to express thoughts in writing due to a central lesion.

Alexia: Visual aphasia or word blindness; inability to read due to a central lesion.

Allele: One of two or more contrasting genes, situated at the same locus in homologous chromosomes, which determines alternative characters in inheritance.

Allergy: A hypersensitive state acquired through exposure to a particular allergen or re-exposure bringing to light an altered capacity to react.

Amaurotic familial idiocy: A disease of infants and children, marked by changes in the macula lutea retinae, increasing failure of vision, paralysis, and death.

Ambivalence: Simultaneous existence of conflicting feelings or attitudes toward an object or person.

Amentia: Mental deficiency.

Anal stage: The stage of pregenital (infantile) libido development in which sexual activity is connected with pleasurable gratification in the anal region.

Analytical mode or style: One type of conceptual style based largely on a breakdown and analysis of the smallest component parts, or units, of any problem or idea.

Anatomical: Pertaining to anatomy or to the structure of an organism.

Anencephaly: A developmental anomaly characterized by absence of the cranial vault and by the cerebral hemispheres completely missing or reduced to small masses attached to the base of the skull.

Anlage: The earliest discernible indication of an organ or part during embryonic development.

Anorexia: Loss of appetite.

Anorexia nervosa: A serious nervous condition in which the patient loses his appetite and systematically takes in little food, so that he becomes greatly emaciated.

Anoxemia: Reduction of oxygen content of the blood below physiological levels.

Anoxia: Deficient amount of oxygen in the tissues of a part of the body or in the blood stream supplying such a part.

Anxiety: An exaggerated state of fear that motivates a variety of behaviors, especially defensive behaviors.

Anxiety reaction: A neurotic reaction with diffuse anxiety and physiological anxiety indicators, such as sweating and palpitation.

Apathy: Lack of feeling or response.

Aphasia: A condition in which the individual suffers from an organic impairment resulting in inability to use symbolic processes.

Apraxia: Inability to carry out purposeful movements in the absence of paralysis or other motor or sensory impairment.

Arthritis: Inflammation of a joint.

Articulation: The enunciation of words and sentences.

Art therapy: A type of psychotherapy using art as a therapeutic device.

Assimilation: The reception and correct interpretation of sensory impressions.

Assimilation-recall disparity: The difference between what is recalled and what is actually understood.

Asthma: A disease marked by recurrent attacks of wheezing coughs, labored breathing, and a sense of constriction due to spasmodic contractions of the bronchi.

Ataxia: A form of cerebral palsy resulting in marked inability to coordinate bodily movement.

Athetosis: A form of cerebral palsy marked by slow, recurring, weaving movements of the limbs.

Atony: Deficient muscular tone.

Audiogram: Graphic record of hearing acuity obtained by the use of an instrument known as an audiometer.

Audiometer: An instrument for testing the hearing acuity of an individual.

Aura: Premonitory sensations or hallucinations that may warn of an impending epileptic seizure.

Autism: Disorder characterized by extreme withdrawal, inaccessibility, inability to relate to other persons, and language difficulties.

Automatism: Mannerism peculiar to severely handicapped children, like ritualistic movements of the hand; any act performed by a person without his being aware of it.

Autonomic nervous system: That system concerned with visceral activities, smooth muscles, and endocrine glands. It is a functional division of the nervous system.

Autosomal recessive gene: A recessive gene that is in an ordinary paired chromosome, as distinguished from a sex chromosome.

Autotelic: (1) Related to self-teaching or self-thought. (2) Pertaining to an environment that helps the child learn by himself through exploration or trial and error without the help of anyone else.

Aversive stimulus: A stimulus which a person tends to avoid if at all possible.

Barrier (Kurt Lewin): Hurdle or obstacle which is in the way of an individual's reaching his goals.

Baseline: Beginning observations prior to intervention; level of functioning established or measured without any active intervention from the observer.

Baseline observation: An operant conditioning procedure in which an initial rate of some response is established. It can be used for descriptive purposes or as a control condition prior to the introduction of behavior modification procedures and subsequent response rate comparisons.

Baserate: Percentage or frequency of occurrence of any behavior within a particular amount of time.

Behavior modification: Application of Skinner's principles of reinforcement learning (1953) to changing and shaping behavior. A technique of modifying another person's behavior by use of systematic reinforcement which may be positive or negative.

Behavior therapy: A method of psychotherapy based on learning principles. It uses such techniques as counterconditioning, reinforcement, and shaping to modify behavior.

Bibliotherapy: A type of psychotherapy in which reading selected works is therapeutic.

Bielschowsky-Jansky disease: The late infantile form of amaurotic familial idiocy.

Bilaterality: From bilateral, meaning both sides. Especially related to hemispheric functioning and the two sides (right-left) of the body.

Bilingual: Use of or ability to use two languages.

Binaural: Involving the use of both ears.

Binocular: Relating to the use of both eyes.

Body image: Awareness of one's own body as it relates to the total environment.

Brain damage: Any damage to the brain that results in varying degrees of dysfunctioning.

Cardiovascular system: Pertaining to the heart and blood vessels.

Carrier: A person who possesses a defect but shows no evidence of it and can pass it to his offspring.

Carry-over: The process of transferring information from one setting to another.

Catalytic force: A force which accelerates or decelerates a reaction.
Cataract: An opaque area on the crystalline eye lens or on its capsule.
Catastrophic reaction: Extreme helplessness, despair, or anxiety experienced when an individual is confronted with a task beyond his ability.
Catatonic schizophrenia: A condition in which negativistic reactions as well as stupor or excitement are conspicuous.
Catharsis: A method used to obtain discharge of strong emotions which is intended to achieve abreaction. Psychodynamically oriented clinicians assume that by bringing emotionally laden fears and problems to the conscious level, therapists can deal with them.
Central nervous system: The total neural tissue which comprises the brain and spinal cord.
Centroencephalic region: Pertaining to the center of the encephalon, which is a mass of nerve tissue contained within the cranium, including the cerebrum, cerebellum, pons, and medulla oblongata.
Cephalalgia vasomotoria: Vascular headache of the nonmigrainous type.
Cerebral cortex: The gray matter composing the external layer of the brain.
Cerebral dominance: The condition in which one hemisphere of the brain is more involved in governing an individual's function than the other hemisphere.
Cerebral palsy: Any one of a group of conditions in which motor control is affected because of lesions in various parts of the brain.
Cerebral vascular disease: Disease in the vessels of the brain.
Cerebrum: The main portion of the brain, occupying the upper part of the cranium and the two cerebral hemispheres. It is united by the corpus callosum and forms the largest part of the central nervous system in man.
Channels of communication: The sensory-motor pathways through which language is transmitted.
Chromosomal anomaly: An irregularity in the chromosomes, which are small rod-shaped bodies that carry hereditary factors.
Chromosome: One of the basic units in the nucleus of the cell which carries the genes or hereditary factors.
Chronological age (C.A.): The real age of an individual in years and months.
Clubfoot: A congenitally deformed foot.
Cognitive processes: Modes of thought, knowing, and symbolic representation, including comprehension, judgment, memory, imagining, and reasoning.
Cognitive style: A certain approach to problem-solving, based on intellectual, as distinguished from affective, schemes of thought.
Colic: Acute abdominal pain.
Compensation: An ego defense mechanism against feelings of inferiority and inadequacy; an attempt to substitute or compensate for a real or imagined defect by emphasizing a more positive trait, skill, or attribute.
Conceptual style: (1) An approach that characterizes individuals. It may vary from impulsive to reflective, from rational to irrational, or from systematic to disorderly. (2) The manner in which one expresses his ideas.
Concrete mode: (1) One of the styles of cognitive functioning that describes the child's approach to problem-solving at a simple, ele-

mentary level. (2) The use of tangible objects in instruction, as opposed to purely verbal instruction.

Conditioned response: A learned or acquired response to a conditioned stimulus, i.e., to a stimulus that did not originally evoke the response.

Congenital: Existing since birth or possibly prenatal (i.e., the individual is born with the condition, defect, or disease).

Consanguineous: Of the same blood; usually related to blood types and to blood relationships.

Conscious: (1) In possession of awareness or mental life or having sensations and feelings. (2) The condition of an organism that is receiving impressions or having experiences.

Constitutional: Pertaining to all conditions present at birth, plus any additions after birth.

Continuous reinforcement: A schedule by which reinforcement is given after each response; a 1:1 relationship between response and reinforcement.

Convulsive disorder: A clinical syndrome, the major symptom of which is loss of consciousness or recurrent seizures or convulsions.

Coping: Use of a dysfunctioning component in spite of its dysfunction.

Correlation coefficient: The degree of correspondence between two variables; a statistical index of covariation that varies from +1.00 to −1.00.

Cranial anomaly: Malformation of the cranium.

Cretinism: A chronic condition due to congenital lack of thyroid secretion. It is marked by arrested physical and mental development with dystrophy of the bones and soft parts and lowered basal metabolism.

Cross-modal: Including more than one sensory modality.

Culture-free test: A type of intelligence test that has been constructed to minimize bias due to ethnic background or to the differing experiences of children raised in rural rather than urban cultures or in lower-class rather than middle- or upper-class cultures.

Cumulative deficit: Addition to former underachievement to the point that the further the child goes in his scholastic career, the further behind he falls in his educational achievement.

Cystic fibrosis: A pathological change in an organ, involving overgrowth of fibrous tissue and accompanied by the development of cystic spaces.

Death wish: According to Freudian theory, the unconscious wish for or drive toward death.

Decibel: A unit of hearing or audition. One decibel is equal approximately to the smallest difference in loudness that the human ear can detect.

Decoding: The receptive habits in the language process, e.g., sensory acuity, awareness, discrimination, and vocabulary comprehension.

Defense mechanism: An adjustment made, often unconsciously, through either action or avoidance of action, in order to escape recognition by oneself of personal qualities or motives which might lower self-esteem or heighten anxiety.

Deficit: (1) Inadequacy in functioning due to general immaturity and developmental lag. (2) Malfunctioning due to irregularities, such as specific lesions.

Delayed speech: Speech which is out-of-phase with other normal development.

Denial: Defense mechanism by which unpleasant thoughts or feelings are denied from the consciousness.

Dermal system: Pertaining to the skin.

Desensitization: A therapeutic technique, based on learning theory, in which a client is first trained in muscle relaxation and then imagines a series of increasingly anxiety-provoking situations, until he no longer experiences anxiety while thinking about the stimuli. The learning principle involved is reciprocal inhibition, according to which two incompatible responses cannot simultaneously be made by a person.

Diabetes mellitus: A disorder of carbohydrate metabolism characterized by an excessive amount of glucose in the urine and in the blood.

Digestive system: The system which converts food into materials fit to be absorbed and assimilated.

Disability: The behavior resulting from an impairment which causes an individual to lack an adequate physical tool for behavior, so that his culture perceives this lack as making him less able.

Discrimination: The act of distinguishing differences among stimuli.

Disinhibition: Disruption of an inhibitory process by a distracting stimulus; lack of emotional control.

Displacement: The substitution of one object for another as a target for aggression or as a source of gratification.

Dissociation: An unconscious mechanism by which an idea or group of ideas is split off from the main body of the mental contents and becomes inaccessible to consciousness.

Distractability: Overresponsiveness to extraneous stimuli.

Dominant gene: A gene which can determine a characteristic by itself.

Down's syndrome: A broad term referring to mongolism.

Dyad: Any prolonged interpersonal relationship between two individuals (parent-child, husband-wife, sibling-sibling, etc.).

Dysarthria: Imperfect articulation in speech.

Dysfunction: Abnormal or imperfect functioning of an organ.

Dyslexia: Usually related to ,the idea of reading difficulties due to cerebral lesions.

Dyspraxia: Partial loss of ability to perform coordinated movements.

Echolalia: Meaningless repetition by an individual of words addressed to him.

Educable mental retardate (EMR): A mentally retarded individual whose IQ is in the 60 to 80 range and who can benefit from special education programs.

Ego: The individual's conception of himself; the superficial part of the id which has been modified by the direct influence of the external world through the senses and which has been imbued with consciousness. Its functions are the testing of reality and the acceptance (through selection and control) of part of the demands of the id.

Egocentricity: Disposition to dwell on oneself and to view every situation from a personal angle; self-centeredness.

Electroencephalogram (EEG): A graphic record of minute electrical impulses arising from brain cells, as measured by an electronic device called an electroencephalograph.

Electrophysiology: The science of physiology in its relations to electricity; the study of the electrical reactions of the body.

Electroshock: Treatment for psychotic patients in which shock is produced by application of electric current to the brain.

Embryo: The early or developing stage of any organism, especially the developing product of fertilization of an egg. In a human, the embryo is generally considered to be the developing organism from one week after conception to the end of the second month.

Emetic: A substance that causes vomiting.

Emotional lability: In psychiatry, emotional instability; a tendency to show alternating states of gaiety and somberness.

Empathy: A projection of one's own personality into the personality of another in order to understand him better.

Encephalitis: Inflammation of the brain.

Encephalopathy: Any degenerative disease of the brain.

Encopresis: Incontinence of feces which is not caused by organic defect or illness.

Endocrinological: Pertaining to the glands of internal secretion.

Endogenous: Developing within or originating from causes within the organism.

Endomorphic (build): A type of body build in which there is a relative preponderance of soft roundness throughout the body, with large digestive viscera and accumulations of fat, the body usually presenting a large trunk and thighs and tapering extremities.

Enuresis: Involuntary nocturnal discharge of urine. Also known as bedwetting.

Epidemiological: Pertaining to a disease which attacks a great many people and spreads rapidly.

Epilepsy: A disease characterized by one or more of the following symptoms: paroxysmally recurring impairment or loss of consciousness, involuntary excess or cessation of muscle movements, psychic or sensory disturbances, and perturbation of the autonomic nervous system.

Equilibrium: A state of balance; a condition in which opposing forces exactly counteract each other.

Etiology: The investigation of the causes or significant antecedents of a given phenomenon.

Eugenics: The study and control of various possible influences as a means of improving the hereditary characteristics of a race.

Euthenics: The science of race improvement through the regulation of environment.

Exogenous: Developing or originating outside the organism.

Expatiation: To speak or write at length or in detail.

Experience method: An approach to reading involving the practice of using the natural experiences of a child in developing his or her ability to read. The student may be asked to write words or to use words verbally which come from his own experiences.

Expressive aphasia: Defect in or loss of the power of expression by speech, writing, or signs, due to injury or disease of the brain centers.

Expressive language: The ability to express or communicate verbal, written, or symbolic language.

External control: Control of an individual by others' opinions and influences.

Extinction: The weakening of a response following removal of reinforcement.

Factor analysis: Statistical technique for reducing a large number of correlations into a few manageable dimensions or factors that represent the underlying sources of similarities and differences among correlations.

Familial retardation: A culturally induced, mild mental retardation, usually characterized by IQ's between 50 and 80.

Family therapy: A specialized type of group therapy in which the members of a given family constitute the group.

Feeblemindedness: A generic term covering all grades of mental inferiority or backwardness.

Feedback: Return to a control center of information regarding events under its control; in psychology, the return of sensory information from the periphery, used in the control of movement and analogous processes; the loop of information going back from output to input.

Fenestration: The surgical creation of a new opening in the labyrinth of the ear for the restoration of hearing.

Feral children: Children raised by nonhuman parents.

Fetus: (1) The unborn offspring of any viviparous animal. (2) The developing young in the human uterus after the end of the second month. Before eight weeks it is called an embryo; it becomes an infant when it is completely outside the body of the mother, even before the cord is cut.

Figure-ground: Tendency of one part of a perceptual configuration to stand out clearly, while the remainder forms a background.

Fissure of Rolando: A division on the right and left hemispheres, grossly separating the frontal and parietal parts of the brain.

Form constancy: Persistence in the perception of a shape, object, or figure when, from a physical viewpoint, a change should take place or may be expected or predicted.

Galactose: A chemical obtained from lactose or milk sugar by the action of an enzyme or by boiling with a mineral acid. It is a white crystalline substance, resembles glucose in most of its properties, but is less soluble and less sweet. It forms mucic acid when oxidized with nitric acid.

Galactosemia: An inherited disorder of carbohydrate metabolism causing an error in the metabolism of galactose in milk. The condition leads to malnutrition in early infancy.

Gargoylism (Hurler's disease): A rare hereditary condition characterized by a peculiarly shaped head and skeletal system. It is thought to result from inability of the body cells to metabolize certain substances of high molecular weight, which consequently accumulate in the body.

Gastrointestinal: Pertaining to the stomach and intestine.

Gaucher's disease: A familial disorder characterized by enlargement of the spleen, skin pigmentation, and the presence of distinctive kerasin-containing cells in the liver, spleen, and bone marrow.

Gene: The biological unit of heredity. It is self-reproducing and located in a definite position on a particular chromosome.

Generalization: (1) In concept formation, problem-solving, and transfer of training, the detection by the learner of a characteristic or principle common to a class of objects, events, or problems. (2) In conditioning, the principle that once a conditioned response has been established for a given stimulus, other similar stimuli will also evoke that response.

Genetic: Pertaining to inherited factors.

Genotypical level of functioning: The level of functioning which explains behavior and must be inferred. It includes self-esteem, affect, and other sources of behavior that must be conjectured.

Gestalt: A structure or configuration of physical, biological, or psychological phenomena which is integrated to constitute a functional unit with properties not derivable from its parts in summation.

Glaucoma: Diseased condition of the eye characterized by increasing intraocular pressure and opacity of the crystalline lens.

Global aphasia: Aphasia which involves all the functions which make up speech or communication.

Grand mal seizure: A type of epilepsy characterized by considerable neural discharge and usually lasting about five minutes. It begins with the severe contraction of the muscles and proceeds to rhythmic movements and tremors.

Grapheme: A basic unit of the writing system consisting of all written symbols or sequences that represent a single phoneme.

Group therapy: Psychotherapy of several persons at the same time in small groups.

Habit hierarchy: An arrangement or ordering of activities on the basis of importance.

Handedness: The hand preference of an individual.

Handicap: Impairment of a particular kind of social and psychological behavior. It is the extent of the individual's subjective interpretation of his disability and impairment.

Haptic: Pertaining to the sense of touch.

Hartnup syndrome: A condition characterized by oversensitivity to light and excessive excretion of amino acids and indole derivatives. It is caused by malfunction in the metabolism of tryptophan.

Hedonism: Philosophical school of ancient Greece, emphasizing pleasure and sensual gratification as primary life goals.

Hematological disorder: Blood disorder.

Hemiplegia: Paralysis of one side of the body.

Hemophilia: A hereditary condition characterized by delayed clotting of the blood with consequent difficulty in checking hemorrhage.

Hepatolenticular degeneration: Degeneration of the liver.

Heredity: Those factors acquired from parents as the result of the action of a single gene or a complex of genes.

Heuristic: Serving to discover or to stimulate investigation.

Histamine cephalalgia: Recurring headaches over the region of the external carotid artery, with local temperature elevation, lacrimation, and rhinorrhea, caused by the administration of histamine or by the release of histamine in the body.

Historical level of functioning: The background of an individual which explains the historical events that lead to a particular genotype.

Homeostasis: Maintenance of equilibrium and constancy among the bodily processes.

Homogeneity: The state of being composed of similar or identical elements or parts; uniformity.

Huntington's chorea: The chronic occurrence of a wide variety of rapid, jerky, but well-coordinated movements performed involuntarily.

Hydrocephaly: A condition involving excess cerebrospinal fluid within the ventricular and subarachnoid spaces in the cranial vault.

Hyperactivity (hyperkinesis): A personality disorder of childhood or adolescence characterized by overactivity, restlessness, distractability, and limited attention span.

Hypoactivity: Insufficient motor activity characterized by lack of energy.

Hypoglycemia: An abnormally diminished content of glucose in the blood.

Hypoparathyroidism: The condition produced by defective action of the parathyroids or by the removal of those bodies.

Hypothalamus: The portion of the diencephalon which forms the floor and part of the lateral wall of the third ventricle. It includes the optic chiasm, mamillary bodies, tuber cinereum, infundibulum, and hypophysis. The nuclei of this region exert control over visceral activities, water balance, temperature, sleep, etc.

Id: The impersonality of the mind apart from its ego; the true unconscious or deepest part of the mind which is the reservoir of instinctual impulses and is dominated by the pleasure principle and blind impulsive wishing.

Identification: An emotional tie unconsciously causing a person to think, feel, and act as he imagines the person with whom he has the tie does. Viewed as both a developmental process and a defense mechanism.

Idiot: Old term for a severely mentally retarded person.

Imbecile: A feebleminded person whose mental age is between two and seven years.

Impairment: Actual physical defect. (Refers to the biological forces.)

Impulsivity: Behavior engaged in without sufficient forethought or care.

Indole: A compound which gives part of the peculiar odor to the feces. It is found in large quantities in the urine and accumulates in the intestine in cases of intestinal obstruction.

Inhibition: Restraint or control exercised over an impulse, drive, or response tendency.

Innate: Those factors present at birth which result from the genetic component inherited from the parents plus any mutations.

Intellectualization: Defense mechanism related to isolation. The emotional bond or link between symbols and their emotional charges is broken by this process.

Interference: With reference to the sensory modalities, a detracting from one modality by a deficit in another modality.

Intermittent reinforcement: A schedule of reinforcement in which the reward is delivered on the basis of some specified ratio of responses. Reinforcement is not delivered after every desired response.

Internal control: Control which is initiated within the individual and is based on his own feelings and beliefs.

Intersensory integration: A workable, interdependent relationship between the sensory modalities, occurring in the positive aspects of channel multiplication and addition.

Inter-test scores: Comparisons among scores of different tests.

Intervening variable: A factor, inferred to be present between stimulus and response which accounts for one response rather than another to a certain stimulus. The intervening variable may be inferred without further specification, or it may be given concrete properties and may become an object of investigation.

Introjection: The act of absorbing the environment or the personality of others into one's own psyche to the extent of reacting to external events as though they were internal ones, thus producing identification of oneself with other persons or objects.

Introspection: Contemplation or observation of one's own thoughts and feelings; self-analysis.

Isolation: Defense mechanism by which inconsistent or contradictory attitudes and feelings are "walled off" from each other in the consciousness. Similar to repression, but different because in isolation the impulse or wish is consciously recognized but is separated from the present behavior (in repression neither the wish nor its relation to action is recognized).

Isolation mechanism: A symptom peculiar to the compulsion neurosis in which after an unpleasant event or any personal activity significant in the sense of a neurosis, a pause is interpolated during which nothing happens and no action is carried out.

Jacksonian epilepsy: A form of epilepsy in which the seizure manifests no loss of awareness but involves a definite series of convulsions affecting a limited region of the body.

Kinesthetic: Pertaining to the senses that yield knowledge of movements and location of the body.

Klinefelter's syndrome: A condition characterized by the presence of small testes. The individual looks like a male but has a genetic construction of XXY. This condition is generally accompanied by mental retardation.

Kufs's disease: The late juvenile form of amaurotic familial idiocy which occurs after age 15.

Labyrinth: The structural part or bony cavity of the inner ear.

Lactose: A white crystalline disaccharide, which on hydrolysis with acids or certain enzymes yields glucose and galactose.

Language: An arbitrary system of symbols by which ideas are conveyed.

Latency stage: A period of middle childhood, roughly the years from 6 to 12, when both sexual and aggressive impulses are said to be in a somewhat subdued state, so that the child's attention is directed outward and his curiosity about the environment makes him ready to learn.

Lateral dominance: The preferential use, in voluntary motor acts, of ipsilateral members of the different paired organs, such as the right ear, eye, hand, and leg, or the left ear, eye, hand, and leg.

Lateralization: A relationship to one side, such as a tendency in voluntary motor acts to use preferentially the organs (hand, foot, ear, eye) of the same side.

Lattices: Form of classification in which the focus is on the connective links and the parts which they link together.

Lesion: Any hurt, wound, or local degeneration.

Leukemia: A cancer affecting the balance of cells in the blood.

Level of aspiration (Kurt Lewin): A term referring to what an individual would like to achieve.

Libido: Sexual desire or energy; the dynamic expression or aspect of the sexual instinct which may attach itself to the ego or to external objects or persons.

Life space (Kurt Lewin): A term referring to a person's interaction with his environment.

Life style (Alfred Adler): A term referring to how an individual wants to live his life.

Linguistics: The science of language.

Longitudinal study: A research strategy based on observation and recording the behavior of subjects over periods of time. It involves obtaining measurements of the same subjects either continuously or at specific or regular intervals.

Lowe's disease: A deficiency of vitamin D which causes rickets and is associated with glaucoma, mental retardation, and renal tubule reabsorption dysfunction as evidenced by hypophosphatemia, acidosis, and aminoaciduria.

Malfunction: Failure to operate in the normal or usual manner; inadequate use of a function.

Mania: A heightened state of euphoria; increased mental and motoric activity.

Manual method: Method of teaching communication to deaf or hard-of-hearing patients by finger spelling and hand gestures.

Maple syrup urine disease: A genetotrophic disease involving an enzyme defect. The name is derived from the characteristic odor of the urine.

Masochism: A deviation in which sexual pleasure is attained from pain inflicted on oneself, from being dominated, or from being mistreated.

Matriarchal: Characteristic of a family ruled by the mother.

Mean: The arithmetical average; the sum of all scores divided by the number of scores.

Memory: The function of reviving past experiences related to objects, places, people, or events.

Meningitis: Inflammation of the membranes that envelop the brain and spinal cord.

Mental age (M.A.): The numerical equivalent of an individual's intelligence; one of the elements used in determining the intelligence quotient.

Mental retardation: A level of intellectual functioning that is significantly below average, that is apparent early in life, and that is characterized by behavioral deficiencies over a wide range of abilities.

Metabolic dysfunction: Dysfunction in the chemical processes and activities of the body.

Metabolism: The physical and chemical processes in living cells by which energy is provided.

Metronome: An instrument designed to mark exact time by a regularly repeated tick.

Microcephaly: Abnormal smallness of the head.

Migraine: A syndrome characterized by periodic headaches, often one sided, and accompanied by nausea, vomiting, and various sensory disturbances.

Minimal brain damage: Borderline cerebral deficit characterized mostly by behavioral rather than neurological signs.

Modality: An avenue of acquiring sensation; the visual, auditory, tactile, kinesthetic, olfactory, and gustatory modalities are the most common sense modalities.

Model: A diagrammatic representation of a concept.

Mongolism: A condition characterized by a small, anteroposteriorly flattened skull, short, flat-bridged nose, epicanthus, short phalanges, and widened space between the first and second digits of hands and feet, with moderate to severe mental retardation, and associated with a chromosomal abnormality.

Montessori method: A program of sensorimotor and perceptual training methods used with exceptional children.

Moron: A feebleminded person whose mental age is between 8 and 12 years.

Mosaicism: A form of Down's syndrome (mongolism) in which adjacent cells are found to contain different numbers of chromosomes.

Motor: Related to the origin or execution of muscular activity.

Motor aphasia: Aphasia in which the patient knows what he wishes to say but cannot utter the words because of inability to coordinate the muscles due to disease of the speech center.

Multiple sclerosis: A disease marked by hardening in sporadic patches throughout the brain or spinal cord, or both. Among its symptoms are weakness, incoordination, strong jerking movements of the legs and arms, abnormal mental exaltation, scanning speech, and nystagmus.

Multisensory: A term generally applied to training procedures which simultaneously utilize more than one sense modality.

Muscular dystrophy: One of the more common primary diseases of the muscles. It is characterized by weakness and atrophy of the skeletal muscles with increasing disability and deformity.

Music therapy: A type of psychotherapy in which music is used as a therapeutic aid.

Mutism: Inability or refusal to speak.

Myelin: The covering of the nerves in the central nervous system.

Negative feedback: Communication to the subject that his response was incorrect. It tends to reduce the chances of repetition of the behavior.

Negative reinforcement: A stimulus which, by producing a painful, or unpleasant reaction, strengthens the probability of an operant response. A loud noise, a very bright light, extreme heat or cold, and electric shock classify as negative reinforcers.

Neocortex: That portion of the pallium showing stratification and organization characteristic of the most highly evolved type.

Neoplasm: Any new and abnormal growth, such as a tumor.

Nephrogenic diabetes insipidus: Diabetes in which the kidneys fail to respond properly, caused by failure of the renal tubules to reabsorb water. The symptoms are excessive thirst, excessive urination, vomiting, dehydration, and erratic fever.

Nesting: A descriptive term for classifying an internal relationship between smaller parts and their all-inclusive whole.

Neurodermatitis: Chronic itching due to a nervous disorder.

Neurological lag: Neurological or nervous system development which is slower than other physical development.

Neuron: A structural unit of the nervous system consisting of the cell body, the nucleus, and the cell membrane.

Neurotic reaction: A form of maladjustment in which the individual is unable to cope with his anxieties and conflicts and develops abnormal symptoms. The disturbance is not severe enough to produce a profound personality derangement, as with psychotic reactions.

Niemann-Pick disease: A metabolic disorder characterized by enlargement of the liver and spleen. It often results in deafness and visual problems.

Noise: Any interference that reduces auditory intake; used in the field of communication to denote any extraneous signal in a communication system.

Nondirective therapy: A method of therapy developed by an American psychologist, Carl Rogers. It stresses psychotherapy as an opportunity for self-actualization and allows the client to guide the therapy.

Norm: An average, common, or standard performance under specified conditions, e.g., the average achievement test score of nine-year-old children or the average birth weight of male children.

Normal curve: The plotted form of the normal distribution.

Normal distribution: The standard, symmetrical bell-shaped frequency distribution, whose properties are commonly used in making statistical inferences from measurements derived from samples.

Nystagmus: An involuntary rapid movement of the eyeball, which may be horizontal, vertical, rotatory, or mixed.

Obesity: An increase in body weight beyond the limitation of skeletal and physical requirements as the result of an excessive accumulation of fat in the body.

Obsessive-compulsive (personality disorder): A disorder characterized by extreme concern with conformity and adherence to standards and moral dictates in a wide variety of behaviors. Persons with the disorder are generally overconscientious, rigid, inhibited, and unable to relax.

Occipital lobe: The posterior portion of the cerebral hemisphere.

Ocular: Pertaining to the eye.

Oedipus complex: Sexual attachment to the parent of the opposite sex, originating as the normal culmination of the infantile period of development.

Olfactory: Pertaining to the sense of smell.

Ontogeny: The developmental history of an organism.

Operant conditioning: The strengthening of a response by presenting a reinforcing stimulus if, and only if, the response occurs.

Operational: Based on empirical and measurable phenomena.
Oral method: Method of teaching communication of language to deaf or hard-of-hearing patients by spoken words.
Oral stage: The stage of pregenital (infantile) libido development in which sexual activity has not yet become separated from the taking in of nourishment.
Organic approach: A method of reading developed by Sylvia A. Warner, which she explains in her book, Teacher.
Organic inferiority: A term used by Adler which assumes an organic or biological basis for feelings of inferiority; there is a neurological relationship between organic inferiority and behavioral mechanisms of a compensatory nature.
Organicity: Dysfunction due to structural deficits in the central nervous system.
Orthopedic defect: Defect in the skeletal system.
Ossicular chain: The small bones of the middle ear.
Osteomyelitis: Inflammation of bone caused by a pyogenic organism. It may remain localized, or it may spread through the bone to involve the marrow, cortex, cancellous tissue and periosteum.
Otological: Pertaining to the ear.
Oval window: The junction between the stapes and the bony labyrinth of the inner ear.
Overcompensation: An attempt to excel in the very area in which one judges oneself to be inferior or weak. It is an attempt to overcome one's inferiority.

Parallel play period: The period during which children play alongside one another but not *with* each other. It usually lasts until age four.
Parietal lobe: The upper central lobe or portion of the brain.
Pathology: The study of diseased or abnormal conditions of an organism or any of its parts.
Peptic ulcer: An ulceration of the mucous membrane of the esophagus, stomach, or duodenum, caused by the action of the gastric juice.
Perception: Recognition of a quality without distinguishing meaning, which is the result of a complex set of reactions including sensory stimulation, organization within the nervous system, and memory.
Perinatal: The period of life from the twenty-first week of gestation to the second month after birth.
Perseveration: The tendency for one to persist in a specific act or behavior after it is no longer appropriate.
Petit mal seizure: A type of epilepsy which is characterized by short lapses of consciousness and commonly begins in early childhood.
Phallic stage: That stage of psychosexual development in which gratification is associated with sex organ stimulation and in which the sexual attachment is to the parent of the opposite sex.
Phenomenal field: The totality of objects or events which are directly experienced at any one moment.
Phenotype: The outward, visible expression of the hereditary constitution of an organism.
Phenotypical level of functioning: The way in which an individual actually functions underneath the outside facade or self-presentational state.
Phenylketonuria (PKU): Inherited faulty metabolism resulting in a

lack of the necessary enzyme for oxidizing phenylalanine which, in turn, promotes accumulation of phenylpyruvic acid and may cause mental retardation.

Phobia: An excessive or inappropriate fear of some particular object or situation which is, in fact, not dangerous.

Phobic reaction: A neurotic condition involving irrational and highly specific fears (e.g., of dirt, water, or high places) as the outstanding features of the neurotic pattern.

Phonation: The production of speech sounds.

Phoneme: Basic unit of sound by which the more complex parts of language (morphemes, like words or sentences) are formed.

Phonics: The system of relating speech sounds to specific letters or letter combinations.

Phylogeny: The origin and development of a species, as distinguished from ontogeny.

Pica: A craving for unnatural articles of food; a depraved appetite, such as is seen in hysteria and in pregnancy.

Plasticity: Characteristic behavior of some children with brain damage or schizophrenia which represents an extremely moldable state, not possessing definite boundaries.

Plate of the stapes: A bone in the ear which attaches to the oval window.

Play therapy: A treatment approach used with children which is based on the assumption that the young child can express thoughts and fantasies more directly in play than through verbal means.

Poliomyelitis: A common, acute viral disease characterized clinically by fever, sore throat, headache, and vomiting, often with stiffness of the neck and back. The major illness is characterized by involvement of the central nervous system.

Polygenes: Genes which produce hereditary characteristics through their interaction.

Polygenic: Pertaining to or influenced by several different genes.

Positive feedback: Communication to the subject that his response was correct. This information reinforces the individual so that he will continue or will increase the behavior.

Positive reinforcement: A stimulus which, when added to a situation, increases the probability of an operant response. Food, water, and sexual contact classify as positive reinforcers.

Postnatal: Occurring after birth.

Preconscious: Latent mental processes of which the individual is not aware at a given moment, but which he may call to consciousness more or less readily.

Prenatal: Existing or occurring prior to birth.

Primary process thinking: The primitive cognitive mode characteristic of infants and children, which is not based on rules of organization or logic. A characteristic of the id is the presence of primary process thinking. It is illogical, pleasure-oriented, has no sense of time or order, and does not discriminate between reality and fantasy.

Programmed instruction: Instruction through information given in small steps, each requiring a correct response by the learner before the next step is presented.

Projection: A defense mechanism by which a person protects himself from awareness of his own undesirable traits by attributing those traits excessively to others.

Projective test: Personality test based on the assumption that any vague, unstructured stimulus will reveal unconscious aspects of one's perception and personality. Such tests include the Rorschach ink blots, drawings, the Thematic Apperception Test, picture completion, and story and sentence completion tests.

Prophylaxis: The prevention of disease; preventive treatment.

Proprioception: Relating to stimuli arising within the organism.

Prosthesis: The replacement of a part of the body by an artificial substitute.

Protocol: The original records of the results of testing.

Psychoanalysis: A dynamic system of psychology originated and developed by Freud, which attributes behavior to repressed factors in the unconscious, for the investigation of which it provides an elaborate technique, utilized especially in the treatment of nervous mental disorders or personality flaws, as well as in the interpretation of a variety of cultural phenomena.

Psychoanalytic psychotherapy: Intensive, long-term treatment based on Freudian methods and techniques, aimed at a significant restructuring of large segments of the personality.

Psychogenic: Traceable to psychological experiences and learning.

Psycholinguistics: The study of the processes by which the intentions of speakers are transformed into signals and by which these signals are transformed into interpretations of hearers.

Psychometrician: A psychologist who administers batteries of tests.

Psychomotor: Pertaining to the motor effects of psychological processes.

Psychomotor seizure: A type of epilepsy characterized by automatisms which range from the unconscious continuing of normal activity to bizarre, inappropriate, and obsessive behavior.

Psychopathology: The study of the causes and nature of mental disease.

Psychosexual: Pertaining to sex life in its broadest sense, including the mental and emotional aspects.

Psychosis: Any abnormal or pathological mental condition which tends to constitute a disease entity.

Psychosomatic disorder: An ailment with organic symptoms attributable to emotional or other psychological causes. The disorder is aggravated by or results from continuous states of anxiety, stress, and emotional conflict.

Psychotherapy: The treatment of disorders by psychological methods; these methods may differ widely, including such approaches as nondirective psychotherapy, re-education, persuasion, psychoanalysis, and gestalt.

Pure tone audiometer: An instrument used to measure hearing ability. A tone is emitted, and the patient responds if it is heard.

Q-sort: An assessment technique consisting of a number of descriptive sentences or phrases, usually typed on individual cards, which the subject is required to sort into a number of discrete categories from very characteristic to very uncharacteristic of himself or others. Numbers of items in each category usually conform to a forced normal distribution.

Ratiocinative: Pertaining to reasoning or drawing deductive conclusions.

Rationalization: A defense mechanism by which logical, socially approved reasons for one's behavior are presented that, although plausible, do not represent the "real" reasons or motives behind one's actions.

Reaction formation: A defense mechanism by which a subject denies a disapproved motive by giving expression to its opposite.

Receptive aphasia: Inability to understand the meaning of written, spoken, or tactile speech symbols, due to disease of the auditory and visual word centers.

Receptive-auditory language: The ability to understand spoken, written, or symbolic language.

Receptive-expressive distinction: The difference between the ability to receive and understand information and the ability to express knowledge of this information.

Recessive gene: A gene which requires another gene like itself to be manifested in a trait. If it is paired with a dominant gene, the dominant gene will be manifested.

Reciprocal inhibition: Concept formulated by Wolpe, stating that anxiety responses can be eliminated by training an individual to make an antagonistic response. Reciprocal inhibition occurs through counterconditioning.

Regression: A return to more primitive or infantile modes of response, either (1) retrogression to behavior engaged in when younger, or (2) primitivation, i.e., more infantile or childlike behavior, but not necessarily that which occurred in the individual's earlier life.

Reinforcement: A procedure to strengthen or weaken a response by the administration of immediate rewards (positive reinforcement) or punishment (negative reinforcement).

Relational mode: A conceptual style characterized by considering one object or entity in connection with another.

Representational level: According to Osgood, the highest level of language organization.

Repression: A defense mechanism by which an impulse or memory which might provoke unpleasant feelings is denied by its removal from awareness.

Reproductive system: The reproductive or sexual organs.

Respiration: The function of breathing; taking air in and expelling it from the lungs.

Response: An overt action resulting from a stimulus.

Reticular formation: Intermingled fibers and gray substance that fills the interspaces of the brain.

Retrocochlear: Behind the cochlea.

Retrolental fibroplasia (RLF): A disease of the retina in which a mass of scar tissue forms in the back of the lens of the eye and results in blindness. It occurs chiefly in infants born prematurely who receive excessive oxygen.

Rheumatic fever: An acute disease occurring chiefly in children and young adults and characterized by fever, inflammation and pain in and around the joints, and inflammatory involvement of the pericardium and heart valves.

Rheumatism: A disease marked by inflammation of the connective tissue structures of the body, especially the muscles and joints, by pain in these parts, by vegetations on the valves of the heart, and by the presence of Aschoff bodies in the myocardium and skin.

Rhinencephalon: A name given the part of the brain that is homologous with the olfactory portions of the brain in lower animals.

Rhinorrhea: The free discharge of a thin nasal mucus.

Rhythm disorder: Speech disorder characterized by hesitation, repetition, prolongations, and stoppages of speech sounds.

Rickets: A condition caused by a vitamin D deficiency, especially in infancy and childhood, with disturbance of bone formation. The disease is marked by bending and distortion of the bones under muscular action, by the formation of nodular enlargements on the ends and sides of the bones, and by delayed closure of the fontanels, pain in the muscles, and degeneration of the liver and spleen.

Rigidity: A tendency for the muscles to become very stiff after they have been extended.

Rogerian technique: A method of psychotherapy developed by an American psychologist, Carl Rogers. It stresses psychotherapy as an opportunity for self-actualization and employs a nondirective or client-centered approach.

Role playing: In psychotherapy, a technique which requires the individual to enact a social role other than his own or to try out new roles for himself.

Rorschach ink blots: One of the first personality tests developed by Swiss psychiatrist Hermann Rorschach to study the unconscious aspects of personality. It consists of 10 ink blots of various shapes and color combinations.

Rotation: An act of faulty written reproduction in which a subject inverts or reproduces a figure in any other position than that of its original one.

Rubella: An acute viral disease causing an eruption similar to the measles. Also called German measles.

Sadism: A sexual deviation in which sexual gratification is obtained through inflicting physical pain on others.

Sanitarium: An institution for promotion of health.

Scapegoating: The act of transferring blame for behavior to others.

Schema: See Model.

Schizophrenia: A group of psychotic reactions characterized by fundamental disturbances in reality relationships.

Schizophrenogenic mother: A term used by those who believe that the attitude of the mother toward her child is the basic determinant of schizophrenia.

Secondary process thinking: Psychoanalytic concept referring to organized, logical, and reality-oriented adult thinking. It is an ego function based on the reality principle.

Self-concept: A person's idea of himself.

Self-esteem: Valuation of one's self.

Self-gestalt: Configuration of the self; self-concept which includes perception of the total self.

Self-presentational level of functioning: The impression one makes on others; the superficial facade.

Semantic: Pertaining to meaning and interpretation of words.

Semicircular canal: The sense organ of equilibrium in the inner ear. Postural changes result in disturbance of the fluids of this canal.

Sensory aphasia: Inability to understand the meaning of written, spoken, or tactile speech symbols, due to disease of the auditory and visual word centers.

Sensory-motor: Pertaining to the combined functioning of the sensory modalities and motor mechanisms.

Shaping: A basic process of operant conditioning involving the reinforcement of successively closer approximations to the desired behavior.

Sinusitis: Inflammation of a sinus. The condition can be acute or chronic.

Socialization: Shaping of individual characteristics and behavior through the stimuli and reinforcements that the social environment provides.

Sociometry: A method for mapping relationships of attraction and rejection among members of a social group. Each member expresses his choices for or against other members. The social map is constructed from the data provided by these choices.

Somatic: Pertaining to the physical body.

Somatotype: Physique or body build. Term used by some theorists (e.g., Sheldon) in relating personality to physical characteristics.

Spastic: Characterized by sudden, violent involuntary contraction of a muscle or group of muscles, attended by pain and interference with function, and producing involuntary movement and distortion.

Spatial orientation: Awareness of space with regard to direction, form, and position.

Speech: Audible communication through a system of arbitrary vocal symbols.

Spielmeyer-Vogt disease: The juvenile form of amaurotic familial idiocy.

Spina bifida: A developmental anomaly characterized by a defect in the bony encasement of the spinal cord.

Spontaneous recovery: The return of a conditioned response after a lapse of time following extinction.

Spontaneous remission: The disappearance of symptoms or maladaptive behaviors in the absence of therapeutic intervention.

Spread of effect (Thorndike): The influence that an anticipatory rewarding state of affairs has on adjacent connections both before and after its occurrence. The effect diminishes with each step that the connection is removed from the rewarding one.

Standard deviation: A measure of variation of a group of scores or values; the square root of the mean of the amount by which each case departs from the mean of all the cases.

Stanford-Binet: The American version of one of the first intelligence scales, developed originally in France by Binet and revised by Terman at Stanford University.

Stapes: Name meaning stirrup which refers to a stirrup-shaped bone in the ear.

Stereognostic discrimination: The faculty of perceiving and understanding the form and nature of objects by the sense of touch.

Stereotyping: A biased generalization, usually about a social or national group, according to which individuals are falsely assigned traits they do not possess.

Stereotypy: The persistent repetition of certain phrases or words that do not make sense. It may also be a persistent maintaining of bodily attitude or of senseless movements.

Steroid: A group name for substances chemically resembling cholesterol. Examples are sex hormones, cardiac aglycones, bile acids, and toad poisons.

Stimulus: An external event, act, or influence which causes physiological change in a sense organ.

Stimulus-response theory (S-R): A psychological view that all behavior is in response to stimuli and that the appropriate tasks of psychological science are those which identify stimuli, the responses correlated with them, and the processes intervening between stimulus and response. There are several varieties of stimulus-response theory, depending on the kind of intervening processes inferred.

Strabismus: Visual defect in which the glance is out of focus; the individual is unable to control the two visual axes relative to each other.

Strauss syndrome: The group of symptoms characterizing the "brain-injured" child; named after A. Strauss for his work with the hyperactive child.

Streptococcus: Nonmotile, chiefly parasitic gram-positive bacteria that divide only in one plane, occur in pairs or chains but not in packets, and include important pathogens of man and domestic animals.

Stuttering: A problem of speech behavior involving three definitive factors: (1) speech disfluency, (2) reactions of the listeners to the speaker's disfluency, and (3) the reactions of the speaker to the listeners' reactions.

Subarachnoid space: The space below the arachnoid layer of the brain.

Sublimation: A form of the defense mechanism of substitution, whereby socially unacceptable motives find expression in socially acceptable ways. It is most commonly applied to sexual desires.

Successive approximation: The procedure used in shaping a behavior. The subject is reinforced for successively closer approximations to the desired behavior until that behavior is emitted.

Superego: That part of the mental apparatus which criticizes the ego and produces distress, anxiety, or punishment whenever the ego tends to accept impulses emanating from the id.

Suppression: A conscious tendency to dismiss the memory of unpleasant or undesirable thoughts or actions.

Syllogistic: A form of logic using a systematic division of propositions into sequential arguments.

Symbiotic psychosis: A close relationship between two individuals, usually mother and son, with a break from reality ties; a feeding of one person on another in terms of psychological strengths.

Symbol: Something that represents another thing.

Symbolization: Using language abstractly.

Symptom: A manifestation of disordered functioning, including both the physical and psychological aspects.

Symptomatology: A branch of medical science concerned with the symptoms of diseases.

Symptom substitution: Appearance of a new symptom when one is taken away if the true "cause" is not treated.

Syndrome: A pattern of symptoms which characterizes a specific disorder.

Synergy: The combining of elementary motor processes to form a complex coordinated movement.

Syntactic: Dealing with grammar and rules governing sentence structure and sequence.

Synthesis: A "putting together."

Syphilis: A contagious venereal disease leading to structural and cutaneous lesions. It is caused by the spirochete *Treponema pallidum.*

Tactile: Referring to the sense of touch.
Tay-Sachs disease: The infantile form of amaurotic familial idiocy.
Teleological development: Growth according to a purpose or end goal; a vitalistic doctrine stating that the processes of behavior are not determined only by the past or present but by the future as well.
Temperament: Constitutional disposition to react emotionally.
Temporal lobe: The lower lateral lobe of the cerebral hemisphere.
Test-retest: A measure of reliability in which the same test is given at two different times, and the scores are correlated.
Threshold of discrimination: The least amount of difference between two stimuli which is necessary before a discrimination can be made.
Time out: An experimental procedure in which the subject is isolated from all reinforcing stimuli for a specified period of time.
Tinnitus: A noise in the ears, as ringing, buzzing, roaring, clicking, etc.
Token reinforcement: A type of reinforcement in which a token (e.g., a poker chip), as a secondary reinforcer, can be exchanged for a primary reinforcing stimulus.
Tokens: The total number of words in a message. The type-token ratio suggested by W. Johnson (1953) consists of the number of different words (types—nouns, pronouns, adjectives) in proportion to the total number of words (tokens).
Toxemia: A general intoxication due to the absorption of bacterial products (toxins) formed at a local source of infection.
Trainable mental retardate (TMR): A mentally retarded individual who is likely to show distinct physical pathology and for whom training programs are directed primarily at self-care rather than vocational development.
Transaction: A two-way interchange between two or more information systems.
Transduce: The conversion of received information from one sensory modality to another.
Transfer of training: The effect of previous learning on present learning. If learning a new task is facilitated, transfer is positive; if the new learning is interfered with, transfer is negative.
Translocation: A type of chromosomal aberration found in some cases of Down's syndrome (mongolism) in which a chromosome has broken and becomes attached to another chromosome.
Trauma: (1) Physical—any wound or injury, especially a structural injury. (2) Psychic—an emotional shock which may cause a lasting disturbance in mental functions.
Tremor: Uncontrollable rhythmic movements.
Trisomy 21: Mongolism caused by having three instead of a pair of number 21 chromosomes.
Tryptophan: An amino acid existing in proteins from which it is set free by tryptic digestion. It is essential for optimal growth in infants and for nitrogen equilibrium in adults.
Tuberculosis: An infectious disease characterized by the formation of tubercles in the tissues which spread in all directions and cause degeneration. It is attended by symptoms due to the destruction it produces and varying with the location of the infection.
Turner's syndrome: A set of symptoms including retarded growth and sexual development, webbing of the neck, low posterior hair line margin, increased carrying angle of the elbow, and cubitus ralgus. It is associated with an abnormality of the sex chromosomes.
Tympanic drum: Also known as the eardrum. The membrane separating the middle ear from the external ear.

Ulcerative colitis: Chronic ulceration in the colon.

Unconscious: In the strictly Freudian sense, that part of mental activity characterized by certain dynamic processes (not merely latent thoughts) which do not reach consciousness in spite of their effectiveness and intensity, and which cannot be brought into conscious experience by any effort of the will or act of memory.

Unsocialized aggressive reaction: Personality disorder of childhood or adolescence characterized by overt or covert hostility, quarrelsomeness, vengefulness, temper tantrums, physical and verbal aggressiveness, and frequent lying and stealing.

Unsocialized delinquent: A delinquent personality type characterized by impulsivity, agressiveness, weak moral controls, and a propensity for sociopathic acting-out. Similar to sociopathic personality.

Valence: The attracting or repelling value of objects or activities. It may be positive (toward) or negative (away from), depending on the object or activity.

Vasovegetative functions: Functions of canals carrying fluids (e.g., the lymph vessels).

Verbal conditioning: Application of conditioning principles to speech. Verbal behavior can be controlled by the systematic application of reinforcement to specific aspects of speech.

Vestibular functioning: The mechanism for reception and integration of sensory data from the static sense and for the resulting responsive adjustment of the organism's posture and movements with respect to gravity.

Vicarious learning: The acquisition of response capabilities without practice. Learning by observation of the behavior of others (modeling) is an example of vicarious learning.

Visual aura: A visual sensation or phenomenon that often precedes the onset of a paroxysmal attack.

Visual-closure: Process of perceptual completion of incomplete forms; i.e., reading "O" instead of "C."

Visual-motor: Pertaining to the relation of visual stimuli to motor responses in an appropriate way.

Wilson's disease: Also known as hepatolenticular degeneration. It involves the depositing of copper in the brain, liver, and other organs, with severe retardation usually resulting.

APPENDIX

TEST DESCRIPTIONS

APTITUDE TESTS

Academic Promise Tests (APT)
The Psychological Corporation
Testing time: 90–120 minutes
Range: Grades 6–9

Includes four subtests: (1) abstract reasoning, (2) numerical, (3) verbal, and (4) language usage. Should be useful for guidance counselors and for placing students in academic settings.

Differential Aptitude Test Battery
The Psychological Corporation
Testing time: 300–330 minutes
Range: Grades 8–12

Multiple test battery which assesses aptitude in abstract, mechanical, numerical, and verbal areas. Practical and easy to administer; good for use by high school counselors.

Flanagan Aptitude Classification Tests (FACT)
Science Research Associates, Inc.
Testing time: 210–328 minutes
Range: Grades 12–16 and adult

Test battery composed of 19 tests largely directed toward the area of vocational guidance. Due to lack of adequate validity data, test results should be used with caution. Suitable for use by high school counselors.

General Aptitude Test Battery
U.S. Employment Service
Testing time: 120–150 minutes
Range: Grade 12 and adult

Limited to administration by the U.S. Employment Service. A general aptitude test series somewhat similar to such batteries as the Differential Aptitude Test Battery with additional manual tests.

PERSONALITY ASSESSMENT

California Psychological Inventory
Consulting Psychologists Press, Inc.
Testing time: 45–60 minutes
Range: Ages 13 and over

Consists of 480 items to be answered true or false. Includes many items from other personality tests, such as the MMPI. Provides 18 scores, with reliability of about 0.80. May be a danger of students answering this test in accordance with socially approved factors. Best used by trained counselors and psychologists.

California Test of Personality
California Test Bureau
Testing time: 45–60 minutes
Range: Grades k–3, 4–8, 7–10, 9–17, and adults

One of the few personality tests designed for use with the elementary school student. Validity data poor and scores on most subtests not stable. Doubtful that this device should be used by the regular classroom teacher.

Edwards Personal Preference Schedule
The Psychological Corporation
Testing time: 40–55 minutes
Range: College and adults

Construct validity in terms of agreement with the Murray Needs System. Uses a forced choice format. Reliability of 0.83. Poor validity data provided by test manual.

Gordon Personal Inventory
Harcourt, Brace & World, Inc.
Testing time: 15–20 minutes
Range: Grades 8–16 and adults

Inventory yields four scores: (1) cautiousness, (2) original thinking, (3) personal relations, and (4) vigor. Lack of adequate validity data to support extensive use of this device.

The IPAT Anxiety Scale
Institute for Personality and Ability Testing
Testing time: 5–10 minutes
Range: Ages 14 and over

Scale constructed as a result of extensive factor analytical studies. Reliability range 0.30–0.40. Too few items in many areas to provide a basis for testing individuals. Best used as a research instrument or as a simple screening device for literate adults.

Minnesota Multiphasic Personality Inventory
The Psychological Corporation
Testing time: 30–90 minutes
Range: Ages 16 and over

Oriented toward the clinical classification system used in psychiatry. Provides nine clinical scales with many other supplemental scales being available. Many researchers use this instrument for a number of purposes. Instrument to be used only by highly skilled examiners.

Mooney Problem Check List
The Psychological Corporation
Testing time: 20–40 minutes
Range: Grades 7–9, 9–12, 13–16, and adults

Serves as a self-report instrument to assist in organizing one's thinking in basic problem areas, such as courtship, sex, and marriage.

Omnibus Personality Inventory (OPI)
The Psychological Corporation
Testing time: 50–70 minutes
Range: College students

Test items taken from a variety of other personality tests. Particularly adapted for the bright college student. Inventory provides 14 scores, with reliability of 0.79–0.94. An excellent research instrument, but extensive validity studies are needed before individual application is made.

Study of Values
Houghton Mifflin Company
Testing time: 20 minutes
Range: Grades 13 and over

Designed to measure six types of values: (1) theoretical, (2) economic, (3) esthetic, (4) social, (5) political, and (6) religious. Reliability of 0.82. Criticized for lack of factor analytical data, indicating that each value is distinct.

Vineland Social Maturity Scale
The Psychological Corporation
Testing time: 5–20 minutes
Range: Best used with children under 12

A scale, not a test, used to assess the social maturity of children. Information collected from an informant, usually the mother, and checked against a scale of items which, in turn, yields a social age.

INTELLIGENCE TESTS

Arthur Point Scale of Performance Test
C. H. Stoelting Company
Testing time: 60 minutes
Range: Ages 4 to adult

A nonlanguage performance test for measuring intelligence. Especially useful for cases in which the child is unable to respond normally to performance type of items. Best administered by trained examiners.

California Short Form Test of Mental Maturity, 1963 Revision (CTMM)
California Test Bureau
Testing time: 40–45 minutes
Range: Grades k–5, 1–3, 3–4, 4–6, 6–7, 9–12, and 12–16

Provides three scores: (1) language IQ, (2) nonlanguage IQ, and (3) total IQ. Only one form of the test available for each level. Language portion of test emphasizes vocabulary with relatively small amounts of sampling of other areas. Fair predictive validity for upper grades. Suitable for administration by the classroom teacher.

Chicago Nonverbal Examination
The Psychological Corporation
Testing time: 40–50 minutes
Range: Ages 6 and over

Provides for minimal verbal output and has been standardized with both verbal and pantomime directions. Not a culture-free test. Most appropriate for deaf children or for children with severe language problems.

Cognitive Abilities Test (CAT)
Houghton Mifflin Company
Testing time: 40–50 minutes
Range: Grades k–1 and 2–3

Directly related to the primary level of the Lorge-Thorndike Intelligence Tests with norms being derived directly from the Multi-Level Edition of these tests. Makes use of pictorial materials and includes oral instructions. Reliability coefficients range from 0.89 to 0.91. Suitable for administration by the classroom teacher.

Columbia Mental Maturity Scale
World Book Company
Testing time: 15–20 minutes
Range: Ages 2 years, 5 months to 16 years, 3 months

Especially useful for examining subjects with verbalization problems. Test weighted with visual discrimination and visual decoding items. Should be given by fully trained test administrator.

Cooperative School and College Ability Tests (SCAT)
Cooperative Test Division, Educational Testing Service
Testing time: 60–75 minutes
Range: Grades 4–6, 6–8, 8–10, 10, 12, and 14

Test gives three scores: (1) verbal, (2) quantitative, and (3) total. Correlates well with other standard group intelligence tests and with school grades. Reports results in terms of a percentile band and provides an excellent form for reporting results to parents. Suitable for administration by the classroom teacher.

Draw-A-Man Test (Harris-Goodenough)
World Book Company
Testing time: 5 minutes
Range: Ages 3 years to 13 years, 2 months

Consists of having a child draw a picture of a man and then, through the use of a scale provided in the manual, a number of parts of the drawing are translated into an IQ score. Best used for a quick, informal assessment of very young children. Validity of test is much less for older range of ages. May be given by teachers after a short training period.

Full Range Picture Vocabulary Test
Educational Tests Specialists
Testing time: 10 minutes
Range: Ages 2½ to adult

A nonverbal test using pictures associated with vocabulary. Designed to assess the verbal intelligence of nonspeaking children. Relatively easy to administer; may be given by the teacher after a brief training period.

Henmon-Nelson Tests of Mental Ability, Revised Edition
Houghton Mifflin Company
Testing time: 30–45 minutes
Range: Grades 3–6, 6–9, 9–12, and 13–14

Provides an overall score for the elementary and secondary forms of the test. The college level test includes (1) verbal, (2) quantitative, and (3) total scores. Reliability coefficients range from 0.87 to 0.94. Total scores correlate well with other group tests and with teacher grades.

IPAT Culture Fair Intelligence Test
Institute for Personality and Ability Testing
Testing time: 20–30 minutes
Range: Scale 2, ages 8–13 and average adults; scale 3, grades 10–16 and superior adults

Relatively free from environmental influence. Stresses what is typically called the "g" factor—the generalized intelligence factor. Low reliability of 0.50 and norming sample small.

Kuhlmann-Anderson Intelligence Tests (K-A)
Personnel Press, Inc.
Testing time: 25–60 minutes
Range: Grades k, 1–4, 4–5, 5–7, 7–9, and 10–12

Consists of eight subtests at all levels. Lower levels provide a single score while upper levels provide three scores: (1) verbal, (2) quantitative, and (3) total. Examiners must pay particular attention to the time for subtests which tend to be very short. Reliability of total scores appears adequate. Appropriate for administration by the classroom teacher.

Leiter International Performance Scale
Western Psychological Service
Testing time: 40–50 minutes
Range: Ages 2 to adult

Administered without the use of language. An effective assessment device for use in cases in which there is a language problem. A clinical tool to be used by highly trained administrators.

Lorge-Thorndike Intelligence Tests, Multi-Level Edition
Houghton Mifflin Company
Testing time: 35–45 minutes
Range: Grades 3–13

Good norming procedures with reliability coefficients of 0.80–0.92. Correlations with school grades show variance of 0.56–0.65. Appropriate for teacher administration.

Ohio State University Psychological Test
Ohio College Association
No time limit
Range: Grades 9–16 and adults

A power test essentially devised to predict success in college. Correlates approximately 0.60 with college grades. Reliability is high. Emphasizes verbal ability. One of the standard college entrance examinations.

Otis-Lennon Mental Ability Tests
Harcourt, Brace & World, Inc.
Testing time: 30–50 minutes
Range: Grades k, 1–1.5, 1.6–3.9, 4.0–6.9, 7.0–9.9, and 10.0–12.9

A revision of the Otis Quick Scoring Test. Excellent technical manual. Reliability coefficients of 0.81–0.92. Correlates well with other group tests and with elementary school grades.

Peabody Picture Vocabulary Test (PPVT)
American Guidance Service
Testing time: 10–15 minutes
Range: Ages 3–18

Especially appropriate for nonspeaking children. Attempts to provide a standardized estimate of a subject's verbal intelligence through use of vocabulary. Test may be given by the regular classroom teacher after a relatively small amount of training.

Quick Test (QT)
Educational Test Specialists
Testing time: 5–15 minutes
Range: Ages 2 through adult

A picture vocabulary test designed to assess the verbal intelligence of a subject without using verbal responses. Excellent for use with subjects having physical limitations and with nonverbal children. Ease of administration makes this a good screening device for use by teachers after a short training course.

Raven's Progressive Matrices
The Psychological Corporation
Testing time: 30–60 minutes
Range: Ages 5 and over

May be obtained in a black and white or in a colored form. Attempts to measure the general factor of intelligence "g." Designs provided with parts missing which are to be supplied by the person being tested. Norms largely based on English populations. Reliability low and inconsistent. Best used in a clinical setting by a skilled test administrator.

Slosson Intelligence Scale
Slosson Educational Publications
Testing time: 15–20 minutes
Range: Ages 2 to adult

An intelligence test based essentially on the items used in the Binet. Designed for ease of administration. Correlates well with both the WISC and the Binet. A good screening device for cases in which a total IQ is the major goal. May be used by the regular classroom teacher after a brief training course.

Stanford-Binet Intelligence Test, Combined 1-M Form (1960)
The Psychological Corporation
Testing time: 40–60 minutes
Range: Ages 2 to superior adult

The standard individual intelligence test upon which all other intelligence tests are normed and validated. Especially appropriate for the very young child, for the exceptionally bright, or for the very retarded. A clinical tool which should be given only by fully trained examiners.

Wechsler Adult Intelligence Scale (WAIS)
The Psychological Corporation
Testing time: 40–60 minutes
Range: Ages 16 through adult

A continuation of the WISC, especially designed to examine adults. Tends to reach a ceiling of 140 IQ. Form identical to that of the WISC. Designed for clinical use and should be given only by fully trained examiners.

Wechsler Intelligence Scale for Children (WISC)
The Psychological Corporation
Testing time: 40–60 minutes
Range: Ages 5–15

The most widely used individual intelligence test. Composed of 12 subtests divided into two major areas: (1) verbal and (2) performance. Also includes a total score. A clinical tool to be administered only by fully trained examiners.

Wechsler Preschool and Primary Scale of Intelligence (WPPSI)
The Psychological Corporation
Testing time: 50–75 minutes
Range: Ages 4–6½

An extension of the WISC for preschool children. Designed according to the same format as the WISC, but meets the needs of younger children. A clinical tool to be used by fully trained examiners.

VISUAL-MOTOR PERCEPTUAL TESTS

Bender Visual-Motor Gestalt Test
The Psychological Corporation
Testing time: 5–10 minutes
Range: Ages 5–10

Composed of nine geometric figures on individual cards. Subjects asked to copy a form as accurately as possible. Used to assess brain damage and personality defects. A clinical tool which should be used by fully trained psychological examiners.

Frostig Developmental Tests of Visual Perception
Consulting Psychologists Press
Testing time: 15–20 minutes
Range: Ages 3–10

Consists of five subtests: (1) eye-motor coordination, (2) figure-ground, (3) form constancy, (4) position in space, and (5) spatial relations. Many materials available to correlate with test analysis. Device suitable for use by classroom teacher after brief training course.

Harris Test of Laterality
The Psychological Corporation
Testing time: 10–15 minutes
Range: Ages 7 to adult

A collection of standard tasks designed to assess eye, hand, and foot dominance. A simple device to use which may be given by classroom teachers after a brief course in testing.

Purdue Perceptual Motor Survey
Charles E. Merrill Publishing Company
Testing time: 30–40 minutes
Range: Grades 1–4

Yields an indication of a child's perceptual-motor level of development. Useful to assess gross motor development as well as fine motor development. May be administered by classroom teacher after a short training course.

Visual-Motor Integration Test
Follett Publishing Company
Testing time: 10–15 minutes
Range: Ages 2–15

A series of designs and forms to replicate or complete. Designed to measure integration of visual and motor factors. May be used by classroom teacher after short training course.

READING TESTS

Auditory Blending Test
Essay Press
Testing time: 5 minutes
Range: Grades 1–5

A test of the ability of a subject to blend sounds individually and into words. Appropriate test for use by the classroom teacher.

Auditory Discrimination Test (Wepman)
J. M. Wepman
Testing time: 2–3 minutes
Range: Ages 2–8

Presents a list of terms in pairs and requires the subject to identify which terms are the same and which are different. An informal assessment of the ability to detect sound difference. Suitable for use by the classroom teacher.

Davis Reading Test
The Psychological Corporation
Testing time: 45–55 minutes
Range: Grades 8–11 and 11–12

Test provides two scores: (1) level of comprehension and (2) speed of comprehension. Well constructed test with adequate reliability. Correlation between grades and test scores is approximately 0.50. Easy test for teacher administration.

Diagnostic Reading Test of Word Analysis Skills
Essay Press
Testing time: 5 minutes
Range: Grades 2–4

A test of the knowledge of letter sounds and how these combine to form words. Assesses the ability to apply phonics. Appropriate test for use by the classroom teacher.

Diagnostic Reading Test: Survey Section
Science Research Associates, Inc.
Testing time: 60–70 minutes for grades 4–8; 175 to 200 minutes for grades 7–13

Five scores are provided: (1) word recognition, (2) comprehension, (3) vocabulary, (4) story reading, and (5) total for grades 4–8. The five score areas for grades 7–13 are: (1) rate of reading, (2) story comprehension, (3) vocabulary, (4) comprehension, and (5) total. Manuals accompanying tests are not very clear and are difficult to use.

Durrell Analysis of Reading Difficulty
Harcourt, Brace & World, Inc.
Testing time: 30–90 minutes
Range: Grades 1.5–6.5

Exceptionally complete reading analysis test. Somewhat difficult to administer, but provides exhaustive information concerning specifics of reading difficulty. Appropriate for use by the classroom teacher after a brief course in teaching reading.

Gates-MacGinite Reading Tests
Teachers College Press
Testing time: 40–60 minutes, depending on level
Range: Grades 1, 2, 3, 4–6, and 7–9

Provides for measures of vocabulary comprehension for grades 1–3, with the addition of speed measurement for grades 4 and above. Well constructed test widely used. Ideal for classroom teacher administration.

Gray Oral Reading Test
The Bobbs-Merrill Company, Inc.
Testing time: 10–15 minutes
Range: Grades 1.0–12.0

One of the standard oral reading tests. Good for screening of possible reading problems. Basically a test of word recognition. Appropriate for administration by the classroom teacher.

Iowa Word Recognition
Institute for Juvenile Research
Testing time: 5 minutes
Range: Grades 1.0–5.8

Test of oral reading of individual words. Appropriate as a screening device to identify possible reading problems. Suitable for use by the classroom teacher.

A Quick Phonics Readiness Check for Retarded Readers
Vita G. Schach
Testing time: 10 minutes
Range: All ages

Includes tests of auditory discrimination, sound blending, and auditory memory. Informal device suitable for use by the classroom teacher.

Spache Diagnostic Reading Scales
California Test Bureau
Testing time: 30–40 minutes
Range: Grades 1–8

Complete battery of reading tests, each of which measures a specific component of reading, including the area of silent reading. An excellent series for the use of the classroom teacher.

Stanford Diagnostic Reading Test
Harcourt, Brace & World, Inc.
Testing time: 160–180 minutes
Range: Grades 2.5–4.5 and 4.5–8.5.

Test battery which assesses vocabulary, reading comprehension, and word recognition skills. Good reliability of about 0.94. A useful test for the classroom teacher in terms of assisting him in locating reading problem areas.

ELEMENTARY ACHIEVEMENT TEST BATTERIES

California Test of Basic Skills (CTBS)
California Test Bureau
Testing time: 240–260 minutes
Range: Grades 2.5–5.9, 4.0–6.9, and 6.0–8.9

A revision of the California Achievement Tests, consisting of 10 subtests: (1) reading vocabulary, (2) reading comprehension, (3) language mechanics, (4) language expression, (5) language spelling, (6) arithmetic computation, (7) arithmetic concepts, (8) arithmetic application, (9) study skills using reference materials, and (10) study skills using graphic materials. Test involves many problems with norms and should be used with care.

Iowa Test of Basic Skills (ITBS)
Houghton Mifflin Company
Testing time: 280–335 minutes
Range: Grades 3–9

One test form used for all grades, with starting and stopping points determining grade level. Provides 15 scores including: vocabulary, reading comprehension, language (4 subscores and 1 total score), work study skills (3 subscores and 1 total score), arithmetic skills (2 subscores and 1 total score), and a composite score. Concerned with knowledge needed to succeed in the regular elementary school.

Metropolitan Achievement Tests
Harcourt, Brace & World, Inc.
Testing time: 95–290 minutes, depending on grade level of test

Range: Primary I, grades 1.5–2.5; Primary II, grades 2.0–3.5; Elementary, grades 3–4; Intermediate, grades 5–6; Advanced, grades 7–8

All the batteries measure vocabulary, reading comprehension, and arithmetic skills. Good norming procedures with good reliabilities. Revised Fall, 1970.

Sequential Tests of Educational Progress (STEP)
Cooperative Test Division
Educational Testing Service
Testing time: 450–500 minutes
Range: Grades 4–6 and 7–9

Test battery composed of six tests: (1) reading, (2) writing, (3) mathematics, (4) science, (5) social studies, and (6) listening. Provides a continuous record of progress from grade 4 through grade 14. Includes data on modern mathematics as well as late social studies materials. Reports to parents and staff in the form of percentile bands.

SRA Achievement Series, 1971 Revision
Science Research Associates, Inc.
Testing time: 270–450 minutes, depending on grade level of test
Range: Grades 1–2, 2–4, and 4–9

Test battery presented in color and well designed. Excellent achievement battery for the use of the regular classroom teacher.

Stanford Achievement Test
Harcourt, Brace & World, Inc.
Testing time: 160–285 minutes, depending on grade level of test
Range: Grades 1.5–2.4, 2.5–3.9, 4.0–5.4, 5.5–6.9, and 7.0–9.9

All levels cover reading, spelling, and arithmetic. Reliability good. Test well normed and easy to administer. Suitable for administration by the regular classroom teacher.

Wide Range Achievement Test (WRAT)
The Psychological Corporation
Testing time: 5–15 minutes
Range: Kindergarten through college

A survey test of reading, spelling, and arithmetic. Excellent for screening purposes. Essentially a test of word recognition. Suitable for use by the classroom teacher.

HIGH SCHOOL ACHIEVEMENT TESTS

Comprehensive Test of Basic Skills (CTBS)
California Test Bureau
Testing time: 240–260 minutes
Range: Grades 8.0–12.9

A continuation of the elementary battery previously described. May attempt to cover too wide a range in too few items. No reliability or other technical data available.

Iowa Test of Educational Development
Science Research Associates, Inc.
Testing time: 330–540 minutes
Range: Grades 9–12

The battery is composed of nine subtests: (1) understanding of basic social concepts, (2) general background in the natural sciences, (3) correctness and appropriateness of expression, (4) ability to do quantitative thinking, (5) ability to interpret reading materials in the social studies, (6) ability to interpret material in the natural sciences, (7) ability to interpret literary materials, (8) general vocabulary, and (9) uses of sources of information. Good reliability, and interreliability coefficients high. High interreliability of some subtests may restrict the diagnostic value of the test battery.

Metropolitan Achievement Tests: High School Battery
Harcourt, Brace & World, Inc.
Testing time: 315–330 minutes
Range: Grades 9–13

Consists of 11 subtests, including reading, spelling, language arts, language study skills, social studies study skills, information, mathematical computation and solving, scientific concepts and understanding, and science information. Reliability coefficients of 0.72 to 0.90. Correlates well with results from the Otis Quick-Scoring Mental Ability Tests.

Sequential Test of Educational Progress (STEP)
Educational Testing Service
Cooperative Test Division
Testing time: 450–500 minutes
Range: Grades 10–12 and 12–14

A continuation of the elementary school battery. (See previous section for discussion.)

Stanford Achievement Test: High School Test Battery (SAT)
Harcourt, Brace & World, Inc.
Testing time: 320–350 minutes
Range: Grades 9–12

Composed of seven subtests: (1) English, (2) numerical competence, (3) mathematics, (4) reading, (5) science, (6) social studies, and (7) spelling. Excellent for college preparatory students. Correlates with results form the Otis Quick-Scoring Mental Ability Tests. An excellent test for administration by the regular classroom teacher.

INTEREST INVENTORIES

Brainard Occupational Preference Inventory
The Psychological Corporation
Testing time: 30 minutes
Range: Grades 8–12 and adults

Covers six broad occupational areas: (1) commercial, (2) mechanical, (3) professional, (4) athletic, (5) scientific, and (6) personal service. Ranked on a scale of "like very much" to "dislike very much" for some 20 items per area. Evidence of validity lacking.

Gordon Occupational Check List
Harcourt, Brace & World, Inc.
Testing time: 20–25 minutes
Range: High school students not planning on college

Consists of 240 statements of job duties and tasks. Statements classified in five broad groupings. Reliability coefficient of 0.8. Validity data lacking.

Kuder Preference Record-Occupational
Science Research Associates, Inc.
Testing time: 25–35 minutes
Range: Grades 9–16 through adult

Provides scores for 50 occupational groups. Median reliability correlation of 0.85. More data needed on validity. Tends to correlate low with comparable portion of the Strong Inventory.

Kuder Preference Record-Vocational
Science Research Associates, Inc.
Testing time: 40–50 minutes
Range: Grades 9–16 and adults

Inventory of vocational preferences.

Minnesota Vocational Interest Inventory
The Psychological Corporation
Testing time: 40–45 minutes
Range: High school and adults

Empirically constructed series of 58 brief statements (in threes) describing tasks or activities used in a variety of trades and nonprofessional occupations. Provides scores for 21 occupations. Reliability of 0.64–0.88. Suitable for use with the student who is not college-bound.

Strong Vocational Interest Blank
Consulting Psychologists Press, Inc.
Testing time: 30–60 minutes
Range: Ages 17 and over

The most widely used occupational inventory. Much research and good reliability. Provides many scales and groupings of vocations.

LANGUAGE TESTS

Illinois Test of Psycholinguistic Ability (ITPA)
University of Illinois Press
Testing time: 30–40 minutes
Range: Ages 6 months to 9 years

Complex device designed to assess a variety of language areas including memory, word discrimination, and language utilization. Composed of 12 subtests. May be used by the classroom teacher after intensive training in the mechanics of the test; however, probably best left to administration by test specialists.

Detroit Test of Learning Aptitude
The Bobbs-Merrill Company, Inc.
Testing time: 30–60 minutes
Range: Ages 4 through adult

Ten subtests measuring various elements of mental processing. An excellent test covering many areas of importance to the elementary teacher. Appropriate for use by the classroom teacher.

Engleman Concept Inventory
Follett Publishing Company
No time limit
Range: All ages

Based on the idea of educational defect rather than on remediation.

Parsons Language Sample
The University of Kansas Research Division
No time limit
Range: All ages

Samples language behavior according to the Shinmorian system. Vocal and nonvocal responses tested in seven subtests.

TEST PUBLISHERS

American Guidance Service
Publishers Building
Circle Pines, Minnesota 55041

Publishers of the Peabody Picture Vocabulary Test.

The Bobbs-Merrill Company, Inc.
1720 East 38th Street
Indianapolis, Indiana 46322

Publishers of the Gray Oral Reading Test.

California Test Bureau
Del Monte Research Park
Monterey, California 93940

Publishers of the California Achievement Test batteries and of the California Test of Mental Maturity.

Consulting Psychologists Press, Inc.
577 College Avenue
Palo Alto, California 94306

Publishers of the Gain-Levine Social Competency Scale, the California Psychological Inventory, and other personality and adjustment tests and inventories.

Cooperative Test Division
Educational Testing Service
Princeton, New Jersey 08540

Publishers of the Cooperative General Achievement Tests, the Sequential Tests of Educational Development, and the Cooperative English Tests.

Essay Press
Box 3
New York, New York

Publishers of the Diagnostic Reading Test.

Follett Publishing Company
1000 West Washington
Chicago, Illinois 60607

Publishers of the Visual-Motor Integration Test and the Frostig Developmental Tests of Visual Perception.

Houghton Mifflin Company
2 Park Street
Boston, Massachusetts 02107

Publishers of the Lorge-Thorndike Tests and the Cognitive Abilities Test.

Institute for Personality and Ability Testing
1602 Coronado Drive
Champaign, Illinois 61822

Publishers of the IPAT Culture Fair Intelligence Test.

Charles E. Merrill Publishing Company
1300 Alum Creek Drive
Columbus, Ohio 43216

Publishers of the Purdue Perceptual-Motor Survey.

The Psychological Corporation
304 East 45th Street
New York, New York 10017

General test publishers and distributors. Distribute the Wechsler Intelligence Tests, the Differential Aptitude Test Battery, the Rorschach Inkblots, the Thematic Apperception Test, and many other achievement, personality, and vocational aptitude tests.

Psychological Tests Specialists
Box 1441
Missoula, Montana 59801

Publishers of the Full Range Picture Vocabulary Test, the Quick Test, and the Memory for Designs Test.

Science Research Associates, Inc.
259 East Erie Street
Chicago, Illinois 60611

Publishers of the Iowa Test of Educational Development, the National Educational Development Tests, the SRA Achievement Series, and many other achievement, reading, and vocational aptitude tests.

Slosson Educational Publications
140 Pine Street
East Aurora, New York 14052

Publishers of the Slosson Intelligence Test.

C. H. Stoelting Company
424 North Homan Avenue
Chicago, Illinois 60624

Publishers of the Arthur Point Scales.

Test Department
Harcourt Brace Jovanovich, Inc.
757 Third Avenue
New York, New York 10017

Publishers of the Stanford Achievement Test series as well as many other achievement tests.

Western Psychological Services
Box 775
Beverly Hills, California 90213

Publishers of the Hooper Visual Organization Test (to detect organic damage) and the Leadership Ability Evaluation (deals with social climate influencing others) and distributor of many personality and mental ability tests.

World Book Company
Yonkers on Hudson, New York

Publishers of the Columbia Mental Maturity Scale and the Goodenough Draw-A-Man Test.

TEACHING RESOURCES

ABC School Supply, Inc.
437 Armour Circle, N.E.
P.O. Box 13084
Atlanta, Georgia 30324

Carry all types of school supplies for the use of elementary and secondary school teachers, including arts and crafts and instructional materials. Publish an annual catalogue listing available supplies.

ACI Films
35 West 45th Street
New York, New York 10036

Distribute many instructional films and filmstrips. Of note are the materials on language arts, such as the Look, Listen, and Read series and the Children's Storybook Theater Series.

American Guidance Service, Inc.
Publishers Building
Circle Pines, Minnesota 55014

Publishers of the Peabody Language Development Kits, the Peabody Individual Achievement Test, and the Goldman-Lynch Sounds and Symbols Development Kit. An annual catalogue is available from the publisher.

Behavioral Research Laboratories
Ladera Professional Center
Box 577
Palo Alto, California 94302

Publishers of the Sullivan Programmed Reading programs as well as a number of instructional materials designed to assist the teacher of the learning disabled child.

Bob and Jill, Inc.
Educational and Recreational Services
55 Lyncroft Road
New Rochelle, New York 10804

Distributors of many instructional aids, such as the Califone Card Reader, the Telor Learning System, and the Makuhi Rhythmic Sticks.

Bowmar
622 Rodier Drive
Glendale, California 91201

Distribute many audiovisual programs involving reacting, such as the Reading Incentive Language Program, the Gold Cup Reading Games, and the Primary Reading Series.

Bro-Dart, Inc.
Eastern Division
1609 Memorial Avenue
Williamsport, Pennsylvania 17701

Repository of over 53,000 textbooks and supplemental books for all grade levels. Issue an annual catalogue.

Caedmon C.
Charles W. Clark Company, Inc.
564 Smith Street
Farmingdale, New York 11735

Publishers of many sound recordings on records and tape. Publications tend to deal with the literary classics, and a number of their poetry recordings have been recorded by the poets themselves.

CCM School Materials, Inc.
2124 West 82nd Place
Chicago, Illinois 60620

Publishers of the threshold program and materials.

The Continental Press, Inc.
127 Cain Street, N.W.
Atlanta, Georgia 30303

Publishers of many ditto masters for use with the child who has learning disabilities.

Cuisenaire Company of America
12 Church Street
New Rochelle, New York 10805

Publishers of many instructional aids for teaching mathematics, such as the Cuisenaire rods.

Developmental Learning Materials
7440 Natchez Avenue
Niles, Illinois 60648

Publishers of many materials devised to aid in teaching basic concepts to children with learning disabilities. Catalogue available from the publisher annually.

The Economy Company
Individualized Instruction, Inc.
P.O. Box 25308
1901 North Walnut
Oklahoma City, Oklahoma 73125

Publishers and distributors of many instructional materials, including Kindergarten Keys, Stepping Stones, Ears Spacetalk, and Keys to Reading.

Educational Achievement Corporation
P.O. Box 7310
Waco, Texas 76710

Publishers of materials related to teaching vocational education, including the Inquiry Based Systems for Teaching Processes Essential in Career Education. Publish an annual catalogue.

Educational Activities, Inc.
P.O. Box 392
Freeport, New York 11520

Publishers and distributors of records, filmstrips, and cassettes for instructing young children and also for teaching the slow learner.

Educational Development Corporation
202 Lake Miriam Drive
Lakeland, Florida 33803

Publishers and distributors of many materials to be used with the Audio Flashcard Reader and readiness aids.

Educational Projections Corporation
3070 Lake Terrace
Glenview, Illinois 60025

Carry all types of multimedia materials, including films, filmstrips, records, and reading programs.

Educational Teaching Aids Division
A. Daigger and Company
159 West Kinzie Street
Chicago, Illinois 60610

Distributors of many Montessori learning aids which stress perceptual-motor development.

Field Enterprises Educational Corporation
Merchandise Mart Plaza
Chicago, Illinois 60654

Publishers of the Childcraft series designed to assist in educating children. Also, distributors of the teaching device called Cyclo-Teacher, a modified programmed instructional device suitable for use in both special and regular elementary school classrooms.

Follett Publishing Company
1010 West Washington Boulevard
Chicago, Illinois 60607

Publishers of materials dealing with movement education for young children, visual perception and auditory perception development, and enrichment for bright children.

General Electric
Instructional Industries, Inc.
Executive Park
Ballston Lake, New York 12019

Distribute the learning system called PAL-Programmed Assistance to Learning. A total program with projector for instruction in basic school subjects.

The Instructor Publications, Inc.
P.O. Box 6108
Duluth, Minnesota 55806

Publish a fine magazine called the Instructor, in addition to many instructional materials, including a large assortment of duplicating masters covering all basic primary level reading and language.

Mead School Products
1391 Chattahoochee Avenue, N.W.
Atlanta, Georgia 30318

Publishers of many activity materials for use with children during the early developmental stage, including materials for development of psychomotor-perceptual abilities. Also distribute many materials for use in physical developmental activities. Publish annually a series of catalogues available to teachers.

Miller-Brody Productions, Inc.
342 Madison Avenue
New York, New York 10017

Publishers and distributors of many instructional aids, including books, audiovisual materials, and developmental materials. Distribute the Newberry Award books.

J. A. Preston Corporation
71 Fifth Avenue
New York, New York 10003

Publishers of many materials suitable for use in developing perceptual-motor abilities in early childhood.

Research Press
Box 31775
Champaign, Illinois 61820

Publishers of many excellent books and films on behavior modification. Some particularly appropriate publications are: New Methods for Parents and Teachers by Dr. Gerald R. Patterson and M. Elizabeth Gullion; and Who Did What to Whom?—a 16-mm. film by Dr. Robert F. Mager. Useful for starting a discussion on factors underlying behavior in the home and school. Publish an excellent annual catalogue.

Science Research Associates, Inc.
259 East Erie Street
Chicago, Illinois 60611

Publishers of the Lift Off to Reading programmed reading system as well as many other reading and mathematics teaching systems.

Spellbinder, Inc.
33 Bradford Street
Concord, Massachusetts 01742

Publishers of an extensive series of programmed and instructional materials for teaching reading and spelling.

Stanwix House, Inc.
3020 Chartiers Avenue
Pittsburgh, Pennsylvania 15024

Publishers dealing with specialized readers, spellers, and arithmetic texts devised to teach the mentally retarded, the visually impaired, and the emotionally disturbed.

Steck-Vaughn Company
P.O. Box 2028
Vaughn Building
Austin, Texas 78767

Publishers of the Human Values Series, Today's Language Series, Reading Essentials Series, and Gateways to Correct Spelling.

Teaching Resources Corporation
100 Boylston Street
Boston, Massachusetts 02116

Publishers of the Fairbanks-Robinson Program, the Dubnoff School Program, the Vanguard School Program, and the Erie Program.

Trend Enterprises
P.O. Box 3073
St. Paul, Minnesota 55165

Publishers of many materials for bulletin board displays, including illustrations, letters, and forms suitable for designing original bulletin boards.

MOTION PICTURE FILM DISTRIBUTORS AND SOME AVAILABLE FILMS*

AIMS Instructional Media Services, Inc.
P.O. Box 1010
Hollywood, California 90028

Just for the Fun of It—19 minutes
A series of physical activities suitable for mentally handicapped children.

The Madison School Plan—17 minutes
A method of placing handicapped children in the regular classroom.

The Santa Monica Project—28 minutes
Demonstration of the engineered classroom.

Appleton-Century-Crofts
440 Park Avenue
New York, New York 10016

*Interested persons should write to the distributors for complete lists of films on the exceptional child.

Behavior Theory in Practice, Part II—20 minutes
A comprehensive discussion of the application of behavior theory to learning.

Association Films, Inc.
600 Grand Avenue
Ridgefield, New Jersey 07657

If These Were Your Children, Parts I and II—28 minutes
Focuses on the behavior of young children to help interpret early clues to possible emotional problems.

Billy Budd Films
235 East 57th Street
New York, New York 10022

Mimi—12 minutes
A young woman copes with her physical handicap and learns to cope with the attitudes of others toward such a condition.

Bradley Wright Films
309. N. Duane Avenue
San Gabriel, California 91775

Learning Is Observing—20 minutes
A training film for teachers of young children with perceptual and learning problems.

Central Educational Films
1621 West 9th Street
Lawrence, Kansas 66044

Leo Beurman—13 minutes
Story of a multiply handicapped adult living in American society.

Churchill Films
662 N. Robertson Boulevard
Los Angeles, California 90069

Kevin—16 minutes
The experience of blindness.

Encyclopedia Britannica Education Corporation
1822 Pickwick Avenue
Glenview, Illinois 60025

Only Benjy Knows—4 minutes
A conflict situation is presented which forces a child to make a decision. He sees a theft by a peer. Should he tell?

H & H Enterprises
P.O. Box 3342
Lawrence, Kansas 66044

All My Buttons—28 minutes
Problems of integrating the handicapped as citizens.

Holt, Rinehart and Winston, Inc.
383 Madison Avenue
New York, New York 10017

A Child Who Cheats—10 minutes
How should the problem of cheating be treated?

Indiana University
Audio-Visual Center
Bloomington, Indiana 47401

Autism's Lonely Children—29 minutes
Dr. Frank Hewitt of the University of California at Los Angeles explains his techniques in working with autistic children.

Mrs. N. Landy
Home for Crippled Children
1426 Denniston Avenue
Pittsburgh, Pennsylvania 15217

Children and Language Disorders, Part I Diagnosis—40 minutes
Methods appropriate to use in exploring language deficiencies.

Lauren Productions
P.O. Box 1542
Burlingame, California 94010

If a Boy Can't Learn—28 minutes
The story of a 17-year-old boy with a learning disability.

McGraw-Hill Films
Princeton Road
Highstown, New Jersey 08520

From Cradle to Classroom—25 minutes
Methods of early stimulation of developmental processes.

National Association for Retarded Children
420 Lexington Avenue
New York, New York 10017

Arts and Crafts for the Slow Learner—27 minutes
Eighteen types for use with the educable mentally retarded are demonstrated.

National Audio-Visual Center
National Archives and Records Services
Washington, D.C. 20409

Early Recognition of Learning Disabilities—30 minutes
The identification of learning disabled children in the regular class from grades k–2.

NBC Educational Enterprises
30 Rockefeller Plaza
New York, New York 10020

My Brother's Keeper—15 minutes
An extended care facility for the retarded with maximum community involvement.

New York University Film Library
26 Washington Place
New York, New York 10003

Behavior Modification: Teaching Language to Psychotic Children—40 minutes
The use of behavior modification procedures in teaching speech to the psychotic young.

Jennifer Is a Lady—26 minutes
Teaching techniques for use with autistic children.

Michael: A Mongoloid Child—12 minutes
A mongoloid teenager integrated and accepted in a rural New England community.

Pennsylvania State University
Audio-Visual Services
University Park, Pennsylvania 16802

Acquisition of Language by a Speechless Child—17 minutes
An eight-year-old child who has never used words is taught how to respond accurately to oral directions.

Louise Sandler
Preschool Center, Franklin Institute Research Laboratories
20th and Race Streets
Room 469
Philadelphia, Pennsylvania 19103

Children at Risk—30 minutes
An experimental program in preschool education is demonstrated.

Smith, Kline and French Laboratories
1500 Spring Garden Street
Philadelphia, Pennsylvania 19101

Toymakers—29 minutes
A survey of mental retardation.

Stanfield House
900 Euclid Avenue
Santa Monica, California 90403

The Undifferentiated Lump: A Film About the Shaping Process—10 minutes
An illustration of one principle of operant conditioning-shaping.

Sterling Educational Films
241 East 34th Street
New York, New York 10016

What Do You See Now? Parts I and II—10 minutes each
Teaches children to identify and use various geometric shapes.

Swank Motion Pictures
201 South Jefferson Avenue
St. Louis, Missouri 63166

Various films aimed at stimulating early identification of and planning for learning disabled children.

Time-Life Films
43 West 16th Street
New York, New York 10011

Broken Bridge, Therapy for Autistic Children—40 minutes
Actual therapy sessions over a six-month period to establish communication with autistic children.

Total Communications Laboratory
Western Maryland College
Westminster, Maryland 21157

Listen—30 minutes
A documentary film dealing with hearing loss and the psychological meaning of such loss.

United Cerebral Palsy Association
66 East 34th Street
New York, New York 10016

Testing Multiply Handicapped Children—30 minutes
The Else Hausserman film demonstrating techniques to be used in assessing very handicapped children.

University of California Educational Film Sales
Berkeley, California 94720

Felicia—13 minutes
A 15-year-old black girl's perceptive inquiry into her life.

Western Behavioral Sciences Institute
Film Library
1150 Silverado Street
La Jolla, California 92037

Journey into Self—47 minutes
Film of an actual group therapy session.

BIBLIOGRAPHY*

Abeson, A. Movement and momentum: Government and education of handicapped children. In S. Kirk and F. Lord, (Eds.). Exceptional Children: Educational Resources and Perspectives. Boston: Houghton Mifflin, 1974.

Abraham, W. Common Sense About Gifted Children. New York: Harper & Row, 1958.

Abrams, J. C., and Belmont, H. S. Different approaches to the remediation of severe reading disability in children. Am. J. Orthopsychiatry, 1965, *35*: 351–352.

Abt, L. E., and Weisman, S. L. (Eds.) Acting Out. New York: Grune & Stratton, 1965.

Ackerman, N. W. The Psychodynamics of Family Life: Diagnosis and Treatment of Family Relationships. New York: Basic Books, 1958.

Adams, H. Mental illness or interpersonal behavior. Am. Psychol., 1964, *19*: 191–217.

Adams, R. L. Personality and behavioral differences among children of various birth positions. Dissertation Abstracts, 1967, *28*: 1697.

Adler, A. The Practice and Theory of Individual Psychology. (Trans. P. Radin) New York: Harcourt, Brace, 1927.

Adler, A. Superiority and Social Interest. London: Routledge, 1964.

Adler, A. The Science of Living. Garden City. N. Y.: Doubleday, 1969.

Ahmann, J. S., and Glosk, M. D. Evaluating Pupil Growth. (3rd ed.) Boston: Allyn and Bacon, 1967.

Aichorn, A. Wayward Youth. New York: Viking, 1965.

Alexander, E. School-centered play-therapy. In N. J. Long, W. Morse, and R. Newman (Eds.), Conflict in the Classroom. Belmont, Calif.: Wadsworth, 1971.

Alexander, F. G., and Selesnick, S. T. The History of Psychiatry: An Evaluation of Psychiatric Thought and Practice from Prehistoric Times to the Present. New York: Harper & Row, 1966.

Allbright, M. Mental health of children with hearing impairments. J. Except. Children, 1952, *19*: 110–113.

Allen, D. E., and Sandhu, H. S. Alienation, hedonism, and life vision of delinquents. Journal of Criminal Law, Criminology, and Police Science, 1967, *58*: 325–329.

Allen, E. A. Attitudes of children and adolescents in school. Educational Research, 1960, *3*: 65–80.

---

*Journal titles are abbreviated according to Index Medicus.

Allen, F. H. Psychotherapy with Children. New York: Norton, 1942.

Allen, G. Patterns of discovery in the genetics of mental deficiency. Am. J. Ment. Defic., 1958, *62*: 840–849.

Allen, R. J., and Gibson, R. M. Phenylketonuria with normal intelligence. Am. J. Dis. Child., 1961, *102*: 115–123.

Allen, R. M. The cerebral palsied, the rehabilitation team, and adjustment: An overview. J. Rehabil., 1960, *26*: 22–25, 42–44.

Alley, G. R., and Snider, B. Comparative perceptual motor performance of Negro and white young mental retardates. Developmental Psychology, 1970, *2*: 110–114.

Allport, G. W. Patterns and Growth in Personality. New York: Holt, Rinehart and Winston, Inc., 1961.

Almeida, C. H. Children's perceptions of parental authority and love, school achievement, and personality. Dissertation Abstracts, 1969, *29*: 3863.

Altus, G. T. A WISC profile for retarded readers. J. Consult. Psychol., 1956, *20*: 155–156.

Amble, B. R., and Butler, G. Phrase-reading training and the reading achievement of slow learners. Journal of Special Education, 1967, *1*: 119–126.

American Psychological Association. Psychological assessment and public policy. Am. Psychol., 1970, *25*: 264–266.

American Psychological Association. Psychology and mental retardation. Am. Psychol., 1970, *25*: 267–268.

Ammons, C. H., Worchel, P., and Dallenbach, K. M. "Facial vision": The perception of obstacles out of doors by blindfolded-deafened subjects. Am. J. Psychol., 1953, *66*: 519–553.

Anastasi, A. (Ed.) Testing Problems in Perspective. Washington: American Council on Education, 1966.

Anastasi, A. Psychological Testing. (3rd ed.) New York: Macmillan, 1968.

Anderson, E. G. A comparison of emotional stability in stutterers and non-stutterers. Dissertation Abstracts, 1968, *28* (8-B): 3511.

Anderson, R. M. Hearing impairment and mental retardation: A selected bibliography. Volta Review, 1965, *67*: 425–432.

Anthony, E. J. The behavior disorders of childhood. In P. H. Mussen (Ed.), Manual of Child Psychology, Vol. 2. New York: Wiley, 1970.

Aronson, S. M., Valsamis, M. P., and Volk, B. W. Infantile amaurotic family idiocy. Pediatrics, 1960, *26*: 229–242.

Arthur, B. Role perceptions of children with ulcerative colitis. Arch. Gen. Psychiatry, 1963, *8*(6): 536–545.

Ausubel, D. Theories and Problems of Child Development. New York: Grune & Stratton, 1958.

Ausubel, D. Maori youth: A psychoethnological study of cultural deprivation. New York: Holt, Rinehart and Winston, Inc., 1965a.

Ausubel, D. Psychological factors in juvenile delinquency. Paper presented at the Seminar on Juvenile Delinquency, Marylhurst College, Oregon, October 1965b.

Ausubel, D., and Ausubel, P. Ego development among Negro children. In A. H. Passow (Ed.), Education in Depressed Areas. New York: Teachers College Press, 1963.

Axelrod, S. Token reinforcement programs in special classes. Except. Child., 1971, *1*: 371–379.

Axline, V. M. Play Therapy. Boston: Houghton Mifflin, 1947.

Ayllon, T., and Azrin, N. H. The measurement and reinforcement of behavior in psychotics. J. Exp. Anal. Behav., 1965, *8*: 357–383.

Ayres, J. The development of perceptual-motor abilities: A theoretical basis for treatment of dysfunction. Am. J. Occup. Ther., 1963, *18*: 221–225.

Ayres, J. Patterns of perceptual-motor dysfunction in children. Percept. Mot. Skills, 1965, *20*: 335–368.

Azrin, N. H., and Lindsley, O. R. The reinforcement of cooperation between children. In L. P. Ullman and L. Krasner (Eds.), Case Studies in Behavior Modification. New York: Holt, Rinehart and Winston, Inc., 1965.

Baer, P. E. Problems in the differential diagnosis of brain damage and childhood schizophrenia. Am. J. Orthopsychiatry, 1961, *31*: 728–737.

Balow, B. A program of preparation for teachers of disturbed children. Except. Child., 1966, *32*: 455–460.

Balser, B. Psychiatric problems in secondary schools: A symposium. Psychology in the Schools, 1966, *3*: 3–29.

Balsur, B. H. Predicting mental disturbance in early adolescence. Am. J. Psychiatry, 1965, *121*:11–15.

Bandura, A. Modeling approaches to the modification of phobic disorders. In R. Porter (Ed.), The Role of Learning in Psychotherapy. Boston: Little, Brown, 1968.

Bandura, A., and Walters, R. H. Adolescent Aggression. New York: Ronald, 1959.

Bandura, A., and Walters, R. H. Social Learning and Personality Development. New York: Holt, Rinehart and Winston, Inc., 1963.

Barker, R. G., and Wright, H. F. Midwest and Its Children. Evanston, Ill.: Row, Peterson, 1955.

Barnard, J. W., and Orlando, R. Behavior modification: A bibliography. LIMRID Papers and Reports, 1967, *4*: 3.

Barraga, N. Increased Visual Behavior in Low Vision Children. New York: American Foundation for the Blind, 1959.

Barry, W. A. Marriage research and conflict: An integrative review. Psychol. Bull., 1970, *73*: 41–54.

Barsch, R. Achieving Perceptual-Motor Efficiency. Vol. 1. Seattle: Special Child Publications, 1967.

Barsch, R. H. Enriching Perception and Cognition: Techniques for Teachers. Vol. 2. Seattle: Special Child Publications, 1968.

Bartel, N. R. Locus of control and achievement in middle class and lower class children. Dissertation Abstracts, 1968, *29*: 4725.

Bartel, N. R., and Guskin, S. L. A handicap as a social phenomenon. In W. M. Cruickshank (Ed.), Psychology of Exceptional Children and Youth. Englewood-Cliffs, N.J.: Prentice-Hall, 1971.

Barter, J. T., Swaback, D. O., Todd, D. Adolescent suicide attempts: A follow-up study of hospitalized patients. Am. J. Psychiatry, 1968, *19*: 523–527.

Bateman, B. Reading and psycholinguistic processes of partially sighted children. Unpublished doctoral dissertation, University of Illinois, 1963.

Bateman, B. Learning disabilities: An overview. Journal of School Psychology, 1965, *3*(3): 1–12.

Bateson, G., Jackson, D. D., Haley, J., and Weakland, J. Toward a theory of schizophrenia. Behav. Sci., 1956, *1*: 251–264.

Bauerfeind, R. H. Building a School Testing Program, 1969 Impression. Boston: Houghton Mifflin, 1969.

Baumeister, A. A. Mental Retardation. Chicago: Aldine, 1967.

Bayley, N. On the growth of intelligence. Am. Psychol., 1955, *10*: 805–818.

Beach, F. A., and Jaynes, J. Effects of early experience upon the behavior of animals. Psychol. Bull., 1954, *51*: 239–263.

Bean, W. J. The isolation of some psychometric indices of severe reading disability. Dissertation Abstracts, 1968, *28*(8-A): 3012–3013.

Beard, R. M. An investigation of concept formation among infant school children. Unpublished doctoral dissertation, University of London, 1957.

Bearn, A. G. Wilson's disease: An inborn error of metabolism with multiple manifestations. Am. J. Med., 1957, *22*: 747.

Becker, H. S. Marihuana use and social control. Social Problems, 1955, *3*: 36–37.

Bee, H. L., and Walker, R. S. Readings regarding experimental modification of the lag between perceiving and performing. Psychonomic Science, 1968, *11*: 127–128.

Beers, C. The Mind That Found Itself. New York: Longmans, Green & Company, 1908.

Bell, R. Q. A reinterpretation of the direction of effects in studies of socialization. Psychol. Rev., 1969, *75*: 81–95.

Benda, C. E. Personality factors in mild mental retardation. Am. J. Ment. Defic., 1963, *68*: 24–30.

Bender, L. Childhood schizophrenia. Am. J. Orthopsychiatry, 1947, *17*: 40–56.

Bender, L. Psychological problems of children with organic brain disease. Am. J. Orthopsychiatry, 1949, *19*: 404–415.

Bender, L., and Helme, W. H. A quantitative test of theory and diagnostic indicators of childhood schizophrenia. AMA Archives of Neurological Psychiatry, 1953, *70*: 413–427.

Benton, A. L. Personal communication, 1963.

Bentzen, F. Sex ratios in learning and behavior disorders. Am. J. Orthopsychiatry, 1963, *33*: 92–98.

Berecz, J. M. Phobias in childhood: Etiology and treatment. Psychol. Bull., 1968, *70*: 694–720.

Bereiter, C., and Englemann, S. Teaching Disadvantaged Children in the Preschool. Englewood Cliffs, N.J.: Prentice-Hall, 1966.

Berenbaum, H. L. Validation of the non-achievement syndrome: A behavior disorder. Dissertation Abstracts, 1968, *29*: 1502.

Bergin, A. E. Some implications of psychotherapy research for therapeutic practice. J. Abnorm. Psychol., 1966, *71*: 235–246.

Bergin, A. E., and Garfield, S. L. (Eds.) Handbook of Psychotherapy and Behavior Change. New York: Wiley, 1971.

Berlin, I., and Dill, A. C. The effects of feedback positive reinforcement on the Wepman Auditory Discrimination Test scores of lower-class Negro and white children. J. Speech Hear. Res., 1967, *10*: 384–388.

Berlin, S., and Berlin, C. Acceptability of stuttering control patterns. J. Speech Hear. Disord., 1964, *29*: 436–441.

Bernstein, L., and Purcell, K. Institutional treatment of asthmatic children. In H. I. Schneer (Ed.), The Asthmatic Child, Psychosomatic Approach to Problems and Treatment. New York: Harper & Row, 1963.

Bernstein, M. Life space interview in the school setting. In R. G. Newman and M. M. Keith (Eds.), The School-Centered Life Space Interview. Washington, D.C.: Washington School of Psychiatry, 1963.

Berry, M. F. Language Disorders of Children: The Basis of Diagnosis. New York: Appleton-Century-Crofts, 1969.

Bertrand, A. L. School attendance and attainment: Function and dysfunction of school and family social systems. Social Forces, 1962, *40*: 228–233.

Bettelheim, B. The Empty Fortress: Infantile Autism and the Birth of the Self. New York: Free Press, 1967.

Bijou, S. W. Environment and intelligence: A behavioral analysis. In R. Cancro (Ed.), Intelligence: Genetic and Environmental Influences. New York: Grune & Stratton, 1971.

Bille, B. Juvenile headaches: The maternal history of headaches in children. In A. P. Friedman and E. Harms (Eds.), Headaches in Children. Springfield, Ill.: Charles C Thomas, 1967.

Biller, B. An exploratory investigation of masculine development in kindergarten age boys. Dissertation Abstracts, 1968, *28*: 4290–4291.

Bills, R. E. Nondirective play therapy with retarded readers. J. Consult. Psychol., 1950, *14*: 140–149.

Birch, H. G. Brain Damage in Children. Baltimore: Williams & Wilkins, 1964.

Birch, H. G. Health and the education of socially disadvantaged children. Dev. Med. Child Neurol., 1968, *10*: 580–599.

Birch, H. G., and Belmont, L. Auditory-visual integration in normal and retarded readers. Am. J. Orthopsychiatry, 1963, *34*: 852–861.

Birch, H. G., and Gassow, J. D. Disadvantaged Children: Health, Nutrition and School Failure. New York: Harcourt, Brace & World, 1970.

Birch, H. G., and Hefford, A. Intrasensory development in children. Monogr. Soc. Res. Child Dev., 1963, *28*(5): 48.

Birch, H. G., Richardson, S. C., Baird, D., Horobin, G., and Illsley, R. Mental Subnormality in the Community. Baltimore: Williams & Wilkins, 1970.

Birch, W., and Stuckless, E. Programming instruction in written language for deaf children. Am. Ann. Deaf, 1963, *68*: 317–336.

Birch, W., and Stuckless, E.: Programmed instruction in written language for the deaf. Except. Child., 1964, *30*: 296–303.

Blair, G. M., Jones, R. S., and Simpson, R. H. Educational Psychology. (2nd ed.) New York: Macmillan, 1962.

Blau, A. The master hand: A study of the origin and meaning of right and left sidedness and its relation to personality and language. Journal of the American Orthopsychiatry Association, 1946, *16*:455–480.

Blewett, D. B. An experimental study of the inheritance of intelligence. J. Ment. Sci., 1954, *100*: 922–933.

Blitzer, J. R., Rollins, N., and Blackwell, A. Children who starve themselves: Anorexia nervosa. Psychosom. Med., 1961, *5*: 369–383.

Bloch, H. A., and Niederhoffer, A. The Gang: A Study in Adolescent Behavior. New York: Philosophical Library, 1958.

Bloch, J., Jennings, P. H., Harvey, E., and Simpson, E. Interaction between allergic potential and psychopathology in childhood asthma. Psychosom. Med., 1964, *26*: 308–320.

Bloodstein, O. A. A Handbook on Stuttering for Professional Workers. Chicago: National Society for Crippled Children and Adults, 1959.

Bloom, B. S. Stability and Change in Human Characteristics. New York: Wiley, 1965.

Bloom, B. S., Hastings, J. T., and Madaus, G. F. Handbook on Formative and Summative Evaluation of Student Learning. New York: McGraw-Hill, 1970.

Blustein, E. S.: The relationship of sibling position in the family constellation to school behavior variables in elementary school children from two-child families. Dissertation Abstracts, 1968, *28*: 346.

Book, J. A., et al. A clinical and genetic study of microcephaly. Am. J. Ment. Defic., 1953, *57*: 637–660.

Bourne, H. Propherenia: A study of perverted rearing and mental dwarfism. Lancet, 1955, 6901: 1156–1163.

Bousfield, W. A., and Orbison, W. D. Ontogenesis of emotional behavior. Psychol. Rev., 1952, *59*: 1–7.

Boutourline-Young, H., Younes, H., Tesi, G., and Jessor, R. Relationships between child growth and environment in a developing country. Paper presented at the 37th Annual Meeting of The American Academy of Pediatrics, Chicago, October, 1968.

Bower, D. Academic underachievement: A suggested theory. J. Psychol., 1967, *66*: 299–302.

Bower, E. M. The school psychologist. Bulletin of the California State Department of Education, 1955, *24*: 1308.

Bower, E. M. The psychologist in the school. Bulletin of the California State Department of Education, 1958, *27*: 43.

Bower, E. M. The emotionally handicapped child and the school. Except. Child., 1959, *26*: 6–11.

Bower, E. M. Early Identification of Emotionally Disturbed Children in School. (2nd ed.) Springfield, Ill.: Charles C Thomas, 1969.

Bower, E. M., and Lambert, N. The Education of Emotionally Disturbed Children. Sacramento, Calif.: State Department of Education, 1961.

Bowlby, J. Maternal care and mental health. Bull. W. H. O., 1951, *3*: 355–533.

Bradley, R. W. Birth order and school-related behavior: A heuristic review. Psychol. Bull., 1968, *70*: 45–51.

Brady, J. P. Brevital-relaxation treatment of frigidity. Behav. Res. Ther., 1966, *4*: 71–78.

Brady, J. P. A behavioral approach to the treatment of stuttering. Am. J. Psychiatry, 1968, *125*: 843–848.

Braley, W. T., Konick, G., and Leedy, C. Daily Sensorimotor Training Activities. Freeport, N.Y.: Freeport Educational Activities, 1968.

Brannon, J. B. Linguistic work classes in the spoken language of normal hard of hearing and deaf children. J. Speech Hear. Res., 1968, *11*: 279–287.

Braun, S., Holzman, M. S., and Lasher, M. G. Teachers of disturbed pre-school children: An analysis of teaching styles. Am. J. Orthopsychiatry, 1969, *39*: 617.

Breger, L., and McGaugh, J. L. Critique and reformulation of "Learning Theory" approaches to psychotherapy and neurosis. Psychol. Bull., 1965, *63*: 338–358.

Brendtro, L. K., and Stern, P. R. A modification in the sequential tutoring of emotionally disturbed children. Except. Child., 1967, *33*: 517–521.

Brereton, B. L. The Schooling of Children with Impaired Hearing. Sidney: Commonwealth Office of Education, 1957.

Brewer, W. F., Jr. Paired-associate learning of dyslexic children. Dissertation Abstracts, 1968, *28*: 3467.

Bricker, C. A. Experimental analysis of auditory discrimination skills in the developmental structure of pre-school children. Dissertation Abstracts, 1969, *29*: 3454–3455.

Brieland, D. M. A comparative study of the speech of blind and sighted children. Speech Monographs, 1966, *17*: 99–103.

Briggs, P. F., and Wirt, R. D. Prediction. In H. C. Quay (Ed.), Juvenile Delinquency. Princeton, N.J.: Van Nostrand, 1965.

Brill, R. B. Hereditary aspects of deafness. Volta Review, 1961, *113*: 168–175.

Brim, O. G., Jr., Glass, D. C., Neulinger, J., and Firestone, I. J. Beliefs and Attitudes About Intelligence. New York: Russell Sage Foundation, 1969.

Brink, T. D. Critique of Hirshoren's ITPA validity study. Except. Child., 1970, *36*: 351–356.

Broca, P. Remarques sur le siège de la faculté du langage articulé, suivies d'une observation d'aphémie (perte de la parole). Bull. Soc. Anat. de Paris (2nd series), 1861, *6*: 330–357.

Brower, D. Academic underachievement: A suggested theory. J. Psychol., 1967, *66*: 299–302.

Brown, E. C. A humanistic model. In L. L'Abate (Ed.), Models of Clinical Psychology. Atlanta: Georgia State University, 1969.

Brown, E. C., and L'Abate, L. An appraisal of teaching machines and programmed instruction. In C. M. Franks (Ed.), Behavior Therapy: Appraisal and Status. New York: McGraw-Hill, 1969.

Brown, R. A., and Pace, Z. S. Treatment of extreme negativism and autistic behavior in a six year old boy. Except. Child., 1969, *36*: 115–122.

Browning, R. M., and Stover, D. O. Behavior Modification in Child Treatment. Chicago: Aldine-Atherton, 1971.

Bruch, H.: Obesity. Pediatr. Clin. North Am., 1958, *5*: 613–627.

Brumbaugh, F. N., and Roshco, B.: Your Gifted Child: A Guide for Parents. New York: Holt, Rinehart and Winston, Inc., 1959.

Bruner, J. S. The Process of Education. Cambridge: Harvard University Press, 1960.

Buell, B. Motor performance of visually handicapped children. Except. Child., 1950, *22*: 69–72.

Buhler, C. B. Theoretical observations about life's basic tendencies. Am. J. Psychother., 1959, *13*: 561–581.

Buktenica, N. A. Perceptual mode dominance: An approach to assessment of first grade reading and spelling. Proceedings: 76th Annual Convention, American Psychological Association, 1968, *3*: 585–586.

Bullock, L. M., and Whelan, R. J. Competencies needed by teachers of the emotionally disturbed and socially maladjusted: A comparison. Except. Child., 1971, *37*: 485–489.

Burdock, E. I., and Hardesty, A. S. Contrasting behavior patterns of mentally retarded and emotionally disturbed children. In Z. Zubin and G. A. Jeris (Eds.), Psychopathology of Mental Development. New York: Grune & Stratton, 1967.

Bureau of Education for the Handicapped. Better education for the handicapped. Annual Reports FY 1969, 1970.

Burks, B. S. The relative influence of nature and nurture upon mental development: A comparative study of foster parent-foster child resemblance and true parent-true child resemblance. In L. M. Therman (Ed.), Yearbook National Social Studies Education, Pt. 1, 1928.

Burnes, D. K. A study of relationships between measured intelligence and non-intellective factors for children of two socioeconomic groups and races. Dissertation Abstracts, 1969, *29*: 4839.

Buros, O. K. (Ed.) Personality Tests and Reviews. Highland Park, N.J.: Gryphon Press, 1970.

Buros, O. K. (Ed.) The Sixth Mental Measurements Yearbook. Highland Park, N.J.: Gryphon Press, 1965.

Burt, C. Inheritance of general intelligence. Am. Psychol., 1972, *27*: 175–190.

Butler, R. A., and Naunton, R. F. The effect of stimulus sensation level on the directional hearing of unilaterally deafened persons. Journal of Auditory Research, 1967, 7: 15–23.

Cain, L. F., and Levine, S. A. A study of the effects of community and institutional school classes for trainable mentally retarded children. Cooperative Research Project No. SAE8256, 1961, San Francisco State College, U.S. Office of Education.

Cameron, D. E. Psychotherapy in Action. New York: Grune & Stratton, 1968.

Cancro, R. Genetic contributions to individual difference in intelligence: An introduction. In R. Cancro (Ed.), Genetics and Environmental Influences. New York: Grune & Stratton, 1971.

Caputo, D. V., Edmonston, W. E., L'Abate, L., and Ronberg, S. R. Type of brain damage and intellectual functioning in children. J. Consult. Psychol., 1963, *27*: 184.

Carlin, A. S., and Armstrong, H. E. Aversive conditioning: Learning or dissonance reduction? J. Consult. Clin. Psychol., 1968, *32*: 674–678.

Carpenter, V. F. Motivational components of achievement in culturally disadvantaged Negro children. Dissertation Abstracts, 1968, *28*: 3991–3992.

Carr, L. J. Delinquency Control. (Rev. ed.) New York: Harper & Row, 1950.

Cattell, R. B. The structure of intelligence in relation to the nature-nurture controversy. In R. Cancro (Ed.), Intelligence: Genetic and Environmental Influences. New York: Grune & Stratton, 1971.

Cautela, J. R. Covert sensitization. Psychological Record, 1967, *20*: 459–468.

Cazden, C. B. Subcultural differences in child language: An interdisciplinary review. Merrill-Palmer Q. Behav. Dev., 1966, *12*: 185–219.

Chalfant, J. C., and Scheffelin, M. A. Central Processing Dysfunctions in Children: A Review of Research. Bethesda, Md.: U.S. Department of Health, Education, and Welfare, 1969.

Chance, J. E. Independence training and first graders' achievement. In M. Kornrich (Ed.), Underachievement. Springfield, Ill.: Charles C Thomas, 1965.

Chapman, A. H., and Loeb, D. G. Psychosomatic gastrointestinal problems in children. Journal of Diseases in Children, 1955, *91*: 717–724.

Charles D. C. Ability and accomplishment of persons earlier judged mentally deficient. Genet. Psychol. Mongr., 1953, *47*: 3–71.

Charters, W. W., Jr. The social background of teaching. In N. L. Gage (Ed.), Handbook of Research on Teaching. Skokie, Ill.: Rand McNally, 1963.

Chase, R. H. Evolutionary aspects of language development and functions: A discussion of Lenneberg's presentation. In F. Smith and G. A. Miller (Eds.), The Genesis of Language: A Psycholinguistic Approach. Cambridge, Mass.: M.I.T. Press, 1966.

Chess, S., Thomas, A., and Birch, H. G. Behavior problems revisited: Findings of an anterospective study. J. Am. Acad. Child Psychiatry, 1967, *6*: 321–331.

Cheves, R. The Ruth Cheves Program of Visual-Motor Perception Teaching Materials. Boston: Teaching Resources, 1963.

Chomsky, N. The formal nature of language. In E. H. Lenneberg (Ed.), Biological Foundations of Language. New York: Wiley, 1967.

Chomsky, N. Language and Mind. New York: Harcourt, Brace & World, 1969.

Churchill, E. M. The number concepts of the young child. Research Studies, 1958, *17*: 34–49.

Cicarelli, V., and Granger, R. The Impact of Headstart. Vols. I, II. An Evaluation of the Effects of Headstart on Children's Cognitive and Affective Development. Blandenburg, Md.: Westinghouse Learning Corporation, 1969.

Clarizio, H., and McCoy, G. F. Behavior Disorders in School Age Children. Scranton, Pa.: Chandler, 1970.

Clark, J., and Wenninger, E. Socio-economic class and area as correlates of illegal behavior among juveniles. Am. Sociol. Rev., 1962, *27*: 826–834.

Clarke, A. D. B., and Clarke, A. M. Cognitive changes in the feebleminded. Br. J. Psychol., 1954, *45*: 173–179.

Clarke, A. D. B., and Clarke, A. M. Some recent advances in the study of early deprivation. Child Psychology and Psychiatry, 1960, *1*: 26–36.

Clarke, A. D. B., Clarke, A. M., and Reiman, S. Cognitive and social changes in the feebleminded—three further studies. Br. J. Psychol., 1958, *49*: 144–147.

Clarke, A. M., and Clarke, A. D. B. Learning transfer and cognitive development. In J. Zubin and G. A. Jervis (Eds.), Psychopathology of Mental Development. New York: Grune & Stratton, 1967.

Clausen, J. Assessment of behavior characteristics in mental retardates. In J. Zubin and G. A. Jervis (Eds.), Psychopathology of Mental Development. New York: Grune & Stratton, 1967.

Clawson, A. The Bender Visual-Motor Gestalt Test. Beverly Hills, Calif.: Western Psychological Services, 1969.

Clement, P. W., and Milne, D. C. Group play therapy and tangible reinforcers used to modify the behavior of eight year old boys. Behav. Res. Ther., 1967, *5*: 301–302.

Clements, H. M., Duncan, J. A., and Taylor, W. M. Toward effective evaluation of the culturally deprived. Personnel and Guidance Journal, 1969, *47*: 891–896.

Clements, S. D. Minimal brain dysfunction in children. NINDB Monograph, U.S. Department of Health, Education, and Welfare, 1966, No. 3.

Clements, S. D., and Peters, J. E. Minimal brain dysfunctions in the school age child. Arch. Gen. Psychiatry, 1962, *6*: 185–197.

Cloward, R., and Ohlin, L. Delinquency and Opportunity: A Theory of Delinquent Gangs. New York: Free Press, 1960.

Cohen, A. Delinquent Boys. Glencoe, Ill.: Free Press, 1955.

Cohen, J. Factorial structure of the WISC at ages 7–6, 10–6, and 13–6. J. Consult. Psychol., 1959, *23*: 285–299.

Cohen, R. Primary group structure, conceptual styles and school achievement. Dissertation Abstracts, 1968a, *28*: 5151–5152.

Cohen, R. The relation between socioconceptual styles and orientation to school requirements. Sociology of Education, 1968b, *41*: 220.

Cole, M., and Bruner, J. Cultural differences and inferences about psychological processes. Am. Psychol., 1971, *10*: 867–876.

Coleman, R., and Deutsch, C. Lateral dominance and right-left discrimination: A comparison of normal and retarded readers. Percept. Mot. Skills, 1964, *19*: 43–50.

Coles, R. The poor don't want to be middle class. The New York Times Magazine, 1965, *12*: 58.

Collman, R. D., and Stoller, A. A. A survey of mongoloid births in Victoria, Australia, 1942–1957. Am. J. Public Health, 1962, *52*: 813–829.

Conant, J. Slums and Suburbs: A Commentary on Schools in Metropolitan Areas. New York: McGraw-Hill, 1961.

Conger, J., and Miller, W. C. Personality, Social Class, and Delinquency. New York: Free Press, 1961.

Conger, J., Miller, W., and Walsmith, C. Antecedents of delinquency: Personality, social class and intelligence. In P. H. Mussen, J. Conger, and J. Kagan (Eds.), Readings in Child Development and Personality. New York: Harper & Row, 1965.

Conn, A. Socioeconomic status and verbal output. Unpublished manuscript. Child Development Laboratory, George State University, 1967.

Connally, C. G. The psychosocial adjustment of children with dyslexia. Dissertation Abstracts, 1969, *29*(10-A): 3456–3457.

Connor, E., and Muldoon, J. F. Resource programming for emotionally disturbed teenagers. Except. Child., 1968, *12*: 261–265.

Connor, F., Rusalem, H., and Cruickshank, W. M. Psychological considerations with crippled children. In W. M. Cruickshank (Ed.), Psychology of Exceptional Children and Youth. Englewood Cliffs, N.J.: Prentice-Hall, 1971.

Coppersmith, S. The Antecedents of Self-Esteem. San Francisco: Freeman, 1967.

Cowen, E. L., Zax, M., Izzo, L. D., and Trost, M. A. Prevention of emotional disorders in the school setting: A further investigation. J. Consult. Psychol., 1966, *30*: 381–387.

Cowles, M., Daniel, K. B., Durant, T., and Parler, J. Psycholinguistic behaviors of isolated, rural children with and without kindergarten. Paper presented at the Southeastern Meeting on Child Development, Athens, Georgia, April, 1970.

Craig, M. M., and Glick, S. J. Ten years experience with the Glueck Prediction Table. Crime and Delinquency, 1963, *9*: 249–261.

Cratty, B. J. Perceptual-Motor and Educational Processes. Springfield, Ill.: Charles C Thomas, 1968.

Cratty, B. J. Movement, Perception, and Thought. Los Angeles: Peek Publications, 1969.

Cratty, B. J. Physical Expressions of Intelligence. Englewood Cliffs, N.J.: Prentice-Hall, 1972.

Cravioto, J., Goana, C. E., and Birch, H. G. Early identification and auditory-visual integration in school-age children. Journal of Special Education, 1967, *2*:75–82.

Creak, M., and Stephen, J. M. The psychological aspects of asthma in children. Pediatr. Clin. North Am., 1958, *5*: 731–747.

Crome, L. A. Critique of current views on acrocephaly and related conditions. J. Ment. Sci., 1961, *107*: 459–474.

Cromwell, R. L. Hull-Spence theory and mental deficiency. In N. R. Ellis (Ed.), Handbook of Mental Deficiency. New York: McGraw-Hill, 1963.

Cronbach, L. J. Essentials of Psychological Testing. (3rd ed.) New York: Harper & Row, 1970.

Cronbach, L. J., and Gleser, G. C. Psychological Tests and Personnel Decisions. (2nd ed.) Urbana: The University of Illinois Press, 1964.

Crotzin, M., and Dallenbach, K. M. Facial vision: The role of pitch and loudness in the perception of obstacles by the blind. Am. J. Psychol., 1950, *63*: 485–515.

Cruickshank, W. M. Learning and physical environment: The necessity for research and research design. Except. Child., 1968, *37*: 261–268.

Cruickshank, W. M. (Ed.) Psychology of Exceptional Children and Youth. (3rd ed.) Englewood Cliffs, N.J.: Prentice-Hall, 1971.

Cruickshank, W. M., Bentzen, F. A., Ratzeburg, F. H., and Tannhauser, M. T. A Teaching Method for Brain-Injured and Hyperactive Children. Syracuse, N.Y.: Syracuse University Press, 1961.

Cruickshank, W. M., Bice, H. V., and Wallen, N. E. Perception and Cerebral Palsy. Syracuse, N.Y.: Syracuse University Press, 1957.

Cruickshank, W. M., and Cowen, E. L. Group therapy with physically handicapped children: Report of study. J. Educ. Psychol., 1948, *39*: 193–215.

Cruickshank, W. M., and Johnson, G. O. Education of Exceptional Children and Youth. (2nd ed.) Englewood Cliffs, N.J.: Prentice-Hall, 1967.

Cruickshank, W. M., and Trippe, M. J. Services to Blind Children in the State of New York. Syracuse, N.Y.: Syracuse University Press, 1959.

Curtis, L. T. A comparative analysis of the self-concept of the adolescent mentally retarded in relation to certain groups of adolescents. Unpublished doctoral dissertation, University of Oregon, 1964.

Dalton, M. M. A visual survey of 5000 school children. Journal of Educational Research, 1943, *37*: 81–94.

Daniels, J. C. Children with reading difficulties. Slow Learning Child: The Australian Journal on the Education of Backward Children, 1967, *13*: 138–144.

Daniels, M. The dynamics of morbid envy in the etiology and treatment of the chronic learning disability. Psychoanal. Rev., 1964, *51*: 45–56.

Daniels, M. Further observations on the development of the vindictive character. Am. J. Psychother., 1967, *21*: 822–831.

Dansinger, S., and Madow, A. A. Verbal, auditory screening with the mentally retarded. Am. J. Ment. Defic., 1966, *71*(3): 387–392.

Darke, R. A. Late effects of severe asphyxia neonatorum. J. Pediatr., 1944, *24*: 148–158.

Davis, A., and Havighurst, R. J. Social class and color differences in child rearing. Am. Sociol. Rev., 1946, *11*: 698–710.

Davis, B. J. Differential language behavior patterns and diagnostic evaluation. Journal of Learning Disabilities, 1970, *3*: 264–275.

Davison, G. C. Systematic desensitization as a coun-

terconditioning process. J. Abnorm. Psychol., 1968, *73*: 91–99.
De Francis, V. Protecting the Child Victim of Sex Crimes Committed by Adults: Final Report. Denver: American Humane Association, Children's Division, 1969.
Delacato, C. H. The Treatment and Prevention of Reading Problems. Springfield, Ill.: Charles C Thomas, 1959.
Delacato, C. H. The Diagnosis and Treatment of Speech and Reading Disorders. Springfield, Ill.: Charles C Thomas, 1963.
Denenberg, K. The effect of seat instability on perception of the vertical. Dissertation Abstracts International, 1969, *30*(1-B): 402–403.
Dennis, W. Causes of retardation among institutional children: Iran. J. Genet. Psychol., 1960, *90*: 47–59.
Dennison, G. Lives of Children. New York: Random House, 1969.
Deutsch, M. The disadvantaged child and the learning process. In H. Passow (Ed.), Education in Depressed Areas. New York: Bureau of Publications, Teachers College, 1963.
Deutsch, M. Facilitating development in the preschool child: Social and psychological perspectives. Merrill-Palmer Q. Behav. Dev. 1964, *10*: 249–263.
Deutsch, M., and Brown, B. R. Social influence in Negro-white intelligence differences. Journal of Social Issues, 1964, *20*: 20–35.
Deutsch, M., et al. The Disadvantaged Child. New York: Basic Books, 1967.
Deutsch, M., Katz, I., and Jensen, A. R. Social Class, Race, and Psychological Development. New York: Holt, Rinehart and Winston, Inc., 1968.
Dexter, R., Leuke, A., Masterson, V., and Sanderson, R. E. The mental retardate with severe somatic growth failure, a special group: Amino acid studies—a pilot study. California Mental Health Research Digest, 1965, *3*: 28.
Dingman, H. F., and Tarjan, G. Mental retardation and the normal distribution curve. Am. J. Ment. Defic., 1960, *64*: 991–994.
Dobzhansky, T. Heredity, environment, and evolution. Science, 1950, *111*: 161–166.
Dobzhansky, T. Genetics of the Evolutionary Process. New York: Columbia University Press, 1970.
Dobzhansky, T. Genetics and the diversity of behavior. Am. Psychol., 1972, *27*: 523–538.
Dollard, J., and Miller, N. E. Personality and Psychotherapy. New York: McGraw-Hill, 1950.
Drews, E. M. What about the gifted child? College of Education Quarterly, 1957, *11*: 3–6.
Drews, E. M., and Teahan, J. E. Parental attitudes and academic achievement. In M. Kornrich (Ed.), Underachievement. Springfield, Ill.: Charles C Thomas, 1965.
Dreyer, A. S., and Rigler, D. Cognitive performance in Montessori and nursery school children. Journal of Educational Research, 1969, *62*: 411–416.
Dubnoff, B., and Chambers, I. The Dubnoff School Program of Sequential Perceptual-Motor Exercises. Boston: Teaching Resources, 1967.
DuBois, P. Varieties of psychological test homogeneity. Am. Psychol., 1970, *25*: 532–536.
Dudek, S. Z., and Lester, E. P. The good child facade in chronic underachievers. Am. J. Orthopsychiatry, 1968, *38*: 153–160.
Duff, M. M. Language functions in children with learning disabilities. Dissertation Abstracts, 1969, *29*: 3958–3959.
Dugdale, R. L. The Jukes: A Study of Crime, Pauperism, Disease, and Heredity. New York: Putman, 1877.
Dunn, L. M. (Ed.) Exceptional Children in the Schools. New York: Holt, Rinehart and Winston, Inc., 1963.
Dunn, L. M. Minimal brain dysfunction: A dilemma for educators. In H. C. Haywood (Ed.), Brain Damage in School Children. Washington, D.C.: Council for Exceptional Children, 1968a.
Dunn, L. M. Special education for the mildly retarded: Is much of it justifiable? Except. Child., 1968b, *35*: 5–24.

Eaton, E., and Menolascino, F. J. Psychotic reactions of childhood: A five-year follow-up study of experiences in a mental retardation clinic. Am. J. Orthopsychiatry, 1967, *37*: 521–529.
Eaton, J., and Polk, K. Measuring Delinquency. Pittsburgh: University of Pittsburgh Press, 1961.
Edmonson, B., DeJung, J. E., and Leland, H. Social perceptual (nonverbal communication) training of retarded adolescents. Ment. Retard., 1965, *3*: 7–9.
Edmonson, B., Leland, H., DeJung, J. E., and Leach, E. M. Increasing social interpretations (visual decoding) by retarded adolescents through training. Am. J. Ment. Defic., 1967, *21*: 1017–1024.
Eickhoff, L. F. The etiology of schizophrenia in childhood. J. Ment. Sci., 1952, *98*: 229–234.
Einhart, C. B., Graham, F. K., Eichman, F. K., Marshall, J. M., and Thurston, D. Brain injury in the pre-school child: Some developmental considerations. II. Comparisons of brain injured and normal children. Psychol. Mongr., 1963, 77: 17–33.
Eisenberg, L. Preventive psychiatry. In D. Rytand and W. P. Creger (Eds.), Annual Review of Medicine. Stanford, Calif.: Annual Reviews, 1962.
Eisenberg, L. Role of drugs in treating disturbed children. Children, 1964, *11*: 167–173.
Ekstein, R. Children of Time and Space: Impulse and Action. New York: Appleton-Century-Crofts, 1966.
Elkind, D., and Deblinger, J. A. Perceptual training and reading achievement in disadvantaged children. Child Dev., 1969, *40*: 11–19.
Ellis, N. R. (Ed.) Handbook of Mental Deficiency. New York: McGraw-Hill, 1963a.
Ellis, N. R. The stimulus trace and behavioral inadequacy. In N. R. Ellis (Ed.), Handbook of Mental Deficiency. New York: McGraw-Hill, 1963b.
Ellis, E. R., and Allen, G. N. Traitor Within: Our Suicide Problem. Garden City, N.Y.: Doubleday, 1961.
Elonen, A. S., Polzien, M., and Zwarensteyn, S. B. The uncommitted blind child. Except. Child., 1967, *33*: 301–306.

Elstad, L. H., Frampton, M. E., and Gall, E. D. The Deaf in Special Education for the Exceptional. Boston: Porter, Sargent, 1955.

Empey, L. T., and Erickson, M. L. Hidden delinquency and social status. Social Forces, 1966, *44*: 546–554.

Engel, M. Some parameters of the psychological evaluation of children. American Medical Association, Arch. Gen. Psychiatry, 1960, *2*: 6.

Entwisle, D. R. Developmental sociolinguistics: Inner-city children. Am. J. Sociol., 1968, *74*: 37–49.

Erickson, E. H. The problem of ego identity. J. Am. Psychoanal. Assoc., 1946, *4*: 56–121.

Erickson, E. H. Identity and the Life Cycle: Psychological Issues. New York: International Universities Press, 1959.

Erikson, E. H. Childhood and Society. New York: Norton, 1950.

Ernhart, C. B., Graham, F. K., Eichman, P. L., Marshall, J. M., and Thurston, D. Brain injury in the preschool child: Some developmental considerations: II. Comparisons of brain injured and normal children. Psychol. Mongr., 1963, *77*: 17–33.

Escalona, S. K. The Roots of Individuality: Normal Patterns of Development in Infancy. Chicago: Aldine, 1968.

Eysenck, H. J. The Dynamics of Anxiety and Hysteria. London: Routledge, 1957.

Eysenck, H. J. Learning theory and behavior therapy. J. Ment. Sci., 1959, *105*: 61–75.

Eysenck, H. J. (Ed.) Behavior Therapy and the Neuroses. New York: Pergamon, 1960.

Eysenck, H. J. Experiments in Behavior Therapy. New York: Pergamon, 1964.

Eysenck, H. J., and Rachman, S. The Causes and Cures of Neurosis. London: Routledge, 1965.

Fagen, S., Long, N., and Stevens, D. Teaching Children Self-control in the Classroom. Columbus, Ohio: Charles E. Merrill Books, Inc., 1971.

Fairbanks, J., and Robinson, J. The Fairbanks-Robinson Program of Perceptual Motor Development. Boston: Teaching Resources, 1967.

Falstein, E. I., Feinstein, S. C., and Judas, I. Anorexia nervosa in the male child. Am. J. Orthopsychiatry, 1956, *26*: 751–769.

Farber, B. Effects of a severely retarded child on family integration. Mongr. Soc. Res. Child Dev., 1960:*25*, No. 1.

Farber, B. Mental Retardation. Boston: Houghton Mifflin, 1968.

Farber, I. E. The role of motivation in verbal learning and performance. Psychol. Bull., 1955, *52*: 311–327.

Farragher, M. E. Therapeutic tutoring as an approach to psychogenic learning disturbances. Journal of Special Education, 1968, *2*: 117–127.

Fenichel, O. The Psychoanalytic Theory of Neurosis. New York: Norton, 1945.

Ferguson, N. U. The Frostig: An instrument for predicting total academic readiness and reading and arithmetical achievement in first grade. Dissertation Abstracts, 1967, *20*: 2090.

Ferrier, E. E. An investigation of the ITPA performance of children with functional defects of articulation. Except. Child., 1966, *32*: 625–629.

Ferster, C. B. Reinforcement and punishment in the control of human behavior by social agencies. In Social Aspects of Psychiatry, Psychiatr. Res. Rep., 1958, *10*: 101–118.

Ferster, C. B. Positive reinforcement and behavioral deficits in autistic children. Child. Dev., 1961, *32*: 437–456.

Ferster, C. B., and Perrot, M. C. Behavior Principles. New York: Appleton-Century-Crofts, 1968.

Ferster, C. B., and Simons, J. Behavior therapy with children. Psychological Record, 1966, *16*: 65–71.

Feshbach, S. Aggression. In P. H. Mussen (Ed.), Carmichael's Manual of Child Psychology. New York: Wiley, 1970.

Feshbach, S., and Singer, R. Television and Aggression: An Experimental Field Study. San Francisco: Jossey-Bass, 1971.

Fiedler, M. F. Deaf Children in a Hearing World. New York: Ronald, 1952.

Filep, R. T. Prospectives in Programming. New York: Macmillan, 1963.

Finch, S. G., and Hess, J. H. Ulcerative colitis in children. Am. J. Psychiatry, 1962, *118*: 819–826.

Finch, S. M., and Poznanski, E. O. Adolescent Suicide. Springfield, Ill.: Charles C Thomas, 1971.

Fink, M. B. Self-concept as it relates to academic underachievement. In M. Kornrich (Ed.), Underachievement. Springfield, Ill.: Charles C Thomas, 1965.

Fisher, S., and Cleveland, S. E. Body Image and Personality. Princeton, N.J.: Van Nostrand, 1958.

Fitts, W. H., and Hammer, W. T. The self-concept and delinquency. Nashville Mental Health Center Monographs, 1969, No. 1.

Fitzelle, G. T. Personality factors and certain attitudes toward child rearing among parents of asthmatic children. Psychosom. Med., 1959, *21*: 208–217.

Fitzhugh, L., and Fitzhugh, K. The Fitzhugh Plus Program. Galein, Mich.: Allied Education Council, 1966.

Flanagan, J. C., Dailey, J. T., Shaycroft, M., Gorham, W., Orr, D. B., and Goldberg, I. Design for a Study of American Youth. Boston: Houghton Mifflin, 1962.

Flavell, J. H. The Developmental Psychology of Jean Piaget. Princeton, N.J.: Van Nostrand, 1963.

Fleming, C. M. Teaching, A Psychological Analysis. New York: Wiley, 1958.

Flory, Donald L. Intellectual development, social class, and the child's activities in the home. Dissertation Abstracts, 1969, *29*: 3217.

Fodor, Y. A. How to learn to talk: Some simple ways. In F. Smith and G. A. Miller (Eds.), The Givens of Language: A Psycholinguistic Approach. Cambridge, Mass.: The M.I.T. Press, 1966.

Fogel, M. L. Picture description and interpretation in brain-damaged patients. Cortex, 1967, *3*: 433–448.

Folling, A. Über Asusscheidung von Phenylbrenztraubensäure in den Harn als Stoffwechselanomalie in Verbindung mit Imbezillität. Hoppe Seylers Z. Physiol. Chem., 1934, *227*: 169–176.

Folsom, A. T. The epilepsies. In H. C. Haywood (Ed.), Brain Damage in School Age Children. Washington, D.C.: Council for Exceptional Children, 1968.
Footlik, S. W. Perceptual-motor training and cognitive achievement: A survey of the literature. Journal of Learning Disabilities, 1970, *3*: 40–49.
Ford, C. E., Jones, K. W., Muller, O. J., Mittwoch, U., Ridler, M., and Shapiro, A. The chromosomes in a patient showing both mongolian and the Klinefelter syndromes. Lancet, 1959, *1*:709–710.
Forness, S. R., and Millan, D. L. The origins of behavior modification with exceptional children. Except. Child., 1970, *37*: 93–100.
Foster, J. C. As the child sees the teacher. Childhood Education, 1933, *9*: 283–288.
Foucault, M. Madness and Civilization. (Trans. R. Howard) New York: Random House, 1965.
Fox, F. H. A description of language and perceptual function of culturally deprived children. Dissertation Abstracts, 1969, *29*: 4323.
Fox, R., Luski, M. B., and Schmuck, R. Diagnosing Classroom Learning Environments. Chicago: Survey Research Association, 1966.
Frampton, M., and Gall, E. (Eds.) Resources for Special Education. Boston: Porter Sargent, 1965.
Franks, C. M. Behavior therapy: Psychology and the psychiatrist: Contributions, evaluation, and overview. Am. J. Orthopsychiatry, 1965, *35*: 141–151.
Franks, C. M. (Ed.) Behavior Therapy: Appraisal and Status. New York: McGraw-Hill, 1969.
Frazier, S. H.; and Carr, A. C. Introduction to Psychopathology. New York: Macmillan, 1964.
Freeberg, N. Assessment of disadvantaged adolescents: A different approach to research and evaluation measures. J. Educ. Psychol., 1970, *61*: 229–241.
Freeberg, N. E., and Payne, D. T. Parental influence on cognitive development in early childhood: A review. Child Dev., 1967, *38*: 65–87.
Freedman, M. Background of deviancy. In W. W. Wattenberg (Ed.), Social Deviancy Among Youth. Chicago: The University of Chicago Press, 1966.
Freeman, E. H., Feingold, B. F., Schlesinger, K., and Gorman, F. J. Psychological variables in allergic disorders: A review. Psychosom. Med., 1964, *26*: 543–575.
French, F. E., et al. Congenital and acquired handicaps of ten-year-olds—report of a follow-up study, Kauai, Hawaii. Am. J. Public Health, 1968, *58*: 1388–1395.
Freud, A. The Ego and the Mechanisms of Defense. New York: International Universities Press, 1946a.
Freud, A. The Psychoanalytical Treatment of Children. London: Imago Publishing, 1946b.
Freud, A. Diagnosis and assessment in early childhood difficulties. Paper presented at the meeting of the Philadelphia Association for Psychoanalysis, Philadelphia, May, 1954.
Freud, S. An Outline of Psychoanalysis. New York: Norton, 1949.
Freud, S. Analysis terminable and interminable. In J. Strachey (Ed.), Collected Papers of Sigmund Freud. New York: Basic Books, 1959.
Freud, S. Civilization and Its Discontents, 1930. (Trans. and Ed. J. Strachey) London: The Hogarth Press, Ltd., 1961.
Friedenberg, E. Z. The Vanishing Adolescent. Boston: Beacon Press, 1965.
Friedlander, K. The Psychoanalytic Approach to Delinquency. New York: International Universities Press, 1947.
Friedman, T. Prenatal diagnosis of genetic disease. Sci. Am., 1971, *225*: 34–42.
Friersin, B. Educating Children with Learning Disabilities: Selected Readings. New York: Appleton-Century-Crofts, 1967.
Frost, J. L., and Hawkes, G. R. (Eds.) The Disadvantaged Child. Boston: Houghton Mifflin, 1966.
Frostig, M. Visual perception in the brain-injured child. Am. J. Orthopsychiatry, 1963, *32*: 271–280.
Frostig, M., and Horne, D. The Frostig Program for the Development of Visual Perception. Chicago: Follett, 1964.
Frostig, M., Lefever, D. W., and Whitteseley, J. R. B. A developmental test for evaluating normal and neurologically handicapped children. Percept. Mot. Skills, 1961, *12*: 283–394.
Frostig, M., and Marlow, P. Language training: A form of ability training. Journal of Learning Disabilities, 1968, *1*: 105–114.
Fry, D. B. The development of the phonological system in the normal and the deaf child. In F. Smith and G. A. Miller (Eds.), The Genesis of Language: A Psycholinguistic Approach. Cambridge, Mass.: The M.I.T. Press, 1966.
Fry, M. The Borstal System. In Penal Reform in England. London: Macmillan, 1946.
Fuller, G. B., and Shaw, C. R. Visual orientation in reading disability: Diagnostic considerations. J. Child Psychiatry, 1963, *2*: 484–494.
Fuller, J. L. Behavior genetics. Annu. Rev. Psychol., 1960, *11*: 41–70.
Fuller, J. L., and Thompson, W. R. Behavior Genetics. New York: Wiley, 1960.
Furman, R. A., and Katan, A. The Therapeutic Nursery School. New York: International Universities Press, 1969.
Furth, H. G. Research with the deaf: Implications for language and cognition. Psychol. Bull., 1964, *62*: 145–164.
Fusfield, I. S. A Cross Section Evaluation of the Academic School for the Deaf. Washington, D.C.: Gallaudet College, 1954.

Gaasholt, M. Precision techniques in the management of teacher and child behaviors. Except. Child., 1970, *37*: 129–135.
Gage, N. L. Theories of teaching. In E. R. Hildegard, Theories of Learning and Instruction. Chicago: The University of Chicago Press, 1964.
Gaines, R. Children's selective attention to stimuli: Stage or set? Child Dev., 1970, *41*: 779–991.
Gallagher, J. J. Teaching the Gifted Child. Boston: Allyn and Bacon, 1964.
Gardner, R. A., and Gardner, B. T. Teaching sign language to a chimpanzee. Science, 1969, *165*: 664–672.

Garfield, S. L. Abnormal behavior and mental deficiency. In R. Ellis (Ed.), Handbook on Mental Deficiency. New York: McGraw-Hill, 1963.

Garmezy, N. Vulnerable children: Implications derived from studies of an internalizing-externalizing symptom dimension. In J. Zubin and A. M. Freeman (Eds.), Psychopathology of Adolescence. New York: Grune & Stratton, 1970.

Garvey, W. P., and Hegrens, J. R. Desensitization techniques in the treatment of school phobia. Am. J. Orthopsychiatry, 1966, *36*: 147–152.

Gerard, M. W. Genesis of psychosomatic symptoms in infancy. In F. Deutsch (Ed.), The Psychosomatic Concept in Psychoanalysis. New York: International Universities Press, 1953.

German, J. L., Harrison, P. A., Rankin, J. K., Donovan, D. J., Hogan, W. J., and Bearn, A. G. Autosomal trisomy of a group of 16–18 chromosomes. J. Pediatr., 1962, *60*: 503–512.

Gersh, M., and Roland, N. Preparation of teachers for the emotionally disturbed. Except. Child., 1969, *35*: 633–639.

Gesell, A., and Ilg, F. L. Infant and Child in the Culture Today. New York: Harper, 1942.

Getman, G. N. Pathway-Eye-Hand Coordination Exercises. Boston: Teaching Resources, 1971.

Getzels, J. W., and Jackson, P. W. Creativity and Intelligence. New York: Wiley, 1962.

Giannini, M. Diagnostic approach to mental retardation. In J. H. Rothstein (Ed.), Mental Retardation. New York: Holt, Rinehart and Winston, Inc., 1963.

Gibbons, H., and McCaslin, M. F. Prevention of blindness—the contributions of medical, social and statistical research. Educating the Blind, 1962, *11*: 116–120.

Gibson, D., and Pozsonyi, J. Morphological and behavioral consequences of chromosome subtype in mongolism. Am. J. Ment. Defic., 1965, *69*: 801–804.

Gibson, D., Pozsonyi, J., and Zarfas, D. E. Dimensions of mongolism: II. The interaction of clinical indices. Am. J. Ment. Defic., 1964, *118*: 503–510.

Gibson, E. The ontogeny of reading, Am. Psychol., 1970, *25*: 136–143.

Gibson, E. J., and Walk, R. D. The effect of prolonged exposure to visually presented patterns and learning to discriminate them. J. Comp. Physiol. Psychol., 1956, *49*: 239–242.

Gill, L. J., and Spilka, B. Some nonintellectual correlates of academic achievement among Mexican American secondary school students. In M. Kornrich (Ed.), Underachievement. Springfield, Ill.: Charles C Thomas, 1965.

Gilula, M., and Daniels, D. Violence and man's struggle to adapt. Science, 1969, *164*: 396–405.

Ginott, H. G. Group Psychotherapy with Children. New York: McGraw-Hill, 1961.

Ginsberg, B. E., and Laughlin, W. S. Race and intelligence, what do we really know? In R. Cancro (Ed.), Intelligence: Genetic and Environmental Influences. New York: Grune & Stratton, 1971.

Ginsburg, G. P., and Hood, R. W. Associative clustering and performance on the Remote Associates Test. Journal of Experimental Research in Personality, 1970, *4*: 171–175.

Giuliani, G. A. The relationship of self-concept and verbal-mental ability to levels of reading-readiness among kindergarten children. Dissertation Abstracts, 1968, *28*: 3866.

Glaser, D. Criminality theories and behavioral images. Am. J. Sociol., 1956, *61*: 440.

Glaser, W. Reality Therapy. New York: Harper & Row, 1965.

Glavin, J. P., Quay, H. C., and Werry, J. S. Behavioral and academic gains in conduct of problem children in different classroom settings. Except. Child., 1971, *37*: 441–446.

Glover, E. Medico-psychological aspects of normality. In E. Glover, On the Early Development of the Mind. Vol. I. Selected Papers on Psychoanalysis. New York: International Universities Press, 1956.

Glueck, E. Efforts to identify delinquents. Federal Probation, 1960, *34*: 49–56.

Glueck, S., and Glueck, E. Unraveling Juvenile Delinquency. New York: Commonwealth Fund, 1950.

Glueck, S., and Glueck, E. Physique and Delinquency. New York: Harper & Row, 1956.

Glueck, S., and Glueck, E. Predicting Delinquency and Crime. Cambridge, Mass.: Harvard University Press, 1959.

Glueck, S., and Glueck, E. Potential juvenile delinquency can be identified: What next? British Journal of Criminology, 1964, *4*: 215–226.

Glueck, S., and Glueck, E. 1000 Juvenile Delinquents. New York: Kraus, 1965.

Goddard, H. H. The Kallikak Family. New York: Macmillan, 1912.

Goldfarb, W. Effects of psychological deprivation in infancy and subsequent stimulation. Am. J. Psychiatry, 1945, *102*: 18–33.

Goldfarb, W. Emotional and intellectual consequences of psychologic deprivation in infancy: A re-evaluation. In P. Hoch and J. Zubin (Eds.), Psychopathology of Childhood. New York: Grune & Stratton, 1955.

Goldfarb, W. A. Follow-up investigation of schizophrenic children treated in residence. Psychosocial Process: Issues in Child Mental Health, 1970, *1*: 9–64.

Goldman, J. A. Comparison of sensory modality preference of children and adults. Dissertation Abstracts, 1967, *28*: 2123.

Goldman, R., and Sanders, J. Cultural factors and hearing. Except. Child., 1969, *35*: 488–490.

Goldstein, A. P. Psychotherapeutic Attraction. New York: Pergamon, 1970.

Goldstein, A. P., Heller, K., and Sechrest, L. B. Psychotherapy and the Psychology of Behavior Change. New York: Wiley, 1966.

Goldstein, H. Population trends in U. S. public institutions for the mentally deficient. Am. J. Ment. Defic., 1959, *63*: 599–604.

Goldstein, H. Social and occupational adequacy. In R. Heber and H. A. Stevens, Mental Retardation. Chicago: The University of Chicago Press, 1964.

Goldstein, H., Jordan, L., and Moss, J. The Efficacy of Special Class Training on the Development of Mentally Retarded Children. Cooperative Research Project No. 619. Urbana, Ill.: The University of Illinois Press, 1965.

Goldstein, H., and Seigel, D. A Curriculum Guide

for the Teachers of the Educable Mentally Handicapped. Springfield, Ill.: State of Illinois Circular No. B-3, 12, 1958.

Goldstein, K. The Organism. New York: American Book, 1939.

Good, C. V. Dictionary of Education. New York: McGraw-Hill, 1945.

Goodenough, F. L. Measurement of Intelligence by Drawings. New York: Harcourt, Brace & World, 1926.

Gordon, E. Methodological problems and pseudo-issues in the nature-nurture controversy. In R. Cancro (Ed.), Intelligence: Genetic and Environmental Influences. New York: Grune & Stratton, 1971.

Goshen, C. E. Mental retardation and neurotic maternal attitudes. Arch. Gen. Psychiatry, 1963, *9*: 168–175.

Gottesfeld, H. Professionals and delinquents evaluate professional methods with delinquents. Social Problems, 1965, *13*: 45–59.

Gottsman, I. Genetic aspects of intelligent behavior. In N. R. Ellis (Ed.), Handbook on Mental Deficiency. New York: McGraw-Hill, 1963.

Gould, R. E. Suicide problems in children and adolescents. Am. J. Psychother., 1965, *19*: 228–246.

Graham, F. K., Ernhart, C. B., Thurston, D., and Craft, M. Development three years after perinatal anoxia and other potentially damaging newborn experiences. Psychol. Monogr., 1962, *76*(3) (whole No. 522).

Graham, P., Chir, B., and Rutter, M. Organic brain dysfunction and child psychiatric disorder. Br. Med. J., 1968, *3*: 695–700.

Grambs, J. D. The roles of the teacher. In L. Stiles (Ed.), The Teacher's Role in American Society. Yearbook John Dewey Society, 1957, *14*: 73–93.

Graubard, P. Children Against Schools: The Education of Disturbed and Delinquent Children. Chicago: Follett, 1969a.

Graubard, P. Utilizing the group in teaching disturbed delinquents to learn. Except. Child., 1969b, *36*: 267–272.

Gray, S. The Psychologist in the Schools. New York: Holt, Rinehart and Winston, Inc., 1963.

Graziano, A. M. Stimulus response: In the mental health industry, illness is our most important product. Psychology Today, 1972, *8*: 12–23.

Green, H. I Never Promised You a Rose Garden. New York: New American Library, 1964.

Greenspoon, J. The effect of verbal and nonverbal stimuli on the frequency of members of two verbal response classes. Unpublished doctoral dissertation, Indiana University, 1951.

Greenspoon, J. The reinforcing effect of two spoken sounds on the frequency of two responses. Am. J. Psychol., 1955, *68*: 409–416.

Grier, W. H., and Cobb, P. M. Black Rage. New York: Basic Books, 1968.

Grinker, R. R., Sr., et al. Psychiatric Diagnosis, Therapy, and Research on the Psychotic Deaf. Chicago: Institute for Psychosomatic and Psychiatric Research and Training, Michael Reese Hospital and Medical Center, 1969.

Gronlund, N. E. Sociometry in the Classroom. New York: Harper & Row, 1959.

Grossman, H. Teaching the Emotionally Disturbed: A Casebook. New York: Holt, Rinehart and Winston, Inc., 1965.

Grotberg, E. (Ed.) Critical Issues in Research Related to Disadvantaged Children. Princeton, N.J.: Educational Testing Service, 1969.

Grunebaum, M. G., Hurwitz, I., Prentice, N. M., and Sperry, B. M. Fathers of sons with primary neurotic learning inhibitions. Am. J. Orthopsychiatry, 1962, *32*: 460–470.

Guilford, J. P. The Nature of Intelligence. New York: McGraw-Hill, 1967.

Guilford, J. P. Intelligence, Creativity, and Their Educational Implications. San Diego: Robert K. Knapp, 1968.

Guskin, S. Social psychologies of mental deficiencies. In N. R. Ellis (Ed.), Handbook of Mental Deficiency. New York: McGraw-Hill, 1963.

Gutheil, E., et al. Music and Your Emotions. New York: Liveright, 1952.

Guthrie, E. R. The Psychology of Learning. New York: Harper, 1935.

Guthrie, G. M., Gorlow, L., and Butler, A. T. The attitude of the retardate toward himself: A summary of research. The Laurelton State School and Hospital. Pennsylvania Psychiatric Quarterly, 1967, *7*: 24–34.

Guthrie, G. M., and Jacobs, P. J. Child Rearing and Personality Development in the Philippines. University Park: Pennsylvania State University, 1966.

Guthrie, R., Whitney, S. B., and Stucky, R. B. PKU screening program progress. Report No. 4. Buffalo, N.Y.: University of New York, Department of Pediatrics, 1963.

Haddad, H. M., and Wilkins, L. Congenital anomalies associated with gonadal aplasia: Review of 55 cases. Pediatrics, 1959, *22*: 885–887.

Hafner, M. S. Motor controls and first grade reading difficulties. Dissertation Abstracts, 1969, *29*(11-A): 3913.

Haley, J. The art of being a failure as a therapist. Am. J. Orthopsychiatry, 1969, *39*: 691–695.

Hall, R. V., Lund, D., and Jackson, D. Effects of teacher attention on study behavior. Journal of Applied Behavior Analysis, 1968, *1*: 1–12.

Halpern, F. Diagnostic methods of childhood disorders. In B. B. Wolman (Ed.), Handbook of Clinical Psychology. New York: McGraw-Hill, 1965.

Halpern, H., and Halpern, T. Four perspectives on antiachievement. Psychoanal. Rev., 1966, *53*: 83–93.

Halstead, W. C. Brain and Intelligence. Chicago: The University of Chicago Press, 1947.

Hammer, E. F. (Ed.) Use of Interpretation in Treatment. New York: Grune & Stratton, 1968.

Hanbrich, V. The culturally different new context for teacher education. Journal of Teacher Education, 1963, *14*: 163–167.

Handbook on Work Experience Education. Sacramento, Calif.: State Department of Education, 1953.

Handlin, O. The Newcomers. Cambridge, Mass.: Harvard University Press, 1959.

Harbert, W. K. Some results from specific techniques in the use of music with exceptional children. Music Educators National Conference, Washington, D.C. Music Therapy, 1952, *2*: 147–151.

Hardy, J. C. Intraoral breath pressure in cerebral palsy. J. Speech Hear. Dis., 1961, *26*: 309–319.

Hardy, J. C., Rembolt, R. R., Spriestersbach, D. C., and Jayapathy, B. Surgical management of palatal paresis and speech problems in cerebral palsy: A preliminary report. J. Speech Hear. Dis., 1961, *26*: 320–325.

Hare, R. D., and Quinn, J. Psychopathy and autonomic conditioning. J. Abnorm. Psychol., 1971, *77*: 223–235.

Haring, N. G., and Fargo, G. A. Evaluating programs for preparing teachers of emotionally disturbed children. Except. Child., 1969, *11*: 157–162.

Haring, N. G., and Hayden, A. H. (Eds.) Proceedings of Workshop in Instructional Improvement: Behavior Modification. Seattle, Wash.: Special Child Publications, 1968.

Haring, N. G., and Lakin, E. P. Educating Emotionally Disturbed Children. New York: McGraw-Hill, 1961.

Harlow, H. F. Social deprivation in monkeys. Sci. Am., 1962, *207*: 136–146.

Harlow, H. F. The maternal affectional system. In B. M. Foss (Ed.), Determinants of Infant Behavior: II. New York: Wiley, 1963.

Harms, E. Essentials of Abnormal Child Psychology. New York: Julian Press, 1953.

Harper, R. A. Psychoanalysis and Psychotherapy: 36 Systems. Englewood Cliffs, N. J.: Prentice-Hall, 1959.

Harper, R. S. Variability, conformity, and teaching. Teachers Collective Record, 1962, *63*(8): 642–648.

Harrell, R. F., Woodward, E., and Gates, A. I. The Effects of Mothers' Diets on the Intelligence of the Offspring. New York: Bureau of Publications, Teachers College, Columbia University, 1955.

Harrington, M. The Other America. New York: Macmillan, 1962.

Harris, I. D. Emotional Blocks to Learning. New York: Free Press, 1961.

Harth, R. Changing attitudes toward school, classroom behavior, and reactions to frustration of emotionally disturbed children through role playing. Except. Child., 1966, *33*: 119–126.

Harth, R., and Glavin, J. P. Validity of teacher rating as a subtest for screening emotionally disturbed children. Except. Child., 1971, *4*: 605–606.

Hartlage, L. L. Deficit in space concepts associated with visual deprivation. Journal of Learning Disabilities, 1968, *1*: 649–651.

Hartmann, H. Ego Psychology and the Problem of Adaptation. New York: International Universities Press, 1958.

Hartmann, H. Towards a concept of mental health. Br. J. Med. Psychol., 1960, *33*: 243–248.

Hartung, J. E. Visual perceptual skills, reading ability, and the young deaf child. Dissertation Abstracts, 1968, *29*(12-A): 4184.

Harvey, O. J. Conceptual systems and attitude change. In M. Sherif and C. W. Sherif (Eds.), Attitude, Ego-involvement and Change. New York: Wiley, 1967.

Harvey, O. J., and Felknor, C. Parent-child relations as an antecedent to conceptual functioning. In R. A. Hoppe, G. A. Milton, and E. C. Simmel (Eds.), Early Experiences and the Process of Socialization. New York: Academic Press, 1970.

Hatfield, E. M. Causes of blindness in school children. Sight Sav. Rev., 1963, *33*: 218–233.

Hathaway, S. R., and Monachesi, E. D. Analyzing and Predicting Juvenile Delinquency with the MMPI. Minneapolis: University of Minnesota Press, 1953.

Hathaway, S. R., and Monachesi, E. D. The personality of predelinquent boys. Journal of Criminal Law, Criminal Police Science, 1957, *48*: 149–163.

Hattan, A., Pizzat, J., and Pelkowski, M. The Erie Program of Perceptual-Motor Teaching Materials. Boston: Teaching Resources, 1967.

Havighurst, R. J. Minority subcultures and the law of effect. Am. Psychol., 1970, *25*: 313–322.

Havighurst, R. J., and Neugarten, B. L. Society and Education. (2nd ed.) Boston: Allyn and Bacon, 1962.

Haywood, H. C. (Ed.) Brain Damage in School-Age Children. Washington, D.C.: Council for Exceptional Children, 1968.

Healy, W., and Bronner, A. F. New Light on Delinquency and Its Treatment. New Haven, Conn.: Yale University Press, 1936.

Hebb, D. O. The Organization of Behavior. New York: Wiley, 1949.

Hebb, D. O. The mammal and his environment. Am. J. Psychiatry, 1955, *111*: 826–831.

Heiner, W. H. An analysis of the speech of nine year old Negro children from Syracuse, New York. Dissertation Abstracts, 1968, *28*(10-A): 3889.

Hellmuth, J. (Ed.) Learning Disorders. Vol. I. Seattle, Wash.: Special Child Publications, 1965.

Hellmuth, J. (Ed.) Learning Disorders. Vol. 2. Seattle, Wash.: Special Child Publications, 1966.

Hellmuth, J. (Ed.) Disadvantaged Child. New York: Brunner/Mazel, 1967.

Hellmuth, J. (Ed.) Disadvantaged Child: Headstart and Early Intervention. Seattle, Wash.: Special Child Publications, 1968a.

Hellmuth, J. (Ed.) Learning Disorders. Vol. 3. Seattle, Wash.: Special Child Publications, 1968b.

Hellmuth, J. (Ed.) Disadvantaged Child: Compensatory Education: A National Debate. New York: Brunner/Mazel, 1970.

Herron, C. J. Some effects of instrumental music training on cerebral palsied children. Journal of Music Therapy, 1970, *7*: 55–58.

Herron, W. G., and Psaila, J. Diagnosing children's problems. Psychology in the Schools, 1970, *7*: 397–403.

Hertzig, M., et al. Class and ethnic differences in the responsiveness of preschool children to cognitive demands. Mongr. Soc. Res. Child Dev., 1968, *33*: No. 117.

Hester, M. S. Manual communication. Report of the proceedings of the International Congress on Education of the Deaf and the 41st meeting of the Convention of the American Instructors of the Deaf. Washington, D.C.: Government Printing Office, 1964. Pp. 356–361.

Hesterly, S. O. Deviant response patterns as a function of chronological age. J. Consult. Psychol., 1963, *27*: 210–214.

Heston, L. The genesis of schizophrenia and schizoid disease. Science, 1970, *167*: 249–256.

Hewett, F. M. Educational engineering with emotionally disturbed children. Except. Child., 1967, *3*: 459–467.

Hewett, F. M. Introduction of the behavior modification approach to special education: A shaping procedure. In N. Haring and A. H. Hayden (Eds.), Proceedings of Workshop in Instructional Improvement: Behavior Modification. Seattle, Wash.: Special Child Publications, 1968.

Hewett, F. M. The Emotionally Disturbed Child in the Classroom. Boston: Allyn and Bacon, 1968.

Hewett, F. M., Taylor, F. D., and Artus, A. A. The Santa Monica Project: Evaluation of an engineered classroom design with emotionally disturbed children. Except. Child., 1969, *35*: 523–529.

Hicks, J. S. Introversion and extroversion and their relationship to academic achievement among emotionally disturbed children. Dissertation Abstracts, 1969, *29*(10-A): 3462.

Hildreth, G. H. Introduction to the Gifted. New York: McGraw-Hill, 1966.

Hilgard, E. R. Human motives and the concept of self. Am. Psychol., 1949, *4*: 374–382.

Hilgard, E. R., and Bower, G. H. Theories of Learning. New York: Appleton-Century-Crofts, 1966.

Hill, S. D., et al. An exploratory study of the use of two response keyboards as a means of communication for the severely handicapped child. Percept. Mot. Skills, 1968, *26*: 699–704.

Hirsch, J. Behavior-genetic analysis and its biosocial consequences. In R. Cancro (Ed.), Intelligence: Genetic and Environmental Influences. New York: Grune & Stratton, 1971.

Hirsh, I. J. Teaching the deaf child to speak: A discussion of Fry's presentation. In F. Smith and G. A. Miller (Eds.), The Genesis of Language: A Psycholinguistic Approach. Cambridge, Mass.: M.I.T. Press, 1966.

Hirsh, I. J. Information processing of input channels for speech and language: The significance of serial order of stimuli. In F. L. Darley (Ed.), Brain Mechanisms Underlying Speech and Language. New York: Grune & Stratton, 1967.

Hirshoren, A. A comparison of the predictive validity of the revised Stanford-Binet intelligence scale and the Illinois Test of Psycholinguistic Abilities. Except. Child., 1969, *3*: 417–521.

Hogan, R. A. The implosive technique. Behav. Res. Ther., 1968, *6*: 423–431.

Holland, J. L., and Baird, L. L. The preconscious activity scale: The development and validation of an originality measure. Journal of Creative Behavior, 1968, *2*: 217–225.

Hollingshead, A. B., and Redlich, F. C. Social Class and Mental Illness: A Community Study. New York: Wiley, 1958.

Hollingworth, L. S. Gifted Children: Their Nature and Nurture. New York: Macmillan, 1926.

Holtzman, W. H. The changing world of mental measurement and its social significance. Am. Psychol., 1971, *26*: 546–554.

Horner, R. D. A factor analysis comparison of the ITPA and PLS with mentally retarded children. Except. Child., 1967, *11*: 183–189.

Horrocks, J. E., and Schoonover, T. I. Measurement for Teachers. Columbus, Ohio: Charles E. Merrill Books, Inc., 1968.

Horton, K. B. Organic disorders in children. In H. C. Haywood (Ed.), Brain Damage in School Age Children. Washington, D.C.: Council for Exceptional Children, 1968.

Hottel, J. V. An Evaluation of Tennessee's Day Class Program for Severely Retarded Children. Nashville: George Peabody College for Teachers, 1958.

Howard, J. Please Touch. New York: McGraw-Hill, 1970.

Howard, M. J., Hoops, H. R., and McKinnon, A. J. Language abilities of children with differing socio-economic backgrounds. Journal of Learning Disabilities, 1970, *3*: 328–335.

Hsia, D. Y., Paine, R. S., and Driscoll, K. W. Phenylketonuria. J. Ment. Defic. Res., 1957, *1*: 53.

Hsu, E. H. On the application of Viennese infant scale to Peiping babies. J. Genet. Psychol., 1946, *69*: 217–226.

Hulton, L. F. The Residential Treatment Center: Children, Programs, Costs. New York: Child Welfare League of America, 1964.

Humphreys, L. G. Theory of intelligence. In R. Cancro (Ed.), Intelligence: Genetic and Environmental Influences. New York: Grune & Stratton, 1971.

Hunt, D. E. Conceptual systems assessment in planning differential educational treatment and in measuring developmental change. Paper presented at the meeting of the American Psychological Association, Chicago, September, 1965.

Hunt, D. E. Adolescence: Cultural deprivation, poverty, and the dropout. Review of Educational Research, 1966, *36*: 463–473.

Hunt, J. M. Intelligence and Experience. New York: Ronald, 1961.

Hunt, J. M. Motivation in information processing and action. In O. J. Harvey (Ed.), Motivation and Social Organization: Cognitive Determinants. New York: Ronald, 1963.

Hunt, J. M. The psychological basis for using preschool enrichment as an antidote for cultural deprivation. Merrill-Palmer Q. Behav. Dev., 1964, *10*: 236.

Hunt, J. M. The impact and limitations of the giant of developmental psychology. In D. Elkind and H. Flavell (Eds.), Studies in Cognitive Development: Essays in Honor of Jean Piaget. New York: Oxford University Press, 1969.

Hunt, J. M., and Girvin, E. K. Social aspects of intelligence: Evidence and issues. In R. Cancro (Ed.), Intelligence: Genetic and Environmental Influences. New York: Grune & Stratton, 1971.

Hurley, L. Perceptual integration and reading problems. Except. Child., 1968, *35*: 207–213.

Hurlin, R. G. Estimated prevalence of blindness in the United States and in the individual states. Sight Sav. Rev., 1962, *32*: 162–165.

Hutt, M. L. Patterns of Abnormal Behavior. Boston: Allyn and Bacon, 1957.

Hutt, M. L., and Gibby, R. G. The Mentally Retarded Child. (2nd ed.) Boston: Allyn and Bacon, 1965.

Hyde, D. M. An investigation of Piaget's theories of the development of the concept of number. Unpublished doctoral dissertation, University of London, 1959.

Ingram, C. P. Educating the Slow-Learning Child. (3rd ed.) New York: Ronald, 1960.

Inhelder, B. Le Diagnostic du Raisonement Cher les Mentaux Neuchateli Delachaue. Neuchâtel: Delachaux and Niestlé, 1944.

Irwin, O. C. Infant speech: Effect of systematic reading of stories. J. Speech Hear. Res., 1960, *3*: 187–190.

Itard, J. M. G. The Wild Boy of Aveyron. (Trans. G. Humphrey and M. Humphrey) New York: Appleton-Century-Crofts, 1932.

Iversen, T. Psychogenic obesity in children. Acta Paediatrica, 1953, *42*: 8–19.

Jackson, D. D. The study of the family. Family Process, 1965, *4*: 1–20.

Jackson, D. D., and Satir, V. Family diagnosis and family therapy. In N. Ackerman et al. (Eds.), Exploring the Base for Family Therapy. New York: Family Service Association, 1961.

Jackson, D. N., and Guthrie, G. M. Multitrait-multimethod evaluation of the personality research form. Proceedings of the 76th Annual Convention of the American Psychological Association, 1968, *3*: 177–178.

Jackson, P. W., and Messick, S. The person, the product, and the response: Conceptual problems in the assessment of creativity. In J. Kagan (Ed.), Creativity and Learning. Boston: Houghton Mifflin, 1967.

Jacobs, J. Adolescent Suicide. New York: Wiley-Interscience, 1971.

Jacobs, J. C. Effectiveness of teacher and parent identification of gifted children as a function of school level. Psychology in the Schools, 1971, *8*: 140–142.

Jacobziner, H. Attempted suicides in adolescence. J.A.M.A., 1965, *191*: 7–11.

Jarvick, L. A., Falek, A., and Pierson, P. Down's syndrome (mongolism): The heritable aspects. Psychol. Bull., 1964, *61*: 388–398.

Jenkins, L. Psychiatric syndromes in children and their relation to family background. Am. J. Orthopsychiatry, 1966, *36*: 450–457.

Jenkins, R. L., and Glickman, S. Patterns of personality organization among delinquents. The Nervous Child, 1947, *6*: 329–339.

Jensen, A. R. Culturally disadvantaged and the heredity-environment uncertainty. In J. Hellmuth (Ed.), Disadvantaged Child: Head Start and Early Intervention. New York: Brunner/Mazel, 1968.

Jensen, A. R. How much can we boost IQ and scholastic achievement? Harvard Educational Review, 1969, *39*: 123.

Jensen, A. R. The race and sex ability interaction. In R. Cancro (Ed.), Intelligence: Genetic and Environmental Influences. New York: Grune & Stratton, 1971.

Jensen, A. R. Educability and Group Differences. New York: Harper & Row, 1973.

Johnson, C. E. A comparison of the spelling study behavior of two groups of third grade children. Dissertation Abstracts, 1953, *13*: 44.

Johnson, C. S. Growing Up in the Black Belt. Washington, D.C.: American Council on Education, 1941.

Johnson, D. J., and Myklebust, H. R. Learning Disabilities: Educational Principles and Practices. New York: Grune & Stratton, 1967.

Johnson, G. B. Bilingualism as measured by a reaction-time technique and the relationship between a language and a non-language intelligence quotient. J. Genet. Psychol., 1953, *82*: 3–9.

Johnson, G. F. Programmed instruction and the exceptional learner. Except. Child., 1968, *34*: 453–457.

Johnson, G. O. Special education for the mentally handicapped—a paradox. Except. Child., 1962, *29*: 62–69.

Johnson, J. C. Educating Hearing Impaired Children in Ordinary Schools. Manchester, England: Manchester University Press, 1962.

Johnson, J. J. Teacher preparation for educating the disturbed: Graduate, undergraduate, or functional. Except. Child., 1968, *34*: 345–351.

Johnson, K. B. Meeting the training needs of the delinquent girl. Training and Scholastic Bulletin, 1941, *38*: 6–14.

Johnson, W. People in Quandaries. New York: Harper & Brothers, 1946.

Johnson, W. Diagnosis as a cause of stuttering. In C. Van Riper (Ed.), Speech Therapy: A Book of Readings. Englewood Cliffs, N.J.: Prentice-Hall, 1953.

Johnson, W., and Fretz, B. Changes in perceptual motor skills after a children's physical developmental program. Percept. Mot. Skills, 1967, *24*: 610.

Johnston, J. M., and Johnston, G. Modification of consonant speech-sound articulation in young children. Journal of Applied Behavior Analysis, 1972, *5*: 233–246.

Jolles, I. A teaching sequence for the training of visual and motor perception. Am. J. Ment. Defic., 1958, *63*: 252–255.

Jones, E. The concept of the normal mind. In S. D. Schmalhausen (Ed.), Our Neurotic Age; A Consultation. New York: Farrar & Rinehart, 1932.

Jones, H. E. The environment and mental development. In L. Carmichael (Ed.), Manual of Child Psychology. (2nd ed.) New York: Wiley, 1954.

Jones, R. L., and Gottfried, N. W. Psychological needs and preferences for teaching exceptional children. Except. Child., 1966, *32*: 313–321.

Jordan, J. E., and Cessna, W. C. A comparison of attitudes of four occupational groups toward education and toward physically disabled persons in Japan. J. Soc. Psychol., 1969, *78*: 283–284.

Jung, C. G. Basic Writings of C. G. Jung. New York: Modern Library, 1959.

Kagan, J. Individual differences in the resolution of response uncertainty. J. Pers. Soc. Psychol., 1965, *2*: 154–160.

Kagan, J., and Moss, H. A. Birth to Maturity. New York: Wiley, 1962.

Kahn, J. H., and Nursten, J. P. School refusal: A comprehensive view of school phobia and other failures of school attendance. Am. J. Orthopsychiatry, 1962, *32*: 707–718.

Kallman, F. J. The use of genetics in psychiatry. J. Ment. Sci., 1958, *104*: 542–549.

Kallos, G. L., Grabow, E., and Guarino, A. The WISC profile of disabled readers. Personnel and Guidance Journal, 1961, *39*: 476–478.

Kanner, L. Early infantile autism. J. Pediatr., 1944, *25*: 211–217.

Kaplan, H. B., and Pokorny, A. D. Self-derogation and psychosocial adjustment. J. Nerv. Ment. Dis., 1969, *149*: 421–434.

Kass, C. Conference on Learning Disabilities. Lawrence, Kansas, November, 1966.

Kaufman, C. Use of application and intake groups to relieve community pressures. Am. J. Orthopsychiatry, 1963, *33*: 547–550.

Kaufman, I. C., and Rosenblum, L. A. The reaction to separation in infant monkeys: Anaclitic depression and conservation-withdrawal. Psychosom. Med., 1967, *29*: 648–675.

Kaufman, M. E., and Levitt, H. A study of three stereotyped behaviors in institutionalized mental defectives. Am. J. Ment. Defic., 1965, *69*: 467–473.

Kelin, M. Narrative of a Child Analysis. New York: Basic Books, 1960.

Kelley, C. M. Crime in the United States. Uniform Crime Reports. Washington, D.C.: U.S. Government Printing Office, 1974.

Kelley, E. O. Some observations on relationships between delinquent girls and their parents. Br. J. Med. Psychol., 1956, *28*: 59–66.

Kellog, W. N. Sonar system of the blind. Science, 1962, *137*: 309–404.

Kelly, G. A. The Psychology of Personal Constructs. New York: Norton, 1955.

Kendler, H. Environmental and cognitive control of behavior. Am. Psychol., 1971, *26*: 962–974.

Kennedy, W. A. A follow-up normative study of Negro intelligence and achievement. Monogr. Soc. Res. Child Dev., 1969, *34*: 1–40.

Kephart, N. Perceptual-motor correlates of learning. In S. Kirk and W. Becker (Eds.), Conference on Children with Minimal Brain Impairment. Chicago: Easter Seal Research Foundation, National Society for Crippled Children and Adults, 1963.

Kephart, N. C. The Slow Learner in the Classroom. Columbus, Ohio: Charles E. Merrill Books, Inc., 1971.

Kephart, N. C., and Strauss, A. A. A clinical factor influencing variations in I.Q. J. Orthopsychiatry, 1940, *10*: 343–350.

Kesey, K. One Flew Over the Cuckoo's Nest. New York: Viking, 1962.

Kessler, J. W. Psychopathology of Childhood. Englewood Cliffs, N.J.: Prentice-Hall, 1966.

Kety, S. Biochemical theories of schizophrenia. I. Science, 1959, *129*: 1528–1532.

Khan, S. B. Affective correlates of academic achievement. J. Educ. Psychol., 1969, *60*: 216–222.

Kidd, A. H., and Rivoire, J. L. Perceptual Development in Children. New York: International Universities Press, 1966.

Kidd, J. W. Perspectives for a classroom for disturbed children. Except. Child., 1967, *33*: 577–581.

Kilman, G. Psychological Emergencies of Childhood. New York: Grune & Stratton, 1968.

Kilpatrick, W. H. The Montessori System Examined. Boston: Houghton Mifflin, 1914.

Kirk, S. A. Educating Exceptional Children. (2nd ed.) Boston: Houghton Mifflin, 1972.

Kirk, S. A., McCarthy, J. J., and Kirk, W. D. Illinois Test of Psycholinguistic Abilities. (Rev. Ed.) Urbana, Ill.: The University of Illinois Press, 1968.

Kirman, B. H., Black, J. A., Wilkinson, R. H., and Evans, P. R. Familial Pitressin-resistant diabetes insipidus with mental defect. Arch. Dis. Child., 1956, *31*: 59.

Kisker, G. W. The Disorganized Personality. New York: McGraw-Hill, 1964.

Klein, J. Head start: Intervention for what? Educational Leadership, 1971, *29*: 16–19.

Klein, M. On mental health. Br. J. Med. Psychol., 1960, *33*: 237–241.

Kline, C. L., and Lee, N. A transcultural study of dyslexia: Analysis of reading disabilities in 425 Chinese children simultaneously learning to read and write in English and Chinese. Am. J. Orthopsychiatry, 1970, *40*: 313–314.

Kline, P. The anal character: A cross-cultural study in Ghana. Br. J. Soc. Clin. Psychol., 1969, *8*: 201–210.

Klineberg, O. Negro Intelligence and Selective Migration. New York: Columbia University Press, 1935.

Kluever, R. C. A study of Guilford's memory factors in normal and reading disabled children. Dissertation Abstracts, 1969, *29*: 3875–3876.

Kluger, J. M. Childhood asthma and the social milieu. J. Am. Acad. Child Psychiatry, 1969, *8*: 353–366.

Knights, R., and Thompson, A. Training Suggestions for Teaching Children with Specific Learning Deficits. Toronto: Canadian Association for Children with Learning Disabilities, 1967.

Knobloch, H., and Pasamanick, B. Exogenous factors in infant intelligence. Pediatrics, 1960, *26*: 210–218.

Knobloch, H., and Pasamanick, B. The developmental behavioral approach to the neurological examination in infancy. Child Dev., 1962, *33*: 181–198.

Knoblock, P. Critical factors influencing educational programming for disturbed children. Except. Child., 1963, *30*: 124–129.

Knoblock, P. (Ed.) Educational Programming for Emotionally Disturbed Children. Syracuse, N.Y.: Syracuse University Press, 1965.

Knoblock, P. Intervention approaches in educating emotionally disturbed children. In P. Knoblock (Ed.), Proceedings of the Second Annual Conference on the Education of Emotionally Disturbed Children. Syracuse, N.Y.: Syracuse University Press, 1966.

Knoblock, P., and Garcea, R. A. Toward a broader concept of the role of the special class for emotionally disturbed children. Except. Child., 1965, *31*: 329–337.

Knox, W. E. An evaluation of the treatment of phenylketonuria with diets low in phenylalanine. Pediatrics, 1960, *26*: 1–11.

Kobrin, S. The Chicago Area Project: A 25 year assessment. Annals of the American Academy of Political and Social Science, 1959, *322*: 19–29.

Kohlberg, L. Montessori with the culturally disadvantaged: A cognitive-developmental interpretation of some research findings. In R. D. Hess and R. M. Bear (Eds.), Early Education. Chicago: Aldine, 1968.

Kohlberg, L. Stage and sequence: The cognitive-developmental approach to socialization. In D. A. Goslin (Ed.), Handbook of Socialization Theory and Research. Chicago: Rand McNally, 1969.

Kopp, H. G. (Ed.) Curriculum: Cognition and content. Volta Review, 1968, *70*: 372–516.

Kosofsky, S. Directive therapy with female juvenile delinquents. J. Clin. Psychol., 1955, *11*: 356–361.

Kotkov, B. Emotional syndromes associated with learning failure. Dis. Nerv. Syst., 1965, *26*: 48–55.

Kramer, E. Art therapy at Wiltwyck school. School Arts, 1959, *58*: 5–8.

Krasner, L., and Ullmann, L. P. (Eds.) Research in Behavior Modification. New York: Holt, Rinehart and Winston, Inc., 1965.

Kretschmer, E. Koerperbau und Charakter. (Aufl. Berlin) Springer, 1955.

Kretschmer, E. Medizinische Psychologie, II. Aufl. Stuttgart, G. Thieme, 1956.

Kubie, L. S. Neurotic Distortions of the Creative Process. Lawrence: University of Kansas Press, 1958.

Kugel, R. B., and Mohr, J. Mental retardation and physical growth. Am. J. Ment. Defic., 1963, *68*: 41–48.

Kvaraceus, W. C. KD Proneness Scale and Checklist. New York: Harcourt, Brace & World, 1953.

Kvaraceus, W. C. Prediction studies of delinquent behavior. Personnel and Guidance Journal, 1955, *34*: 147–149.

Kvaraceus, W. C. Prediction of maladjustive behavior. Proceedings of the 1958 Invitational Conference on Testing Problems. Princeton, N.J.: Educational Testing Service, 1959. Pp. 26–34.

Kvaraceus, W. C. Helping the socially unadapted pupil in the large city schools. Except. Child., 1962, *28*: 399–404.

Kvaraceus, W. C. Problems of early identification and prevention of delinquency. In W. W. Wattenburg (Ed.), Social Deviancy Among Youth. National Society Study of Education, 65th Yearbook. Chicago: University of Chicago, 1966.

Kvaraceus, W. C. Dynamics of Delinquency: Anxious Youth. Columbus, Ohio: Charles E. Merrill Books, Inc., 1970.

Kvaraceus, W. C., and Miller, W. B. Delinquent Behavior, Culture, and the Individual. Washington, D.C.: National Education Association, 1959.

L'Abate, L. Principles of Clinical Psychology. New York: Grune & Stratton, 1964.

L'Abate, L. A communication-information model. In L. L'Abate (Ed.), Models of Clinical Psychology. Atlanta: Georgia State College, 1969a.

L'Abate, L. An input-output approach to psychodiagnosis of children. World Journal of Psychosynthesis, 1969b, *1*: 68–73.

L'Abate, L. The bankruptcy of the child guidance clinic movement. World Journal of Psychosynthesis, 1969c, *2*: 35–40.

L'Abate, L. The continuum of rehabilitation and laboratory evaluation: Behavior modification and psychotherapy. In C. M. Franks (Ed.), Behavior Therapy: Appraisal and Status. New York: McGraw-Hill, 1969d.

L'Abate, L. Receptive-expressive functions in kindergarten children and adolescents. Psychology in the Schools, 1971, *8*: 253–259.

L'Abate, L., Norman, M. A., and Aurandt, H. P. Modality Preference, Temporality, and School Performance. Georgia State University. Unpublished research, 1970.

L'Abate, L., Timms, R., and Smith, D. A study of the usefulness of the Montessori method in upper-class children. Unpublished research, 1969.

Lambert, N. M. The prediction of school adjustment. Am. J. Orthopsychiatry, 1964, *34*: 340–342.

Lang, P. J. The mechanics of desensitization and the laboratory study of fear. In C. M. Franks (Ed.), Behavior Therapy: Appraisal and Status. New York: McGraw-Hill, 1969.

Langdell, J. I. A psychosomatic approach to obesity in childhood and adolescence. In S. J. Szurek and I. N. Berlin (Eds.), Psychosomatic Disorders and Mental Retardation in Children. Palo Alto, Calif.: Science and Behavior Books, 1968.

Lange, J. Crime as Destiny. London: Allen and Unwin, 1931.

Langner, T. S., et al. Psychiatric impairment in welfare and non-welfare children. Welfare in Review, 1969, 7: 10–22.

Lantz, B. Some dynamic aspects of success and failure. Psychol. Monogr., 1945, *59*: 40.

Lapouse, R., and Monk, M. Fears and worries in a representative sample of children. Am. J. Orthopsychiatry, 1959, *29*: 803–818.

Lapouse, R., and Monk, M. Behavior deviations in a representative sample of children. Am. J. Orthopsychiatry, 1964, *34*: 436–446.

LaPray, A. J., and Downing, L. N. Child rearing attitudes of mothers of emotionally disturbed children. Selected Papers, 46th Annual International Convention. Washington, D.C.: Council for Exceptional Children, 1968.

Laughlin, H. P. The Neurosis in Clinical Practice. Philadelphia: W. B. Saunders Company, 1956.

La Vietes, R. The teacher's role in the education of the emotionally disturbed child. Am. J. Orthopsychiatry, 1962, *32*: 854–862.

La Vietes, R., Cohen, R., Reens, R., and Roland, R. Day treatment center and school: Seven years' experience. Am. J. Orthopsychiatry, 1965, *35*: 160–169.

Laycock, S. R. Counseling parents of gifted children. Except. Child., 1956, *23*: 108–110.

Lazarus, A. A. Group therapy of phobic disorders by systematic desensitization. J. Abnorm. Psychol., 1961, *63*: 505–510.

Lazarus, A. A. Crucial procedural factors in desensitization therapy. Behav. Res. Ther., 1964, *2*: 65–70.

Lazarus, A. A. Broad spectrum behavior therapy and the treatment of agoraphobia. Behav. Res. Ther., 1966, *4*: 95–97.

Lazarus, A. A. Behavior therapy in groups. In G. M. Gazda (Ed.), Basic Approaches to Group Psychotherapy and Group Counseling. Springfield, Ill.: Charles C Thomas, 1968a.

Lazarus, A. A. Learning therapy and the treatment of depression. Behav. Res. Ther., 1968b, *6*: 83–89.
Lazarus, A. A. Behavior Therapy and Beyond. New York: McGraw-Hill, 1971.
Lazarus, A. A., and Davison, G. C.: Clinical innovation in research and practice. In A. E. Bergin and S. L. Garfield (Eds.), Handbook of Psychotherapy and Behavior Change. New York: Wiley, 1971.
Lazarus, R. S. (Ed.) Personality and Adjustment. Englewood Cliffs, N.J.: Prentice-Hall, 1963.
Leahy, A. M. Nature-nurture and intelligence. Genet. Psychol. Monogr., 1935, *17*: 235–308.
Leary, T. Interpersonal Diagnosis of Personality: A Functional Theory and Methodology for Personality Evaluation. New York: Ronald, 1957.
Leaver, J., McKinney, B., Roe, E., and Verhoeks, J. Manual of Perceptual Motor Activities. Johnstown, Pa.: Mafex Associates, 1968.
Leavitt, F. Drugs and Behavior. Philadelphia: W. B. Saunders Company, 1974.
Lehrer, B. E. An investigation of the role of intellectual, motivational, and other nonintellectual factors in the prediction of educational achievement and efficiency. Dissertation Abstracts, 1969, *29*: 3876.
Leib, J. W., et al. Teaching machines and programmed instruction: Areas of application. Psychol. Bull., 1967, *67*: 12–26.
Leighten, D., and Kluckhorn, C. Children of the People: The Navaho Individual and His Development. Cambridge, Mass.: Harvard University Press, 1947.
Leighton, A. H., Prince, R., and May, R. The therapeutic process in cross-cultural perspective: A symposium. Am. J. Psychiatry, 1968, *124*: 1171–1183.
Lejeune, J., Gautier, M., and Turpin, R. Le mongolisme: Premier exemple d'aberration autosomique humaine. Ann. Hum. Genet., 1959, *1*: 41.
Leland, H., Walker, J., and Taboada, A. N. Group play therapy with a group of nursery male retardates. Am. J. Ment. Defic., 1959, *63*: 848–851.
Lemmon, A. Visual perceptual characteristics of groups of educable mental retardates. Dissertation Abstracts, 1968, *28*: 2901–2902.
Lenneberg, E. H. The natural history of language. In F. Smith and G. A. Miller (Eds.), The Genesis of Language: A Psycholinguistic Approach. Cambridge, Mass.: The M.I.T. Press, 1966.
Lenneberg, E. H. (Ed.) Biological Foundations of Language. New York: Wiley, 1967.
Lennox, W. G. Epilepsy and Related Disorders. Boston: Little, Brown, 1960.
Lesser, G. S., Fifer, G., and Clark, D. H. Mental abilities of children from different social-class and cultural groups. Monogr. Soc. Res. Child Dev., 1965, *30*: No. 12.
Lesser, L. I., Ashenden, B. J., Debuskey, M., and Eisenberg, L. Anorexia nervosa in children. Am. J. Orthopsychiatry, 1960, *30*: 572–580.
Levi, A. Treatment of a disorder of perception and concept formation in a case of school failure. J. Consult. Psychol., 1965, *29*: 289–295.
Levine, E. The Psychology of Deafness. New York: Columbia University Press, 1960.
Levine, E. S. Studies in psychological evaluation of the deaf. Volta Review, 1963, *65*: 496–512.
Levine, M. Psychotherapy in Medical Practice. New York: Macmillan, 1942.
Levinson, P. The next generation: A study of children in AFDC families. Welfare in Review, 1969, *7*: 1–10.
Levitt, E. E. The results of psychotherapy with children: An evaluation. J. Consult. Psychol., 1957, *21*: 189–196.
Levitt, E. E. Psychotherapy with children: A further evaluation. Behav. Res. Ther., 1963, *1*: 45–51.
Levy, D. Release therapy in young children. Psychiatry, 1938, *1*: 387–389.
Levy, D. M. Release therapy. Am. J. Orthopsychiatry, 1939, *9*: 713–736.
Levy, D. M. Maternal Overprotection. New York: Columbia University Press, 1943.
Levy, R. Effects of institutional vs. boarding home care on a group of infants. J. Pers., 1947, *15*: 233–241.
Lewis, H. Deprived Children: A Social and Clinical Study. London: Oxford University Press, 1954.
Lewis, N. D. C. A Short History of Psychiatric Achievement. New York: Basic Books, 1941.
Lewis, O. The Children of Sanchez. New York: Random House, 1961.
Lichten, S. O. The Drop Outs. New York: Free Press, 1962.
Lillie, L. The effects of motor development lessons on mentally retarded children. Am. J. Ment. Defic., 1968, *72*: 803–808.
Lindeman, B., and Kling, M. Bibliography: Definitions, uses, and studies. Journal of School Psychology, 1969, *7*: 36–41.
Lindsley, O. R. Operant conditioning methods applied to research in chronic schizophrenia. Psychiatr. Res. Rep., 1956, *5*: 118–153.
Lindvall, C. M. Measuring Pupil Achievement and Aptitude. New York: Harcourt, Brace & World, 1967.
Lippitt, R., and Radke, M. New trends in the investigation of prejudice. American Academy of Political and Social Science, 1946, *244*: 167–176.
Livingston, S., and Escala, P. Headaches and epilepsy in children. In A. P. Friedman and E. Harms (Eds.), Headaches in Children. Springfield, Ill.: Charles C Thomas, 1967.
Loban, W. Language ability in the middle grades of the elementary school. Unpublished doctoral dissertation, University of California, 1961.
Loevinger, J. On the proportional contributions of differences in nature and in nurture to differences in intelligence. Psychol. Bull., 1943, *40*: 725–756.
Loevinger, J. Theories of ego development. In L. Breger (Ed.), Clinical-Cognitive Psychology: Models and Integrations. Englewood Cliffs, N.J.: Prentice-Hall, 1969.
London, P. The Modes and Morals of Psychotherapy. New York: Holt, Rinehart and Winston, Inc., 1964.
Long, K. K. Transfer from teaching to learning. J. Educ. Psychol., 1971, *62*: 167–178.
Long, N. J. Direct Help to the Classroom Teacher. Washington, D.C.: Washington School of Psychiatry, 1966.

Long, N. J., Alpher, R., Butt, F., and Cully, M. Helping children cope with feelings. Childhood Education, 1969, *45*: 367–372.

Long, N. J., and Morse, W. C. Special classes for children with social and emotional problems in public school. In W. Wattenberg (Ed.), Social Maladjustment. Chicago: National Society for the Study of Education, 1965.

Long, N. J., Morse, W. C., and Newman, R. G. (Eds.) The WOC Student and the WOC Program: An Introduction and Interpretation for the Teacher. In Conflict in the Classroom. Belmont, Calif.: Wadsworth, 1971.

Long, N. J., and Newman, R. G. Managing surface behavior of children in school. In N. J. Long, W. C. Morse, and R. G. Newman (Eds.), Conflict in the Classroom. Belmont, Calif.: Wadsworth, 1965.

Long, N. J., and Newman, R. G. The teacher and his mental health. In N. J. Long, W. C. Morse, and R. G. Newman (Eds.), Conflict in the Classroom. Belmont, Calif.: Wadsworth, 1971.

Lorenz, M. H. Follow-up studies of the severely retarded. In M. C. Reynolds, J. R. Kiland, and R. E. Ellis (Eds.), A Study of Public School Children with Severe Mental Retardation. Research Project No. 6, St. Paul, Minn., 1953.

Lourie, N. V. Orthopsychiatry and education. Am. J. Orthopsychiatry, *1967*, *37*: 836–842.

Louittit, C. M. Clinical Psychology of Exceptional Children. (3rd ed.) New York: Harper & Brothers, 1957.

Lovaas, O. I. Program for establishment of speech in schizophrenic and autistic children. In J. Wing (Ed.), Early Childhood Autism. New York: Pergamon, 1966.

Lovaas, O. I., Freitag, G., Gold, C. J., and Kassorla, I. C. Experimental studies in childhood schizophrenia: I. Analysis of self-destructive behavior. J. Exp. Child Psychol., 1965, *2*: 67–84.

Lovaas, O. I., Freitas, L., Nelson, K., and Whalen, C. The establishment of imitation and its use for the development of complex behavior in schizophrenic children. Behav. Res. Ther., 1967, *5*: 171–181.

Lovell, K. A. A follow-up study of Inhelder and Piaget's The Growth of Logical Thinking. Br. J. Psychol., 1961, *52*: 143–153.

Lovitt, T. Assessment of children with learning disabilities. Except. Child., 1968, *35*: 233–239.

Lovitt, T. Behavior modification: The current scene. Except. Child., 1970a, *37*: 85–91.

Lovitt, T. Behavior modification: Where do we go from here? Except. Child., 1970b, *37*: 157–167.

Lowe, G. U., Terry, M., and MacLachan, E. A. Organic-aciduria, decreased renal ammonia production, hydrophthalmos and mental retardation. Am. J. Dis. Child., 1952, *83*: 164.

Lowenfield, B. Psychological problems of children with impaired vision. In W. M. Cruickshank (Ed.), Psychology of Exceptional Children and Youth. Englewood Cliffs, N.J.: Prentice-Hall, 1963.

Lucito, L. J. Gifted children. In L. M. Dunn (Ed.), Exceptional Children in the Schools. New York: Holt, Rinehart and Winston, Inc., 1963.

Lulow, W. V. Headaches in children: Psychopathological aspects and psychotherapeutic approach. In A. P. Friedman and E. Harms (Eds.), Headaches in Children. Springfield, Ill.: Charles C Thomas, 1967.

Lumbe, A. S., and Vogman, S. K. Occupational Conditions Among the Deaf. Washington, D.C.: Gallaudet College, 1959.

Luria, A. R. Psychological studies of mental deficiency in the Soviet Union. In N. R. Ellis (Ed.), Handbook of Mental Deficiency. New York: McGraw-Hill, 1963.

Luria, A. R. Higher Cortical Functions in Man. New York: Basic Books, 1966.

Lurie, R. S. The contribution of child psychiatry to the pathogenesis of hyperactivity in children. Clinical Proceedings Children's Hospital (Washington, D.C.), 1963, *19*: 247–251.

Lyle, J. G. Problems of T.A.T. interpretation and the diagnosis of delinquent trends. Br. J. Med. Psychol., 1958, *31*: 51–59.

Lyle, J. G. The mentally retarded and institutionalized. J. Ment. Defic., 1959, *3*: 121–128.

Lyness, S. L. The relationship of auditory perception to primary grade reading abilities. Dissertation Abstracts, 1968, *28*: 3028–3029.

Maccoby, E. E. Selective auditory attention in children. In L. P. Lipsett and C. C. Spiker (Eds.), Advances in Child Development and Behavior. New York: Academic Press, 1967.

MacDonald, A. P., Jr. Manifestations of differential levels of socialization by birth order. Developmental Psychology, 1969, *1*: 485–492.

Machover, K. Personality Projection in the Drawing of the Human Figure: A Method of Personality Investigation. Springfield, Ill.: Charles C Thomas, 1949.

Macmillan, D. L., and Fornes, S. R. Behavior modification: Limitations and liabilities. Except. Child., 1970, *37*: 291–297.

Maes, W. R. The identification of emotionally disturbed elementary school children. Except. Child., 1966, *5*: 607–609.

Magaro, P. A. Perceptual discrimination performance of schizophrenics as a function of censure, social class, and premorbid adjustment. J. Abnorm. Psychol., 1967, *72*: 415–420.

Magary, J. F., and McIntyre, R. B. (Eds.) Fifth Annual Distinguished Lectures in Special Education: Summer Session, 1966. Los Angeles: University of Southern California, School of Education, 1967.

Maher, B. A. Intelligence and brain damage. In N. R. Ellis (Ed.), Handbook of Mental Deficiency. New York: McGraw-Hill, 1963.

Maher, B. A. Principles of Psychotherapy. New York: McGraw-Hill, 1966.

Mahler, M. S. On symbiotic child psychosis. In R. S. Eissler et al. (Eds.), Psychoanalytic Study of the Child. Vol. 2. New York: International Universities Press, 1955.

Mahler, M. S. On Human Symbiosis and the Vicissitudes of Individuation. New York: International Universities Press, 1968.

Maier, N. R. Innovation in education. Am. Psychol., 1961, *26*: 722–726.

Makita, K. The rarity of reading disability in Japanese children. Am. J. Orthopsychiatry, 1968, *38*: 599–614.

Malone, C. A. Some observations on children of disorganized families and problems of acting out. J. Child Psychiatry, 1963, *2*: 22–49.

Mann, L. Perceptual training. Am. J. Orthopsychiatry, 1970, *40*: 30–38.

Marks, I. M. Fears and Phobias. London: Academic Press, Inc., 1969.

Marquis, J. M., and Morgan, W. K. A Guidebook for Systematic Desensitization. Palo Alto, Calif.: Veterans Administration Hospital, 1969.

Marshall, H. H. The effect of punishment on children: A review of the literature and a suggested hypothesis. J. Genet. Psychol., 1965, *106*: 22–33.

Martinson, R., and Lessinger, L. Problems in identification of gifted children. Except. Child., 1960, *26*: 227–231.

Martmer, E. E. The Child with a Handicap. Springfield, Ill.: Charles C Thomas, 1959.

Masland, R. J., Sarason, S. B., and Gladwin, T. Mental Abnormality. New York: Basic Books, 1958.

Maslow, A. Toward a Psychology of Being. Princeton, N.J.: Van Nostrand, 1962.

Maslow, A., and Mittelmann, B. Principles of Abnormal Psychology. New York: Harper & Brothers, 1951.

Massimo, J., and Shore, M. Comprehensive vocationally oriented psychotherapy: A new treatment technique for lower class adolescent delinquent boys. Psychiatry, 1967, *30*: 229–236.

Masterson, J. F., Tucker, K., and Berk, G. The symptomatic adolescent: Delineation of psychiatric syndromes. Compr. Psychiatry, 1966, *7*: 166–174.

Masterson, J. F., Jr., and Washburne, A. The symptomatic adolescent: Psychiatric illness or adolescent turmoil? Am. J. Psychiatry, 1966, *122*: 1240–1248.

Mayer, C. R., et al. The use of punishment in modifying student behavior. Journal of Special Education, 1968, *2*: 323–328.

Mayer, M. The role of residential treatment for children. Am. J. Orthopsychiatry, 1955, *25*: 667–668.

McCabe, B. F. The etiology of deafness. Volta Review, 1963, *65*: 471–477.

McCandless, B. R. Environment and intelligence. Am. J. Ment. Defic., 1952, *56*: 674–691.

McCandless, B. R. Relation of environmental factors to intellectual functioning. In H. Stevens and R. Heber (Eds.), Mental Retardation. Chicago: The University of Chicago Press, 1964.

McCarthy, D. Language development in children. In L. Carmichael (Ed.), Manual of Child Psychology. (2nd ed.) New York: Wiley, 1954.

McCarthy, J. J., and McCarthy, J. F. Learning Disabilities. Boston: Allyn and Bacon, 1969.

McCarthy, J. M. Psychoeducational Diagnosis—A Derivative of Classroom Behavior. Hoffman Estates, Ill.: Community Consolidated School District 54.

McCarthy, J. M., and Paraskevopolus, J. Behavior patterns of learning disabled, emotionally disturbed, and average children. Except. Child., 1969, *36*: 69–74.

McClanahan, L. J. The effectiveness of perceptual training for slow learners. Dissertation Abstracts, 1968, *28*: 2560.

McCorkle, L. W., Elias, A., and Bixby, F. The Highfields Story: An Experimental Treatment Project for Youthful Offenders. New York: Holt, Rinehart and Winston, Inc., 1958.

McDaniel, T. W. Physical Disabilities and Human Behavior. New York: Pergamon, 1969.

McDermott, J. F., Jr., Harrison, S. I., et al. Social class and mental illness in children: The diagnosis of organicity and mental retardation. J. Am. Acad. Child Psychiatry, 1967, *6*: 309–320.

McDonald, A. P., Jr. Manifestations of differential levels of socialization by birth order. Developmental Psychology, 1969, *1*: 485–492.

McDonald, C. W. Neurological organization: An evaluative review of the theories and procedures of Doman and Delacato. In H. C. Haywood (Ed.), Brain Damage in School Age Children. Washington, D.C.: Council for Exceptional Children, 1968.

McGehee, W., and Lewis, W. D. The socioeconomic status of homes of mentally superior and retarded children and the occupation rank of their parents. J. Genet. Psychol., 1942, *60*: 375–380.

McGuire, L. L., and Meyers, C. E. Early personality in the congenitally blind child. New Outlook for the Blind, 1971, *65*: 137–143.

McIntire, M. S., Menolaschino, F. J., and Wiley, J. H. Mongolism: Some clinical aspects. Am. J. Ment. Defic., 1965, *69*: 794–800.

McKenzie, H. S., Clark, M., Wolf, M. M., Kothera, R. K., and Benson, C. Behavior modification of children with learning disabilities using grades as tokens and allowances as backup reinforcers. Except. Child., 1968, *34*: 745–752.

McNeil, D. Developmental psycholinguistics. In F. Smith and A. Miller (Eds.), The Genesis of Language: A Psycholinguistic Approach. Cambridge, Mass.: The M.I.T. Press, 1966.

McNeil, T. F., and Wiegerink, R. Diagnostic categories and obstetric complication histories in disturbed children. Except. Child., 1971, *37*: 751–752.

Medicine, B. The native American. In D. Spiegel and P. Keith-Spiegel (Eds.), Outsiders USA. San Francisco: Rinehart, 1973.

Meeker, M. N. The Structure of Intellect: Its Interpretation and Uses. Columbus, Ohio: Charles E. Merrill Books, Inc., 1969.

Mehlman, B. Group play therapy with mentally retarded children. J. Abnorm. Soc. Psychol., 1958, *48*: 53–60.

Mehrens, W. A., and Lehmann, I. J. Standardized Tests in Education. New York: Holt, Rinehart and Winston, Inc., 1969.

Meier, J. H., Nimnicht, G., and McAlfee, O. An autotelic responsive environment nursery school for deprived children. In J. Hellmuth (Ed.), Disadvantaged Child. Vol. 2. New York: Brunner/Mazel, 1968.

Menninger, K. The Human Mind. (3rd ed.) New York: Knopf, 1945.

Merton, R. K. Social Theory and Social Structure. Glencoe, Ill.: Free Press, 1957.
Mesinger, J. F. Emotionally disturbed and brain damaged children—should we mix them? Except. Child., 1965, *32*: 237–238.
Meyerson, L. A psychology of impaired learning. In W. M. Cruickshank (Ed.), Psychology of Exceptional Children and Youth. (2nd ed.) Englewood Cliffs, N.J.: Prentice-Hall, 1963a.
Meyerson, L. Somatopsychology of physical disability. In W. M. Cruickshank (Ed.), Psychology of Exceptional Children and Youth (2nd ed.) Englewood Cliffs, N.J.: Prentice-Hall, 1963b.
Michael, W. B. A short evaluation of the research reviewed in educational and psychological testing. Journal of Educational Research, 1965, *31*: 92–99.
Michal-Smith, H. Psychotherapy for the mentally retarded. In H. Michal-Smith and S. Kastein (Eds.), The Special Child: Diagnosis, Treatment, Habilitation. Seattle, Wash.: New School for the Special Child, 1962.
Michal-Smith, H., and Morgenstern, M. Learning disorders—an overview. In J. Hellmuth (Ed.), Learning Disorders. Vol. I. Seattle, Wash.: Special Child Publications, 1965.
Michaux, L. A. The Physically Handicapped and the Community: Some Challenging Breakthroughs. Springfield, Ill.: Charles C Thomas, 1970.
Miller, H., and Baruch, D. W. Emotional problems and their relation to asthma. Journal of Diseases of Childhood, 1957, *93*: 242–245.
Miller, H. L. Education for the Disadvantaged. New York: Free Press, 1967.
Miller, N. Language therapy with an autistic nonverbal boy. Except. Child., 1969, *35*: 555–558.
Miller, T. P. Peptic ulcers in children. Can. Psychiatr. Assoc. J., 1965, *10*: 43–49.
Miller, W. The impact of a total community delinquency control project. Social Problems, 1962, *10*: 168–191.
Miller, W. B. Lower class culture as a generating milieu of gang delinquency. Journal of Social Issues, 1958, *14*: 5–10.
Minuchin, S., Montalvo, B., Gurney, B. G., Jr., and Schumer, F. Families of the Slums. New York: Basic Books, 1967.
Mira, M. P. Individual patterns of looking and listening preferences among learning disabled and normal children. Dissertation Abstracts, 1968, *28*: 3499.
Mischel, W. Personality and Assessment. New York: Wiley, 1968.
Money, J. (Ed.) The Disabled Reader: Education of the Dyslexic Child. Baltimore: The Johns Hopkins Press, 1966.
Moore, A. B. Reasoning ability and verbal proficiency in deaf and hearing children. Dissertation Abstracts, 1969, *3*: 4381.
Moore, J., Charnell, E., and West, M. J. T. Television as a therapeutic tool. Arch. Gen. Psychiatry, 1965, *12*: 217–220.
Moore, N. Behavior therapy in bronchial asthma: A controlled study. J. Psychosom. Res., 1965, *9*: 257–276.
Moore, O. K. Autotelic responsive environments and exceptional children. In J. Hellmuth (Ed.), The Special Child in Century 21. Seattle, Wash.: Special Child Publications, 1964.
Moorehead, M. M. Speech recognition and production in young children and adults. Dissertation Abstracts, 1968, *28*: 3668.
Moorehead, P. S., Mellman, W. J., and Wenar, C. A familial chromosome translocation associated with speech and mental retardation. Am. J. Hum. Genet., 1961, *13*: 32–46.
Morrill, C. S. Teaching machines: A review. Psychol. Bull., 1961, *58*: 363–375.
Morse, W. Crisis intervention in school mental health and special classes for the disturbed. In N. J. Long, W. Morse, and R. Newman (Eds.), Conflict in the Classroom. (2nd ed.) Belmont, Calif.: Wadsworth, 1971a.
Morse, W. Education of maladjusted and disturbed children. In N. J. Long, W. Morse, and R. Newman (Eds.), Conflict in the Classroom. (2nd ed.) Belmont, Calif.: Wadsworth, 1971b.
Morse, W. C. The education of socially maladjusted and emotionally disturbed children. In W. M. Cruickshank and G. O. Johnson (Eds.), Education of Exceptional Children and Youth. Englewood Cliffs, N.J.: Prentice-Hall, 1958.
Morse, W. C., Cutler, R. L., and Fink, A. H. Public School Classes for the Emotionally Handicapped: A Research Analysis. Washington, D.C.: Council for Exceptional Children, NEA, 1964.
Moser, H., Efron, M., and Young, D. New screening method for amino acid disorders. Paper presented at the Joseph P. Kennedy, Jr. Foundation, New York, February 1964.
Moss, S. Z. How children feel about being placed away from home. Children, 1966, *13*: 153–157.
Mowrer, O. H. A stimulus-response analysis of anxiety and its role as a reinforcing agent. Psychol. Rev., 1939, *46*: 553–565.
Mowrer, O. H. Learning theory and the neurotic paradox. Am. J. Orthopsychiatry, 1948, *18*: 571–610.
Mowrer, O. H. Learning Theory and Personality Dynamics. New York: Ronald, 1950.
Moynihan, D. P. Employment, income, and the ordeal of the Negro family. In T. Parsons and K. B. Clark (Eds.), The Negro American. Boston: Houghton Mifflin, 1966.
Muehl, S. Relation between word-recognition errors and hand-eye preference in preschool children. J. Educ. Psychol., 1963, *54*: 316–321.
Mullen, B. N. A perceptual and cognitive taxonomy of character disorders. Dissertation Abstracts, 1967, *28*: 2145.
Muma, J. R. A comparison of certain aspects of productivity and grammar in speech samples of fluent and nonfluent four-year-old children. Dissertation Abstracts, 1967, *28*: 2658–2659.
Muma, J. R. Unpublished research. Center for Hearing Disabilities, University of Alabama, Tuscaloosa, 1970.
Mundy, L. Environmental influence in intellectual functions as measured by intelligence tests. Br. J. Med. Psychol., 1957, *30*: 194–201.
Murphy, G. Personality. New York: Harper & Brothers, 1947.
Murray, E. J., and Jacobson, L. I. The nature of learning in traditional and behavior psychother-

apy. In A. E. Bergin and S. L. Garfield (Eds.), Handbook of Psychotherapy and Behavior Change. New York: Wiley, 1971.

Murray, H. A., et al. Explorations in Personality: A Clinical and Experimental Study of Fifty Men of College Age. New York: Oxford University Press, 1938.

Myklebust, H. R. Auditory Disorders in Children. New York: Grune & Stratton, 1954.

Myklebust, H. R. Toward a new understanding of the deaf child. In M. Frampton and E. D. Gall (Eds.), Special Education for the Exceptional. Boston: Porter Sargent, 1955.

Myklebust, H. R., and Boshes, B. Minimal Brain Damage in Children. Final Report, 1969, Neurological and Sensory Disease Control Program, Washington, D.C., Contract No. 108-65-142, Department of Health, Education, and Welfare.

Nagi, S. Z. Disability and rehabilitation: Legal, clinical, and self-concepts and measurement. Columbus: Ohio State University Press, 1969.

Nagy, I. B., and Framo, J. L. (Eds.) Intensive Family Therapy: Theoretical and Practical Aspects. New York: Harper & Row, 1965.

Nash, H. Mixed metaphor in personality theory. J. Nerv. Ment. Dis., 1965, *140*: 384–388.

Nass, M. L. The effect of three variables on children's concepts of physical causality. J. Abnorm. Psychol., 1956, *53*: 191–196.

Naumberg, M. Dynamically Oriented Art Therapy: Its Principles and Practice. New York: Grune & Stratton, 1966.

Naville, S. Psychomotor therapy. Newsletter: The Marianne Frostig Center of Educational Therapy, 1970, *10*: 25.

Nehaus, M. The relationship between parental attitudes and the emotional adjustment of deaf children in early childhood, late childhood and adolescence. Dissertation Abstracts, 1968, *28*: 4299.

Nelson, C. M. Techniques for screening conduct-disturbed children. Except. Child., 1971, *37*: 501–507.

Netter, F. H. Nervous System. Vol. I. of CIBA Collection of Medical Illustrations. Summit, N.J.: CIBA Pharmaceutical Company, 1962.

Neville, D. A. A comparison of the WISC patterns of male retarded and non-retarded readers. Journal of Educational Research, 1961, *54*: 195–197.

Nevis, S. M. A longitudinal study of visual preferences in the first six months of life and implications for perceptual-cognitive growth. Dissertation Abstracts, 1967, *28*: 2629.

Newbert, N. A study of certain personality correlates of the middle child in a three child family. Dissertation Abstracts, 1969, *29*: 4333–4334.

Newland, T. E. Psychological assessment of exceptional children. In W. M. Cruickshank (Ed.), Psychology of Exceptional Children and Youth. (2nd ed.) Englewood Cliffs, N.J.: Prentice-Hall, 1963.

Newman, R. G. Psychological Consultation in the Schools. New York: Basic Books, 1967.

Newton, E. Planning for the language development of disadvantaged children and youth. Journal of Negro Education, 1964, *33*: 210–217.

Noland, C. Y., and Morris, J. E. Development and validation of the Roughness Discrimination Test. International Journal for the Education of the Blind, 1965, *15*: 1–6.

Nolen, P., Kunzelmann, H. P., and Haring, N. C. Behavioral modification in a junior learning disabilities classroom. Except. Child., 1967, *33*: 163–168.

O'Connor, N., and Hermelin, B. Speech and Thought in Severe Subnormality. New York: Pergamon Press, 1963.

O'Gorman, G. The Nature of Childhood Autism. London: Butterworth, 1967.

Ojemann, R. H. Developing a Program for Education in Human Behavior. Iowa City: State University of Iowa, 1959.

O'Leary, K. D., and Becker, W. C. Behavior modification of an adjustment class: A token reinforcement program. Except. Child., 1967, *33*: 637–642.

O'Leary, K. D., Kaufman, K. F., Kass, R. E., and Drabman, R. S. The effects of loud and soft reprimands on the behavior of disruptive students. Except. Child., 1970, *37*: 145–155.

Olson, D. R., and Pagliuso, S. (Eds.) From perceiving to performing: An aspect of cognitive growth. Ontario Journal of Educational Research, 1968, *10*: 155–231.

Orton, S. T. Specific reading disability—strephosymbolia. J.A.M.A., 1928, *90*: 1095–1099.

Osgood, C. E. Method and Theory in Experimental Psychology. New York: Oxford University Press, 1953.

Osgood, C. E. Motivational dynamics of language behavior. In M. R. Jones (Ed.), Nebraska Symposium on Motivation. Lincoln: University of Nebraska Press, 1957.

Osgood, C. E. The psychologist in international affairs. Am. Psychol., 1964, *19*: 111–118.

Ostfeld, A. M. Mechanisms of headaches in children. In A. P. Friedman and E. Harms (Eds.), Headaches in Children. Springfield, Ill.: Charles C Thomas, 1967.

Painter, G. B. The effect of a rhythmic and sensory-motor activity program on perceptual motor-spatial abilities of kindergarten children. Except. Child., 1966, *33*: 113–116.

Palmer, F. H. Inferences to the socialization of the child from animal studies: A view from the bridge. In D. A. Goslin (Ed.), Handbook of Socialization Theory and Research. Chicago: Rand McNally, 1969.

Parsons, O. A. Clinical neuropsychology. In C. D. Spielberger (Ed.), Current Topics in Clinical and Community Psychology. Vol. 2. New York: Academic Press, 1970.

Parsons, R. W. Convergence in psychotherapy with delinquent boys. J. Consult. Psychol., 1966, *13*: 329–333.

Pasamanick, B. Some misconceptions concerning differences in the racial prevalence of mental diseases. Am. J. Orthopsychiatry, 1963, *33*: 72–86.

Pasamanick, B., Knobloch, H., and Lilienfeld, A. M. Socioeconomic status and some precursors of neuropsychiatric disorder. Am. J. Orthopsychiatry, 1956, *26*: 594–601.

Pasamanick, B., and Knobloch, H. Brain damage and reproductive causality. Am. J. Orthopsychiatry, 1960, *30*: 208.

Pasamanick, B., and Knobloch, H. Epidemiologic studies on the complications of pregnancy and the birth process. In G. Caplan (Ed.), Prevention of Mental Disorders in Children. New York: Basic Books, 1961.

Patterson, C. H. Counseling and Psychotherapy: Theory and Practice. New York: Harper & Brothers, 1959.

Patterson, C. H. A current view of client-centered or relationship therapy. The Counseling Psychologist, 1969, *1*: 2–25.

Patterson, G. R. An empirical approach to the classification of disturbed children. J. Clin. Psychol., 1964, *20*: 326–337.

Patterson, G. R., Jones, J. W., and Wright, M. A. A behavior modification technique for the hyperactive child. Behav. Res. Ther., 1965, *2*: 217–226.

Patterson, G. R., McNeal, S., Hawkins, N., and Phelps, R. Reprogramming the social environment. J. Child Psychol. Psychiatry, 1967, *8*: 191–195.

Patterson, G. R., Ray, R. S., and Shaw, D. A. Direct intervention in families of deviant children. Oregon Research Institute Bulletin, 1968, *8*: 1–62.

Patterson, G. R., and Reid, J. B. Reciprocity and coercion: Two facets of social systems. In C. Neuringer and J. Michaels (Eds.), Behavior Modification for Clinical Psychology. New York: McGraw-Hill, 1969.

Paul, G. L. Insight vs. Desensitization in Psychotherapy. Stanford, Calif.: Stanford, 1966.

Pavenstedt, E. A comparison of the child-rearing environment of upper-lower and very-lower lower-class families. Am. J. Orthopsychiatry, 1965, *35*: 89–98.

Pearson, J. S., and Kley, I. B. On the application of genetic expectancies as age-specific base rates in the study of human behavior disorders. Psychol. Bull., 1957, *54*: 406–420.

Peck, H. Delinquency: A laboratory for public health psychiatry. Am. J. Orthopsychiatry, 1958, *18*: 134–146.

Peck, J. R., and Sexton, C. L. Effect of various settings on trainable children's progress. Am. J. Ment. Defic., 1961, *66*: 62–68.

Peel, E. A. Experimental examination of some of Piaget's schemata concerning the child's perception and thinking and a discussion of their educational significance. Br. J. Educ. Psychol., 1959, *29*: 89–103.

Pegnato, C. W., and Birch, J. W. Locating gifted children in junior high schools: A comparison of methods. Except. Child., 1959, *25*: 300–304.

Penfield, W., and Roberts, L. Speech and Brain Mechanism. Princeton, N.J.: Princeton University Press, 1959.

Penrose, L. S. The Biology of Mental Defect. (3rd ed.) New York: Grune & Stratton, 1963.

Persons, R. W. Relationship between psychotherapy with institutionalized boys and subsequent community adjustment. J. Consult. Psychol., 1967, *31*: 137–141.

Peter, L. Prescriptive Teaching. New York: McGraw-Hill, 1965.

Peterson, D. Behavior problems in middle childhood. J. Consult. Psychol., 1961, *25*: 205–209.

Pettigrew, T. F. Race, mental illness and intelligence: A social psychological view. Eugenics Quarterly, 1964, *11*: 189–215.

Philips, I. Children, mental retardation, and emotional disorder. In I. Philips (Ed.), Prevention and Treatment of Mental Retardation. New York: Basic Books, 1966.

Phillips, E. L. Parent-child psychotherapy: A follow-up study comparing two techniques. J. Psychol., 1960, *49*: 195–202.

Phillips, E. L., and Wiener, D. N. Short-Term Psychotherapy and Structured Behavior Change. New York: McGraw-Hill, 1966.

Piaget, J. Judgment and the Reasoning of the Child. New York: Harcourt, Brace, 1928.

Piaget, J. The Child's Concept of Physical Causality. New York: Harcourt, Brace, 1930.

Piaget, J. The Moral Judgment of the Child. New York: Harcourt, Brace, 1932.

Piaget, J. Logic and Psychology. Manchester, England: Manchester University Press, 1953a.

Piaget, J. The Origins of Intelligence in the Child. (Trans. M. Cook) London: Routledge, 1953b.

Pick, H. L., Jr., Pick, A. P., and Klein, R. E. Perceptual integration in children. In L. P. Lipsett and L. L. Spiker (Eds.), Advances in Child Development and Behavior. Vol. 3. New York: Academic Press, 1967.

Pierson, G., Cattell, R., and Pierce, J. A. A demonstration of the HSPQ of the nature of the personality changes produced by institutionalization of delinquents. J. Soc. Psychol., 1966, *70*: 229–239.

Pimm, J. B., and McClure, G. Working with emotionally disturbed children in the public school setting. Except. Child., 1967, *33*: 633–655.

Pintner, R., and Patterson, B. G. The Binet scales and the deaf child. J. Educ. Psychol., 1915, *6*: 201–210.

Polenz, R. J. An analysis of performance of second grade boys with visual perceptual deficiencies and second grade boys with satisfactory visual perception on the Gray oral reading test. Dissertation Abstracts, 1969, *29*: 2447–2448.

Posner, C. A. Some effects of genetic and cultural variables on self-evaluations of children. Dissertation Abstracts, 1969, *29*: 4833–4834.

Powledge, F. To Change a Child. Chicago: Quadrangle Books, Inc., 1967.

Premack, D. Language in chimpanzee? Science, 1971, *172*: 808–822.

Price, B. Primary biases in twin studies: A review of prenatal and natal difference-producing factors in monozygotic pairs. Am. J. Hum. Genet., 1950, *2*: 293–352.

Prigmore, C. Correctional manpower. Rehabil. Rec., 1965, *6*: 22–23.

Provence, S., and Lipton, R. C. Infants in Institutions. New York: International Universities Press, 1962.

Purcell, K. Distinctions between subgroups of asthmatic children: Children's perceptions of events associated with asthma. Pediatrics, 1963, *42*: 486–494.

Quay, H. C. Some basic considerations in the education of emotionally disturbed children. Except. Child., 1963, *30*: 27–31.

Quay, H. C. Dimensions of personality in delinquent boys as inferred from the factor analysis of case history data. Child. Dev., 1964, *35*: 479–484.

Quay, H. C. Juvenile Delinquency: Research and Theory. Princeton, N.J.: Van Nostrand, 1965a.

Quay, H. C. Personality and delinquency. In H. C. Quay (Ed.), Juvenile Delinquency. Princeton, N.J.: Van Nostrand, 1965b.

Quay, H. C. Personality dimensions in preadolescent delinquent boys. Educational Psychological Measurement, 1966, *26*: 99–110.

Quay, H. C., Morse, W. C., and Cutler, R. L. Personality patterns of pupils in special classes for the emotionally disturbed. Except. Child., 1966, *32*: 297–301.

Quay, H. C., and Peterson, D. R. Behavior Problem Checklist and Manual for the Behavior Problem Checklist. Champaign, Ill.: University of Illinois, 1967.

Quay, H., and Quay, L. Behavior problems in early adolescence. Child Dev., 1965, *35*: 215–220.

Quigley, S., Jenne, W., and Phillips, S. Deaf Students in Colleges and Universities. Washington, D.C.: Alexander Graham Bell Association for the Deaf, 1968.

Rabinovitch, R. D., et al. A research approach to reading retardation. Neurology and Psychiatry in Childhood, 1956, *34*: 363–396.

Rabinow, B. The role of the school in residential treatment. Am. J. Orthopsychiatry, 1955, *25*: 685–691.

Radke, M. J. The relation of parental authority to children's behavior and attitudes. University of Minnesota Child Welfare Monograph, 1946, No. 22.

Rae-Grant, Q. A. F., Gladnin, T., and Bower, E. M. Mental health, social competence, and the war on poverty. Am. J. Orthopsychiatry, 1966, *36*: 652–664.

Rank, B. Adaptation of the psychoanalytic technique for the treatment of young children with atypical development. Am. J. Orthopsychiatry, 1949a, *19*: 130–139.

Rank, B. Aggression. In A. Freud et al. (Eds.). The Psychoanalytic Study of the Child. New York: International Universities Press, 1949b.

Rank, O. The Artist and Other Contributions to the Psychoanalysis of Poetical Creation. (4th ed.) Leipzig: Internationaler Psychoanalytischer Verlag, 1925.

Rank, O. Art and Artist. New York: Knopf. 1932.

Rankin, R. J. Measurement of cognitive development. Paper presented at the NDEA Advanced Study Seminar on Improvement of Education for Disadvantaged Children, University of Oregon, July, 1968.

Ransom, G. A. Aural-visual independent activities in first-grade reading programs. Dissertation Abstracts, 1968, *28*: 2454–2455.

Rasoff, B. Sensory preference and intersensory functioning in children. Dissertation Abstracts, 1969, *29*: 3514–3515.

Reckless, W., Dinitz, S., and Kay, B. The self-component in potential delinquency and potential nondelinquency. Am. Sociol. Rev., 1957, *22*: 566–571.

Redl, F. Children Who Hate. New York: The Free Press of Glencoe, 1951.

Redl, F. The concept of a therapeutic milieu. Am. J. Orthopsychiatry, 1959, *29*: 721–734.

Redl, F. When We Deal with Children. New York: Free Press, 1966.

Redl, F., and Wineman, D. The Aggressive Child. New York: Free Press, 1957.

Redlich, F. C. The concept of health in psychiatry. In A. H. Leighton, J. A. Claussen, and R. N. Wilson (Eds.), Explorations in Social Psychiatry. New York: Basic Books, 1957.

Register, M., and L'Abate, L. The clinical usefulness of an objective nonverbal personality test for children. Psychology in the Schools, 1972, *9*: 378–387.

Reiss, A. J. Social correlates of psychological types of delinquency. Am. Sociol. Rev., 1952, *26*: 720–732.

Reiss, A. J., Jr., and Rhodes, A. L. The distribution of juvenile delinquency in the social class structure. Am. Sociol. Rev., 1961, *26*: 720–732.

Riessman, F. The Culturally Deprived Child. New York: Harper & Row, 1962.

Reitan, R. M. Psychological deficit. Am. Rev. Psychol., 1962, *13*: 415–446.

Reitan, R. M. The neurological model. In L. L'Abate (Ed.), Models of Clinical Psychology. Atlanta: Georgia State University, 1969.

Repucci, N. D. Social class, sex differences, and performances on cognitive tasks among two-year-old children. Proceedings, 77th Annual Convention, American Psychological Association, 1969, *4*: 553–554.

Resnick, R. J. A developmental and socioeconomic evaluation of perceptual integration. Developmental Psychology, 1969, *1*: 691–696.

Reynolds, M. C. The capacities of children. J. Except. Child., 1965, *31*: 344–345.

Rhodes, W. C. Institutionalized displacement and the disturbing child. In P. Knoblock (Ed.), Educational Planning for Emotionally Disturbed Children: The Decade Ahead. Syracuse, N.Y.: Syracuse University Press, 1965.

Rhodes, W. C. The disturbing child: A problem of ecological management. Except. Child., 1967, *33*: 449–455.

Rhodes, W. C. A community participation analysis of emotional disturbance. Except. Child., 1970, *36*: 309–314.

Rice, C. E., Fenstein, S. H., and Schasterman, R. J. Echo detection ability of the blind: Size and distance factors. J. Exp. Psychol., 1965, *70*: 246–251.

Richards, J. E. Techniques used in a school program for children emerging from early infantile autism. Except. Child., 1963, *29*: 348–357.

Rickard, H. C., and Dinoff, M. Behavior modification in a therapeutic summer camp. In H. C. Rickard (Ed.), Behavioral Intervention in Human Problems. New York: Pergamon, 1971.

Rimland, B. Infantile Autism. New York: Appleton-Century-Crofts, 1964.

Rioch, M. J. The work of Wilfred Bion on groups. Psychiatry, 1970, *33*: 56–66.

Robbins, M. P., and Glass, G. V. The Doman-Delacato rationale: A critical analysis. In J. Helmuth (Ed.), Educational Therapy. Seattle, Wash.: Special Child Publications, 1969.

Robbins, S. D. One thousand stutterers: A personal report of clinical experience and research with recommendations for therapy. J. Speech Hear. Disord., 1964, *29*: 178–186.

Robeck, M. C. Subtest patterning of problem readers on WISC. California Journal of Educational Research, 1960, *11*:110–115.

Robeck, M. C. Intellectual strengths and weaknesses shown by reading clinic subjects on the WISC. Journal of Developmental Reading, 1964, 7: 120–129.

Robins, L. N. Deviant Children Grow Up: A Sociological and Psychiatric Study of Sociopathic Personality. Baltimore: Williams & Wilkins, 1966.

Robinson, H., and Robinson, N. M. The Mentally Retarded Child. New York: McGraw-Hill, 1965.

Robinson, S. A. A study of delinquency among Jewish children in New York City. In M. Sklare (Ed.), The Jews: Social Patterns of an American Group. Glencoe, Ill.: Free Press, 1957.

Rogers, C. R. The Clinical Treatment of the Problem Child. Boston: Houghton Mifflin, 1939.

Rogers, C. R. Client-Centered Therapy. Boston: Houghton Mifflin, 1951.

Rogers, C. R. A theory of therapy, personality and interpersonal relationships, as developed in client-centered framework. In S. Koch (Ed.), Psychology: A Study of Science. Vol. 3. New York: McGraw-Hill, 1959.

Rogers, D. The Psychology of Adolescence. New York: Appleton-Century-Crofts, 1962.

Rogers, M., and Quigley, S. P. Identification of researchable rehabilitation problems of the deaf. Am. Ann. Deaf, 1960, *105*: 335–364.

Rogers, M. E., Lilienfeld, A. M., and Pasamanick, B. Prenatal and perinatal factors in the development of childhood behavior disorders. Acta Psychiatr. Neurol. Scand., 1955, *102*: 1–158.

Rokeach, M. The Open and Closed Mind. New York: Basic Books, 1960.

Romano, M. Reaching Delinquents Through Reading. Springfield, Ill.: Charles C Thomas, 1957.

Rose, D. M., Butler, C., and Eaton, F. L. Play therapy with psychotic adolescent girls. Int. J. Group Psychother., 1954, *4*: 303–311.

Rosen, B. C. Race, ethnicity, and the achievement syndrome. In M. Kornrich (Ed.), Underachievement. Springfield, Ill.: Charles C Thomas, 1965.

Rosen, B. M., Bahn, A. K., and Kramer, D. Demographic and diagnostic characteristics of psychiatric clinic outpatients in the U.S.A., 1961. Am. J. Orthopsychiatry, 1964, *34*: 455–468.

Rosen, E., Fox, R., and Gregory, I. Abnormal Psychology. (2nd ed.) Philadelphia: W. B. Saunders Company, 1972.

Rosen, J. The community speech and hearing center as a representative of the profession. American Speech and Hearing Association, 1961, *31*: 117–119.

Rosenberg, P. H., and Latimer, R. Suicide attempts by children. Ment. Hyg., 1966, *50*: 354–359.

Rosenblum, L. A., and Kaufman, I. C. Variations in infant development and response to maternal loss in monkeys. Am. J. Orthopsychiatry, 1968, *38*: 418–426.

Rosenow, E., and Whyte, A. H. The ordinal position of problem children. Am. J. Orthopsychiatry, 1931, *1*: 430–434.

Rosenthal, R., and Jacobson, L. Teachers' expectancies: Determiners of pupils' I.Q. gains. Psychol. Rep., 1966, *19*: 113–118.

Rosenthal, R., and Jacobson, L. Pygmalion in the Classroom. New York: Holt, Rinehart and Winston, Inc., 1968.

Rosenzweig, C. Maternal attitude and latency-age school achievement: A study of mother-child interaction in the developmental phases. Dissertation Abstracts, 1969, *29*: 4121–4122.

Ross, A. Learning difficulties of children: Dysfunctions, disorders, disabilities. Journal of School Psychology, 1967, *5*: 82–92.

Ross, A. O. The Exceptional Child in the Family. New York: Grune & Stratton, 1964.

Ross, S. L., Jr., DeYoung, H. G., and Cohen, J. Confrontation: Special education and the law. Except. Child., 1971, *38*: 5–12.

Ross, S. L., DeYoung, H. G., and Cohen, J. Confrontation: Special education placement and the law. In S. Kirk and F. Lord (Eds.), Exceptional Children: Educational Resources and Perspectives. Boston: Houghton Mifflin, 1974.

Roswell, F. G., and Natchez, G. Reading Disability: Diagnosis and Treatment. New York: Basic Books, 1964.

Roth, R. M., and Meyersburg, H. A. The nonachievement syndrome. In M. Kornrich (Ed.), Underachievement. Springfield, Ill.: Charles C Thomas, 1965.

Rothney, J. W. M. Methods of Studying the Individual Child. Waltham, Mass.: Blaisdell Publishing Company, 1968.

Rotter, J. Generalized expectancies for internal versus external control of reinforcement. Psychol. Monogr., 1966, *80*: 1–28.

Rotter, J. B. Beliefs, social attitudes, and behavior: A social learning analysis. In R. Jessop and S. Feschbach (Eds.), Cognition, Personality, and Clinical Psychology. San Francisco: Jossey-Bass, 1968.

Rowe, E. D. Speech Problems of Blind Children. New York: American Foundation for the Blind, 1958.

Rubin, E. Z., Simson, C. B., and Betwee, M. C. Emotionally Handicapped Children and the Elementary School. Detroit: Wayne State University Press, 1966.

Rubin, T. I. The Angry Book. London: Macmillan, 1969.

Rudnick, M., Sterritt, G. M., and Flax, M. Auditory and visual rhythm perception and reading ability. Child Dev., 1967, *38*: 581–587.

Rumbaugh, D. M., et al. A computer-controlled language training system for investigating the language skills of young apes. Behavior Research Methods and Instrumentation, 1973, *5*: 385–392.

Rundle, A. T. Etiological factors in mental retardation: I. Biochemical. Am. J. Ment. Defic., 1964, *67*: 61–68.

Russell, E. W. Neuropsychological keys for assessing the localization and process status of cerebral damage. Dissertation Abstracts, 1968, *29*: 2196.

Russell, R. W. Psychology: Noun or adjective? Am. Psychol., 1970, *25*: 211–218.

Rutter, M. Children's behavior questionnaire for completion by teachers: Preliminary findings. J. Child Psychol. Psychiatry, 1967, *8*: 1–11.

Rutter, M. Concepts of autism: Review of research. J. Child Psychol. Psychiatry, 1969, *9*: 1–25.

Rutter, M., Greenfeld, D., and Lockyer, L. A five to fifteen year follow-up study of infantile psychosis: II. Social and behavioral outcome. Br. J. Psychiatry, 1967, *113*: 1183–1199.

Ryckman, D. B., and Wiegerink, R. The factors of the Illinois Test of Psycholinguistic Abilities: A comparison of 18 factor analyses. Except. Child., 1969, *36*: 107–113.

Rynders, J. E. Alternatives to special class placement. In E. L. Meyer (Ed.), Strategies for Teaching Exceptional Children. Denver: Love Publishing Company, 1972.

Sabatino, D. A. The information processing behaviors associated with learning disabilities. Journal of Learning Disabilities, 1968, *1*: 440–450.

Sabatino, D. A. Auditory and visual perceptual behavior function of neurologically impaired children. Percept. Mot. Skills, 1969a, *29*: 244–259.

Sabatino, D. A. Identifying neurologically impaired children through an auditory test of perception. J. Consult. Clin. Psychol., 1969b, *33*: 184–188.

Saenger, G. The Adjustment of Severely Retarded Adults in the Community. Albany, N.Y.: New York State Interdepartmental Health Resources Board, 1957.

Safilios-Rothschild, C. The Sociology and Social Psychology of Disability and Rehabilitation. New York: Random House, 1970.

Salter, A. The Case Against Psychoanalysis. New York: Medical Publications Ltd., 1953.

Sampson, E. E., and Hancock, F. R. An examination of the relationship between ordinal position, personality, and conformity: An extension, replication, and partial verification. J. Pers. Soc. Psychol., 1967, *5*: 398–407.

Sandler, A. M., Daunton, E., and Schnurmann, A. Inconsistency in the mother as a factor in character development: A comparative study. Psychoanalytic Study of the Child. Vol. XII. New York: International Universities Press, 1957.

Santoro, R. M. The relationship of reading achievement to specific measures of visual perception, visual motor perception, and intelligence. Dissertation Abstracts, 1968, *28*: 4010–4011.

Santostefano, S. Construct validity of the Miniature Situations Test: I. The performance of public school, orphaned, and brain damaged children. J. Clin. Psychol., 1965, *21*: 418–421.

Santostefano, S. Cognitive controls versus cognitive styles: An approach to diagnosing and treating cognitive disabilities in children. Seminars in Psychiatry, 1969, *1*: 291–317.

Sapon, S. M. Receptive and expressive language. Paper presented at the 1965 annual meeting of the American Psychological Association, Chicago, September, 1965.

Sarason, S. B., and Doris, J. Psychological Problems in Mental Deficiency. New York: Harper & Row, 1969.

Scanlon, R. G. Individually Prescribed Instruction: A System of Individualized Instruction. Philadelphia: Research for Better Schools, Inc., 1971.

Schachter, S. Birth order and sociometric choice. J. Abnorm. Soc. Psychol., 1964, *8*: 453–456.

Schaefer, C. E. The Similes Test: A new measure of metaphorical thinking. Proceedings of the Annual Convention of the American Psychological Association, 1970, *5*: 169–170.

Schaefer, H. H., and Martin, P. L. Behavior Therapy. New York: McGraw-Hill, 1969.

Schellenberg, E. D. A study of the relationship between visual-motor perception and reading disabilities of third grade pupils. Unpublished doctoral dissertation, University of Southern California, 1962.

Scheuer, A. The relationship between personal attributes and effectiveness in teachers of the emotionally disturbed. Except. Child., 1971, *37*: 723–731.

Schiffer, M. The Therapeutic Play Group. New York: Grune & Stratton, 1965.

Schilder, P. The Image and Appearance of the Human Body. New York: International Universities Press, 1950.

Schiller, J. J., and Deigman, M. L. An approach to diagnosis and remediation of learning disabilities. Journal of Learning Disabilities, 1969, *2*: 509–519.

Schloesser, P. T. The abused child. Bull. Menninger Clin., 1964, *28*: 260–268.

Schmuck, R. A. Helping teachers improve group processes. Journal of Applied Behavioral Science, 1968, *4*: 401–437.

Schneer, H. I., Kay, P., and Brozovsky, M. Events and conscious ideation leading to suicidal behavior in adolescence. Psychiatr. Q., 1961, *35*: 507–515.

Schneider, K. Clinical Psychology. New York: Grune & Stratton, 1959.

Schofield, W. Psychotherapy: The Purchase of Friendship. Englewood Cliffs, N.J.: Prentice-Hall, 1964.

Schofield, W. Clinical and counseling psychology: Some perspectives. Am. Psychol., 1966, *21*: 122–131.

Schooler, C. Birth order effects: Not here, not now. Psychol. Bull., 1972, *78*: 161–175.

Schopler, E. Parents as cotherapists with psychotic children. Paper presented at the meeting of the American Psychological Association, Washington, D.C., September, 1969.

Schrut, A. Suicidal adolescents and children. J.A.M.A., 1964, *188*: 1103–1107.

Schulman, J. L., Kaspar, J. C., and Throne, F. M. Brain Damage and Behavior: A Clinical-

Experimental Study. Springfield, Ill.: Charles C Thomas, 1965.

Schwartz, A. S. Eating problems. Pediatr. Clin. North Am., 1958, *5*: 595–611.

Schwartz, L. Preparation of the clinical teacher for special education: 1866–1966. Except. Child., 1967, *10*: 117–124.

Schwesinger, G. C. Heredity and Environment. New York: Macmillan, 1933.

Schwitzgebel, R. Short-term operant conditioning of adolescent offenders on socially relevant variables. J. Abnorm. Psychol., 1967, *72*: 134–142.

Scott, P. Gangs and delinquent groups in London. The British Journal of Delinquency, 1956, *7*: 4–26.

Scott, R. A. The socialization of blind children. In D. A. Goslin (Ed.), Handbook of Socialization Theory and Research. Chicago: Rand McNally, 1969.

Scott, T. H., Bexton, W. H., Heron, W., and Doane, B. K. Cognitive effects of perceptual isolation. Can. J. Psychol., 1959, *13*: 200–209.

Searle, L. V. The organization of hereditary maze-brightness and maze-dullness. Genet. Psychol. Monogr., 1949, *39*: 279–325.

Sears, R., Whiting, J., Nowlis, V., and Sears, P. Some child rearing antecedents of aggression and dependency in young children. Genet. Psychol. Monogr., 1953, *47*: 135–236.

Sears, R. R., Maccoby, E. E., and Levin, H. Patterns of Child Rearing. Evanston, Ill.: Row, Peterson, 1957.

Sechrest, L., and Jackson, D. N. Social intelligence and accuracy of interpersonal predictions. J. Pers., 1961, *29*: 167–182.

Seguin, E. Idiocy: And Its Treatment by the Physiological Method. Albany, N.Y.: Brandow, 1866.

Seltzer, R. A. Computer assisted instruction—what it can and cannot do. Am. Psychol., 1971, *26*: 373–378.

Senn, M. J., and Hartford, C. (Eds.) The Firstborn: Experiences of Eight American Families. Cambridge, Mass.: Harvard University Press, 1968.

Sharder, W. K., and Leventhal, T. Birth order of children and parental report of problems. Child Dev., 1968, *39*: 1164–1175.

Shaw, C. R. The Psychotic Disorders of Childhood. New York: Appleton-Century-Crofts, 1966.

Shaw, C. R., and McKay, H. D. Juvenile Delinquency and Urban Areas. Chicago: The University of Chicago Press, 1942.

Shaw, C. R., and Schelkun, R. F. Suicidal behavior in children. Psychiatry, 1965, *28*: 157–169.

Shaw, M. E., and Wright, J. M. Scales for the Measurement of Attitudes. New York: McGraw-Hill, 1967.

Sheard, M. H. The influence of patients' attitudes on their response to antidepressant medication. J. Nerv. Ment. Dis., 1964, *139*: 195–197.

Shearer, W. M. Speech: Behavior of middle ear muscle during stuttering. Science, 1966, *152*: 1280.

Sheldon, W. H. Varieties of Delinquent Youth. New York: Harper & Row, 1949.

Sherrington, C. S. The Brain and Its Mechanisms. New York: Cambridge University Press, 1933.

Shockley, W. Offset analysis description of racial differences. Paper presented at the autumn meeting of the National Academy of Sciences, Dartmouth College, Hanover, N.H., 1969.

Shockley, W. Models, mathematics, and the moral obligation to diagnose the origin of Negro IQ deficits. Review of Educational Research, 1971, *41*: 369–377.

Shores, R. E., and Haubrich, P. A. Effects of cubicles in educating emotionally disturbed children. Except. Child., 1969, *36*: 21–24.

Short, J. F., and Nye, F. I. Extent of unrecorded delinquency, tentative conclusions. Journal of Criminal Law, Criminology, Police Science, 1958, *49*: 296–302.

Sidowski, J. B., Kopstein, F., and Shillestad, I. L. Prompting and confirmation variables in verbal learning. Psychol. Rep., 1961, *8*: 401–406.

Siegel, E. Learning disabilities: Substance or shadow. Except. Child., 1968, *2*: 433–438.

Siegel, I. E., and Perry, C. Psycholinguistic diversity among "culturally deprived" children. Am. J. Orthopsychiatry, 1968, *38*: 122–126.

Signori, E. I., Smordin, M. M., Rempel, H., and Sampson, D. L. G. Comparison of impulse, ego, and superego functions in better adjusted and more poorly adjusted delinquents. Percept. Mot. Skills, 1964, *18*: 485–488.

Silver, A. A., and Hagin, R. A. Specific reading disability: Follow-up studies. Am. J. Orthopsychiatry, 1964, *34*: 95–102.

Silver, A. A., Hagin, R. A., and Hersh, M. F. Reading disability: Teaching through stimulation of deficit perceptual areas. Am. J. Orthopsychiatry, 1967, *37*: 744–751.

Silver, L. B. Frequency of adoption in children with the neurological learning syndrome. Journal of Learning Disabilities, 1970, *3*: 306–310.

Silverman, C. The epidemiology of depression: A review. Am. J. Psychiatry, 1968, *124*: 883–891.

Silverman, T. R. Categorization behavior and achievement in deaf and hearing children. Except. Child., 1967, *34*: 241–250.

Simon, E. I. Short term parent-group education. Journal of Psychiatric Nursing, 1966, *4*: 16–29.

Simon, H. A., and Newell, A. Human problem solving: The state of the theory in 1970. Am. Psychol., 1971, *2*: 145–160.

Sinclair-de-Zwart, H. Developmental psycholinguistics. In D. Elkind and J. H. Flavell (Eds.), Studies in Cognitive Development: Essays in Honor of Jean Piaget. New York: Oxford University Press, 1969.

Skeels, H. M. Effects of adoption on children from institutions. Children, 1965, *12*: 33–34.

Skeels, H. M. Adult status of children with contrasting early life experiences. Monogr. Soc. Res. Child Dev., 1966, *31*: 1–56.

Skeels, H. M., and Harms, I. Children with inferior social histories: Their mental development in adoptive homes. J. Genet. Psychol., 1948, *72*: 283–294.

Skinner, B. F. Science and Human Behavior. New York: Macmillan, 1953.

Skinner, B. F. Cumulative Record. New York: Appleton-Century-Crofts, 1959.

Skinner, G. T. Single versus multiple modality in visual and auditory discrimination training. Dissertation Abstracts, 1968, *21*: 1172–1173.

Skodak, M., and Skeels, H. M. A final follow-up study of one hundred adopted children. J. Genet. Psychol., 1949, *75*: 85–125.

Slaughter, C. H. Cognitive style: Some implications for curriculum and instructional practices among Negro children. Journal of Negro Education, 1969, *38*: 5–111.

Slobin, D. I. Comments on developmental psycholinguistics. In F. Smith and G. A. Miller (Eds.), The Genesis of Language: A Psycholinguistic Approach. Cambridge, Mass.: The M.I.T. Press, 1966.

Small, J. G. A psychiatric survey of brain injured children. Arch. Gen. Psychiatry, 1962, 7: 120–124.

Smith, B. O. A concept of teaching. Teachers College Record, 1960, *61*: 229–241.

Smith, D. E., and Carrigan, P. M. The Nature of Reading Disability. New York: Harcourt, Brace & World, 1959.

Smith, D. W., Blizzard, R. M., and Wilkins, L. The mental prognosis in hypothyroidism of infancy and childhood. Pediatrics, 1957, *19*: 1011–1020.

Smith, F., and Miller, G. A. (Eds.) The Genesis of Language: A Psycholinguistic Approach. Cambridge, Mass.: The M.I.T. Press, 1966.

Smith, H. Motor activity and perceptual development, some implications for physical educators. Journal of Health, Physical Education, Recreation, 1968, *39*: 28–33.

Smith, J. O., and Mueller, M. W. Research and development of the Peabody language development kits. In J. Hellmuth (Ed.), Educational Therapy. Seattle, Wash.: Special Child Publications, 1969.

Smith, M. B. The revolution in mental health care—a bold new approach? Trans-Action, 1968, *5*: 19–23.

Smith, R. M. Clinical Teaching: Methods of Instruction for the Retarded. New York: McGraw-Hill, 1968.

Smith, R. M. Teacher Diagnosis of Educational Difficulties. Columbus, Ohio: Charles E. Merrill Books, Inc., 1969.

Snyder, S. H. The true speed trip: Schizophrenia. Psychology Today, 1972, *5*: 42–45.

Snygg, D. The relation between the intelligence of mothers and of their children living in foster homes. J. Genet. Psychol., 1938, *2*: 401–406.

Sollenberger, R. T. Chinese-American child-rearing practices and juvenile delinquency. J. Soc. Psychol., 1968, *24*: 13–23.

Speer, G. S. The mental development of children of feeble-minded and normal mothers NSSE Thirty-ninth Yearbook, 1940, *2*: 309–314.

Speers, R. W., and Lansing, C. Group Therapy in Childhood Psychoses. Chapel Hill: The University of North Carolina Press, 1965.

Speery, B. M., and Gardner, G. E. Clinically derived constructs concerning the learning of letters and word forms. Am. J. Orthopsychiatry, 1963, *33*: 348–349.

Spencer, J., Walton, W. S., Miller, F. J. W., and Court, S. D. A Thousand Families in Newcastle Upon Tyne. New York: Oxford University Press, 1954.

Sperry, B., et al. Renunciation and denial in learning difficulties. Am. J. Orthopsychiatry, 1958, *28*: 98–111.

Sperry, R. W. Hemisphere deconnection and unity in conscious awareness. Am. Psychol., 1968, *23*: 723–733.

Spitz, H. H. Field theory in mental deficiency. In N. R. Ellis (Ed.), Handbook of Mental Deficiency. New York: McGraw-Hill, 1963.

Spitz, R. A. Hospitalism: A follow-up report. Psychoanal. Study Child, 1946, *2*: 113–117.

Spivack, G. Perceptual processes. In N. R. Ellis (Ed.), Handbook of Mental Deficiency. New York: McGraw-Hill, 1963.

Spradlin, J. E. Language and communication of mental defectives. In N. R. Ellis (Ed.), Handbook of Mental Deficiency. New York: McGraw-Hill, 1963.

Staats, A. W., and Staats, C. K. Complex Human Behavior: A Systematic Extension of Learning Principles. New York: Holt, Rinehart and Winston, Inc., 1963.

Stabler, J. R., and Johnson, E. E. Instrumental performance as a function of reinforcement schedule, luck versus skill instructions, and sex of child. J. Exp. Child Psychol., 1970, *9*:330–335.

Staffieri, R. Birth order and creativity. J. Clin. Psychol., 1970, *26*: 65–66.

Stansfield, W. D. Theory and Problems of Genetics. Schaum's Outline Series. New York: McGraw-Hill, 1969.

Stein, S. L. The interrelationships among self-esteem, personal values, and interpersonal values. Dissertation Abstracts Int., 1970, *30*: 3803.

Stennet, R. G. Emotional handicap in the elementary years: Phase or disease? Am. J. Orthopsychiatry, 1966, *36*: 444–449.

Stephens, E. Defensive reactions of mentally retarded adults. Social Casework, 1953, *34*: 119–124.

Stephens, J. M. The Psychology of Classroom Learning. New York: Holt, Rinehart and Winston, Inc., 1965.

Stephenson, B. L. A study of sex and race variables and psycholinguistic abilities of lower socioeconomic status first grade children. Dissertation Abstracts, 1969, *29*: 3475.

Stern, C. Principles of Human Genetics. (2nd ed.) San Francisco: Freeman, 1960.

Stevens, H. A., and Heber, R. Mental Retardation. Chicago: The University of Chicago Press, 1964.

Stevenson, H. W. Social reinforcement with children as a function of CA, sex of E., and sex of S. J. Abnorm. Soc. Psychol., 1961, *63*: 147–154.

Stevenson, H. W. Discrimination learning. In N. R. Ellis (Ed.), Handbook of Mental Deficiency. New York: McGraw-Hill, 1963.

Stevenson, H. W., Williams, M., and Coleman, E. Interrelations among learning and performance tasks in disadvantaged children. J. Educ. Psychol., 1971, *62*: 179–184.

Stiles, L. The teacher's role in American society. In L. Stiles (Ed.), Yearbook of John Dewey Society. New York: Harper & Row, 1957.

Stodolsky, S. S., and Lesser, G. Learning patterns in the disadvantaged. Harvard Educational Review, 1967, *37*: 546–593.

Stone, L., and Church, J. Childhood and Adolescence. (2nd ed.) New York: Random House, 1968.

Stott, D. H. Studies of Troublesome Children. New York: Humanities Press, 1966.

Stranahan, M., Schwartzman, C., and Atkin, E. Group treatment for emotionally disturbed and potentially delinquent boys and girls. Am. J. Orthopsychiatry, 1957, *27*: 518–528.

Strauss, A. A. The development of conceptions of rules in children. Child. Dev., 1954, *25*: 193–208.

Strauss, A. A., and Lehtinen, L. E. Psychopathology and Education of the Brain-Injured Child. New York: Grune & Stratton, 1947.

Strauss, A. A., and Werner, F. Disorders of conceptual thinking in the brain injured child. J. Nerv. Ment. Disord., 1942, *96*: 153–172.

Stringer, L. A., and Glidewell, J. C. Early Detection of Emotional Illness in School Children: Final Report. Clayton, Mo.: St. Louis County Health Department, 1967.

Strodtbeck, F. The hidden curriculum in the middle-class home. In J. D. Krumboltz (Ed.), Learning and the Educational Process. Chicago: Rand McNally, 1965.

Strupp, H. H., and Bergin, A. E. Critical evaluation of some empirical and conceptual bases for coordinated research in psychotherapy: A critical review of issues, trends, and evidence. Int. J. Psychiatry, 1969, 7: 116–168.

Sullivan, E. V., McCullough, G., and Stager, M. A developmental study of the relationship between conceptual, ego, and moral development. Child Dev., 1970, *41*: 399–411.

Sumption, M. R., and Lueckins, E. M. Education for the Gifted. New York: Ronald, 1960.

Supa, M. M., Cotzin, M., and Dallenbach, K. M. Facial vision: The perception of obstacles by the blind. Am. J. Psychol., 1944, *62*: 133–183.

Sutherland, E. Principles of Criminology. Philadelphia: Lippincott, 1947.

Sutton, E. Knowing and Teaching the Migrant Child. Washington, D.C.: Department of Rural Education, National Education Association, 1954.

Swift, M. S., and Spivack, G. Achievement related classroom behavior of secondary school normal and disturbed students. Except. Child., 1969a, *35*: 677–684.

Swift, M. S., and Spivack, G. Clarifying the relationship between academic success and overt classroom behavior. Except. Child., 1969b, *36*, 99–104.

Switzer, J. Developmental differences in place and name sequence learning in normal, hyperactive, and hypoactive eight and twelve year old boys. Dissertation Abstracts, 1962, *22*: 2482.

Switzer, J. A genetic approach to the understanding of learning problems. J. Am. Acad. Child Psychiatry, 1963, *2*: 653–666.

Szasz, T. S. The Myth of Mental Illness. New York: Harper & Brothers, 1961a.

Szasz, T. S. The uses of naming and the origins of the myth of mental illness. Am. Psychol., 1961b, *16*: 59–65.

Talkington, L. W. Frostig visual perception training with low-ability-level retarded. Percept. Mot. Skills, 1968, *27*: 505–506.

Tapp, J. T., and Simpson, L. L. An overview of the organization of the central nervous system. In H. C. Haywood (Ed.), Brain Damage in School Age Children. Washington, D.C.: NEA, 1968.

Taylor, D. M. The Consistency of the Self-Concept. Unpublished doctoral dissertation, Vanderbilt University, 1960.

Taylor, J. G. The Behavioral Basis of Perception. New Haven, Conn.: Yale University Press, 1962.

Taylor, P. H. Children's evaluations of the characteristics of a good teacher. Br. J. Psychol., 1962, *32*: 258–266.

Tedeschi, J. T., Schlenker, B. R., and Bonoma, T. V. Cognitive dissonance: Private ratiocination or public spectacle. Am. Psychol., 1971, *8*: 685–696.

Teicher, J. D., and Jacobs, J. Adolescents who attempt suicide: Preliminary findings. Am. J. Psychiatry, 1966, *122*: 1248–1257.

Telford, C. W., and Sawrey, J. M. The Exceptional Individual. (2nd ed.) Englewood Cliffs, N.J.: Prentice-Hall, 1972.

Templin, M. Norms on a screening test of articulation for ages three through eight. J. Speech Hear. Disord., 1953, *17*: 323.

Terman, L. M. Genetic studies in genius. Mental and Physical Traits of a Thousand Gifted Children. Vol. I. Stanford, Calif.: Stanford University Press, 1925.

Terman, L. M., and Merrill, M. A. Stanford-Binet Intelligence Scale. Boston: Houghton Mifflin, 1960.

Thomas, A., Chess, S., and Birch, H. Temperament and Behavior Disorders in Children. New York: New York University Press, 1968.

Thomas, A., Chess, S., Birch, H., Hertzig, M., and Korn, S. Behavioral Individuality in Early Childhood. New York: New York University Press, 1964.

Thomas, D. R., et al. Social reinforcement and remedial instruction in the elimination of a classroom behavior problem. Journal of Special Education, 1968, *2*: 291–306.

Thompson, L. A. Role playing ability and social adjustment in children. Dissertation Abstracts, 1969, *29*: 3499.

Thompson, W. R., and Heron, W. The effects of restricting early experience on the problem solving capacity of dogs. Can. J. Psychol., 1954, *8*: 17–31.

Thrasher, F. M. The Gang. Chicago: The University of Chicago Press, 1927.

Thurstone, T. G., Thurstone, L. L., and Strandskov, H. H. A psychological study of twins. University of North Carolina Laboratory Monograph, No. 4, 1953.

Tijo, J. A., and Levan, A. The chromosome number in man. Hereditas, 1956, *42*: 1–6.

Tischer, S. Psycho-motor reeducation for children with reading difficulties. Canadian Psychologist, 1968, *9*: 187–195.

Tisdall, W. A follow-up study of trainable mentally handicapped children in Illinois. Am. J. Ment. Defic., 1960, *64*: 11–16.

Titchener, J. L., and Emerson, R. The family in psychosomatic process. Psychosom. Med., 1960, *22*: 127–142.

Tolor, A., and Griffin, A. M. Group therapy in a school setting. Psychology in the Schools, 1969, *6*: 59–62.

Toolan, J. M. Suicide in childhood and adolescence. In H. L. Resnick (Ed.), Suicidal Behaviors: Diagnosis and Management. Boston: Little, Brown, 1968.

Torpey, C. R. Operant conditioning and verbal behavior in behaviorally impaired children: An experimental analysis. Dissertation Abstracts, 1969, *29*: 4426.

Torrance, E. P. Rewarding Creative Behavior. Englewood Cliffs, N.J.: Prentice-Hall, 1965.

Torrance, E. P. The Torrance Tests of Creative Thinking: Norms Technical Manual. (Research ed.) Princeton, N.J.: Personnel Press, 1966.

Truax, C. B., and Carkhuff, R. R. Toward Effective Counseling and Psychotherapy: Training and Practice. Chicago: Aldine, 1967.

Tryon, R. C. Genetic differences in maze learning ability in rats. Yearbook of National Social Studies Education, 1940, *39*: 111–119.

Tuckman, J., and Connon, H. E. Attempted suicide in adolescents. Am. J. Psychiatry, 1962, *119*: 228–232.

Tulkin, S. R. Race, class, family, and school achievement. J. Pers. Soc. Psychol., 1968, *9*: 31–37.

Turner, C. Effects of race of tester and need for approval on children's learning. J. Educ. Psychol., 1971, *62*: 240–245.

Turner, D. R. Predictive efficiency as a function of amount of information and level of professional experience. J. Proj. Tech. Pers. Assess., 1966, *30*: 4–11.

Tyler, R. W. Educational evaluation: New roles, new means. In R. W. Tyler (Ed.), Sixty-eighth Yearbook of the National Society for the Study of Education, Part II. Chicago: The University of Chicago Press, 1969.

Ullman, E. Art therapy. Bulletin of Art Therapy, 1961, *1*: 10–20.

Ullmann, L. P., and Krasner, L. (Eds.) Case Studies in Behavior Modification. New York: Holt, Rinehart and Winston, Inc., 1965.

Ullmann, L. P., and Krasner, L. A. A Psychological Approach to Abnormal Behavior. Englewood Cliffs, N.J. Prentice-Hall, 1969.

Ussery, L. E. An experimental investigation of learning and performance in children with academic disabilities. Dissertation Abstracts, 1968, *29*: 1514.

Vacc, N. A. A study of emotionally disturbed children in regular and special classes. Except. Child., 1968, *35*: 197–204.

Valentine, C. A. Deficit, difference, and bicultural models of Afro-American behavior. Harvard Educational Review, 1971, *41*: 137–157.

Vallett, R. E. A social reinforcement technique for the classroom management of behavior disorders. Except. Child., 1966, *33*: 185–189.

Vallett, R. E. The evaluation and programming of basic learning abilities. Journal of School Psychology, 1968, *6*: 21–27.

Vallett, R. E. Programming Learning Disabilities. Palo Alto, Calif.: Feron, 1969.

Vance, P. C. Motor characteristics of deaf children. Dissertation Abstracts, 1968, *29*: 1145–1146.

Vandenberg, S. G. The hereditary components in a psychological test battery. Am. J. Hum. Genet., 1962, *14*: 220–237.

Vandenberg, S. G. What do we know today about the inheritance of intelligence and how do we know it? In R. Cancro (Ed.), Intelligence: Genetic and Environmental Influences. New York: Grune & Stratton, 1971.

Vane, J. Implications of the performance of delinquent girls on the Rosensweig Picture-Frustration Study. J. Consult. Psychol., 1954, *18*: 414.

Vane. J. Relation of early school achievement to high school achievement when race, intelligence, and socioeconomic factors are equated. Psychology in the Schools, 1966, *3*: 124–129.

Van Witsen, B. Perceptual Training Activities Handbook. New York: Teachers College Press, 1967.

Van Wyk, M. K. Integration—a look at the total picture. Volta Review, 1960, *62*: 69–70.

Verville, E. Behavior Problems of Children. Philadelphia: W. B. Saunders Company, 1967.

Vosk, J. S. A study of Negro children with learning difficulties at the outset of their school careers. Am. J. Orthopsychiatry, 1966, *36*: 32–41.

Walker, H. M. Empirical assessment of deviant behavior in children. In N. J. Long, W. C. Morse, and R. G. Newman (Eds.), Conflict in the Classroom. Belmont, Calif.: Wadsworth, 1971.

Walker, R. N. Body build and behavior in young children: Body build and nursery school teachers' ratings. Monogr. Soc. Res. Child Dev., 1962, *27*: No. 84.

Wallach, M. A., and Wing, C. W., Jr. The Talented Student: A Validation of the Creativity-Intelligence Distinction. New York: Holt, Rinehart and Winston, Inc., 1969.

Wallin, J. E. W. Education of Mentally Handicapped Children. New York: Harper & Row, 1955.

Ward, A. J. Early infantile autism, diagnosis, etiology, and treatment. Psychol. Bull., 1970, *73*: 350–362.

Warkentin, J., and Whitaker, C. A. The secret agenda of the therapist doing couples therapy. In G. H. Zuk and I. Boszormenyi-Nagy (Eds.), Family Therapy and Disturbed Families. Palo Alto, Calif.: Science and Behavior Books, 1967.

Wattenberg, W. Recidivism among girls. J. Abnorm. Psychol., 1955, *50*: 405–406.

Webb, P. K. A comparison of the psycholinguistic abilities of Anglo-American, Negro, and Latin-American lower class preschool children. Dissertation Abstracts, 1969, *29*: 3351–3352.

Webb, R. G. Sensory-motor training of the profoundly retarded. Am. J. Ment. Defic., 1969, *74*: 283–295.

Wechsler, D. WISC Manual: Wechsler Intelligence Scale for Children. New York: The Psychological Corporation, 1949.

Wechsler, D. WIPPSI Manual: Wechsler Preschool and Primary Scale of Intelligence. New York: The Psychological Corporation, 1967.

Wechsler, D. Concept of collective intelligence. Am. Psychol., 1971a, *26*: 904–907.

Wechsler, D. Intelligence, theory, and the IQ. In R. Cancro (Ed.), Intelligence: Genetic and Environmental Influences. New York: Grune & Stratton, 1971b.

Weeks, H. Youthful Offenders at Highfields. Ann Arbor: The University of Michigan Press, 1963.

Weener, P., Barritt, L. S., and Semmel, M. A critical evaluation of the Illinois Test of Psycholinguistic Abilities. Except. Child., 1967, *33*: 373–380.

Weikart, D. P. Preschool programs: Preliminary findings. Journal of Special Education, 1967, *1*: 163–182.

Weinstein, L. Project Re-Ed schools for emotionally disturbed children: Effectiveness as viewed by referring agencies, parents, and teachers. Except. Child., 1969, *35*: 703–711.

Wepman, J. M. Neurology romantic style. Contemporary Psychology, 1968, *3*: 591–592.

Wepman, J. M., Jones, L. V., Bock, R. D., and Van Pelt, D. Studies in aphasia: Background and theoretical formulations. J. Speech Hear. Disord., 1960, *25*: 323–332.

Werner, H., and Wapner, S. Perception. In F. H. Allport (Ed.), Theories of Perception and the Concept of Structure. New York: Wiley, 1955.

Werry, J. S. Developmental hyperactivity. Pediatr. Clin. North Am., 1968, *15*: 581–599.

Werry, J. S., and Quay, H. C. Observing the classroom behavior of elementary school children. Except. Child., 1969, *34*: 461–470.

Werry, J. S., and Wollensheim, J. L. Behavior therapy with children: A broad overview. J. Am. Acad. Child Psychiatry, 1967, *6*: 346–370.

Wertheimer, P. A. School climate and student learning. Phi Delta Kappan, 1971, *11*: 527–531.

West, R. M. The Rehabilitation of Speech. New York: Harper & Row, 1957.

Westman, J. C., Rice, D. L., and Bermann, E. Nursery school behavior and later school adjustment. Am. J. Orthopsychiatry, 1967, *37*: 725–731.

Wheeler, L. R. A comparative study of East Tennessee mountain children. J. Educ. Psychol., 1942, *33*: 321–334.

Whelan, R. J., and Haring, N. G. Modification and maintenance of behavior through systematic application of consequences. Except. Child., 1966, *32*: 281–289.

Whipple, G. M. Report of the society's committee on the education of gifted children. In G. M. Whipple (Ed.), Twenty-third Yearbook of the National Society for the Study of Education, Part I. Bloomington, Ill.: Special Studies, Public School Publishing Company, 1924.

White, M. A., and Charry, J. (Eds.) School Disorder, Intelligence, and Social Class. New York: Teachers College Press, 1966.

Whitehurst, M. W. Hearing rehabilitation. In E. Froeshels (Ed.), Twentieth Century Speech and Voice Correction. New York: Philosophical Library, 1948.

Whiting, J. W. M., and Child, N. Field Guide for a Study of Socialization in Five Societies. Cambridge, Mass.: Harvard University Press, 1953.

Whitten, P., and Kagan, J. Jensen's dangerous half-truth. Psychology Today, 1969, *8*: 66–68.

Wiest, W. M. Some recent criticism of behaviorism and learning theory with special reference to Breger and McGough and to Chomsky. Psychol. Bull., 1967, *67*: 214–225.

Wilderson, F. B. A concept of the ideal therapeutic relationship in classes for emotionally disturbed children. Journal of Special Education, 1966, *1*: 91–99.

Williams, J. R., and Scott, R. B. Growth and development of Negro infants: Motor development and its relationship to child-rearing practices in two groups of Negro infants. Child Dev., 1953, *24*: 103–112.

Williams, M. E. K. Help for the teacher of disturbed children in the public school: The use of consultation for problem solving and personal growth. Except. Child., 1967, *39*: 87–92.

Williams, R. J., and Siegel, F. L. Propetology, a new branch of medical science. Am. J. Med., 1961, *31*: 3.

Wilson, G. T., and Davison, G. C. Aversion techniques in behavior therapy: Some theoretical and metatheoretical considerations. J. Consult. Clin. Psychol., 1969, *33*: 327–329.

Wilson, J. A. R. Diagnosis of Learning Difficulties. New York: McGraw-Hill, 1971.

Wilson, J. A. R., and Robeck, M. C. The Kindergarten Evaluation of Learning Potential (KELP): A Curricular Approach to Evaluation. Santa Barbara, Calif.: Sabox Publishing Company, 1965.

Wilson, R. C., and Morrow, W. R. School and career adjustment of bright high-achieving and under-achieving high school boys. In M. Kornrich (Ed.), Underachievement, Springfield, Ill. Charles C Thomas, 1965.

Winchester, A. M. Heredity: An Introduction to Genetics. New York: Barnes & Noble, 1966.

Winebrenner, D. K. Finding the visually inadequate child. Visual Digest, 1952, *16*: 21–34.

Wing, J. K. Early Childhood Autism: Clinical, Educational, and Social Aspects. New York: Pergamon, 1966.

Wirt, R. D., and Briggs, P. F. Personality and environmental factors in the development of delinquency. Psychol. Monogr., 1959, *73*: 47.

Witty, P. (Ed.) The Gifted Child. American Association for Gifted Children, Boston: Heath, 1951.

Wolins, M. Young children in institutions: Some additional evidence. Developmental Psychology, 1970, *2*: 99–109.

Wolman, M. J. Preschool and kindergarten child attitudes toward the blind in an integrated program. New Outlook for the Blind, 1958, *52*: 128–133.

Wolpe, J. Psychotherapy by Reciprocal Inhibition. Stanford, Calif.: Stanford University Press, 1958.

Wolpe, J. The systematic desensitization treatment of neurosis. J. Nerv. Ment. Dis., 1961, *132*: 189–203.

Wolpe, J. Parallels between animal and human neurosis. In J. Zubin and H. F. Hunt (Eds.), Comparative Psychopathology. New York: Grune & Stratton, 1967.

Wolpe, J. The Practice of Behavior Therapy. New York: Pergamon, 1969.

Wolpe, J., and Lazarus, A. A. Behavior Therapy Techniques. New York: Pergamon, 1966.

Wood, F. H. The educator's role in team planning of therapeutic educational placements for children

with adjustment and learning problems. Except. Child., 1968, *34*: 337–340.
Wood, N. E. Delayed Speech and Language Development. Englewood Cliffs, N.J.: Prentice-Hall, 1964.
Woodruff, A. D. Basic Concepts of Teaching, with Brief Readings. San Francisco: Chandler, 1962.
Woodward, K. F., Brown, D., and Bird, D. Psychiatric study of mentally retarded preschool children. A.M.A. Arch. Gen. Psychiatry, 1960, *2*: 156–170.
Woodward, K. F., Siegel, M. G., and Eustis, M. J. Psychiatric study of mentally retarded children of preschool age: Report on first and second years of a three year project. Am. J. Orthopsychiatry, 1958, *28*: 376–393.
Woodward, M. The behavior of idiots interpreted by Piaget's theory of sensorimotor development. Br. J. Educ. Psychol., 1959, *29*: 60–61.
Woodward, M. Early experiences and later social responses of severely subnormal children. Br. J. Med. Psychol., 1960, *33*: 123–132.
Woodward, M. Concepts of space in the mentally subnormal studied by Piaget's method. British Journal of Clinical Psychology, 1962, *1*: 25–37.
Woodward, M. The application of Piaget's theory to research in mental development. In N. R. Ellis (Ed.), Handbook of Mental Deficiency. New York: McGraw-Hill, 1963.
Woodworth, R. S. Heredity and environment: A critical study of recently published material on twins and foster children. Social Science Research Council Bulletin, 1941, *47*: 95.
Woody, R. H. The use of electroencephalography and mental abilities tests in the diagnosis of behavior problem males. Unpublished doctoral dissertation, Michigan State University, 1964.
Woody, R. H. Intra-judge reliability in clinical electroencephalography. J. Clin. Psychol., 1966, *12*: 150–154.
Woody, R. H. Behavioral Problem Children in the Schools. New York: Appleton-Century-Crofts, 1969.
Worchel, P., and Dallenbach, K. M. Facial vision: Perception of obstacles by the deaf-blind. Am. J. Psychol., 1947, *60*: 502–553.
Worchel, P., and Mauney, J. The effect of practice on the perception of obstacles by the blind. J. Exp. Psychol., 1951, *60*: 646–751.
Worchel, P., Mauney, J., and Andres, J. The perception of objects by the blind. J. Exp. Psychol., 1950, *40*: 170–176.
Wright, H. L. A clinical study of children who refuse to talk in school. Am. J. Orthopsychiatry, 1966, *36*: 305.
Wright, P., and L'Abate, L. Reinforcement procedures with Head Start children. Research in progress.
Wunsch, W. L. Some characteristics of mongoloids evaluated at a clinic for children with retarded mental development. Am. J. Ment. Defic., 1957, *62*: 122–130.
Wyatt, G. L. Language, Learning, and Communication Disorders in Children. New York: Free Press, 1969.
Wyatt, R., Termini, B., and Davis, J. Biochemical and sleep studies of schizophrenia: A review of the literature – 1960–1970. Part I. Biochemical studies. Schizophrenia Bulletin, 1971, No. 4.
Wyden, P. Suburbia's Coddled Kids. New York: Avon, 1962.

Yates, A. Frustration and Conflict. Princeton, N.J.: Van Nostrand, 1966.
Yates, A. J. Behavior Therapy. New York: Wiley, 1970.
Young, F. M. Response of juvenile delinquents to the Thematic Apperception Test. J. Genet. Psychol., 1956, *88*: 25–29.

Zax, M., and Cowen, E. L. Early identification and prevention of emotional disturbance in public schools. In E. Cowen, E. Gardner, and M. Zax (Eds.), Emergent Approaches to Mental Health Problems. New York: Appleton-Century-Crofts, 1967.
Zeaman, D., and House, B. J. The role of attention in retardate discrimination learning. In N. R. Ellis (Ed.), Handbook of Mental Deficiency. New York: McGraw-Hill, 1963.
Zedler, E. Y. Public opinion and public education for the exceptional child – Court decisions 1873–1950. In S. Kirk and F. Lord (Eds.), Exceptional Children: Educational Resources and Perspectives. Boston: Houghton Mifflin, 1974.
Zeilberger, J., and Sloane, H. Modification of a child's problem behaviors in the home with the mother as therapist. Journal of Applied Behavior Analysis, 1968, *1*: 47–53.
Zigler, E. Familial mental retardation: A continuing dilemma. Science, 1967, *20*: 292–298.
Zigler, E., and Butterfield, E. C. Motivational aspect changes in I.Q. test performance of culturally deprived nursery school children. Child Dev., 1968, *29*: 1–14.
Zigler, E. F. Social reinforcement, environment and the child. Am. J. Orthopsychiatry, 1963, *33*: 614–623.
Zigler, E. F., and Harter, S. The socialization of the mentally retarded. In D. A. Goslin (Ed.), Handbook of Socialization Theory and Research. Chicago: Rand McNally, 1969.
Zilboorg, G., and Henry, G. W. A History of Medical Psychology. New York: Norton, 1941.
Ziller, R. C. The alienation syndrome: A triadic pattern of self-other orientation. Sociometry, 1969, *32*: 287–300.
Zivitz, N. Evaluation of intractable asthma of children in a new residential treatment center. J. Asthma Res., 1966, *3*: 291–297.
Zuckerman, M., Lubin, B., and Robins, S. Validation of the multiple affect adjective checklist in clinical situations. J. Consult. Psychol., 1965, *29*: 594.
Zuk, G. H. Clinical differentiation of patterns of distractability in young retarded children. J. Clin. Psychol., 1962, *18*: 280–282.
Zukerman, G., and Berkowitz, P. Creative arts with emotionally handicapped children. Paper presented at the Thirty-sixth Annual Convention of the International Council for Exceptional Children, Kansas City, Mo., August, 1958.

AUTHOR INDEX

SUBJECT INDEX

Page numbers in *italics* refer to illustrations; (t) refers to tables.